READING DIFFICULTIES
THEIR DIAGNOSIS AND CORRECTION

READING DIFFICULTIES
THEIR DIAGNOSIS AND CORRECTION

BY

Guy L. Bond

Professor of Education and
Director of the Reading Clinic

AND

Miles A. Tinker

Professor of Psychology
and Education

UNIVERSITY OF MINNESOTA

New  York

APPLETON-CENTURY-CROFTS, Inc.

372.4
B64n
c.6

PREFACE

THIS BOOK was written because the authors firmly believe that the children who get into difficulty with reading need immediate help. Such children need to have their reading problems diagnosed and corrected if they are to gain the reading ability needed today. *Reading Difficulties: Their Diagnosis and Correction* is written for three groups who are vitally concerned with the problem of reading difficulties—the classroom teacher, the school remedial teacher, and the clinician—whether in training or in service. The authors wish to direct their discussion to all who would give aid to a child who is in minor difficulty in his reading or whose reading has become or is becoming so impaired that he needs detailed attention in order to be enabled to grow comfortably and securely in reading again. Such a child needs expert help if he is to receive many of the desirable results from education.

The aim of this book is to help classroom teachers, remedial workers, and clinicians diagnose and correct the various kinds of problems which are grouped under the heading of reading disability. The authors are keenly aware of the fact that learning to read is complex and that there are many possible confusions along the route. The early detection and correction of these difficulties by the classroom teacher will do much to prevent the accumulation of minor problems that may lead to major reading disability. This book is designed to give the teacher specific help by describing how to diagnose and correct reading difficulties in the formative stages.

Certain children will persist in their reading difficulties to the point that they will need more detailed diagnosis and highly individualized remedial training. The classroom teacher cannot be expected to make these more detailed and complex analyses, but the various problems of reading disability are discussed in this book in a sufficiently detailed and direct manner so that a thorough understanding of the most complex cases is possible. Specific suggestions for correcting the various kinds of problems of disabled readers have been given so that all who are concerned with disabled readers will have the information necessary to diagnose and correct the most stubborn cases.

The authors have utilized extensively the results of research on reading instruction and reading disability. They wish to thank all of the research workers who have made this book possible. The authors have drawn heavily on their own and many of their co-workers' clinical experience at the University of Minnesota Psycho-Educational Clinic. They wish to thank specifically Bruce Balow, Theodore Clymer, and Maynard Reynolds, associates of the authors on the faculty of the University of Minnesota, for many practical suggestions.

Lastly, the authors wish to express their deep gratitude to Dr. R. M. Elliott for his careful, extensive, and helpful editorial suggestions.

G. L. B.
M. A. T.

CONTENTS

Contents

Part V: SPECIAL PROBLEMS

PART I
Principles of Reading Instruction

1 INTRODUCTION

THE IMPORTANCE OF PROFICIENT READING

THE ABILITY to read well constitutes one of the most important skills a person can acquire. In fact, satisfactory adjustment to living in the complex modern world requires effective reading. Our world is a reading world. It is difficult to discover any activity, whether in school, in business, even in recreational pursuits and daily life, that does not require more or less reading in order to do it as well as it should be done. In many situations, reading constitutes the indispensable avenue of communication.

Even casual observation of people's activities reveals the prominent role of reading in their lives. What they do is made possible or at least expedited by tremendous quantities of reading matter in the form of magazines, newspapers, books, directories, pamphlets, and catalogues. People read to get information, in order to buy economically or to arrive at a decision, for recreation, and for a host of other reasons. There is more reading done today than ever before.

The importance of proficient reading becomes clearer when its role in various aspects of a person's life is considered. Among many others the following are well worth special notice: (a) daily life activities; (b) progress in school; (c) recreation; (d) personal and social adjustment; and (e) citizenship.

Reading in Daily Life Activities

Proficient reading implies clear comprehension of the communication presented in print or writing whether the message is a short one such as a safety sign, or a long complicated one such as rules for parliamentary procedures in a state legislative assembly. Efficiency in most daily life activities depends to some degree upon accurate comprehension in reading. The housewife reads recipes, directions for clothing construction and for using household appliances. Farmers read agricultural journals and pamphlets as well as directions for assembling and using specialized machinery. The contractor reads the building rules and regulations of his community. The printer, the advertiser, and the publisher must read the trade journals and other publications dealing with their work in order to keep up with new developments. Similarly, an examination of almost any other occupation or

3

activity will reveal that somewhere it demands reading. Today it is scarcely thinkable that one can achieve success along any line without the ability to read. Most people spend few hours during their waking lives without reading something. Much of this reading is done to meet a definite need. Beyond all these specific situations where reading is required, it is universally agreed today that in order to lead a full and satisfying life one must be able to read with understanding.

Reading in School

Reading is generally recognized to be the most important subject taught in the elementary school. Proficient reading is essential as a tool for learning a large portion of subject matter throughout the successive school levels. Moreover, in recent years greater recognition is being given to the importance of proficient reading in high school and college. These trends are shown by two facts. (1) For over 25 years a relatively large number of investigations in the field of reading have been reported each year and during recent years, nearly 100 investigations per year have been published. (2) Much more time, effort, and material are devoted to the teaching of reading in the elementary school than in the past. As to secondary schools, Strang (158) estimates that 80 to 90 per cent of all study activities in typical high schools require reading. Although, contrary to some writers, "learning to read" continues to have an important place in the modern school, "reading to learn" or the use of reading as a tool becomes more and more prominent as the child progresses through the grades.

The present trend is to co-ordinate reading to learn with learning to read from the beginning of reading instruction. Children begin reading science and social studies materials early. This trend increases through the primary grades and becomes very prominent in the intermediate grades. By the time high school is reached, a large portion of the reading is concerned with content subjects. To an increasing degree the pupil must be a skillful reader to succeed in the subject matter fields. For instance, the results reported by Lee (121) indicate that satisfactory achievement in grades four, five, and six requires at least fourth-grade reading ability. Similarly, Elden Bond (16) demonstrated the need of proficient reading in the tenth grade. He found that general reading comprehension was significantly related to achievement in each of the content subjects except mathematics. Also, to a considerable degree, reading content subjects is related to proficiency in the basal reading program. In fact, Swenson (164) shows that there is considerable overlapping in the acquisition of abilities required for reading general and science materials. Artley (4) reports similar relationships between comprehenson of general and social studies materials. To some degree the skill acquired in one area shows transfer to another.

Mastery of the basic reading skills, however, is not enough for best achievement in the content areas. Reading content materials is a complex task. For this, in addition to the basic skills, the reader must apply special expertness, some of which is unique to the specific subject matter. The need of these special skills is shown by the studies of Shores (150) and Fay (66). Achievement in the content areas, therefore, requires proficient use of both basic and special reading abilities. Furthermore, the pupil must learn to adjust the abilities, skills, and procedures at his disposal to the specific requirements of each subject matter. It becomes obvious that to read well at any level, the pupil must be proficient in numerous ways.

Reading for Enjoyment

Reading as a leisure-time activity has an important role in the lives of both children and adults. The proficient reader is able to satisfy important emotional and intellectual needs. The trends of leisure-time reading activities vary from person to person and from time to time for the same individual. For the one who reads much and widely, the rewards in terms of personal enrichment are great. The imagination is stimulated, healthy emotional responses are aroused, and a better understanding of himself and others is achieved. Skillful reading also increases one's enjoyment of both the characters and the plot of a story and an appreciation of the achievements of the great men and women, past and present, in our civilization. It is not too much to say that the more extensive the leisure-time reading, the greater the enrichment of one's personal life.

To enjoy reading extensively, one must be a proficient reader. It is true of course, that other factors, such as opportunity in terms of time and availability of materials, are involved. Attitudes and interests also play an important part. But the inefficient reader cannot and will not engage in extensive leisure-time reading.

Reading and Adjustment

There are several ways that degree of reading proficiency may influence the personal and social adjustment of a person. Emotional disturbances are likely to accompany reading disability. In many cases, such maladjustment is due to frustration in the learning situation. The need of successful achievement is fundamental at all educational levels. When there is severe reading retardation, normal personality development is likely to be inhibited. The frustration due to continued failure in reading may manifest itself in any one of several ways. The child may compensate for his feeling of inferiority by exhibiting bullying and blustering behavior. Or he may retire from active participation in school or play activities and seek the satisfaction he desires through daydreaming. Continued frustration in the learning situation may lead to truancy and even juvenile delinquency. In fact, evidence presented by Gates (76), Gates and Bond (83), Fendrick and Bond (69), and by Polmantier (139) indicates that in certain instances, failure in reading tends to contribute to juvenile delinquency. In general, the evidence indicates that the person with a reading disability tends also to be the person with other adjustment problems. Happily, correction of his reading disability actually tends to improve his personal and social adjustment.

Proficient reading should contribute to the development of insight both into one's own attitudes and patterns of behavior and into those of others. This wholly desirable outcome is achieved as a by-product of increased ability to participate in self-reliant and discriminating interpretation of what is read. The selection of a reading program best suited to promote desirable personal and social development springs from a clear recognition of the need for participating in the social community. It is then only a natural consequence that proficient reading aids in the estimation of one's own abilities and limitations as well as a better understanding of human conduct in one's self and in others.

Reading and Civic Responsibility

To be a good citizen in a democracy, proficient reading is essential. Competency in one's community and in the nation implies that the citizen be well informed concerning local and national issues. He must be able to think clearly, to exercise critical evaluation in discriminating facts and opinions, to reconcile conflicting views, and to detect and evaluate propaganda. To think clearly concerning the critical issues involved in the vital problems encountered, the citizen must be able to arrive at conclusions that take into account all the relevant factors. Among all the avenues of communication available, proficient reading is the most effective tool for this purpose.

The health of a democracy depends to some degree upon the functional literacy of its adult citizens. Persons with less than fourth-grade reading ability are considered to be functionally illiterate. They are unable to assimilate ideas effectively from printed material. Census data of 1947 indicate that 10.4 per cent or about 8.6 million adults 25 years of age and older received less than five grades of schooling. One duty of a good citizen is to be qualified to become a good soldier. Selection of men for the army during the Second World War revealed an alarming number of functional illiterates. Data cited by Russell (144) and by Harris (94) show that several hundred thousand men were unable to pass a simple reading test. A special training program, described by Witty and Goldberg (187), demonstrated that over 90 per cent of such cases can develop sufficient skill in reading and writing to qualify for army duties.

The Role of Proficient Reading

When all aspects of the situation are considered, it is not difficult to appreciate the important role played by reading ability. If one can read well, he can function more effectively in daily activities, achieve more satisfactorily in school learnings, satisfy emotional and intellectual needs, maintain better personal and social adjustment, appreciate better our cultural heritage, and be a better citizen. Furthermore, the importance of good reading ability becomes immediately obvious when we examine the handicaps of those who fail to learn to read. In addition to being handicapped in practically all walks of life, they all too often tend to become frustrated individuals who are prevented from satisfying many of their important emotional and intellectual needs.

THE EXTENT OF READING DISABILITY

During recent years the teaching of reading, especially in the elementary grades, has achieved a position of prime importance in our schools. Research has forged ahead, teachers are better trained, reading materials have become abundant, and techniques and devices for teaching have improved. As a result of all this, pupils, on the whole, tend to be better readers than in the past. Nevertheless, a surprising number of pupils fail to make the progress in reading to be expected from their capacities. Disabled readers turn up at all school levels from the latter part of grade one into the university. Witness the evidence for this statement in the recognition that is today given remedial reading and the widespread establishment of reading clinics.

Amount of Reading Disability

The role of reading deficiency in school failures around 1926 was made clear by figures cited by Gates (79). Pupils who failed in the primary grades were mostly failures in reading, ranging from 99.15 per cent in grade one to about 70 in grade three. From grade to grade, these percentages became gradually less until in grade eight it dropped to about 25.

More recent figures and estimates indicate that reading disability still constitutes a serious problem in the school. According to Betts (8), various authorities estimate that 8 to 15 per cent of the school population have varying degrees of reading disability. The percentage cited by Durrell (56) is 15.2 and by Monroe (132) is 12 to 15. McCallister (125) points out that a large proportion of the pupils who enter junior and senior high school have not attained sixth-grade reading ability. The picture presented by Witty (185) and Lazar (120) is similar. About 16 and 22 per cent of eighth-grade pupils were more than two years retarded in reading. Comparable results could be cited from other studies. Every survey completed at any grade level beyond the first reveals numerous cases of retarded readers. The percentages of seriously retarded readers (one year in the lower grades and two years or more at the higher levels) range from about 10 to 25.

Reports of surveys reveal that boys become retarded readers much more frequently than girls. Durrell (56) found that twice as many boys as girls were retarded: 20 per cent of boys and 10 of girls in one study, and 18 per cent of boys and 9 of girls in another. In clinical cases the percentages are higher. The ratio of boys to girls referred to Durrell's clinic was ten to one. Similar findings are reported by Monroe (131). Of the reading disability cases she studied, 84 to 94 per cent were boys. The reason for these sex differences is by no means clear. We shall turn our attention to possible explanations for these sex differences in a later chapter.

A final word of caution, however, is necessary in interpreting these figures. In the first place, not all pupils whose reading is appreciably below their grade level are disability cases. Some who are slow learners may be reading up to their capacity. Secondly, there is some failure among authorities to agree on the definition of a retarded reader. Harris (94) estimates that between 10 and 15 per cent of elementary school children have reading disabilities which should be classified as mild. In any case, whether 5, 10, or 15 per cent of pupils are disabled readers, the problem is serious and remedial work is indicated.

EFFECTS OF READING DISABILITY

The effects of reading disability are numerous and in many instances tragic for the child involved. Three factors in the problem deserve special mention. These are the kind of classroom teaching, the child's personality structure, and the form of school administration. About the first of these we note at once that the presence of disability cases in a class places an added burden upon the teacher. The well-trained teacher provides for instructional adjustment of procedures to individual differences. In any reading program certain pupils will encounter now and then minor difficulties such as inability to master the use of verbal context as an aid to word recognition. Bond and Handlan (27) state that the detection and correction of such difficulties should be an essential part of individualized instruction in reading. Teachers rather consistently do remedial instruction to take care of such minor deficiencies. In any classroom, at any time, more serious difficulties may occur. This happens whenever a child fails to respond to the best efforts of the teacher. The teacher, in addition to being frustrated, may devote time to the disability case that should be employed in other teaching activities. Special training in diagnosis, remedial teaching and clinical practice is required to deal with these severe disability cases. Just as soon as any such case is identified, the pupil should be referred to the appropriate specialist. Since there tends to be considerable lag both in referring disability cases and in obtaining specialized aid, difficulties of classroom instruction are increased.

Next, there is the child's personality. Surely most important of all is the effect of a child's personality in producing reading difficulty and then, reciprocally, the effect of reading disability upon the personality of the child.

Which of these is cause and which is effect is often hard to determine. Sornson (155), as one instance, found that children who became retarded readers in the first two grades felt more insecure and had less satisfactory personal and social adjustment than good readers. Frequently this trend becomes tragic. The disability prevents normal progress in learning. The need for successful achievement is fundamental in all children. When this is prevented, various forms of personality maladjustment are apt to appear. The child's feeling of inferiority tends to produce either unfortunate compensatory behavior or a retreat into daydreaming. The antisocial compensatory behavior, motivated largely by a desire for attention, disrupts classroom procedures and also prevents normal participation in activities outside school. The asocial behavior manifested by daydreaming and by other aspects of the shut-in personality can become fully as serious as the antisocial behavior noted above. Furthermore, various social pressures from parents, teachers, and other children may increase the tendency to retreat from reality. Additional details of the effects of antisocial and asocial behavior will be dealt with in a later chapter.

Third, there is the relation of reading disability to the school's organization and plan of operation. The presence of reading disability cases in every schoolroom certainly raises administrative problems. The school system must plan how to deal with its disability cases most advantageously. Any remedial program should be pupil-centered in the sense that it is geared to the needs of the pupils concerned. In addition, from the administrative side there must be provision for supervision, for trained clinical personnel, for space where individual teaching may be done, and for an abundance of appropriate materials. The extent of the administrative problem is revealed by the report of Lazar (120) concerning retarded readers in junior high schools in New York City. A summary of the views of 88 school principals showed that the retarded reader was a problem in 99 per cent of their schools, that proper remedial materials were lacking in 51 per cent of schools, that 88 per cent of the junior high school teachers were not equipped to teach elementary basic reading skills, that 91 to 99 per cent of the classroom teachers are not trained to meet the needs of severely retarded readers, and that in 96 per cent of the schools it was felt that special teachers should be provided to instruct retarded readers outside the regular classrooms. Obviously, reading disability complicates the tasks of the school administrator.

RESULTS OF TRAINING TO CORRECT DISABILITY

There is every reason to adopt a favorable view concerning what can be accomplished with reading disability cases by the application of appropriate remedial procedures. Like any skill, reading will show improvement with practice. With good motivation and sufficiently individualized instruction based upon careful diagnosis, progress will result. Obviously the improvement in reading with remedial training will be more rapid in some cases than in others. Nevertheless, if the pattern of difficulties has been discovered by accurate diagnosis, one rarely has a case that does not respond satisfactorily.

Reports in the literature give ample evidence that well-conceived remedial programs are effective at any grade level. It may be assumed that normal children under average conditions of learning will gain approximately one grade in reading ability each school year. Instruction in remedial reading should result in gains in reading achievement that are greater than at this rate of one grade per year. Durrell (56) cites results obtained in the Boston University Reading Clinic. The 12 children in his group ranged in chronological age from 8 years and 4 months to 12 years and 6 months. From October to May individual children gained from 2.0 to 3.8 grades in reading.

Lazar (120) reports the results of a remedial program in three junior high schools involving 233 pupils. The average numbers of classroom periods devoted to remedial instruction in the three schools were 19, 27, and 42. The mean gains in reading grade during the special instruction were respectively 1.8, 2.2, and 2.3. In comparison to normal rates (100 per cent), the rates of learning to read by these remedial cases during the periods of training were 225, 314, and 288 per cent. Additional data were obtained from an extension of the remedial program to 10 additional junior high schools where the average reading abilities and I.Q.'s were lower than in the original experiment cited above. In this instance, children on the average gained from one to two reading grades per school year. "Average rate of learning to read was two to three times what it had been prior to the child's placement in the reading program." (Page 40.) Other data reveal similar trends.

Even relatively short programs of remedial instruction yield gratifying results. Bond and Fay (25) report the results of a five-week program with 23 children at the University of Minnesota Reading Clinic. The average gain was 0.50 grade which was four to five times as much as would be expected for these children under good classroom teaching.

The results of remedial instruction in reading, even when the cases are relatively severe problem children, are highly gratifying. Monroe (131) reports a study of 89 children who were referred to the Institute of Juvenile Research for many other difficulties as well as for poor reading. The children had a variety of environmental and behavioral problems in addition to their reading difficulties. They represent the more complex type of clinical cases. Consequently, to improve their reading ability is a correspondingly harder task. The 89 cases received on the average 26.9 hours of remedial instruction which resulted in an average gain in reading grade of 1.39. Those with higher I.Q.'s made greater gains: I.Q.'s of 110 and above gained

1.72 reading grades; I.Q.'s of 90-109 gained 1.55 reading grades; and I.Q.'s below 90 gained 0.96 of a reading grade.

Less systematic remedial instruction will also produce better than normal gains in reading ability. Monroe (131) cites results on another group of 50 children who were referred by their teachers to the Institute of Juvenile Research for diagnosis of reading difficulties. The findings of the diagnosis were discussed with the teachers who then helped their pupils before or after school or during free periods. Since the classroom teachers were not trained remedial instructors and were hampered by lack of time, the remedial work was neither intensive nor well controlled. Nevertheless an average of 18.1 hours of treatment over a stretch of about seven months resulted in a gain of 0.79 of a reading grade.

Numerous other studies reported in the literature reveal the important relationship between remedial instruction and increased skill in reading. Especially important is the fact that a remedial program that is based upon careful diagnosis of difficulties tends to produce improvement at a rate which is two to four times the normal rate. With individual cases the rate of improvement may be greater or less than this. Increase in reading skill is not the only gain achieved. In most instances the child's personality undergoes a desirable change, and the child tends to develop better personal and social adjustments in all his activities. He becomes a happier child and may now develop a genuine interest in reading and other learning.

NEED FOR PREVENTING READING DISABILITY

The presence of reading disability cases in our schools constitutes a serious problem at all levels of the academic ladder. Perhaps because the need for remedial work, once it is present, constitutes such a pressing problem, it usually tends to receive more attention than preventive measures. It is not uncommon to find school administrators pointing with pride to their remedial programs while at the same time little emphasis is placed upon prevention of reading disability before it occurs.

Many reading difficulties can be forestalled. Others can be corrected in their initial stages by the classroom teacher at a time when correction is relatively easy. The preventive program implies at least three kinds of emphasis in instruction: (1) a thoroughgoing reading readiness program in preparing the child for initial reading and for reading at successive higher levels; (2) proper adjustment of instruction to individual differences; and (3) systematic developmental programs at all levels.

In the well-organized instructional program, therefore, there will be a natural emphasis upon prevention of reading disability. If it were possible in day-to-day teaching to provide for each pupil's progress in terms of his capabilities, less occasion for remedial work would arise. Such an ideal educational environment cannot be achieved yet. Even with the best of teaching and the best organized systematic program, certain children will be in difficulty serious enough to require remedial instruction which is outside the capabilities of the classroom teacher to provide. With less than the best teaching, the incidence of disability cases will increase. In any case, there will be found in our present-day schools an appreciable number of pupils who are in serious difficulty with their reading. A remedial program must be provided to correct these difficulties.

POINT OF VIEW

It is the point of view of the present book that a reading case develops because one or more factors in a child's make-up or in his environment have been such that he has not achieved up to the learning capacity which he possesses. Further, the writers believe that reading disability can be corrected by the application of proper diagnosis and remedial instruction. Nothing of value is accomplished by blaming the disability on low intelligence or on lack of interest and laziness on the part of the child. Such a view is unrealistic. For one reason or another, school instruction has not in these cases capitalized on the child's mental ability nor developed motivation through successful appeal to his potential interests.

View on Causes

The writers know that the causes of reading disability tend to be complex. In the more difficult cases, there is usually a pattern of interacting factors operating, each contributing its part to the disability and each impeding future growth. The problem of the remedial clinician is to search out as many as possible of the limiting conditions that are operating in a particular case and apply the proper corrective measures.

In general, the writers believe that most disability cases are made rather than born that way. Reading disabilities are sometimes the result of predisposing conditions within the child that are unrecognized, but for the most part they are brought about by factors in the child's environment at home, at play, and in school. Without appropriate guidance and without proper instruction given at the right time, the child will fail to acquire the skills essential for normal development of reading ability.

Reading difficulties vary from minor to very severe. When minor difficulties occur and are not recognized and promptly corrected, their deleterious effects tend to become cumulative and frequently result in severe disability.

Although the writers emphasize educational factors as causes of reading disability, they also recognize that various other factors may and often do constitute more or less serious handicaps and thus contribute as parts of a complex pattern of causes. Immaturity in various aspects of reading readiness, basic emotional instability, physical deficiencies (vision, etc.), social pressures at home or in school, and other factors may be involved. A single factor seldom causes reading disability, but one factor may be relatively more important than other factors in the pattern.

The writers are keenly aware that failure to recognize a child's handicaps and failure to adjust instructional procedures to minimize their effects on learning may contribute to reading disability. That is, unless all educational, physical, and emotional factors which may hinder normal progress in learning to read are identified early and proper instructional adjustments made, a disability case is apt to develop.

View on Remedial Instruction

The writers hold to the view that remedial instruction in reading is essentially the same as good classroom teaching that is individualized. The teacher works with the specific case, employing regular teaching methods but concentrating more intensely upon the skill wherein the child is deficient. Concentration of effort is on the pupil's needs. A thoroughgoing diagnosis of abilities and difficulties is presupposed.

Effective remedial instruction is done by a good teacher of reading. She must be familiar with the principles and practices underlying sound reading instruction. Above all she must be versatile in adapting materials and techniques to the specific needs of a particular case and she must apply them with patience, understanding, and sympathy. Successful remedial work can be achieved only when there is good rapport between pupil and teacher.

The writers are convinced that well-conceived remedial instruction will result in improvement of reading ability. Theoretically, the instruction should bring the child up to the reading grade that is in line with his learning capacity. This should be possible except in a small number of cases that are complicated by factors beyond the ability of the teacher to correct. It is, however, a rare case where a skilled teacher is not able to bring about significant improvement in reading ability.

PLAN OF THIS BOOK

This book aims to present a discussion of a practical program for the improvement of reading based upon research findings and sound instructional procedures. Our chief concern will be the individual child who is in difficulty in his attempts to learn to read. The first major section of the book deals with fundamental principles of reading instruction. In Chapter 2 of this section is an over-all view of the nature of reading growth. Included are sections dealing with the nature of the reading process, normal reading growth, goals of reading instruction, contemporary trends in reading instruction, and a statement of what constitutes a good reader. Chapter 3 is concerned with adjusting instruction to individual differences. After considering various aspects of the problem and their implications, current approaches to these problems and approved modern practices are discussed.

The second major section of the book is devoted to the nature and causes of reading disability. Chapter 4 is a discussion of the general nature of reading disability. After describing the nature of a disabled reader, the considerations involved in classifying a reader as disabled are described. This is followed by the descriptive characteristics of a disabled reader. Chapters 5 and 6 are concerned with causes of reading deficiencies. The role of physical, emotional, intellectual, and educational factors are described and evaluated.

Part III deals with diagnosis. After considering the general nature of diagnosis in Chapter 7, the various questions which must be answered by the diagnostician in his analysis of reading difficulties are discussed in Chapter 8. Chapter 9 presents a survey of specific approaches to diagnosis. The instruments used in diagnosis and representative detailed techniques are described.

Part IV of the book is devoted to remedial treatment. The basic principles of remedial instruction are described in Chapter 10. In Chapters 11 through 16, various aspects of remedial treatment are taken up. Separate chapters are devoted to developing basic comprehension abilities, word identification and recognition, developing left-to-right progression in perceptual orientation, overcoming specific reading defects, reading in the content fields, and developing rate of comprehension. Each of these areas is dealt with in the following manner: (1) The essential learnings for adequacy in the area are reviewed. (2) Techniques for detecting failure to establish these learnings are described. (3) Remedial methods are given, with illustrative exercises for correcting deficiencies for each essential learning. (4) The relevant interrelationships of deficiencies that may occur in each area are discussed.

The final section of the book is concerned with certain special problems. Chapter 17 is devoted to the special problems that are involved in developing interests and tastes. Essential learnings, detection of difficulties, and suggestions for a developmental program are discussed. Chapter 18 is devoted to the specially handicapped child. Emphasis is placed upon the need for highly individualized treatment in the case of several types of handicapped children. Specialized aspects of diagnosis and remedial treatment are gone over. In the final chapter a number of case studies are listed.

The appendices contain lists of (1) intelligence and reading tests, (2) books on reading, (3) sources of graded books, (4) references on sources of materials, and (5) bibliographies of reading literature.

SUMMARY

Proficient reading is important to the individual for many reasons. It is essential for effective adjustment in a multitude of everyday life activities as well as for learning in school. Furthermore, reading for enjoyment has an important place in leisure-time activities of both children and adults. Ability to read well frequently promotes one's personal and social adjustment in a variety of situations. The proficient reader tends to be better informed and hence a better citizen.

The prevalence of reading disability in our schools is surprising in view of the time, energy, and money devoted to the teaching of reading. Reports show that from 10 to 25 per cent of pupils are seriously retarded and a large portion of these are disability cases. Boys become disability cases much more frequently than girls.

The effects of reading disability are numerous and frequently tragic for the person involved. Normal progress in school is blocked for the disabled reader. Perhaps most important of all are the deleterious effects of reading disability upon the personality of the child concerned. The feelings of inferiority produced by lack of success frequently lead to various forms of maladjusted behavior. In addition, the presence of disability cases in the school produces certain administrative problems concerned with classroom teaching and the provision for remedial programs.

Evidence shows that remedial training produces desirable results. A remedial program based upon proper analysis of a child's difficulties brings improvement in reading ability in nearly every case. Frequently the child can be brought up to his full potential learning capacity. Of equal importance are the desirable changes in personality that occur with correction of reading difficulties.

More emphasis than now occurs should be placed upon the prevention of reading disability. A program of reading instruction which provides for adjustment to individual differences will reduce the incidence of disability cases. With the best of teaching, however, there will be an occasional pupil who is in trouble in his efforts to learn to read.

The writers hold to the view that reading disability is due to a multiplicity of causes. There is a pattern of these operating together rather than a single cause. They also believe that most disability cases are produced by factors in the child's environment at home, at play, and in school. It is recognized, however, that other factors such as emotional instability and physical deficiencies are contributing causes. The writers hold to the view that properly conceived remedial training will result in improvement of reading ability.

The aim of this book is to present the fundamental principles of reading instruction together with discussions of causes, diagnosis, and remedial treatment of cases with varying degrees of disability.

SELECTED READINGS

BLAIR, Glenn M., *Diagnosis and remedial teaching*, rev. ed. New York: The Macmillan Company, 1956, Chap. 1.

DOLCH, Edward W., *Problems in reading*. Champaign (Ill.): The Garrard Press, 1948, Chap. 13.

GATES, Arthur I., *The improvement of reading,* 3rd ed. New York: The Macmillan Company, 1947, Chap. 1.

HARRIS, Albert J., *How to increase reading ability,* 3rd ed. New York: Longmans, Green & Company, 1956, Chap. 1.

STRANG, Ruth, *Problems in the improvement of reading in high school and college,* rev. ed. Lancaster (Pa.): The Science Press, 1940, Chap. 1.

————, McCULLOUGH, Constance M., and TRAXLER, Arthur E., *Problems in the improvement of reading,* 2nd ed. New York: McGraw-Hill Book Company, Inc., 1955, Chaps. 1-2.

2 NATURE OF READING GROWTH

COMMUNICATION between people is achieved by means of the language arts. These are customarily listed as speaking, listening, writing, and reading. Prior to going to school the child develops in his listening and speaking abilities and the greater this development, the greater is his ability to carry on communication with others. Extensive and varied experiences with objects, situations, and people, together with guidance provided by parents, promote verbal facility in both listening and speaking. All this constitutes essential preparation for reading. As the child grows older, enters school and progresses through the grades, more and more communication can and should be by means of reading printed and written material. The effectiveness of such communication depends upon the reading skills and abilities acquired by the child.

THE READING PROCESS DESCRIBED

Even before formal reading instruction, frequently before his going to school, the child begins to sense that printed words "talk." The transition from this to the realization that reading is "talk wrote down" is rapid. The child notes his father and mother absorbed in looking at the print in newspapers and books. And when a parent reads a story to the child, he notes that the parent's gaze is directed at the print. If placed where he can watch the pictures while the reading is done, the child may note and ask questions about the printed words below the pictures.

To read, following the usual approaches, the child must learn the relationship of printed language to oral language. That is, he must understand that a printed word stands for a spoken word and has the same meaning as the spoken word. In beginning reading, the printed word should always be in the speaking and understanding vocabulary of the child. He associates the printed word with the sound of the spoken word and also with the meaning of the spoken word.

The printed words in any story or other product of writing are merely symbols which stand for meanings intended by the author. A writer can only put down symbols that stand for meanings. These symbols serve as cues to the reader who must organize an understanding of what is meant. The ease with which a child can do this depends largely upon his past experiences.

17

For beginning readers, the meanings are in terms of his experience as represented by previously acquired facility in understanding and using speech. In other words, the child reads with his experience, with experiences "behind his eyes," as it were.

To a large degree, the thinking which a child does involves verbal manipulations. When he begins to read, this becomes important, for thinking is an essential aspect of reading at all stages of development. In fact, reading as a tool for learning may be ineffective unless thinking accompanies it. Learning to read and reading to learn should develop hand in hand throughout the school years.

Reading is both a subject of instruction and a tool employed in studying in the subject matter fields. During recent years, an increased emphasis has been placed upon reading to learn. The writers of this book, however, intend to avoid an overemphasis upon either learning to read or upon reading to learn. Both views have a place and should be co-ordinated in the balanced program of instruction. Though we know that the skillful teaching of reading is of the highest importance in the primary grades, we recognize that it is still important in the upper grades and in high school where additional skills and abilities are required to cope successfully with new reading situations. And at all grade levels, proper instruction should be given in adapting the skills acquired to the reading of subject matter material.

The special skills should be taught as they are needed. Furthermore, they should be taught in the appropriate context, which means, for example, that the special skills needed for the reading matter of science should be taught with material similar to that used in science instruction. Even though such a procedure places emphasis upon reading as a tool, it is teaching of reading. Also, as pointed out by McKee (127), skillful teaching of the content subjects can make an important contribution to the improvement of the child's reading ability in addition to developing his tastes and broadening his interests.

Definition of Reading

Concepts concerning the nature of reading have changed during the past fifty years (see below). A generation ago, reading was considered to be a relatively simple process. Now it is recognized both by authorities in reading and by experienced teachers to be a very complex process. In addition to mastering the mechanics of reading (simpler aspects), the pupil must understand and reflect on what he reads (complex aspects). In other words, in addition to mere recognition of words, clear enunciation, and proper phrasing, there must be comprehension and thinking. Because reading is an aspect of written communication which implies both a writer and a reader, the effective reader endeavors to grasp the ideas expressed by the writer. If this is to be achieved, reading must be taught by one who is aware of the complexities involved. Only when the nature of reading is understood and the teacher is competent can the child's reading abilities develop to the extent called for by his intellectual capacities, which means he becomes a mature reader.

The definition of reading here adopted may be summed up as follows: Reading involves the recognition of printed or written symbols which serve as stimuli for the recall of meanings built up through the reader's past experience. New meanings are derived through manipulation of concepts already in his possession. The organization of these meanings is governed by the clearly defined purposes of the reader. In short, the reading process involves both the acquisition of the meanings intended by the writer and the reader's own contributions in the form of interpretation, evaluation, and reflection about these meanings.

DESCRIPTION OF NORMAL READING GROWTH

In order to detect those children who, for one reason or another, have failed to make satisfactory progress in reading, it is necessary to have in mind some norms of reading growth. There are, of course, marked individual differences in rate of progress in learning to read. Some children will begin to read early and progress rapidly. Others will start late and move forward slowly. Between these are the average learners. It should be noted also that a given child may progress at different rates at different stages in his development of reading abilities. In general, however, normal growth in reading tends to be fairly continuous and developmental in nature. At each stage, the abilities essential for success at the succeeding level are acquired. When this progress is continued without serious interruption, the child eventually becomes a fairly mature reader.

Although a discussion of growth in reading may refer to steps or stages of development, this is done for convenience of exposition. There are no discrete steps of development involved. Whether one is speaking of reading readiness, word knowledge, or specific reading abilities, growth is more or less continuous throughout the successive school grades. For instance, reading readiness is not confined to the period preceding reading instruction, nor is development of the special reading skills limited to the upper grades.

For convenience of exposition the present discussion may be organized under the following topics: the pre-reading period, progress in reading readiness, introduction to reading, progress in the primary grades, progress in the intermediate grades, progress in the basic reading skills, and progress in the special reading skills.

The Pre-reading Period

Soon after birth the child begins to acquire experience essential for learning to read. With further growth in mental ability, in emotional adjustment, in acquiring interests and having all sorts of experience with objects and people, the child eventually is ready to begin reading. An understanding and speaking vocabulary develops gradually. In time, sentences are comprehended and properly used. As this is going on, the child develops skill in auditory and visual discrimination. Varieties of concepts are formed. Under favorable circumstances, the child develops attentive attitudes which permit listening to and comprehending of stories. If experience is extensive, if many clear concepts have been acquired, and if adequate facility in the understanding and use of language has been achieved, the child will have a distinct advantage in getting ready for reading.

Many environmental factors condition the rate of development up to the time when the child is ready to read. To acquire auditory and visual skills together with language facility, there must be opportunity and guidance. In addition to his meeting a broad range of experiences, the child must be stimulated to discriminate sounds and objects, and to listen to and use words. It is important for older persons to talk to and with the child. Stories should be told and they should be read together with the child while he looks at pictures and talks about them. Also, his own extensive experience with such materials as picture books, crayons, paper, scissors, paint brushes, etc. plays a role in his preparation for reading.

Under favorable circumstances, and provided that mental growth, emotional adjustment, and physical status are normal, in time, the child not only will be ready to read but also he will be eager to read. Obviously there are marked differences in the rate with which children acquire reading readiness. A few are ready even before reaching the first grade, many are ready soon after beginning the first grade, but a few are not ready until later.

Progress in Reading Readiness

Since, for one reason or another, all children are not ready to begin reading when they enter the first grade, a program for developing reading readiness is in order. Details of such a program are given in Bond and Wagner (28) and in Tinker (175). Only the general nature and implications of such a program will be discussed here.

The child is ready to begin a specific reading program only when he has reached a certain stage of mental maturity, has a satisfactory emotional adjustment, and has acquired an adequate background of experiences and attitudes. Mental maturity, of course, comes only through natural growth, i.e., at its own pace. As already noted, there are many degrees of readiness among children at the beginning of grade one. After an evaluation of each child's background, the teacher provides a program to offset whatever deficiencies in reading readiness she discovers. With proper guidance and instructional procedures, each child will soon, or in some cases after some delay, be ready to read.

Some authors seem to imply that the readiness program is completed when the child has acquired those experiences and skills which assure success in beginning reading. Many teachers hold to the same view. Such a viewpoint is unfortunate. The concept of reading readiness is basic to the development of reading ability at all levels, from the kindergarten on. With each new unit of instruction, the child should be prepared so that he will be able to carry out effectively the reading and thinking activities involved in the unit. To be successful in any reading task, the pupil must possess the necessary concepts, vocabulary knowledge, and ability to handle the language relationships involved. The pupil must also select and organize those meanings which are in line with his purpose. All this implies instruction and guidance so that the pupil will be *ready to read* each new unit proficiently. Various aspects of reading readiness will be considered later at appropriate places.

Introduction to Reading

After proper preparation, the child is introduced to reading in grade one. He begins the accumulation of a sight vocabulary and at the same time learns that printed and written symbols stand for meanings in a variety of situations. Training in auditory and visual discrimination continues. New word meanings are acquired. His teacher gives him help in the elementary use of techniques and clues for word identification. In the meantime he is progressing naturally from the reading of labels, words standing for actions, and short signs and notices to reading a book, the pre-primer. Systematic training in reading a book then becomes a reality with progress to the primer level and so on to the first reader. All along the line, learnings are reinforced through exercises suggested in manuals, through the use of workbooks and other supplementary materials.

There will be marked individual differences in the reading progress made by first-grade pupils. By the end of the first grade, the average learners will have acquired a considerable stock of sight words, some independence in using techniques of word recognition, and considerable skill in both the oral and silent reading of easy materials. The children will also have developed desirable attitudes toward reading through their newly acquired skill in the use of books, and will, it is hoped, find interest and enjoyment in independent reading of other books outside the basic materials, including those in the public library.

Progress in Primary Grades

To a large degree the reading instruction in grades two and three consists of an extension, refinement, and amplification of the program begun in grade one. New techniques are introduced and the child begins to learn them at whatever time he is ready and just at the proper stage of development. Throughout the primary grades there are no abrupt distinctions in progressing from one part of the program to the next. Under favorable circumstances, the average child will have achieved the following goals by the end of grade three: he will have made marked progress toward mastering techniques of word recognition and the other fundamentals of reading, developed considerable independence in reading situations, acquired a fair degree of flexibility in the use of reading skills, laid a sound foundation for study-type of reading and for the special sorts of reading ability and study, achieved greater speed in silent than oral reading, and acquired desirable positive attitudes toward books and reading. With normal progress, by the end of grade three the child will have acquired a sound foundation for all future reading, notwithstanding that there are still many basic skills in word recognition, comprehension, and techniques of study to be developed later.

Progress in the Intermediate Grades

Reading instruction in grades four through six becomes pretty much an extension of the developmental program begun in the primary grades. In addition to perfecting the basic abilities, there is closer concentration upon developing the specialized abilities and study skills required for reading subject matter in content fields and other work-type materials. Beginning with grade four, children move into a period of ever-increasing diversification of learning wherein reading is the essential tool. To an accelerating degree, reading becomes a means of achieving information and pleasure. When there has been normal progress in the earlier grades, the consolidation of basic reading abilities and the extension of these abilities in specialized directions in the intermediate grades will proceed at a relatively rapid pace. The child becomes a more independent and extensive reader. Although the relative emphasis upon silent reading increases, oral reading should not be neglected. By the time the sixth grade is finished, the child who has made normal progress will have acquired a solid foundation for reading in later years. Additional instruction in reading in the junior and senior high school years, however, is necessary to assure most proficient reading. This is particularly true with regard to perfecting the special abilities and skills employed in serious study and in the comprehension of difficult material.

Progress in the Basic Reading Abilities

Throughout the successive grades there is more or less steady growth in the acquisition of word knowledge, skill in word recognition, and ability to comprehend printed matter. Progress is developmental or sequential in nature. Each feature of a learning provides a basis for subsequent growth in features similar to it. Reading readiness plays an important role in these learnings. A child is ready to advance to a succeeding level of a learning sequence only when his mastery of what comes before is sufficient to insure success with the more mature learning. In word recognition, for example, he learns letter and phonogram sounds in the early years. This equips him to acquire the more mature features of word recognition which involve syllabication, prefixes, suffixes, and word roots taught in the intermediate grades. It can be demonstrated that many qualities of a mature reader can be detected in the early reading responses of the beginner. As a matter of fact, they can be detected in the pre-reading program. Each succeeding learning builds on and utilizes the skill acquired in what came earlier. These basic reading abilities are not acquired in splendid isolation but as part of a well-integrated sequential reading program.

Progress in the Special Reading Abilities

The acquisition of the special abilities necessary for proficient reading in the content areas begins early and progresses at a gradual pace for most pupils. Since the reading of some content material is introduced in grade one in the better reading programs, it is necessary to teach the elementary features of the special abilities during the primary grades. By grade three, such guidance should become fairly prominent. If this is done, the progress of the average pupil in reading to learn will have advanced far enough by the end of the primary grades so that the transition to the major reading tasks in the intermediate grades will be smooth and effective rather than abrupt and difficult.

As the child moves through grade three and into and through the intermediate grades, the study skills are added to the special reading abilities. Mastery of the basic reading abilities together with continuing improvement in the special reading abilities and study skills become co-ordinated into proficient reading habits. With normal progress, the child will have acquired considerable flexibility in adapting these abilities and skills to the purposes and subject-matter requirements in each of the content areas. In addition, he will have learned the supplementary skills necessary to meet the reading problems which are unique to a particular subject matter. Although complete mastery of the special reading abilities cannot be achieved by the end of grade six, good progress in this direction will have been made. The child will have a sound foundation for further progress in dealing with the reading tasks in the junior and senior high school years. It is justified at any grade level to assume that the reading growth required for effective learning can be completed by an earlier grade when and only when the reading materials used are not more advanced than those the child met in the earlier grade. Such is rarely if ever the case. The materials to be read in high school are obviously more mature than those used in the elementary school. Consequently the child must be taught to meet the new demands placed upon him.

GOALS OF READING INSTRUCTION

An effective reading program does more than develop the abilities and skills, both basic and special, outlined in the preceding section. Nevertheless, the broader goals of the reading program are built upon these foundations.

Reading involves more than ability to identify and recognize words, more than ability to group words into thought units, more than ability to note details and follow directions, more than ability in each and all the skills and techniques. The reading program must attain for every possible child a number of specific goals. As an introduction to these goals of reading instruction, we cite the list made up by Bond (19) which emphasizes the many advantages that the printed page has over other means of mass communication:

(*a*) Reading enables a person to be more critical. He can at any time stop and reflect upon what has been or is being read. This encourages more rigorous thinking about a given subject.

(*b*) The reader can organize more effectively the contributions from many sources. What other authorities assert can be consulted by taking one book after another from the shelf. Naturally one should ascertain that the authorities consulted are well qualified to express an opinion.

(*c*) Reading permits adjustment to individual needs and understandings. Books can be chosen to help solve any problem or satisfy any interest. Only such authorities as he desires and chooses to communicate with and as he can understand need be selected.

The over-all goal of reading instruction is to help each pupil to become as able and as diversified a reader as his capabilities, the available facilities, and the instructional program permit. To achieve this, certain subgoals must be considered. These goals are present during early reading experiences and grow more apparent as reading matures up through the grades. It should be recognized that there is interdependence among the goals of reading instruction. One goal is not necessarily more important than another. The following goals (except the first) have been outlined by Bond (19).

The Basic Understandings of Words, Sentences, Paragraphs, and Stories. Growth in these understandings is essential if the pupil is to progress toward becoming a mature reader. Word meanings are at first derived from experience. As language facility increases and words are used in connection with newly experienced objects, situations, and events, concepts become clarified and enriched. Growth tends to be continuous but slow. The instructional program employed for developing a child's vocabulary for expressing meanings will provide varied and rich experiences both at firsthand and vicariously, wide and extensive reading, and study of words in context. It will also develop the habit of attending to the meaning of words so that if an unusual or expressive word is used, the child will note it and its meaning. An understanding of words is basic for the understanding of sentences, paragraphs, and stories.

The understanding of sentence structure affects reading comprehension. In addition to knowing the meaning of words in a sentence, the reader must grasp the relations between words and groups of words. The kind and amount of instruction is determined by individual needs. With one or another child the instruction may involve guidance in proper phrasing, interpretation of punctuation, interpretation of figures of speech, use of a word whose meaning is appropriate to the verbal context, and sorting out and properly relating several ideas incorporated in one sentence.

In addition to understanding words and sentences, proper comprehension of a paragraph requires an understanding of the relations between sentences in that paragraph. The instructional task involves guidance in identifying the topical sentence containing the key idea and in interpreting its relation to the explanatory or amplifying sentences. In a similar manner, some attention should be devoted to the relation between paragraphs in longer selections.

Obviously, one set of learnings involved in comprehending a story consists of word, sentence, and paragraph understanding. Also involved is the degree to which a child has the ability to listen to and follow the sense of the story. Some children by the time they begin school have made considerable progress along this line. Others have acquired little or no story sense at that time. These will need preliminary guidance in learning, prior to formal reading instruction, how to listen carefully to what is said and how to follow a sequence of events in stories. The story sense cannot be developed to its maximum efficiency for any child by the time reading is begun. Since the acquisition of several important reading techniques is facilitated by ability to comprehend stories, continued instruction is in order. Guidance in listening attentively and in following sequences of events should be an integral part of reading instruction at least through the primary grades. After the primary grades, more complex plots and more complicated organization of ideas are encountered. The child must learn to sense the author's organization in order to grasp the meanings of the longer selections.

Maturity in Reading Habits and Attitudes. Development of reading habits and attitudes begins early and continues as long as the child is growing in reading capability. The child learns to appreciate and to care for books. He develops the attitude of intellectual curiosity and the realization that books can help him to satisfy this curiosity as he employs them to solve his own problems and to contribute to group enterprises in which he takes part. As he gradually learns that reading is a part of written communication, he develops the attitude of wanting to share what the author has to say. The habit of attending to words and of demanding an understanding of their meanings grows and should be encouraged at all levels. Finally, developing the habit of relying on one's own resources and of energetically attacking reading material should be encouraged early in the hope that it will be strengthened throughout the instructional program.

Independence in Reading. In order to begin to read well and to be able to continue his intellectual growth after formal education is finished, the child must develop independence in reading. Several features are involved in achieving this independence. He must be able to recognize words rapidly and with a minimum of effort if he is to grasp and think over the content of what is read. Growth in reading ability implies the ability to work out the pronunciation and understanding of new words. The independent reader will also know about various sources where he can search out new material, he will know how to select relevant subject matter from these sources, and he will possess appropriate techniques for judging the suitability of that subject matter. Independence in reading is also manifested by the ability to initiate one's own reading activities, to appreciate reading problems, and to set one's own reading purposes. Reading programs organized into important experience units that require related reading and activities encourages growth in independence. Teacher guidance plays an important role in the development of independence in reading.

Efficiency in the Use of the Basic Study Skills. A number of skills are requisite for attaining this goal. Development of efficiency in locating information through such aids as tables of contents, indexes, and card catalogues constitute one group of these skills. Instruction in the elementary techniques of locating information begins early. The more complex features are taught in a sequential order.

Acquiring proficiency in the use of general reference material constitutes a second group of study skills. Beginning with simple alphabetizing, the child goes on to use dictionaries, encyclopedias, and the like.

A third group of these skills deals with interpretation of pictures, maps, graphs, and charts. Teaching how to do this begins in the kindergarten and progresses in a developmental manner through the school years. This set of skills is relatively important though frequently it receives little emphasis.

A final group of skills is especially essential. They are the techniques of organizing materials, including such things as outlining, classifying materials under main and subheadings, organizing sentences in experience charts in sequential order, and ordering selected materials in proper sequence for a report to the class. Constructing time lines, two-way charts, and classification tables are additional examples. Acquisition of the ability to organize materials is essential for well-rounded growth in reading proficiency.

Maturity in Five Major Classes of Comprehension Abilities. The development of five highly interrelated types of comprehension, each corresponding to a different though related ability, constitute major goals of reading instruction. Listed, they are as follows: (*a*) reading for specific information, (*b*) reading to organize, (*c*) reading to evaluate, (*d*) reading to interpret, and (*e*) reading in order to appreciate. These varieties of comprehension are the ever-present goals of reading instruction. They should not be postponed so that they have to be initiated at more advanced school levels. Detailed consideration will be given to these ways of learning in a later chapter.

Maturity in Adjusting to the Reading Demands of Each Discipline of Human Experience. In order best to impart their ideas to readers, authors develop ways of writing that are appropriate for their purpose and for what they have to say. For steady growth in reading proficiency, the child must learn to adjust his reading to the requirements of the type of material he is reading. One thinks, for instance, of the contrast between the kind of adjustment needed for reading and solving a verbal or formulated arithmetical problem and that for reading an easy short story. Such adjustments are achieved through a close-knit co-ordination of the basic reading proficiencies, the different abilities involved in comprehension and the study skills. The reader must choose from his repertory of abilities and skills just the ones which are most appropriate for reading effectively a particular selection for a specific purpose. Since the adjustment must be taught, it becomes a goal of reading instruction. A young child starts to develop a differential attack upon various types of reading material as soon as he reads a science unit in his basic reader or in a supplementary book. Versatility in this sort of adjustment improves from grade to grade. Teacher guidance should step in to help in making these adjustments. The achievement of facility in this differential attack becomes a goal of reading instruction at all instructional levels.

Breadth of Interest in Reading and Maturity of Taste in All Fields of Human Experience. This objective will seem obvious to teachers. To be successful, a reading program must go beyond development of both the basic and special abilities and the study skills. The child must also desire to read widely for enjoyment and profit. The amount, the variety, and the quality of what is read is the truest test of the quality of the teaching program. Guidance, beginning early and continuing through the instructional levels, should aim to provide the child with broad, permanent interests and good taste.

CONTEMPORARY TRENDS IN READING INSTRUCTION

Consideration of the changing concepts of reading during the past 50 years as well as of modern approaches to reading should result in better understanding of contemporary trends in reading instruction.

Changing Concepts of Reading

Concepts both of reading and of instructional practice have undergone changes during the past half century (Tinker, 175). The concepts of reading instruction considered desirable have shown greater changes than classroom practices. Around 1900 there was heavy emphasis upon mastering the mechanics of word recognition and fluent oral reading. By 1920 the emphasis was changing to teaching the attitudes and skills concerned with clear and rapid comprehension in silent reading. Further changes were evident by 1937. Writers on reading were then insisting that, in addition to perceiving words and grasping essential ideas, the proficient reader must reflect on their significance, interpret what is read, and grasp implications. That is, the reflective side of reading was receiving emphasis. Concepts of reading were expanding still further by 1948. It was then recognized that reading consists of a relatively large number of skills which vary in their application depending upon reading purpose, kind of material read, and values sought. Significance of attitudes in the pupil's interpretation of what is read, and the role of reading in personality development were also stressed. Throughout these years actual classroom practice in reading has lagged behind the kind of reading instruction considered desirable in terms of current needs. Many schools are 50 years behind the currently defined needs.

Modern Approaches to Reading Instruction

A variety of approaches to reading instruction are employed in present-day classroom practice. No one specific approach is suitable for all children or in all reading situations. As a matter of fact, teachers do not tend to confine themselves to a single approach in practice. Bond and Wagner (28) have described the six modern approaches listed below.

Reading instruction may consist primarily of teaching word recognition. Here the major task of reading instruction is assumed to be training which will promote effective recognition of isolated words. Realizing the important role of word recognition in reading, many teachers concentrate their instruction almost solely upon techniques for developing this. Placing major emphasis upon drill in word recognition has many serious limitations. The child tends to become overanalytical, and to lack fluency and understanding because he concentrates upon words rather than upon meanings. Since the method tends to be tedious and uninteresting, motivation for reading to learn is difficult to develop. Nevertheless, this method, in combination with other methods, is widely and effectively used in present-day reading instruction.

A second approach consists primarily of oral instruction. Here the assumption is that the words a child learns to read are a part of his oral vocabulary. Therefore instruction in reading is best achieved by relating reading to oral language. The child is urged to read aloud on all possible occasions. There is no attempt to suppress vocalization, particularly in the primary grades. The method has several weaknesses. Vocalization tends to become a fixed habit, the child reads aloud to himself, and encounters emotional blocking when asked to read material that is difficult. When we say this we do not mean that no oral reading should be done. An appropriate amount and kind of oral reading is desirable in any well-balanced program of reading instruction.

A third approach may consist of totally silent reading instruction. This completely non-oral approach excludes the use of any oral reading even in beginning instruction. It assumes that it is not necessary to relate visual symbols to spoken words in teaching reading. It is further held that inner speech is a serious handicap to effective silent reading. Buswell's study (32) demonstrated that non-oral reading instruction can be as effective as methods which make use of some oral reading, though it is no better. An important contribution of the non-oral method is the demonstration of ways to get children to read silently for meaning. Its main drawback is that very little use is made of the oral language which has developed during the pre-school period.

In a fourth approach, beginning instruction may be based primarily upon reading experience charts. A series of simple related sentences are organized by pupils with the guidance of the teacher. An experience chart is made which reports some recent experience of the pupils. Advantages include learning through doing, dealing with experiences real to the children and with words used in everyday conversation of the children. Certain weaknesses are inherent in the use of experience charts. The vocabulary burden is heavy, it is difficult to achieve enough repetition of words to make them a part of the sight vocabulary, and too frequently the quality of the material in the charts is rather poor. Experience charts, when used, should be employed only as a supplementary aid to learning.

In a fifth approach, reading becomes a thought-getting process centered around purposeful activities. Here reading instruction is organized into topical units. Purposes are clearly defined. The units are organized with materials of various levels of difficulty to facilitate adjustment of instruction to individual differences. Progress toward a goal is evident to the reader. Thoughtful and critical reading as well as interest are stimulated. The method permits development of versatility in applying abilities and skills according to kind of material read and according to the reading purposes.

Although this can be an effective instructional method, certain weaknesses may creep in. The program may become too difficult if too many units are included. Also there may be a tendency for the teacher to place insufficient emphasis upon development of effective word-recognition techniques and other skills. Tendencies to overemphasize fact-getting materials to the sacrifice of imaginative materials should be guarded against.

In a sixth approach, reading instruction consists of a well-organized co-ordination of all the other methods. The well-trained teacher will be familiar with the strengths and weaknesses of the methods discussed above. She will be able to integrate into her well-balanced instructional program, as the occasion demands, the strong points of each approach. By this means, she will be able to adjust her teaching to the needs of each and every pupil. It is this integration of approaches that the writers of this book advocate as most promising for developing proficient reading and at the same time keeping down the number of remedial cases.

THE "HALLMARK" OF A GOOD READER

The good reader is the one who has achieved a satisfactory degree of maturity in the development of his reading abilities, skills, interests, and tastes. By the time the sixth grade is finished, maturity in reading is indicated by the following accomplishments:

1. The essential techniques of word identification and recognition will have been mastered.

2. Vocabulary understanding will be extensive.

3. Comprehension will be effective.

4. A high degree of proficiency in the basic study skills will have been achieved.

5. The child will be versatile in adjusting his reading habits to variation in purposes and materials.

6. He will have acquired the attitude of demanding of himself an understanding of what is read.

7. He will have learned to interpret, evaluate, and reflect on what he has read.

8. Reading interests will be large and varied.

9. Progress will have been made in development of taste and appreciation along desirable lines.

10. The child's oral reading will be adequate for giving pleasure to others.

11. Reading will be employed extensively to satisfy the child's needs.

12. The foundations essential for building new skills needed in higher grades will have been established.

13. Since greater maturity is to be demanded in the high school grades, further learnings will be needed to perfect and extend those already acquired by the end of grade six.

SUMMARY

Reading involves the recognition of printed or written symbols which serve as stimuli for the recall of meanings acquired through past experience. New meanings are also obtained through manipulation of the concepts already possessed by the reader. The reading process involves, therefore, the acquisition of the meanings intended by the writer and, beyond these, certain interpretations, evaluations, and reflections about these meanings on the part of the reader.

Normal reading growth is developmental in nature. It begins with the acquisition of experience, facility in language, and a good emotional adjustment prior to entering school followed by training in readiness factors after school is begun. After proper preparation, the child is introduced to reading in grade one. He continues his progress in the basic reading abilities through the primary grades. In the intermediate grades the child perfects the basic reading abilities. This is accompanied by a greater concentration upon growth in the specialized abilities and skills needed for reading content subject matter.

Effective reading instruction involves progress toward several goals. Such goals include the basic understanding of words, sentences, paragraphs, and stories; maturity in reading habits and attitudes; independence in reading; efficiency in the use of the basic study skills; maturity in comprehension, which requires the use of several special abilities; maturity in adjusting to a variety of reading demands; breadth of reading interests and maturity in reading tastes.

Concepts of what constitutes adequate reading instruction have changed over the past 50 years. However, classroom practice in reading instruction has lagged behind what is considered desirable in terms of current needs.

There is variation in the modern approaches to reading instruction. The writers of this book consider that the best results will be obtained by instruction based upon an integration of several of the modern emphases.

SELECTED READINGS

BOND, Guy L., and WAGNER, Eva W., *Teaching the child to read,* rev. ed. New York: The Macmillan Company, 1950, Chaps. 1-4.

GATES, Arthur I., *The improvement of reading,* 3rd ed. New York: The Macmillan Company, 1947, Chap. 2.

HARRIS, Albert J., *How to increase reading ability,* 3rd ed. New York: Longmans, Green & Company, 1956, Chaps. 3, 4.

McKEE, Paul, *The teaching of reading in the elementary school.* Boston: Houghton Mifflin Company, 1948, Chaps. 1-4.

McKIM, Margaret G., *Guiding growth in reading.* New York: The Macmillan Company, 1955, Chaps. 1-2.

STRANG, Ruth, McCULLOUGH, Constance M., and TRAXLER, Arthur E., *Problems in the improvement of reading,* 2nd ed. New York: McGraw-Hill Book Company, Inc., 1955, Chaps. 1-6.

TINKER, Miles A., *Teaching elementary reading.* New York: Appleton-Century-Crofts, Inc., 1952, Chap. 1.

YOAKAM, Gerald A., *Basal reading instruction.* New York: McGraw-Hill Book Company, Inc., 1955, Chaps. 1-6.

3 ADJUSTING INSTRUCTION TO INDIVIDUAL DIFFERENCES

DEVELOPING the reading abilities described in the preceding chapter is a task which is neither easy nor simple. The acquisition of all the skills and abilities required for growth toward reading maturity necessitates a motivated and energetic learner. The maintenance of the most desirable balances among the skills and abilities essential to efficient growth demands an organized instructional program attuned to the needs and characteristics of each individual child being taught. The classroom teacher needs to be a keen student of the reading growth of each child so that any faulty learnings can be detected and corrected early, and in order that any omissions or overemphases can be avoided.

Importance of Awareness That Children Differ

A class made up of 30 to 40 children cannot be taught as though all members of the class had the same interests, desires, intellectual capabilities, or physical characteristics; nor can they be taught as though they had reached the same levels of attainment in reading or possess identical instructional needs. Any one child must be given material that is as nearly suitable to his level of reading growth as is possible. He must be taught by methods compatible with his characteristics and capabilities. For him, in addition, those phases of reading instruction must be emphasized that demand immediate attention. Reading instruction, to be effective, must proceed on an individual basis.

The teacher, however, is teaching a class and not just one child. Her problem is one of so organizing instruction that a class may be taught as a community with all members doing educationally worthwhile things. At the same time instruction must be adjusted to meet the needs and characteristics of individuals. In addition, instruction must be organized so that, for at least part of the time, the teacher is free to devote attention to those children needing special guidance. The problem of adjusting instruction to individual differences in large classes is probably the most difficult one faced by the teacher.

IMPROVED METHODS AND MATERIALS

Fortunately, today's elementary teachers are better prepared to adjust instruction to individual differences in reading than were teachers in the past. As a result of laboratory research and classroom tryouts, the teacher is equipped with teaching techniques far superior and more diversified than was the teacher just a few years ago. The teacher knows that reading skills and abilities are developed gradually over the years of elementary school in an orderly, systematic sequence. She also knows that a basic program of skill development is needed. The study of practices and procedures in classrooms in recent years has shown that progress in reading is not satisfactorily nurtured in an opportunistic or haphazard manner. The teacher of today is aware that reading growth is best developed in a classroom atmosphere which is businesslike, energetic, and knows where it is going. Learning situations which are based on a recognition of the complexity of the art of reading and which develop systematically the skills involved are the rule in today's classrooms.

Teachers of today are more aware of the individual instructional needs of children than were the teachers of the past. It was not unusual, in the past, to label a child as dull or mentally incompetent when really he was in a learning difficulty. Today teachers have better means of diagnosing individual needs than were formerly available. They are far better trained in the use of diagnostic procedures and can, as a result, prevent many serious reading problems from occurring. Teachers can better diagnose and correct those learning difficulties that do develop. Because teachers who have been recently trained have more refined measures of reading growth available than did the teachers of the past, they have more accurate information upon which to adjust the materials of instruction to whatever levels of competence exist in their classes. The results of testing programs are being made increasingly available to teachers so that instructional programs can be adjusted to meet the known needs of a class.

Basic reading materials have improved markedly over the last few years. They are much broader in types of reading experiences used to develop the skills and abilities. Programs designed a few years back, for example, were composed entirely of narrative type of content. More modern books show the child how to read what he is actually expected to read in other phases of the curriculum. They give him instruction in reading both narrative content and factual materials of science, social studies, and mathematics. The newer basic reading programs train the child in the study skills and they help him plan his own reading in all areas. In addition, an increasing number of basic and supplementary materials, written at varying levels of reading difficulty, suitable in interest to children of a given age, are being made available in recent publications.

The manuals and workbooks accompanying basic reading programs have more carefully planned exercises for developing skills and abilities than did those of just a few years ago. Not so long ago, it was assumed that the child could discover by himself the most effective ways of identifying new words and of organizing the material he was reading. Writers of modern manuals and workbooks are aware that few, if any, children develop well-balanced skills and abilities in reading unaided. Therefore the modern teacher not only has better materials available but also she is encouraged to use them to meet individual needs of the children in her class.

Teachers of today have a greater supply of supplementary reading materials than did their predecessors. Classroom and central libraries are well stocked with both narrative and factual materials dealing with the major topics introduced in basic readers. This fortunate circumstance is increasingly apparent at the more advanced levels of the elementary grades. The teacher in grade one, for the most part, must depend upon carefully controlled basal readers for both her basic and supplemental materials. But as the children mature in reading, there are an increasing number of related books available to supplement the basic reading program.

REASONS FOR INCREASED ATTENTION TO DIFFERENCES IN READING

It is fortunate indeed that the contemporary teacher is better equipped to adjust instruction to individual differences than was the teacher of the past. There are several reasons why it is well that this is so. First, awareness of the importance of education and of reading ability in modern society has made for a greater concern about the reading capability of the growing child than has ever been felt before. Second, children who get into difficulty in reading are no longer allowed to drop out of school, as of course they should not be. Therefore, every child who enters the first grade is expected to go on developing reading proficiency up to the level of his capabilities as he progresses through the elementary and secondary schools. Third, in addition to the fact that practically all children are retained in the schools, is the fact that reading ability is no longer used as the sole criterion for promotion. Children now, for the most part, are promoted in school so that they will be with other children of their own age, interests, and stage of total development. This policy in some respects makes the problem of adjusting reading instruction to individual differences more difficult. Fourth, improved instruction has increased the need for adjusting instruction to individual rates of growth. The only way to make children equal in reading ability is not to teach any of them. Then they would all have the same stature in reading— none of them would be able to read. But instruction that allows each child to grow as rapidly as he is able encourages differences in reading capability. Under improved instruction, a wide range in reading ability can be expected at any grade level. It would be unrealistic to expect children with divergent interests, with different backgrounds, and with unequal linguistic ability, physical stamina, hearing ability, vision, and intellect to grow at the same rate in such a complicated set of skills and abilities as those involved in learning to read.

A WIDE RANGE IN READING ABILITY IS
TO BE EXPECTED

At any grade level, then, it is reasonable to expect that there will be a wide range in reading ability. In the fifth grade, for example, it is quite normal to find a six- or seven-year difference between the least and the most competent reader. Such a range of reading ability within a fifth-grade class cannot and should not be prevented but it must be recognized and the appropriate adjustments made.

Failure to adjust the material and the instruction to the range of reading capability found within the classroom is probably the most important single cause of reading disability. Such failure limits the usefulness of the printed page as a tool of learning throughout the curriculum. The teacher, then, must know the reading capability and the varying instructional needs of each child. In addition, she must know the methods of making appropriate adjustments in class organization and in instruction to meet the range of reading talent and the variety of instructional needs.

Every teacher is aware of the fact that children grow in reading capability at different rates and that in any class there is a wide range of reading capabilities to be found. She knows that there is a vast difference in the difficulty of a paragraph that can be read and understood by the most able and the least able child within the class. Teachers know that some children read extensively and that others read very little. They know that many children initiate their own reading activities and that others must be urged to read. They know that some children read books of high quality and others appear to be satisfied with relatively immature writings. They are aware that some children read broadly and others confine themselves to a single type of reading or what satisfies a single interest.

It is small wonder that children grow at different rates. A child learns to read with his eyes, his ears, his energy output, his background of experience, his interests, drives, emotional stamina, and of course with the application of his intelligence. Any differences found within the children in any of these traits will make for differences in the rate at which they learn to read. The teachers know that it is quite normal for the children to have differences in auditory acuity, in physical stamina, and in intelligence. The problem of adjusting to individual differences is one of recognizing these differences as well as the varying rates of growth and of so adjusting materials and instruction that the child may be an energetic learner who is at ease, and it is hoped, absorbed in the learning situation. The instructional program should allow the child neither to dawdle nor to be placed in situations that are so difficult that he may become confused and discouraged.

Unfortunately, many teachers do not recognize the extent to which individual differences exist within their classrooms nor do they know the normal range of differences in reading to be expected in a typical class at the various grade levels. However, teachers are aware that each child varies in his own reading capabilities. They know that a certain boy, for example, is able to read and understand science at a relatively high level but that his oral reading of poetry is uninspired to say the least. They know that his speed of reading is not equal to his accuracy in reading. It is often evident that a given child is able to use the meaning of a sentence to help him recognize unfamiliar words, while his knowledge of phonetic elements may be limited. Another child may have a high degree of independence in working out words but he is unable to group them into thought units. The extent of these variations and their importance in making an adjustment to individual differences is frequently not fully understood.

How to adjust instruction to the individual differences that exist in any class will now be discussed under the following major headings:

1. Normal range of reading ability found in classrooms at different grade levels.
2. Basic considerations in adjusting to individual differences.
3. Current approaches in meeting individual differences in reading.

NORMAL RANGE OF READING ABILITY FOUND IN CLASSROOMS AT DIFFERENT GRADE LEVELS

In considering the normal range of reading ability at the different levels of instruction, it is important to recognize that what will be described is the range to be found in an average classroom, with ordinary children, using regular instructional methods and the usual materials. To the degree that any of the above are superior, the average reading capabilities of the children will be increased, as will also the range of reading ability found within the class. For example, if the materials used for instruction of an average class are considerably better than is usual, it can be expected that the class will achieve above average in reading performance. It can also be expected that the difference between the least able and the most able reader within the classroom will be increased. If the methods of instruction used by the teachers are superior and are adjusted to individual differences more than is customary, not only will the average reading performance of the class be bettered, but also the range of reading ability within the class will become greater. If the instruction is meager and restricted, the range of reading capabilities will also be restricted and the reading ability of the class in general can be expected to be inferior.

Figure 1 illustrates the normal range of reading ability found within typical classrooms at the various grade levels indicated. The figure is made by taking the distribution of grade scores achieved by several classes at each grade level at the beginning of the school year. The frequency distributions are superimposed one upon the other at each grade level and the characteristics of the frequency distribution determined. While the figures for each grade level were empirically arrived at, in certain instances, adjustments had to be made to force the observations to indicate the range at the start of a given year. For example, at fourth-grade level, the classes in question were slightly superior to the typical fourth-grade class and had a median score of 4.2. Therefore the distribution had to be corrected to make the median score 4.0, i.e., one typical for a beginning fourth-grade class. The authors do not feel that such minor adjustments alter the accuracy or value of the figure.

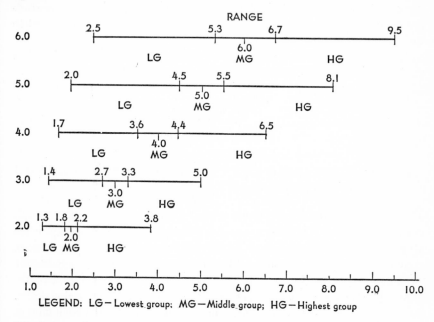

FIG. 1. Normal range of reading ability found in typical classrooms of grades two through six at the beginning of the school year.

The figure indicates the median of the scores made by the best readers of all of the classes at a given grade level. For example, in the class beginning the second grade, the class representing the 2.0 distribution, the median grade score of the best reader in each of the several classes was determined and the resultant score was 3.8 (eight months through the third grade). The figure illustrates also the median score of the poorest readers of the several classes at each grade level. In grade two, the median score made by the poorest readers was 1.3. Inasmuch as many teachers adjust to individual differences through grouping procedures and since the customary number of groups into which a class is divided is three, each distribution has been divided into thirds to show the typical make-up of the three groups the teacher has to handle. In the second grade, the middle third of the class ranges in reading ability from 1.8 to 2.2. Thus there is typically a four-month spread between the best and poorest reader in the middle group of readers in grade two.

In studying the figure, it should be noted that the range of reading capability increases as children progress through the elementary school. The total range between the best and poorest reader in the *generalized* second-grade class is two years and five months; in the third grade, the range is three years and six months; in the fourth grade, the range is four years and eight months; in the fifth grade, it is six years and one month; and in the sixth grade, it is seven years. These data approximate the range in reading ability that is usually found and that the teacher must be prepared to handle at the various grade levels.

Comparison of the ranges in reading ability shown in Figure 1 reveals a large degree of overlap in the reading capabilities of the children found in the various grades. For example, there are children entering grade two who read as competently as some of the children in the upper third of the children in grade three. There are also children in grade two who are reading approximately as well as children in the middle group of grade four. In addition there are some pupils in grade four who would be relatively poor readers in the lowest group of grade three, and they would be somewhat less than average readers in grade two. There are even children in grade six who read no better than the children in the poorest group of grade three, that is, those reading at grade 2.5.

In grade two, it should be noted that the range of reading ability in the upper third of the class is much greater than the range in the lower third. It should be observed also that as children progress through the grades, the distributions become progressively less restricted in the lower end of the distribution. It is likely that this condition is the result of starting slow-learning youngsters in the reading program relatively early. By the beginning of the second grade, they have made some progress in reading and therefore they are able to read as well as the usual youngster after three months of reading instruction. In a way, this is an artificial growth on their part. These youngsters have learned to read only a few words over the period of a year's time and therefore they are able to demonstrate about as much competence on a reading test as the typical child learns in three months. Probably it is questionable whether this is as permanent a learning as is that made by the typical child. As the years go on, these slow-learning children approach more nearly their true rate of growth.

Probably the most important information to be derived from Figure 1 is *the great range in reading talent that is to be found in the upper and lower groups when the class is divided into thirds.* Also, the fact that the middle group is relatively homogeneous in reading capability is important. In grade five, for example, it can be seen that the difference between the best and poorest reader in the upper third of the distribution is spread over two years and six months (2.6). Some members of this upper group will find themselves comfortable in books suited to typical children half-way through the fifth grade while others can read with profit books appropriate for the early part of grade eight (8.1).

The problem of adjusting to this wide range of reading capability in this upper group makes it important for the teacher to diversify instruction within the group. Likewise, the lower third of the fifth-grade class has a great range in reading ability—a range of two years and five months (2.5). Within this group there are youngsters who will find material suited to the typical beginning second-grader somewhat difficult. There are other youngsters within this same lowest group who can read with profit material suited to youngsters half way through the fourth grade. This lowest reading group, therefore, also needs a diversification of instruction to meet the wide range of reading capability.

The problem of adjusting instruction to fit the large range of reading ability found in the upper third and in the lower third of a fifth-grade class is, however, quite different. The children in the upper third of the distribution are competent, independent readers and the teacher, in adjusting to their individual differences, can lean heavily upon their proficiency and their independence. In adjusting to the large range found in the lower third of the distribution, the teacher finds the problem complicated by the fact that these children are somewhat less than competent and are not independent readers. The problem is made still more difficult in handling the lower reading group by the fact that there is not a wealth of reading materials which are suitable to their age level and their interest level, while remaining suitable to their reading level. This is not true for the upper group. There is an abundance of reading materials suitable for them.

Consider adjustment to the lower third of a typical fifth-grade class. If we use a textbook of fourth-grade difficulty in the basic reading instruction, it would be as suitable to the vast majority of the lower third of the class as the typical fifth-grade book is for the middle reading group.

Most of the children in the lower group read at between the 3.5 and 4.5 grade level, whereas the reading of the children in the middle group is btween the 4.5 and 5.5 level. There are only one or two children within a typical fifth-grade class who are reading at a lower level than 3.5. Under proper instruction, with suitable introduction of words, suitable building of readiness, and suitable establishing of purposes, the child with 3.5 reading ability can read a book suitable for the typical child with fourth-grade reading ability. There will be one or two children at the bottom of the distribution in the fifth-grade class who will require even more marked adjustments in their material and instruction.

Another interesting fact revealed by an examination of Figure 1 is that the best readers in any given group are always reading material that is, for them, relatively easy. Therefore, within any group, the more able readers in that group should be challenged to read more difficult materials through extending the reading program into supplemental and personal development reading activities.

BASIC CONSIDERATIONS IN ADJUSTING TO INDIVIDUAL DIFFERENCES IN READING

The problem of adjusting to the wide range in reading capability resulting from the different rates of growth found in any classroom has many dimensions. Each of these dimensions must be considered in formulating workable programs for adjusting to the individual differences in reading. Some of the current approaches to the problem of adjusting to individual differences in reading fail to take into account one or more of the important dimensions of the problem and are therefore to some degree inadequate or are an incomplete solution. Among the more important facts to be taken into account in formulating an instructional approach to individualization which will be discussed in the paragraphs that follow, are:

1. Children are alike in many ways.
2. Children grow in many ways other than in reading capability.
3. A given child's general growth curve in reading is not necessarily uniform.
4. Reading is a complex learning with many dimensions.
5. The problem and its solution change as we advance through the curriculum.
6. The problem changes according to the phase of the reading curriculum being considered.
7. The problem changes with changes in school organization.
8. The solution must be realistic in respect to the time it requires.
9. The adjustment must be based on a recognition that the teacher's energy and time for preparation are not unlimited.

The above facts must be recognized in formulating classroom organization and procedures to adjust to individual differences in reading. They are so crucial that the neglect of any one of them will seriously limit the adequacy of the adjustment. Quite obviously, an adjustment which so dissociates one child from another that the interplay of learnings is impossible, is unfortunate; or the approach that takes more of the teacher's time in preparation than is reasonable must be rejected; or the method that so freezes a child in a less advanced group that he cannot advance if his rate of learning accelerates, cannot be recommended. The suitability of adjustments to individual differences in reading, then, will be workable to the extent that the many dimensions of the problem are recognized and provided for.

Children Are Alike in Many Ways

A program of adjustment to individual differences in reading must recognize the similarities as well as the differences among children. Each child within the classroom is an important individual. He has many drives, motives, and desires. Children of any given age, for example, are quite likely to be interested in much the same things. Each child within a class needs to be recognized as an important member of this little community in which he spends such a large portion of his day. The poor reader as well as the good one must have friends and feel that he is an integral part of the class; that he has contributions to make to the class; and that he is not forced aside into any position of inferiority. Every child, then, should be helped to preserve his feelings of his own personal worth. Moreover, every child needs to feel that he is progressing in the important learnings that are taking place within the class. He needs to feel that he is becoming, day by day, a better reader even though he may recognize that his rate of growth in reading is somewhat slower than that of some other children. To the extent that the adjustment recognizes the personal worth of each child, allows the child to participate in important enterprises within the class, gives him a feeling of confidence, security, and well-being, and to the extent that it avoids stigmatizing the child, will it encourage comfortable, efficient growth in reading for all children.

Children Grow in Many Ways Other Than in Reading Capability

Children grow in many ways other than in reading and therefore any adjustments provided to allow for individual differences must take into account many characteristics of child growth and development other than level of attainment in reading. The elementary school child is changing in physical size, in social adaptability, and in interests. He is continually developing proficiencies in many skills and abilities.

It is sometimes asserted that the school system could regroup children so as to house all of those with the same reading needs within the same classroom so that the teacher could then use fairly uniform approaches in teaching them. This would not be a workable solution. The problem of adjusting to individual capabilities in reading would soon develop. Children might be equal in reading capability at the onset of instruction, but they would soon become heterogeneous. The differences in rates of reading growth would almost immediately show up. Moreover, these children so grouped would not be similar in any other characteristic if they were grouped according to reading ability. For example, in a class composed of children with fifth-grade reading ability, there would be great variation in their arithmetic ability; their interests would range from those of children of second- to ninth-grade age; the size of the chairs would need to range from those suitable for second-graders to those suitable for ninth-graders. There would be almost as great a range in chronological age within such a group of children classified according to reading ability as there is now in reading ability for children classified according to chronological age. They would not even be able to play together because of differences in age, size, and interests. Methods of adjustment, then, which place children of different ages and different interest levels within the same classroom are indeed unfortunate. Programs of adjustment that keep children, as nearly as possible, with other children of their own levels of over-all development are the ones that are most likely to be successful. Adjustment to individual differences in reading will have to be taken care of in ways other than homogeneous grouping according to reading ability.

A Child's General Growth Curve in Reading Is Not Necessarily Uniform

A given child's general growth curve in reading is not necessarily uniform, and any adjustment which does not provide for the possibility of moving the child from one group to another is unfortunate. One child, for example, may find reading a very difficult undertaking at the outset, but as he progresses he may accelerate his rate of growth. Such a child may have high general intelligence but be limited in auditory acuity. In such a case, the child would at the beginning find establishment of word-recognition techniques somewhat difficult. As a result his growth in reading would be slow. But as the program advanced and as the role of reasoning became increasingly important, the child's rate of growth in reading would become accelerated. Another child might start out being relatively good in the reading program as long as the building of basic sight vocabulary and word-recognition techniques were the important determiners of success. But were this child somewhat limited in the more complex reasoning abilities, such as ability to make accurate judgments and to visualize what is read, his rate of growth would taper off as the program at more mature levels began to place emphasis on these capabilities.

The correlation between intelligence and reading ability at the end of the first grade is relatively low, approximately .35. At the sixth-grade level, studies show this relationship has risen about .65. The difference between these correlations shows that the rate at which many children are attaining competence in reading is altering. To the extent that the organization within the classroom allows the child to grow in reading capacity comfortably and energetically and remains flexible enough to adjust for these varying rates of growth, good progress can be expected.

Reading Is a Complex Learning with Many Dimensions

Reading ability is not a specific or single attribute. It is made up of a hierarchy of many skills and abilities, attitudes, and tastes. A well-rounded basic reading program is designed to encourage relatively uniform growth for any given child in the many components of reading ability. Nonetheless, a study of the reading profiles of children indicates that no child develops the numerous skills, abilities, attitudes, interests, and tastes in a uniform manner. There will be marked differences in degree of maturity of reading development in the various outcomes of reading instruction for any given child.

A fifth-grade child, for example, may show as much as a difference of three or four years between his most mature reading capability and his least mature one. He may have a high degree of proficiency in using word-recognition techniques, but his ability to read to understand the fundamental idea in a selection may be relatively immature. Or he may, given an unlimited time, be able to work out words independently as well as the usual seventh-grader, while his fluency in understanding what the passage is about may be equal only to that of the beginning third-grader. Another child may be relatively efficient in reading material of the narrative type, but he may be relatively ineffective in reading materials in the content fields. Such uneven profiles of reading, brought about through the complex nature of the learning, are unfortunate and indicate the need for corrective work with these children.

That child would be rare indeed whose area of best performance and area of worst performance in the complex task of learning to read is separated by less than a year. The adjusted reading program, therefore, must be flexible enough to adjust to the differences in reading capabilities found within the individual child. The program of individualization cannot be so formalized that the adjustments cannot vary according to the type of reading done at a given time. The child with poor ability to understand the general idea of a passage should get considerably more exposure to that type of reading than he does to the word-recognition exercises in the basic program. And the child who reads narrative material satisfactorily but is poor at reading study-type material of a content field must have the level of difficulty of the latter material adjusted to his ability to read it. His basic reading program should be adjusted to emphasize the development of the study-type comprehension abilities and the application of these in reading content material.

A reading program designed to meet the individual needs of children, then, must not only take into account the range of general reading capability found within a classroom, but it must also take into account the characteristics of the growth pattern in the reading of each child. Programs of measurement should be able to detect such differences and programs of adjustment should allow for these differences within children. Undoubtedly, the complex nature of reading and the resultant unevenness in the growth patterns of individuals make the task of adjusting to individual differences in reading a difficult one. The teacher can hope for success in this task only by knowing the reading profiles of the students she is teaching and by utilizing materials and methods which facilitate individual adjustments.

The Problem and Its Solution Change as We Advance Through the Curriculum

The problem of adjusting to individual differences changes in at least three ways as we advance through the school years. In the *first place,* the range of reading capability found within any classroom increases as the children become more and more proficient in reading. For example, it will be recalled that in Figure 1, the beginning second-grade class had a range of reading capability of two and a half years; while the beginning sixth-grade class had a range of approximately seven years. This difference in range does not necessarily mean that the sixth-grade teacher has a more difficult problem of adjusting to individual differences than does the second-grade teacher. It does mean, however, that there will have to be a greater difference between the level of difficulty in the materials used in the sixth-grade class than there will in the materials of the second-grade class. An inspection of the difference between the material that the average fourth-grader can read and the material that the average sixth-grader can read will not be as apparent as is the difference between material that an average second-grade child can read and material that a child approximately half-way through the first grade can read. The amount of reading growth that takes place in the early grades is startling indeed and the fineness of adjustment required to meet the reading capabilities within a second-grade class is more demanding than is the adjustment needed to meet the range of reading capabilities in the sixth grade.

The *second way* in which adjustment to individual differences changes through the grades will be found in the relative independence of children in the sixth grade as contrasted with children in the second grade. The teacher in the second grade has very few readers within her class who can be called independent readers, while the teacher in the sixth grade will find that the upper two-thirds of her class are relatively independent readers and that only the lower third of the class lacks some degree of independence. The fact that there are many independent readers in a sixth-grade class does not mean that adjustment to individual needs is not necessary, but it does mean that the teacher there can rely more upon individual assignments that can be done independently. In the basic reading program, however, where skills and abilities are being developed, the problem of the sixth-grade teacher is very similar to that of the second-grade teacher.

The need for basic reading instruction is not lessened as the child advances through his school years. The teacher of the intermediate grades must be alert to the need for adjusting to the level of development in reading skills and abilities of each child. She must be aware of the need for adjusting to the range of capabilities within the individual child and she must be aware of the importance of identifying the reading needs of each child and of giving systematic instruction to insure balanced growth. It cannot be overemphasized that a systematic, well-organized basic program of instruction in reading is essential in the intermediate grades and that the teacher will cause reading disabilities if this systematic reading instruction is not given. Incidental reading instruction with social studies material, for example, will not suffice.

Another way in which adjustment to individual differences changes as children progress through the grades is in the amount of suitable reading material that is available. The teacher in the intermediate grades has a greater wealth of material available, at various levels of readability, suitable to the range of reading talent found within these grades than does the primary teacher. It must be remembered that the poorest group of readers in a sixth-grade class are as mature readers as the children who are the most competent readers in a beginning second-grade class. Many materials are available in the upper elementary grades which are suitable even to the poorest readers in the class, whereas, in a second-grade class, there are very few, if any, materials outside of basic pre-primers and primers that can be read by children in the lower third of the class in reading competency.

In formulating programs for adjusting to individual differences, it is essential to recognize the changes in the problem that take place throughout the school years. It is fortunate indeed that as the range of reading capability increases, the independence of the children within the class is increasing also and that there is more suitable material available. Another thing that should be remembered is that at all levels of instruction there is an abundance of materials suitable for the capable readers. The problem is a difficult one only in the case of the poor readers. Fortunately, the number of books suitable for poor readers increases in the higher grades.

The Problem Changes According to the Phase of the Reading Curriculum Being Considered

The child must, at all levels of advancement, have at least four types of reading experiences if he is to become a proficient reader. *First,* he must progress through a carefully controlled set of reading experiences and exercises designed to show him how to go about reading. This is the basic program of reading instruction. It is composed of a set of well-organized materials with suggested exercises that enable a competent teacher to develop in her pupils the essential skills and abilities. *Second,* he must participate in those reading experiences in which he is using reading as an aid to developing understandings and knowledges within other subject-matter areas. *Third,* he must have reading experiences designed to enhance his own personal development, his own interests and tastes. These are experiences designed to give him broad contacts with children's literature, to enhance his understanding of himself, to increase his awareness of social relationships, and to develop his aesthetic appreciations. *Fourth,* he must have experiences designed to correct reading faults he may have established.

This phase of the program can be described as re-educative or corrective. There is probably no child who, from time to time, does not make faulty learnings in regard to reading, or who does not need a greater emphasis on some reading skill or ability.

The adjustment to individual needs and capabilities in each of these phases of the reading program constitutes a different problem. Adjustments that are suitable to one phase of the broad reading curriculum are not necessarily suitable to another. The task of adjusting to individual differences in reading is different, for example, if we are considering that part of the child's reading experiences in which the fundamental purpose is to develop skills and abilities in reading than it is if the fundamental purpose of reading is to develop an understanding of the content of the social studies. The goals set by the teacher in these two situations would be somewhat different. When the teacher is teaching social studies, her primary concern is with developing the outcomes of social studies instruction even though the children are using books for this purpose. When the teacher is teaching reading, her primary concern must be the development of skills and abilities in reading even though the children may be reading in their basic readers material of the social studies type. It would be unfortunate indeed if teachers thought that reading skills and abilities could be developed incidentally while the basic purpose was learning the subject matter of any of the content fields. It would be equally unfortunate if the basic reading program failed to give systematic instruction in the skills and abilities necessary to read materials of the social studies.

In summary, adjustment in the four types of reading experience, then, is dictated by the nature of the outcomes expected and the use to which reading is to be put. In the basic reading program, some form of group instruction is advisable. In the second type, reading in the other branches of the curriculum, it is likely that the experience curriculum or topical unit approach is desirable. In reading for personal development, a highly individualized approach emphasizing the "right book for the right child" is most feasible.

In the re-education or remedial phase of the program, the nature of the skill that needs attention prescribes the type of instruction needed and who among the children should work together at it. Much of the controversy over the most effective way to adjust to individual differences stems from the fact that proponents for one type of adjustment over another are actually concerned with one particular phase of the reading program which especially interests them. Of course it should be borne in mind that these different phases are not completely discrete. For example, when the children are engaged in a social studies lesson, the teacher may discern that certain children are having difficulty in locating places on a map and she may surmise that the cause of their difficulty is that they are ineffective in interpreting the marginal key numbers and letters. The teacher would call these children aside and give them re-education in regard to this skill needed in map reading. Although this particular skill was taken up in the basic reading program in an orderly and systematic way, for some reason or other these children failed to learn it.

It is not necessary to go into all the interrelationships among the four phases of the reading curriculum. Sufficient to say at this time that the adjustment to individual differences varies according to each phase of the reading curriculum.

The Problem Changes With Changes in School Organization

As the child progresses through the grades, the school organization changes. The almost universal type of organization found in the primary grades is a self-contained classroom. The teacher is responsible for all of the learning activities in which the primary classes are engaged. In the intermediate grades, there are slight modifications of this approach. Though for the most part, these classes are self-contained, just as in the primary grades, in some school systems there are special teachers to handle music, art, physical education, or other specialized areas. In some school systems, there are platoon arrangements where teachers devote their entire day to teaching arithmetic, reading, or some other subject. In most junior high schools, the children have a different teacher for every subject.

The problem of adjusting to individual differences in reading is different depending upon the way the school is organized. The task in a graded elementary school is somewhat different from that in a one-room rural school. It may well be that the teacher in a one-room rural school is forced to face the problem of adjusting to individual differences more realistically than is, for example, the teacher in a fifth-grade classroom, even though the fifth-grade class will encompass practically all the levels of reading growth that are usually found in the typical one-room school. The graded classroom teacher has one advantage, however, and that is, that the interests of the children, the size of the children, and the ages of the children are more uniform.

In the junior high school, the problem of understanding a child as fully as is necessary for adjusting to his reading needs is more difficult than it is in the primary grades. This is so because the junior high school teacher may be teaching as many as 150 different children in five classes for an hour a day, while the primary teacher lives rather closely with some 30 or 35 children during the whole day. It is fortunate, indeed, that the onset of reading growth takes place in a situation in which the teacher and 30 children live and work together throughout the entire school day because a detailed understanding of the child's interests, his needs, drives, and levels of reading competency are necessary if proper provision for his reading needs is to be made. The application of this detailed information is especially crucial when the child is a relatively immature and dependent learner.

The problem of adjusting to individual differences in the graded elementary school is somewhat complicated by the fact that the teacher has the children for only one year and each succeeding teacher must learn the needs of each child. The rural teacher has the advantage of developing the child's growth for a period of years.

As was said, differences in school organization can complicate the problem of making recommendations for adjusting to individual differences. In the junior and senior high schools, the need for guidance programs to collect information about the children and to see that it reaches the teachers who must make the adjustments must be met. This is not so essential a recommendation in the primary grades, for the teacher in this case can closely observe her 30 children throughout the year. The recommendation for collecting and disseminating cumulative information in the graded elementary school is probably more pertinent than it would be in the rural elementary school where the teacher has the same children over a period of years.

The Solution Must Be Realistic in Respect to the Time It Requires

In considering suitable methods of adjusting to individual differences in reading, the question of the time it requires becomes exceedingly important. The time that can be devoted to basic instruction in reading, for example, is limited. At all levels of instruction, other learnings are taking place during the school day and the efficient use of time in all of the school activities is serious business—reading is no exception. Those methods of adjustment then, that make undue demands either on the teacher's instructional time or the class's working time must be rejected. A teacher with 35 children must organize her class in the most efficient way. She cannot, for example, devote her entire time to developing reading skills and abilities for just one child at the expense of the other members of the class, no matter how urgent his need.

Programs that recommend that each child should have a different book suitable to his individual needs for basic instruction are unrealistic in their time requirements. It is necessary for the teacher, in developing reading skills and abilities, to introduce the material, to establish purposes, to develop the background, to introduce the new vocabulary, to guide the reading through the asking of pertinent questions, to discuss the selection after it is read, and to utilize comprehension exercises related to the selection read. In addition, the new words must be used in relationship to previously learned words in order to develop word-recognition techniques, and the selection must be used in a creative fashion so that the children feel they have completed the experience. Faced with such instructional demands, it is apparent that the teacher cannot have each child reading a different book while she is teaching the class to develop the skills and abilities in reading. There simply would not be enough time. If we were to assume that the teacher devoted an hour a day to systematic instruction in reading development, she would have somewhat less than two minutes in which to accomplish the fundamentals of reading instruction for each different selection that some 35 children were reading.

Because of the time factor, some form of grouping the children for basic reading instruction is often recommended. It must be recognized that even if the class is divided into three groups, each reading a different topic, the teacher who devotes one hour a day to basic reading instruction can spend only twenty minutes in instructing each of the three groups. In order to make instruction more efficient, it is recommended that the three groups of children read on a common topic in materials written at different levels of difficulty. Since the whole class is dealing with one topic rather than three, the time used for developing readiness, developing backgrounds, developing interest, introducing new words, doing the creative activities, discussing and evaluating what has been accomplished can be utilized more effectively.

Whatever method of adjusting to individual differences in reading is adopted, the efficient use of teacher and class time must receive careful consideration.

The Adjustment Must Be Based on a Recognition That the Teacher's Energy and Time for Preparation Are Not Unlimited

The methods of adjusting to individual differences and the class organization adopted must be realistic in limiting demands placed upon the teacher. Sometimes it is suggested, for example, that teachers prepare the specific exercises to correct a faulty learning or to reinforce skills and abilities that the children have only partially learned. Such recommendations are justified. But, if the teacher were to prepare materials to meet all of the re-educative or reinforcing needs of a class of 35 youngsters, she would need more than a 24-hour day. The use of workbooks accompanying basal readers, suitable to the child's level of development, is recommended as one means of saving the teacher's energy and preparation time.

Under certain methods of group instruction in the basal reading program, the teacher is expected to be teaching three rather discrete classes in reading and is therefore expected to make three preparations. This preparation involves the collection of pictures and other means of developing readiness, background, interest, and understanding of word meanings. Her preparation also includes the analysis of the stories or selections to be read by each group. In addition, it involves the preparation necessary to develop the specific comprehension abilities and word-recognition techniques for three separate lessons. It involves the collection of three separate sets of related reading materials and planning three separate activities related to what is being read. It is questionable whether this method of group instruction uses the teacher's energy and preparation time effectively. It is easy to see, on the other hand, that when children read the same identical content in material at different levels of reading difficulty, a more efficient use is made of both class time and teacher time.

Though there are many plans for adjusting to individual differences in reading, whatever plan is used, the fact that the teacher is a person whose time and energy are not unlimited must be taken into account. Also the fact that the children like to work and do things together must be recognized. It must be remembered when formulating the approach to basic reading instruction that the children are growing in many ways other than in reading capability; that their growth curves are not necessarily uniform; that reading is a very complex learning; and that class time is not unlimited. All these considerations have to be taken into account when planning adjustments to individual rates of growth in reading.

CURRENT APPROACHES IN MEETING INDIVIDUAL DIFFERENCES IN READING

A major responsibility of the school is to develop each child up to the limit of his own capability. Any failure in the teaching program to adjust to individual differences in reading thwarts this aim in two ways: *first,* failure to adjust materials and methods in reading instruction to the range of reading capability found within any classroom will impede growth in reading; *second,* failure to adjust the difficulty of reading material to the known reading capabilities of the individual pupils in the classroom reduces the usefulness of printed material as an aid to learning in all of the curricular areas. In addition, material which does not challenge the capable learners in the various content areas, limits the possibility of superior achievement within those areas for the brighter children and also it limits their growth in reading. Exposing the less able readers to materials that are too difficult, cuts down for them the usefulness of printed material as an aid to learning and it can cause serious confusions and rejection of reading as well, thereby causing disability in learning to read.

The entire reading curriculum of the children within a classroom must be adjusted to their individual reading capabilities if the printed page is to become an effective tool of learning and if reading disability is to be prevented. A fifth-grade child, for example, who can read material of seventh-grade difficulty with ease and profit, should have many reading experiences at that level of difficulty. A fifth-grade child who is unable to read third-grade material comfortably will not profit much from holding a fifth-grade book in his hands and staring at it. He would profit from reading a book more in keeping with his reading capabilities.

Individual differences in reading must be provided for throughout the curriculum if printed material is to become an effective aid to learning for all the members of the class and if maximum growth in reading is to be achieved. The adjustment of instruction to individual differences in reading is much more than an approach. It is a combination of approaches and adaptations of methods of instruction that encourages individual rates of growth. According to Bond and Wagner (28),[1] adjustment of instruction must be based on

an attitude in which the teacher assumes that each child has the right to progress as rapidly as he is capable, that each child can expect the school to provide for his rate of learning be it slow or fast, and that each child can expect the school to study him as an individual and to help him when he is in difficulty. Anyone with a belief in individualized instruction would have but little in common with the teacher who said that her greatest problem in teaching a class in reading was to keep the children on the same lesson in the same book; with the teacher who has the children read aloud in turn, paragraph after paragraph, page after page; or, with the teacher who penalizes the good reader who reads ahead because he cannot wait for a slow reader to unfold the story for him; or with the teacher who assumes that there is one best method for teaching all children. The attitude of adjustment of instruction to individual differences can be accomplished only with methods and classroom procedures which are in keeping with and which make possible the full use of differences in ability to learn. It becomes the teacher's responsibility, then, to select and to adjust her methods so that they make possible adaptations of instruction in reading to individual differences, which are so apparent among children.

The adjustment to differences must recognize the fact that a given child has many differences within himself and that he has strengths as well as weaknesses. Lazar (119) says,

It implies, too, a positive attitude toward individual differences, a respect for them, a realization that since society is enriched by the diversity of talents, interests, aptitudes, and skills of its people, the schools should serve to cultivate rather than to level these differences.[2]

The various approaches to meeting individual differences in the teaching of reading are difficult to discuss and to evaluate because each phase of the reading curriculum constitutes a special set of problems. The basic program in reading is probably the most complex one in the curriculum in the matter of adjusting to individual differences. This phase of the curriculum must assume the responsibility for developing in an orderly, sequential manner the skills and abilities needed for success in all the other reading activities. The adjustment to individual differences in the basic reading program must be such that there is little chance for gaps in learning, for overemphases resulting in loss of balance among the skills and abilities, and for the per-

[1] From G. L. Bond and E. B. Wagner, *Teaching the child to read,* rev. ed. New York: The Macmillan Company, 1950. Used with the permission of The Macmillan Company.

[2] May Lazar, *Individualization of instruction in reading.* Educational Research Bulletin No. 1. New York: Board of Education of the City of New York, 1941.

sistence of faulty habits with consequent confusions and deterioration of reading progress. In those situations in which reading is used as an aid to learning, the task of adjusting to individual differences in reading is considerably less complex and resolves itself into bringing children and books realistically together so that the topics under consideration can be effectively studied. In personal development reading, the problem is still less complex. This phase of the reading curriculum can be made a highly individual matter with guided reading programs where children and books are individually brought together according to a child's level of reading maturity, interest, personal growth, needs, and the like. In this case, neither the maintenance of an orderly sequence of skill development nor the development of the knowledges and understandings of a curricular field need to be considered. The sole problem here is that of guiding each child into books that he can read comfortably and with pleasure and that develop him as a person.

In adjusting to individual differences in reading, the importance of finding suitable material for every reading situation cannot be overemphasized. In all of his reading experiences, the child must have material that he can read and read effectively. Naturally, at times, there should be material with which he must tussle, but he must be able to win the tussle. In this way he will increase his stature in reading. At other times, and probably more often, he must read material which causes him little or no difficulty. It is through such reading experiences that he gains fluency and the ability to attend to the ideas of the author rather than to the reading task.

In the basic reading program, the difficulty of the material is ever increasing and as soon as the child is really comfortable, the difficulty is increased so that the learner is challenged to grow. Fortunately, this material is well introduced, the difficulties are anticipated, and instruction on how to proceed is given.

Materials that the child reads independently in other phases of the curriculum should be somewhat less difficult, for the most part, than those in his basal reading program. This is especially true of the guided reading program. The teacher does not have time to give the necessary instruction in reading for 35 different references to the extent that this instruction is given for the basic readers; nor can there be 35 individual discussions of the results of reading and clarification of ideas. The teacher would find it difficult indeed to so appraise the independent reading of each of 35 children that she could locate every misunderstanding, find the causes of each, and give the necessary instruction to overcome the confusions, whereas this is a necessary part of basic instruction in reading. The materials, then, for both the content fields and for personal development reading should be at such a level of difficulty that they can be studied and read independently without the likelihood of faulty reading.

There are many ways in which the problem of adjusting to individual differences in the program of basic instruction in reading can be attacked.

As yet a fully adequate solution to the problem has not been found and maybe it never will be found. The approaches are becoming broader and more successful, however. Among those that warrant consideration are the following:

1. Retardation and acceleration
2. Curriculum adjustment plans
3. Fixed grouping plans
4. Flexible grouping plans,

Retardation and Acceleration

In the past, retardation and acceleration was considered an effective and sensible approach to solving the problem of individual differences in reading. If a child were quick in learning to read, he was skipped a grade. If he found reading difficult and progressed slowly, he was retained in the grade for another year. The main criterion for retardation or acceleration was the child's success in learning to read. According to Percival (138), over 99 per cent of the failures in the first grade were in reality reading failures and 90 per cent of retardation in the first three grades was due to the child's slow progress in reading.

There are two immediately apparent results of inflexible promotion policies based upon achievement. The first is that the teachers need to make adjustments to children with a wide range in chronological ages. In Table 1, Goodenough (88) indicates the age range that was found in

Table I

AGE-GRADE DISTRIBUTION
OF 11,769 CHILDREN IN THE ELEMENTARY SCHOOLS OF
DAYTON, OHIO, DURING THE SCHOOL YEAR OF 1912-1913

| | AGE | | | | | | | | | | | | | % 3 OR MORE YEARS OVER-AGE |
GRADE	5	6	7	8	9	10	11	12	13	14	15	16	17	
I	309	1308	451	128	52	11	6	4	2	1	..	..	..	3.3
II	..	203	906	372	115	52	30	8	..	2	..	..	..	5.5
III	..	..	188	823	455	169	73	45	19	2	2	..	..	7.9
IV	..	..	..	168	621	414	224	133	43	19	2	2	..	11.1
V	..	..	..	2	179	475	307	236	111	51	6	1	..	12.3
VI	..	..	..	..	4	148	439	344	166	69	16	5	1	7.6
VII	..	..	..	..	..	8	158	430	318	159	26	5	..	2.8
VIII	..	..	..	..	..	..	8	104	334	221	84	10	2	1.6

Used with permission of the Research Division of the Board of Education, Dayton, Ohio.

Dayton, Ohio, for the school years 1912-1913 when this promotion practice was the custom. While the children of grade three, for example, may have been somewhat comparable in regard to reading ability, there was a wide range of variation in all the other aspects of their growth and development. The teacher's problem of adjustment was more difficult then than is the problem confronted by the present-day teacher where chronological age is more constant and the adjustment is made to achievement. The second result of inflexible promotion policies according to achievement is that as the children become more and more overage they drop out of school without having achieved an adequate education.

Under such promotion policies, the child who learned to read rapidly was advanced in keeping with his general reading ability. He might have been of fourth-grade age, but he sat in a sixth-grade classroom. He might in general have had as much ability as some of his classmates, and certainly more than others, but he was not of the same age, emotional and physical development, nor did he have the same interests. He would not have been able to work independently as well as the older children and almost certainly he would not have had as broad experiences as the other members of the class. It is questionable whether he would have been suited to the more advanced class in reading because he lacked breadth of experience in reading and he would have been suited to the class in few if any other respects. The problem of the overage child was just as great. If, for example, a 13-year-old boy, because of low achievement, found himself in a class situation in which most of the children were 8 years old, he would have been unacceptable to the group and would have been misplaced in all other respects.

Few modern educators would assume that these promotion policies could have anything other than unfortunate effects. Even more moderate degrees of retardation and acceleration have not proven effective in adjusting to individual differences in achievement. The findings of W. W. Cook (38),[3] showing how futile it is to base a promotion policy on varying rates of growth in reading and other achievements, were summarized as follows:

1. The evidence supports rather conclusively the contention that schools with a relatively high percentage of failures tend to have a relatively high proportion of overage, slow-learning pupils.

2. In these schools, the high percentage of overage pupils who have been retained through failure reduces both the average intelligence of the classes and the achievement averages of the grades, when compared with schools having more lenient standards of promotion.

3. When the achievements of pupils of equal chronological age and mental age in the two groups of schools are compared, no difference is found.

4. When the variability of classes is compared with respect to mental age and eleven educational achievement fields, no significant difference is found between the two groups of schools.

5. The evidence supports the conclusion that by failing slow-learning pupils a school cannot increase its grade achievement averages or reduce the variation of achievement found in individual classes.

[3] From Walter W. Cook, *Grouping and promotion in the elementary schools.* Series on individualization of instruction, No. 2. Minneapolis: University of Minnesota Press, 1941.

Cook concluded that

The hypothesis that pupils of low achievement accomplish more when retained in grade groups more nearly representative of their level of ability is not supported by the evidence presented in this study. As far as achievement and personality development are concerned, the crucial issue appears to be not whether the slow-learning pupil is passed or failed but how adequately his needs are met wherever he is placed. No promotion practice, be it universal promotion or the maintenance of high achievement standards, really comes to grips with the vital problem of educational and personality adjustment, with the problem of furnishing each teacher suitable instructional materials, teaching procedures, and point of view to enable her to cope with a range of ability of from six to ten years in her class.[4]

Retardation and acceleration will not solve the problems of adjustment to individual differences. Wherever a child is placed, the teacher must adjust the instruction to him and whether he is retarded or accelerated, procedure must be justified upon criteria much broader than achievement alone.

A specialized type of retardation and acceleration is sometimes recommended. This suggestion is that children can be placed in reading classes according to their reading achievement while for the rest of the time they meet in their regular classes. For example, all the children who can read at fourth-grade level are placed in one class for reading instruction. They are taught with fourth-grade material. Children so assigned would come from grades ranging from second to sixth. As a method of adjusting to individual differences in reading, this program has serious limitations. Some of its limitations are:

1. The teacher of the regular class will still have the problem of adjusting to individual differences in reading in all other areas of the curriculum.

2. The reading program would not be synchronized with the curriculum as a whole. For example, fourth-grade social studies units in the reading program do not deal with topics of importance to the sixth-grade social studies curriculum.

3. The age range is unfortunate. Children of second-grade age and those of sixth-grade age have little in common.

4. As time goes on, differences in reading ability among children so grouped would increase, and before long they would not be a homogeneous fourth-grade reading group.

5. Even at the start, the instructional needs of the second-grade child who has general fourth-grade reading ability are quite different from those of the sixth-grader who has general fourth-grade reading ability.

Any policy of retardation and acceleration based on achievement neglects many of the basic considerations necessary to a proper adjustment to individual differences in reading. In the first place, it neglects the fact that

4 *Ibid.*

children of a given age level will be alike in many ways, that children grow in many particulars other than in reading capability, and that a given child's growth curve is not necessarily uniform. Because of these facts, he may be drastically misplaced. It also neglects the fact that reading is a complex learning with many dimensions and that the child needs breadth in the types of reading he can do as well as altitude in level of general comprehension. Any plan of adjustment that neglects so many important considerations is unworkable.

Curriculum Adjustment Plans

Many plans of manipulating the curriculum have been used to adjust to individual differences in reading. Some of these approaches to the problem were unsuccessful because they failed to take into account some of the basic considerations in adjusting to differences in reading. Some of them were not effective because they assumed a smaller range of reading capability than is actually found within the typical class.

Plans such as the *Dalton, Winnetka,* and *Pueblo* separated the content of the curriculum into specific lessons and permitted each child to progress at his own rate. These plans neglected to note the fact that children are alike in many ways and that they learn better when sharing experiences and that the problem and its solution change at different levels of the curriculum. Such plans might be better suited to the college level than to the early elementary school grades. Children at the primary level cannot work independently for long periods of time when developing basic skills and abilities in reading and they must work under the close direction of the teacher. Therefore, these approaches were unrealistic because they did not take child growth and development into account nor the changes at different levels of the curriculum. Likewise they did not face up to the limits of the teacher's time and energy.

Plans such as the *Cambridge, Denver,* and *North Portland* plans attempted to solve the problems of adjustment with a uniform curriculum, uniform goals, and using uniform materials, but varying the length of time used by the slow, medium, and fast students. The fundamental objective of these plans was to bring the slower students up to grade, that is, to restrict the range of capability within the class. These plans neglected to take into account the wide range of reading ability and the differential rate of growth found within a class. Children within a classroom are so vastly different in reading capability that materials suitable in difficulty to the able group would be so difficult for the least able group that it would be impossible for them to read these materials no matter how much time was made available during the day. These plans of adjustment are based on the assumption that the materials and the outcomes of instruction are fixed and cannot be altered. Such assumptions are erroneous—neither the outcomes nor the materials of instruction need to be inflexible. Many children cannot be expected to equal all the reading achievements of the average child. Other children will be certain to achieve much greater maturity and breadth in reading programs than can be expected of the average child. Therefore, some of the adjustments to individual differences in reading will come through recognizing the inevitability of differential outcomes. The materials are not necessarily fixed in difficulty either. Studies in readability have shown the many factors that make materials difficult. The same basic ideas and concepts can be written at various levels of reading difficulty. An acceptance of these differences in materials and outcomes will open new approaches to solving the problem of individual differences in reading within a classroom.

Grouping Plans

Many plans for grouping individuals for reading instruction have been used. Methods of grouping children according to their reading ability have followed three general patterns.

1. Children may be grouped into classes according to general mental ability.
2. Children may be placed in fixed reading groups within a class.
3. Children may be placed in flexible groups within a class.

Grouping according to general mental ability is a method of adjustment that is frequently used. In schools having several classes at any grade level, children have been allocated within classes according to their intellectual capability. For example, one class would be composed of very able students; a second class, of the average children; and a third class, of children with less than average ability. The basis of these groupings is usually intelligence. There is no question that such a procedure does limit, to some extent, the range of reading capability found within the classroom. However, the reduction in range is not as great as might be expected. Research by both Hull (106) and Hollingshead (104) shows that such grouping restricts the range of reading ability only about 20 per cent, so that the teacher still has the problem of adjusting her instruction to individual differences within the class. This approach to adjustment to individual differences has several serious limitations:

1. It is suitable only to larger schools.
2. It is probably more suitable to advanced levels of education than it is to the elementary school.
3. It is based on the assumptions that the groups will be homogeneous in such characteristics as reading ability and that the teacher can teach the class as a whole. Research has shown this assumption to be unwarranted.
4. It does not recognize that children grow in many ways and that they vary considerably in trait differences.

If proper adjustments and methods are used in heterogeneous classes, the progress of all the children is stepped up when they work together, no matter what their level of capability is. Able children learn to use their creative ability and their investigative talents for the benefit of the entire group. They discover that even though they may be able to read somewhat better than another child, the other child may be able to sing better or to construct nicer things. The less able child can gain much from the class discussions and can profit from the enrichment brought to him by the more able children in his class. Of course such outcomes result only if the class is working on problems in common and if the children are not set apart too drastically in instructional groups within the class.

Fixed reading groups within a class is the most common practice followed by teachers who want to individualize instruction in reading. Fixed grouping within the class may have serious limitations that must be avoided if grouping procedures are not to cause more difficulties than they correct. A first disadvantage is that the groups are so separated that the class can rarely find an opportunity to work together as a whole. This sort of separation has unfortunate results for the lower and upper groups. The children in the lower groups cannot help but develop feelings of inferiority. When the teacher, day after day, turns to the top group to obtain a correct answer to a question, these feelings are going to be increased. Seating the children in groups according to their reading capabilities tends to make such an occurrence more apparent and even more frequent. This also tends to dramatize unwisely the class grouping. Calling the groups by names which indicate superiority is certainly unfortunate. Such names as the oaks, the willows, and the saplings should be avoided.

A second disadvantage of fixed grouping arises out of the fact that the reading materials used, in many instances, are dealing with different content. In a third-grade class, for example, the teacher might have the lower group reading in a book of second-grade difficulty. These children might be reading a unit on community helpers. The teacher would find it necessary to build readiness for the unit on this topic, to introduce the new words that would be met, to plan with the group the reading and activities that were to be related to the unit, and to initiate independent discussions about the material read. As suggested in the second-grade manual, the children might, for example, wish to culminate the unit with a grocery store activity. At the same time, the middle group of children, in a third-grade reader, might be reading a unit on Indians and Indian life. Again the teacher would find it necessary to develop the readiness for reading about Indians, to introduce the new words that would be used in the unit, and to establish and plan with the children the purposes for reading and the related experiences. The discussions about Indian life would have to be specific to the middle group of children and the activities for culminating this unit would be participated in only by the middle group. They might, for example, choose to build a tepee for their culminating activity. At the same time, the upper group, in a fourth-grade reader, might be reading a unit concerned with man's adaptation to extreme conditions in nature. Again the teacher would find it necessary to keep this group instructionally separate from the other groups that she is teaching. This group might choose to build an igloo for their culminating activity. Since the class as a whole would not be considering problems in common, the advantages of having children of various levels of ability working together would not be realized. The use of materials which separate the children into three distinct groups is destructive of the social dynamics within a classroom.

A third disadvantage of fixed grouping for reading instruction is that it tends to make the groups inflexible. Frequently the groups are not altered for different types of instructional activities during the day. Also it becomes difficult to move a pupil who is achieving well into a more advanced group because the reading requirements are too great. Likewise it is difficult to move a child from a more advanced group to a lower group because this emphasizes for him his failure.

A fourth disadvantage of the fixed-group approach is that the teacher assumes that the grouping solves the problem of individual differences. This assumption is erroneous. In a fifth-grade class, for example, there is likely to be a two-and-a-half-year difference between the best and poorest reader in both the upper and the lower groups. While under good instructional conditions most of these children may profit from using a similar textbook, readiness must be carefully developed for the poorer readers within the groups, aid must be given to them as they read the selection through instructional questions and through some rereading, and immediate help must be given to them when they get into difficulty. The better readers within the groups need to have the program considerably enriched. They need to have comprehension questions that demand reflection and critical reading. Some differentiation in assignment and differentiation in methods according to the child's characteristics is required. Modifications in emphasis according to the reading needs of the individual child are essential. No method of grouping within the class brings about homogeneity within the groups. The teacher must face the fact that under any method of organization in the classroom, differential approaches to reading instruction are necessary if she is to meet the individual needs of each child.

Flexible grouping plans is another and very likely the best approach to adjusting to individual differences in reading. The difficulties that arise when grouping is too drastic, when it separates the children and their activities too widely, or when it becomes too rigid indicate that adjustment to individual differences is no simple matter. There can be no method of promotion nor any uniform method of grouping that will solve the problem. When grouping is made flexible, many of the difficulties are avoided and grouping becomes one of the best single means of individualizing instruction in reading.

Grouping procedures must be flexible in three ways. *First,* the group formed for basic reading instruction should be used for that phase of the curriculum only and the children should be regrouped according to need in other phases of the curriculum. *Second,* the children who need instruction in a specific reading skill or ability should form a temporary instructional group even if they come from different basic reading groups. *Third,* a child should be able to move readily from one group to another if he improves in reading ability enough to be better suited to a more advanced group. On the other hand, he should be able to move to a less advanced group without stigma if he has been absent, or if he for any other reason, needs to be with a less mature reading group. He may even meet with two groups for a time. We must remember that movement between groups is almost impossible in the traditional three-group, three-track method.

In general, grouping seems most effective if the following principles are adhered to:

1. *The groups are not fixed and their number depends on the nature of the outcome expected.* In the basic reading program two or three groups might be established for systematic instruction, but in the enrichment reading related to the basic program as many as six or seven interest groups might be formed. While using reading as an aid to learning in an experience unit in the content fields, several interest groups or committees might be formed or children might even read independently about their phase of the topic. In the personal development or recreational phase of reading, independent reading may be the rule with the child guided into a selection chosen for its value to him and him alone. However, even in this phase, a unit organization with interest groups might be beneficial from time to time. For re-educative or remedial work, a small group of two or three children having a common instructional need, might be drawn aside for concentrated work on a specific reading problem.

2. *The number and size of groups depends on the maturity and independence of the children.* As the children get older, as they become more experienced in working in groups, and more independent in their reading, a larger number of groups can be used effectively. When children are able to initiate their own reading activities in the study of a topic, find their own material in the library, and independently study and discuss the material, the number of groups may be increased. Such independence is gradual in development and cannot be expected too early in the sequence nor can it blossom overnight if the children have been in restricted reading programs. In the elementary grades, such growth in independence is encouraged by having the basic reading program organized in real topical units, letting the children help with the planning of the extension of the unit, encouraging them to read the related supplementary material independently, and having them participate in creative activities culminating the unit.

3. *In most situations, the groups should be reading about a topic that is the concern of the entire class.* Each child needs to feel that he is a member of the class community in which he resides for about six hours a day. Every

child in a fourth-grade class, for example, should know that he is an important member of that class. The fundamental dignity of each child must be maintained, be he a mature or an immature reader. The current practice of dividing the class into three distinct basic reading groups studying three separate reading programs is extremely detrimental to the social dynamics of the class and to the personal adjustment of its individual members. It is likewise an inefficient arrangement for very busy teachers to have to make three separate preparations. How much better it would be if materials the same in content and suited to the varying reading levels of the children were used in the basic reading program. Then the children could comfortably develop skills in reading at their own levels and participate together in all phases of the basic program. A good amount of such material (23), is already available and more should be developed.

If material of this kind is used in basic reading instruction, the teacher needs to make only one preparation, to assemble related reading material for only one topic rather than three, to develop readiness for one topic, and to conduct one culminating activity for the entire class. This saves both class time and the teacher's preparation time. It also liberates the teacher so that she can work with small groups needing specific re-educative or remedial help.

This same approach would be highly desirable for reading in the content fields because the children could start their reading of a topic together in a systematic manner and then they could break up into subgroups or work independently in order to extend the treatment of the topic. This approach is not necessary for the personal development or recreational phase of the reading program because it is not the function of this phase of the reading program to develop systematically either the skills and abilities in reading or the understanding of the concepts in the content fields.

4. *Frequently the group organization should be abandoned and the class should work together.* In the basic reading program, wherein an orderly introduction of reading skills and abilities is essential and an orderly and gradual expansion of vocabulary load is demanded, it is likely that for certain parts of the instruction about three reading groups are desirable. The current plan of having different editions of basal readers dealing with the same content but written on different levels of reading difficulty proves extremely helpful in meeting individual differences in reading. All the children in the class can be reading on the same topic, whether they be mature, average, or immature readers. The teacher is at liberty to teach the class as a whole or to work with them in groups. Some of the time, all the children would work together, while at other times, those children using different editions might better work as groups.

For reading related material, in order to explore more fully some phases of the topic introduced in the basic reader, the formation of committees would be wise. Under this plan, the teacher works with the class as a whole when introducing the unit, developing readiness for the unit, and co-opera-tively planning with the children the expansion of the unit in related activi-ties. While the children are reading the material in the simplified and more advanced editions of the basic readers, the teacher can either form groups or work with the class as a whole. In the committee work, the class can be divided according to interests, with perhaps the best and poorest readers in the class working on the same committee. The teacher brings the class together again for the activities relating the various selections to the unit, for the creative activities in culminating the unit, and for evaluating the unit. This approach has all the advantages of group instruction, it takes only a reasonable amount of teacher time, and it builds up the personal self-respect of each child.

In those reading experiences where the children are using reading as an aid to learning in the content fields, the class will at times profit from work-ing together as well as in groups. There is a great need for material differen-tiated in difficulty in the content fields so that the individual differences in reading can be realistically and practically met. In the children's literature phase of the reading program, many times it is wise to have the entire class working together. When a book is shared through individual oral reading of parts of favorite stories would be one such time; the showing of new books added to the room library would be another. In the re-educative phase of the reading program, the entire class might profit from a demonstration of a word-recognition technique and could profitably be taught together.

Such individualization of instruction with multiple, flexible grouping, with materials that allow the class to participate together while each child is working with material he can read, will do much to allow children to grow in reading at the rate most suitable to each one. Such instruction will do much to prevent a child's minor misunderstandings from accumulating until he gets into a major confusion and becomes a complex reading disability case.

A realistic approach to individual rates of growth, good basic reading instruction, and a wise use of reading as an aid to learning and to personal development must be supplemented, for every child who needs it, by a diagnostic and remedial program. The classroom teacher with approxi-mately 35 children cannot be expected to spend the time necessary to correct a marked reading confusion for one child at the expense of the other 34. Therefore, every school should have the services of a remedial teacher to work with the more difficult educational disability problems. Flexible grouping, coupled with material realistically planned to meet the individual levels of reading ability, overcomes most of the difficulties. If adequate re-education programs are carried on by the teacher and reinforced by remedial programs when necessary, most serious reading problems can be avoided. Only under these conditions can we expect every child who enters the first grade to develop reading ability to the fullest of his potential.

SUMMARY

One of the most complex problems confronting the teacher is that of adjusting instruction to individual differences in reading. The children within any classroom vary greatly in reading maturity, reading habits, intellectual capabilities, and physical characteristics. The teacher must organize the class and the instruction so that each child can work up to his capacity. All told, the teachers of today are better equipped with better professional training, with improved materials and with more penetrating measurements necessary for making adjustments to individual differences than were the teachers of the past.

The range of reading ability found in any classroom is large. The better the instruction and the longer it continues, the greater will be the range in reading ability. If instruction is excellent not only will the average reading performance of the class be raised but also the range of reading ability within the class will become greater. Each succeeding year of instruction increases the range of reading ability within the class so that by the sixth grade, the difference between the best and the poorest reader will be about seven years in reading growth, i.e., from grade 2.5 to grade 9.5. Furthermore, there will be extensive overlap in the reading capabilities found in the various grades. Indeed, there is so much overlap that the teacher, at any grade level, must be able to meet the reading instructional needs of the children for grades above and below the one she is teaching. If the teacher organizes the class into three instructional groups, the range within the upper and lower groups will still be so great that further individualization is required. The problem of adjustment to the upper group is somewhat easier than it is to the lower group because of the reading competence and independence of the children and the greater availability of suitable materials.

Among the more important considerations in meeting individual differences in reading are: the similarities and differences in children, the nature of individual learning curves, the complexities involved in learning to read, the changes of approaches brought about by differences in curriculum and school organization differences at the various grade levels, and the need for realistic use of class time and teachers' energies.

The need for adjusting to individual differences in reading throughout the entire curriculum makes the problem somewhat more complicated than the problem of adjusting to the basic reading program alone. The methods and class organization that are suitable for one type of reading experience will not always be suitable for another type. The types of reading experiences children have may be roughly classified as: basic instruction in reading, reading and study in other phases of the curriculum, independent personal development or recreational reading, and re-educative or remedial reading. However, these phases of reading are not altogether discrete. In general, the approaches to individual differences used in these phases of the entire reading curriculum are different and much of the seeming controversy on methods stems from the fact that the proponents of one approach over another are emphasizing different phases of reading instruction.

Some approaches that have been tried, include: retardation and acceleration, curriculum adjustment plans, fixed grouping plans, and flexible grouping plans. Among these, the flexible grouping plans, reinforced by materials written on multiple levels of difficulty, seem to hold the most promise. Whatever approach is used, the teacher should be sure that groups are not fixed but are adjustable to the outcomes expected from the reading, and also that the number and size of the groups are compatible with the maturity and independence of the children. In many instances the groups should be reading about a topic of concern to the entire class, and the best and the poorest readers should have opportunities to work together.

SELECTED READINGS

BETTS, Emmett A., Adjusting instruction to individual needs. *Reading in the elementary school*. Forty-eighth Yearbook of the National Society for the Study of Education, Part II. Chicago: University of Chicago Press, 1949, Chap. 13.

BOND, G. L., and HANDLAN, B., *Adapting instruction in reading to individual differences*. Minneapolis: University of Minnesota Press, 1948.

COOK, Walter W., *Grouping and promotion in the elementary schools*. Minneapolis: University of Minnesota Press, 1941.

DURRELL, Donald D., *Improvement of basic reading abilities*. Yonkers (N. Y.): World Book Company, 1940, Chaps. 3, 4.

HARRIS, Albert J., *How to increase reading ability,* 3rd ed. New York: Longmans, Green & Company, 1956, Chap. 5.

LAZAR, May, *Individualization of instruction in reading*. Educational Research Bulletin No. 1. New York: Board of Education of the City of New York, 1941.

RUSSELL, David H., *Children learn to read*. Boston: Ginn and Company, 1949, Chap. 15.

STRANG, Ruth, MCCULLOUGH, C. M., and TRAXLER, A. E., *Problems in the improvement of reading*, 2nd ed. New York: McGraw-Hill Book Company, Inc., 1955, Chap. 11.

TINKER, Miles A., *Teaching elementary reading*. New York: Appleton-Century-Crofts, Inc., 1952, Chap. 11.

PART II

Nature and Causes of Reading Difficulties

4

GENERAL NATURE
OF READING DISABILITY

IN THE PRECEDING chapter we considered the extent of individual differences in reading ability and the approaches to meeting the range of reading ability to be expected within a typical classroom. There are some children whose reading growth is so different from the usual child that they constitute a troublesome instructional problem. Often the classroom teacher can diagnose these difficulties and give these children the corrective or re-educative help that they need so that they can continue to progress in reading growth. At other times, the disabled readers are so confused educationally that they require more time for individual help than the classroom teacher can devote to them. In both instances the child is a disabled reader, but the nature and severity of the disability makes one approach more suitable than the other.

In order to consider the nature of reading disability, it is necessary to isolate the group of children to be discussed, define the disabled reader, explain the characteristics that set him apart from the general population, and describe the over-all categories into which disabled readers fall. The nature of reading disability will be considered under the following headings:

1. The disabled reader
2. Considerations involved in classifying a child as a disabled reader
3. General descriptive categories of disabled readers

THE DISABLED READER

Reading disability is a subtle and difficult condition to describe. This is true since there are no two cases which are exactly alike and no two cases are caused by the same set of circumstances. Disabled readers have enough in common, however, so that they do form a distinct group in the educational scene. The first characteristic of the disabled reader is that he does not read as well as he should. Not all children who cannot read well are disabled readers. Just some of them are. On the other hand, some of the children who are seemingly progressing fairly well are, in reality, reading disability cases. Further, all children in the lower third of a class are not necessarily disabled readers. Indeed, most such children are not. Many truly disabled readers will be found among the average readers and a few may be in the upper third of the class in reading ability. The extent of retardation in reading on the basis of chronological age or grade placement is insufficient evidence upon which to classify a child as a disabled reader.

The child who is a disabled reader cannot be described as one whose reading ability is below his achievement in other school subjects in general. For while some disabled readers can be so described, the vast majority will be low both in reading and in general achievement. This is true because poor reading ability so limits other achievement that it is the rare child who can attain success in school in spite of having a reading disability. It is also important to note that the child who is low in both reading and in general achievement may or may not be a disabled reader. A child may be poor in reading and the other school subjects for a variety of reasons other than disability in reading.

The disabled reader is the child who is so handicapped in reading that his educational career is in jeopardy. Not only is his educational growth impeded but frequently his reading patterns are so confused that future growth in reading becomes improbable. He is ineffective in using print as an aid to learning. He is often a discouraged student who thoroughly dislikes reading. In many cases, the child becomes so frustrated over his inability to read that his personal adjustment suffers a severe shock. He is, therefore, quite apt to show emotional tensions in reading situations. Sometimes these tensions upset him completely and he demonstrates unfortunate adjustment patterns in general. Such unfortunate adjustment patterns may vary all the way from unfounded excuses for his trouble with reading to rather severe functional emotional disorders.

George illustrated the former type of poor adjustment when he said, "I don't want to learn to read because it is all make-believe. I don't want to read about a boy that has a boat. I want to have one myself." Many children who get into trouble with reading complain about the material not meeting their needs, but when they are successful in reading that same material, they find a new interest.

Henry displayed a functional disorder when it became apparent that he could not attempt to read even for two or three minutes without developing a sick headache and an upset stomach. He claimed to have eye trouble although this could not be detected by thorough examination. He would work on puzzle-type material and numbers for long periods of time with no sign of visual discomfort or stomach unrest. After he attained success in reading by careful, individually planned work based on a complete diagnosis, he showed no signs of his former functional disorders. Naturally not all children, however, who have both poor reading and poor personal adjustment can be said to have them as a result of poor growth in reading. Quite frequently the child is disturbed for other reasons and his reading suffers along with his other achievements.

Typically, the disabled reader is a child of intellectual capability who has for a variety of reasons that will be discussed in the chapters that follow, failed to grow in reading. He is not living up to his potential as a learner at least in reading. He is quite likely to be ineffective in all that is expected of him in school. He may reject reading, become a discouraged person, acquire unfortunate adjustment patterns, and become increasingly less able to learn. He is a child in need of educational help.

CONSIDERATIONS INVOLVED IN CLASSIFYING A CHILD AS A DISABLED READER

The problem now confronting us is different than was the one of detecting the range of reading ability in a class in order to make adjustments to varying rates of growth in reading as discussed in the preceding chapter. The identification of reading disability cases is much more complicated than is the sectioning of a class into reading groups or even of locating the suitable level at which to start instruction for each child within a class. A reading test alone will not be enough to find the reading disability cases within a school. There are many poor readers in every class who cannot be classified as disabled readers. A study of the data taken from research in progress by G. L. Bond and T. Clymer will show the conditions that exist. These data were obtained from the measurement of randomly selected fifth-grade classes in a large midwestern city and are rather typical of what can be expected in elementary classes in general.

Table 2

SCATTERGRAM BASED ON STANFORD-BINET I.Q.
AND GATES READING SURVEY LEVEL OF COMPREHENSION
GRADE SCORE OF 379 FIFTH-GRADE CHILDREN

READING GRADES	INTELLIGENCE QUOTIENTS									
	55-64	65-74	75-84	85-94	95-104	105-114	115-124	125-134	135-144	145-154
9.0 or above						1	1			1
8.5-8.9						1	3	2	1	1
8.0-8.4						4	7	7	1	
7.5-7.9					2	6	2	4		
7.0-7.4				1	3	7	9	6	2	
6.5-6.9			1	1	8	11	7	4	2	1
6.0-6.4				3	8	9	15	2	1	
5.5-5.9				3	14	8	5			
5.0-5.4		1		11	16	8	7	1		
4.5-4.9		3	4	11	12	5	4	1		
4.0-4.4	1	2	12	12	9	3	1			
3.5-3.9	2	7	9	14	7	4	2			
3.0-3.4		2	9	10	4		1			
2.5-2.9		2	2	3	2					

Table 2 shows the scattergram representing the Stanford-Binet I.Q.'s and the reading scores of 379 fifth-grade children whose average I.Q. is 105 and whose average reading grade is 5.5 (five months through the fifth grade). The scattergram shows that while there is a positive relationship between reading and I.Q., there is also a considerable range in reading to be found among the fifth-grade children at any I.Q. level. The Table shows that the able children are learning to read much more effectively than are the less able children. It also shows that the children with I.Q.'s between 95 and 124 account for much of the heterogeneity. The groups above and below those levels have a somewhat restricted range of reading ability. That is, superior children with an I.Q. of 125 or higher are not to be found among the poor readers. Likewise, it is rare for a child with an I.Q. below 95 to be among the very able readers of the class.

Table 3

PER CENT OF CHILDREN FROM THREE
I.Q. RANGES IN VARIOUS READING GROUPS

READING GROUPS	I.Q. RANGES		
	55-94	*95-114*	*115-154*
HIGH Group I	3	39	58
MIDDLE Group II	24	52	24
LOW Group III	73	24	3

Table 3 shows the I.Q. composition of the upper, middle, and lower thirds in reading in these fifth-grade classes. It will be noticed that about three out of every four of the children in the lowest reading group had I.Q.'s of 94 or lower. These children, although poor readers, cannot, for the most part, be considered disabled readers. They are reading about as well as can be expected in view of their limited intellectual ability. Approximately one out of four of the children in this lowest reading group has an I.Q. between 95 and 114. Some of these children may be disabled readers and others will be found to be poor readers but not retarded enough to be classified as disabled. Very few children with I.Q.'s above 125 were in the lowest reading group, but it is likely that the 3 per cent who were in this group would be classified as disabled readers.

The middle reading group was found to be fairly well balanced. About half of its members had I.Q.'s between 95 and 114, one-fourth of the members were the intellectually more able children and one-fourth were intellectually less able. Some of the more able children in this middle reading group would very likely be classified as disabled readers because they could be expected to be doing much better. This middle reading group did not contain many children with I.Q.'s below 85 nor many with I.Q.'s above 125 (see Table 2).

More than half the children in the highest reading group had I.Q.'s of 115 or higher and more than one-third were children with I.Q.'s between 95 and 114. These latter children are doing a superior job of learning to read. Only three children, out of over 100 with I.Q.'s below 95, were in the highest reading group. The children with I.Q.'s below 95 in this reading group must have profited from favorable learning conditions indeed, to be reading so well.

These data alone are not sufficient to locate all the children who should be classified as disabled readers. Therefore we must discuss the factors that need to be considered in order to determine whether a child is disabled in reading or whether he is just a poor reader.

Opportunity to Learn

The child who is to be classified as disabled in reading must be distinguished from the child who has not had an opportunity to learn. If we did not take into account the opportunity of a child to learn, we would have to say that nearly all children would be disabled readers before they entered the first grade. While it is true that their ability to get meaning from the printed page is negligible and in no way in keeping with their ability to listen, they cannot be disabled because they have not been taught. They have had no opportunity to learn. They may have a relatively large listening vocabulary but the typical child entering the first grade cannot read many more words than his own name. Most children cannot, for example, read the word *STOP* if it is taken off the octagonal sign where they are accustomed to seeing it. In a way, they have had the opportunity to learn because there has always been printed matter before them. However, they did not receive systematic organized instruction, so, in reality, they have not had the opportunity to learn. Even though the child entering the first grade is not able to read as well as he can listen, he is not disabled because he is doing as well as could be expected of him.

The older child who has come from a non-English-speaking country to the United States would not be considered a reading disability case even though he did constitute an instructional problem. He may need to start learning to read English at the beginning, but he cannot be called a disabled reader. He should have material different than that used for the six-year-old beginner and he will need methods of instruction that are suitable to his unique needs. Nonetheless, he is not a disabled reader. He is a child who cannot read English because of lack of opportunity to learn.

The role of lack of opportunity to learn is even more complicated than is indicated in the case of the child who has not yet entered school or the child from another country. Some children will be retarded in reading in comparison to their other intellectual achievements because they did not start to learn to read as early as they started building other verbal learnings. A gifted child, for example, who is just entering the third grade may have the verbal facility of the usual sixth-grade child. He could not be expected to read as well as a typical sixth-grade child because he has been given reading instruction for only two years while his general language development has taken place over a period of eight years. He has, therefore, not had the opportunity to develop reading capability up to his general verbal ability. He may have been ready intellectually to read at the age of four, but because of educational practice and his own developmental needs he did not receive systematic instruction in reading until he entered the first grade at the age of six and, therefore, he cannot be expected to read up to his general verbal achievement level.

Verbal Competency

The aural verbal ability of a child is frequently used as an indication of the level at which we could expect him to read. If the child has a superior listening vocabulary, he may be expected to read at a higher level than can other children of his age. If the child is able to understand paragraphs of more than usual difficulty read aloud to him, he should be able to read better than those children who have less aural verbal ability. The child's verbal ability, as measured by a test such as the Durrell-Sullivan Reading Capacity Test [1] gives a good indication of the level at which he should be reading. A marked discrepancy between his aural verbal and his reading ability is an indication that a child may be a disabled reader.

There are, however, two considerations that must be taken into account before a child who is reading below his general verbal ability is classified as a disabled reader or before seemingly low verbal ability may be said to indicate poor reading rather than a true natural mental limitation. This relationship can be accounted for by the fact that the child has had one avenue of developing verbal ability closed to him. A child, for example, who has been a poor reader from the first grade to the sixth will not have had an opportunity to develop language equal to that of his natively equal counterpart who always has been a good reader. The poor reader will not have had as much experience with words because he has not read as widely. Nor will he have had as much experience in understanding paragraphs as his able-reading counterpart. Bond and Fay (26), among others, have shown that poor readers are considerably lower in the vocabulary items in the Stanford-Binet Intelligence Tests than are good readers of equal intelligence. Of course, these findings could indicate either that these children have native limitations in verbal ability as compared with their general intelligence and are therefore poor readers, or that they are limited in developing language because they are poor readers and therefore lack verbal experience. The authors, through experience with hundreds of reading cases, tend to take the latter point of view, namely, that an able child who is a poor reader cannot be expected to develop as extensive a vocabulary nor to be as

[1] See Appendix I for list of reading tests.

experienced in interpreting paragraphs as can his able-reading counterpart. Therefore, the use of aural verbal ability alone as a criterion for classifying children as reading disability cases might classify certain children among the verbally inept who are really reading disability cases and who would profit much from remedial instruction.

The second problem involved in using a discrepancy between aural verbal ability and reading as a means of classifying a child as a disabled reader is that it does not take into account the opportunity of the child to learn. Two children, for example, may have the same measured verbal ability. One, however, is only a second-grade child while the other is a sixth-grade child. The second-grader has had only one year of reading instruction while the other has had five. The younger child cannot be expected to read as well as the older child who has had five times as much reading instruction, even though they measure the same on an oral vocabulary test or a test of ability to understand paragraphs read orally.

Verbal competency should be one of the considerations involved in classifying a child as a disabled reader but it will often mislead the teacher or diagnostician if used as the sole criterion. The length of time in school and the opportunity to learn to read must also be considered. The accuracy of the estimate of verbal aptitude also must be taken into account if all the children who are in need of specific help in reading are to be located and if a given child is not to be misjudged.

Success in Nonreading Fields

In determining the classification of a child as one who is a disabled reader, teachers often compare his reading achievement with his success in subjects requiring a minimum of reading. Arithmetical computation is frequently used as one of the subjects less influenced by reading ability. If the child is doing well in arithmetic and doing poorly in reading, he is likely to be a disabled reader. Such information adds considerably to the accuracy of locating children who are disabled readers rather than poor readers who are doing as well as can be expected.

In cases where the child appears to be emotionally disturbed, for example, the comparison between reading ability and success in arithmetic gives some evidence of the relationship between the personality problem and reading ability. If the disturbed child is intellectually capable and still is poor in both reading and arithmetic, it is likely that his lack of achievement is the result of a more deep-rooted personality problem. If, however, such a child's reading achievement is considerably below his arithmetic, it is likely that his personality difficulty centers around his lack of success in reading. This judgment of the situation cannot always be accepted because in some few cases the disturbed child may have achieved a feeling of success in arithmetic and therefore applied himself with unusual vigor to that field. The child's lack of outstanding success in reading may have irritated an existing insecurity so that reading was rejected in favor of the more satisfy-ing field in which he found more immediate success.

Success in nonreading fields does indicate in the vast majority of cases how well the child is able to apply himself to learning situations other than reading. If he has a general personality problem, he is likely to give evidence of ineffective learning in these fields as well as in reading. Also, if he has limited general capability he will show poor success in nonreading fields as well as in reading. But, when a child is highly successful in nonreading fields, yet has difficulty in reading, he is likely to be an intelligent, well-adjusted child who is a disabled reader because of some faulty learning. Such a child can usually be helped a great deal by remedial instruction in reading. While success in nonreading fields is insufficient evidence in itself to classify a child as a disabled reader, it is often used as one of the facts to be taken into account in making such a classification. Monroe (131), for example, uses arithmetic achievement as one of the criteria for selecting children who will profit from remedial instruction in reading.

Mental Ability

The mental ability of the child is most often used as the basic criterion against which to compare his reading ability in order to judge the existence of a reading disability. The customary method of making this comparison is to use the mental age or grade of the child as the key to reading expectancy. When the child's average reading age is felt to be significantly lower than his mental age, he is thought to be a disabled reader. While undoubtedly the true mental ability of the child should be used as a basic consideration in classifying a child as a disabled reader, marked caution is necessary for two reasons. First, the determination of mental capacity of a poor reader is difficult. Second, the problem is further complicated by the fact that although mental age is calculated from birth, the child is not introduced to systematic instruction in reading until he is six or more years old.

Assessing Mental Age. There are many types of tests which may be used to assess the mental age of children. Four general types of measurement are in common use. They are: verbal group mental tests, nonverbal group mental tests, individual mental tests, and individual performance mental tests. Each of these tests has its advantages and limitations. In classifying a child as a disabled reader, the particular measure of mental ability used must be carefully considered.

Verbal Group Mental Tests. These are of little use in selecting children who will profit from remedial work in reading. These tests are themselves, to a great extent, reading tests and therefore the poor reader cannot demonstrate his true mental ability. Clymer (36) has shown that at the fifth-grade level, certain group intelligence tests give no measure whatsoever of the mental ability of the children who are reading in the lowest 40 per cent of the class. To show the extent of misinterpretation possible by uncritical use of such tests for disabled readers, the case of Mary can be cited. Mary was brought to the University of Minnesota Clinic for study. In the course of diagnosis, her cumulative record was assembled. At the end of kindergarten, she was given a Stanford-Binet mental test which indicated that she had an I.Q. of 115. In grade four, she was given a verbal group test and was appraised to have an I.Q. of 80. Inasmuch as her reading ability and general school performance were consistent with the 80 I.Q., no mismeasurement was suspected. She went into junior high school and in the ninth grade was given another and this time a more verbal group test, one that was almost a power of comprehension reading test. At least it was for one who read as poorly as Mary. She obtained an I.Q. of 56. This measurement, while somewhat consistent with her scholastic performance, seemed unreasonable to the counselor, so a complete study of Mary seemed in order. When an individual Stanford-Binet mental test was given, the results indicated that she had an I.Q. of 104. Mary, in reality, was a marked reading disability case. Her reading score indicated only third-grade ability. She was found to have a spelling attack on words. She seemed to be attempting to learn all the 800,000 words in the language by memorizing the spelling of each. She could comprehend but little and therefore could not show her true mental ability on a test that required reading. Such tests are all too frequently used in making comparisons between reading growth and mental growth. The one advantage to such tests is that they can be given to large groups. The results are useful in making most comparisons for able readers. But they are worse than worthless in the case of poor readers because the results are often considered accurate.

Nonverbal Group Tests. Such tests are often used as a criterion for determining reading expectancy of children. These tests can be given to large groups and therefore save a great deal of testing time. They are useful in selecting children who have a marked discrepancy between their mental age and their reading age. These tests, while paper and pencil tests, do not require reading matter as a means of presenting the items. Therefore the disabled reader can take these tests unhampered by his poor reading ability. The major difficulties with these tests are two: first, they are not as accurate in measurement as would be desirable for individual diagnosis; second, they do not appear to measure the type of mental ability needed for success in reading. They are, to some degree, performance tests rather than tests of reasoning ability. Nonetheless they are useful in saving testing time. In doubtful cases, however, the results should be checked by more accurate individual tests.

Individual Mental Tests. These are the most suitable measures of mental growth to be used with reading cases. The Stanford-Binet [2] and the Wechsler Intelligence Scale for Children [3] are the most popular and useful

[2] See Appendix I for list of intelligence tests.
[3] *Ibid.*

tests of this type. Such tests give an accurate measure of mental ability for able readers and are only slightly affected by the lack of reading ability of disabled readers. Bond and Fay (26) have shown, however, that the disabled readers do have appreciable difficulty with the items in the Binet directly related to reading growth such as: vocabulary, reading and memory, minkus completion, abstract words, and dissected sentences. This handicap may make for as much as from 5 to 20 I.Q. points underestimation for poor readers of fifth-grade age. In the case of Mary, cited above, the difference between the 115 I.Q. at kindergarten age and the 104 I.Q. when she was in the ninth grade could be accounted for by this tendency of the test to underestimate the mental ability of the disabled reader. Providing the clinician is alert to this possibility, individual mental tests are accurate. Of course, the worker can only say that the I.Q. of Mary at ninth grade is at least 104, while in all likelihood it is from 5 to 20 points higher. Individual mental tests are the most desirable measures to use in estimating reading expectancy. They are limited, however, by the fact that they are time-consuming and require trained examiners.

Individual Performance Tests. These are useful additions to other tests for supplying information to be used in the diagnosis of certain types of reading problems. They aid in getting a measure of the mental ability of children who are hard-of-hearing, who have marked speech difficulties, or who have other handicaps. These tests have the same limitations as other individual tests, since they are time-consuming and require trained examiners. One further important limitation is that they do not emphasize the verbal aspects of intellectual growth.

Relating Mental Growth to Reading Expectancy

The problem of relating a child's mental growth to his reading growth in order to estimate the level at which he should be able to read is a complicated one. The usual way in which this judgment is made is to consider that the child should have reached a reading age or grade roughly comparable to his mental age or grade. Then, if a given child's reading grade is significantly lower than his mental grade, he is classified as a disabled reader. The amount of discrepancy between reading grade and mental grade considered significant increases as the child grows older. In the primary grades, from one-half to three-fourths of a grade difference is taken to be enough to classify the child as a disabled reader. In the intermediate grades, a difference of one to one and a half grades is used. A second-grade child, whose mental grade is 2.8 (i.e. equal to the average child eight months through the second grade) and whose reading grade is 2.2, would be thought a disabled reader. Likewise, in the second grade, a very able child whose mental grade is 4.0 and whose reading grade is 3.4, would be considered disabled. There is serious question as to whether this latter comparison is justified.

The child of high ability, 150 I.Q., who enters the first grade at the age of 6.5, cannot be expected to read at a 4.3 grade level even though that would be about his mental grade. As a matter of fact, such a child would typically be able to read little, if anything, because he has not yet been taught. He has had no real opportunity to learn to read.

There are many possible ways to use the general intelligence of the child as a yardstick against which to judge his reading growth. The use of results of mental tests in classifying a child as a disabled reader has been done by using the mental age or grade as the level at which the child is expected to read. Most studies of over- and underachievement have used the mental age criterion to estimate who were the good and who were the poor achievers. These studies have universally found that bright children underachieve and dull children overachieve in comparison to their mental age.

The assumption that a child should be achieving up to his mental age needs careful inspection. While it is true that such learnings as listening or speaking vocabulary can be so adjudged, other learning cannot be expected to be related in the same way. The child of 150 I.Q. who is 10 years old has a mental age of 15. This means that he should, on the basis of his mental grade, be doing mathematics, for example, equal to that of about a tenth-grader instead of a fifth-grade child. But it is doubtful if such a child typically knows algebra and geometry because he has not yet met them. Reading achievement acts the same way. The child with 150 I.Q. is mentally ready to read when he is 4 years old but he is not ready in many other ways, so he does not start to read until two years later. This is probably as it should be. While his mental age has continued to advance, his reading ability remains at the level of being mentally ready. By the time he enters the first grade, he is so mentally equipped for reading instruction that he can be expected to learn faster than the other, less able children.

We might assume that, under average conditions, he would learn reading as he has learned everything else, at about one and a half times the rate of the usual child. To the extent that all the other elements that influence reading success are favorable, he would learn somewhat faster than the other children of his mental capability and if these other conditions are unfavorable, he would learn somewhat slower. But on the whole, it can be assumed that the usual child with 150 I.Q. can be expected to learn new things, when presented, about one and a half times as fast as the average child. Likewise, the child with a 75 I.Q. can be expected to learn them only about three-fourths as fast as the average child. If we assume that the I.Q. is an index of rate of learning each new experience, a child, at the end of the first grade, will have learned to read according to the formula: I.Q. times years in school plus 1.0 equals reading grade. The 1.0 is added because the child starts school at grade 1.0 and after a year in school, the average child is at grade 2.0 or just entering the second grade.

By this formula, the typical child with an I.Q. of 70 could be expected to read at 1.7 at the end of one year of instruction. Similarly, at the end of two years, he should read at 2.4. Using this same formula, the child with 100 I.Q. would be expected to read at 3.0 and the able child with 150 I.Q. would be expected to read at 4.0. At the end of four years, the child with 150 I.Q. could be expected to read at 7.0.

These data from a study in progress by G. L. Bond and T. Clymer indicate that such a relationship between I.Q. and reading achievement is most probably the one that exists. The data were secured from randomly selected classes in a large midwestern city. The classes were measured at the middle of the fifth grade with the Stanford-Binet Intelligence Test and the Gates Reading Survey Test. The average reading ability of the 379 children measured was 5.5 and the average I.Q. was 105.

Table 4

TWO ESTIMATES OF READING EXPECTANCY OF VARIOUS STANFORD-BINET I.Q. GROUPS COMPARED WITH THE OBSERVED READING ABILITY AMONG 379 CHILDREN HALF-WAY THROUGH THE FIFTH GRADE

I.Q.	Estimated Reading Expectancy by the Mental Grade Method	Observed Reading Ability among Fifth-Grade Pupils (Av. R. G. 5.5)	Estimated Reading Expectancy by formula (Years in School × I.Q. + 1.0 = Expected Reading Grade)	Percentage of Disabled Readers by the Mental Grade Method	Percentage of Disabled Readers by Formula Method
150	10.8	8.2	7.8	66	0
140	9.8	7.3	7.3	70	0
130	8.7	7.4	6.9	40	7
120	7.6	6.4	6.4	42	14
110	6.6	6.1	5.9	30	14
100	5.5	5.2	5.5	24	14
90	4.4	4.4	5.0	4	20
80	3.4	3.9	4.6	0	16
70	2.3	3.8	4.2	0	5
60	1.2	3.8	3.7	0	0

Table 4 shows a comparison between the observed reading scores of these children at various I.Q. levels and the estimation of reading expectancy on the bases of Mental Grade and on the formula (years in school × I.Q.) + 1.0. The reading expectancy score by the Mental Grade Method in this table was calculated by assuming that the typical child enters the first grade at 6.2 years of age. Then under continuous promotion, he would be 10.7 years old when he was half-way through the fifth grade. His reading expectancy score, is therefore, (10.7 × I.Q. − 6.2) + 1.0. In calculating the reading expectancy score by the Mental Grade

Method for a child with an I.Q. of 150 half-way through the fifth grade, his reading expectancy score would be $(10.7 \times 1.50 - 6.2) + 1.0$, or $(16.0 - 6.2) + 1.0$, which equals $9.8 + 1.0$, or 10.8.

The reading expectancy grade scores calculated by the formula (years in school $\times$ I.Q.) $+ 1.0$ is worked out by taking the number of years the child has been in school and multiplying that number by his I.Q. and then adding 1.0 because his grade score was 1.0 when he entered school. In calculating the reading expectancy score by the formula (years in school $\times$ I.Q.) $+ 1.0$ for a child with an I.Q. of 150 half-way through the fifth grade, his reading expectancy score would be $(4.5 \times 1.50) + 1.0$, or $6.8 + 1.0$ which equals 7.8.

A study of the Table indicates that the formula applied at the fifth-grade level gives estimates of reading expectancy that are startlingly close to the observed reading averages for almost every level of I.Q. The Table also shows that the Mental Grade Method used as a means of determining expected reading level is quite unrealistic when compared with the observed reading scores. It approximates observed reading scores for only the I.Q. range of 90-110. Able children cannot be expected to achieve in four and one-half years, reading ability equal to their general mental ability based on growth of over ten and one-half years. Nor should we be satisfied with the expected achievement in reading of the slower-learning children as indicated by their mental grades. They evidently learn to read at nearly the same rate that they have learned other things all of their lives.

Included in Table 4 are the percentages of fifth-grade children who would be classified as reading disability cases by each of the methods used. You will recall that a child in the latter part of the intermediate grades (i.e., 5.5 grade and above) is usually classified as a disabled reader if his reading grade is one and a half years or more below his reading expectancy level. It can be seen in Table 4 that the children who would be selected as disabled readers would be different, depending on the method of classification used. The classification on the basis of mental age would lead us to select children, for the most part, who came from the superior groups. Classification by the formula method that assumes that the able child would learn faster once he was introduced to systematic instruction in reading, would select reading cases more often from the 80 to the 120 I.Q. range and with almost equal frequency at the various levels within this range. This latter sort of selection may be more in accord with practical diagnosis.

Figure 2 shows the relationship graphically and is based on the data given in Table 4. A study of the Figure shows that the line of estimated reading ability by the formula (years in school $\times$ I.Q.) $+ 1.0$ is much closer to the observed reading ability than is the line of estimated reading ability calculated from the Mental Grade of the child.

The disabled reader is, in general, one who has had an opportunity to

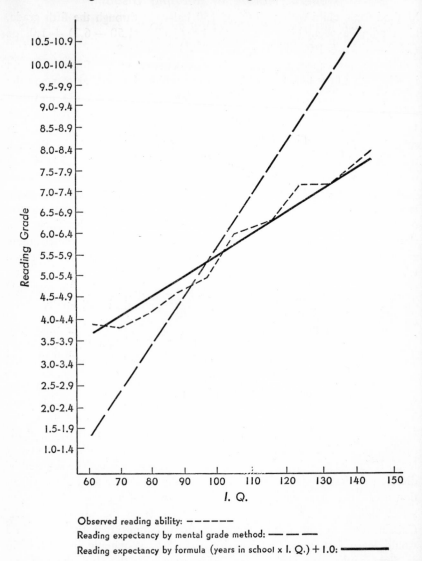

FIG. 2. Graphic presentation of reading expectancies as compared with observed reading ability.

learn to read, but who is not reading as well as could be expected by his aural verbal ability, his mental capacity, and his success in nonreading learnings. He is, in reality, the child who is at the lower end of the reading distribution when compared with other children of his general capability. He is at the lower end of the reading distribution for a variety of reasons which will be discussed in the chapters that follow. It should be noted, however, that there are other children of his general capability who are as far advanced in the reading distribution as the disabled reader is retarded.

GENERAL DESCRIPTIVE CATEGORIES OF DISABLED READERS

The children who have been classified as disabled readers can be grouped into descriptive categories which help to give an understanding of the general nature of reading disability. There are, among the children who are disabled readers, the following groups:

1. Simple retardation cases
2. Specific retardation cases
3. Limiting disability cases
4. Complex disability cases

Simple retardation cases are those disabled readers who lack general maturity in reading. They are significantly retarded in reading when compared with other children of their general reading expectancy, but there is no unusual or limiting characteristic about their reading pattern. They are immature in reading, but there is nothing especially wrong with their reading. A fifth-grade boy of average intelligence, for example, who has not been as interested in reading and who has read only about half as much as the typical child, may be reading at only third-grade level. He is a good reader of third-grade material and his entire profile on a diagnostic battery of tests looks like any normal third-grade pattern. Such a case would be one of simple retardation. The problem can be answered by giving the child more experience in reading and systematic instruction at his level of reading ability. Such cases are frequent among disabled readers. These children do not constitute a re-education problem, but they do need marked adjustment of material and instruction. If they are forced into reading books too difficult for them or if they are not given systematic instruction in reading development at their level, they will very likely become more complex reading disability cases. There are many reasons, other than conflicting interests, which result in the prevalence of such reading cases.

Specific retardation cases are those children who have specific limitations in their reading profiles. In general, these children are competent readers and may or may not be classified as disabled readers. They are classified as disabled if they are weak in enough areas of reading to lower their average performance sufficiently. One such child, for example, might be a reader who is able to read and understand the general significance of paragraphs difficult enough to challenge the reading capacity of children of his age and intelligence. He cannot, however, read to follow directions or to organize longer interrelated selections. He has the general basic reading skills and abilities, but he has not learned to adapt them to all of his reading purposes. He may be inexperienced in reading to note relationships and to organize what he has read. He needs training in the areas where he is weak and not re-education in the basic skills and abilities. He is fundamentally an able reader, but he is retarded in specific ways that do not limit his general growth in reading.

Limiting disability cases are those disabled readers who have serious deficiencies in their basic skills and abilities which limit their entire reading growth. Children who have a word-recognition deficiency, limiting mechanical habits or inability to sense thought units, etc., would fall into this descriptive category. The essential fact about the children in this group is that they need re-education. They need to unlearn some of the things they have learned or to learn some new basic approaches to reading. They have either failed to make some essential learning that is necessary for reading growth, or have acquired a detrimental form of learning, or have overemphasized a needed skill so much that there is a lack of balance in their reading attack. These children need well-planned remedial programs to correct their faulty reading patterns and to develop the skills they need.

Complex disability cases are really a subgroup of limiting disability cases, i.e., children who have deficiencies in their reading patterns which limit further growth in reading. Also, their reading is complicated by unfortunate attitudes toward reading and by undesirable adjustments to their failure to progress. Re-educating these children may be further complicated by sensory, physical, or other handicaps. Each of these children needs a remedial program carefully devised to meet the complexities of his entire problem. The conditions that bring about such reading cases will be discussed in the chapters that follow.

SUMMARY

The disabled reader is more than just a child who cannot read well. He can be found among children at almost any level of general intellectual capability. He is a child who is not reading as well as could be expected for one of his intellectual or verbal maturity. No two disabled readers are the same and it is likely that no two were caused by the same set of circumstances. Many disabled readers become discouraged and frequently develop emotional tensions when in reading situations.

The classification of a child as a disabled reader rather than just a poor reader must be based upon his opportunity to learn, his verbal ability, his demonstrated ability to apply himself in learning situations other than reading, and his general mental ability. The mental ability of the child is most often used in assessing the reading expectancy of the child. Care must be taken in measuring the mental ability of the disabled reader because taking most tests requires reading ability. For this reason individual mental tests are the most suitable instruments.

The problem of using mental growth as a means of assessing reading expectancy is a complicated one. The use of mental age or grade as the sole criterion of expected attainment in reading is of questionable validity. A more sensible and useful approach would seem to be to depend upon calculations based on years in school and the I.Q. of the child.

Disabled readers can be grouped into descriptive categories according to the seriousness of the problem and the nature of the adjustment needed. Simple retardation cases are those children whose reading ability is generally immature but otherwise well balanced. Children with specific retardation are low in one or more types of reading but are competent in basic reading skills and abilities. Children with limiting disability are deficient in basic reading abilities that preclude further growth in reading. Children with complex disability in reading are those who cannot grow further in reading because of deficiencies in basic reading abilities, complicated by their rejection of reading, accompanying personality problems, and frequently by sensory or physical handicaps.

SELECTED READINGS

BRUECKNER, L. J., and BOND, G. L., *Diagnosis and treatment of learning difficulties.* New York: Appleton-Century-Crofts, Inc., 1955, Chap. 6.

GATES, Arthur I., *The improvement of reading,* 3rd ed. New York: The Macmillan Company, 1947, Chap. 1.

TINKER, Miles A., *Teaching elementary reading.* New York: Appleton-Century-Crofts, Inc., 1952, Chap. 12.

5

CAUSES OF READING
DISABILITY:
I. PHYSICAL DEFICIENCIES

READING DISABILITY may be mild, moderate or severe, but whatever its degree, it must be assumed that there is present a cause or pattern of causes which so handicaps a child that he cannot make normal progress in reading. The program of instruction most effectively designed to relieve a case of reading difficulty is based upon a knowledge of this cause or these causes. If we want to identify these we must make an inquiry into a large number of possible impeding factors. These factors may be constitutional, environmental, or both. If a difficulty is but relatively minor and of such a nature that it can be diagnosed by the classroom teacher, proper adjustment of instructional procedures ordinarily will remedy the situation. Techniques for doing this have been outlined by Tinker (175). In more severe cases, the causes must be searched out through a more intensive diagnosis by specialists.

Causes of reading disability are numerous. Some, which in the past were considered important, now receive less emphasis. A number of these will be mentioned later. The search for a single factor or cause of disability has rarely proved to be sufficient. Seldom if ever does a single factor cause disability in reading. The writers of this book strongly emphasize multiple causation. They maintain that all but the very mildest cases of reading disability are caused by a composite of related conditions. Ordinarily several factors are involved, each contributing to the difficulty as part of a pattern. In a search for causes, therefore, the clinician attempts to discover those factors, which in stubborn cases almost seem to conspire to operate together to prevent a child from making expected progress in reading.

In addition to the stress we have laid on the many causes of reading disability that may become contributing factors, there is one *general* fact about reading which should be spotlighted. This fact, emphasized by Gates (79), is the highly complex nature of the reading process. Proficient reading depends upon the acquisition and versatile application of several intricately co-ordinated skills. These skills or abilities are acquired only through long, motivated practice under good guidance. Because the reading process is so complex, there are many opportunities for unfortunate complications to impede its growth. Various factors, operating singly or

84

more often together, may hold up further progress in reading. It is the task of the diagnostician to discover these factors so that they can be eliminated or so that corrective instructional procedures can be devised to adjust to, or to circumvent their bad effects.

It is the purpose of this chapter to discuss and evaluate the role of various physical deficiencies or conditions as contributing causes of reading disability. We shall turn our attention to visual, hearing, and speech deficiencies, motor adjustments, glandular deficiencies, general health, brain damage and congenital word-blindness, and lateral dominance.

VISUAL DEFICIENCIES

It seems axiomatic that ocular comfort and visual efficiency are desirable prerequisites for easy reading. When a child shows signs of becoming a disability case, the tendency of both teachers and parents is to think of the possibility of visual deficiencies. It is true, of course, that a child's eyesight may be so poor that it is practically impossible to read. And there seem to be a number of less severe eye defects which constitute handicaps to children in the reading situation. When these pupils attempt to read, they become uncomfortable, squirmy, fatigued, and distraught to such a degree that they can continue the reading activity for only a short time. Or they may refuse to read at all. Although certain mild defects may not interfere with learning to read, they may make reading for a lengthy period fatiguing. It is not surprising, therefore, that many studies have concentrated upon visual deficiencies as causes of reading disability.

These investigations are too numerous to survey in detail. Furthermore, neither the investigators themselves nor other writers who have attempted evaluation of the studies are in complete agreement concerning the role of visual deficiencies as causes of reading disability. All writers do agree, however, that visual deficiency may be a factor in specific cases and that every child who is a reading disability case should have an eye examination.

In spite of the inconclusiveness of the published reports, certain trends in the findings seem important. The remedial worker should be familiar with these trends. With this in mind, we shall now proceed to run through certain representative findings in this section.

Survey Studies of Visual Deficiencies

Any well-conducted survey reveals a large incidence of visual problems among school children. Betts and Austin (10) made an intensive study of all 126 pupils in a fifth-grade population of one school. In addition to reading tests and the Keystone Telebinocular screening test, a complete eye examination was given by a qualified ophthalmologist. Only about 38 per cent of the children were not in need of lens correction by glasses.

However, no significant relation was found between the visual findings and reading achievement. Nevertheless, those children with a visual handicap have to compensate for this by putting excessive strain on their eyes during prolonged reading.

As part of an extensive investigation, Robinson and Huelsman (142) studied 53 pupils in grade four and 52 pupils in grade seven. The correlation between individual reading tests and individual visual tests revealed very slight and inconsistent relationships. These relationships were essentially the same when the effects of intelligence were eliminated.

In a study of 611 college freshmen, Imus, Rothney, and Bear (107) discovered similar conditions. The measurements of visual status made by ophthalmologists revealed that all but 16 per cent had either mild, moderate, or severe ocular defects. No significant relation was discovered between ocular defects and either reading ability or scholastic achievement. Furthermore, since this is true, it is not surprising to learn that correction of ocular defects did not guarantee improvement in reading or in college grades.

The results cited above are typical for the survey type of study. The studies reveal a large incidence of visual defects in both school and college students. Correlations between reading ability and scores on visual tests tend to be negligible.

Comparison of Good and Poor Readers

The most frequently used method in studying the relationship between visual efficiency and reading ability is to compare the visual characteristics of groups of successful and unsuccessful readers. Here the findings are not in complete agreement. While a few reports suggest that a large per cent of poor readers have some degree of eye defect, others appear to find little difference in visual characteristics between poor and good readers. It is more common to find trends somewhere between these extremes.

Fendrick (68) compared the visual characteristics of 64 poor readers with 64 good readers in grades two and three. The pupils were matched in pairs on the basis of chronological age, years in school, and I.Q. The average difference between groups in reading grade was 1.85. Visual status was determined by the Telebinocular screening tests and by optometrical examinations. The results of the screening tests revealed relatively inferior performance on measures of visual acuity for the reading disability group. This difference was accentuated when only pupils taught by look-and-say (visual) techniques were considered. There was no important difference in acuity for pupils taught by phonetic (auditory) methods. The same trends were found for astigmatic anomalies. The optometric examination (100 cases) showed that 44 per cent of the disability group had defective vision in comparison with 30 per cent for the normal group. The difference was most striking for serious defects, i.e., 16 vs. 6 per cent. Other visual characteristics did not differentiate the groups. Although the trends in this study are suggestive, the differentiation of poor from good readers on the basis of their visual equipment is not impressive.

Employing the Telebinocular screening test with college students, Swanson and Tiffin (163) examined poor readers, unselected readers, and stutterers. Their findings indicated that differences in visual efficiency are not causally related to differences in reading ability among college students. Similar conclusions are reached in other studies.

In her intensive analytical study of 22 clinical reading cases, Robinson (141) discovered that 14 had visual anomalies. Analysis indicated that in 11 of the 22 cases, visual difficulties were probably contributing causal factors of reading disability.

Reports from other studies do not agree with each other. For instance, Farris (65) and Witty and Kopel (188) fail to demonstrate any differentiation of poor and good reading groups on the basis of one or another single visual deficiency. And Edson (62) failed to find that achievement in reading in the fourth grade is limited by visual anomalies. On the other hand, Selzer (149) seemed to find important differences.

The evidence suggests that certain refractive errors (faulty focus of light rays that enter the eyes) are more apt to be associated with reading disability than others. The three kinds of refractive errors are *hyperopia* or farsightedness, *myopia* or nearsightedness, and *astigmatism* or blurring of vision due to uneven curvature of the front of the eye.

There appears to be a high incidence of *hyperopia* among reading disability cases. In comparing poor with good readers or with unselected cases, a greater per cent of poor readers had hyperopia in studies by Eames (60), Farris (64), and Taylor (165). *Myopia,* on the other hand, is seldom associated with reading disability. Studies by Eames (60), Taylor (165), and Farris (65) revealed myopia among good readers as often as or more often than among disability cases. It must be kept in mind, however, that the more severe degrees of myopia will prevent clear vision of materials on charts and blackboards when viewed from a distance. Also myopia will tend to produce undue fatigue of the eye muscles in those children who need to hold their book closer to the eyes than normal (14 inches) for clear vision during prolonged reading.

Astigmatism does not appear to be closely related to reading disability. In fact, as pointed out by Robinson (141), in some instances it may be associated with better than average reading.

Binocular Difficulties

Certain visual difficulties may occur due to the fact that normally we employ our two eyes together for seeing. They are *strabismus, fusion difficulties,* and *aniseikonia.* To see only one image of an object, it is necessary to focus the two eyes precisely and simultaneously on the object. When this is impossible because of muscular imbalance of one or both eyes, the person has *strabismus* or lack of binocular co-ordination. When this condition is mild, the visual image of words or other objects is blurred, and when more severe, two images are seen. Lack of co-ordination between the two eyes may contribute to reading disability. Many writers such as Betts (8), Harris (94), Taylor (165), Farris (64), and Robinson and Huelsman (142) emphasize the handicap of binocular in-co-ordination in reading activities. Eames (58) discovered a significantly greater degree of exophoria (lack of co-ordination in which the eyes turn outward from the desired position) in reading disability cases than in controls. The blurring and double images produced confusion and fatigue in attempts to identify letters and words. Selzer (149) reported that 90 per cent of his reading disability cases had muscle imbalance. When he examined 100 unselected cases, 9 had muscle imbalance and 5 of these were poor readers. Two of these 5 were fitted with proper glasses and their reading improved. According to Farris (64), one-eyed pupils do better in reading than those with muscle imbalance. He also noted that there was greater improvement in reading among pupils with lens corrections than for those without. At the college level, Stromberg (162), Swanson and Tiffin (163), and Bear (6) found no relation between eye-muscle imbalance and reading performance. This finding may be due to the fact that students who reach college have achieved a measure of adaptation to the imbalance or achieve well due to good motivation even though they may have visual fatigue. Witty and Kopel (188) also consider that muscle imbalance is not a factor in reading disability. In contrast, Park and Burri (137) found that ocular defects among elementary school pupils most closely associated with poor reading were binocular in-co-ordination and fusion difficulties (see below). Summing up these somewhat confusing data, it will at least be evident that ocular imbalance may be an important reading handicap to some pupils.

In addition to binocular co-ordination, there must be precision of accommodation or focus of the eye lens if there is to be *fusion* of the images in the two eyes so that the object or word is seen clearly. Taylor (165) reports that 25 per cent of reading failures and only 12.4 per cent of the normal controls had difficulty in fusing retinal images. The most extensive study was done by Eames (60). He reported that 44 per cent of poor, in comparison with 26 per cent of good readers, had fusion difficulties. Although Witty and Kopel (188) found that 29 per cent of their poor readers and 1 per cent of the normal controls exhibited slow fusion, they tend to minimize its relation to reading disability.

Aniseikonia is present when the ocular images of an object fixated are unequal either in size or shape in the two eyes. This makes it difficult for the reader to fuse the incongruent images. The result is visual discomfort, headache, or general fatigue which decreases the length of time a reader can effectively concentrate on visual work. In an extensive study, Dearborn and

Anderson (50) compared 100 retarded readers with 100 unselected cases matched on the basis of mental age. They found that 51 per cent of the poor readers and 23 per cent of the control group had significant amounts (1 per cent and over) of aniseikonia. Aniseikonia at near vision (reading distance), which would produce visual discomfort in reading, was present in 56 per cent of the poor readers and in 22 per cent of controls (68 children in each group). These are statistically significant differences. They conclude that aniseikonia is one of the many factors which may contribute to the causation and persistence of disability in reading.

Eye Movements

Extensive investigation of eye movements in reading reveal that the efficient reader tends to employ relatively few fixations per line of print and that the fixations progress from left to right with few regressions. In contrast to this, the poor reader uses many fixations and many regressions or backward movements. These findings have led many writers to conclude that faulty eye-movement patterns cause reading disability. Tinker (174) has demonstrated that this is an erroneous viewpoint. Examination of the available data reveals that eye-movement patterns merely reflect the degree of proficiency in the cerebral processes involved in reading, i.e., they are symptoms of reading disability, not causes. The role of eye movements in reading will be considered in more detail in a later chapter.

Implications of These Studies

As you have seen, the evidence concerning the relation between specific eye defects and reading disability is not unequivocal. Numerous investigations reveal greater incidence of ocular defects among reading disability cases than among good readers or unselected pupils. But some studies fail to show such a difference. Furthermore, groups of selected good readers include some pupils with ocular defects. These pupils learn to read well in spite of what might have been supposed to be handicaps.

What shall we say? In the first place, one should recognize that eye defects *may* be a handicap to both good and poor readers. Optimum conditions for learning to read do require comfortable and efficient vision. The presence of eye defects which can be corrected should not be condoned. It is the responsibility of the school to do whatever is possible to assure effective vision.

Second, there is sufficient positive evidence to indicate that such defects as farsightedness, binocular in-co-ordination, fusion difficulties, and aniseikonia may contribute to reading difficulties in certain cases. In fact, most writers admit that in individual cases visual defects may impede reading progress.

Third, severe reading disability in most instances is the result of the accumulated influence of many factors operating together in a complex pattern. Consequently it is difficult to evaluate the influence of one factor alone. The point that should be emphasized is that several factors may contribute to failure in reading. It seems obvious that one or another visual defect may be among the contributing factors and therefore must be taken into account. In other words, where visual defects are present, the child is more likely to get into difficulty in reading and is more difficult to teach. It is now generally accepted that visual examinations are essential in diagnosing the causes of reading disability. The clinician should realize, however, that correction of a visual defect is very rarely sufficient to relieve reading disability. Once the correction has occurred, other aspects of the disability which have arisen through handicapped learning must be identified also and appropriate remedial training instituted to achieve the total improvement in reading that now has become possible.

Identification of Visual Defects

To detect possible visual defects, school nurses and reading clinicians use a variety of screening devices. If the screening indicates a visual deficiency is present, the child is referred to a competent specialist for expert diagnosis. None of these screening devices is meant to take the place of a regular eye examination by a specialist. Several screening devices are briefly described below:

The Keystone Visual Survey Telebinocular (distributed by the Keystone View Company, Meadville, Pa.) consists of a binocular viewer and a series of slides. It is employed to detect indications of nearsightedness, farsightedness, astigmatism, muscular imbalance, lack of near-point and far-point fusion, as well as binocular efficiency and stereopsis level (depth perception). No specialized training is needed for its use. It has the advantage of yielding a fairly comprehensive visual inventory and of appraising the co-ordination of the eyes under conditions similar to those in reading activities. Although not all persons referred to specialists on the basis of a Telebinocular testing turn out to have visual defects, it remains a useful screening device.

The Eames Eye Test (distributed by World Book Company, Yonkers-on-Hudson, N. Y.) is intended to detect certain gross classes of eye trouble. It screens for deficiency in visual acuity, nearsightedness, farsightedness, astigmatism, lack of binocular co-ordination, and lack of fusion. According to Eames (61), the tests have high reliability, and a large per cent (97) of the referrals check with oculists' examinations. Since it is easy to give, this test is particularly appropriate for use in schools and clinics. It is inexpensive, and detects most of the visual defects found in school children.

The Ortho-Rater (distributed by Bausch and Lomb, Rochester, N. Y.) originally designed for industrial visual screening, is now being adapted (Robinson and Huelsman) for use with school children. It screens for deficiencies in visual acuity, binocular co-ordination, and depth perception.

It is an expensive apparatus and scoring of the tests is not yet adequately adapted for use with school children.

The Massachusetts Vision Test (Sloane, 152) is good for measuring acuity and binocular co-ordination. It is not practical in the reading clinic since it requires a permanent installation and a trained technician.

The Snellen Chart (distributed by American Optical Company, Southbridge, Mass.) may be used if a more comprehensive test is not available. It measures visual acuity at a distance of 20 feet and will detect nearsightedness. This test is of little use for detecting farsightedness and astigmatism. The *E Chart* is a modification of the Snellen Chart in which the response is made by having the child indicate in which direction he sees the *E* pointing. This can be used to advantage with young children and illiterates. In any testing program, visual acuity at the reading distance should also be measured. This can be done with the *A.M.A. Rating Reading Card* (distributed by the American Medical Association, 535 North Dearborn St., Chicago, Ill.). This test is somewhat similar to the Snellen Chart, but is designed to be read at 14 inches from the eyes. Failure on this test and success on the Snellen Chart indicates farsightedness, while success on this test and failure on the Snellen Chart indicates nearsightedness. Both near- and far-point acuity are measured by the Telebinocular, the Ortho-Rater and the Eames Test.

The diagnostician should keep in mind that poor visual acuity by itself does not specify what the eye defect is. The trouble may be due to nearsightedness, farsightedness, astigmatism, binocular in-co-ordination, or something more serious. The exact defect must be determined by an eye specialist on referral.

Classroom Symptoms of Visual Difficulty

Certain writers, among them Harris (94) and Betts (8), suggest that the teacher should be alert in observing signs of visual discomfort in the appearance or behavior of children. Betts and Austin (10) conclude that a substantial percentage of pupils can be referred to an eye specialist on the basis of such symptoms. Knox (115) attempted to determine the accuracy with which a check-list of symptoms could be used as a basis of referral. She noted that a total of 94 symptoms of visual difficulty was cited by various writers. After consulting with eye specialists, a list of 30 symptoms was selected for study. A group of 126 pupils in the third grade was observed and 47 children referred on the basis of symptoms alone. All 126 pupils were also given visual screening tests and a limited number were examined by an eye specialist. An analysis of results led to the identification of the following 11 symptoms as most significant: facial contortions; book held close to face; tense during visual work; tilting head; head thrust forward; body tense while looking at distant objects as blackboard and charts; assuming poor sitting position; moving head excessively while reading; rubbing eyes frequently; tending to avoid close visual work; and tending to lose place in reading. When two to four of these symptoms persist, a child is more likely to need visual care. A combination of screening tests plus observation of symptoms yields greater accuracy in referral than either alone.

HEARING DEFICIENCIES

Although the relation of hearing deficiency to progress in reading is not obvious, there are ways in which it can be a handicap. Since learning to read under most methods depends to a substantial degree upon speech, any appreciable speech retardation due to hearing impairment may become a contributing factor in reading disability. If auditory difficulties are severe enough to prevent satisfactory discrimination between word sounds, the child may be in trouble with his reading. It is well known that hearing impairment frequently leads to emotional maladjustment which may become tragic in its effect upon a child's personality. Such a condition can prevent satisfactory progress in learning to read as it can any other learning.

Frequency of Hearing Difficulties

Dahl's survey (41) makes clear that there is a wide range from one group to another in the percentage of children with impaired hearing. Various studies have reported from about 3 to about 20 per cent of children with hearing deficiencies, with a median of 10 per cent. The wide disparity in reported incidence of impaired hearing is apparently due to lack of uniform techniques of measurement and to lack of uniform standards for differentiating hard-of-hearing from the normal. Various investigators consider a child has normal hearing if the loss is no greater than 15, 10, 9, or 6 decibels. In any case, the basic facts reveal that a large number of school children—perhaps around 5 per cent in the general population—have serious hearing impairment. Apparently, many additional children have slight hearing losses which may later develop into serious impairment unless proper medical treatment is given.

Relation of Hearing Impairment to Reading Disability

The consensus of the reports summarized by Dahl (41) reveal that the I.Q. measured by a verbal or Binet type of test is about 7 points lower for the hard-of-hearing child than for the child of normal hearing. But when measured on nonlanguage tests, there are no significant differences between the two groups. Apparently language development is retarded somewhat among hard-of-hearing children.

It is well-established that hard-of-hearing children tend to be educationally retarded. For instance, Waldman, Wade, and Aretz (180) found on the average that deafened children were approximately one year behind normal children in educational achievement. It was in the school subjects which involved oral instructions that hearing impairment was most evident.

Obviously, reading achievement depends considerably upon language development and speech facility. Instruction in reading usually involves a large oral component. There the child needs to follow oral activities of both the teacher and other pupils, associate oral speech with printed and written words, make rather fine auditory discriminations between certain words, and use auditory techniques in word analysis. The child who does not hear satisfactorily will be handicapped in these activities.

In general, however, the hearing ability of school children tends not to be correlated with reading ability. Thus, Reynolds (140) found no significant relation between various auditory measures and general reading ability among unselected fourth-grade pupils. It is inevitable that the effect discussed above will be obscured in group studies such as this.

Most studies fail to find greater incidence of hearing deficiency among large groups of reading disability cases than among normal readers. In such investigations, however, the individual clinical case who is handicapped by a hearing defect may have no effect on the group comparison. Betts (8) states that impaired hearing may be causally related to poor reading, or it may reveal merely another difficulty for which the non-achievers must compensate. Kennedy (113), Henry (98), and Robinson (141) found that children with hearing deficiencies for high frequencies tended to be poor readers. The conclusion of Witty and Kopel (190) is that auditory factors appear related to reading disability in individual cases of gross defect and under special conditions of instruction, i.e., a predominantly oral-phonetic type of instruction. In Bond's study (18), the auditory characteristics of 64 poor readers were compared with those of 64 good readers. Significant differences appeared between the two groups. Auditory acuity, blending, and auditory perception difficulties were significantly more frequent among the poor than among the good readers. These differences were even greater between pupils taught by the phonetic (auditory) method. The same trend was found for auditory discrimination although the differences were not as significant. Bond concluded that if a pupil is exposed to an oral-phonetic type of instruction, auditory ability seems to be an important factor in reading disability. This relation appears to be less certain for children taught by predominantly look-and-say (visual) techniques.

In the cases of certain children, even when no hearing deficiency can be found by tests, there is difficulty in auditory discrimination or in auditory blending. Some are unable to distinguish fine differences in sounds as in *shall* and *shell,* or in *mountain* and *fountain.* Other children are not able to blend the component sounds of a word into a word unit. For instance, when the separate sounds *dr* and *ink* are given, he cannot blend them together into *drink.* Such difficulties will be given further attention in later chapters.

Implications of the Findings

There is ample evidence to indicate that certain children are handicapped by hearing impairment. This seems particularly true of cases with severe hearing loss, with high tone deafness, or when pupils with hearing loss are taught by auditory methods. Certainly, every child who is a reading disability case should have a hearing test. While impairment of hearing seldom appears to be the sole cause of reading disability, it may be an important contributing factor in a pattern of causes. Proper instructional adjustments will in most cases minimize the effects of hearing impairment on learning to read. Classroom adjustment to hearing difficulties will be considered more in detail in later chapters.

Testing Hearing

Hearing impairment is most accurately determined by means of an audiometer. Several are available.[1] Western Electric Company's 4C model is similar to a portable phonograph. Each child hears the sounds through a telephone receiver connected to the apparatus. As many as 40 pupils can be tested simultaneously. Children who cannot write numbers cannot be tested by this apparatus. Otherwise the 4C model is a fairly good screening device. If this audiometer is not available, or is inapplicable, as when testing young children, the watch-tick or whisper (or low voice) test may be used for preliminary screening.

A loud-ticking watch, such as an Ingersoll or a Westclox Pocket Ben is employed for the watch-tick test. The child with normal hearing will hear the usual ticking at a distance of about 48 inches. Testing is done in a quiet room. The child stands with one ear toward the examiner and puts his finger in the other ear. The examiner holds a card beside the child's head so that he cannot see the watch. Then the watch is held close to the child's ear and gradually withdrawn until it can no longer be heard. The distance at which the sound disappears is recorded. Similarly, the watch is held at about 48 inches away and slowly moved toward the ear. The distance at which the ticking is first heard is recorded. An average of the two distances is taken. If this average is less than 20 inches, the child requires further checking.

The following method has been used successfully by the writers for administering the whisper or low-voice test: Four or five children are lined up in a row in a quiet room about 5 feet from the examiner and with their backs to him. The latter remains in a fixed position and gives directions to the children, speaking in a distinct, low tone of voice. Directions such as the following are given: "Take five steps forward; raise your right arm; take two steps forward; hold up three fingers"; etc. By watching the children, the

---

[1] Western Electric audiometers are distributed by Graybar Electric Company, New York City; Maico audiometers by the Maico Company, Minneapolis, Minn.

examiner can note those who hesitate, turn to see what other children do, look back at the examiner, or fail to follow directions. The children who get to a position approximately 20 feet from the examiner without signs of seeking help have normal hearing. Hard-of-hearing children are readily detected. Whisper tests may be given by softly saying single words while the child stands about 20 feet away with one ear turned toward the examiner, i.e., a distance at which the majority of children can hear in the particular room used. The child attempts to repeat each word as he hears it. If necessary, the examiner moves closer until responses are correct. Each ear is tested separately.

Any children who do not pass the group audiometer (4C) test or who evidence signs of hearing impairment by the watch-tick or whisper test, should be given the individual and more precise test by means of the Western Electric 6BP or a comparable audiometer. Such an audiometer provides precise measurements over the range of frequencies ordinarily covered by oral speech, i.e., 128 to 8192 vibrations per second by octave steps (128, 256, etc.). High tone deafness mentioned above, is readily detected by this apparatus. The measurements are made in terms of significant hearing loss in comparison with the normal. Zero decibel loss means exactly at normal. Since there is some variation in normal hearing, significant loss is set at various amounts from 6 to 15 decibels. However, a loss of 10 decibels or more may be used as a practical standard. When a child has a significant hearing loss in one or both ears, he should be referred to a medical specialist for diagnosis and treatment. Dahl's book (41) is a comprehensive and practical manual devoted to the measurement and evaluation of hearing.

The alert teacher will note signs of hearing difficulty in a child's behavior. Hearing impairment may be suspected if a child is inattentive and frequently asks to have statements repeated or constantly misunderstands even simple directions. Other signs include reports of ringing and buzzing in the head, tilting of the head, turning one ear toward the speaker, cupping a hand behind the ear, sitting with a blank expression on face, scowling plus strained posture in listening, and turning radio or phonograph on unusually loud. Persistence of any of this behavior suggests the need of a screening test of hearing efficiency.

MOTOR, SPEECH, AND GLANDULAR DISTURBANCES

An appreciable number of disabled readers exhibit poor motor co-ordination. This is manifested by awkwardness in walking, running, writing, and athletic activities. Tests of motor precision tend to yield better scores for superior readers than for nonreaders. Monroe (131) noted that some of her reading disability cases exhibited lack of precision in motor control, in making motor adjustments required in reading, and in bodily adjustments needed to attend persistently to selected stimuli. She suggests that in certain cases, lack of precise motor control may be an important concomitant of reading disability. Although direct causal relation between poor motor control and reading disability has not been clearly established, Gesell and Amatruda (86) mention that muscular in-co-ordination and speech and reading disabilities may be due to slight birth injuries to the brain. Further evidence on this point is needed.

Speech defect is a prominent type of motor in-co-ordination often associated with reading disability. There appears to be a reciprocal relation between facility in speech and reading. Monroe (131) notes that faulty articulation may directly affect reading by presenting a confusion in the sounds of words to be associated with written and printed words. A child with faulty speech hears a word one way when spoken by others and another way when spoken by himself. Thus either of two associations may be aroused on presentation of a printed word. For instance, if the child substitutes *d* for *g* in his speech, he may read "bed" for "beg." Such mistakes would tend to produce confusions in both word recognition and word comprehension.

The unfortunate emotional involvement created by defective speech may contribute to reading disability. Real or fancied reactions of the teacher and classmates to errors of articulation during oral reading may cause the child embarrassment and accentuate his self-consciousness. This may in turn lead to resentment toward the teacher, the school, and particularly toward reading and other language activities. It may make the child unwilling to engage in oral reading and talking in class. Gates (79) points out that, in some instances, these difficulties spread to silent reading. This general emotional stress due to speech defects may, therefore, be responsible in some cases for difficulty in learning to read.

The experimental evidence of a relation between speech defects and reading disability is not unequivocal. Bond (18) found no important differences in incidence of speech defects among poor and good silent readers. However, he did find that 35 per cent of those children that were retarded in oral but good in silent reading had speech defects. This was 11 to 13 per cent greater than when the children were consistently either good or poor in both oral and silent reading. But Monroe (131), who used oral reading as one of her measures of reading ability, discovered that her reading disability cases had many more speech defects than the controls. She concludes that defective speech may be considered a factor in reading disability. In an intensive investigation, Robinson (141) found speech or auditory discrimination difficulty to be contributing causes of reading disability in 4 of the 22 cases. According to most studies and the views of authorities, defective articulation (formation of speech sounds) rather than stuttering seems to be the type of speech defect most frequently associated with reading disability.

Monroe (131) has suggested that inaccurate articulation and reading disability may come from other basic factors, particularly the inabilitv to discriminate successfully the sounds of words. Robinson (141) admits there is some evidence for this. According to Witty and Kopel (190), the observed association of these motor inefficiencies and reading disability found in some children suggests a common basic cause as dysfunction of the endocrine glands. This claim should be viewed with caution. Further evidence is needed to establish any assumption that associated speech and reading difficulty are both symptoms of other more basic factors. Severe speech difficulties should, of course, be referred to a speech specialist for remedial treatment.

Glandular disturbances may be associated with reading disability in specific cases. The evidence in this area, however, must again be interpreted with caution because various mental, physical, and emotional deviations are involved in malfunctioning of the endocrine glands. The most satisfactory evidence comes from reports of case studies of thyroid dysfunction. Harris (94) found signs of endocrine disturbances more frequently among disabled reading cases than among normal children. Olson (135) noted delayed progress in reading cases with underfunctioning of the thyroid. Witty and Schacter (191) found noteworthy improvement in reading over a period of time when thyroid medication was provided where indicated. Hypothyroidism was considered a cause of reading difficulty in 9 per cent of Robinson's cases (141). There has been no confirmation of Mateer's contention (124) that reduced function of the pituitary gland is a common cause of reading disability.

Thyroid deficiency (hypothyroidism) is usually manifested by obesity and mental sluggishness. But a child with an overactive thyroid (hyperthyroidism) tends to lose weight, is overactive and easily fatigued, and is irritable. Neither condition is conducive to effective learning. A child suspected of symptoms of glandular difficulties should be referred to a physician.

Implications of the Findings

Apparently motor in-co-ordination is a concomitant in certain reading disability cases. Causal relationship, however, has not been established. The suggestion that the motor in-co-ordination together with reading disability are merely symptoms of some basic condition such as glandular dysfunction or minor birth injury seems probable but needs confirmation.

Defects in articulation, which complicate word discrimination and word recognition, appear to constitute a form of speech difficulty which contributes to reading difficulty in certain cases. The emotional involvement created by defective articulation may hinder progress in reading. Stuttering does not itself appear to be a primary cause of reading disability. However, if stuttering induces embarrassment in the child or if it is so severe that it blocks smooth progress along lines of print, it may disturb the reading process.

The evidence indicates that glandular dysfunction, particularly hypothyroidism, may contribute to reading disability in certain specific cases. The factors discussed in this section emphasize the importance of individual case study in reading disability. A factor, such as a speech defect, may be a contributing cause in one case but not in another. Further attention will be given to the values of the case studies approach in a later chapter.

GENERAL HEALTH

Learning to read is a complicated and, more often than not, an arduous task. For success, the child must be alert, attentive, and able to concentrate and participate vigorously in the classroom reading activities. Any physical condition which lowers a child's vitality so that he is in a continuous state of fatigue makes it impossible for him to give sustained attention to the task at hand. Malnutrition and loss of sleep are examples. The child who is in a state of chronic fatigue may become almost continuously, or at least intermittently, inattentive. When this happens, the child fails to learn what he should or only learns slowly. In particular, he fails to learn words or techniques which are necessary for progress in later lessons. These effects are cumulative so that eventually he becomes a disabled reader. In addition, such a child is disposed to develop nervous tensions and a negative attitude toward reading.

In some cases, extensive and frequent periods of absence for whatever cause lead to reading disability. When the new words and techniques taught during his absences are vital for later learnings, a child may become severely handicapped in subsequent assignments. Unless special help is provided in school or at home, he slips back farther and farther with each extended absence. As this continues, the child may become a disabled reader.

BRAIN DAMAGE AND CONGENITAL "WORD-BLINDNESS"

Brain injury may occur at birth. The more severe cases among the surviving, such as those with severe paralysis or marked mental retardation, are easy to classify. According to the mature judgment of such authorities as Ford (73), Gesell and Amatruda (86), and Jensen (110), however, many children who receive minor birth injuries betray no clinical symptoms, or else their symptoms are so slight that they escape notice. The prevalence of motor in-co-ordination, minor speech difficulties, or a history of a difficult birth among disabled readers suggests that brain damage may be a basic causal factor. It is probable, however, that reading disability due to brain injury is relatively rare. An occasional very severe case may have a neurological origin. Sometimes a retarded reader who fails to respond to the best clinical treatment has a history of a difficult birth, motor in-co-ordination, or delayed speech development though he possesses normal intelligence. Such a child should be referred to a medical specialist for diagnosis.

Evidence indicates that brain damage is seldom or never the cause of ordinary reading disability. In rare cases, minor brain injury may lead to a series of symptoms such as motor in-co-ordination and slight speech defects associated with difficulties in learning to read. When these symptoms are present in a severely retarded reader unresponsive to remedial instruction, he should be referred to a medical specialist. There is such a thing as an acquired defect in adults known as word-blindness, or alexia, that is attributable to a pathological condition in certain areas of the brain.

The term *word-blindness* denotes a well-recognized condition in adults in which the patient is without memories for word-forms as seen. It usually occurs as a sequel to brain hemorrhage which destroys part of the visual area of the brain. The patient can see black marks on paper but fails to recognize that they stand for words, i.e., specific sounds and ideas. They appear to him the way Greek text might appear to a second-grade American child. Hinshelwood (103), designates this condition "acquired word-blindness." Re-education of such cases is a slow and laborious task.

The child who has experienced extreme difficulty in learning to recognize printed and written language exhibits symptoms analogous to disabilities caused by known cerebral lesions in acquired word-blindness. Because of this, Hinshelwood (103) has, in the opinion of most authorities, wrongly and unwisely, applied the term *congenital word-blindness* to very young nonreaders. His attempt to distinguish two varieties of word-blindness (even if it can be sustained) is not of value to students of reading deficiencies.

LATERAL DOMINANCE

The role of lateral dominance in reading disability is a controversial issue. The literature on the subject is extensive and largely equivocal. It is possible here to indicate only the trends of the evidence and to attempt some evaluation of it.

Lateral dominance refers to the consistent preference for using and for more skillful use of the muscles on one side of the body. Lateral dominance is illustrated by handedness which involves preferred use of either right or left hand for skilled manipulations, and by eyedness which involves preferred use of right or left eye for such tasks as aiming or examining things through a monocular microscope. Crossed dominance, which is less common, occurs when the preferred eye and hand are on the opposite sides. A few individuals are neither dominantly right- nor left-sided, i.e., the ambidextrous person is as skillful with one hand as with the other.

Orton (136), a neurologist, has proposed a much discussed cerebral dominance theory of laterality in relation to reading disability. It is well-established that the right cerebral hemisphere controls movements of the left side of the body and that the left hemisphere controls the right side of the body. He suggests that memory images or records of letters and words exist in the brain in both right and left orientations, one in each hemisphere like mirror images. Orton claims that learning to read involves selecting the memory images in one hemisphere, the dominant one. Where there is marked cerebral dominance, usually manifested by either dominant right- or left-handedness, the child ordinarily has no difficulty in learning to read. However, if the child has not developed either right or left dominance at the time he begins to learn to read, difficulties will arise. There will be conflict between the two sides of the brain. Either right or left orientation of letter sequences may be aroused upon looking at a word, according to which hemisphere happens to take the lead. The result is a tendency to make reversals in reading. Although Orton's theory is generally accepted by neurologists, it is not by most psychologists. As pointed out by Jastak (109), Orton fixed his attention on a group of symptoms and then worked out an *ad hoc* neurological theory to explain them. There is, of course, an excessive incidence of reversals among certain reading disability cases, but they are better explained in other ways as we shall see in a later chapter.

Dearborn has been one of the most vigorous exponents of a relationship between laterality and reading disability (44, 46, 47, 48). Among his clinical cases he found a greater incidence of left dominance, crossed dominance, and lack of dominance than among good readers. He notes that reading difficulties are most likely to appear among children who have been changed over in handedness or whose lateral dominance has never been well-established. In a summary statement, Dearborn (45) suggests that to avoid difficulties in reading, one should be either left-eyed and left-handed or right-eyed and right-handed, preferably the latter. Dearborn's view finds support in certain other facts. Eames (59) found lateral dominance anomalies much more frequently among poor readers than among unselected cases. Crosland's results (40) suggest an association between left-eyedness and reading failure. Although Witty and Kopel (189) tend to minimize the influence of dominance anomalies, they concede that left-eye dominance may induce right-to-left eye movements in reading, i.e., wrong direction. The findings of Teagarden (166) indicate that lack of dominance or crossed dominance may hinder reading progress. Finally, Monroe (131) had more mixed dominance (right hand-left eye, and vice versa) among disability cases than with normal readers.

In a number of more recent investigations, no relation of lateral dominance to reading disability has been found. Noteworthy are the studies of Bennett (7), Haefner (92), Gates and Bond (84), and Witty and Kopel (189).

The equivocal evidence in this area needs further analysis. Most investigations have compared the incidence of dominance anomalies in reading disability groups with the incidence in groups of normal readers. Left-handedness, mixed dominance, or lack of dominance occurs in both groups. It seems reasonable to assume that (1) the dominance anomalies of the good readers when not accompanied by other handicaps were overcome, but (2) these anomalies among poor readers constituted only one of several handicapping conditions and that the constellation of factors produced reading disability. As a matter of fact, such writers as Dearborn (48), Harris (94), Robinson (141), and Gates (79) suggest that dominance anomalies can be a contributing cause of reading disability in *certain clinical cases*. They provide for measuring dominance in diagnosis. Furthermore, certain secondary conditions arising from laterality should not be neglected. The naturally left-handed child who has been forced to change over to his right hand, may be laboring under sufficient emotional tension to hinder effective learning. Even without a change over, the left-handed child may develop considerable nervous tension in adapting to school and play activities. *He has to learn to adjust to a right-handed world.* The awkwardness involved in these adjustments tends to produce self-consciousness. The left-handed child should receive sympathetic guidance in the special adjustments he has to make. Certainly, the naturally left-handed child should not be forced to change over to the right hand.

Implications of the Findings

The evidence that left-handedness, mixed dominance, or lack of dominance may be involved in reading disability is equivocal. Careful analysis of data and conclusions indicates that, in certain rare clinical cases, one or another of these anomalies may contribute to reading disability as part of a pattern of hindering factors.

Measurement of Lateral Dominance

Detailed programs for determining handedness and eyedness are given in descriptions of diagnostic procedures. The following tests should be adequate:

Tests of handedness include noting which hand is used to throw a ball, cut paper with scissors, pick up a small object from the floor, hammer a nail, erase the blackboard, and thread a needle. The tests should be given in such a way that there is equal opportunity to use either hand. Both hands must be free and an object is presented so that it is equally convenient to pick it up with either hand. Several trials should be given, and the results should be tabulated. Examination of the records will reveal definite handedness, or a tendency to use both hands at least nearly equally well.

Sighting tests are usually employed to determine eyedness. A homemade cardboard tube for this purpose is readily constructed. It will yield reliable results. Use one-half of a manila folder. Cut off about ¾ inch from one end to make it 9 by 11 inches. On one long edge, place a dot 1½ inches from each end. On the other long edge, place a dot 4½ inches from each end. Connect the two dots near one end of cardboard by an oblique line. Do the same at the other end. Start at the long edge that has the oblique lines meeting the edge 1½ inches from the end and measure down 2 inches from the corner along the short ends of cardboard and place dots. Now draw lines from end of the oblique lines to the dots just made. Cut off the corner triangular areas formed by these new lines. On the other long edge,

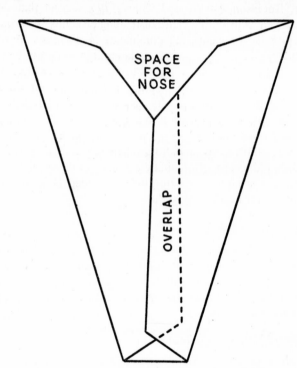

FIG. 3. V-shaped tube for determining eyedness.

measure off 2½ inches from the corners and make dots. From the same corners, measure off along one short edge of the cardboard 4½ inches, and along the other short edge, 3½ inches. Draw lines connecting dots so as to make a triangle at each corner. Cut off these corner triangular areas. Now fold the cardboard along the two long oblique lines and glue the edges together where the ends overlap to make a V-shaped tube. The finished product is shown in the accompanying diagram.

The V-shaped tube is used as follows to determine eyedness of a child: The child is told that you want to find how well he can see things through this tube (show it). Then he is asked to hold the tube between his two hands with the cut-out V at the wide end upward and toward his face. Then he is directed to squeeze the tube open by pressing the hands toward each other and to peek through the tube and tell what you are holding up in front of your nose. The examiner stands about 10 feet away and holds a pencil tip, a crayon, a finger, or some other small object in front of his nose right after the child puts the cone to his face. The object can be seen with only one eye. This eye is easily identified by the examiner as right or left by looking into the open end of the cone as the child looks at him. Several trials are taken with a different object held up at each trial.

The results are tabulated. Examination of these results will readily show whether the child is dominantly right-eyed, or left-eyed, or uses one eye and then the other (lack of dominance) in sighting. The Miles *A-B-C Vision Test of Ocular Dominance* is a device similar to the homemade V-tube. It is sold by the Psychological Corporation, New York City. The Harris *Tests of Lateral Dominance* (same company) provide measures of hand and eye preferences. The relative efficiency of each eye in reading when both eyes are open can be determined by either the *Keystone Tests of Binocular Skill* (Keystone View Company, Meadville, Pa.) or by the Spache (156) *Binocular Reading Test*. These latter two tests will furnish useful supplementary information but this is not essential for determining eyedness.

SUMMARY

This survey suggests that any one of a number of physical conditions may or may not be involved as a contributing factor in reading disability. Much of the evidence is equivocal. It becomes obvious that any single factor by itself seldom if ever causes reading disability. As emphasized throughout this chapter, reading disability tends to be due to multiple causation. Several hindering factors co-operate as a pattern in producing the disability.

A more detailed summary together with selected readings will be found at the end of the next chapter.

CAUSES OF READING DISABILITY: II. EMOTIONAL, INTELLECTUAL, AND EDUCATIONAL FACTORS

6

IN THE PRECEDING CHAPTER, a number of physical conditions which may be involved in reading disability were surveyed. In this chapter, various emotional, intellectual, and educational factors will be examined and their possible roles in helping to produce reading disability appraised.

PERSONAL AND SOCIAL ADJUSTMENT

The personal and social adjustment of the child is intimately linked with his emotional adjustment. In fact, when we say that a child having a reading disability tends to be a personality case, we imply that the child is having difficulty in his emotional adjustment. Emotional maladjustment and personality maladjustment are used synonymously by persons discussing personal and social adjustment in relation to reading disability.

In working with reading disability cases, it soon becomes obvious that most children in difficulty are laboring under some disturbing emotional stress. Emotional tension in the classroom is manifested by symptoms such as shyness or retiring behavior, lack of attentive concentration, habitual nail-biting, a tendency to stutter, lack of self-confidence shown by symptoms of discouragement or by giving up easily, irritability, or aggressive compensatory behavior which draws the attention of other children and disrupts class activities.

There is a wide range in the kind of personal and social adjustment which children manifest when they first begin school. Some are confident, well-poised, cheerful, and co-operative. Such children adjust to the school situation with a minimum of conflict. They respond well to guidance in schoolroom activities. Other children are relatively immature emotionally. They are shy and timid, self-centered, un-co-operative in routine school activities, unable to get along with other children in either play or work, and are easily upset emotionally. Between these two extremes there are many degrees of maturity in personal and social adjustment. Inadequate emotional stability, insufficient self-reliance, and inability to co-operate may handicap a child in his efforts to learn to read.

As the school years go by, certain children will become reading disability cases Most of them will manifest emotional involvement and instability. Naturally, the teacher should be alert to detect symptoms of this. However, as pointed out by Gates (79), one should always be cautious and not assume that a child's instability is permanent or constitutional until other possible sources of his symptoms are ruled out. On the other hand, the signs of personal and social maladjustment may be only surface symptoms of fundamental causes that are indeed relatively difficult to search out. Furthermore, many a child with symptoms of emotional maladjustment does not necessarily become a reading case at all. Many such children learn to read well. However, since most reading cases are also personality cases, it is necessary to explore the role of emotional difficulties as possible causes. To do this, we turn first to representative research studies.

Research Studies

When groups of poor readers are compared with good readers, the results usually show a somewhat larger percentage of pupils with unfavorable signs of personality adjustment among the retarded readers. In most instances the differences are not conspicuous. Bennett (7) discovered that poor readers more frequently were inclined to a solitary life, found adjustment to school life difficult and unpleasant, and were subject to emotional upsets, fears, indecision, and loneliness. These differences, however, between groups of normal and poor readers were not highly reliable. Ladd (117) found a slight but unreliable tendency for poor readers to have less satisfactory personality adjustment. According to Sornson (155), children who become retarded readers in the primary grades develop feelings of insecurity and manifest a less satisfactory form of personal and social adjustment. In Gann's study (74), the behavior of the poor readers manifested a greater number of unfavorable signs. Since Gann depended largely upon rating techniques and the Rorschach Test which have questionable reliability, the discovered trends may not be of great significance. Her view that any secure and stable person, with the usual school arrangements, will learn to read at least with average success has not been substantiated.

The group comparisons in these studies do reveal a somewhat greater incidence of behavior troubles among the poor readers. It should be kept in mind that they also show that many children with adjustment difficulties become good readers.

There is some evidence that certain types of disabled readers exhibit more unfavorable traits than others. For instance, Karlsen (112) found that word-by-word readers rated low in attention, motivation, and social confidence, while context readers rated high on these characteristics.

Reports of clinical studies such as those of Robinson (141), Gates (77), Bird (13), Blanchard (15), Monroe (131), and Witty and Kopel (190) indicate that the incidence of emotional problems among clinical cases of disabled readers is high. The listed personality handicaps which interfere with learning include introversion or preoccupation with one's own thoughts, shyness, lack of self-confidence, fear of the reading task, antagonism toward reading, overdependence upon approval, nervous tensions, compensatory obnoxious behavior, withdrawal from ordinary associations, truancy, and giving up easily. In only a few instances was there evidence of constructive compensatory behavior such as intensive devotion to drawing or dramatics or some other activity.

Effects of Lack of Success

Inability to learn to read satisfactorily usually means severe frustration for the child. When his unsuccessful attempts to read make him conspicuous in a socially unfavorable way, the child is hurt and ashamed. His continued lack of success with attendant frustration and feelings of insecurity bring on emotional maladjustment (Sornson, 155). Some of these children become easily convinced that they are stupid. This feeling is frequently enhanced by the attitudes of their classmates, their parents, and even the teacher, if she fails to understand the true situation. Reading becomes disliked and they seek opportunities to avoid it. Sometimes failure leads children to become timid and withdrawn. Excessive daydreaming is indulged in. In other cases, insecurity is manifested by nervous habits such as nail-biting, or the appearance of hysterically motivated illnesses such as headaches. Still others may compensate for their feelings of inferiority by developing various forms of antisocial behavior.

Most children who enter school with well-integrated personalities are eager to learn to read. They will thrive on success and approval. When some of these meet only failure and frustration, the resulting emotional upset practically always leads to personal and social maladjustment. The reading case has become a personality case.

Emotional Maladjustment as a Cause

Occasionally a child has become emotionally unstable before he ever begins school. The basis of this maladjustment may be either constitutional or home environment or a series of unfortunate incidents during his early pre-school years. Whatever the basis, such a child exhibits impulsive responses, negativistic attitudes, irritability, fluctuation of attention, and lack of energy. These children are unable to achieve the co-operation and sustained effort required in learning to read. Until their emotional adjustments are improved, little progress in learning to read may be expected. Psychiatric aid is indicated.

Emotional Maladjustment: Cause and Effect

When reading disability is accompanied by emotional involvement, it becomes a question of whether the personality maladjustment is primary or secondary. There is no consensus among writers and investigators on this point. At one extreme is Gann (74). She believes that every personality tension unfavorable to learning to read has arisen prior to entering school. The view that personality maladjustment may be due to reading disability is discarded by her. At the other extreme is Fernald (70). Her analysis of the school histories of 78 cases of extreme reading disability treated in her clinic revealed only 4 children who had given evidence of emotional instability before entering school. The other 74 cases were happy, well-balanced, and eager to learn when they entered school. With these, the emotional upset occurred only when they were frustrated in their attempts to learn to read. When they did learn to read, the personality maladjustment disappeared. Similarly, Wilking (184) reviewed 30 studies and discovered only one case reported in which the reading disability was caused by prior emotional maladjustment.

Gates (79) stands in an intermediate position. First he estimated that about 75 per cent of severe cases of reading disability will exhibit personality maladjustment. Then he further estimated that, of those showing personality maladjustment, in about 25 per cent, some emotional difficulty is a contributing cause of the reading failure, i.e., 19 per cent of total group. Harris (94) considers this estimate to be too low. Out of 22 cases, Robinson (141) found that 41 per cent had emotional difficulties, but in only 32 per cent were the emotional difficulties considered to be causes of reading failure. Social problems, many of which involved emotional difficulties, were listed separately. In a large proportion of these cases, the emotional difficulty was considered to be both effect and cause of reading disability.

It is not surprising that the emotional maladjustment associated with reading disability can be both cause and effect. Examination of reported evidence and the views of writers and clinical workers suggests that in only a few cases does the personality maladjustment existing prior to reading experience prevent a child from learning to read. In a larger number of cases, the emotional difficulties appear to be due to failure in reading. There are no data available which permit one to assign exact percentages to the proportion of instances in which the emotional difficulties are causes rather than effects. Examination of all the evidence, however, does make it pretty clear that the emotional maladjustment is much more frequently the effect than the cause of reading disability. This view is strongly supported by the fact that in most instances, the emotional difficulties clear up when the reading disability is relieved by remedial instruction.

When the·emotional and personality maladjustment involves both cause and effect of reading disability, the interaction tends to become circular. In many cases, it is highly probable that there is a reciprocal relationship. Lack of success during early attempts to learn to read produces unfortunate emotional conditioning. The frustration brings feelings of inferiority accompanied by personality and behavior deviations. The emotional maladjustments developed in this way are then a handicap to further learning. In this way, a vicious circle is formed. The reading disability and the emotional reactions interact, each making the other more intense. Robinson (141), Bennett (7), and Monroe (131) concur in this view. In fact, some of the evidence obtained in Robinson's study suggest this reciprocal relationship.

The Home Environment and Adjustment

Success in learning to read depends, in some cases, then, upon the personal and social adjustment of the child. As noted above, the child who is happy, has a well-integrated personality, and feels secure is more likely to make normal progress in his reading than the insecure child. Conditions in the home have an important effect upon a child's personality adjustment before he goes to school and during the school years. A child is fortunate indeed if the home environment provides love, understanding, an opportunity to develop individuality, and a feeling of security. On the other hand, a number of unfortunate home conditions may bring about emotional maladjustment in the child. Quarreling parents, broken homes, neglect of the child, overprotection or domination or anxiety on the part of parents, hostility of parents, and unhealthy rivalry among children in the family are likely to produce nervous tensions and develop feelings of insecurity. Crane (39) has considered reading difficulties as a social work problem. He conducted an intensive case study of 23 children who were reading at least one year below capacity and who were referred as problem cases to a social worker. The parent-child relations were disturbed in 21 of the 23 cases, and there was marked sibling jealousy in 15 cases. Also, 15 manifested unfavorable attitudes toward school. Gates (79) has ably discussed the personality maladjustments which may arise from unfortunate home conditions. When a child becomes the center of a conflict between parents, his unsuccessful attempts to maintain loyalty to both produce emotional reactions with feelings of insecurity unfavorable to learning. The conflict due to divided loyalty in a broken home may produce a similar personality maladjustment in the child.

Sheer neglect or lack of sympathetic understanding makes the child feel that he is not loved or not wanted. Apparent indifference on the part of the parent or overconcern about his difficulties in learning gives rise to anxiety, lack of confidence, and perhaps unfortunate compensatory behavior to get attention.

Overprotection and domination of the child by parents leads to adjustment difficulties. The parent may insist upon exercising intimate and detailed guidance in all activities of the child. The child, prevented from developing initiative, becomes so dependent on others that he is unable to proceed on his own in any learning situation. The overprotective parent may attempt to dominate all activities of the child including his efforts to learn to read. If the child rebels against this domination, as frequently occurs, emotional conflict arises which is deleterious to effective learning.

A mother may be excessively anxious that her child learn to read well. Marked solicitude of the parent about every phase of the child's reading activities may produce anxiety. The cumulative effect of all this may so interfere with learning that the child may even neglect reading entirely.

When a child's reading achievement is compared unfavorably with that of a brother or sister, the effect may be disastrous. Inability to compete successfully is likely to develop a feeling of inferiority. In an attempt to escape from competition and maintain his self-esteem, the child may refuse to cope with difficulties and even cease all efforts to learn to read.

If any conflict between parent and teacher over the child arises, it may have deleterious effects upon the adjustment of the child. For instance, when a child dislikes his teacher, fails to get ahead satisfactorily in reading, and carries his complaint home, if one of the parents vociferously condemns the teacher and her methods of teaching in the presence of the child, the child may make no further effort to learn to read in his desire to prove that the teacher is wrong and that his parent is right.

Any one or a combination of the home situations mentioned in this section may result in unfortunate personality adjustment in the child. Under such stresses as these he all too often develops nervous tension and becomes a chronic worrier. Or he may adopt a defeatist attitude and give up trying to learn to read. In other instances, the child may assume various aggressive and obnoxious forms of compensatory behavior which disrupt classroom activities. In some happier instances, however, these adverse conditions work just the other way, spurring the child on to increased effort so that he becomes an excellent reader. The gratifications achieved through reading may even provide him a way of escape from trying environmental pressures. But in general, of course, unfavorable home conditions hinder rather than help reading progress.

Attitudes

It is of great importance that the child develop favorable attitudes toward school, his teacher, the other school children, and toward reading. While favorable attitudes foster progress in learning to read, unfavorable attitudes may result in reading disability. Satisfactory personal and social adjustment provide the background for the development of favorable attitudes toward the school situation. Home conditions, amount of pleasure obtained from playing with other children, teacher-pupil relations, and the instructional program all influence attitudes toward reading.

Although under favorable circumstances most children begin school eager to learn to read, a few children will come feeling antagonistic toward the whole idea of reading. Occasionally there will be a beginner, who for one reason or another, is so emotionally disturbed that positive attitudes toward reading are difficult to develop in him. These negative children need sympathetic understanding and guidance from the teacher if they are to achieve proper attitudes toward reading.

In most instances, unfavorable attitudes toward reading arise after rather than before the child is exposed to reading instruction. A consensus of investigators, including Ladd (117) and Sandin (147), report that successful achievers form positive attitudes toward reading and the school while slow-progress pupils and reading disability cases hold unfavorable attitudes. From the first day in school, the child should receive sympathetic guidance and the kind of instruction which will assure success in reading. When this happens, most children will maintain their approving attitudes toward reading and other school activities—in short, they will like school.

Implications of the Evidence

Reading disability is generally accompanied by emotional involvement which adversely influences the personal and social adjustment of the child. This personality maladjustment may be due to constitutional factors, to one or more of a variety of pressures in the child's environment, or to failure in reading. The degree to which reading disability is a cause or an effect of personality or emotional maladjustment is often not clear. Examination of the available data suggests the following.

1. In a relatively small proportion of the cases, children are emotionally upset and maladjusted when they arrive at school. The origin of their personality difficulties may be something constitutional or may come from unfortunate environmental conditions. Many of these children will encounter difficulties in their attempts to learn to read.

2. In a relatively large proportion of reading cases, the children will have formed well-adjusted personalities before they arrive at school. The frustration from failure to learn to read results in some degree of personality maladjustment. In these cases, reading disability causes the emotional difficulty.

3. Emotional maladjustment may be both an effect and a cause of reading disability in many cases. The emotional disturbance produced by failure to learn to read may then become a handicap to further learning. A vicious circle is formed, i.e., there is a reciprocal relationship between the emotional conditioning and the reading disability.

4. If the personal and social maladjustment is due to reading disability, it tends to disappear in most cases when the child becomes a successful reader.

5. A few children need to be referred to a psychiatric social worker, a

clinical psychologist, or a psychiatrist for psychotherapy. These include two types of reading disability cases. First, there are the children who are so emotionally upset that they do not respond to the best efforts of the remedial teacher. They must achieve better adjustment through specialized aid before they are ready to learn effectively. Second, with a few children, the emotional maladjustment associated with reading is so ingrained in their responses that it remains after they learn to read well. They continue to feel nervous and insecure about their reading ability. Special therapy is needed to help them achieve more satisfactory emotional adjustment.

6. Adverse attitudes toward reading, the teacher, and school activities are due frequently to failure in reading. These undesirable attitudes are symptoms of personal and social maladjustment.

Identification of Emotional Maladjustment

Usually the presence and degree of emotional maladjustment are ascertained from systematic observations by the teacher and the clinician. All the symptoms mentioned above are readily detectable by the alert and trained observer. Carefully kept cumulative records which include comments on each child's behavior traits and his apparent adjustment to the school situation are also helpful. Home inventories such as the *Minnesota Scale of Parents Opinions* (130) may provide useful information on tension producing factors in the home. Witty and Kopel's *Diagnostic Child Study Record,* Forms V, VI and VII (190) may be used to advantage. Harris (94, p. 239) provides a list of questions to be used in a home inventory. Coordination of the information from observation, records, and a survey of home conditions should give a fair picture of a child's personal and social adjustment together with some information about factors that seem to be involved in maladjustment.

INTELLIGENCE

Reading achievement tends to be related to intelligence at all academic levels. In the elementary school, Strang (159) found correlations of .80 to .84 between the language score on the *California Tests of Mental Maturity* and scores on the *Gates Basic Reading Tests.* But for the nonlanguage intelligence score and the reading tests, the correlations were only .36 to .56. Using the same mental test with ninth-grade pupils, Traxler (176) found a correlation of .69 between the language score and score on the *Iowa Silent Reading Test;* and a correlation of .36 between the nonlanguage score and the reading. Similarly, with university freshmen, Wheeler and Wheeler (183) obtained a correlation of .70 between intelligence test scores where language is used in the tests and reading ability; and .36 between quantitative scores and reading ability. Thus verbal group intelligence tests usually correlate fairly high with reading comprehension while nonlanguage group intelligence tests correlate much lower. Neither the language group test nor the nonlanguage type of test seems very appropriate for getting at the relation between intelligence and reading performance with reading disability cases. The mental age derived from a verbal group intelligence test tends itself to be largely a reading score. Although nonlanguage intelligence test scores may be of considerable help in predicting the reading potentiality of retarded readers, such tests probably do not measure satisfactorily the intellectual abilities employed in reading. Karlsen (112) found that, although the *Wechsler Intelligence Scale for Children* appears to be a promising test in clinical work with children, the mental ages obtained were lower than on the Stanford-Binet Test. Data from a variety of sources, especially Clymer's study (36), suggest that the best measure of mental ability to use with retarded readers is the *Revised Stanford-Binet Intelligence Test.* This is an individual test which must be administered by a trained examiner. According to Monroe's findings (131), mental age derived from this test correlates from .56 to .65 with reading ability. Even the individual Stanford-Binet Test is not entirely free from reading factors. Bond and Fay (26) made a comparison of the performance of good and poor readers on the individual items in two forms of this test. The responses to verbal items, some of which must be read, indicated that reading ability is likely to distort the mental age by favoring the child with superior reading ability and by penalizing the child with poor reading ability. In any case, as pointed out by Durrell (56), neither the Stanford-Binet mental age nor any other measure of reading capacity necessarily sets a limit to a child's reading achievement.

At the present time, the Stanford-Binet seems to be the best intelligence test for use with retarded readers. The correlations cited above, obtained by Monroe, indicate considerable relationship between mental level and ability to learn to read in the ordinary classroom situation. Although children of high intelligence are likely to become able readers and those of low intelligence tend to be poor readers, there are many exceptions. As we shall see later, these data do not mean exactly that low intelligence is a cause of reading disability.

To a certain degree, less than normal intelligence places a limit on attainment in learning to read. After making a survey of the literature, Kirk (114) estimated the maximum reading achievement that should be expected at the completion of school for children of different intelligence levels. He also presented evidence that though dull children may become reading disability cases, they can be taught to read up to the level indicated by their mental capacity. See our later chapter on the specially handicapped child for additional details.

Intelligence seems to play a role in how well a pupil continues to gain in reading ability after a short period of intensive clinical training. Schummers (148) checked the reading status of 52 cases four years after they had spent a five-week period in the University of Minnesota Reading Clinic. Thirteen of these with an average I.Q. of 110, and with little or no special help (zero to 51 hours during the four years), gained 2.5 grades in reading during these four years. Another 13 with an average I.Q. of 103 and with a large amount of special help (216 to 900 hours during the four years), gained only 3.0 grades in reading during these four years. Although other factors may have been operating, these data supply evidence that the aftereffects of clinical training are greater for the brighter children.

Low Intelligence as a Cause of Reading Disability

It is pertinent to inquire whether low intelligence really causes reading disability. In answer, perhaps it is most accurate to say that low intelligence is not itself a direct cause but that it may lead indirectly to reading disability. This occurs when reading instruction of the slow learner during the early school years is not adapted to his needs. The dull child is not ready to read as soon as the one with normal intelligence and he must of necessity proceed at a slower pace after he does begin. In the regular classroom situation, the slow learner is likely not to learn enough at each lesson for effective handling of the next assignment. He drops farther and farther behind as time goes on in the developmental program. If these handicaps are allowed to accumulate, he becomes a reading disability case.

Implications of the Evidence

The possession of less than normal intelligence need not be a cause of reading disability. However, when instructional methods are not adjusted to his slow learning ability, an accumulation of partial learnings will eventually make it impossible for such a child to profit by ordinary classroom instruction. Methods of adapting reading instruction to the slow learner will be described in a later chapter.

EDUCATIONAL CAUSES

Among all the factors which are considered as possible causes of reading disability, the group of conditions that are classed as educational stand out as tremendously important. The vast majority of our disability cases are brought about through faulty learning or lack of educational adjustment of one sort or another. As the child progresses up through the reading program, he fails to acquire the essential learnings or he gets into difficulty because of faulty learnings. The complexity of the reading process, as discussed earlier, is a complicating factor. When we try to get at these educational causes, several areas of educational procedure must be considered. Although they are discussed separately, it must be supposed that they do not operate in isolation. Rather they tend to be related and interacting.

School Administrative Policies

To a large degree, proficient instruction in reading depends upon the teacher. Just because this is true, we must turn our attention to the role that certain administrative policies play in determining how effectively a teacher can organize and carry out her reading program. Some of the policies which handicap even the best of teachers will be considered briefly.

Reading versus Pupil Development. Whether reading or child development should be the chief concern of the school during the early grades is a controversial issue (Dolch, 53). In earlier years the emphasis was almost entirely upon development of reading skill. Recently, many educators have objected to this emphasis. They hold the view that the chief concern of the school should be the happy, balanced development of each child's personality. Many teachers are not only aware of the issue between these two emphases, but also may be under pressure to stress one approach at some sacrifice of the other. The prime argument of those who oppose development of effective reading in the primary grades, is that putting pressure on the children to read sometimes produces personality maladjustments. They claim that emphasis upon reading destroys interest in learning since, as they claim, reading is an activity foreign to the real interests of children in these grades. Actually, there need be no serious conflict between well-balanced child development and all-around development which includes reading, if the reading is taught properly. With individualized instruction, which takes into account reading readiness, development of reading can become an integral part of the program to develop a balanced personality. Such a program means that only those who are ready begin to read early in grade one. Other children start at some later time and only when they are capable of succeeding. Where frustrations arise, it is likely to be due to the method of instruction rather than to reading as such. In any case, reading instruction is bound to suffer when administrative pressure tends to overemphasize or to underemphasize reading in the primary grades.

Promotion Policy and Curriculum Rigidity. In 1938, Cole (37) stated that the basic cause for the prevalence of remedial reading classes was the failure of schools to adjust the curriculum to the current promotion policy. To some degree, this indictment is still valid. She was referring to promoting children mainly by age rather than by achievement with no accompanying change in curriculum requirements. This produces a wider and wider range in reading ability in successively higher grades. At the same time, the curriculum requirements have remained fairly rigid. Consequently, much of the material assigned to pupils in the higher grades is too difficult for the reading ability possessed by many pupils. Material at a fixed level of difficulty, e.g., the grade four level, tends to be used rather than materials on the same topic but at different difficulty levels. Too frequently we try to force the child to adjust to the curriculum rather than adjusting the curriculum to the child. As the poorer readers are promoted from grade to grade, they drop farther and farther behind, and eventually become disabled readers. Although such a promotion policy coupled with rigid curriculum requirements may be detrimental to reading achievement, it is not the only problem involved. Another is the lack of a satisfactory reading readiness program which provides for adjustment of instruction to individual differences. It is lack of this, forced by rigid curriculum requirements, rather than year-by-year promotions as such, that brings about reading disability.

Lack of Reading Readiness

Success in learning to read depends largely upon the stage of all-around development which the child has achieved. The pattern of growth involved embraces a complex of abilities, acquired behavior, and information. In general, a child is ready to be taught to read by a given program when he has attained a certain stage of mental maturity, an adequate background of experience, and satisfactory personal and social adjustments. Some aspects of reading readiness, as intelligence, come with inner maturation. But many important ingredients are learned and therefore are susceptible to guidance. To a large degree, therefore, reading readiness can be and should be taught. An appreciable number of children who arrive at the first grade are not ready to learn to read in the typical program. These children will range from those who need a few weeks of readiness work to those who may need from a semester to a year or more of this training in addition to the intellectual development to be gained during that length of time. It is always desirable to recognize that the program of instruction can be modified to adjust to differences in intelligence.

Reading disability is frequently caused by starting a child in a standard reading program before he has acquired the readiness which will assure success in classroom reading activities. Due to his lack of experience, verbal facility, intellectual or emotional maturity, or a combination of these, he is unable to achieve enough of the learnings day by day to handle satisfactorily what is coming next. He gets farther and farther behind as time goes on. Inability to cope with the assignments produces frustration which leads to feelings of inadequacy, inferiority, insecurity, and perhaps even rebellion. Such a child is likely to develop an attitude of indifference to reading. He may even come to hate reading and all persons and activities connected with reading activities.

The large incidence of failures in reading during the primary grades is due in part to lack of reading readiness. Any educational program or administrative policy which provides the same formal reading instruction for all pupils at the beginning of grade one can only lead to disaster for many pupils.

Lack of Adjustment to Individual Differences

Beginning in grade one and in every grade thereafter, reading instruction can be effective for all pupils only when there is satisfactory adjustment to individual differences. Without such adjustment, reading difficulties arise. This topic has been considered in detail in an earlier chapter.

Methods of Teaching

The vast majority of reading cases are brought about through failure on the part of the child to acquire the necessary learnings, or through faulty learnings as he progresses up through the reading program. The extreme complexity of the reading process provides numerous opportunities for the child to get into difficulties. Coupled with this is the factor of *ineffective teaching.* For one reason or another there occurs a lack of educational adjustment to the needs of certain pupils so that they fail to acquire the essential learnings.

A number of factors may lead to ineffective teaching. Curriculum requirements may take so much of the teacher's time that she is unable to individualize the program satisfactorily. At the same time, the methods or materials used may be too difficult for certain youngsters. Coupled with these conditions, it is probable that certain pupils are pushed through the program too rapidly to acquire the learnings the program is designed to teach.

Use of materials and methods that appear dull and unimportant *to the pupil* constitutes another aspect of ineffective teaching. In beginning reading, for instance, it is important that the child develop the attitude of insisting upon understanding what is read. To achieve this, the reading material should either tell him a story (have a plot) or give him some information he desires. This cannot be achieved by excessive use of ill-constructed and insipid experience charts, nor by the reading of the dull and anemic materials made up of almost meaningless sentences in many primers, or isolated drill on word parts. One youngster, on being exposed to such material said to his teacher, "That sounds silly." It is not surprising that some children react strongly against such reading activities, and develop unfortunate attitudes which harden into obstacles to learning to read.

In a similar way, procedures which do not tie up class activities with the reading program may lead to reading disability. When reading is taught as something apart, as something of little consequence in the class scene, it is small wonder that the child sees no reason for learning to read. In contrast to this, if there is a vital relationship between reading and class activities so that reading itself is an essential tool in those activities, the child is more inclined to become motivated to learn to read. In other words, it is desirable that reading activities stem from some of the important things the child is doing in the class, and that many of the class activities stem from the reading program. Then the child can see a reason for reading. His interest and motivation are maintained at a high level.

It should be emphasized here that interest is not synonymous with being entertained. Real interest with strong motivation back of it is not achieved by flitting from one amusing incident or story to another. Much more fundamental is a program in which reading is tied up in a carefully co-ordinated manner with important enterprises going on in the classroom.

Such a program implies an intimate co-ordination of the language arts in general, i.e., speaking, writing, listening, spelling, and reading. Difficulties arise, for instance, when a youngster is expected to spell a word and use it in his writing when he has not learned to recognize it in his reading.

Excessive emphasis upon isolated drill tends to kill interest. As we shall see later, a certain amount of appropriately conducted drill is desirable and necessary. Sometimes, however, drills are separated so far from the real act of reading that the child is not able to bridge the gap. Not only is he unable to transfer what is learned in the drill to actual reading, but also he does not see the reason for the drill. For him, the drill may kill his interest in learning to read. Methods which concentrate upon isolated drill with phonetic elements, or excessive devotion to reading and recitation of isolated facts rather than sharing stories and experiences lead to loss of interest and inhibit the desire to learn to read.

Inappropriate emphasis upon the basic reading skills may prevent effective reading. The basic skills include such things as development of a sight vocabulary, word-recognition techniques, word meanings, reading by thought units or phrasing, comprehension, and study skills. Either under-emphasis or overemphasis may lead to difficulties. Probably more children are in difficulties due to underemphasis than to overemphasis. The basic skills are the things which underlie efficiency in reading. Stories and other reading matter in books are simply materials which make it possible for the teacher to show the child how to do the job of reading. In doing this, the skills and abilities should be properly stressed and systematically ordered.

Many youngsters are in trouble because progressive tendencies in teaching are not well thought out. It should not be forgotten that progressive tendencies which ignore systematic, orderly development of the essential skills and abilities are unfortunate for the pupils. The methods used, the creative drive, and the use of reading as an important tool within a progressive program, are good as long as the orderly development of reading skills and abilities is duly attended to. It is difficult to conceive of proper emphasis upon the basic skills and abilities without an orderly, sequential, basic reading program. It is impossible to keep the sequence in mind and have reading a by-product of something other than an important reading program. Some of the cases referred to the Minnesota Reading Clinic appear to be the result of teaching reading as a by-product of the social studies and other content studies. McKee (127) concurs in our view. He points out that the perfunctory, unorganized, and meaningless teaching of the content subjects as carried out in many schools is partially responsible for the retardation in reading ability found among pupils. Teaching of the content subjects can contribute to effective reading if training in the basic skills and abilities is an integral part of that instructional program. The initial introduction to reading content materials should be made in a well-organized basic program which shows the child how to go about reading and teaches him the essential skills and abilities.

When the emphasis upon mechanics of reading leads to neglect of meanings, the child is in difficulty. Undue stress upon word recognition, perfection of enunciation, and speed may lead to verbalism, i.e., the pronunciation of words without understanding their meanings. A girl in one of our remedial reading groups could do a beautiful job of orally reading fourth-grade materials, but she could comprehend practically nothing of what she "read." To pronounce words without understanding their meaning is not reading. It is merely word-calling. This girl was a reading disability case.

Overemphasis upon phonetic analysis as a word-recognition technique frequently causes disability. The child is so intent upon sounding out most of the words he encounters that he is unable to attend to meanings. Or he laboriously separates a new word into its component sounds and then is unable to blend the separate sounds into a recognizable pronunciation of the word. Such cases usually have an insufficient sight vocabulary and are unable to make adequate use of verbal context clues to word recognition.

To progress satisfactorily in learning to read there must be a proper balance maintained in the growth of a large number of skills and abilities. Such things as the development of a sight vocabulary, the various techniques for word recognition, concepts and word meanings, reading in thought units, the comprehension and study skills, and many other abilities must not be done in splendid isolation one after another. They are all part of an integrated sequential program. There is a balanced relationship between them that must be striven for. The pupil who gets into difficulty is quite frequently the child for whom the balance has not been maintained.

We grant that it is difficult to imagine a teacher who is able to handle a class of 30 to 40 children and at the same time keep account of all the essential balances while carrying out her sequential program in a systematic and orderly fashion. But in any case, the teacher should never forget the importance of the balanced program and do what is possible to achieve it. The smaller the class, the greater the possibility of maintaining the balance.

Role of the Teacher

Heed should be given to the role of the teacher herself. She can have a positive or negative influence upon progress in learning to read. Pupils are fortunate indeed if their teacher is so able, well-trained, and sympathetic that she maintains good pupil-teacher relationships and is able to achieve a proper balance in the orderly development of skills and abilities in the sequential reading program. When teachers deviate from this high standard, reading instruction is apt to suffer. The teacher who is inept due either to poor training, lack of experience, or a slavish devotion to inflexible routine, will be unable to adjust reading instruction to the numerous and varied needs of pupils in her class. Under such conditions, certain pupils will be in difficulty.

Gates (79) and Witty and Kopel (190) have stressed the unfortunate effects of unsatisfactory teacher-pupil relationships. A teacher's personality, especially when she forms some unfortunate attitude toward a particular pupil, may cause or intensify the emotional stress associated with his failure in reading. Apparent indifference, hostility, or any obvious anxiety on the part of the teacher when a pupil is having difficulty in reading, intensifies the child's emotional reactions and feelings of insecurity. We have to face it—in many cases, the teacher is not without blame when a child becomes a reading disability case.

Implications of the Evidence

Educational factors play an important role in the causation of reading disability. Any administrative policy which prevents either adjustment of instruction to individual differences or proper emphasis upon reading readiness hinders effective progress in reading. By far the most important educational cause of reading disability is ineffective teaching. Failure of the child to acquire the necessary learnings, or his acquisition of faulty learnings may block later progress. Factors which bring this about may be such things as too rapid progress in the teaching schedule, inappropriate materials or inappropriate methods, unhappy isolation of reading from other class activities, the wrong kind of emphasis upon a technique or skill, or treating reading as a by-product of content studies. Ordinarily two or more of these factors are involved, and sometimes a physical deficiency as well. In many cases, the disability arises because the instructional program has failed to maintain a proper balance in the growth of a large number of skills and abilities. When ineffective teaching is specified as the cause of reading disability, what is meant is a pattern of interacting factors. The principle of complex causation is operating.

Identification of Educational Causes

The effects of these things we refer to as school administrative policies upon reading disability are not readily measured. Evaluation of curriculum requirements as related to individualization of instruction may be worked out within the school system itself or it may be carried out by a qualified expert from the outside.

Inadequate learnings, faulty learnings, and lack of balance among abilities are discovered through diagnostic tests described in a later chapter.

SUMMARY

This summary will cover materials discussed in this and the preceding chapter.

The possible causes of reading disability are numerous. A single factor seldom causes reading disability. In all but the mildest cases the difficulty is due to a composite of related conditions. The contributing factors interact as parts of a pattern. The view taken in this book, therefore, is that reading disability is due to multiple causation.

Although the evidence concerning the relation between specific eye defects and reading disability is not unequivocal, certain relevant trends appear. (1) Eye defects appear frequently among both good and poor readers and can be a handicap to a child in either group. Comfortable and efficient vision should be provided for all children whenever possible. (2) Positive evidence indicates that farsightedness, binocular in-co-ordination, fusion difficulties, and aniseikonia may contribute to reading disablity in certain cases. When a visual defect is present, there are usually other associated contributing causes. (3) Visual examinations are essential in diagnosing causes of reading disability.

Hearing impairment can be a handicap in learning to read. This is particularly true when the hearing loss is severe enough to interfere with normal auditory discrimination. The evidence indicates that hearing impairment may be associated with reading disability as a contributing cause when (*a*) the hearing loss is severe, (*b*) the child has high tone deafness, and (*c*) pupils with hearing loss are taught reading by predominantly auditory methods. All pupils who become reading cases should have a hearing test.

Although motor in-co-ordination is sometimes associated with reading disability, causal relationship has not been established. Both the motor in-co-ordination and reading disability may be due to some basic condition such as minor birth injuries. Defects in articulation which complicate word discrimination and recognition may contribute to reading disability. Any severe emotional involvement created by speech defects tends to inhibit effective progress in learning to read. In certain cases, glandular dysfunction, particularly hypothyroidism, may contribute to reading disability.

Various conditions associated with poor health can be detrimental to normal progress in reading. Apparently, brain damage is seldom a cause of reading disability but when it is present, a very difficult instructional problem exists.

Reading disability is usually accompanied by emotional involvement which adversely affects the personal and social adjustment of the child. This personality maladjustment may be due to constitutional factors, to pressures in the child's environment, or to failure in reading. In a relatively small number of cases, the child is emotionally upset when he arrives at school.

Such a child is apt to encounter difficulty in reading. In many cases, the frustration arises from failure to learn to read. In these cases the reading difficulty causes the emotional upset. It seems that, in many cases, emotional maladjustment may be both effect and cause. When emotional disturbance arises from reading disability, it may then become a handicap to further learning. There is in such cases a reciprocal relationship between emotional conditioning and the reading disability. In those cases where personality maladjustment is due to reading failure, it tends to disappear when the child learns to read satisfactorily. With certain cases, when the emotional maladjustment is deep-seated, psychiatric help will be needed.

Lower than normal intelligence need not be a cause of reading disability. But when instructional procedures are not adjusted to a child's slow learning ability, an accumulation of partial learnings will eventually make it impossible for him to profit by regular classroom instruction.

Frequently, reading disability is largely due to educational factors. Any administrative policy which prevents proper individualization of instruction including proper emphasis upon reading readiness will prevent effective progress in reading. Failure to acquire the necessary learnings or the acquisition of faulty learnings is most frequently due to ineffective teaching. One or more of the following factors may be involved in the ineffective teaching which brings about reading disability; too rapid progress in the instructional schedule, isolation of reading instruction from other school activities, inappropriate emphasis upon some technique or skill, or treating reading as a by-product of content studies. Frequently, the difficulty occurs because the instructional program has failed to maintain a proper balance in the growth of a large number of skills and abilities.

It should be obvious from our discussion of causes of reading disability that the case study is of great importance. Watkins' study (181) gives definite support to this view. No pattern of causes is valid for disability cases in general. Each case is unique. An intensive diagnosis must be made of each child referred to the clinic. Only when this is done will the clinician have a sound basis for his recommendation of a specific remedial program that will relieve the disability.

SELECTED READINGS

BLAIR, Glenn M., *Diagnostic and remedial teaching,* rev. ed. New York: The Macmillan Company, 1956, Chap. 3.

GATES, Arthur I., *The improvement of reading,* 3rd ed. New York: The Macmillan Company, 1947, Chap. 4.

HARRIS, Albert J., *How to increase reading ability,* 3rd ed. New York: Longmans, Green & Company, 1956, Chaps. 9, 10.

MONROE, Marion, *Children who cannot read.* Chicago: The University of Chicago Press, 1932, Chap. 5.

ROBINSON, Helen M., *Why pupils fail in reading.* Chicago: The University of Chicago Press, 1946, Chaps. 2-8.

STRANG, Ruth, McCULLOUGH, Constance M., and TRAXLER, Arthur E., *Problems in the improvement of reading,* 2nd ed. New York: McGraw-Hill Book Company, Inc., 1955, Chap. 12.

WITTY, Paul, and KOPEL, David, *Reading and the educative process.* Boston: Ginn and Company, 1939, Chaps. 7-8.

PART III

Diagnoses of
Reading Difficulties

7 GENERAL PRINCIPLES OF DIAGNOSIS

THE COMPLEX NATURE of the reading act makes it possible for a wide variety of faulty reading habits to become established. There are also many chances for the child to fail to develop sufficiently one or more of the numerous essential skills or abilities involved in proficient reading. There is the additional hazard of a child developing some overemphasis of a particular skill, thus preventing him from employing the diversified approach to reading that is so much needed for success.

The problem of helping the disabled reader is further complicated by the many characteristics of the child and his learning environment that have a bearing on his reading growth. It is necessary to adjust to some of the variations within the physical, emotional, educational, intellectual, and environmental factors if reading growth is to progress smoothly or at all. Sometimes these same factors need to be corrected before remedial programs can be expected to be effective.

It is small wonder, then, that the classroom teacher, attempting to correct disabilities in this intricate learning for a wide variety of children who are in trouble, finds that no two cases have the same instructional needs. Any attempt to give a child remedial instruction must be based on a thorough diagnosis of his unique reading needs and personal characteristics. Such a diagnosis is the very core of successful programs of correction, whether they are for the less complex problems met in the classroom or for the more complicated problems of the clinic.

Diagnosis of reading difficulties is an essential part of classroom instruction. The better classroom teachers are constantly studying the reading strengths and weaknesses of their children. They are also on the alert for any signs of physiological or sensory limitations among them. Being well aware of the need for adjusting methods to the differences noted, teachers are becoming increasingly familiar with modern diagnostic procedures and with the relationship of the findings to varied programs of re-education or to altered ways of training their pupils. They are quick to detect and correct many learning difficulties before they become serious and they are becoming well equipped to cope with the milder degrees of reading difficulties.

The classroom teacher may need special help in diagnosing or correcting some of the more complex disabled readers or when limitations in reading are so subtle that a diagnosis, more detailed and more penetrating than the

125

teacher has time or training to give, is required. Frequently it is necessary to study the reading pattern of a disabled reader by means of individual appraisals that take several hours to administer. The classroom teacher with 35 children must make a decision as to how much of her time can be devoted to one child at the expense of all the rest. It becomes expedient to have the more detailed diagnoses conducted by someone who can work individually with given children over a long period of time. At times, the diagnosis entails the use of special equipment which is available only in a reading clinic. In many cases of disability in reading, it is necessary to obtain appraisals and corrective help from other specialists, such as social workers, psychologists, physicians, or psychiatrists.

Of course, the teacher should diagnose and correct as many of the reading difficulties as she can. The early detection and correction of such cases will prevent many from becoming more complex reading cases. There are numerous diagnostic procedures that the classroom teacher can use in studying the moderately disabled reader. In the more subtle cases, an outside diagnosis may be needed to help the teacher formulate the kinds of remedial treatment she can provide in the classroom. In some instances, both the detailed diagnosis and the therapeutic treatment will be best given in special reading centers or clinics. But in every reading disability case, whether simple or complex, a diagnosis is necessary. That diagnosis must be directed toward obtaining whatever information about the case is essential for improvement of instruction.

The following general principles of diagnosis in reading warrant discussion:

1. A diagnosis is always directed toward formulating methods of improvement.
2. A diagnosis involves far more than appraisal of reading skills and abilities.
3. A diagnosis must be efficient—going as far as and no farther than is necessary.
4. Only pertinent information should be collected and by the most efficient means.
5. Whenever possible, standardized test procedures should be used.
6. Informal procedures may be required when it is necessary to expand a diagnosis.
7. Decisions in formulating a diagnosis must be arrived at on the basis of patterns of scores.
8. A diagnosis should be continuous.

A DIAGNOSIS IS ALWAYS DIRECTED TOWARD FORMULATING METHODS OF IMPROVEMENT

In studying a disabled reader, whether in the classroom or clinic, the diagnosis should be concerned with the collection of information necessary

for planning a corrective program. There are two types of diagnosis—
etiological and therapeutic. Etiological diagnosis is concerned with finding
out what caused a child to get into difficulty. Such a search is often impossible and frequently useless for formulating a remedial program. It is of
little use, for example, to search the records and find that a child is in
difficulty in reading in the fourth grade because he was absent from school
with the measles when he was in the first grade. Nothing can be done now
to give him the help that should have been available when he returned to
school after a month's absence during the first grade. A body of such information, collected and summarized for research purposes, would be most
useful for the prevention of reading difficulties, but it is not useful now for
the immediate job of correcting a reading disability that began several
years earlier.

Therapeutic diagnosis is concerned with the conditions that are now
present in the child in order to give direction to a program of re-education.
The diagnostician concerned with therapeutic diagnosis searches for the
reading strengths and limitations of a child and for any characteristics
within this child's present environment or make-up that need to be corrected
before remedial instruction can be successful, or for conditions that need
to be adjusted to before he can be expected to make maximum progress.
The diagnostician would be more concerned about a current hearing loss,
for example, than he would be about finding out that the child was in
difficulty because he had had a temporary hearing loss several years ago.

DIAGNOSIS INVOLVES FAR MORE THAN
APPRAISAL OF READING SKILLS AND ABILITIES

The complex nature of reading disability and the large number of factors
that are related to successful achievement in reading make it necessary to
explore many traits in the individual child as well as many reading skills
and abilities in order to arrive at an adequate diagnosis. In addition to
locating the deficiencies in reading that are at the root of the disability, it is
frequently necessary for the diagnostician to appraise the physical, sensory,
emotional, and environmental factors that could impede progress. In some
cases, the diagnosis will require other expert help. The diagnostician needs
to be on the alert to the possible effect of conditions within the child or his
environment that require such specialized help as the services of a social
case worker, psychologist, physician, otologist, ophthalmologist, psychiatrist, or neurologist. All appraisals made in more complex cases should be
extensive enough to locate the existence of such limitations. The measurements employed in a reading diagnosis will be discussed in chapters that
follow. It is enough to say here that the diagnosis should supply all the
information pertinent for correcting the disability.

THE DIAGNOSIS MUST BE EFFICIENT—GOING
AS FAR AS AND NO FARTHER THAN IS NECESSARY

The diagnosis of some disabled readers is often a lengthy and intricate process. In other cases, the instructional needs of a child can be isolated with relative ease and in a minimum of time. A diagnosis, therefore, should proceed as far, and only as far, as is necessary to formulate a remedial program for each specific case. The diagnosis should proceed from group measurements to the more detailed individual measurements which are needed for the specific case under study. Also, the diagnosis should be arrived at by measuring first the relatively common types of problems and proceeding toward the more unusual ones.

It would be expected, for example, that one would give routinely to all suspected reading disability cases measurements of general reading capability and of general mental ability. On the other hand, it would be only in an unusual case that a complete neurological examination would be required. The procedures in diagnosis are, therefore, much like successive screenings in which only the more complex and subtle cases are retained for further measurement and study. It turns out that there are, then, various levels of diagnosis: (1) appraisals which are routinely made for all children in the schools or for all children referred for special study; (2) appraisals which are more detailed in character and are made only in those instances in which more analytical study is warranted; and (3) appraisals which are highly individual in nature which are made only when confronted by more subtle cases.

In reading diagnosis, as in all educational diagnosis, three levels of study, as described in Brueckner and Bond (31) are apparent. The level of diagnosis reached in any one case depends on the characteristics of that particular case. The three levels through which some cases must be carried are: general diagnosis, analytical diagnosis, and case-study diagnosis.

Many children's learning problems may require only a general study of their educational achievement and intellectual capacity. Other children's difficulties may require more differential or analytical study in order to locate the specific areas of limitation. Some of these children's problems may be so subtle or complex that a detailed case study is required before a remedial program can be designed.

General Diagnosis

General diagnosis is made by studying the results of general survey or achievement tests in order to locate areas of weakness. Such a diagnosis is used to identify children who are doing relatively poor work in reading as compared with their other achievements. When the general diagnosis includes adequate measures of mental ability, the instructional problem of some of the poor readers may be isolated and corrective educational procedures outlined. The information for general diagnosis is usually obtained by the use of group tests and other sources of information which supply the teacher with data on the achievement levels of the children in the major curricular fields, their general intelligence, their ages, and any other facts needed to run an individualized educational program. The information recorded in the cumulative records of the children could be used in making a general diagnosis. A study of that record would show any unusual or unexplained changes in the general progress of a student. If, for example, a child was seen to have a consistent rate of growth, and if this rate of growth was within the expected range for a child of his general intelligence, albeit somewhat slow, the teacher would know that she need not explore his case further. This child's educational problem would have been diagnosed and it is unlikely that further diagnosis would supply valuable additional information.

A general diagnosis might indicate that the child was doing better work in reading than he was in the other areas of the curriculum. The problem would then be to explore these other areas and a further assessment of the child's reading strengths and weaknesses would be unnecessary. General diagnosis of another pupil might reveal that the child was relatively capable, that he was doing well in nonreading subjects, but that he was low in general reading capability. In such a case, further diagnosis would be essential. The child would need a more analytical diagnosis of his poor reading ability.

The general diagnosis can serve three major purposes. First, it gives information necessary to adjust instruction to meet the needs of groups of children in general. For example, a fifth-grade class as a whole may be found to be relatively weak in reading ability. If so, the conclusion may be reached that more attention should be given to reading instruction than had been given in the past. Second, the general diagnosis can give the information necessary for adjusting instruction to individual differences in reading found within the class. It can, for example, indicate the range of general reading capability with which the instruction must cope and also indicate the individuals that would profit from such modifications as are usually made within a class to adjust to individual differences. Third, a general diagnosis can help to locate the children who are in need of a detailed analysis of their reading disability.

Analytical Diagnosis

Analytical diagnosis explores systematically specific strengths and weaknesses in reading. This level of diagnosis locates the nature of the reading disability. It indicates the skills and abilities wherein the child's weakness lies. The diagnosis identifies such problem cases as: the inefficient reader, the child limited in word recognition, the child with general comprehension difficulty, or the child limited with respect to some specific type of comprehension, etc.

This level of diagnosis may indicate the instructional needs of the first two types of reading cases, i.e., general retardation or specific retardation. A rather detailed analytical diagnosis might indicate that a given child had a rather uniform profile in reading and was, on the whole, a good reader of material at his own level of reading advancement, although a year or so less mature than he should be in reading. Such a child would be likely to need some adjustment through an organized basic program at his level of reading capability and also through supplying more stimulation to read. He does not need re-education nor a modified remedial program, nor does he need a still more thorough case-study diagnosis. The original analytical diagnosis would have discovered all one would need to know about his instructional needs.

Another child may be found low in reading through a general diagnosis, but the analytical study of his reading strengths and weaknesses shows that most of his skills and abilities have already been developed adequately. Limited experience in a specific type of reading comprehension was found to have caused his poor general performance. Such a case would require no further diagnosis. All that is needed is a remedial program designed to give training and experience in the type of comprehension in which the child was found to be limited.

Analytical diagnosis has two important contributions to make to the correction of reading disability. *First,* it locates those areas of limited ability that need to be explored more fully. *Second,* it is often sufficiently diagnostic to indicate by itself the instructional adjustments required. Many cases, however, will need more detailed study of their reading problems and specific characteristics than can be made at the analytical level.

Case-Study Diagnosis

All disabled readers who have not been adequately diagnosed by general or analytical diagnosis will need careful case studies made of their reading skills and abilities. In addition, they may need appraisals made of their mental, physical, and sensory characteristics; their attitudes toward reading; their adjustment to the reading problem; and their environmental surroundings. When dealing with the more involved cases of limiting disability or complex disability, all the requisite information must be collected if an adequate program is to be formulated.

The first type of information that it is necessary to obtain for case-study diagnosis is secured from standardized reading diagnostic tests or procedures. This phase of the case-study diagnosis is undertaken to find out the nature of the deficiency in reading. If in the analytical diagnosis it was discovered that a child had poor ability in word recognition, the case study would determine the nature of his word-recognition problem. By means of appraising and comparing the various elements involved in word recognition, an understanding of the specific character of any particular word-recognition problem can be discovered. Detailed study of a child's approach to word recognition would show if his trouble is a lack of knowing how to use context clues, an insufficient sight vocabulary, a lack of flexible visual analysis of words, insufficient knowledge of word parts, inability to synthesize words, a tendency to be overanalytical, a tendency to lean too much upon striking characteristics of words, or whichever one of the many types of confusion is at the base of the word-recognition problem. Not until a detailed study of this special area is made can a proper remedial program be formulated.

The second type of information that it is necessary to obtain requires a study of the child. Appraisals of his mental capability, vision, hearing, and physical characteristics may reveal corrections that should be made before successful re-education is likely to occur. These appraisals would show what adjustments should be made in the remedial program as well. If, for example, the child with a word-recognition problem were found to have poor vision, certain modifications in remedial instruction would obviously be in order, in addition to having his vision helped by means of glasses. Rather than train this child in the use of smaller word parts, it would be better to emphasize larger word elements and to increase his sight vocabulary.

The third type of information needed in a case-study diagnosis takes into account the child's reactions to his reading disability. If he has rejected reading, if he has found excuses for not learning to read, or if he demonstrates a keen aversion to anything involving print, the program of remediation must be carefully planned to provide immediate demonstrable success and strong motivation. If the child shows signs of emotional upset, regardless of whether they are the cause or the result of reading disability, he must be closely studied.

The fourth type of information that sheds light on problems in case-study diagnosis is derived from an evaluation of environmental factors bearing upon children, such as home conditions, school conditions, and community relationships which relate directly to the likelihood of successful re-education. If, for example, it is found that a child's parents do not use good judgment in dealing with his reading problem, if they try to shame him or punish him in order to get greater effort out of him, it will be necessary to have home consultations in order to explain to his parents some of the more successful means of motivating the child so as to assist his re-education program.

In the other situation, where a school has been unaware that a child's entire reading program must be adjusted in order to help him correct his reading disability, it may be necessary for a reading diagnostician to meet with his teachers so that the reasons for these adjustments may be explained and so that the best ways of modifying his program may be suggested. The authors have never found either a teacher or a parent who has been unwilling to make every effort to improve the environment in which the over-all learning of the child must go on when the entire problem was explained to him or her and when appropriate suggestions were made.

A case-study diagnosis is necessary for many disabled readers and it might even be valuable for all of them. But since such a diagnosis is expensive and requires time and materials, a more reasonable approach might be to consider reading diagnosis as a series of screenings which enables the diagnostician to go as far as and no farther than is necessary to formulate a remedial program.

ONLY PERTINENT INFORMATION SHOULD BE COLLECTED AND BY THE MOST EFFICIENT MEANS

There is a tendency for clinicians and teachers to add tests to their routine diagnostic programs on an experimental basis. This is as it should be, but when such tests are found to have little diagnostic value, they should be discontinued. The time, energy, and expense involved in getting the necessary information is so great that everyone making diagnoses should appraise the measuring instruments being used to make sure they are efficient and that they add to the understanding of the children's instructional needs. There should be grave concern lest unnecessary overlap in testing occurs. The more reliable and valid measures should be used. A test that provides group measurement should be employed whenever the results justify its use. While it is true in a diagnosis that anything worth measuring at all should be measured well, it is equally true that the diagnosis should avoid wasteful and nonessential methods. This does not mean that cutting down on the information needed to correctly diagnose a case should be condoned. It does mean that undiscriminating and inefficient measurement must be avoided.

WHENEVER POSSIBLE, STANDARDIZED TEST PROCEDURES SHOULD BE USED

In diagnosing the learning difficulty of a disabled reader, an analysis of his reading, his physical and sensory characteristics, and various personality and environmental factors must be made. The authors of this book wish to make it clear that they fully appreciate the interrelationships which exist between the child's development, his other achievements, his personal qualities, his environment both in and out of school, and his reading capabilities. However, after a child has had reading disability identified as his major problem, it becomes necessary to thoroughly investigate his reading pattern in order to locate the root of his difficulty. This is always one of the major concerns of the diagnostician when studying a reading disability case, because without locating the particular reading anomalies, little if anything can be done to correct the reading disability.

It may be, for example, that a disabled reader is found to be farsighted and the appropriate correction is made with glasses. He is now comfortable visually. He stands a more reasonable chance of learning to read, but he is still a disabled reader. There is need for analyzing his reading to locate the faulty learnings, which perhaps were brought about in part by his visual difficulty, in order to plan the instruction which will correct his reading disability. No matter what physical, environmental, or personality problem brought the reading difficulty about, it is necessary to study and correct the reading disability. The other factors associated with the reading difficulty also need to be studied so that the correction in reading can be made most efficiently and so that the other conditions may be improved.

There are two general types of appraisals used in diagnosing reading disability. *First,* there are those which involve the application of precise units and numerically expressed norms, such as age or grade norms, percentile norms, or standard score norms which require measurement by standard procedures. *Second,* there are appraisals which are qualitative in character and for which norms expressed in numerical terms either are not available or are inappropriate. This second type of appraisal is often called an evaluation. This kind of appraisal is limited in one sense in that the procedures involved are not systematic and in another, to the varying degrees to which the personal bias of the diagnostician may enter into the appraisal. Such appraisals gain their merit from the fact that they allow the diagnostician to obtain information about things for which no standardized measures are available.

Standardized measurements are the most valuable instruments for analyzing the child's reading strengths and weaknesses. They are also needed for collecting many of the related facts that enter into the formulation of a remedial program. Methods of appraisal involving accurate measurement should be used whenever possible. When using standardized tests it is necessary for the diagnostician to follow precisely the procedures for giving and scoring the instruments that are outlined in the manuals that accompany them. Any variation from standard procedures may seriously affect the use of the norms supplied.

When interpreting the results of normative data obtained from standardized tests, both survey and diagnostic, care must be exercised. The norms supplied for such tests indicate the performance of a large number of typical pupils on a sample of typical learnings within the field that is being measured. Therein the standardized tests have their strength and also their weakness. Disabled readers are far from being typical learners. They are designated disabled readers because they are atypical. Standardized tests allow the diagnostician to compare a disabled reader with his more fortunate typical counterpart. In this way, strengths and weaknesses can be located with a minimum of clinical bias.

Much caution and considerable insight must be used in interpreting the results of the measurements. A child of sixth-grade age, for example, with a reading expectancy of 6.0 may measure 3.0 in reading. An uninitiated examiner might assume that such a child needs reading materials and methods suitable for the typical third-grade child. This is usually not the case. This sixth-grade child is not a typical third-grade reader. He is a sixth-grade child with sixth-grade interests, drives, motives, and friends. Moreover, he is not even a third-grade reader, for further study would very likely indicate that his basic reading skills and abilities, and therefore his instructional needs, are closer to those of a second-grade child. His degree of mental maturity enables him to use his limited basic reading skills better than does the typical child with 2.0 reading ability. He has 6.0 potential with which to apply his 2.0 reading skills. Therefore, he is able to measure somewhat higher, namely, 3.0, because of his greater mental maturity than the second-grade child with 2.0 reading ability, 2.0 potential, and 2.0 chronological age and experience. This is but one illustration of the care with which the diagnostician of reading cases must work. The standardized test is, however, his most reliable instrument of measurement for many of the appraisals which must be made. They give him typical basic facts upon which to make his judgments as to what is best for the case of atypical learning he is trying to remedy. A reading diagnosis is likely to be accurate to the extent that the diagnostician obtains numerical data upon which to base his judgments. A list of useful standardized tests may be found in Appendix I. Diagnostic methods will be described in the chapters that follow.

INFORMAL PROCEDURES MAY NEED TO BE USED WHEN IT IS NECESSARY TO EXPAND THE DIAGNOSIS

Even though the diagnosis is based on standardized data, there is often the need to explore areas for which standardized tests have not been developed. A diagnostician collecting information from sources of evaluation rather than measurement, should follow certain procedures which will enable the data he gets to be as accurate as possible. These suggestions may prove helpful for collecting evaluative data:

1. *Isolate specific outcomes or characteristics to be evaluated.* If, for example, information is desired on the method of attack a child uses on words in isolation when working orally, the observer should be alert to all of the approaches that might be used by the child.

2. *The diagnostician should define the observable outcomes or characteristics in exact terms.* The diagnostician should have before him, for example, a check-list of possible methods that the child might use when he is orally solving a word-recognition problem.

3. *The informal situation in which the characteristic is to be observed should be well planned and suitable to the outcomes to be observed.* The child whose methods of word study are to be observed should be given a list of words of increasing difficulty and he should be requested to work out the unknown words orally so that the diagnostician may note which word-recognition approaches the child is using.

4. *A record should be made of what he finds with illustrative samples of the performance on which the judgment was made.* Using the example of methods of word study just described, the child might be found to be attempting a phonetic approach to the problem, but his knowledge of word elements may be weak. Sample words should be listed to show: (*a*) visual separation of the words; (*b*) the elements miscalled; (*c*) any difficulty in synthesis that results; and (*d*) the final pronunciation of the word. In addition, a formulation of the diagnostician's opinion, at the time, should be recorded.

5. *A judgment as to the significance of the observed behavior or characteristic should be made.* The diagnostician, in the example cited above, should indicate the importance of the information obtained to the understanding of the instructional needs of the child he is studying.

The usefulness of the information obtained by informal procedures depends on the experience of the observer, the number of observations made, the degree to which the sample of observations is unbiased, and the relevance of the information to the understanding of the case. Many elements in reading diagnosis must be obtained by informal procedures.

The information acquired by informal approaches should be obtained as systematically as possible and it must be interpreted and used with caution. Many misjudgments are made if the personal biases of the diagnostician are allowed to influence the judgments he makes, even on normative data. Such misjudgments are even more prevalent when the data are collected by informal approaches. For example, a diagnostician may have a special interest in reversals of words. When a child makes a few reversals, as most children do, they may be overemphasized by the diagnostician. As a result, the child may be classified as a reversal case while his true difficulty is something quite different.

Informal procedures have merit because they allow the diagnostician to explore further some characteristic suspected from more standardized measurement situations. Many times, when giving a standardized diagnostic reading test, the examiner notices some reading tendency of the child which he wishes to study further. He may complete the test as designed so that he can use the norms, but then he may explore further, informally, the items he wishes to check because of his "hunch." For example, the diagnostician may be giving a standardized list of isolated words to find out how well a child can work out the pronunciations in an untimed situation. He gives this child the list of words according to directions and determines the child's score. He may have noted, however, that the child seemed to have trouble in visually separating the words into usable elements. The diagnostician may wish to go back to some of the words missed and by covering up parts of the words, show the child the correct way to analyze them. He might then see whether the child could have recognized the words, had his visual analysis been correct. This information would be recorded but would not enter into the application of the normative data.

Informal appraisals also have value in that they are, at times, the only or the most appropriate methods of gaining information. There are no suitable standardized tests, for example, to measure the child's attitude toward reading. Probably the diagnostician has to ask the child what he thinks of reading or informally watch the child's reactions to reading situations. Such information may be of real significance in formulating a remedial program and therefore should be collected, even though at times it may be of questionable validity. The good diagnostician will probably be aware of the amount of confidence to be placed in such information.

DECISIONS IN DIAGNOSIS MUST BE BASED UPON PATTERNS OF SCORES

When the information about a disabled reader has been collected, it must be arranged so that the various numerical scores can be compared with one another. Adequate diagnosis is based on such comparisons. High as well as low scores must be taken into account in making estimates of the instructional needs of the disabled reader. Often, disability is the result of an unfortunate overemphasis on some part of the reading program. One child's sight vocabulary may be low because he has always been so effective in employing word-recognition techniques that he has found little need to remember words at sight. Another child may have such a compulsive need to be accurate in reading that he cannot become a fluent reader. He always measures 100 per cent in accuracy, but even if more detail about a passage had been required, he would have known that, too. No minutiae escape him, but this takes up too much reading time. These lacks of balance in outcomes can only be detected by making comparisons between standardized norms.

If the diagnostician fails to compare the child's performance in the separate skills with his general reading ability, many mistakes in planning remedial work will ensue. For example, when a fifth-grade child has only third-grade ability in syllabication, the diagnostician may think his lack of ability to break words into syllables is at the root of the difficulty. But when it is noted that the child's general reading ability is only that of the typical second-grade child, his ability to syllabify becomes a strength rather than a weakness.

Most standardized diagnostic tests in reading are so arranged that such comparisons are made easily. Even the range of tolerance is frequently indicated so that the diagnostician will not be disposed to place too much emphasis upon some low or high score which is not significantly out of range as compared with the over-all reading capability of the child.

After the numerical data are compared and judgments are made, decisions should be modified in accordance with the qualitative data acquired by means of evaluative techniques and other informal approaches. The diagnostician will do well, however, to be careful not to let isolated observations or bits of information alter drastically the judgments he has made on the basis of reliable and valid measurements.

THE DIAGNOSIS SHOULD BE CONTINUOUS

Occasionally, a case fails to respond to remedial instruction based upon the original diagnosis. In such a case, after two or three weeks of instruction, there should be a re-evaluation of the diagnosis, perhaps with additional measurements and other appraisals. Some vital factor in the case may have been overlooked in the original diagnosis.

When the remedial program is successful, reading disability is dynamic rather than static. The original diagnosis indicated the instructional needs of the disabled reader at the time remedial instruction was undertaken. The remedial program based on it was designed to alter the child's reading profile in ways that would encourage better over-all growth in reading. As remedial work progresses, however, study of the child should be continued further. If the remedial instruction has been effective, the needs of the child will have changed and the remedial program may require modification. Diagnosis must therefore be continuous.

At the start of remedial instruction, a child may have been insecure in reading situations. The diagnostician may have recommended that a chart be kept to show him his progress. After a time, as the child gains security, the chart can be discontinued. Another child may have been relatively poor at using context clues as an aid to word recognition and was depending solely upon analytical approaches. The remedial instruction may have been directed toward encouraging the use of context. After a time, it may be noted that the child was neglecting careful inspection of the words and making seemingly random guesses. The guesses made sense but not the correct sense. By continuous diagnosis, the remedial worker could detect when the problem changed and thus maintain a better balance between the word-recognition techniques. In these two examples, the remedial work had to be altered because the instructional needs of the child had changed.

SUMMARY

The correction of reading disability is complicated by the complex nature of the reading process and by the many differences in children and their environments which influence reading growth. It is small wonder that no two cases of reading disability confront the teacher or diagnostician with exactly the same problem. It is, therefore, apparent that any attempt to give remedial instruction must be based on an adequate diagnosis. The more complex and the more subtle cases of reading disability often require more detailed and more penetrating study than the classroom teacher has the time or training to give. At times the services of a clinical diagnostician are required. In such instances, it is sometimes necessary to enlist the services of other specialists a well, such as social case workers, psychologists, physicians, or psychiatrists.

The diagnosis of a disabled reader must be directed toward improvement of instruction. Therefore, the therapeutic type of diagnosis is more essential than is the etiological, i.e., the one that seeks causes only. The diagnosis involves more than an appraisal of reading skills and abilities. It must also assess the mental, physical, sensory, emotional, and environmental factors that could impede progress.

The diagnosis must be efficient and, therefore, it should proceed only as far as is necessary to formulate a remedial program and no farther. Some children's instructional needs can be appraised by general diagnosis, others will need a more thorough study by analytical means, and still others may need a complete clinical case study of their reading disability. Since diagnosis of reading disability is detailed and time-consuming, only pertinent information should be collected and it should be obtained by the most efficient means available.

The use of standardized measurements is essential for reliable diagnosis of reading disability. Even the results of standardized tests must be interpreted with care because the disabled reader constitutes an atypical and subtle problem. It may be necessary to resort to informal procedures in order to obtain information that cannot be obtained by standardized measurements. The diagnostician must be cautious in collecting data by informal procedures because it is easy for him to lean too heavily upon clinical insight alone.

The remedial program is planned by first taking into account the numerical data and then modifying it in accordance with whatever other information is obtained. The diagnostician should treat the data objectively so that the case can be accurately judged. If after a reasonable period the remedial work proves unsuccessful, a reappraisal should be made to find the correct diagnosis. Even in successful cases, diagnosis should be continuous because reading disability is one aspect of a dynamic process and it alters during remedial instruction, whereupon the remedial program must be changed to meet the new needs of the disabled reader.

SELECTED READINGS

BRUECKNER, L. J., and BOND, G. L., *Diagnosis and treatment of learning difficulties.* New York: Appleton-Century-Crofts, Inc., 1955, Chaps. 2, 4.

GATES, Arthur I., *The improvement of reading,* 3rd ed. New York: The Macmillan Company, 1947, Chap. 3.

HARRIS, Albert J., *How to increase reading ability,* 3rd ed. New York: Longmans, Green & Company, 1956, Chaps. 7, 8.

TINKER, Miles A., *Teaching elementary reading.* New York: Appleton-Century-Crofts, Inc., 1952, Chaps. 17, 18.

8 ANALYSIS OF READING DIFFICULTIES

THE LAST CHAPTER discussed, in general terms, some basic principles of diagnosis. The concern of this chapter is the application of these principles to specific problems involved in locating and diagnosing disabled readers. The amount of diagnostic effort that needs to be expended in order to formulate remedial programs for disabled readers varies widely. Some children who are suspected of being disabled readers are later found not to fit this classification but to have other problems. This chapter will not go into the diagnosis necessary to solve the many types of problems sometimes confused with reading disability. Our present concern is limited to the diagnostic procedures needed to locate and to analyze reading disability cases of various kinds.

At times, the case-study diagnosis of reading disability will point out other areas that need exploration because, if not tended to, they will interfere with the correction of the reading problem. Under such circumstances, the appropriate course of action will be indicated, but in certain instances the diagnoses in related fields will be left to discussions in references dealing with those specific problems. For example, a child's reading disability may be difficult to correct because of an emotional disturbance of deep-seated origin. It is not the province of this book to describe how the emotional problem should be diagnosed or treated. Nevertheless, the reading diagnostician has to be alert to such problems and should include in his case study, observations that will identify related problems which need further study by other specialists. In formulating a remedial program, the diagnostician must always take into account the presence of conditions that need treatment elsewhere.

The screening approach, in related problem areas, should be such that if any error is made it should be in the direction of referring false positives rather than in neglecting a case which requires specialized diagnosis. For example, the reading diagnostician does not diagnose visual defects, but he does screen for the possibility of visual handicaps. It is better for him to refer, for expert attention, two possible cases who do not need visual correction than it is to miss one who does.

A reading diagnostician needs to find the answers to some specific questions concerning the disabled reader before an effective remedial program can be formulated. Our discussion of the analysis of reading difficulties will be in terms of the following questions which must be answered for each case:

1. Is the child correctly classified as a disabled reader?
2. Who can most effectively give the remedial work?
3. What is the nature of the training needed?
4. How can improvement be brought about most efficiently?
5. Are there any limiting conditions within the child which must be considered?
6. Are there any environmental conditions that might interfere with progress in reading?

IS THE CHILD CORRECTLY CLASSIFIED AS A DISABLED READER?

Poor reading ability is so interrelated with other characteristics of child growth and development that it is often extremely difficult to determine whether the reading disability or some other condition is the basic problem. Not all children who are poor readers are in reality reading disability cases. There are many children low in reading ability who can in no way be considered reading disability cases. A few children who are disabled readers have a problem of greater importance that should be attended to prior to any attempt to correct the reading. First of all, the teacher or diagnostician must identify the true general nature of the child's problem and decide whether the child will profit from remedial instruction in reading or whether some other adjustment is required.

The child who is considered disabled because he is not as effective in reading as other children of his age, may be reading better than could be expected of him. The most obvious example of this erroneous classification is the child who has low verbal intelligence. Such a child cannot be expected to grow as rapidly as can other children in reading. His problem will not be solved by a remedial reading program but it can be eased by curricular changes and by using methods more suited to his limited learning ability. He cannot be classified as a disabled reader but rather he should be considered a slow learner. For this reason no child should ordinarily be considered disabled in reading unless there is a discrepancy between his learning capacity or general verbal intelligence and his reading performance.

Physical anomalies may cause a child to be misclassified as a disabled reader when what he needs is to see a doctor, not the remedial teacher. Among the more common physical conditions that make for erroneous classification are glandular conditions which limit the amount of energy a child has. The child with a glandular limitation, even though he is bright enough, may not be able to sustain the high level of concentration needed to read intently during a testing period or long enough to finish an assignment. Such a child would measure low in reading performance even though he might have well-developed skills and abilities in reading. Even if he has not been able to develop reading competency, his basic problem is still medical. Reading instruction, properly adjusted, should be continued while the physical limitation is being treated, but a concentrated program in remedial reading for many of these cases could prove unfortunate. To instill a sense of inadequacy in the child would seriously limit his future reading growth.

Children with neurological limitations such as spastic conditions, epilepsy, or chorea resulting from rheumatic fever cannot be expected to develop reading capabilities as rapidly as can their equally intelligent but neurologically sound contemporaries. Spastic children, for example, can learn to read but because of difficulties in co-ordination, they may be expected to learn more slowly than normal children. As long as he maintains a relatively even reading profile, a spastic child cannot be considered a disabled reader even when there is a discrepancy between his mental grade or level of learning ability and his reading grade.

Some neurological problems are more difficult for the educational diagnostician to detect and are only suspected after considerable remedial instruction has been given with unsatisfactory results. The diagnostician should be on the alert to the possibility of neurological limitations, especially in those cases that are high in intelligence and low in other organized learnings such as arithmetical computation. The reading diagnostician and remedial worker must be well aware of the fact that all human deficiencies cannot be corrected by education.

In cases where children have neurological limitations, the teacher of reading must often be satisfied with less than usual results. In many of these cases, attention to both the neurological limitation and the reading problem can be given simultaneously. The remedial reading program in such cases is designed to give the child the highly individualized help he needs. His problem usually is not unfortunate reading growth patterns, but rather that of a restricted over-all reading development brought about by the neurological limitation.

The relationship between reading disability and emotional maladjustment often causes difficulty in classifying a child's major problem as one of reading disability. The fact that a dual relationship between reading disability and emotional insecurities exists has been discussed in a previous chapter. At times, the poor reader is an emotionally disturbed child and reading ability suffers along with other school learnings. At other times, and more often, the emotional disturbance is brought about by the failure to make normal progress in reading. In the latter situation, immediate attention to the reading problem will correct both the reading and the emotional problems. Sometimes, however, the child is so confused that the help of a specialist in emotional problems may be needed. The specialist may decide that the basic emotional problem must be treated before further reading instruction is given. More often, however, even in those cases where deep-seated emotional tensions are suspected of making the child an inefficient learner, emotional therapy and remedial instruction in reading can be given concurrently, to the mutual benefit of both.

The reading diagnostician should study the emotional reactions of a child who is reading below expectancy in terms of his learning ability. The child who is inefficient in learning in general and who is emotionally disturbed is more likely to have a basic emotional problem than is the child who is low in reading and reading-related subjects alone. The emotionally tense child who is achieving better in nonreading subjects than he is in reading and who is considerably better in silent reading than in oral reading may be suspected of having his emotional problem reading-centered. Unless a qualified expert in the field of emotional problems has recommended a delay of the reading instruction, it is the opinion of the writers that the child, whether the emotional disturbance is the cause or the result of the reading disability, should be considered a reading disability case and treated as suggested in Chapter 18 on the specially handicapped child.

The determination of the basic problem of a child is frequently difficult and requires an alert diagnostician. A careful study of his achievement scores and mental ratings, the parental interview blanks, physiological records, and personality inventories is often necessary to determine correctly whether the child should be classified as a disabled reader or not. This problem alone may have been what has led some psychologists with a flair for sweeping statements to claim that to understand reading disability in all of its ramifications is to know all there is to know about psychology and reading instruction.

WHO CAN MOST EFFECTIVELY GIVE THE REMEDIAL WORK?

There are three places in which remedial work can be given, namely, the classroom, the school reading center, and the clinic. The regular classroom teacher can and should give remedial instruction to the majority of children moderately disabled in reading. The size of the class, her other responsibilities, and her training limit the teacher to the solution of the less complicated reading problems. She must always decide just how much attention can be given to one child at the expense of the many. If adequate programs of measurement, efficient class management, and materials realistically designed to aid the teacher in adjusting to individual differences are used, most reading difficulties can be detected early and corrected by the classroom teacher. Even under these fortunate circumstances, however, the teacher may frequently need the help of an expert diagnostician to aid her in the formulation of the classroom remedial program.

The second place in which remedial work in reading is given is at a reading center within the school. This center is usually a room well stocked with materials for reading and for special practice exercises. The remedial teacher works with groups of children needing more specialized and individual attention than can be given by the classroom teacher. The size of the groups given reading instruction in these centers varies from about 6 children to 15, depending on the needs of the children and the number of children requiring specialized instruction.

In general, the smaller the groups, the greater the returns for each child. There seems to be little advantage in having groups with less than 6 children when instruction is given to moderately disabled readers. The remedial teachers working in school reading centers need special training in order to be qualified to handle the problems they meet. Also, these remedial teachers should be able to diagnose the less complex reading cases and offer remedial suggestions for those children who are to be treated by the classroom teachers. The teachers in charge of remedial rooms or centers within a school should be successful classroom teachers who have had additional training in reading and in diagnosing and treating reading disability leading to an advanced degree. Reading disability is no simple thing to be solved by a novice or merely by a set of exercises purporting to be suitable for all cases.

The third place in which remedial work is given is at an educational or reading clinic. Such clinics are frequently located in the major universities or teachers colleges. An increasing number of school systems are developing child study clinics which include sections devoted to educational disability and reading difficulty. This trend is indeed fortunate because there will be many children who develop learning difficulties as long as we are trying to teach all children to read. The more complex problems are best diagnosed and treated in such clinics. However, the demand for the services of these educational clinics so far exceeds the available personnel and facilities, that only those children who cannot be taken care of in the other two places should be retained in the clinic for remedial work. In a complex case, the child should be excused from part of his regular class work and given careful individual clinical attention. The teacher and parents must be informed of the child's problem so that his entire reading environment may be attuned to his needs.

The clinic's greatest aid to a public school system is in making more thorough diagnoses than can be obtained elsewhere. Only the more subtle and complex reading cases need clinical remedial training. To sum up, many disabled readers should be corrected in the classroom; some of them, however, will be given remedial instruction in a school reading center; and others will be referred to a clinic for treatment. However treated, every case must be diagnosed well.

In order to decide where the child with a reading difficulty can most effectively be treated, the diagnostician needs first to decide into which of the general descriptive categories the child fits. These categories are described in Chapter 4.

Recommendations for Simple Retardation

Children, who are significantly retarded in reading but who show no unusual or limiting characteristics about their reading patterns and also no personal rejection of reading and no disturbance about it, can be effectively treated in the regular classroom. They are cases of simple retardation. They are immature in reading but need no marked re-education. They do need instruction suited to their level of advancement, a rigorously motivated reading program and an opportunity to read a lot.

At times, some children in this category will be better treated in the school reading center. The amount of retardation and the grade level of the child will determine which location is more suited to his needs. If the child were so low in reading ability that he could not profit from most of the instruction given in the lowest reading group in the class, he would be more effectively taught by the remedial teacher in the school reading center. Most reading cases of secondary school age, however, might be assigned to a remedial teacher. It is difficult for the secondary teacher, who works with perhaps two hundred pupils a day, to know any one child well enough to overcome an extreme case of even simple retardation.

The impersonal nature of the secondary school makes the problem of helping the disabled reader by the classroom teacher more difficult than it is in the elementary school where the teacher works the entire day with thirty or so children. No case of simple retardation in the elementary school needs to be referred to the reading clinic for individual treatment.

The child with simple retardation in reading can usually be located by general diagnosis, using achievement tests and nonverbal group mental tests. At times, he may not be isolated until the analytical level of diagnosis is reached. The child with simple retardation in reading is one who has a low but relatively uniform reading profile and who has no unfortunate reactions to his poor reading. He is a disabled reader only because he is not reading as well as he could be expected to read. A study of his reading scores shows that he has normal reading patterns for the typical child of equal reading attainment. There is no interfering habit nor faulty attitude present to impede future growth.

Recommendations for Specific Retardation

Children best described as cases of specific retardation are those who are severely limited in one or more areas of reading but who demonstrate that they have developed the general basic skills and abilities well enough to be able readers in other areas. Practically all of these cases can be given the remedial work they need by the classroom teacher. The skills or abilities in which the child needs further training and experience have been located. Then, as the child participates in the regular developmental reading program, the teacher places increased emphasis on specific areas where the child is weak. If there are two or three children needing the same emphasis, the teacher can give them remedial training as a small group, from time to time. In some instances, children with specific limitations from several classes of about the same grade level can be sent to the school remedial center for group instruction, but for the most part, they should be given needed training by the classroom teacher. The prognosis for overcoming specific retardation is exceedingly good even though the degree of retardation is sometimes great.

A child with specific retardation in reading is located by the use of reading tests that are more analytical than are those customarily used in general diagnosis. Tests that give scores in various important areas of reading are needed to diagnose the child with specific retardation. Indications of attainment in the more common types of comprehension and study skills are needed to locate an area of specific limitation. If a child is high in some of the comprehension tests but low in other tests, he is correctly described as a case of specific retardation and no further diagnosis is needed. The child's high scores indicate that there is no basic limitation in his reading. His low scores isolate the areas needing attention.

Recommendations for Limiting Disability

The child who has serious deficiencies in basic reading skills and abilities which impede his entire reading growth is best described as having a limiting disability. Such a child is low in all types of reading because he has acquired interfering habits or has failed to learn one or more essential skills. His reading profile does not indicate the healthy reading growth of the simple retardation case but rather an unfortunate reading pattern.

Most children with limiting disability should be given remedial work in a school reading center. A few could be corrected by the classroom teacher but usually re-education takes more time and careful planning than she is able to devote to it. Some of the more difficult cases of this type should be referred to the reading clinic for remedial work. Any decision must rest on a thorough case-study diagnosis. This should usually be conducted at a child study center or psycho-educational clinic. The results of the complete diagnosis and recommended remedial program should be discussed with the remedial teacher in a case conference. However, in practice, the clinics are frequently so overcrowded that case reports are sent to the remedial teacher who, in turn, discusses the problem with the school personnel concerned.

Recommendations for Complex Disability

Children who are best described as complex disability cases include the disabled readers whose problems are more subtle and complicated. These children are always severely retarded in reading. They are frequently bright, capable youngsters who demonstrate antagonism toward reading and who feel embarrassed about their inability to read. They sometimes make a wholesome adjustment to their reading difficulty by doing outstanding work in fields such as art or arithmetic computation which do not require reading ability. More often, however, they merely take on unfortunate modes of adjustment to their lack of success in reading and from this spreads a general ineffectiveness in other school work. In many cases, they exhibit a lack of persistence and a tendency to retreat from school in general and from reading situations in particular. They are absent from school frequently and sometimes they become delinquent.

Many children with complex reading disability become blocked and so tense that they are ineffective learners. They get into a downward spiral that increases tensions and causes ever greater inefficiency in learning. A child with a complex disability in reading is often found to have anxiety and worry about reading and fear of reading. He tends to be insecure and defeated. Children who are classified in this category need careful individual clinical attention. A complex reading disability case needs clinical diagnosis of his problem and often the reading diagnostician must enlist the services of other specialists in order to appraise the child's needs accurately and thoroughly.

Often the remedial work for such children should be done in the clinic. In some cases, of course, it can be done at the school reading center when there is time to give the child the necessary individual help that he requires.

WHAT IS THE NATURE OF THE TRAINING NEEDED?

The nature of the training needed by a disabled reader is indicated by his reading strengths and weaknesses. Locating the reading limitation is the most important phase of a diagnosis for formulating a program of correction. The diagnostician's fundamental problem is that of finding just what, in the reading pattern of the disabled reader, is retarding his reading growth. The diagnostic appraisal of what is really wrong with the child's reading, what faulty techniques he is using, what abilities he is overemphasizing, what abilities he lacks, is essential for formulating a remedial program.

There are some limitations in the child's reading profile which have little effect on his reading growth in general. A child may be unable to read the materials of science or he may be weak in one of the study skills. Under such circumstances, the limitation can readily be located and effective work instituted so as to overcome the specific limitation. Many children have these minor and easily corrected reading limitations. A general and analytical diagnosis can and should locate such problems. Once located, the nature of the training needed becomes clear. The child should have training in the weak area pointed out by the diagnosis. This type of limitation is specific and has no unfortunate repercussions on other aspects of the child's reading growth. The diagnosis and planning of remedial instruction is relatively simple in such cases.

There are other limitations in the reading patterns of disabled readers that have more far-reaching and devastating effects. Failure to establish some skills and abilities, the overemphasis of others, failure to learn some of the essential knowledges, or the adoption of faulty approaches may interfere with the child's entire reading development. The lack of a sufficient degree of flexibility and adaptability may seriously limit the child's ability to adjust his reading skills to the needs of specific types of reading material or to certain purposes for reading. The following classification of the more prevalent reading difficulties includes the types of defects that must be located if a diagnosis is to indicate clearly the precise kinds of instruction that are needed:

CLASSIFICATION OF READING DIFFICULTIES

A. Deficiencies in basic comprehension abilities.
   1. Limited meaning vocabulary.
   2. Inability to read by thought units.
   3. Insufficient sentence sense.
   4. Lack of the sense of paragraph organization.
   5. Failure to appreciate the author's organization.
B. Faulty word identification and recognition.
   1. Failure to use context and other meaning clues.
   2. Ineffective visual analysis of words.
   3. Limited knowledge of visual, structural, and phonetic elements.
   4. Lack of ability in auditory blending or visual synthesis.
   5. Overanalytical.
      a. Analyzing known words.
      b. Breaking words into too many parts.
      c. Using letter by letter or spelling attack.
   6. Insufficient sight vocabulary.
   7. Excessive locational errors.
      a. Initial errors.
      b. Middle errors.
      c. Ending errors.
C. Inappropriate directional habits.
   1. Orientational confusions with words.
   2. Transpositions among words.
   3. Faulty eye movements.
D. Poor oral reading.
   1. Inappropriate eye-voice span.
   2. Lack of phrasing ability.
   3. Unfortunate rate and timing.
   4. Emotionally tense oral reader.
E. Limited in special comprehension abilities.
   1. Inability to isolate and retain factual information.
   2. Poor reading to organize.

3. Ineffective reading to evaluate.
4. Insufficient ability in reading to interpret.
5. Limited proficiency in reading to appreciate.
F. Deficiencies in basic study skills.
   1. Inability to use aids in locating materials to be read.
   2. Lack of efficiency in using basic reference material.
   3. Inadequacies in using maps, graphs, tables, and other visual materials.
   4. Limitations in techniques of organizing material read.
G. Deficient in ability to adapt to needs of content fields.
   1. Inappropriate application of comprehension abilities.
   2. Limited knowledge of specialized vocabulary.
   3. Insufficient concept development.
   4. Poor knowledge of symbols and abbreviations.
   5. Insufficient ability in the use of pictorial and tabular material.
   6. Difficulties with organization.
   7. Inability to adjust rate to suit the purposes and the difficulty of material.
H. Deficiencies in rate of comprehension.
   1. Inability to adjust rate.
   2. Insufficient sight vocabulary.
   3. Insufficient vocabulary knowledge and comprehension.
   4. Ineffectiveness in word recognition.
   5. Being an overanalytical reader.
   6. Insufficient use of context clues.
   7. Lack of phrasing.
   8. Using crutches.
   9. Unnecessary vocalization.
  10. Inappropriate purposes.

The above list of defects in reading patterns that must be appraised in a thorough diagnosis shows that reading disability is no simple condition that can be corrected by a single approach. The information concerning the child's strengths and weaknesses in these areas is obtained by a variety of techniques. A competent diagnostician uses both standardized and informal procedures in studying the nature of reading deficiencies so that appropriate remedial programs can be designed.

The whole field of tests and testing procedures is used by the reading diagnostician. He usually starts by giving survey and achievement tests, individual mental tests, personality appraisals, and may continue until he has measured such details as how many independent letters are unknown to the child or which of the important digraphs he does not know. A study of the possible limitations should go as far as and no farther than is necessary to formulate the nature of reading instruction needed. A list of standardized tests useful in making such appraisals is given in Appendix I. In the next chapter, the specific approaches to diagnostic answers to the question concerning the nature of instruction needed are described. It is enough to say here that the diagnostician must search out the nature of the defects in the child's reading if remedial work is to be successful.

HOW CAN IMPROVEMENT BE BROUGHT ABOUT MOST EFFICIENTLY?

The answer to this question is extremely important because the corrective program must be efficient in order to develop reading capability at an accelerated rate. Extensive diagnosis of the nature of the reading problem will have pointed out the type of instruction that is necessary. The purpose of the remedial program is to overcome unfortunate approaches to reading that have already limited or are likely to impede the child's reading growth. The information gained from the study of the child must enable the diagnostician to make several decisions which will increase the efficiency of the remedial instruction. First, the decision must be made as to the proper level of difficulty of the material; second, the material must deal with topics that are interesting to the child, or at least, as compatible as possible with interests of children of his age and general capability; third, the diagnostician must suggest the methods by which the child will be informed of his progress; fourth, the diagnostician must estimate the appropriate length of the instructional period; and fifth, he must give the necessary information for planning the types of independent work that the child needs.

Determining the Proper Level of Difficulty of Material to Be Used in Remediation

The diagnostician must make a careful estimate of the level of difficulty of the material that is to be used at the start of remedial instruction. Usually the child who is in difficulty with his reading has been having trouble for some time. It thus becomes vital to select material for him at the appropriate level of difficulty. This material should be such that the child can get some sense of being competent to handle it. The problem of selecting material suitable in difficulty is complicated by the fact that the disabled reader cannot read as well as would be expected of a child of his age and mental maturity. Some diagnosticians think that the correct approach for estimating the difficulty of material is to study the results of standardized tests and thus ascertain the child's general reading level. They think that if a child measures, for example, 2.5 (middle of the second grade) he should start his remedial instruction in material suitable for the typical child half-way through the second grade. But research and experience have shown that for most disabled readers this would be an overestimation of the level at which their instruction should start.

Let us suppose that a child who measures 2.5 on a standardized reading test is one with a mental grade of 5.0. Such a child is really not a typical 2.5 reader. He is often a reader with considerably less skill development than a typical 2.5 child. Such a child is able to bring to the reading scene a much broader background of experience, a keener appraisal of the concepts, a higher level of reasoning ability than can the typical child who is half-way through the second grade. He may, therefore, measure as much as a year higher in general comprehension than he would in such basic reading abilities as the ability to recognize words or to phrase them effectively for comprehension.

In judging the level of difficulty suitable for initial remedial instruction, the diagnostician must consider, in addition to standardized tests, other evidences of the child's level of skill development. Such evidence as his ability to read material orally should be investigated. In oral reading situations, does he make more than one error in every twenty running words? What is his skill in phrasing? What word-recognition techniques does he use? What about his ability to answer various types of comprehension questions about the material read? The level at which the child can read comfortably and effectively can be estimated by trying the child out in a series of basic readers and locating the particular level that seems suitable for him. He may be started, for example, in a book at second-grade level of difficulty. If this book proves to be too difficult, a first-grade book can be tried. If this is still too difficult, a primer could be used. The diagnostician may find, on the other hand, that the first book he chooses is too easy, that the child can read the second-grade book with great fluency. Then he would try a third-grade reader. The diagnostician would sample books in the series until the level was found at which the child could read with reasonable ease. This informal approach gives a rough estimate of the level of difficulty that is suitable for a given child.

It is possible to get this estimate in another way. Some of the results of standardized diagnostic tests will indicate the level at which remedial instruction should be started. If it is found, for example, that in the skill areas the child tends to measure around 2.0, even though his general reading level on the basis of comprehension tests is 2.5, the appropriate level at which to start the child's remedial instruction is likely to be toward the end of a first-grade reader, or approaching the 2.0 level. Such appraisals will give the diagnostician a general estimate of the level of material suitable for beginning instruction, but it must be modified in accordance with the type of remediation the child most needs.

A second consideration in selecting material for a child having difficulty with his reading takes into account the nature of the disability. The diagnostician must consider the instructional outcomes to be gained from its use. For example, if the child's major problem is one of developing greater speed, the material selected should be considerably easier than that normally appropriate for the child's general level of attainment. If the child can comfortably read material of fourth-grade level, then material that is from a half-year to a year easier should be selected for increasing speed of reading. Material that would be suitable should contain no more than one word that would cause the child difficulty in every hundred running words. On the other hand, if the child's problem is one of developing knowledge of visual, structural, and phonetic elements, he should be given material that is rather difficult, material in which he is likely to meet one word that he needs to analyze in every twenty running words. He may be given exercises that require the phonetic analysis of a high percentage of the words. Such exercises would be too difficult for general reading purposes but would be highly suitable for the specific problem at hand. It should be noted, however, that in these exercises, the child must have a reasonable chance for success.

The selection of materials at the appropriate level of difficulty for a specific case is probably one of the most important decisions the diagnostician makes.

Estimating What Material Is Suitable in Interest and Format

An important consideration in selecting material to be used for remedial treatment is that it should be suitable to the child in both interest and format. Securing such material for remedial instruction is a major problem of the remedial teacher. The diagnostician must make an estimate of the type of material the child will be interested in and the format that will be suitable. The problem resolves itself into finding material that will be relatively mature in content and format but which requires only the reading ability that the disabled reader has. Under certain circumstances, workbooks accompanying the basal readers may contain the material with which it will be necessary to start the remedial instruction. In other circumstances, it may be that the teacher will have to prepare her own materials. More frequently, the problem can be handled successfully by using material that is appropriate in level of difficulty and making it possible for the child to utilize the results of his reading in ways that are important to him. For example, a boy of high school age may be willing to read in a fourth-grade science book an account of the way to connect a battery to a bell in order to make it ring, if he is allowed to actually do the job.

The task of the diagnostician is that of estimating the level at which the child should be expected to read from the point of view of difficulty, the areas of interest that seem to be most acceptable to him, and the degree to which he will be adaptable to somewhat immature format. Estimates of all these conditions are made on the basis of reading tests, interest inventories, informal appraisals, and work samples with various types of materials. See Appendixes III and IV for sources of graded book lists and materials.

Selecting Means of Showing Progress

The diagnostician should suggest appropriate means of demonstrating to the child that he is making progress in reading. He should also estimate the amount of attention that should be given to demonstrating to the child that now he is learning to read. The method of demonstrating such growth will be determined by the nature of the remedial training to be given. If, for example, the child's problem is one of oral reading, the diagnostician may suggest that a tape recording of the child's oral reading be taken at intervals throughout the remedial instruction. Then, from time to time, the child should be allowed to listen to his recordings and note the growth that is taking place.

The amount of time that should be devoted to making his growth in reading apparent to the child depends upon the child himself. If he is insecure in the reading situation, or if he has demonstrated personality problems which are coupled with his lack of success in reading, more time should be devoted to this phase of the remedial work than would be necessary with a child who is not so insecure.

These judgments will be based upon an inspection of the child's reading profile and also upon appraisals of the child's attitude toward reading or his emotional adjustment.

Estimating the Desirable Length and Frequency of Remedial Lessons

The diagnostician must make estimates of the appropriate length of time for each training period and also the frequency with which training periods should be given. These estimates are made on the basis of three types of appraisals. *First,* consideration must be given to the type of outcome expected from remedial instruction. If the child needs to increase his speed of reading, the actual remedial lesson should be relatively short and highly motivated. Then between lessons the child may continue to emphasize speed of reading independently.

The second consideration used in judging the length of the remedial sessions allows for the physical stamina of the child. If he is one who tires easily, or if he is emotionally upset, the length of the training periods should be short. If he is physically robust and emotionally relaxed, the training periods can be longer.

Third, any condition such as poor vision that limits the child's ability to give close attention to reading instruction over a period of time will shorten the length of remedial sessions. It is often better to have two short sessions a day than to have one longer one.

A careful inspection of all of the information available about the youngster is necessary in order to make a reasonable estimate of the length of time for each training period and the frequency of the remedial lessons.

Planning for Independent Work

The final consideration in determining how improvement can be brought about most efficiently is the planning of independent work for the student. The child's reading disability will not be corrected in the remedial periods alone. He must extend his remedial reading experiences into his independent work. The level of difficulty of material used for independent work should be considerably easier than that which is studied during the remedial lessons. The nature of the independent work will be somewhat different than when work is done in remedial lessons. In planning independent work, the diagnostician must judge how best to motivate it and what type of exercises might be most profitable for the child to engage in independently. We may ask, for example, if the child is trying to build a larger sight vocabulary, would it be best for him to have a pack of word cards upon which he drills himself, or stories that contain words in contextual settings, or would workbook-type exercises be best? These decisions are made by the diagnostician on the basis of the nature of instruction needed, the characteristics of the child, and the characteristics of his general environment.

ARE THERE ANY LIMITING CONDITIONS WITHIN THE CHILD THAT MUST BE CONSIDERED?

In formulating a remedial program, all causes of reading disability considered in Chapters 5 and 6 must be appraised by the diagnostician and he must decide what expert help is needed. For the re-education program to be effective, any limitations within the child which might influence his reading growth detrimentally must be located. If the child has poor vision, an examination by a competent expert is required. Whenever possible, the visual defect should be corrected. Whether corrected or not, modifications in the remedial program will be necessary. Such modifications are described in a later chapter dealing with the specially handicapped child.

If poor hearing is suspected, the aid of an otologist should be secured. Again, the mere correction of the auditory limitation will not improve the reading disability. It will, however, make the child more trainable. The child with poor auditory capacity will need modifications in his instructional program. See Chapter 18 on the specially handicapped child.

All of the factors that caused reading disability in the first place may also become conditions within the child which need correction or to which the program must adjust. Whenever possible, such limitations should be corrected prior to the start of remedial training. Where no correction is possible, the program must be altered to make allowance for the known limitation. It should be further recognized that the correction of a limiting condition does not alter the reading needs of the child. If the child, for example, has third-grade reading ability prior to a visual correction, he will still have third-grade skills and abilities in reading after the visual correction. The correction, then, of an unfortunate characteristic within the child will not alter the need for remedial reading instruction. It will, however, make the chances that the child will learn to read efficiently and effectively much greater.

ARE THERE ANY ENVIRONMENTAL CONDITIONS THAT MIGHT INTERFERE WITH PROGRESS IN READING?

The diagnostician must study the entire environment of the child. There may be limitations within the child's environment that influence the success of the remedial program. Sometimes, in understandable zeal to help their children, parents create emotional tensions that do not help the reading and disturb a child greatly. At other times, parents may be undertaking to help their child in ways that are detrimental to his reading growth. Parents can contribute much to the success of a remedial program by remembering that they should.:

1. Take an interest in the independent reading work that the child brings home.
2. Make available to the child a good place in which to work without interruption.
3. On the advice of the remedial teacher, secure materials that are the child's own.
4. Hide their anxieties about the child's reading problem.
5. Tell the child a word if he gets into difficulty while doing his independent reading at home.
6. Read the independent material so that they can discuss it with him.
7. Avoid ridicule or making comparisons between siblings.
8. Let the child know that they appreciate his many accomplishments and that they have confidence in him.
9. Recognize that the child's "don't care" attitude toward reading is often a "do care very much" one and that it is wise to let him adopt this apparent attitude as a "safety valve."

It is not only the home conditions and child-parent relationships that should be appraised, but the school situation should also be studied. All too frequently the improvement of reading for the disabled reader is left to the remedial program alone. At times, the school situation is not conducive to effective reading development for the disabled reader. The child's entire reading environment should be co-ordinated if he is to progress successfully. Sometimes a teacher does not fully recognize the seriousness of having a child try to read material that is so difficult that it can be nothing but frustrating to him. At other times, the teacher is not fully aware of the fact that a child's lack of attention may be the result of a hearing loss. The authors of this book have yet to see the parent or teacher who would not do everything in his power to co-operate in helping a disabled reader if the child's problems were clearly explained.

The diagnostician, then, must make an attempt to locate any irritant within the environment of the child which will impede his progress in learning to read.

AN ILLUSTRATION OF THE ANALYSIS
OF READING DIFFICULTIES

The following illustration of reading diagnosis shows how the study of a fifth-grade class progresses through the various levels from general diagnosis to analytical diagnosis to case-study diagnosis. It also indicates how answers to the various questions the diagnostician seeks are secured.

General Diagnosis in Reading

The first level of diagnosis can be called general diagnosis and concerns itself with securing information about the levels of performance of children in the more common aspects of reading growth. To adjust instruction to individual differences, school systems frequently give periodic achievement tests. Where no such tests are given, the diagnostician will do well to give these as the first step in his diagnosis. A general diagnosis should also include an estimate of the child's intellectual level.

The diagnostician can compare the child's mental grade status, his reading grade status, and his level of performance in other fields. It is then possible to make a judgment of whether or not a child is a disabled reader. If the child's reading grade is about the same as his mental grade and as his success in other fields of learning, we judge him to be progressing as well in reading as can be expected. This is true even if his reading ability is somewhat poorer than the reading of other members of his class. Such a child will need no further diagnosis in reading even though he may need certain adjustments for the slow learner, to be described in a later chapter. The classroom teacher should be a constant student of each child she teaches in the developmental reading program. In regular class work, the teacher systematically studies every child's performance in an analytical, diagnostic manner.

If a child is considerably lower in reading ability than his mental level indicates that he should be and than he is in the subject-matter fields that are independent of reading success, there is need for further diagnosis. The general diagnosis helps the diagnostician to locate, among the children in a class, those few who are educationally handicapped by ineffective reading and those who need curricular adjustments. Standardized survey tests, achievement tests, mental tests, informal objective tests, and general observations are used in making these judgments.

An examination of a typical fifth-grade class of 35 pupils will help to show the outcomes of a general diagnosis. Table 5 gives the results of a survey of reading capabilities, mental ability, and arithmetical computation obtained at the beginning of the school year. The *Gates Reading Survey* for measuring reading ability and the 1937 revision of the *Stanford-Binet* for measuring intelligence were used. The scores in arithmetic were obtained from the norms given in the *Modern School Achievement Test*. The reading

Table 5

TEST INFORMATION ABOUT A BEGINNING FIFTH-GRADE CLASS

Grade Score	CHRONO-LOGICAL GRADE	MENTAL GRADE	GATES READING SURVEY				ARITH-METICAL COMPU-TATION
			Power of Compre-hension	Vocabu-lary	Speed	Average Reading Grade	
Above 9.0					1		
8.5-8.9		1		1	0	1	1
8.0-8.4		2	1	2	1	1	2
7.5-7.9		2	3	1	2	2	3
7.0-7.4		3	2	2	2	1	2
6.5-6.9		2	3	2	3	3	3
6.0-6.4	1	4	2	3	2	4	3
5.5-5.9	10	4	4	5	4	3	4
5.0-5.4	18	5	5	5	5	6	6
4.5-4.9	6	3	4	4	4	4	4
4.0-4.4		4	5	4	5	5	3
3.5-3.9		3	3	2	3	3	2
3.0-3.4		1	1	3	1	1	1
Below 3.0		1	2	1	2	1	1
Median Scores *	5.3	5.5	5.3	5.5	5.4	5.4	5.5

* Calculated on ungrouped data.

grade scores were obtained from the table of norms given in the test booklet. The mental ages and the chronological ages of the children were converted into grade scores. This makes possible comparisons between reading grade, mental grade, arithmetic grade, and chronological grade.

A study of Table 5 will give much useful information. The class is a somewhat better than average one. The average mental grade is 5.5 which is in advance of a typical beginning fifth-grade class. The class grade score in arithmetical computation is 5.5, which is average performance for a class of this general capability. The average reading grade of 5.4 is about the same as the mental grade, which indicates that this class is doing fairly well in reading. A further inspection shows that the class is rather uniform in its average reading attainments. The average power of comprehension is 5.3, average vocabulary is 5.5, and the average speed of reading is 5.4. It seems, then, on the basis of the above average performances of this class that there is no real reading problem here.

A further study of the class, however, reveals that there is a rather large problem of adjusting materials and methods to individual differences. There are 13 children who are instructionally suited to a fifth-grade basal reader. There are 10 children who are below 4.5 in reading ability and therefore need to be taught with simpler material. There are 12 children who are reading at 6.0 or higher and need an expanded reading program.

Figure 4 shows the profiles of three members of this fifth-grade class. The general diagnosis shows that two of them should be considered disabled readers while one of them should not. The figure shows that Alice is a child

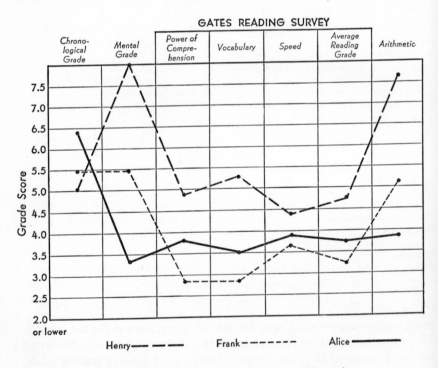

FIG. 4. Profiles of three children beginning fifth grade.

of less than average mental ability. Her chronological grade of 6.2 shows that she is the oldest child in her class. She has been retarded one year in school. Her mental grade is next to the lowest in the class and her I.Q., which is 74, is the lowest. Alice is doing a very creditable job of learning to read. She is reading a half-year higher than would be expected from a child of her mental level. Alice needs the type of instruction described in a later chapter of this book as suitable for a slow-learning child. She is not a disabled reader and needs no further reading diagnosis.

Frank is a disabled reader. He is more than two years behind in his reading development as compared with his mental grade. He is a boy of average intelligence so he should be reading about 5.3. Instead he is reading 3.0. He needs to be studied further in order to plan a remedial program to improve his reading ability. His relatively successful performance in arithmetic shows that he is able to achieve in areas other than reading.

Henry is a reading disability case although he is reading only two months below his grade placement. He is one of the youngest members of the class, but he is also one of the most capable intellectually. His mental grade indicates that he should be reading above seventh-grade level instead of 4.8, his average reading grade. His arithmetic grade is high (7.5) and more in keeping with his mental ability. Henry has a reading disability. A further diagnosis of Henry's reading disability is needed in order to plan his remedial program.

Analytical Diagnosis in Reading

The analytical diagnosis separates the reading act into some of its more specific skills and abilities. It enables the diagnostician to detect the areas in which the child's difficulty lies. This level of diagnosis will show whether the child's difficulty is in a specific type of comprehension, in word-recognition techniques, in reading efficiency, oral reading, or basic study skills. An analytical diagnosis might also indicate how well the child is able to adapt his reading abilities to meet the demands of the specific content fields. There are many tests which give the type of information needed for analytical diagnosis. Some of the more useful ones are listed in Appendix I.

Figure 5 shows the results of an analytical diagnosis for three members of the fifth-grade class under consideration. The general diagnosis, it will be remembered, revealed that Frank and Henry were disabled readers needing further diagnosis. Barbara has not shown such an over-all deficiency. However, an inspection of her relative scores on the analytical diagnosis in Figure 5 shows that she has a specific retardation. Barbara is, in general, a competent reader. Her profile shows that she is low in one type of reading— reading to follow directions—in which she is more than a year and a half lower than would be expected of a girl with her mental capability and general reading ability. This is not a serious matter but it is probable that a short period of emphasis on this type of reading would make Barbara as proficient in reading to follow directions as she is in other comprehension abilities. She needs no further diagnosis.

Figure 5 shows that Henry has a very uneven profile. The analytical diagnosis of Henry shows that he is low in the more general types of reading

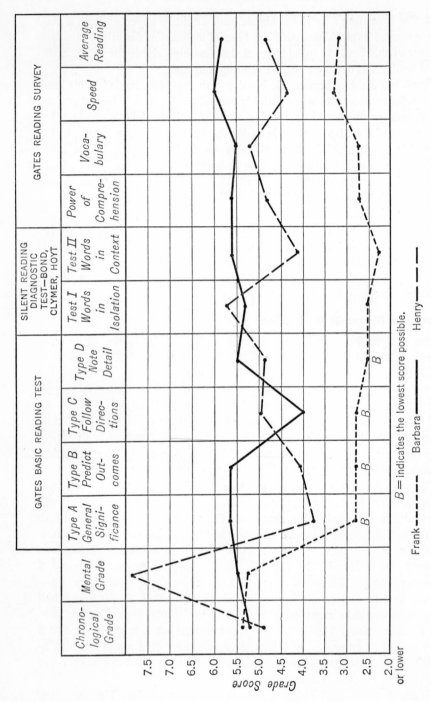

B = indicates the lowest score possible.

Frank ———   Barbara ———   Henry — — —

FIG. 5. An analytical reading diagnosis of three children beginning fifth grade.

comprehension. It also shows that he is considerably better at recognizing words in isolation than he is at recognizing words in context. He is also a very slow reader. It is reasonable to suspect that Henry is an overanalytical reader and that he fails to use the more rapid word-recognition techniques. The precise nature of instruction he needs will have to be found out by further study in a diagnostic case study.

Frank is seen to be low in all types of reading in Figure 5 and he must be studied further. The analytical diagnosis shows Frank to be a reading disability case and that only the speed of reading score (though still low) even approaches what could be expected of him. An inspection of his performance on the speed test shows a high degree of inaccuracy. Even the speed test, therefore, cannot be considered good performance because to obtain speed without accuracy is a questionable attribute. It is apparent, on the basis of the analytical diagnosis, that Frank has something basically wrong with his reading. The difficulty appears to be in the word-recognition area, but even this suspicion awaits case-study diagnosis before it will be verified.

Case-Study Diagnosis in Reading

Standardized tests employed in general and analytical diagnosis, individual standardized tests, detailed silent reading diagnostic tests, and informal study of the child's approaches to the various aspects of reading are used in a thorough case-study diagnosis. Such a diagnosis also includes an analysis of the child's strengths and limitations as an individual—his sensory capacities, his emotional reactions, and his attitudes toward reading. A case-study diagnosis should also appraise the general school environment in which the child is working, the methods of instruction used in his school, and an appraisal of those home conditions that might be specifically related to reading and thus influence his reading growth. The last kind of appraisal should include finding out how the parents feel about their child's reading problem and how much they desire to co-operate in overcoming the difficulty. A case-study diagnosis must give answers to the specific questions concerning the disabled reader that have been discussed in this chapter.

The first question, whether the child is correctly classified as a disabled reader, is frequently answered by the general diagnosis. However, in some cases, the case-study approach will indicate that a child's major problem is something other than disability in reading. The detailed case studies of Henry and Frank did not reveal any existing condition which would lead to a classification other than reading disability. The general diagnosis showed, on the other hand, that Alice's problem was one of low mentality and that she could not be classified as a disabled reader.

The second question, dealing with the problem of who can give the remedial instruction most effectively, can sometimes be answered in the general diagnosis and at other times in the analytical, but frequently it must await the completed case study. The general diagnosis showed that Alice's problem was such that the classroom teacher should adjust to it. The analytical diagnosis showed that Barbara was weak in just one type of reading. She had a specific retardation in reading which could be adequately handled in the typical classroom situation.

As a result of a thorough case study, it was judged that Henry would profit from remedial reading in a group at the school reading center; while Frank's problem was so complex and charged with emotional rejection of reading that it was felt that he would need to get his remedial work at a reading clinic.

The third question, dealing with the nature of the training needed was answered, in the case of Alice, in the general diagnosis. She needed training in reading suitable to a slow-learning child. The nature of the training needed for Barbara was answered by the analytical diagnosis, which showed that Barbara needed training in following exact directions. The case-study diagnosis showed that Henry was, indeed, an overanalytical reader. He had a high score in knowledge of phonetic elements and he attempted to employ this means of word recognition even with words that he could recognize at sight when they were flashed before him with a speed that allowed him only a glance at the word. He also demonstrated a tendency to pay marked attention to word endings and to neglect somewhat the beginning elements of words. In addition, he was very poor at making adequate use of context clues. Henry had a marked limiting disability in word recognition. The remedial work that Henry needs will be described in a later chapter, dealing with word identification and recognition.

The nature of the training needed by Frank was also indicated by the case-study diagnosis. Frank's problem is complex indeed. He has failed to develop a systematic attack on words. He is a marked reversal case and has emotionally rejected reading. In addition, there is evidence that Frank has a visual handicap which should be corrected before remedial work is undertaken. The necessary remedial work for Frank will be of the types discussed in Chapter 13, dealing with left-to-right orientation in reading and word perception, and in Chapter 18 on the especially handicapped child. He also needs some additional emphasis on word recognition as described in Chapter 12.

The fourth question that must be answered by the diagnosis deals with ways in which improvement can be brought about most efficiently. This question could have been answered for Alice in the general diagnosis and for Barbara in the analytical diagnosis. Alice should be given material at approximately the middle of the third-grade level. She needs encouragement, success, and many opportunities to use the results of her reading in constructive activities such as building models or helping make displays and things of that sort. She needs concrete illustrations of what she is reading about. Alice should read for only one well-defined purpose at a time because she has low intelligence and finds it difficult to attend to several purposes at the same time.

For general purposes, Barbara should read material at 5.5 level of difficulty. But in the exercises designed to increase her ability to follow exact directions, her remedial instruction should be started with material that is somewhat easier in level of reading difficulty. The purposes for which Barbara reads this material should be to emphasize reading to organize, to get the sense of a sequence of ideas, and to follow exact directions. Special exercises such as the *Gates-Peardon Practice Exercises, Type C* might be good material with which to start Barbara's corrective instruction. It would be well to keep a chart indicating her speed and accuracy in doing these exercises. As she increases in accuracy, she can be encouraged to read somewhat more rapidly and the difficulty of the material can be increased. Barbara can be expected to develop readily the ability to organize and to follow exact directions.

Complete case-study diagnoses were necessary to find out how improvement could be brought about most efficiently in the cases of Henry and Frank. Henry should have a time chart kept indicating the speed at which he reads during the reading of exercises that are designed to increase his speed. He should be given remedial instruction in material about half-way through the fourth grade in difficulty. There should be considerable recreational reading for Henry. He should be given exercises designed to encourage the use of context clues. These exercises should be approximately fourth-grade in level of difficulty.

The problem of bringing about progress in reading in the case of Frank is much more difficult. He will need to read material approximately at the second-grade level of difficulty. It would be well to use material that is as mature in format as possible. Workbook material might be used to advantage. The remedial teacher must be optimistic and demonstrate to Frank that he is actually growing in his reading capability. Frank should develop a picture dictionary in which he can see that the number of words he recognizes is increasing. He might profit from dictating some stories of his own and if his tendency to reverse words persists, it may be necessary to employ sound tracing methods, described in a later chapter.

The fifth question is concerned with the existence of limiting conditions within a child that must be considered in formulating his remedial program. As a result of a thorough case-study diagnosis, it became clear that Henry had no limiting characteristics to which the program needed to adjust or for which there had to be a correction made prior to remedial instruction. Frank was found to have two limiting conditions. The first was his emotional rejection of reading. This emotional rejection must be taken into consideration in formulating his remedial program, but it was not felt that it was serious enough to warrant treatment by a specialist. The fact that Frank's arithmetic score was nearly equal to his mental grade, indicated that in other learnings Frank was able to apply himself reasonably well. Frank's second limitation was his eyesight. There was some indication that Frank was farsighted and that he found it difficult to focus on the printed page at reading distance. A thorough visual examination was recommended before Frank was to undertake remedial instruction.

The sixth question deals with environmental conditions that might interfere with the progress of remedial work. It was found that for three of the children, Henry, Frank, and Alice, the school would have to make some adjustments to their needs. In the case of Alice, the adjustments would be those that should be expected in general adjustment to the existence of individual differences in any class. It was found, for example, that in science and social studies, the same textbooks were used by all the children in the class. Alice could not be expected to profit from the use of this material.

Henry, who had been in the middle reading group, should be kept there. But it was found that he could not read with profit some of the material of the content fields. Somewhat less mature reference material should be made available for him.

The school adjustments necessary for Frank are more complicated. Frank should not attempt to read the materials in the content fields, but he should use this reading time for reading materials at his level of advancement. He can listen to the discussions in the classroom and he can participate in the creative activities.

There were no indications of unfortunate circumstances in any of the homes of these children with the possible exception of Frank. Frank's parents were very concerned about his poor reading ability. They had attempted to teach him to read by means of a strictly phonetic approach, which had been recommended in a series of articles taken from their local newspaper. After about a month of instruction, they wisely judged that Frank was not only getting worse in reading, but that he was becoming highly disturbed by the instruction they were giving him and his own seeming inadequacy in response. Frank's parents were eager to co-operate with the school and the reading clinic. They agreed to set aside a place for Frank to keep his reading materials and they welcomed the suggestion to discuss with Frank the stories he read and to help him by pronouncing words he found difficult.

Each of the cases from this fifth-grade class was different. Some of the children needed no further study beyond the general and analytical diagnoses. Two of the boys needed detailed case-study diagnoses. The case-study diagnoses were made at a reading clinic. It was necessary for the diagnostician to have consultations with both the classroom teacher and the parents of the two boys.

In making the case-study diagnoses of the reading disability cases, both standardized and informal procedures were employed, and in one case, the services of an outside expert were needed. The reading diagnostic tests most useful in case-study diagnosis will be described in detail in the chapter that follows.

SUMMARY

The reading diagnostician must analyze the reading capabilities of each child in difficulty until he has found wherein the reading problem lies. He must also appraise, by screening methods, those related problems which need to be corrected or to which instructional adjustments must be made. A diagnostician must make recommendations in six areas.

1. He must find out whether the child is correctly classified as a disabled reader or if some other problem of child growth and development is the basic difficulty.

2. He must make recommendations as to just where the remedial work can be given most effectively. Should the child be re-educated in the classroom, in the school reading center, or in the clinic? The answer to this question lies in the nature of the case. Most simple retardation and specific retardation cases should be given remedial training in the classroom or school reading center. Children with limiting disability should be corrected at the school reading center or clinic, while complex disability, for the most part, should be corrected at a clinic.

3. The nature of the training needed must be discovered. Identification of the particular character of the reading limitation is the most important part of the reading diagnosis. The reading pattern of the child must be studied to locate the specific faulty learning impeding his reading progress. This requires a thorough appraisal of the skills and abilities involved in reading.

4. The most efficient methods for improving the child's reading should be recommended. These include recommendations in regard to level and types of material to be used, ways of demonstrating progress in reading to the child, and plans for extending the reading instruction with exercises or assignments that can be done independently.

5. The diagnostician must locate any condition within the child that might influence reading growth detrimentally. He should utilize other expert help whenever it is needed for diagnosis and correction. He should recommend needed modifications in the remedial program to adjust to any limitations.

6. He must appraise the entire learning environment of the child in order to locate any conditions that might interfere with progress in reading. He should make recommendations as to how the parents and the school can contribute to the solution of the child's reading problem.

In order to secure information for planning remedial work, the diagnostician must use many types of measures and appraisals. He should use both standardized and informal procedures. He will find it necessary to progress through general, analytical, and case-study levels of diagnostic procedures. He should diagnose a case only as far as is necessary in order to formulate the remedial instruction.

SELECTED READINGS

BETTS, Emmett A., *Foundations of reading instruction.* New York: American Book Company, 1946, Chap. 11.

BRUECKNER, L. J., and BOND, G. L., *Diagnosis and treatment of learning difficulties.* New York: Appleton-Century-Crofts, Inc., 1955, Chaps. 2, 4.

DOLCH, Edward W., *A manual for remedial reading,* 2nd ed. Champaign (Ill.): The Garrard Press, 1945, Chap. 4.

DURRELL, Donald D., *Improvement of basic reading abilities.* Yonkers (N.Y.): World Book Company, 1940, Chap. 13.

GATES, Arthur I., *The improvement of reading,* 3rd ed. New York: The Macmillan Company, 1947, Chap. 3.

HARRIS, Albert J., *How to increase reading ability,* 3rd ed. New York: Longmans, Green & Company, 1956, Chaps. 7, 8.

9

SPECIFIC APPROACHES
TO DIAGNOSIS

AN INDIVIDUALIZED APPROACH must be adopted in diagnosing reading disability. Watkins (181) has demonstrated convincingly that there are no common patterns of reading deficiency which characterize the proper individuality of disabled readers. Seldom, if ever, does one find even two cases with exactly the same pattern. In a single child, the pattern of reading abilities may be quite uneven and the patterns vary from one disability case to another.

It is customary to designate the reading-grade level of a child in terms of an average derived from scores on several tests. Let us suppose, for instance, that a pupil's average reading grade turns out to be 3.2 when all aspects of his reading are averaged. Actually no one of his test scores may be 3.2. He may be relatively good in word-recognition skills but poor in sentence comprehension; high in vocabulary knowledge but poor in a timed test of comprehension; and good in grasping details but poor in comprehending the general ideas involved. In short, in the case of a particular child, the pattern of reading abilities tends to be quite uneven whether this child is, on the average, a disabled reader or is reading at a grade level that agrees with his learning aptitude.

In general, it may be expected that a retarded reader will exhibit a pattern of reading abilities that is more variable than that possessed by a normal reader. Since these patterns differ from one instance to another, each case must receive individual diagnosis to discover his particular weaknesses and strengths. Only then is it possible to provide a remedial program suitable to relieve a child's difficulties. The emphasis throughout this book is to adjust remedial measures to the individual needs revealed by diagnosis.

INSTRUMENTS USED IN DIAGNOSIS

A variety of tools and techniques are employed for diagnosing reading proficiency. Each has an important function in the diagnostic program. These instruments and techniques may be classified as follows: (1) group survey tests; (2) group diagnostic tests; (3) informal procedures; (4) detailed individual techniques. Only brief mention will be made of the first three at this time since their uses are considered in detail at appropriate places throughout the book.

167

Group Survey Tests

As noted in a previous chapter, survey tests are employed to help identify reading disability cases. The use of satisfactory survey tests yields a fairly adequate measure of the grade level at which a pupil can read. A comparison of this measure with his mental grade or some other adequate criterion of learning capacity will reveal the degree to which a child is retarded in reading, if at all. A survey test usually begins with relatively easy items and progresses to more and more difficult items. Norms for interpreting scores usually extend over a range of several grades. The typical survey test includes measures of vocabulary knowledge, comprehension of sentences or paragraphs or both, and sometimes speed and accuracy. The *Gates Primary Reading Tests* and the *Gates Advanced Primary Reading Tests* [1] are examples of survey tests for use at the primary levels and for retarded readers in the intermediate grades. The *Stanford Reading Test* and the *Gates Reading Survey* are typical examples of survey tests for use at levels above the primary grades.

Group Diagnostic Tests

Although the survey tests are designed primarily for determining a pupil's average reading grade, they are also to some degree diagnostic. Examination of the grade equivalents of scores for the various areas tested (word recognition, vocabulary knowledge, sentence comprehension, paragraph comprehension) will reveal information concerning the individual needs of a pupil who is in difficulty. There are, however, more analytical group tests that are more diagnostic in nature. They are superior to the general survey test for diagnostic purposes in that they provide a profile of silent reading abilities. Examination of such a profile reveals strong and weak areas in a pupil's repertory of the abilities measured in the subtests. Some analytical tests have a small number of subtests, others a large number.

Typical examples of analytical tests which are useful in identifying individual needs are: (1) at the primary level, *Progressive Reading Tests* and *Ingraham-Clark Diagnostic Reading Tests;* (2) at the intermediate and higher levels, the Dvorak and Van Wagenen *Diagnostic Examination of Silent Reading Abilities, Gates Basic Reading Tests,* the *Diagnostic Reading Tests* issued by the Committee on Diagnostic Reading Tests, and the Bond-Clymer-Hoyt *Developmental Reading Tests.*

The analytical type of group test provides valuable information about the strengths and the weaknesses of individual pupils. This information is useful to both the classroom teacher and the remedial teacher. Ordinarily, the giving of a group diagnostic test and a study of the scores obtained constitutes a first step in the analytical diagnosis of reading disabilities. To the

---

[1] See Appendix I for lists of reading tests.

classroom teacher, these scores, within the limitation of the test used, reveal those aspects of reading in which a child is deficient. When a child's retardation in a particular skill, such as some aspect of word recognition or sentence comprehension is not great, a moderate amount of individual instruction by the teacher will ordinarily correct the situation. Again, a teacher may find that her class as a whole tends to be deficient in such an area as reading to appreciate general significance. This probably indicates that she needs to change her emphasis in instruction to maintain a better balance among basic reading abilities.

With a greater degree of deficiency, i.e., a year or more retarded, the case may be referred to a remedial teacher for intensive instruction. If the test results indicate that the deficiency is limited to a single area such as one type of paragraph comprehension, the remedial instruction in the classroom can deal with it. If, however, the group test reveals extensive disability involving several or all reading skills, then additional diagnosis is indicated. In such cases a detailed diagnosis as described below should be carried out.

The use of group diagnostic tests may be summed up in the following statements. Group diagnostic tests (1) are useful to the teacher for sizing up the relative proficiency of her pupils in a variety of reading abilities; (2) reveal the individual needs of specific pupils who can be helped by the classroom teacher; (3) identify pupils who are in difficulty seriously enough to be referred to a remedial teacher for additional diagnosis and remedial instruction; (4) are in general primarily useful for identifying individual needs of pupils with moderate reading deficiencies in the intermediate and higher grades; (5) are also useful in the more severe disability cases in locating the areas that need further diagnosis. For example, if a child is low in the vocabulary section of a test, an intensive case-study diagnosis of his word-recognition techniques is in order. For details of the above, see Chapters 7 and 8.

Informal Procedures

The diagnosis of reading ability and deficiencies is best achieved through using standardized tests and procedures. It is possible, however, and sometimes desirable to make a preliminary diagnosis by less formal procedures. This can be accomplished through the use of a carefully graded series of basic readers. The series should be one which the child has not used before. Selections of 100 to 150 words are chosen from each successive book in the series. For any grade level, e. g., grade 3.0, select material at about 20 pages from the beginning of the first book at that grade. Similarly, for halfway through a grade (grade 3.5, etc.) select material near the beginning of the second book for that grade. A few questions involving both some ideas and some facts are constructed on each selection. After the pupil, starting at a relatively easy level, has read each selection orally to the teacher, or to the examiner in an individual testing situation, he then answers the comprehension questions based upon its content. If the material in the book he starts with is not handled easily, he is moved back to a still easier level. The child then reads the successively more difficult selections until his reading levels are determined. Betts (8) has outlined reading levels as follows:

1. The child's *independent reading level* is ascertained from the book in which he can read with no more than one error in word recognition (pronunciation) in each 100 words and has a comprehension score of at least 90 per cent. At this level the child must read orally in a natural conversational tone. The reading should be rhythmical and well phrased. At the same time he is free from tension and has good reading posture. His silent reading will be faster than his oral reading and free from vocalizations. This is the level at which the child should do extensive supplementary reading for enjoyment or for information in line with his interests. At this *independent reading level,* the child has complete control of experience (concepts), vocabulary, construction, and organization. He has, therefore, maximum opportunity for doing the thinking that is required for a full understanding of what he is reading.

2. The *instructional reading level* is determined from the level of the book in which the child can read with no more than one word-recognition error in each 20 words and has a comprehension score of at least 75 per cent. At this level the child reads orally, *after silent study,* without tension, in a conversational tone, and with rhythm and proper phrasing. Silent reading is faster than oral. The child is able properly to employ word-recognition clues and techniques. This is the level at which a pupil is able to make successful progress in reading under *teacher guidance.* When using challenging materials at this level, and with purposeful reading directed by the teacher, the result should be maximum progress in acquiring reading abilities.

3. The *frustration reading level* is marked by the book in which the child "bogs down" when he tries to read. He reads orally without rhythm and in an unnatural voice. Errors and refusals are numerous. Tensions are manifest. The child comprehends less than half of what he is trying to read. The test should be stopped as soon as it is clear that the child is at his frustration level.

No child should be asked to go on reading at the frustration level when he is being taught or in any other situation. The teacher, however, should recognize that such a level exists. Too frequently children are found to be working at their frustration levels in classes where instruction is not satisfactorily adjusted to individual differences.

4. The *probable capacity reading level* is shown by the highest book in the series in which the child can comprehend 75 per cent of the material when it is read aloud by the examiner. When he answers questions about and discusses the material he has read, the child is able to pronounce and use properly many of the words in the selection. He should also be able to

use in his oral discussion some language structures comparable to those in the selection read to him.

Certain hazards are involved in determining these reading levels. First we may ask how satisfactorily can one determine 90 per cent or 75 per cent comprehension of what is read? Part of the answer depends upon exercising great care in making out the thought and fact questions. It may happen, for instance, that a child can answer correctly all of one set of questions on the material read, and only 50 per cent of another set on the same reading material. The questions, therefore, should be stated in clear and simple language and there must be enough of them to sample thoroughly the content of the reading selection. The experienced teacher should be able to organize such questions and she may refer to the questions on the reading paragraphs in *Durrell Analysis of Reading Difficulty* (World Book Company, Yonkers, N. Y.) to see for herself some good examples. This is a very important matter, for the success of this type of diagnosis is at stake in the way this is done.

Another matter of some consequence in the informal determination of reading levels is the detection of pronunciation errors. Children who depend solely on word-recognition techniques and who have failed to develop an adequate sight vocabulary, will make just about the same number of pronunciation errors regardless of the difficulty of the material they are reading. Concretely, they will mispronounce about as many words in first-grade material as in fourth-grade. The examiner, therefore, must note, record, and evaluate the procedures employed by the child in his reading. This is facilitated by use of the kind of check-list given below.

Additional important information is obtained in the informal diagnosis by having the child read silently some selections from the basic readers. These selections should be comparable in difficulty to those read orally. In addition to checking comprehension as in the oral reading, the examiner must record rate of reading and faulty habits, as indicated in the outline below.

Determination of reading levels as described above is useful to the classroom teacher who is seeking to discover the instructional needs of particular pupils, preliminary to adjusting her instruction to their needs. If an examiner wishes a somewhat more thorough diagnosis of the sources of reading deficiencies of certain pupils, she must introduce a more detailed procedure while these tests are given or she must do some additional testing, using selections of comparable difficulty. In this case what she does is to time the reading of each selection and record every error in the form in which it occurs. Also she notes down her observations on such things as comprehension difficulties, rate variations, voice control, rhythm, word-by-word reading, signs of tension, and the degree to which word-recognition clues and techniques are used. Additional information on word-recognition skills may be obtained by having the child pronounce words from the word lists which are given at the end of the basic readers. Errors should be recorded and analyzed. The following *Informal Diagnosis Blank* has been organized to facilitate the recording of data obtained during informal diagnosis.

INFORMAL DIAGNOSIS BLANK

Basic Data

Name _____ School attending _____

    Chronological age _____ Grade in school _____

    Mental test given _____

    I.Q. _____ M.A. _____ Mental Grade _____

Standardized reading tests given:

    1. _____ Score _____ Reading Grade _____

    2. _____ Score _____ Reading Grade _____

    3. _____ Score _____ Reading Grade _____

    4. _____ Score _____ Reading Grade _____

        Average reading grade _____

Reading Levels

    1. Independent reading level, grade _____

    2. Instructional reading level, grade _____

    3. Frustration reading level, grade _____

    4. Probable capacity reading level, grade _____

Oral Reading from Book

    1. Name and grade level of book _____

    2. Rate: words per minute _____

    3. Degree of comprehension _____

    4. Expression _____

    5. Nature of enunciation _____

    6. Skill in phrasing _____

    7. Word-by-word reading _____

    8. Habits during reading: head movements, following with finger, posture, distractibility, tenseness _____

    9. Attitude toward reading _____

   10. Word-recognition difficulties:

        a. Reversals _____

        b. Wrong beginning _____

        c. Wrong middle _____

        d. Wrong ending _____

        e. Wrong several parts _____

   11. Word-recognition skills:

        a. Use of context _____

        b. Adequacy of sight words _____

        c. Adequacy of procedure in word analysis _____

   12. Other difficulties:

        a. Repetitions _____

        b. Omissions _____

        c. Refusals _____

        d. Other _____

Silent Reading from Book

1. Name and grade level of book _____
2. Rate: words per minute _____
3. Degree of comprehension _____
4. Vocalization (degree of lip movement, whispering, audible speech) _____
5. Finger pointing _____
6. Head movements _____
7. Signs of tenseness _____
8. Posture _____
9. Distractibility _____
10. Other habits _____

Word Pronunciation from Word Lists in Basic Book

1. Name and grade level of book _____
2. Nature of phonetic attack _____
3. Blending skill _____
4. Resorts to spelling attack _____
5. No method of word analysis _____
6. Skill in syllabication _____
7. Recognition of familiar parts _____
8. Recognition of parts of compound words _____
9. Recognition of word roots _____
10. Handling of suffixes _____
11. Handling of prefixes _____
12. Trouble with consonants _____
13. Trouble with vowels _____
14. Sounds omitted _____
15. Sounds added _____

Other Relevant Data

1. Hearing status _____
2. Visual status _____
3. Speech difficulties _____
4. Other physical difficulties _____
5. Fluency in language usage _____
6. Chief interests _____
7. Ability to concentrate _____
8. Persistence in tasks _____
9. Emotional reactions (confident, shy, overaggressive, negativistic, cheerful, etc.) _____
10. Attitudes (toward school, teacher, reading) _____
11. Handedness _____
12. Eyedness _____
13. Home environment _____
14. Other observations _____

Tentative Diagnosis of Case

1. Degree of reading retardation _____
2. Important physical handicaps _____

3. Adjustment difficulties _____

4. Lack of voice control and rhythm in oral reading _____

5. Main word-recognition difficulties _____
_____

6. Comprehension difficulties _____
_____

Suggested Remedial Procedures

1. _____
_____

2., etc. _____

Obviously the more systematic, standardized diagnostic procedures (described below) are more reliable and yield a more thorough diagnosis than any informal procedure, especially with the more severe disability cases. Nevertheless, the informal reading diagnosis as described above has certain advantages. It is inexpensive and lends itself to relatively rapid administration. Several equivalent forms for successive testing are readily assembled from the basic reading series. The informal diagnosis can be applied in the classroom by the teacher as well as in the clinic. The classroom teacher will find it useful for determining strengths and weaknesses of her pupils at periodic intervals. Discovered weaknesses can be remedied before they become more severe. One advantage is that many retarded readers can be handled in this way. The clinician may employ the informal diagnosis as a supplement to the more formal diagnosis. In fact, the informal diagnosis explores some areas not treated in standardized procedures. It is possible to supplement the informal inventory with Gray's *Standardized Oral Reading Paragraphs,* of which several forms are available for use in grades one to eight. To employ the informal diagnostic procedure, the examiner should be professionally competent and have had some supervised training. The able and well-trained teacher should qualify as a competent examiner.

Detailed Techniques

Group tests and informal techniques have their appropriate uses in diagnosing reading deficiencies. With many disability cases, however, a more detailed and extensive procedure appears necessary. This is especially true with the more severe cases of disability, particularly those of long standing. In the next sections several representative detailed techniques of diagnosis will be briefly described.

REPRESENTATIVE DETAILED TECHNIQUES

The techniques of individual diagnosis described here are representative but by no means inclusive of all the programs described in the literature. The reader should bear in mind that each of these techniques (and others not described) have enjoyed successful use in the field. Some of the limitations and strong points of each of the techniques described will be noted.

The descriptions presented in this chapter are designed to give the reader merely a general impression of the main characteristics of the diagnostic tests together with examining procedures and uses. Actual use of any diagnostic test will be based upon the detailed directions accompanying the test.

A. DURRELL ANALYSIS OF READING DIFFICULTY

The Durrell procedure for discovering cases of disability and the diagnosis upon which remedial programs are to be based is outlined in three steps:

1. Discrepancies between mental ability and reading achievement are determined. The *Revised Stanford-Binet Scale* and an appropriate reading test may be employed for this. For children in grades 3 to 6, Durrell suggests use of the *Durrell-Sullivan Reading Capacity Test* and the *Durrell-Sullivan Reading Achievement Test* which are both standardized on the same population. The *Reading Capacity Test* is entirely nonverbal in the sense that no reading is required. This is actually a listening comprehension test. It measures the child's understanding of spoken language both for word meanings and paragraph comprehension. The scores are combined to give grade or age level for hearing comprehension. This is compared with level of achievement on the *Reading Achievement Test* to discover discrepancies which indicate reading disability. These tests may be given by a teacher without specialized training. They provide an economical means of identifying poor readers without major language deficiencies who are capable of improving their reading proficiency. If standardized tests are not available, it is suggested that those children who are in the lowest third of the class in reading ability and who also appear to have normal intelligence be selected for the detailed diagnosis.

2. The next step is a thorough physical examination of those children with a serious discrepancy between their mental ability and their reading achievement. In this examination, special attention is given to hearing and sight as well as to any physical condition which may result in chronic fatigue.

3. The third step consists of a detailed analysis of reading difficulties by means of the *Durrell Analysis of Reading Difficulty,* revised edition (57). This consists of a series of individual tests in oral and silent reading, word perception, visual memory of word forms, auditory analysis of word elements, plus systematic observing and recording of certain responses and forms of behavior which will be described below.

The Test Materials (Durrell)

Materials for the *Durrell Analysis of Reading Difficulty* consist of a manual of directions, a booklet of reading paragraphs, a tachistoscope for quick exposure of words, various series of words on cards to use in the tachistoscope and for word analysis, and an individual record blank. The test is designed for grades 1 to 6. The testing of one child takes from 30 to 90 minutes depending upon the experience of the examiner. Only experienced teachers acquainted with the methods and objectives of teaching reading are qualified to use these tests. Its administration is best learned, however, under the direction of a person with a good deal of clinical experience.

The Individual Record Blank (Durrell)

An individual record blank is provided for each child tested. Included in this are the following: (1) blanks for entering identifying data; (2) a profile chart for recording grade and age, results of reading analysis tests, other reading tests, intelligence test (see outline below); (3) an extensive check-lists of difficulties observed and recorded, psychological factors (special interests, etc.), and home history; (4) blank space with suggestions for outlining remedial plans.

On succeeding pages of the Individual Record Blank are given the examiner's copy of the individual diagnostic tests together with questions to be asked of the pupil and a check-list of difficulties that may be observed during the testing. In addition, grade norms are provided for each test. Difficulties noted on separate tests are summarized in the general check-list on page 2 of the Individual Record Blank.

Tests and Procedures (Durrell)

Oral Reading is the first test in the Analysis series. Eight paragraphs of reading material are printed on cardboard and assembled in a booklet. The child is started with a paragraph on which it is pretty certain he will make no error—a "basal paragraph." The reading is continued with succeeding paragraphs until seven or more errors are made on a single paragraph, or until the time required for reading any paragraph is more than two minutes (upper level). A detailed record is made of all errors such as omitted words, words inserted, mispronunciation, words not known, etc. All behavior symptomatic of reading difficulties is checked on the check-list in the Record Blank. A list of comprehension questions is asked at the end of each paragraph. Grade norms, based on the time required for reading, are provided. High, middle, and low positions within each grade are given. If two or more comprehension questions are failed, the child is rated low on that paragraph.

Silent Reading is the second test. A different set of paragraphs are used. They are graded in difficulty and printed on cards in a booklet as in Test 1. The child reads paragraphs of the same difficulty as he did in the first test. As each paragraph is completed, the child is asked to tell everything he can remember in the story. The material in the examiner's copy is arranged to facilitate recording the ideas recalled. Any relevant reading difficulties are checked in the list accompanying this test. Grade norms based upon time and memory scores are provided.

Listening Comprehension comprises Test 3. Paragraphs of the same levels of difficulty as those in preceding tests are used. Each paragraph is read aloud by the examiner and a set of questions is asked the child. The listening comprehension is ascertained from the level where not more than one question of the eight is missed.

The Word Recognition and Word Analysis Test comes next. For this test, lists of words are printed on strips of cardboard for presenting in a cardboard tachistoscope (short exposure) device. Separate lists of words are employed for grade one and for grades two to six. One of these lists of words suitable to the child's reading ability is presented in the tachistoscope so that the words appear one at a time for one-half second each. Both correct and incorrect pronunciation are checked appropriately. When a child fails to grasp a word in this flash test, the shutter of the tachistoscope is opened so that the child can study and try to work out the pronunciation of the word. This provides a test of word-analysis skills. Correct and incorrect responses during this analysis are recorded. Also difficulties in word analysis and word recognition are noted in the accompanying check-list. Successively more difficult lists of words are presented until the child fails on seven successive words of a single list or the hardest list in the series is completed. There are grade norms both for word recognition (flash presentation) and for word analysis.

The next series of tests is comprised of *Naming Letters, Identifying Letters Named, Matching Letters,* and *Writing Letters.* These tests are designed for the severely retarded reader or for any child when it is suspected that he does not know the names of the letters.

The test for *Visual Memory of Words—Primary* is to be used with children whose reading grade is three or below. *Visual Memory of Words—Intermediate* is for children with reading grades four to six. The child is shown a letter or word in the tachistoscope for two to three seconds. When this is covered, he turns to the record booklet and marks from memory the item shown.

A series of tests deal with the auditory analysis of word elements: *Hearing Sounds in Words—Primary* tests ability to identify beginning sounds, ending sounds, and both beginning and ending sounds in words. A child who fails the preceding test should be given the test on *Learning to Hear Sounds in Words.* This will provide information on the severity of his difficulty in perceiving sounds in words. To discover which letter sounds and blends are not known, the test for *Sounds of Letters* is given to children with less than second-grade reading ability.

The *Learning Rate* test is given to severely retarded readers to discover the degree of difficulty a child has in remembering words taught.

Additional tests are *Phonic Spelling of Words,* a *Spelling Test,* and a *Handwriting Test.*

A form is provided for a detailed analysis of faulty pronunciation or spelling. This will provide information on vowel errors, consonant errors, reversals, addition of sounds, omission of sounds, and substitution of words.

Standardized tests are not available for gathering information on certain reading habits and skills for this can be done just as well informally. Durrell therefore suggests informal tests for the following: (1) reading interest and effort, (2) suitability of the level of reading materials used in the classroom, (3) speed of reading, (4) word skills, and (5) speed and accuracy in locating information.

Summarizing the Diagnosis (Durrell)

The list of difficulties recorded at the end of each test in the analysis is transferred to the summary check-list on page 2 of the Individual Record Blank. In addition, the child's grade level on the Reading Analysis Tests and on additional tests is entered in the Profile Chart on page 1 of the record blank, as shown in Figure 6. (There is no place on the profile for entering scores on some of the diagnostic tests, as visual memory for words, etc.) The scores are entered by making a cross at the appropriate points on each scale of the Profile Chart and then drawing a line connecting the crosses. Examination of the profile reveals grade placement on the various tests plus any discrepancy between achievement and capacity. The nature and extent of specific difficulties involved in the reading deficiency of the child appear in the summary check-list of difficulties on page 2 of the record blank. The remedial program for a child is organized upon the basis of the information in the profile chart and the summary list of difficulties. According to Durrell, the most helpful information will be derived from the check-lists of specific difficulties. Suggestions for organizing remedial teaching based upon the diagnosis are given by Durrell (56).

Advantages of the Durrell Program

The *Durrell Analysis of Reading Difficulty* has certain distinct advantages: (1) Directions for administering the tests are complete and clear. (2) The type of case for which each test is needed is indicated. (3) The series of tests require a reasonable amount of time to administer. (4) Techniques of administration are not complicated. The tests for the moderately retarded reader can be given successfully by a competent, experienced teacher who is acquainted with the methods and objectives of teaching reading. (5) As emphasized by Durrell in the Manual of Directions, "The check-lists of errors are more important than the norms." This check-list is probably the most detailed and complete of its kind. Appropriate use of these check-lists which accompany the diagnostic tests will provide sufficient information for diagnosing reading difficulties in a majority of cases. At

Durrell Analysis of Reading Difficulty

NEW EDITION

BY Donald D. Durrell *Professor of Education and Director of Educational Clinic, Boston University*

NAME _____   DATE _____

SCHOOL _____   EXAMINER _____

AGE _____ GRADE _____   REPORT TO _____

DATE OF BIRTH _____   ADDRESS _____

Profile Chart

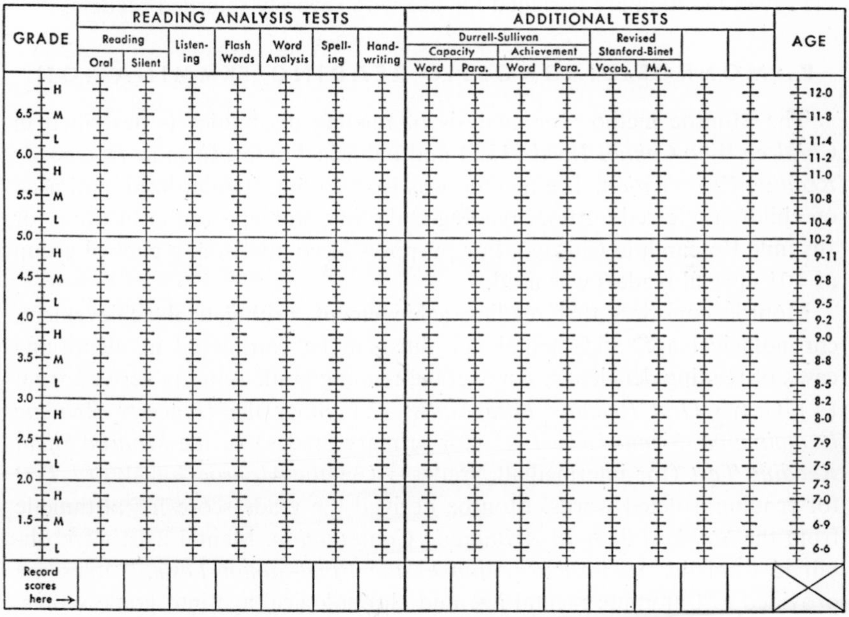

GRADE	READING ANALYSIS TESTS							ADDITIONAL TESTS								AGE
	Reading		Listen-ing	Flash Words	Word Analysis	Spell-ing	Hand-writing	Durrell-Sullivan				Revised Stanford-Binet				
								Capacity		Achievement						
	Oral	Silent						Word	Para.	Word	Para.	Vocab.	M.A.			

Record scores here →

FIG. 6. Durrell cover page. (Reproduced with permission of the publisher.)

times, the grade norms will also be found useful. (6) The Analysis of Reading Difficulty is most useful for diagnosing cases with not more than moderately severe deficiencies.

Limitations of the Durrell Program

The *Durrell Analysis of Reading Difficulty* has certain limitations: (1) Even though the revised test provides also for diagnosis of the severely retarded, it is generally more useful with the less severe cases. (2) The recording of eye movements by direct observation will provide little useful information (see below). (3) There is no provision for recording some of the test results on the profile. (4) Some of the tests for the severely retarded depend upon considerable clinical experience for interpretation. The ordinary classroom teacher is not qualified to do this.

Summary Statement

The Durrell program for diagnosis of reading difficulty provides an excellent means for prompt analysis of those cases which have the less severe reading disabilities occurring frequently in our schools. New tests in the revised edition are designed for use with severely retarded readers.

B. MONROE DIAGNOSTIC READING EXAMINATION

The Monroe method for analysis of reading disabilities is described in *Children Who Cannot Read* (131) and published in test form as *Diagnostic Reading Examination*. The method was worked out, standardized, and used on children referred for poor reading and other problems at the Institute for Juvenile Research in Chicago. For purposes of comparison, a control group of 101 normal readers was used.

Monroe considers that reading achievement, arithmetical achievement, chronological age, and mental age must all be considered in identifying cases of reading deficiency. An average reading grade score is derived from (1) *Gray's Oral Reading Paragraphs;* (2) either the *Haggerty Reading Examination, Sigma 1, Test 2* [2] (for primary grades) or the *Monroe Silent Reading Test* (for intermediate grades); (3) the *Monroe Iota Word Test* for reading isolated words. Monroe derived the grade score for arithmetic from the *Stanford Test In Arithmetic Computation*. Mental ages were obtained from the *Stanford Revision of the Binet-Simon Tests*. Tables are provided to transmute mental age and chronological age into grade scores. With these scores available, the reading index is computed.

The Reading Index (Monroe)

A single measure of reading proficiency is given by the *reading index*. It is obtained by comparing a child's composite reading grade with the average

[2] Apparently other standardized reading tests which yield grade scores may be substituted for those originally used by Monroe.

of his chronological, mental, and arithmetic grades. An example follows (131):

Chronological age grade of *M* is 3.5; mental age grade, 4.0; arithmetic grade, 3.6. The average of these is 3.7 which is his grade expectancy, or the grade level at which *M* should be able to read. The grade average of four reading tests (see above) is 2.1 or the level at which *M* is actually reading. The reading index is obtained by dividing the average reading grade by the average of the arithmetic, chronological, and mental grades. So the reading index for *M* is 2.1/3.7 = 0.56. *M*'s reading is only 56 per cent of the expectation, i.e., 56 per cent of grade 3.7. The reading index of each child is determined in this manner. Test-retest reliability of the index after six months interval is .94, which is very high.

The reading index identifies reading disability cases very well. Reading indices of the control group fall into a normal distribution about their mean of 1.00 (1.02 actually). Experience shows that a child with a reading index of 0.80 or below is practically always a reading case. This is about one standard deviation below the mean of 1.00. Those with indices between 0.80 and 0.90 tend to be borderline. Some of the latter will need remedial instruction, others will not.

Grade	CA	MA	Arith-metic	Spell-ing	O	C	WA	WD
10	15-6							
9	14-6							
8	13-6							
7	12-6							
6	11-6							
5	10-6							
4	9-6							
3	8-6							
2	7-6							
1	6-6							

FIG. 7. Case 16, Reading Index is 0.66. (Reproduced from M. Monroe, *Children Who Cannot Read*, University of Chicago Press, 1932, page 31, with permission of the publisher.)

Monroe's method reveals cases of discrepancy between reading and other accomplishments on a profile. A sample case is shown in Figure 7. Grade scores for a case are plotted for actual grade placement, chronological grade, mental grade, and achievement in arithmetic, spelling, oral reading, silent reading comprehension, word analysis (Iota Word Test), and auditory word discrimination. The spelling grade is obtained from the *Ayers Spelling Scale* and the word discrimination grade from Monroe's test (see below).

Various possible impeding factors which may contribute to a child's failure to learn to read are checked. These include: visual and auditory acuity, visual discrimination of form and orientation, auditory discrimination, hand and eye preferences (laterality), speech defects, motor control, social and emotional adjustment, and difficulties due to faulty learnings. Emphasis is placed upon constellations of impeding factors rather than upon one single cause.

Test Materials and Diagnostic Procedures (Monroe)

Once a reading case has been identified in terms of a low reading index, an analysis of his reading defects is made. This is achieved through a classification of errors made while responding orally in the following three tests:

1. Gray's *Oral Reading Examination* consists of 12 paragraphs of increasing difficulty. Grade scores on this test range from early first grade up to grade eight.

2. Monroe's *Iota Word Test* measures accuracy for reading isolated words. The test consists of 53 words printed on three cards. Many of these words are such that reversals are possible if the child is having orientation difficulties. Grade scores range from 1 to 5.5.

3. Monroe's *Word-Discrimination Test* consists of 47 words. Each word is presented in a group of six other confusion words, or arrangements of letters. The groups of words are printed on a series of six cards, seven or eight groups per card. The key word is given orally by the examiner and the child then points out the word he thinks he heard spoken. Grade scores range from 1 to 5.5.

Errors are carefully recorded on all three tests. These errors are then analyzed, classified, and tabulated as follows:

Faulty vowels. In his mispronunciation the child may have altered one or more vowel sounds as *dig* read *dug*.

Faulty consonants. Here, one or more consonant sounds are altered as *send* read *sent*.

Reversals. A mispronunciation reveals a reversal in the orientation of letters (*dig* read *big*), or in a sequence of letters (*was* read *saw*), or in a sequence of words (*he said* read *said he*).

Addition of sounds. The child wrongly inserts one or more sounds in a word, as *tack* read *track*.

Omission of sounds. The mispronunciation involves omission of one or more sounds in the test word, as *blind* read *bind*.

Substitution of words. The child substitutes a word unrelated in form or sound, as *lived* read *was*.

Repetition of words. Each test word repeated whether read correctly or incorrectly is counted as a repetition as *"a boy a boy had a dog"* (two repetitions).

Addition of words. The child inserts a word into the text, when *once there was* is read *once upon a time there was* (three word additions).

Omission of words. The child omits a word from the text, as *a little pig* read *a pig.*

Refusals and words aided. The child refuses to attempt a word or a word has to be supplied by the examiner after a delay of 15 seconds.

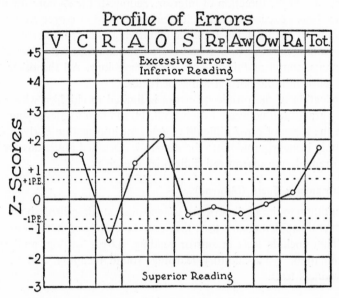

FIG. 8. Case 22, Reading Index is 0.72. (Reproduced from M. Monroe, *Children Who Cannot Read,* University of Chicago Press, 1932, page 62, with permission of the publisher.)

When more than one type of error is found in a mispronunciation, the number under each type is tabulated.

The same number of words is presented to each child in the *Iota Word Test* and in the *Word-Discrimination Test.* In the Gray *Oral Reading Paragraphs,* the child continues until he has at least seven errors in each of two successive paragraphs. Since errors in this test depend upon number of paragraphs read, a table is provided to convert raw scores into the proportions of errors per 500 words (the average number of words read in control group). This provides the same basis of comparison for all children regardless of number of paragraphs read. The number of errors of each type for the three tests together are summated.

Means and standard deviations have been computed for each error type for each reading grade in the control group. Then at each tenth of a grade from grade 1.4 to 5.8, standard scores (scores in standard deviation units), called Z-scores were computed and arranged in tables, one table for each type of error. At each tenth of a grade level the Z-scores ranged from −3 to +5 with the mean at 0. By referring to the appropriate table and looking opposite a child's average reading grade, the Z-score for that type of error is read off and entered on his profile of errors. When the Z-scores for all types of errors are tabulated in this manner, excessive errors which indicate the nature of the difficulties in inferior reading are readily identified. Plus Z-scores are in the direction of inferior reading. If the Z-score for any error type reaches or exceeds +1, this indicates the need of corrective instruction. An example (131) will illustrate the identifying of excessive errors: Case *H*, with a reading index of 0.72 (see Figure 8), had excessive errors of vowels, consonants, sound additions, and sound omissions. All the other types of errors fell within the normal range or better.

Application of the profile of errors is limited to children whose average reading grades fall between 1.4 and 5.8. In addition to identifying from the profile the types of error difficulties, relevant information derived from the case study is incorporated into the diagnosis. Detailed directions for instruction to remedy the discovered difficulties are given.

Supplementary Tests (Monroe)

In addition to the basic series of diagnostic tests described above, Monroe lists several supplementary tests that may be employed if that seems desirable. They include tests of mirror reading, mirror writing, auditory word discrimination, visual-auditory learning, sound blending, and handedness and eyedness tests.

Advantages of the Monroe Program

The Monroe program for the analysis of reading difficulties contains the following favorable features: (1) Directions for giving and scoring the tests and for interpreting the results are clear and are complete in detail. (2) The technique is especially useful for dealing with more severely retarded reading cases. It was originally employed with a group of reading defect cases with a mean reading index of 0.49, i.e., 49 per cent of expectation. (3) The program is readily modified for use with slow-learning children as shown by Kirk (114). (4) Remedial instruction based upon the diagnosis is highly successful in relieving reading disability. This is true for the moderately retarded as well as for the severely retarded.

Limitations of the Monroe Program

The Monroe program of diagnosis has certain limitations: (1) It tends to be time-consuming, exacting, and laborious. (2) It appears not to be the most appropriate technique for dealing with moderately retarded readers. (3) The applicability of the profile of errors is somewhat limited, i.e., to average reading grades 1.4 to 5.8, with greatest accuracy between 2.0 and 4.9. (4) The program of remedial instruction based upon the diagnosis tends to be extremely detailed, exacting, and time-consuming. There is a strong emphasis upon phonetics and other exacting drill. The tests can be used only by a trained clinical worker.

Summary Statement

The Monroe technique of diagnosis provides an excellent method for dealing with the more severely retarded reading cases. However, the extensive analysis involved in the diagnosis is not necessary for a large proportion of the disability cases which occur in our schools. It is one of the most carefully worked-out systems and has proved its value in reading clinics.

C. THE GATES READING DIAGNOSTIC TESTS

The Gates program for analysis of reading disabilities is described in *The Improvement of Reading,* 3rd edition (79) and in *Gates Reading Diagnostic Tests.* The latest revision of the *Manual of Directions* for these tests appeared in 1953. Gates's program of diagnosis is based upon the author's experience at Teachers College, Columbia University, over a period of more than 20 years.

In the Gates procedure, the formal identification of reading disability requires a measure of mental age, actual grade placement, and a measure of silent reading ability. Mental age as determined by the Stanford-Binet Test is considered to provide the best criterion of a child's verbal ability with which to compare his reading. One or more standardized silent reading tests appropriate to the child's reading level are given. The mental age and silent reading scores are converted to grade scores. To determine whether a child is able to keep up with his class, his average silent reading grade is compared with his grade location. Ordinarily, the more important comparison is between average silent reading grade and mental grade. This comparison will reveal the degree of reading retardation in relation to the child's intelligence level or learning ability. Comparison of reading grade with either actual grade placement or with mental grade is made by reference to a table which indicates ratings that are respectively average (or at grade), low, or very low. The degree of retardation which receives a rating of low or very low varies with grade level. For example, at grade 2.0, a child reading at grade 1.5 is rated low, and at 1.3 is rated very low. But at grade 6.0 a reading grade of 4.5 is rated low, and of 4.0 is rated very low. A child whose average silent reading is either low or very low in comparison with his mental grade, is called a reading disability case. To discover the specific kinds of difficulties involved in the reading disability, the detailed diagnostic tests are given. It will not be necessary to give all the diagnostic tests to all reading cases. The skilled examiner will be able to select those tests essential to secure the diagnostic information he needs as a basis for determining the proper remedial instruction for a particular child.

The Test Materials (Gates)

The *Gates Reading Diagnostic Tests* are made up of three types of material: (1) The *Manual of Directions* contains detailed instructions for giving, recording, and scoring the tests. In addition, references are made to suggested remedial procedures in the author's *Improvement of Reading*. Also included are instructions on how to get the proper ratings, how to enter data in the record booklet, and how to use the tables of norms which are given for all tests. Grade equivalents are provided for the scores on each diagnostic test. A table is provided for converting grade scores into age equivalents for those who desire this. Gates considers that grade scores are the most meaningful in the eyes of the majority of workers in the field. (2) Two booklets, of four cards each, contain test materials which are to be presented to the child visually. They constitute Form I and Form II, which are equivalent sets of test materials. The child makes oral responses to these visual materials. (3) The *Pupil's Record Booklet* contains the third set of materials. On the first page are spaces for recording the child's name and other identification data; raw scores, grade scores, and ratings for intelligence, for silent reading tests, and for all diagnostic reading tests. (See Figure 9.) On successive pages are copies of the materials on the test cards and the text for various tests which are to be presented orally to the child. The text of all test materials is arranged in the booklet in a form suitable for recording errors and other aspects of a child's responses. At appropriate places, there are check-lists to facilitate the recording of important characteristics of reading performance identified through an analysis of the errors or observations of other behavior during the reading. Also included in the booklet are spaces for summarizing diagnoses and recommendations for remedial instruction; for data on physical examination, and on social and personal adjustment; and for notes on interests, home conditions, and school history. Since materials for both Form I and II are included, the same booklet can be used for original testing and for retesting after remedial instruction.

Tests and Procedures (Gates)

The diagnostic tests will be briefly described in the order in which they are listed in the test materials. Note will be made of only one form since the two forms are equivalent.

Oral Reading Test. This test is composed of seven paragraphs of increasing difficulty. The child begins with the first paragraph and continues until he makes 11 or more errors in each of two consecutive paragraphs. The time he takes to read it and his errors are recorded for each paragraph. The grade scores range from 1.6 to 8.5. Also information on the child's behavior

GATES READING DIAGNOSTIC TESTS
PUPIL'S RECORD BOOKLET

By Arthur I. Gates, Professor of Education
Teachers College, Columbia University

Pupil's Name...School................................Date..............................

Pupil's Age...............Birthday.....................Grade..............Examiner..................Teacher...........................

	1 Raw Score	2 Grade Score	3 Rating		1 Raw Score	2 Grade Score	Rating
AGE, GRADE, INTELLIGENCE				PHRASE PERCEPTION			
1. Chronological Age				1. Number Phrases Correct			
2. Grade Status				WORD PERCEPTION, ANALYSIS, ETC.			
3. Binet I.Q.........M.A.				1. Flash Presentation			
4. ............I.Q.........M.A.				2. Untimed Presentation			
SILENT READING TESTS				SPELLING			
1.				1. Gates Test			
2.				VISUAL PERCEPTION TECHNIQUES			
3.				1. Syllabication			
4.				2. Recognition of Syllables			
5.				3. Recognition of Phonograms			
Average of Reading Tests				4. Blending Letter Sounds			
ORAL READING				5. Giving Letter Sounds			
1. Gates Oral — Total Score				6. Reading Capital Letters			
a. Omissions, Words				a. Speed			
b. Additions, Words				b. Errors			
c. Repetitions				7. Reading Small Letters			
d. Mispronunciations				a. Speed			
e. Full Reversals				b. Errors			
f. Reversal of Parts				AUDITORY TECHNIQUES			
g. Wrong Order (e+f)				1. Blending Letter Sounds			
h. Wrong Beginnings				2. Giving Letters for Sounds			
i. Wrong Middles				3. Giving Words—Initial Sounds			
j. Wrong Endings				4. Giving Words—Ending Sounds			
k. Wrong Several Parts				OTHER TESTS			
VOCABULARY							
1. Gates Oral Vocabulary							
2.							
REVERSAL TEST							
1. Total Errors							
2. Per Cent Reversals							

BUREAU OF PUBLICATIONS, TEACHERS COLLEGE, COLUMBIA UNIVERSITY
Copyright, 1945, by Teachers College, Columbia University

FIG. 9. Gates cover page. (Reproduced with permission of the publisher.)

while the reading is going on is recorded by means of the check-list or in the form of notes. These data provide an important supplement to the error analysis. Analysis of the errors plus reference to the appropriate tables will indicate whether the child is making excessive errors in each of the following categories: words omitted, words added, repetitions, mispronunciations, full reversals, reversal of parts, all reversals, wrong beginnings, wrong middles, wrong endings, wrong in several parts. Observation of performance during the oral reading yields such information as degree of skill in the use of various word-recognition techniques and clues, signs of nervous tension, ability to phrase, and enunciation habits.

Oral Vocabulary Test. There are 30 items in sentence form which include key words. The items range from very easy to difficult. In each item the child picks out the one of four word choices which he considers best indicates the meaning of the key word. Gates suggests that this test be used chiefly in the fourth grade and above. It is primarily useful as a substitute for an individual intelligence test when the latter is not available. The results must be interpreted with caution, for the vocabulary grade score for a reading case tends to fall between the reading grade and the mental grade derived from the Stanford-Binet Test. Grade scores range from 2.0 to 13.0.

The Reversals Test. The materials consist of 30 printed words such as *ton, saw, team* which make real words when all or part of the letters are in reverse order. The child is asked to pronounce the words in the order printed. All errors are recorded just as made. The tables will reveal any tendency toward excessive reversals.

Phrase Perception. The materials consist of 26 phrases of two to four words each. Starting with short phrases, the examiner exposes each phrase through a window in a card for one-half second. This flash perception test is employed to determine how well a child can recognize phrases of different lengths in a single glance. The total score, converted into a grade score, may be compared with silent reading scores or other test scores available.

Word Perception—Flash Presentation. The materials consist of four columns of 20 words each. In each column, the words progress from short easy ones to longer more difficult ones, such as *so* to *superstition.* The test procedure is the same as in the phrase perception test described above. The first two columns of words are used. The number of correct responses in the one-half second exposure per word is converted to a grade score for comparison with other results such as mental grade and average reading grade.

Untimed Word Perception and Analysis. Columns 2 and 3 of the word lists described just above are used. Words are read horizontally, i.e., the first word in each column, the second word, etc. This test determines the child's ability to recognize words in isolation when he proceeds in his own way to work out the recognition and pronunciation of each word, one after another. Plenty of time is allowed for each word. The child is encouraged to employ whatever techniques of analysis he possesses, but he is not helped in his analysis. The test is discontinued when 10 consecutive words have been missed. Every mispronunciation is written in above the word on the record blank. From observations of a child's behavior and from analysis of his errors, the accompanying check-list of difficulties is filled in. The total score for the test is converted into a grade score for comparison with other results. For instance, a comparison with silent or oral reading grade will provide an estimate of how well the child employs context clues in reading. These clues are, of course, present in silent and oral reading but not in isolated word perception. An appreciably higher score in either silent or oral reading than in either the timed or untimed word perception, therefore, would suggest that the child makes very good use of context clues when they are available.

Spelling. The third and fourth columns of 20 words each, described above in the word perception tests, are used for the spelling test. Each word is pronounced by the examiner and spelled aloud by the child. All misspelled words are written down by the examiner. Methods of attack on words are recorded by filling out the accompanying check-list. The grade score is compared with grades on reading tests and on the word perception test. Analysis of the results may provide clues for improving both reading and spelling.

Tests for Detailed Analysis. In many cases, use of a part or all of the diagnostic tests described above will provide satisfactory information concerning the specific difficulties involved in a child's reading deficiency. These cases are usually those with moderate degrees of reading retardation. For more severe reading cases, especially those with pronounced difficulties in word perception, more detailed testing is in order. For this detailed analysis, Gates provides a series of tests on visual perception techniques and another on auditory techniques.

Visual Word Perception Techniques. Test 1 deals with use of *syllabication* in working out the pronunciation of words. A series of 20 nonsense words such as *inmo* and *indarill* are used. The syllables employed, although in nonsense words, occur frequently in elementary school reading materials. This test is designed to determine the extent to which a child can locate and blend or combine syllables. No credit is given if the individual letters are sounded and blended. If he does rather poorly, he is given the next test.

Test 2, *recognition of syllables,* consists of 20 syllables such as *ick, eep,* and *ight* which occur frequently in children's books. The child is asked to look at each syllable and pronounce it. A syllable must be pronounced as a unit to get credit. If the grade score in Test 2 is considerably higher than in Test 1, a pupil's difficulty apparently consists in finding and combining syllables rather than in recognizing a syllable in isolation.

Test 3 requires the *recognition of phonograms* such as *st, ed,* and *el.* They are word elements, a letter or group of letters forming a speech sound. The test is given and interpreted in the same way as is Test 2.

Test 4 deals with *blending letter sounds*. There are 20 series of letters, separated by dashes, such as *k-o, d-u-r,* and *f-u-r-n.* The letters do not compose real words. The task is to look at the letters, think of their sounds, and then blend the sounds into a unitary word sound. A relatively low grade score on this test may be due to one or more of the deficiencies detected in the following three tests.

Test 5 is a test in *giving letter sounds*. Printed letters are presented, one at a time (not in alphabetic order) and the child is asked to give the corresponding sound. Tests 6 and 7 require *reading of capital and lower case letters*. Names of letters presented in random order are given by the child. Comparison of the grade scores obtained in Tests 5, 6, and 7 will help the examiner to diagnose the difficulty in blending letters presented visually (Test 4).

Auditory Techniques. Proficiency in the auditory techniques needed in word identification and recognition and in word analysis is determined by four tests which are given in the Record Booklet. Test 1 is concerned with *blending letter sounds*. There are 20 words such as *m-e, p-e-n, th-un-d-er.* For each word the examiner gives orally the sounds of the letters or phonograms with a short pause between them. The child listens and then tries to combine the sounds into the total proper word as *me,* etc.

Test 2 is *giving letters for sounds*. The examiner utters the sounds of an individual letter and the child attempts to name the letter of which he has heard the sound. There are 31 items such as *r* in *ray, u* in *up, ch* in *chew.*

Test 3 requires *giving words with stated initial sounds*. The child is asked to supply a word that begins with the sound that is pronounced by the examiner. For example, the examiner speaks the word *saw,* then sounds the initial *s* sound, and asks the child to give other words that begin with the same *s* sound.

Test 4 involves *giving words with stated final sounds*. The child is asked to supply a word that ends with the same sound as the one he hears the examiner pronounce, that is, to supply a rhyming word. For instance, if the word *can* is given, the examiner by speaking it alone directs his attention to the ending *an* sound and the child then tries to give some words that rhyme with *can.*

These detailed tests of visual and auditory techniques are concerned with skills fundamental in word analysis and word recognition. Normally the skills are developed through training activities which begin prior to reading and continue as a part of reading instruction. Marked weaknesses in any of these tests, revealed by an inspection of the scores, indicate deficiencies which handicap a child in working out the identification and recognition of unfamiliar words.

Additional Information. All the diagnostic tests described above were carefully standardized on the same population. The tables of norms presented in the *Manual of Directions* are derived from this standardization. In addition, provision is made for obtaining and recording various kinds of data on vision, hearing, speech, adjustment, school performance, and home conditions. All relevant data for a given child are organized into a case history report. Included are suggestions for remedial instruction based upon the diagnosis.

Advantages of the Gates Program

The Gates program for analysis of reading difficulties possesses the following favorable features: (1) It is perhaps the most complete program of diagnosis available. Apparently the tests are designed to identify any and all types of reading difficulties that may occur. (2) The program is readily adapted to a case of reading disability of any degree of severity by a judicious selection of appropriate tests. (3) The provision for converting raw scores into grade scores is especially helpful in identifying and evaluating difficulties. (4) All tests in the series are carefully standardized. (5) Particularly helpful are the references to specific remedial techniques for each type of difficulty discovered.

Limitations of the Gates Program

The Gates *Reading Diagnostic Tests* have certain limitations: (1) The tests can be used safely only by one who has had a thorough clinical training in administering them and in evaluating the results. This prohibits their use in many school systems. (2) Completion of a diagnosis with these tests is a relatively long and laborious task. (3) The scoring and rating of the test results are complicated. In some instances, the directions to the examiner are not unequivocal. (4) Evaluation of performance on a particular test becomes confusing when the examiner is directed to compare this test performance with performance on a large number of the other tests or ratings with no suggestion as to which are the more important comparisons. For instance, test performance for *Word Perception and Analysis* is to be compared with 25 different scores or ratings. (5) The examiner is given an inadequate amount of help in selecting which tests to use with the less severe cases of disability.

Summary Statement (Gates)

The Gates technique of diagnosis constitutes an excellent comprehensive program. Although complicated and exacting to use, it can be adapted by the *skilled clinician* to any type of disability case. The program assumes use of the author's *The Improvement of Reading* as a supplement to the diagnostic tests when the examiner is looking for explanations, interpretations, and specific remedial measures. Of all the diagnostic techniques available, the Gates program is perhaps the most inclusive and most satisfactorily standardized one for broad usage. It has enjoyed extensive and successful use over the years.

D. THE BOND-CLYMER-HOYT TECHNIQUE

Traditionally, any system for thorough diagnosis of reading difficulties has required individual testing by a skilled examiner. Such a diagnosis tends to become time-consuming and sometimes decidedly complicated and exacting. In the ordinary school system, programs of this kind frequently are not feasible or are actually impossible. Furthermore, the majority of children with reading disabilities in our schools suffer from only moderate degrees of retardation. There is need for a diagnostic technique which will satisfactorily identify the specific difficulties of these pupils and which can be employed by the skilled teacher who lacks clinical training. The Bond-Clymer-Hoyt *Silent Reading Diagnostic Tests* (20) are designed to give the classroom teacher help in diagnosing the reading needs of her pupils. Since they are group tests, a teacher can test all her pupils at once. But at the same time, data for individual diagnosis are obtained. These tests diagnose silent reading abilities, a special feature that is justified by the fact that a large majority of reading is silent reading. The *Silent Reading Diagnostic Tests* are based upon research and experimental use in regular classrooms over a period of five years. They have been carefully standardized and have high reliability. Experience with the tests has demonstrated their usefulness for diagnosing reading difficulties. They are designed for use with elementary school children of second-grade age and above. However, the tests have been found diagnostically useful as early as the end of the second grade. At the same time, teachers in junior and senior high schools have found the tests useful for formulating remedial programs for children with relatively severe reading retardation at these levels.

The disability cases are identified in terms of significant discrepancies between mental grade and average reading grade derived from a series of silent reading tests of appropriate difficulty. The tests that are to do this should measure vocabulary and comprehension. Bond, Clymer, and Hoyt suggest that the *Developmental Reading Tests* published by Lyons and Carnahan be used. These tests measure at the primary level, vocabulary, general comprehension, and specific comprehension; at the intermediate level, they measure vocabulary and four types of comprehension: facts, organization, evaluation and interpretation, and appreciation. If for any reason these *Developmental Reading Tests* are not used, other tests which cover the same areas must be used because certain aspects of the remedial treatment rest upon a comparison of scores on these kinds of tests.

The Silent Reading Diagnostic Tests materials consist of a folder containing the diagnostic tests, a Profile to facilitate interpretation of test results, an outline for summarizing the diagnosis, and a *Manual of Directions*.

Manual of Directions (Bond-Clymer-Hoyt)

This manual contains information concerning the purpose of the diagnostic tests, information on how to choose the school grades where the tests may be used to advantage, descriptions of the tests (to be supplied briefly below), directions for administering the tests, directions for scoring, directions for making the graphic profile (to be described below), and suggestions on interpreting the test results. The materials in the manual are clear and complete in detail.

The Diagnostic Tests (Bond-Clymer-Hoyt)

Eleven diagnostic tests are assembled into one test booklet. A brief description of the tests follows:

Test I. *Word Recognition.* There are 54 items in this test. Each item consists of a picture accompanied by five words. Some of the five are actual words, others consist of letter combinations in the form of a word but so arranged that the child can commit initial, middle, final, or reversal errors. A sample item consists of a picture of a *coat* with the following choices: 1. boat; 2. coal; 3. cost; 4. ceat; 5. coat. A line is to be drawn around the word that tells about the picture. The correct word may identify the picture as in this example, or it may describe an act involving the thing pictured, i.e., *read* is correct for a picture of a book.

Test II. *Recognition of Words in Context.* This test contains 28 items similar to the following:

> We play ball in the _____.
> card   yard   yad   young   yond.

A line is to be drawn around one word which will complete the sentence. Note that the choices are such that various types of errors can be made, as in Test I.

Test III. *Recognition of Reversible Words in Context.* This list consists of a short story in which 23 words (items) can be reversed. Where each of these key words occur in a sentence there are three choices so arranged that a full or partial reversal can be made. Below is an example:

> | | asw (1) | |
> |--------------------------|----------|--------------|
> | Tom was waiting, and he | saw (2) | Jane coming. |
> | | was (3) | |

A line is to be drawn around the one word in each group of three that makes the most sense.

Test IV. *Word-Recognition Techniques: Visual Analysis—Locating Usable Elements.* In each of the 36 items, a picture is accompanied by a long ("large") word which contains the shorter or "little" word identified by the picture. For example, the picture of a dress is accompanied by the word *addressing*. A line is to be drawn around the "little" word shown by the picture.

Test V.   *Word-Recognition Techniques: Visual Analysis—Syllabication*. The 24 items consist of polysyllabic words such as *along, baseball, signature*. A line is to be drawn between syllables.

Test VI.   *Word-Recognition Techniques: Visual Analysis—Locating Root Words*. The items consist of 30 words, each one containing a word root such as *afloat, unlikely*. A circle is to be drawn around the little word, within the larger word, from which the larger one is made.

Test VII.   *Phonetic Knowledge—General Word Elements*. There are 30 items such as:

ur   or   ro   ar   on

The examiner twice reads orally one word element in each item. A line is to be drawn around the one read aloud.

Test VIII.   *Recognition of Beginning Sounds*. There are 30 items similar to the following:

till   sit   that   his

A word is pronounced twice ("this—this") by the examiner. A line is drawn around the word that has the same beginning sound as the word read aloud by the examiner.

Test IX.   *Rhyming Words*. There are 30 items similar to the following:

wand   pay   beg   boy

The examiner pronounces twice the word *way—way*. A line is to be drawn around the word that rhymes with the word read aloud by the examiner.

Test X.   *Letter Sounds*. The 30 items in this test are similar to the following:

z   b   n   f

The examiner twice utters the sound of one of the four letters (as "Fuh—Fuh"). A line is drawn around the letter that stands for the sound.

Test XI.   *Word Synthesis*. This test measures the ability to blend parts of a word into a whole, visually and phonetically. A series of short paragraphs are so printed that an initial consonant or syllable comes at the end of each line with the rest of the word at the beginning of the next line. This arrangement is illustrated by the following:

The mother squir-
rel looked down from a h-
igh tree.

In order to answer the questions after each paragraph, the child must synthesize (blend) the divided word and comprehend the sentences. For instance, for this example the question is:

> This mother was
>   · (*a*) a bird   (*b*) an animal   (*c*) a dog

A line is drawn around the word or words that make the sentence correct.

Blanks are provided at the end of the tests for summarizing the diagnosis. Questions are given as a guide to the diagnosis, identifying the remedial needs, any limiting conditions, and the emotional status of the child, with remedial recommendations.

The Graphic Profile (Bond-Clymer-Hoyt)

The major aspects of diagnosis are derived from the graphic profile located on page 1 of the test folder (see Figure 10). At the top of the profile are entered the basic data such as chronological grade, mental grade, school grade, reading scores, and average reading grade. These are followed by the detailed scores derived from the diagnostic tests described above.

The diagnostic data are in two groups: (1) scores in word recognition and (2) scores in word-recognition techniques (i.e., whether the child uses as he should visual analysis, phonetic knowledge, and word synthesis). Under each grouping, scores on detailed areas of the analysis are listed. For instance the error analysis of the data from Test 1 plus 2 yields scores on initial errors, middle errors, ending errors, orientational errors. In a similar manner, scores are listed for the detailed diagnostic information derived from scoring the other tests.

Plotting the Graphic Profile. A grade equivalent scale is given horizontally across the profile. At the top of the profile the grade equivalents are listed by half-grade intervals from 1.5 to 8.0. A check is placed on this scale at the grade level recorded under *Pupil Score* for each measure of the *Basic Data* and *Reading Abilities*.

The norms are also given for each diagnostic test by half-grade intervals across the grade equivalent scale. For each diagnostic score, the grade equivalent is determined automatically when the test score is checked on the grade equivalent scale. As a guide for this, test score values for each test are listed by intervals along the grade equivalent scale. The location of the check indicates the equivalent grade score.

After the grade equivalent scale has been checked for all basic data, reading tests, and diagnostic tests, the check marks are joined by connecting successive check marks by lines down the profile. The resulting diagnostic profile presents graphically the high and low levels of a pupil's reading skills and abilities. Those skills that are significantly above or below a child's average reading ability should be closely considered in planning the remedial program.

SILENT READING DIAGNOSTIC TESTS—EXPERIMENTAL FORM
Graphic Profile

Name_____School_____Grade____Date_____

BASIC DATA	Pupil Score	Grade Equivalent 1.5 2.0 2.5 3.0 3.5 4.0 4.5 5.0 5.5 6.0 6.5 7.0 7.5 8.0
Chronological Grade		
Mental Grade		
Grade in School		

READING ABILITIES

Vocabulary		
Factual (General)		
Organize (Specific)		
Evaluate-Interpret		
Appreciate		
Average Reading		

RECOGNITION PATTERN

		Perfect Score
Total Right (1+2)	1,0 2,4 3,4 4,8 6,6 7,2 7,7 7,9 8,0 8,2	
Total Errors (1+2)	5,4 4,5 3,8 2,6 1,5 ,9 ,4 ,4 ,2 ,0	
Total Omitted (1+2)	2,0 1,5 1,2 1,0 ,7 ,3 ,3 ,1 ,0 ,0	
Words in Isolation (1)	,9 1,6 2,2 3,2 4,4 4,8 5,1 5,2 5,3 5,4	
Words in Context (2)	,5 ,8 1,2 1,6 2,1 2,4 2,6 2,7 2,7 2,8	
Orientation (3)	,4 ,6 1,0 1,6 2,0 2,1 2,1 2,2 2,2 2,3	

ERROR ANALYSIS (1+2)

Initial Errors	1,2 ,9 ,7 ,5 ,2 ,1 ,0 ,0 ,0 ,0	
Middle Errors	1,5 1,3 1,1 ,8 ,6 ,4 ,2 ,1 ,1 ,0	
Ending Errors	1,4 1,2 1,1 ,7 ,5 ,3 ,2 ,1 ,1 ,0	
Orientation Errors	1,3 1,1 ,9 ,6 ,2 ,1 ,0 ,0 ,0 ,0	

RECOGNITION TECHNIQUES

Visual Analysis (4+5+6)	1,0 1,4 3,0 4,3 5,3 6,3 6,6 6,9 7,2 7,4	
Locating Elements (4)	,6 ,8 1,6 2,3 2,8 3,4 3,4 3,5 3,6 3,6	
Syllabication (5)	,2 ,3 ,5 ,7 ,9 1,0 1,1 1,1 1,2 1,2	
Locating Root Word (6)	,2 ,3 ,9 1,3 1,6 1,9 2,1 2,3 2,4 2,6	
Phonetic Kn. (7+8+9+10)	2,3 3,9 5,5 6,9 7,8 8,8 9,5 102 106 111	
Word Elements (7)	,5 ,8 1,3 1,7 1,9 2,1 2,3 2,4 2,5 2,7	
Beginning Sounds (8)	,8 1,2 1,6 2,0 2,2 2,4 2,5 2,6 2,7 2,8	
Rhyming Sounds (9)	,0 ,3 ,6 ,8 1,3 1,8 2,2 2,5 2,7 2,8	
Letter Sounds (10)	1,0 1,6 2,0 2,4 2,4 2,5 2,6 2,7 2,8 2,8	

WORD SYNTHESIS (11)

	,1 ,2 ,4 ,7 1,3 1,8 2,0 2,2 2,3 2,4	

MISCELLANEOUS DATA

Hearing _____   Other _____

Vision _____

FIG. 10. Graphic profile for the Bond-Clymer-Hoyt *Silent Reading Diagnostic Tests*, copyright 1955, Lyons and Carnahan, Chicago, Illinois. (Reproduced with permission of the publisher.)

To determine the important diagnostic measures, two more vertical lines should be drawn on the profile. These vertical lines should be drawn through the entire profile at an equal distance on either side of average reading grade score. If the average reading grade is between 1.5 and 2.4, the vertical lines should be one-half grade from the average reading grade; if between 2.5 and 3.4, three-fourths grade; if 3.5 to 5.4, one grade; and if 5.5 and above, one and one-half grades. These are called *lines of importance*. An illustrative profile of an actual case is given in the teacher's key and in our Chapter 19.

Interpreting the Test Results (Bond-Clymer-Hoyt)

After the graphic profile is completed, interpretation of the test results is readily made. Identification of a reading disability case is made by comparing mental grade with average reading grade as described above. The intelligence test employed to get the mental grade must be fair to the pupil, i.e., in this instance it must not involve any reading. If the average reading grade is below the mental grade by the amount shown by the lines of importance described above, the child is judged a reading case. That is, when the mental grade reaches or exceeds the line of importance at the *right,* the pupil is a disability case.

Unevenness in the development of reading abilities is determined by comparing scores on the reading tests. Corrective measures are needed where over- or underdevelopment is found.

Examination of the profile formed by scores on the diagnostic tests will reveal areas of difficulty. Any check mark which reaches or falls below the line of importance on the *left* side (below average reading) indicates a need of remedial instruction to correct the difficulty. Any of the check marks for the skills listed under recognition techniques which extend beyond the line of importance drawn on the *right* of average reading represent skills which are overdeveloped in relation to the child's general reading ability. For the time being, there need be no further training in such skills. In fact they should not be further trained because, in many instances, overdeveloped analytical skills cause reading difficulties. Complete details for plotting the profile, for interpreting the results revealed in the profile, and for setting up the remedial program are given in the teacher's manual of directions.

Advantages of the Bond-Clymer-Hoyt Program

Diagnosis of reading difficulties by means of these *Silent Reading Diagnostic Tests* has certain advantages: (1) The tests can be administered and the results interpreted and used by any competent classroom teacher. (2) Directions for scoring and interpretations are clear, direct, and relatively uncomplicated. (3) The tests are economical of time. They can be given to a whole class at once. (4) Identification of reading difficulties is easily and quickly achieved by means of the profile. Use of the profile avoids the laborious task of referring to tables of norms. (5) The technique provides an important practical aid for improving adjustment to individual needs in reading instruction. (6) Emphasis is upon diagnosing *silent* reading abilities and skills in contrast to other detailed diagnostic tests. (7) The tests provide a complete diagnosis of the essential skills. (8) Use of these tests will lessen the need for a reading specialist since many of the reading difficulties can be taken care of more effectively by the classroom teacher. Furthermore, those cases in need of the help of a reading specialist are identified by the tests.

Limitations of the Program

The *Silent Reading Diagnostic Tests* have certain limitations: (1) The technique is not designed for use with cases of extreme reading disability or nonreaders. A more elaborate program of individual testing will be necessary for the diagnosis of their difficulties. (2) The diagnosis is based upon silent reading. Some clinical workers will wish to obtain the supplementary information that is provided by an oral reading test. (3) The tests are most effective for pupils with reading abilities ranging from about grade two to grade six.

Summary Statement (Bond-Clymer-Hoyt)

The Bond-Clymer-Hoyt *Silent Reading Diagnostic Tests* provide a new approach to the diagnosis of reading disabilities. They make it possible for the classroom teacher or the clinician to diagnose in an effective manner the difficulties of a major portion of the retarded readers in our schools. Proper use of the tests should lead to improved reading instruction in the elementary and in the junior high schools. Although these are group tests, they serve the same purpose as individual tests.

USE OF DIAGNOSTIC TESTS

Significant degrees of reading retardation are identified in terms of discrepancy between learning ability (usually mental grade or listening comprehension) and reading ability as measured on standardized tests or by the less formal testing methods already described. Specific difficulties involved in the retardation are determined by detailed diagnostic testing. Several standardized group tests which are analytical in type provide useful information concerning strengths and weaknesses of individual pupils. The use of such tests ordinarily constitutes a first step in diagnosis of reading disability. When reading retardation is relatively severe, a more detailed technique of diagnosis is required. Such testing may become extensive for some of these cases.

When a detailed diagnosis is indicated, the teacher or clinician should choose the most appropriate technique for the case at hand from among a number of techniques which have proved successful. Some of the representative programs have been described above.

The examiner should choose a program of diagnosis which will be most economical of time and at the same time will prove adequate for disclosing the difficulties involved in the retardation. It is not feasible to set up rigid rules on how to make the choice of a diagnostic technique. Through experience, the teacher and the clinician will acquire the ability to choose the best series of tests for a particular case. This implies, of course, that an examiner has become familiar with various available techniques, both informal and standardized.

Although rigid specifications for choosing a technique cannot be made, some general hints and suggestions about doing this are in order. When the degree of reading retardation is moderate, the *Durrell Analysis of Reading Difficulties* or the *Bond-Clymer-Hoyt Silent Reading Diagnostic Tests* or chosen parts of the *Gates Reading Diagnostic Tests* or some comparable program will be found useful. At times, informal techniques of diagnosis may be successfully used with these cases. When the disability is more severe, the complete Gates program or the Monroe program or some comparable program of diagnosis will be needed. Skilled clinicians sometimes employ parts of more than one diagnostic series for their testing.

It will be understood from the above statements that it would be inaccurate to designate any one program as the best technique available. Some are more appropriate for certain children, others more appropriate for others. Although the emphases vary from one technique to another, any one of them is effective in helping those cases for which it is designed. A well-trained clinical worker should be familiar with all the tests discussed.

EYE-MOVEMENT ANALYSIS

The study of eye movements has become an important technique for investigating the reading process. Although the first study was reported by Javal in 1879, research activity in this field did not become vigorous until after 1900. Several hundred studies have now been reported. The literature in this field has been reviewed in two reports by Tinker (171, 174).

The essential characteristics of eye movements in reading are briefly stated. In reading, the eye makes several stops, each a fixation pause, along a line of print. The eye moves from one fixation to the next with a quick jerk known as the saccadic movement. The fixation pauses are the only periods of clear vision. They total on the average about 94 per cent of the reading time. The interfixation movements are so rapid that clear vision is impossible. These total 6 per cent of the reading time on the average. During reading, therefore, the eyes are motionless on fixations a large portion of the time. During the reading of a line of print, the eyes sometimes move backwards toward the beginning of the line and make fixation pauses to get a clearer view of material or to reread it. These backward moves are called regressions. When one line is finished, the eyes make a return sweep to the beginning of the next line.

It was discovered early that the good reader makes relatively few fixation pauses and few regressions in reading a given line of print while the poor reader makes many more fixations and regressions. It was also found that young pupils make a large number of fixations and regressions in reading. As the pupils develop into more mature readers, they make fewer and fewer fixations and regressions. The patterns of eye movements, therefore, furnish clues to the level of one's reading proficiency. This relationship of oculomotor patterns to reading proficiency eventually led to the practice of photographing eye movements in the reading clinic as an aid to diagnosing reading disability. This was followed by attempts to improve reading performance by training eye movements. The necessary assumption underlying and justifying this training was that eye movements are important determinants of reading proficiency. Thus, if a retarded reader were trained to use eye-movement patterns similar to those which characterize efficient reading, his reading proficiency, it was presumed, would improve. We assert that this unfortunate emphasis upon the mechanics of eye movements tended to direct attention to peripheral factors as determinants of reading performance rather than to the important central processes of perception and comprehension.

In a number of clinics, where the eye-movement assumption has been held, it has led to the analysis of eye movements in diagnosing reading disability. Such writers as Harris (94), Taylor (165), Hamilton (93), Broom, Duncan, Emig, and Steuber (30), and others have emphasized and promoted this view. The value of their practices is, in our opinion, very doubtful.

Ineffective eye movements *do not* cause reading deficiency. Ample evidence in research studies indicates that eye-movement patterns during reading are symptoms of the central processes of perception and comprehension. They merely reflect the ability of the reader to interpret what he sees. Those changes in eye movements which occur with improved reading do not mean that the eye muscles co-ordinate better than before. Oculomotor behavior is very flexible and adjusts readily to any change in the perceptual and assimilative processes involved in reading. Investigation of the eye movements of children who are reading disability cases should not be a matter of concern in teaching reading.

So we say that it is best to dispense with the study of eye movements in the reading clinic. If a child is a reading case, we know without photographing his eye movements that he will employ a relatively large number of fixations and regressions and perhaps make pauses of long duration. No additional essential information is gained by an analysis of his eye movements. And if his two eyes do not co-ordinate well, this will be discovered better by a medical eye examination than by eye-movement photography. Standardized diagnostic procedures provide us with all the information we require. The apparatus for photographing eye movements is an expensive gadget whose use is to be classified as a time-consuming luxury rather than a necessity in the reading clinic.

SUMMARY

All group reading tests are somewhat diagnostic in that they reveal to some degree the individual needs of a pupil. Certain analytical group tests which provide a profile of silent reading abilities supply additional diagnostic information. The administering of these analytical tests and a study of their results is ordinarily a first step in the diagnosis of reading disability. In the cases of children with more severe and extensive disability, a still more detailed diagnosis is required. It is possible to make a preliminary detailed diagnosis by use of materials in successive books in a graded series of basic readers. The intensive diagnosis of reading difficulties is best achieved, however, through use of standardized detailed techniques.

Several representative detailed techniques have been described. The Durrell program is most appropriate for use with the less severe cases of disability. It is uncomplicated and takes only a moderate amount of time to administer. Basically, the program consists of a standardized method for observing, recording, and interpreting errors and faulty habits during reading and word perception.

The Monroe program of diagnosis is most useful for dealing with the more severely retarded reading cases. Although effectively organized and clearly described, the technique is complicated. Diagnosis is based largely upon the analysis of errors made during responses on oral reading and word-recognition tests. There is a strong emphasis upon phonetics. The technique is also readily adapted for use with slow learners. The Monroe technique can be used only by trained clinicians.

The Gates program is perhaps the most comprehensive in that it is applicable to any degree of retardation in reading. Only part of the tests is used for the less severe cases. Two equivalent forms of the test are available. The examiner must be a trained clinician. The procedures themselves, the scoring methods, and the final interpretations are complicated. References are given for specific remedial instruction for each kind of difficulty. Although auditory analysis receives some attention, greater emphasis is put on visual analysis. The basic analyses are derived from tests of oral reading and word and phrase recognition. When dealing with more severe cases, visual and auditory skills are examined.

The Bond-Clymer-Hoyt program identifies reading difficulties through group testing of silent reading. The analysis is based upon responses to 11 diagnostic tests. The tests may be given and interpreted by the classroom teacher. The program is particularly useful for children with moderate degrees of reading retardation. Adjustment of instruction to individual needs will be greatly facilitated by use of these tests. They are also useful as a supplementary aid to diagnosis by means of oral reading.

When a detailed diagnosis of reading difficulty is called for, the examiner should choose the most appropriate technique for the case at hand. Skill in choosing the proper technique, in testing, and in interpreting results comes with use.

Eye-movement patterns are symptoms rather than causes of reading disability. The study of eye movements is not of any concern in the reading clinic or to any teacher whose aim it is to teach children to read.

SELECTED READINGS

BLAIR, Glenn M., *Diagnostic and remedial teaching*, rev. ed. New York: The Macmillan Company, 1956, Chap. 2.

BRUECKNER, L. J., and BOND, G. L., *Diagnosis and treatment of learning difficulties*. New York: Appleton-Century-Crofts, Inc., 1955, Chaps. 2, 4, 6.

DOLCH, Edward W., *A manual for remedial reading*, 3rd ed. Champaign (Ill.): The Garrard Press, 1945, Chaps. 3, 4, 7, 13.

DURRELL, Donald D., *Improvement of basic reading abilities*. Yonkers (N.Y.): World Book Company, 1940, Chaps. 2, 13, 15.

GATES, Arthur I., *The improvement of reading*, 3rd ed. New York: The Macmillan Company, 1947, Chaps. 3, 17.

HARRIS, Albert J., *How to increase reading ability*, 3rd ed. New York: Longmans, Green & Company, 1956, Chaps. 7, 8, 19.

MONROE, Marion, *Children who cannot read*. Chicago: University of Chicago Press, 1932, Chaps. 1, 2, 3, 4.

WITTY, Paul, and KOPEL, David, *Reading and the educative process*. Boston: Ginn and Company, 1939, Chaps. 3, 8, 9.

PART IV

Remedial Treatment of
Reading Difficulties

10 BASIC PRINCIPLES OF REMEDIAL INSTRUCTION

THE PREVIOUS CHAPTERS have made it clear that no two cases of reading disability are exactly alike. Four detailed aspects of this general fact have also been shown; no two cases of reading disability result from the same set of circumstances, no two have exactly the same reading patterns, no two cases have the same instructional needs, and no two can be treated in exactly the same manner. Every child is different in many ways from every other child. Because his difficulties in reading stem from a wide variety of causes, the diagnosis of his case involves a study of the child to find out his instructional needs and everything else that may influence a remedial program for him.

The remedial teacher studies the diagnostic findings and then arranges a learning situation that will enable the child henceforth to grow in reading at an accelerated rate. The remedial teacher's problem is to appraise materials, and methods in order to select the combination that will best suit a given disabled reader. The many kinds of reading confusions children manifest indicate that no two disabilities will be corrected exactly the same way. Nonetheless, there are some basic principles underlying remedial instruction irrespective of the specific nature of a particular reading disability. There are certain common elements among corrective programs, whether we are treating a comprehension case, a problem of word recognition, or an oral reading limitation.

Among the more important general categories of basic principles underlying treatment of disabled reading are the following:

1. Treatment must be based on an understanding of the child's instructional needs.
2. Remedial programs must be highly individualized.
3. Remedial instruction must be organized instruction.
4. The reading processes must be made meaningful to the learner.
5. Consideration of the child's personal worth is necessary.
6. The reading program must be encouraging to the child.
7. Materials and exercises must be suitable to the child's reading ability and instructional needs.
8. Sound teaching procedures must be employed.

TREATMENT MUST BE BASED ON AN UNDERSTANDING OF THE CHILD'S INSTRUCTIONAL NEEDS

The remedial program must be designed to emphasize those phases of reading growth that will enable the disabled reader to grow rapidly and solidly. The program designed for each child must be based on a diagnosis of his instructional needs. The purpose of the diagnosis is to obtain information about each child that is necessary in order to formulate a remedial program suited to him. Watkins (181) has shown that the child who is in trouble in reading often has an unequal profile showing an unfortunate pattern of reading skills and abilities. Some phases of reading will be well learned while other phases will be developed poorly. Still other phases may have been overemphasized to the point that they restrict the child's development in reading. The diagnosis must ferret out these inconsistencies in the child's attack on reading.

The child having difficulty in reading will show irregular performances. He may have a large sight vocabulary but he is unable to phrase well. He may be high in word recognition but low in comprehension. A reading diagnosis is designed to locate the inconsistencies that preclude rapid and effective growth in reading. The diagnosis is designed to locate essential areas of growth that have been neglected, those that have been faultily learned, or those that have been overemphasized. It is impractical to start a remedial program in reading until the nature of the instruction needed by the disabled reader has been established. Otherwise, the program may stress areas already overemphasized or omit areas needing attention or perhaps underemphasize such areas.

The remedial program must be based on more than an understanding of the child's reading needs. It must also be based on the child's characteristics. The child who is hard-of-hearing needs a different approach to reading than does his counterpart with normal hearing. The child with poor vision needs marked adjustments in methods and, if his limitation is severe enough, in materials also. The child who is a slow learner needs modified methods and so does the child who is emotionally disturbed. The modifications of instruction for such children will be discussed in a later chapter.

Inasmuch as each case is different, there can be no "bag of tricks" nor can there be a universal approach which will lead to the solution of disabled readers' problems. Many times, remedial training suited to one child would be detrimental to another. If, for example, a remedial program has been planned to develop more adequate phrasing, the child might well be required to do considerable prepared oral reading in order to help him to read in thought units. This same recommendation would do serious harm to the youngster who is already overvocalizing in his silent reading. It would exaggerate the faulty habit he had acquired and increase his disability. To sum up, every remedial program must be made on the basis of a thorough appraisal of the child's instructional needs, his strengths and weaknesses, and the environment in which correction is to take place.

Clearly Formulate the Remedial Program

After the diagnosis has shown the kind of instruction that is needed, the remedial program should be carefully planned. This requires writing down what is to be done for each case. This must be done because it is too difficult to remember each child, his needs, the level of his attainments, and his limitations with the exactness that is necessary in order to conduct an effective corrective program. The written case report should indicate the nature of the disability and the type of exercises recommended to correct the difficulty. It should identify the level of material that is to be used. The written report should state any physical or sensory characteristics of the child that need to be corrected or for which the program needs to be modified. Any indication of faulty personal adjustment or unfortunate environmental conditions should be included. The child's interests, hobbies, and attitudes should become part of the written record. Most important, it should include a description of the remedial program recommended and the type of material and exercises to be used.

The Remedial Program Should Be Modified as Needed

The original plan of remedial work is not to be considered a permanent scheme of instruction. It will need to be modified from time to time as the child progresses in reading. Often a child who is having difficulty in learning changes rapidly in respect to his instructional needs. The better the diagnosis and the more successful the remedial work, the more rapidly will the child's needs change. One disabled reader, for example, may have failed to build analytical word-recognition techniques but is depending on sight vocabulary and context clues as his means of recognizing new words. He would be given remedial work designed to teach him the analytical techniques. After a time, he may develop considerable skill in word study, but he may not make a corresponding gain in rate of reading. His problem would no longer be one of developing word analysis. In fact, emphasis on this phase of the program might become detrimental to his future reading growth. The use of larger word elements and other more rapid word-recognition techniques and further building of sight vocabulary would be advisable. As the problem changes, so must the program of remediation be modified in order to meet the new reading needs of the child.

Inasmuch as the child's instructional needs change rapidly, it is unwise to set him into a remedial program that resembles the production line in a factory. Such a program assumes that once a given child's level of reading performance is identified, all that is needed is to put him through a set of exercises uniform for all children. There is no single method suited to all children even in the developmental reading program. The disabled reader whose needs change rapidly as his limitations are corrected, is in dire need of a program that readily adjusts to every change in his reading pattern. To achieve success, a remedial program must be based upon a continuous diagnosis and it must be modified as the child's instructional needs change.

In some instances, the original program for remediation does not result in improvement. When this occurs, a re-evaluation of the diagnosis and perhaps additions to the diagnosis are in order. A somewhat altered approach to instruction may be necessary to bring success.

A Variety of Remedial Techniques Should Be Used

There is an unfortunate tendency, once a form of remedial instruction has been prescribed, to stick to the use of that specific type of exercise to overcome a known deficiency. Basing a remedial program upon a diagnosis does not imply that a given exercise can be used until the child's reading disability is corrected. There are many ways to develop each of the skills and abilities in reading. An effective remedial program will use a variety of teaching techniques and instructional procedures.

Many sources of help describing teaching techniques are available to the remedial teacher. Professional books on remedial instruction in reading give suggestions for correcting specific types of reading retardation. Russell and Karp (145) have compiled a helpful group of remedial techniques. Manuals and workbooks accompanying basal reading programs are the most fruitful source of teaching techniques. The exercises suggested for teaching the skills and abilities when first introduced in such manuals and workbooks are the sort of things that prove beneficial for remedial programs. If, for example, a fifth-grade child has difficulty with finding root words in affixed words, the teacher can find many and varied exercises in second- and third-grade manuals to teach this skill. The remedial teacher could have the child start with exercises which have simple variant endings on words, such as *walked* or *looking*. As the child improves, the exercises can be increased in difficulty up to those found in fourth- or fifth-grade manuals or workbooks which involve words with prefixes and suffixes, such as *unlikely* or *reworkable*. Teachers' manuals and workbooks accompanying basal readers give exercises and suggested activities that may be used to teach all skills and abilities in reading. The newer basic series of books have lists of these exercises with page references. As she examines the teaching techniques suggested in such materials, the remedial teacher can accumulate a variety of exercises for each of the important types of disabilities listed in Chapter 8. She can keep the program dynamic and interesting to the child by using a variety of teaching techniques and at the same time be sure that the instruction emphasizes the skill development that is needed.

In attempting to use a variety of teaching methods and techniques, care must be taken that the teaching approaches do not confuse the child. The directions given him should be simple and the teaching techniques should not be changed too often. The exercises should be as nearly like the reading act as possible. Artificial or isolated drills should be avoided. The child should not have to spend time learning complicated procedures or directions. Enough variety should be introduced, however, to keep the program stimulating.

An effective and interesting teaching technique should not be used too long nor so often that it loses its value. A fifth-grade child, for example, may be weak in visualizing what is read. For him, the remedial work is planned to emphasize the ability to form sensory impressions and to stimulate the imagination. The teaching techniques used have him read a story and then draw some illustrations for it. This is an effective means of getting this particular child to visualize as he reads. But remember, if he should have to draw pictures of what he reads every day, he may decide that he would rather not read at all. Variety could be introduced by visualizing for different purposes. At one time, pictures for a play television show might be made; at another time, the child might describe how furniture could be arranged for a creative dramatic presentation; at another time, he might read and tell how he thought the scene of a story looked. All of these purposes would require visualization of what is read.

Basing treatment upon an understanding of the child's instructional needs means that the remedial program is planned after a thorough diagnosis has been made. It does not mean that the program becomes fixed or that further study of the child is unnecessary. It is true that if the basic principles of remedial instruction discussed in this chapter are followed, approximately 65 per cent of disabled readers will improve even without diagnosis. However, there will remain somewhere around 35 per cent of disabled readers who will not get along well. Aside from those children who are described as cases of simple retardation, there is no way of knowing which children will be among the successful and which will be among the 35 per cent for whom the remedial work will fail. Whichever children the failures happen to be, they will probably become even more stubborn cases than they were before the remedial instruction started. Those children who did improve without a diagnosis would have improved even more rapidly if the remedial program had been designed to meet their specific needs. Mass training by common methods is unfortunate even if given the label of remedial instruction.

The reason most programs that attempt to correct reading disability meet with some degree of success is because the children are treated individually and many desirable adjustments are made. Even artificial programs, which are basically poor, will demonstrate a modicum of success if they are given by an enthusiastic teacher because they are given to individual children. Well-rounded remedial programs based on careful and continuous diagnosis, using a variety of teaching techniques and taught by an equally enthusiastic teacher, will give far better results.

REMEDIAL PROGRAMS MUST BE HIGHLY INDIVIDUALIZED

The disabled reader is one who has failed to respond to reading programs that are designed to meet the instructional needs and characteristics of the majority of children. The onset of reading disability is usually gradual. The child who becomes a disabled reader gets into a moderate degree of difficulty, misses some instruction, or in some way falls behind or gets confused. The reading curriculum and the class itself go on, while the child is left farther behind. Soon he finds himself hopelessly out of things. He can no longer read well enough to keep up with his group. He may develop an aversion to reading and he is quite likely to develop unfortunate reading habits. All of these things accumulate until it is apparent to the teacher that the child has become a disabled reader. He has not learned the skills and abilities essential to effective reading. Faulty habits and unfortunate modes of reading have become established. He is developing or has already developed an attitude of dislike and antagonism toward reading and his sense of defeat mounts higher and higher.

Such a child's difficulty has been brought about gradually through his failure to progress in the usual fashion. The teacher, confronted with thirty-five other children, at first failed to see the child's need or could not take the time to adjust the instruction to his requirements. The child thus developed an abnormal and unfortunate variation in his reading skills and abilities.

A program designed to treat reading disabilities is based on the assumption that children learn differently and need programs that meet their individual requirements. Such programs must be based on a recognition of a particular child's physical and mental characteristics and must be designed individually to be efficient in overcoming his difficulties.

The Remedial Program Should Be in Keeping With the Child's Characteristics

The expected outcomes of instruction and the methods used in achieving these outcomes will need to conform to the child's characteristics. If the child is lacking in general intelligence, he can neither be expected to reach the ultimate stature in reading of children of greater mental capability nor can he be expected to progress as rapidly. The remedial teacher will be wise to modify the outcomes of the program. The prognosis for rate of gain is usually directly proportional to the general intelligence of the child. In addition to lowering the results she expects, the remedial teacher would be wise to modify the methods of instruction also to meet the slow-learning child's needs. Such children need more concrete experiences, more carefully given directions, and more emphasis on repetition and drill than do children of higher intelligence.

If a child has poor vision or poor hearing, modifications in methods will need to be made. Such limitations make learning to read more difficult but in no way preclude the child from achieving. Deaf children have been taught to read about as effectively as their contemporaries with normal hearing when methods of instruction were adjusted to their needs. Children with marked visual defects have learned to read well, but they are more likely to get into difficulty. The disabled reader with lesser degrees of sensory handicaps can be taught more efficiently if his limitations are known and modifications in methods of instruction are made. The nature of the adjustments in methods that have proven helpful will be discussed fully later in this book.

Remedial Instruction Should Be Specific, Not General

The remedial teacher should focus instruction upon the specific reading needs of the child. The diagnosis has usually indicated that there is something specifically wrong with the pattern of the child's reading performance. One child, for example, may have learned to read with speed but falls short of the accuracy required in certain situations. Such a child should be given material to read that has factual content and he should read it for purposes that demand the exact recall of those facts. Another child may be so overconcerned with detail that he reads extremely slowly, looking for more facts than the author wrote. He becomes so concerned with the detail that he cannot understand the author's over-all intent. The teacher, in this latter case, would be specifically endeavoring to make the child less compulsive so that the rate of reading and its outcomes can become compatible with the purposes of this particular reading.

The principle that remedial instruction should be specific and not general means that the remedial teacher should emphasize those phases of reading development that will correct the child's reading limitation. It does not mean that just one type of exercise should be employed nor does it mean that a specific skill or ability should be isolated and receive drill. In the case of a disabled reader who has an insufficient knowledge of the larger visual and structural elements used in word recognition, the teacher would be making an error if she used a method that gave isolated drill on word elements. A more effective procedure would be to have the child read a basal reader at the proper level of difficulty. He would read for the purposes suggested in the manual, but when he encountered a word-recognition problem, the teacher would help him by emphasizing the larger elements in the word. When the exercises given in the manual for developing basic skills and abilities were studied, the remedial teacher would have this child do the ones that gave him experience in using the larger visual and structural parts of the words. The teacher could construct some additional exercises that would provide experiences with the larger elements in words the child already knew so that he could learn to use these in recognizing new words. Types of exercises suggested in manuals of other basic reading series using vocabulary known to the child could also be used in constructing these teacher-made materials.

The workbook exercises accompanying the basic reader should be used. The disabled reader may need to have certain pages selected for him so that he does not have to do all the exercises. This must be done because the child has an uneven profile and he may have emphasized one phase of reading instruction to the detriment of another. The child who needs a greater knowledge of large visual and structural elements may have failed to develop them because he had overemphasized phonetic letter-by-letter sounding in word recognition. Such a child should avoid for the time being the exercises that teach the knowledge of letter sounds.

Children have been given remedial instruction by various procedures at the University of Minnesota Psycho-educational Clinic. Children who were taught by using a regular developmental reading program, modified to emphasize those skills in which a given child needed further training and to minimize those which he had overemphasized, showed far greater gains than did the children who were taught by isolated drill exercises. It is to be concluded that remedial training is best done in nicely controlled reading programs such as are found in basic readers, but with modifications to meet the instructional needs of each child.

Remedial Instruction Should Be Energetic

Growth in reading presupposes an energetic learner. Of course, the child must learn to read by reading. He must attack the printed page vigorously and often if he is to succeed. A fatigued child cannot be expected to make gains during the remedial period. Therefore, the length of the period for remedial instruction should be such that concentrated work is possible. The disabled reader frequently finds it difficult to attend to reading for any considerable length of time. His lack of attention may be due to a variety of causes. In one case it may be lack of physical stamina, while in another, it may be that he is not getting enough sleep at night, or it may be that his emotional reactions to reading sap his vitality. His inattention or lack of vigor may be due to habits of escaping from an unsuccessful and uncomfortable situation. Whatever the cause, most children if properly motivated can apply themselves to the reading situation at least for a short period of time. Obviously, if the lack of attention and vigor result from a condition that can be corrected, the correction should be made. In any case, the length of the remedial reading period should be adjusted so that an energetic attack can be maintained.

Frequently it is necessary to divide the remedial sessions into short periods. The child may work with the remedial teacher for a period of forty-five minutes. At the start of the remedial training, it may be necessary to have him read from a basic reader for only ten minutes for specific purposes and then have him use the results of his reading in some creative activity, such as drawing, constructing, modeling, discussing, or the like. Then the child might work on some skill development exercises which emphasize the training he needs. These exercises might entail rereading the material he read at the first part of the session or they may be word-recognition drill on new words introduced in the basic reader. Finally, the child might be asked to tell about the book he has been reading independently. As he gains in reading growth, the length of concentrated reading time should be increased. Soon the child who has no physical limitation will be reading longer without interruption. When this is so, the use of creative activities can be less frequent. Then the child can read for several days during the remedial periods before he utilizes the results of reading. He will still need to discuss what he has read and do the exercises suited to him as suggested in the manual or as found in the workbook.

REMEDIAL INSTRUCTION MUST BE ORGANIZED INSTRUCTION

Reading instruction in both the developmental and remedial aspects must be well organized. The skills and abilities grow gradually as the child meets more complex applications of each. There is a tendency for remedial teachers to neglect the sequences involved in teaching the child each of the basic areas. In word recognition, remedial work is often erroneously given in one phase before the child has developed the learning that should precede it. The child may, for example, lack ability to break words into syllables so the remedial teacher gives him exercises to develop that skill. A study of the sequence in word-recognition techniques might show that the child had many other learnings to master before he could be expected to be successful in this relatively mature approach to word recognition.

In order that growth in word recognition may develop smoothly, with no undue burden upon the learner who is already in difficulty, a gradual, orderly sequence must be maintained. Such organization is necessary so that there will be no omissions in developing the essential skills, so that there will be little chance for overemphasis, and so that new skills are introduced to the child when he has the necessary prerequisites for learning them. In learning to recognize words, the child should first establish the habit of left-to-right orientation before he is allowed to employ any detailed analytical attacks. He should also learn to recognize word wholes when he knows them, rather than to employ analysis; to use the context and initial elements before he is encouraged to attend to variant endings; and to form the habit of viewing the word systematically from start to finish before he is required to visually separate the words into syllables.

The child who is in confusion in reading requires even more systematic instruction than does the child who is learning without difficulty. The remedial teacher must either be completely aware what sequence of learning is desirable in all the areas of reading growth or she must use the basal reading material in which the orderly development of skills has been carefully planned out. The remedial teacher cannot afford to use haphazard approaches. She must follow the sequence and explain carefully each new step in it. Therefore, the most successful remedial teachers find it expedient to use basic reading programs, modified to fit the child's specific needs whatever they may be.

THE READING PROCESSES MUST BE MADE MEANINGFUL TO THE LEARNER

One reason why the disabled reader is in difficulty is because he does not understand the processes involved in being a good reader. The remedial teacher has the responsibility not only for maintaining orderly sequences of skill development, but also for making the steps involved meaningful to the child. The teacher should not only teach the child to use context clues in word recognition, but also she should let the child see how helpful such an aid to word recognition can be. The teacher should show the child how to organize the material he reads for effective retention. She should, in addition, let the child understand why such an organization is effective. The child should be led to understand the importance of reading certain material carefully with attention to detail, while other material can be read rapidly to understand the general ideas it advances.

If the remedial teacher expects the child to retain a knowledge of word elements, it is important for her to show him how much they will aid him in recognizing new words. For too long, many remedial teachers have felt that if the child is stimulated to read material at the correct level of difficulty he will automatically develop the needed skills. This point of view can be seriously questioned. A more reasonable assumption is that the child should be shown how to go about his reading and how much use he can make of each added reading accomplishment. Suppose a child, for example, has learned by rote to pronounce prefixed words. How much better it would have been to point out to him the prefixes in those words and show him how they change the meaning of the root words.

The remedial teacher will find that making the processes of reading meaningful to the learner helps to solve his reading confusions. Drill on isolated parts of words is not as effective as is a meaningful approach to reading. Modern developmental reading programs are planned to enable the child to develop the needed skills and abilities and to understand the usefulness of each. The remedial program should be concerned even more with making reading processes meaningful to the child. The day has long since passed when it was assumed that if we but interested the child in reading, he would effectively go ahead on his own to develop skills of which he was unaware.

CONSIDERATION OF THE CHILD'S PERSONAL
WORTH IS NECESSARY

The disabled reader frequently feels insecure and defeated in school. Any remedial program designed to treat reading disabilities must make the child feel his successes from the start. It must also take into account the child's sense of personal worth. The child who is in serious trouble in reading is often antagonistic toward reading and thoroughly dislikes it. He would like to wake up some morning knowing how to read, but he believes there is something wrong with him that precludes his learning to read. Frequently he thinks that he is mentally incapable of learning or that he has some other defect. Often he has a poor estimate of himself as a person.

Remedial programs should consider the fact that the disabled reader builds a barrier between himself and all reading instruction. One of the first tasks of a remedial teacher is to gain the child's confidence. Resistance to the remedial program will be magnified if the child is classified in any unfortunate way. Whenever the remedial work is to be done by the classroom teacher, the child should be a working member of that class. He should be able to enter into the various activities even though his part in them is meager.

If it is necessary to give a child remedial training in the school reading center, great care must be taken when the work starts. Remedial programs should be considered a privilege and should be entered voluntarily. When the remedial groups are made up, it is strategic to include in them the brightest children who are disabled readers. These children are known to be bright and capable in other areas of the school curriculum and so the other children will see that the program is for able children who are having some specific difficulty. Another reason for selecting the more able children to start with, is that in their instances there is a greater chance for rapid improvement. This will enable the program to get off to a good start and will make it possible to do the most service to the greatest number. Besides, such an approach will place the remedial work in its proper perspective of being special instruction in reading rather than a class designed for the mentally inept.

In many schools, cases are selected for remedial work by sending the four or five poorest readers from each room to the reading center. This is an unfortunate practice. As has been previously explained, the poorest readers in the room are not necessarily the children who will profit from remedial instruction in reading. Many such children are essentially slow learners. They are not disabled readers. Only children who are properly classified as reading disability cases should be sent to the school reading center for remedial instruction. Another tendency is to refer disciplinary and delinquent children to the reading center for individual work or for work in the smaller group. While it is true that many delinquent and disciplinary cases are poor readers, it is unwise to give the remedial teacher too large a number of these children at any one time. The correction of reading disability is a difficult task and if too many kinds of problems are concentrated in any one group, the teacher cannot hope to be successful. Also, the reading center will acquire a reputation as a place for misfits.

In general, it is desirable to inaugurate remedial work with children who have the following characteristics:

1. General intelligence of over 90 as measured by suitable tests.
2. Children who have asked to be admitted after the work has been discussed with them.
3. Children whose parents have requested such service.
4. Children who are classified as having reading disability as their major problem.
5. Not too great a proportion of children with behavior problems at any one time.

Frequently the disabled reader is emotionally tense or insecure. He has had no real opportunity to gain confidence in himself because most of the school day involves reading. For some time he has been much less effective in school work than his intellectual level would indicate that he should be. Such a child may become submissive or demanding, aggressive or withdrawing, or show his basic insecurity in a variety of ways. He may develop attitudes of indifference, dislike, or rejection. He may resist help, display few interests, and be antagonistic toward reading instruction. Remedial reading programs must overcome these unfortunate attitudes and compensatory modes of behavior. One of the first responsibilities of the remedial teacher is to develop in the child a need for learning to read. The second is to gain the child's confidence to such a degree that he will know a personal interest is being taken in him and that now his reading problem is going to be solved. A direct attack on the reading problem by a businesslike, considerate adult will do much to overcome tensions and faulty attitudes. When a child recognizes that an interest is taken in him and his problem, it will give him the much-needed sense of personal worth and the confidence in himself that he has hitherto lacked.

THE READING PROGRAM MUST BE ENCOURAGING TO THE CHILD

Most disabled readers are discouraged about their failure to learn to read. They frequently think that they cannot learn. This lack of confidence in their ability to learn is detrimental to possible reading growth. The effective learner is a confident and purposeful learner, one who has a desire to learn and finds pleasure in working toward this goal. In order that a child may go ahead rapidly in learning to read, it is necessary for him to know that he can learn and to see that he is progressing satisfactorily.

There are several principles underlying remedial instruction that give the child this sense of confidence he needs. The following principles will help to give the child the necessary encouragement:

1. The teacher must be optimistic.
2. The child needs group as well as individual work.
3. The child's successes should be emphasized.
4. A positive approach should be used in pointing out errors.
5. His growth in reading should be pointed out to the child.
6. Remedial programs should not be substituted for enjoyable activities.
7. Remedial programs must be pleasant and free from undue pressures.

The Teacher Must Be Optimistic

A teacher who would help a child to overcome a reading disability should be a buoyant, energetic person. She must make the child sense her confidence in him. At times, the problems involved in correcting a complex reading disability may seem to her to entail almost insurmountable teaching problems. Nevertheless, the teacher must approach each disabled reader showing that she knows he will learn to read. Such an attitude is an outgrowth of a thorough understanding of the instructional needs of the child, that is, a sound diagnosis, and of having the remedial program planned well enough in advance so that the general nature of remedial instruction is clearly in mind. In addition, the teacher gains immediate confidence through knowing exactly what is going to be undertaken during each remedial lesson. A well-prepared teacher who knows exactly where each session is going will instill confidence in the child. With this preparation, progress in reading ordinarily takes place.

The teacher may well be optimistic because the vast majority of reading disability cases do show immediate gains from remedial instruction. If the child's reading problem and his characteristics have been carefully appraised and if the program has been carefully formulated, success is almost assured. Of course, the teacher's confidence may sometimes, and from time to time, be shaken. There are periods during the corrective treatment of practically every remedial case when there is little evidence of new growth. But all the same, confidence in the child's ultimate success must be maintained even when things do not appear to be going well. Under some circumstances the remedial program should be restudied and the diagnosis reviewed, but all this need not lessen confidence in the child's ultimate success.

The Child Needs Group as Well as Individual Work

The disabled reader needs to share experiences with other children just as much as, or even more than, the child whose growth in reading is normal. Not only should his classroom work be organized so that he can participate in some of the important activities with which the class is concerning itself, but also it is beneficial for the child who is in difficulty to see that there are other children who are having similar difficulties. It is therefore recommended that whenever it is possible to have disabled readers work in groups, this should be undertaken. Much good can be gained by the disabled reader in seeing other children right around him who are in a like difficulty, and who are making progress in overcoming it. It is sometimes assumed that remedial reading instruction is a formal procedure in which the child is separated from other children and drilled until his disability is corrected. Such instruction is most unwise. It is a boost to the child to know that there are other children who are learning to read and who are able to use their newly gained proficiencies in group situations.

The summer program of the University of Minnesota Psycho-educational Clinic provides a good illustration of how both individual and group remedial work can be made available to the child. Of course, in the school reading center or in the typical reading clinic, slight modifications would have to be made. The children who come to the summer reading clinic at the University of Minnesota are, for the most part, extremely disabled readers. The great majority of them would be described as complex or limiting disability cases. The most successful approach that we have been able to devise for these children has been to separate them into groups or classes of about 15 to 20 children. They work with a classroom teacher for an entire morning. In the classroom work, there is a regular unit of instruction, using topics to be found in readers and selected so as to be at the reading level at which the greatest number in the class can read comfortably. These topics are supplemented by additional reference books in the room. For some of the children, picture books or pictures in books which supply information are used. In addition to the unit the children are reading about, there is group instruction using basal material at the appropriate level for each group within the class. Then for a period of from a half hour to an hour every day, each child is withdrawn from the class, either in small groups of four or five or for individual instruction, whichever is deemed best from the nature of the case. In this situation, the children are given remedial instruction designed to overcome their specific remedial problems. Children in the same major classification of disability form the small groups. Children who do not fit into any groups are handled individually. In a typical school reading center, the remedial reading teacher would not have additional personnel to handle small groups. Therefore the modification recommended for the school reading center would be to have those children who were less seriously retarded or who constituted a very similar type of disability, such as the slow readers, brought together for instruction in relatively large groups. Those children with more complex disabilities could be handled in smaller sections. Such group sessions could be conducted during the morning. Then the remedial teacher would be free in the afternoon to handle smaller groups or work with certain individual children whom she had observed during the morning sessions were in need of additional help.

The Child's Successes Should Be Emphasized

In order that the remedial program may be encouraging to the child, his successes rather than his mistakes should be emphasized. Teachers have a tendency to point out errors to children rather than to make them feel that for the most part they are doing particularly well. A child whose errors are continually focused upon may become overwhelmed by a sense of defeat. A wise teacher will start the child in a remedial program that is somewhat easy for him so that his successful performance will be immediately apparent. As he gains confidence, the difficulty of the reading situations may be increased. The teacher should always be quick to recognize when the child has put forth a real effort and has done something well. Many times, particularly at the start, recognition will have to be given for activities related to the reading rather than the reading itself. Gradually the teacher will find increased opportunities to give praise for the actual reading that is well done. At all times it should be remembered that the effectiveness of remedial instruction depends in no small measure upon the child's gain in confidence. This gain in confidence is brought about through successful experiences with reading which in the past had caused the child so much difficulty.

A Positive Approach Should Be Used in Pointing Out Errors

The emphasis upon success does not mean that errors are to be altogether overlooked. The faulty reading of a child must of course be brought to his attention. Errors in word recognition must be pointed out. Faulty habits in reading which limit his speed must be recognized by him before they can be corrected. Sometimes it is necessary to demand greater exactness in reading on the part of the child. While it is true that the teacher must point out the child's mistakes, she must at all times indicate that the child is improving and that for the most part he is really doing well. If, for example, a child should call the word *house, horse* in the sentence "The dog ran up to the house," the teacher should point out to him that he had the sentence nearly correct, but that in order to be exactly right he should have looked at the center part of the last word a little more carefully. As a matter of fact, the child did recognize most of the words in the sentence. He made an error that indicated that he was using the context well and that his error was a very slight one indeed. The words *house* and *horse* do look much alike.

In a comprehension lesson, the child may give the wrong answer to a question. Instead of saying that the answer is wrong and calling on another child in the group, it would be far better for the teacher to say, "Let's see what the book says about this" and then find out wherein the child made his error. It will frequently be found that he did not understand the meaning of a word or that he failed to notice a key word such as *not,* or that he had not grouped the words into proper thought units. Whatever the cause of his error, it should be located and the child should be shown the correct way to read the passage. The attitude of the teacher should be not one of pointing out errors but one of helping the child learn to read.

Growth in Reading Should Be Demonstrated to the Child

The disabled reader needs to have his growth demonstrated to him. There are many ways in which reading growth can be shown. The diagnostician has isolated the child's needs in this regard and indicated the amount of emphasis that should be given. It will be recalled that the method for demonstrating the progress of the child to him depends upon the nature of the reading problem. If, for example, the child is trying to develop a sight vocabulary, he could make a picture dictionary of the words he was trying

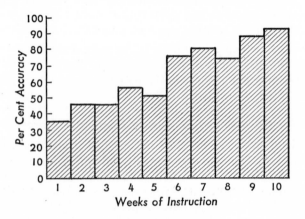

FIG. 11. An accuracy bar chart.

to learn. As the dictionary became larger, the child would recognize that he had increased his sight vocabulary. The child who is working on accuracy of comprehension could develop a bar chart (Fig. 11) in which he would indicate his level of per cent of accuracy on successive periods. If such a child failed to gain over the period of a week, the teacher could simplify the material or ask more general questions so that accuracy would increase. Then as the child gained confidence, the difficulty of the material could be gradually increased again. It is a good plan for the child to go back, from time to time, and reread something that he has read previously. He will discover that material that was difficult for him a short while ago, is now relatively easy for him to read. This will be especially true if the teacher takes time to develop the necessary readiness prior to the reading.

Whatever the nature of the difficulty, it is important for the remedial program to be organized to demonstrate to the child that he is progressing toward his goal of better reading. The child who has been in difficulty for a long time needs whatever encouragement can be given him. He needs not only to be in a comfortable learning situation, but also he needs to see that he is making effective advancement in reading.

Remedial Programs Should Not Be Substituted for Enjoyable Activities

The remedial teacher must so organize the periods of instruction that children are not required to come for training at a time that competes with other activities of great importance to them. For example, it is a frequent practice to have children come to a clinic for remedial instruction after school. This is a decidedly unfortunate time for a boy who enjoys outdoor sports with his friends, and who finds this the only time that such outdoor games are played in his neighborhood. In scheduling summer reading programs, it is wise to delay their start until a week or so after school is out and the children have found that they have time that they do not know what to do with. Even then the better scheduling time for classes is probably in the morning because the majority of things that the child likes to do, such as going swimming or playing baseball, are done in the afternoon.

The busy classroom teacher frequently finds it difficult to give an individual child attention he needs when the class is in session. She may therefore select recess time or the time in which other children have their hobby clubs, or are in the auditorium viewing a movie, for helping a child with his reading. Such a practice is understandable but is unfortunate for the correction of a reading disability. A better time would be to work with the children needing re-education while the rest of the children are busily engaged in studying or reading independently. Whatever time is used for giving remedial help, it is important that it does not conflict with activities which are important to the child.

Remedial Programs Must Be Pleasant and Free from Undue Pressures

An effective remedial program must be one that is satisfying to the child, makes him feel that he is getting along well, and keeps at a minimum any anxiety which he feels about his reading progress. The teacher's responsibility in encouraging the child to read energetically is indeed great. She should neither unduly hurry the child nor allow him to dawdle; she should be sure the child is working hard and yet avoid putting undue pressure on him. Most children, in fact, practically all children can be expected to work intently in developing reading ability. This is especially true if the reading materials are at the right level, if the child is properly motivated, and if he is reading for purposes that are real to him. There should always be a friendly atmosphere, but an atmosphere that keeps uppermost the point of view that the child is there to learn to read.

MATERIALS AND EXERCISES MUST BE SUITABLE TO THE CHILD'S READING ABILITY AND INSTRUCTIONAL NEEDS

The selection of appropriate material for remedial work in reading is one of the most important problems the remedial teacher has to solve. Some teachers feel that the most important element in the problem is that the material should deal with a subject in which the child is interested. Others feel that the level of difficulty of the material is of even greater importance. Still others believe that having the type of material that is compatible with the nature of the remedial instruction is of paramount importance. There can be no doubt that all three of these elements enter into the selection of appropriate material for remedial instruction. Without trying to decide here between them, we may conclude that the more important considerations in selecting material are:

1. The materials must be suitable in level of difficulty.
2. The materials must be suitable in type.
3. The materials must be at the appropriate level of interest and format.
4. The materials must be abundant.

The Materials Must Be Suitable in Level of Difficulty

The child grows in reading by reading, therefore the material that is used for remedial instruction should be of a difficulty level that enables the child to read comfortably and with enjoyment. The diagnostician will have suggested the level of difficulty of the material the child could be expected to read. The remedial teacher must pick out materials at that level to suit the child. The difficulty of material can be judged in many ways. Readability formulas, such as the Lorge formula (123), the formula of Dale-Chall (42), and that of Spache (157) have proven useful in estimating the reading level of materials. Sources of graded book lists are given in Appendix III. Most of the basic readers are carefully graded and indicate the level of reading maturity necessary for their use. In general, of course, books of second-grade level are suitable to the child whose skills are of second-grade maturity. Third-grade books are suitable for the child whose basic skill development is approximately that of a third-grade child. Ungraded books can be estimated by a formula or by using a basic reading series as a difficulty rating scale. The difficulty of an ungraded library book may be judged by comparing it with the various grade levels of a basic reader. For example, a library book can be compared with a third-grade reader. If it is judged to be harder, it may then be compared with a fourth-grade reader, and so forth, until the approximate level of difficulty can be estimated. In making the judgment, the teacher should look at the number of unusual words it contains, the length of its sentences, the number of prepositional phrases, the number of unusual word orders, the complexity of the ideas it includes. In judging level of difficulty, it is important that the remedial teacher remember that the results of standardized survey tests tend to give an overestimation of the skill development of a reading disability case. Therefore, it is usually wise to start remedial instruction with material that is somewhat lower than the child's general reading score as indicated by standardized tests.

The difficulty of the material that is suitable for remedial instruction will vary somewhat with the nature of the child's disability. The teacher should modify the general estimate of level of difficulty according to the outcomes of instruction to be achieved by the use of that material. For example, if the child's major problem is one of developing sight vocabulary, the material should be relatively easy with few new words being introduced. Those that are introduced should be used often in the material. For such a child, a relatively easy level in a basic reading program would be desirable. On the other hand, for the child who is trying to analyze words effectively, a higher concentration of new vocabulary would be desirable. The child could well afford to meet one new word in approximately every 20 running words. This would give him an opportunity to employ the techniques of word analysis that he needs to develop and at the same time it will enable him to maintain the thought of the passage so that context clues can be used as a means of checking the accuracy of his word recognition.

A child who is trying to increase his speed of comprehension, should use material that is for him definitely easy. Such material would have few if any word-recognition problems for him. On the other hand, the child who is trying to increase his power of comprehension should use material with which he must tussle, but he must have a reasonable chance of successfully comprehending the material.

The Materials Must Be Suitable in Type

It is often said that any kind of material that is suitable for teaching reading in the first place is suitable for remedial instruction. While this is true, it is important to recognize that the material must be nicely selected to meet the child's instructional needs. The type of material that is suitable for one kind of disability is not necessarily suitable for another. If the child's major problem is that of increasing his speed of reading, the most suitable material would be short stories whose plots unfold rapidly. The material should not only be easy in regard to reading difficulty, but the nature of the content should be such that the child can read it to gain a general impression or the general significance of the story. If, on the other hand, the child's problem is one in the word-recognition area, a basic reader along with the exercises found in the manuals and the workbooks related to the word-recognition problem would be the most desirable type of reading material to use. If the child's problem is in the comprehension area and it is desired to increase his accuracy in reading, material in science or in social studies that has considerable factual information should be used. In every instance, the material should be at the appropriate level of difficulty, but also in every instance, the material should be of a type that is appropriate to the outcomes of reading expected.

The Materials Must Be at the Appropriate Level of Interest and Format

A relatively mature and intelligent 12-year-old will usually not find first- and second-grade material interesting, nor will he find the format very attractive. Such a child with second-grade reading ability must nevertheless use material that he can read. The problem facing the remedial teacher in this respect is very great. The second-grade book is designed for a child who is 7 or 8 years of age. The pictures in it are of small children and its print looks large and juvenile. The topics dealt with in the book are appropriate to the 7- or 8-year-old and not to a 12-year-old. Therefore, many books that are used for remedial reading instruction lose some of their value because they lack interest and have the wrong format. In such a case, however, there can be no compromise with the need for using material that is at the suitable level of difficulty. The problem resolves itself, then, into how to find material that is of a suitable level of difficulty and is as appealing as possible to a child of more mature age.

An increasingly large number of books suitable for remedial work are being developed. There are those books that are primarily designed for the less capable reader. Such books as the *Gates-Peardon Practice Exercises,* (85) published by the Bureau of Publications, Columbia University, the *American Adventure Series,* (9) published by Wheeler Publishing Company, and *The Everyreader Series,* (63a) published by Webster Publishing Company, are useful. Another source of materials that can be used with remedial cases is the books designed to meet the individual differences in ability within the classroom. Basic reading programs are being developed that have parallel readers, such as the *Regular* and *Classmate Editions* of the *Developmental Reading Series,* (23) published by Lyons and Carnahan. In this series of readers, there are two editions which are alike in all important respects. They have the same covers, the same titles, pictures, content, and interest level. The difference lies in the fact that the *Classmate Edition* is written with a smaller vocabulary load, shorter paragraphs, simpler sentences, and fewer words per page. The classmate editions are considerably easier in reading difficulty than are the regular editions. The sixth-grade book in the regular edition requires sixth-grade reading ability, whereas the same stories can be read in the classmate edition by children who have only third-grade reading ability.

Another source of material that is useful in remedial work is the *Modern Wonder Books* (111) that are published by the American Educational Press. The workbooks that accompany basic readers are also suitable material. The workbooks look considerably more mature than the basal readers they accompany. The pictures are in black and white. The drill exercises give no indication of the maturity level of the children who are expected to read them. There are many lists of books that are suitable for use in remedial work. Many of these lists indicate the level of reading maturity which is required to read the books and also indicate the maximum age of a child who will enjoy reading the material. A list of such bibliographies is given in Appendixes III and IV.

The Materials Must Be Abundant

In selecting material for remedial work, the first and most important consideration is that it must be of the proper level of difficulty. The second is that it should be appropriate in type. The third is that it should be interesting in format and meet the interest level of the child. Another consideration in securing materials to be used in remedial reading is that they should be abundant. There should be a wide variety of material meeting many interests and at various levels of difficulty. For any one child, there should be ample material suitable for him to read. There should be material for his remedial instruction and also material for his independent reading. The independent reading for a remedial reading case should be considerably easier than that used in giving him remedial instruction. The material for independent reading needs to be on a wide variety of topics because the children will have a wide variety of interests. The material that the child is to read independently should fulfill an existing interest which the child already has, while the material that is used for instructional purposes must be such that he can be motivated to take an interest in reading.

SOUND TEACHING PROCEDURES MUST BE EMPLOYED

During the entire discussion of principles for treatment of reading difficulties, it has been implied that remedial instruction is the application of sound teaching procedures directed toward the specific needs of the child. Instruction in remedial reading is not unusual in character nor is it necessary to use expensive and artificial equipment. The skills and abilities should be emphasized in actual reading situations free from isolated drill. Sound teaching procedures such as those used for introducing the reading skills and abilities in the first place should be used. The materials best suited to remedial instruction are those that are best for the developmental program.

The difference between remedial instruction and the developmental program is in the extent of individualization and in the study of the child rather than in the uniqueness of the methods or materials it employs. There are certain principles of reading instruction that are sometimes neglected in remedial work. Readiness should be carefully built for every topic and every selection to be read by the disabled reader. This includes the creation of interest in, the development of background for, and the introduction of new words for each selection the child reads. The child who is in difficulty in reading, just as much as other children who are not, should have the purposes for reading well understood before the reading is done. He should also use the results of his reading in a creative enterprise of one sort or another. If, for example, he has read a selection about flood control to find what techniques are used, it would be important for him to make a diagram of a river bed illustrating what he had learned, just as it would be for children in the developmental reading program. Seeing that children use the results of their reading is a good procedure for all children. It becomes an essential practice, though an often neglected one, for children who are in difficulty in reading. The form of use to which the results of reading are put may be a discussion, a picture drawn, a chart made, a map planned, or any one of many such enterprises. The relative amount of time devoted to these things should be small, however, and above all, the creative work should be the child's own.

Consideration must be given to the learning environment of the child both in and out of school. Whether the remedial work is done in the classroom, the school reading center, or the clinic, only a small segment of the child's reading is done during the corrective lessons. If the remedial program is to be successful, the rest of the child's reading day must be adjusted to his needs and reading capabilities. The effective work of the remedial periods can be destroyed if unfortunate demands or pressures are placed upon the child either in school or at home. As has been stated earlier, both the classroom teacher and the parents will be willing to co-operate if they are given an understanding of the child's reading problem. The parents are often endeavoring to help the child with his reading, and this is as it should be, but the remedial teacher should consult with them so that their work will be of the greatest benefit to the child. Bond and Wagner (29) show many ways in which parents can help a child to grow in reading.

The remedial teacher will find it helpful to keep a cumulative account of the child's progress. The record should include the books read; the type of exercises used, and the success of each; any charts used to show the child his progress; and the results of periodic tests. In this connection, any indications of fields of interests and anecdotal accounts of the child's reactions to the remedial program will be a help. By studying this record, the teacher can compare periods of rapid growth with the type of exercises used and books read at those times. A study of past records will recall to the teacher those approaches that were successful with other similar cases. The teacher can assemble a file of such folders, arranged according to the specific problem involved.

When the child has made sufficient progress so that he can be released from further remedial work, he should be gradually put into situations where he must rely on his own resources. A follow-up with the classroom teacher will be necessary. The child who has had a severe reading limitation may become discouraged again if his work does not go well after he finishes remedial instruction. Any indications of loss of interest or of confusions in learning should get immediate attention by the classroom teacher during the readjustment period.

SUMMARY

Although the remedial work for each disabled reader must be different in certain respects, there are some common elements among the corrective programs. The remedial program must be designed to emphasize the child's instructional needs as shown by the diagnosis, and therefore there can be no universal approach in all cases. The remedial program for each reading case must be carefully planned and what is to be done should be written down. It will be necessary to modify the program from time to time in order to keep abreast of the child's changing instructional needs. Even though the program is well planned to give emphasis on overcoming a specific disability, a variety of remedial techniques should be used. The remedial teacher will find manuals and workbooks that accompany basal reading programs the most fruitful source of teaching techniques.

Remedial reading programs must be highly individualized and they must be designed in keeping with the child's instructional needs and characteristics. It is necessary to modify the approaches to reading in order to adjust to such limitations as poor hearing or poor vision. Remedial instruction should not drill upon one specific skill or ability in isolation, but should provide new experience in whatever skills are needed in connection with purposeful reading. The length of remedial sessions should be so planned that the child will not become fatigued or inattentive.

Reading instruction for the disabled reader must be well organized in order that skills and abilities may be developed smoothly with no undue burden for the child, with little chance for overemphasis, and with no omissions of essential learnings. The teacher should not only maintain an orderly sequence of skill development, but also should make the steps involved meaningful to the child.

The remedial reading program must be encouraging to the child since much of his trouble arose because he had lost confidence in his ability to learn. The teacher should be optimistic; the child's successes should be emphasized; and his progress should be demonstrated to him. Materials must be suitable to the child's reading abilities and instructional needs; they should be suitable in level of difficulty and type of content; they should be as nearly as possible appropriate in level of interest; and they should look "mature" to the child. The materials used for remedial instruction must be of such difficulty that the child can read them and of such maturity that he will be motivated to read them. There can be no compromise with the difficulty level of the material because the child will not be interested in reading material he cannot read, no matter how attractive the subject matter. In all remedial work, sound teaching procedures should be used and artificial devices and isolated drill should be avoided.

SELECTED READINGS

BOND, G. L., and WAGNER, E. B., *Child growth in reading*. Chicago: Lyons & Carnahan, 1955, Chap. 11.

BRUECKNER, L. J., and BOND, G. L., *Diagnosis and treatment of learning difficulties*. New York: Appleton-Century-Crofts, Inc., 1955, Chap. 5.

DOLCH, Edward W., *A manual for remedial reading,* 2nd ed. Champaign (Ill.): The Garrard Press, 1945, Chap. 2.

DURRELL, Donald D., *Improvement of basic reading abilities*. Yonkers (N.Y.): World Book Company, 1940, Chap. 14.

GATES, Arthur I., *The improvement of reading*, 3rd ed. New York: The Macmillan Company, 1947, Chap. 5.

HARRIS, Albert J., *How to increase reading ability*, 3rd ed. New York: Longmans, Green & Company, 1956, Chap. 11.

TINKER, Miles A., *Teaching elementary reading*. New York: Appleton-Century-Crofts, Inc., 1952, Chap. 12.

WITTY, Paul, *Reading in modern education*. Boston: D. C. Heath & Company, 1949, Chap. 7.

11 DEVELOPMENT OF THE BASIC COMPREHENSION ABILITIES

To COMMUNICATE by means of printed or written language involves both meanings and comprehension. Learning to read requires the development of facility in comprehending the meanings represented by printed or written symbols. To recognize printed symbols merely as words encountered previously and to pronounce those words without understanding what is intended by the writer *is not reading*. A child learns to read effectively only to the degree that he acquires a meaningful vocabulary and progresses in ability to understand and interpret printed or written materials.

Word recognition divorced from meaning, or when that meaning is vague and unclear, leads to mere word calling. The result is *verbalism* or the pronunciation and use of words in context without understanding their meanings. Verbalism blocks the way to the manipulation and organization of meanings in purposeful reading. When this occurs, the thinking side of reading is inhibited or eliminated so that true reading has become impossible. This occurs too frequently in the school situation. If the reader associates no satisfactory meanings with his word recognition and if a time comes when he is held responsible for the content of the material he has been "reading," he is forced to try and remember the material verbatim. Under these conditions, comprehension is at best very limited. According to the viewpoint adopted here, there can be no such thing as reading without understanding. That is, if understanding is lacking, reading has not been done.

To become a proficient reader, then, there must have occurred a sequential development of word knowledge and of comprehension skills. These are integral parts of the complex process of reading with understanding. In addition, there must be a mastery of the word-recognition skills discussed in the next chapter and the development of a large sight vocabulary. In the early grades, the meaning-listening vocabulary exceeds by far the child's recognition vocabulary. The acquisition of new word meanings and new sight vocabulary and the development of word-recognition skills progress hand-in-hand. New words are incorporated into the understanding and speaking vocabulary of the child. An increasing number of words becomes so familiar that they are recognized at a glance and their meanings understood. Word-recognition clues and techniques are applied to the association of familiar word meanings with the printed symbols which represent them.

Although the recognition of words and the understanding of word meanings are essential, something more still is needed for comprehension in reading. The elements in a sentence must be evaluated and their organization in relation to each other understood. Word meanings which are in harmony with the rest of the context must be selected. Thus the word *store* has a different meaning when used in the sentence "You may store your cart in the garage," than in "He went to the store for some bread." Many words have a large number of semantic variations or change of meaning according to their context. For instance, in *Webster's New International Dictionary,* seven columns are devoted to semantic variations of the word *set.* In addition, in order to comprehend a paragraph or larger unit, the relations between its elements, i.e., in each sentence and in the relations among sentences and among paragraphs, need to be understood. Evaluation of these relationships necessarily involves thinking. So we find that recognition of words, understandings of word meanings, and comprehension are all interdependent aspects of the reading process. To insure that appropriate word meanings are attached to printed symbols, recognition skills should be taught for the most part in some context. That context may be pictures or sentences.

In good teaching practice, all approaches to basic meaning development will be co-ordinated into the sequential program. This program will include the following: (1) various methods of acquiring word meanings such as experience, context clues, enrichment of meaning through descriptive words, figures of speech and symbolic expressions, the noting of semantic variations, and word study; (2) phrasing into thought units; (3) sentence comprehension; (4) paragraph meaning and organization; and (5) story organization and story sense.

The above basic aspects of comprehension are involved in all reading of stories and descriptive materials. Specific or specialized comprehension abilities and study skills will be considered in later chapters. The present chapter will deal with the development of the basic comprehension abilities which apply to all reading situations.

HOW COMPREHENSION TAKES PLACE

It has been emphasized above that true reading is reading with understanding or comprehension. Basically, comprehension depends upon facility in the use of concepts or meanings evolved through experience. To be of use in reading, the concepts acquired through experience must be attached to words or groups of words as symbols of their meanings. Such words become a part of one's understanding and speaking vocabulary. Then, when a reader recognizes a word or group of words, perception of the printed symbol stimulates the recalling or constructing of meanings for which the symbol stands. Obviously, the meanings recalled are those possessed by the reader and necessarily must have been evolved through past experience. As noted by Harrison (95), the meaning may be derived directly from those past experiences, or it may consist of a newly constructed meaning which results from combining and reorganizing meanings already possessed by the reader. The author brings known ideas together in such a way that the reader senses a new relationship and therefore gains a new idea, concept, or sensory impression. Take for instance the meanings aroused when a fourth-grade city child reads the sentence "The tired rider drooped in his saddle as his spotted horse walked along the mountain trail." Since the reader has not seen such a rider, he may organize the meaning of the sentence from a variety of remembered visual experiences such as: (1) his father napping with his head bent forward as he rests in an easy chair; (2) a bridle path through the park; (3) a mounted policeman who sat erect on his black horse; (4) a spotted black and white coach dog; and (5) the scenery during an auto trip through hilly country. By recombining these concepts, the child may achieve a close approximation of the meaning intended by the writer of the sentence. So one reads primarily with his experiences which are ultimately based upon sensory impressions of all kinds such as hearing, seeing, tasting, smelling, and touching. Also involved is one's behavior in adjusting to all kinds of situations including the accompanying emotional reactions and imagination.

The role of experience in the acquisition of word meanings in early childhood has been well portrayed by the *Literature Committee of the Association for Childhood Education* (122) [1] in the statement:

> Inquiring eyes and eager hands aid them in the discovery of a wealth of meanings. The fitting of names to things becomes an intellectual adventure. Sensitive ears delight in sounds which invite repetition and encourage free experimentation with language as a medium. Out of their world of familiar sights, sounds, smells, and objects large and small, children establish a variety of relationships through enumeration of sounds, objects, names of persons, and repetition of rhythmic phrases.

The development of concepts which carry the meanings begins early in a child's life. Activities at home, hearing the talk of parents and other children and adults, listening to radio and viewing television, trips about the neighborhood, and in some instances, more extended travel are all involved in developing a hearing-meaning vocabulary. Concepts are being acquired. The child begins to use words and later sentences in a correct manner. Precision in the use of oral language forms is gradually acquired. To be serviceable in reading, a meaning must be attached to a word, for it is only by the use of words that meanings can be recalled. If the recalled meanings are to be precise, the words which stand for those meanings must have been

---

[1] Literature Committee of the Association for Childhood Education, *Told under the blue umbrella.* New York: The Macmillan Company, 1947, pp. 158-159. Quoted with permission of The Macmillan Company.

in the usage vocabulary of the reader. The degree to which he is able to use a word in his language and thinking determines to a large extent how effectively he will be able to use it in reading.

In the normal course of development, a child's experiences will lead him to use sentences for oral communication. Sentences are groups of words organized in meaningful relationships. Nearly all reading matter is in the form of sentences. The degree to which a reader has acquired an understanding of sentences and is skillful in using sentence forms determines how well he will be able to read print organized in sentences. Furthermore, the precise meanings of certain words in a sentence are comprehended from the context of the sentence.

The comprehension of sentences is facilitated when reading is done by thought units. A thought unit is a group of words which make up a meaningful sequence in a sentence. For instance, in the sentence "One of the men saw the bricks start to fall," there are three thought units as the spacings indicate. Verbal facility in oral communication leads to phrasing into thought units. Growth in reading sentences by thought units, however, is relatively slow. It is dependent upon increased efficiency in the recognition of single words. Only when the child has developed an adequate sight vocabulary, can he group words into thought units. Some grouping (two-word units) occurs during the latter part of grade one. Progress is more rapid from the third grade on. The average reader is fairly proficient in reading by thought units by the time he reaches sixth grade.

The child with good verbal facility succeeds in having his ideas organized into thought units and his spoken sentences reflect this organization. A similar trend is found in reading. The child who is a word-by-word reader seldom grasps the meaning of a sentence as a whole. But when a child is reading by thought units, the resulting organization of the material promotes comprehension. Proficiency in perceiving words in thought units, therefore, is usually accompanied by good understanding of the material that is being read.

Attention must also be directed to comprehension of paragraphs and larger units. To comprehend the material in a paragraph requires an understanding of the relations between sentences in that paragraph. This involves identifying the topical sentence containing the key idea and an understanding of its relation to the explanatory or amplifying sentences.

We also have to note the relation between paragraphs in longer selections. In a well-written story or article the paragraphs will be arranged in an orderly manner. The introductory paragraph or paragraphs usually present briefly the plan, the central theme, or the purpose of the story or article. Succeeding paragraphs, arranged in logical sequence, present the unfolding of the story through the high point and on to the ending. Or in expository material, the paragraphs follow one another in orderly sequence giving the details needed to explain the event, process or activity outlined in the introduction. To achieve proper comprehension of larger units, the pupil will need to understand this relation between the introductory and subsequent paragraphs.

Satisfactory comprehension of larger units of material involves still further skills. These include the specific comprehension abilities and the study skills. Proper application of such skills as ability to follow printed directions, and ability to locate information is needed for satisfactory comprehension of larger units whether such units consist of one or more paragraphs. These specialized applications of the basic comprehension abilities will be considered in detail in a later chapter.

LISTENING AND READING COMPREHENSION

Essentially the same processes are involved in comprehending printed material and in understanding spoken words. In both cases, perception of words arouses meanings which lead to comprehension. The meanings aroused by the perceived words depend mainly upon two factors: (1) the learner's or the reader's entire background of experience, and (2) his facility in language usage for purposes of communication. There are marked differences between children in the length and complexity of a selection which they can comprehend. Provided a child has made normal progress in the mechanics of reading (word recognition, etc.) he should be able to comprehend just as long and complex a unit that he is reading as he can if precisely the same words are spoken to him. A summary of the experimental evidence on comparison of listening and reading comprehension with the implications for reading instruction are given by Tinker (175). Although the experimental findings are not uniform, certain trends appear: (1) in the lower grades, listening comprehension is equal to or better than reading comprehension. This holds true also for pupils of low ability. (2) However, when pupils have become more skilled in reading, reading comprehension is equal or superior to listening comprehension. The same trend is evident for pupils of relatively high academic ability. Haugh (96) determined the relative effectiveness of reading and listening as methods of acquiring information with eleventh-grade high school pupils. He found that the pupils comprehended more from reading a radio script than from listening to a dramatization of the script.

These results suggest that during the primary grades, while pupils are in the process of mastering the mechanics of reading, listening comprehension tends to be superior to reading comprehension. It must be kept in mind that when a child begins grade one, there is a six-year lag of reading comprehension behind listening comprehension. From birth on, the child has been developing listening comprehension. Furthermore, at the first-grade level, a child would normally hear more running words in two days than he reads in the entire first-grade program. However, word repetition and vocabulary control in first-grade materials constitute an advantageous situation for rapid development in reading comprehension.

As soon as appreciable progress has been achieved in mastering the mechanics of reading, something that occurs sooner for the more able child, the two modes of comprehension become equivalent. Then as greater proficiency and maturity are reached, reading comprehension may become more proficient than listening comprehension. These trends make sense when we think about it. In the primary grades, considerable attention must be devoted to developing word-recognition techniques and the building of a sight vocabulary. As these skills are acquired, there is greater opportunity for the pupil, when he reads, to concentrate on comprehension. Then with the accumulation of a richer background of reading and other experiences, with increasing maturity and improved reading proficiency during progress through the upper grades, reading comprehension gets its opportunity to become superior to listening comprehension. This is because the reader can stop and reflect, evaluate or debate, or of course reread parts of the material.

The implication of these trends for instruction to improve reading comprehension seems clear. Though word-recognition techniques and other mechanics should be developed effectively in the early grades, still they should be relegated to their appropriate place, which is to say they should have become as automatic as possible here, as at all levels. At the same time, there should be a strong emphasis upon comprehension. With the mastering of the mechanics, the major portion of the pupil's attention during reading can be devoted to comprehension. This, with teacher guidance, will become more and more proficient. Thus, the well-balanced program of instruction through the grades plays a dominant role in developing reading comprehension up to a level that is as good as or better than listening comprehension. This balanced program will, of course, give appropriate emphasis to oral language and usage, which have an important role in improving reading.

This development of reading comprehension to a high level of proficiency should receive strong emphasis through the grades. As the child progresses through the school years, his acquisition of information depends more and more upon what he reads. It is highly desirable, therefore, that reading comprehension become as good as or better than listening comprehension.

BASIC COMPREHENSION NEEDS

Comprehension in reading involves certain basic needs. These needs have been considered above. They may now be listed in summary form.

Word Meanings. The acquisition of word meanings is fundamental to all comprehension in reading. When word meanings are ample, precise, and rich, and when semantic variations are understood, adequate concepts are available for the pupil to draw upon in the thinking he must do in effective reading. Without satisfactory word meanings, comprehension of either spoken or printed language is impossible. Comprehension of sentences and paragraphs naturally requires an understanding of the words in them.

Thought Units. To achieve perfect conception of the meaning of a complete sentence, it is necessary for the pupil to read by thought units. When a child has acquired the knack of grouping words into meaningful phrases called thought units, he is organizing the material in the only manner which promotes good reading comprehension. Thus, the inability to group material into thought units—which is the trouble with the child who reads one word at a time or groups words inappropriately—is an obstacle to effective sentence comprehension.

Sentence Comprehension. Materials for reading are nearly always in the form of sentences. In addition to understanding the meanings of the separate words and thought units, there must be the ability to understand the relationships between these in the sentence. The child who cannot sense the relationship between the elements within a sentence and give each its proper weight will experience severe difficulties in comprehension.

Paragraph Comprehension. Satisfactory comprehension of the material in a paragraph is possible only when the reader understands the relations between the sentences which make up the paragraph. Without this ability, which is not easily come by, progress in the application of other comprehension skills will almost always be blocked.

Comprehending Larger Units. To grasp the organization of an expository article or a story, the reader must understand the relation between the theme or purpose presented in the introductory paragraphs and the role of the succeeding supporting paragraphs. Without this ability, a reader will be unable to handle satisfactorily the specialized applications of the basic study abilities described in a later chapter.

Role of the Basic Comprehension Abilities. As already noted, the basic comprehension abilities are interdependent. They are all developed as related parts of the sequential instructional program. An understanding of word meanings is essential in all reading. This skill plus knowing how to group words into thought units are necessary components of sentence comprehension. Sensing the relation between sentences necessary for paragraph comprehension is possible only when word meanings are adequate, words are organized into thought units, and sentences are comprehended. Finally, all the foregoing are needed to grasp the organization of an expository article or to grasp the story sense in larger units.

DIAGNOSIS AND TREATMENT OF COMPREHENSION DIFFICULTIES

As explained in earlier chapters, treatment of reading difficulties must be based upon diagnostic findings. That is, remedial instruction should aim to overcome whatever individual deficiencies have been discovered by the diagnosis. We have just concluded our discussion of comprehension. Our next problem is to describe and explain the techniques for discovering these needs and the proper instructional procedures for treating them. As for the needs which fall under comprehension, we shall take them up in the order presented above: words, thought units, sentences, paragraphs, and larger units.

A preliminary step in any analysis of comprehension abilities is to determine the level at which a child can read with satisfactory comprehension. When this level is significantly lower than his learning capacity, an analysis is undertaken to discover the reasons for this retardation. One aspect of this analysis concerns itself with deficiencies in comprehension. Informal and formal procedures for determining levels of reading ability have been discussed in an earlier chapter. Techniques for diagnosing what is wrong when comprehension is inadequate and what the methods of remedial treatment should be are explained below.

WORD MEANINGS

Basically, the meanings of words are derived from experience. The preciseness of these meanings and of the accompanying concepts is reflected in the verbal fluency employed in communication. An important first step in evaluating word meanings, therefore, is to check on the breadth of a child's experiences, how many words he knows, and his verbal fluency in use of words.

Evaluation of Background of Experience

The development of word meanings or concepts from experience is of high importance at all stages of a child's life from the pre-school period right through the grades and later. Ideally, these life experiences should be rich, real, and varied. Both formal and informal methods for evaluating a child's experience are available.

Formal techniques usually consist of inventories of a pupil's interests and activities. Illustrative inventories are given in Dolch (55, pp. 121-123; 52, pp. 444-446) and Witty and Kopel (190, pp. 185-188; 317-339). These inventories yield information on home environment, play, work, and social activities outside school, association with other children and with adults, excursions to nearby places and travel to other places farther away, church and club activities, possessions and the ways they are used, entertainment, intellectual activities such as special classes and reading, and participation in sports.

Informal evaluation of experience by the teacher is possible. To do this, there must be harmonious and sympathetic relations between teacher and pupil so that the child will be willing to talk freely about himself with complete frankness. Any teacher can devise an outline guide for getting relevant information about a pupil's experience along the lines cited above. A sample outline, adapted largely from Witty and Kopel (190), is given below. This can be modified or expanded to fit a particular case.

SAMPLE INVENTORY OF EXPERIENCES

NAME _____ AGE IN YEARS _____ MONTHS _____

SCHOOL GRADE _____ TEACHER _____ DATE _____

1. *Home Environment:*

    a. What things do you do with your father or mother?...............
    b. Names and ages of brothers and sisters.........................
    c. What things do you do with them?...............................
    d. Do you have parties at home?...................................
    e. Do you have a radio at home?........ and a television set?........
    f. Tools and toys at home...
    g. What are your regular duties at home?..........................
    h. Do you have a weekly allowance?................................
    i. What pets do you have?...
    j. What things do you like best about your home life?.............

2. *Activities Outside School:*

    a. What do you do:
        (1) After school?...
        (2) In the evening?...
        (3) On Saturday and Sunday?...................................
        (4) On vacations?...
    b. Do you work for pay?...
    c. How do you spend your money?...................................
    d. What are the names of your close friends?......................
    e. What do you do with your friends?..............................
    f. What kinds of clubs or youth groups do you belong to and what do you do there?..

3. *Recreational Activities:*

    a. How often do you go to the movies?.............................
    b. What movies do you like best?..................................
    c. What games do you play with neighborhood children?.............
    d. Do you go to:
        (1) Ball games? ....
        (2) Concerts? ....
        (3) Circuses? ....
        (4) Picnics? ....
        (5) Amusement parks? ....
    e. What do you like best, to play with other boys and girls or by yourself? ....
    f. What hobbies or collections do you have?.......................

SAMPLE INVENTORY OF EXPERIENCES (cont.)

4. *Excursions and Travel:*
   - *a.* Have you been to:
     - (1) A museum? ....
     - (2) A zoo? ....
     - (3) A summer camp? ....
     - (4) A farm?
     - (5) A trip by boat, train or airplane? ....
   - *b.* Have you been:
     - (1) Outside your home town? ....
     - (2) To another state? ....
     - (3) To the seashore? ....
     - (4) On a long vacation trip? ....

5. *Intellectual and Special Activities:*
   - *a.* Have you had any special classes in:
     - (1) Music? ....
     - (2) Dancing? ....
     - (3) Church school? ....
     - (4) Art? ....
   - *b.* What kinds of books or stories do you like to read?.............
   - *c.* How frequently do you get books from the library?.............
   - *d.* What books and magazines are there at home?.................

After collecting information about a child's experience, the teacher must decide how satisfactory that experience is. There are no norms for this. However, the teacher should be able to estimate whether a child has had only a meager background of experience, a fair amount, or a very rich experience. Particularly, she should be able to spot those areas in which experience is either lacking or skimpy. When this has been found out, the next problem is to remedy the situation to the extent permitted by the school program.

A Twofold Problem

Providing experience for school children poses a twofold problem. First, there is the problem of developing a broader background of experience which will build the habits and attitudes that come from such experiences. The proper word labels associated with these experiences are acquired. Once the child has formed these habits and attitudes, he pays attention to the words used by other people when they talk or write about their experiences. In general, all this is the outcome of a rich and broad curriculum.

The second problem is much less general. It is the business of enlarging the background of concepts and the vocabulary specific to a section of some unit, or topic or story which the pupils are going to read. The teacher makes sure in advance that each child has the vocabulary and concepts that the author has assumed they have. These preliminary talks and the sharing of experiences lets the teacher know about deficiencies a child may have. She then develops the vocabulary and concepts needed for whatever the specific reading task is going to be about. This is essential to any good instruction, remedial or otherwise. Techniques for providing such experience are described below.

Providing Experiences

An important problem for the school is to provide, as far as possible, a background of normal experiences where this is lacking. This will involve experience with such things as toys, tools, and equipment; with social activities including group participation of many kinds; and with places such as parks, factories, zoos, farms, and the city hall. The extension and enrichment of experience is, of course, valuable at all grade levels and for all pupils, irrespective of previous experience. Repetition of an experience with proper guidance can often be much more valuable educationally than was the initial unguided exposure.

In the present context, the purpose of providing experience is to develop a knowledge of words and concepts which can be employed to advantage in reading. To be of educational value, experience should provide new meaningful words and concepts, and clarify word meanings and concepts already possessed by the child. That is to say, the experience should provide words which can be employed properly in the pupil's thinking and talking. When this is achieved, the child will be better prepared to carry out meaningful reading.

In order to add to the store of meaningful concepts, experiences must extend and enrich knowledge, they must be with real things so that correct associations and meanings are achieved, and they must be varied. Two general types of experience may be employed to develop word meanings: direct or firsthand experiences, and secondhand or vicarious experiences. And the words which symbolize these experiences must be used in discussion and writing.

Firsthand Experiences

Firsthand experiences, which involve direct contact with situations, people, objects, and institutions, are most effective. Ordinarily, these contacts will be in the immediate environment but some may be the result of visits to summer camps, vacation trips with parents, or excursions and other special trips.

An important group of firsthand experiences involves well-planned trips to such an event as a concert planned for children, or to such places as a fire station, a zoo, an art museum or museum of natural history, a farm, a broadcasting station, a manufacturing plant, and an airport. Harrison (95) outlines a number of excursions which have been found profitable with younger children. She also lists references (p. 47) containing suggestions for firsthand experiences.

Firsthand social experiences involving interaction between children in groups develop concepts useful for interpreting a variety of content in reading materials. Such experiences may consist of social activities in the school or at a well-organized playground, and in supervised church activities.

Another form of firsthand experience is provided by a variety of construction activities and by demonstrations and laboratory work in the school. Concepts that may be developed in these ways include what a bird needs for building a nest, if, for example the bird is a wren which will move into some man-made houses but not others, the influence of sunlight on plant growth, and the nature of a vacuum.

Vicarious Experiences

It is not feasible, and frequently not possible, to develop word meanings by direct experience alone. Much worthwhile experience can be provided pupils through secondary media. Among these are visual and auditory aids such as pictures, charts, maps, models, slides, filmstrips, motion pictures, recordings, and radio and television programs. Another group of vicarious experiences are provided by stories told or read by the teacher and pupils, and educational talks by outsiders.

Planning and Discussion

In general, any form of direct or vicarious experience should constitute an activity within a larger unit of study in connection with learning situations. And to achieve maximum profit from an experience, careful planning is necessary. As noted by Dolch (55), experience alone does not educate. Without proper guidance, a child may go to a museum, a concert, or a botanical garden, and return without any meaningful and usable words which he can employ to think with and talk with.

Since the meanings a child achieves in reading are determined by the nature and clearness of his concepts, these experiences should yield as varied and accurate meanings as possible. Acquiring experiences should be a purposeful activity. Children should be thoroughly prepared beforehand so that they may pay attention to and understand as many of its features as possible. They should know what to look for and what questions they would like to have answered.

If experiences are to be profitable, the child must think about them, seek out their meaning and make use of them in subsequent speaking, listening, and reading. To provide maximum motivation toward this end, there must be an opportunity both before and after participating in an experience, for discussion under teacher guidance. During this exchange of ideas and the answering of questions, there will be opportunity to define purposes, extend information, clear up misconceptions, and clarify and enrich meanings. This preparation for experience and the discussion following it, tends to be highly profitable whatever the nature of the experience, whether it is a story read by the teacher, an educational movie, a laboratory experiment, or an excursion. Development of word meanings and concepts is also promoted by the exchange of experiences in informal discussion. In all this planning and discussion, children should be encouraged to seek meaning in everything they encounter and to ask for additional explanations and further clarification of whatever they do not understand.

Growth in word meanings comes with usage. Having acquired new "labels" or words through experience, opportunity should be provided for prompt use of the new vocabulary in speaking, listening, writing, and reading.

Applications in Remedial Instruction

Reading disability cases are frequently deficient in those experiences which furnish a sufficient supply of word meanings to insure reading with understanding. The areas where these deficiencies exist are identified through the procedures outlined above. The role of the remedial teacher is to provide the needed experiences as far as possible. The procedures to be employed are essentially the same as in any good instructional program. The only difference is that the instruction is more highly individualized. It aims to fit the needs of the particular child. Part of the time the teacher will be concerned with a single child. At other times she may be dealing with a small group of children who have similar deficiencies. Furnishing the desired experiences will, of course, be integrated with other aspects of a well-coordinated program of remedial instruction.

The remedial teacher will be concerned primarily with the second part of the twofold problem of providing needed experiences as described earlier, that is, furnishing the words and concepts adequate for reading with understanding a specific topic or story. Too frequently this is overlooked by the remedial teacher. The habits and attitudes of attending to vocabulary and of demanding meaning must be transferred to the specific story or topic to be read. The key words and concepts are listed by the teacher. Through explanations, illustrations, and discussion, the teacher makes sure that these are understood by the child so that the material in the story can be comprehended satisfactorily. Illustrative lessons of this kind are given in the workbooks which accompany basic readers such as Bond and Cuddy or Bond, Dorsey, Cuddy and Wise (21), Russell and McCullough or Russell and Wulfing or Ousley (146), and Betts and Welch (11).

Evaluation of Word Knowledge

The vocabulary tests in most standardized silent reading tests such as the *Gates Reading Survey* may not yield a true measure of word meanings because of the child's inability to read, i.e., identify, those words. In an initial determination of vocabulary knowledge, word-meaning tests should be given orally. This can be achieved by use of such tests as the vocabulary part of the *Durrell-Sullivan Reading Capacity Test,* the vocabulary test in the *Gates Reading Diagnostic Tests,* and by giving orally the vocabulary test in the *Gates Reading Survey* or in other comparable tests. Such tests provide a grade level of vocabulary knowledge.

In the reading situation, an important skill is to grasp the meaning of a word in context. This ability may be checked by a variety of informal tests. Samples of such tests are given by Durrell (56, p. 30); by Strang, McCullough, and Traxler (161, p. 300); and the *Iowa Elementary Teachers Handbook, Volume II, Reading* (108, p. 163). A greater variety of informal vocabulary test items is found in many of the workbooks that accompany basic reader series.

The definition matching test is one favorite type. Five or six of the more difficult words in the passage that is being studied are lined up in one column and the definitions in a second column. The definitions should fit the meaning in the context from which the words are taken and should consist of words understood by the child. (This latter requirement holds for all types of vocabulary test items.) The word to be defined is connected with its definition by a straight line. A more satisfactory variation of matching test is illustrated below. (Since some children can do the exercises but cannot read the directions, the teacher should read the directions aloud and demonstrate how the exercise is to be done.)

Directions: Find in the right-hand column the meaning of each numbered word at the left. Then write the letter in front of the meaning in the space in front of the numbered word.

_____ 1. Shutter	*a.*	a group of buildings where people live
_____ 2. Beaver	*b.*	to lose something
_____ 3. Shoulder	*c.*	part of a body where arm is attached
_____ 4. Settlement	*d.*	a kind of tree
_____ 5. Trade	*e.*	a soft furred wild animal
	f.	shivering
	g.	a movable cover for a window
	h.	an opening in the forest
	i.	to exchange goods
	j.	a small hill

In this type of test, it is best to have more definitions than words to be defined. Otherwise the child makes two errors at a time.

The multiple choice type of question is also useful and easy to construct. For example:

Directions: Read the question and draw a line under the word which is the right answer:

1. What does <u>shutter</u> mean?   much shaking   window-cover
   changing position   large rooster

2. What does <u>beaver</u> mean?   insect   dog   animal   wood

Other types of test items to check word meanings in context follow:

1. Jack planted <u>the shoots</u> in his garden: arrows   tiny plants
   seeds

2. The ship was sailing towards <u>the rising sun:</u>   westward   eastward
   northward

The various checks on word meanings in context are used most profitably during the day-to-day instruction both as a check on comprehension and as teaching devices to promote development of word meanings. The most opportune time to clarify word meanings is in the context where the difficulty occurs.

TECHNIQUES FOR DEVELOPING WORD MEANINGS

Word meanings and the concepts tied in with these meanings are acquired in a variety of ways. As already noted, a child must be able to recognize or identify a word before he can sense its meaning. Although it is discussed separately, it must be kept in mind that development of word recognition and of word meanings are co-ordinated in the instructional program. As emphasized above, word meanings are based primarily either upon firsthand or vicarious experiences at all age levels. Some supplementary techniques for developing word meanings will now be taken up.

Use of Context Clues

The meaning of a new word can frequently be derived from the context in which it occurs. To do this, the child will need to comprehend the rest of the words in the sentence or passage. Many children with reading disability make little or no use of context in trying to discover the meanings of strange words. Such a child should be given practice in "guessing" the meaning of unknown words as they occur in context. He should be taught to read the rest of the sentence or passage and then look back and try to decide what the unknown word probably means. For instance note the sentence:

The Indians in the canoe were from a <u>reservation,</u> the land set aside for Indians who still lived in the northern part of the state.

The word *reservation* acquires meaning from the context which follows in the rest of the sentence. Take another example:

Although Mary was surprised when Jack <u>glared</u> at her, she was not disturbed by his <u>angry look.</u>

If such a sentence is part of a story, other sentences may amplify and clarify the meaning. Although some guesses may be wrong, such training usually brings considerable skill in deriving meaning from context.

Context clues to word meanings frequently come from the author's definitions. Such a definition may be the explanation given in the rest of the sentence, or it may come from another word or phrase in the sentence. Sometimes it is in a separate sentence. A few examples follow:

1. When Mother did not like the <u>retort</u> Harry made, she asked him to <u>answer</u> her more politely.
2. The boys were delighted with the summer <u>cruise</u>—<u>a voyage by steamship</u> on the Great Lakes.
3. Just after we got on the train the <u>conductor</u> gave the engineer the signal to start. In addition to <u>directing the trainmen,</u> the conductor also <u>collects the passengers' tickets.</u>

Another difficulty which disabled readers have is in choosing the correct meaning of a word that has several meanings. For instance, the correct meaning of *paid* in the following sentence depends on the context of the complete sentence: "Jack paid dearly for his mistake." In fact, the correct meaning for such words is sensed *only* in terms of the context. Many and varied examples of exercises to train pupils in use of context clues as aids to working out word meanings are given in workbooks such as those mentioned above.

Wide Reading and Context Clues

The extension and enrichment of word meanings are aided by wide reading of interesting and relatively easy materials. For such reading, not more than one unfamiliar word should appear in 100 to 200 running words. Ordinarily each new book, story, or article that is read will introduce new words to the reader and provide him with generous repetitions of words previously encountered. The use of old words in a variety of contexts broadens and clarifies their meanings. The more important new words will be met with sufficiently often to acquire more and more meaning. It is unrealistic to expect that a clear meaning for every new word encountered will be learned right away. But of course this does not mean that unfamiliar words should be ignored. It is particularly important that the reader should pay attention to whatever unfamiliar words he meets in context. Eventually, many of these words will become commonplace and meaningful. Motivation is maintained by guiding children to material which catches their interest and is pitched at just the proper level of difficulty so that the context will yield a maximum amount of intelligible clues to the meaning of any new words.

In any wide reading program, the proper use of clues from their meaningful contexts is essential if the concepts or meanings of the new words encountered are to be learned satisfactorily. The remedial teacher, therefore, will need to test the child's skill in the use of context clues and to give whatever instruction is necessary, employing the methods described above. For best results, this checking and training in the use of clues must be a continuing program with each disabled reader since this skill is ordinarily slow in developing.

Suggestions for guidance in the use of context in developing word meanings are given by McCullough (126) and Artley (3). For instance, a word may be defined in a sentence, or it may be recognized as a synonym, or it may sum up the particulars of a situation. Sometimes a meaning clue may come from familiar idioms and sayings. Or it may come from the mood or feeling tone reflected in the context.

It is common practice to explain the meanings of new words to a child by using words he already knows. This happens in oral communication, in a context of printed material, and in dictionaries. As the child progresses through school, this technique is employed more and more. Dolch (55) outlines five ways of giving word meanings with words only. The first four of these, (1) synonym or word substitute, (2) classification, (3) pointing out differences, and (4) pointing out similarities, are classified as minimum methods which do not exhaust all available resources. Dolch emphasizes that the school should go as far as possible beyond this minimum with a fifth technique which he calls *the method of many associations*. This is a method that places a desirable stress upon enriching the meaning of a word by presenting to the child anything that can be told about the word, anything he can read about it, plus any other associations that can be built up through reference to direct and vicarious experiences. The more adequately this can be done, the greater will be the depth and breadth of word meaning acquired.

It must be emphasized that the acquisition of verbal meanings alone is not enough. In any program for developing word meanings through reading, the goal should be to go beyond mere verbal meanings. As pointed out by Dolch (55), one way to do this is to appeal to realistically conceived imagination. That is, if the child is aided in exercising his imagination to extend his verbal understanding of words to concrete pictures, instead of being satisfied with a synonym, he will try to recall some of the store of sensory impressions, emotional reactions, ideas, and events suggested by each word.

This is well illustrated by the proper interpretation of descriptive words, figures of speech, and symbolic expressions. The following examples, adapted from Bond, Dorsey, Cuddy and Wise's *Fun to Do Books* (21), suggest ways for developing these skills:

1. Which of the following makes a <u>tinkling sound?</u>   (*a*) an old man's voice   (*b*) a tiny bell   (*c*) an automobile horn

2. What is meant by: As John looked at his new bicycle his eyes were <u>glowing like coals?</u>   (*a*) they were bright   (*b*) they were on fire

3. What is meant by: <u>One should never look a gift horse in the mouth?</u>
(*a*) one must not look in a horse's mouth   (*b*) one should not ask questions about gifts

Many other samples may be found in the teacher's edition of the various *Fun to Do Books* cited above. Appropriate items for this sort of training may also be derived from most reading materials. When using such items, many relevant associations can be brought in by discussing the items and the correct answers with the children. All these exercises provide opportunities to develop further the attitude of demanding that meanings be found in everything read. Another approach is to ask the child to tell everything a word, a phrase, or a symbolic expression makes him think of. Skill in getting a child to extend meanings from mere words to reality through using his imagination may develop slowly in the case of some children. However, once a child gets the knack of doing this, the wide reading program will pay big dividends in developing his understanding of what words mean.

Teaching What Words Mean

The teaching of word meanings is valuable only when it is done properly. We have emphasized right along that direct, systematic, well-planned drill on words in context increases knowledge of vocabulary but that teaching of words in isolation is usually wasteful and ineffective. The correct meaning of a word very frequently depends upon the context in which it occurs. Many times, familiar words are used in an unfamiliar sense. Teaching these new meanings of old words and the relation of the particular meaning to context is a considerable part of vocabulary training. (The teaching of word meanings for technical terms found in the content fields is a topic to be taken up in a later chapter.)

In the present discussion, the authors are defending the view that word study can be profitable in developing meanings only to the degree that it consists in using each word in various contexts, in associating it with concrete experiences, in giving it a sufficient number of oral and written repetitions in a program of wide reading in a variety of situations. First of all, therefore, word study should deal with new words met in context. Learning a word's meaning will then fulfill the child's immediate need, his present desire to understand some passage. This should be followed by using the word in discussion and in oral and written reports. Finally, he should read a considerable body of material in which the word occurs frequently.

Since many words have several meanings or shades of meaning, the initial contact with a new word in context can provide it with only a limited meaning. To extend and enrich the meaning of a new word, the word should also be presented to the child in a variety of contexts selected to bring out and emphasize different shades of meaning or different meanings. Exercises of this kind may be followed by discussions and other exercises specially designed to point up the different shades of meaning of the word. It is also helpful for the remedial teacher to introduce activities which involve the application of meanings of the word to such concrete situations as demonstration and use of equipment, giving titles to pictures or drawings, and the writing of letters. These concrete activities constitute useful techniques for extending and enriching the meaning of a word through association with doing something that is not strictly limited to talking and reading.

Role of the Basic Sight Vocabulary

As already implied, the child can make little progress in reading without a basic sight vocabulary. This becomes especially important for the retarded reader. The Dolch basic sight vocabulary (52) of 220 service words constitutes about 65 per cent of all the words in the reading material of the primary grades and nearly 60 per cent of those in intermediate grades. With normal progress, the child will have mastered these 220 service words during his third grade in school. Many retarded readers are particularly deficient in recognizing and understanding the proper use of these words. When recognition of these words is being taught, emphasis should be placed upon developing an understanding of their meaning when used in context. One way to do this is to organize exercises like the following:

Directions: Read the sentence on the left and then underline the word at the right that gives the idea or meaning of the word underlined in the sentence.

1. He sat under the tree.   (*a*) when   (*b*) where   (*c*) how   (*d*) why
2. He left on July 6.   (*a*) when   (*b*) where   (*c*) how   (*d*) why
3. He ran because he was late.   (*a*) when   (*b*) where   (*c*) how   (*d*) why
4. Jack has a brown coat.   (*a*) color   (*b*) wood   (*c*) cloth   (*d*) straw
5. Ann has the right box.   (*a*) odd   (*b*) wooden   (*c*) correct   (*d*) small

The meanings of some of these service words can be taught best in terms of usage in context rather than a defining word. For instance:

1. When John and Bill reached home, Mother gave them some cookies.

Children are taught that *them* means the persons, animals or things talked or written about.

A variety of sentences to illustrate this meaning should be presented to the child. Similar treatment should be employed to teach the meanings of such words as *they, could,* and *what.*

Many of the basic sight words are particularly difficult for retarded readers to learn and retain. It is a cardinal principle that those words are remembered best which carry the most meaning. This emphasizes the need for developing as much meaning as possible for the words in the basic vocabulary (or for any other words for that matter). Without teacher guidance, such words as *where, their, by, myself, which,* and the like are not particularly meaningful for many children.

Systematic Study of Words

Direct, systematic, well-organized drill on words has value in developing word meanings when this drill is on words in context or is related to the usage of words in context. When teacher guidance produces sufficient motivation to lead to a general interest in words, the teacher will find it profitable to devote some study to the meanings suggested by common prefixes, suffixes, and word roots, and to synonyms and antonyms. This approach to word study should be used when a word that lends itself to analysis is met in context. A few examples will illustrate:

1. The sailors went aboard the ship (prefix and word root).
2. He has a kingly appearance (word root and suffix).
3. The army was undefeated (prefix, root, suffix).

In addition to identifying the root word and prefix or suffix with their meanings, the possibility of making other words by adding other prefixes or suffixes may be explored at appropriate times. The meanings of the more common word roots, prefixes, and suffixes may be worked out in this manner. This instruction in the use of structural aids to meaning should accompany and be co-ordinated with use of structural aids to word recognition in the sequential reading program. That is, it should be introduced at the appropriate place and taught with structural analysis in word recognition. Training for identifying and understanding word roots, prefixes, and suffixes can be done by the following types of exercises:

1. Draw a line under the root word in each of the following and tell what the root word means:
   worker   untie   kindly
2. Draw a line under the prefix in each of the following and tell how the prefix changes the meaning of the root word:
   unlike   return   displace
3. Draw a line under the suffix in each of the following and tell how the suffix changes the meaning of the root word:
   slowly   worker   doubtful

After roots, prefixes, and suffixes have been identified, their uses in developing meanings should be brought out through discussion and supplementary exercises. One way of doing this is to rewrite sentences. The pupil is given a sentence containing words with prefixes. He is asked to identify the word with a prefix and then told to rewrite the sentence with a new word or phrase that will replace it without changing the meaning of the sentence. Example:

Your bicycle is <u>unlike</u> mine.
Your bicycle is <u>different from</u> mine.

In a similar way, the exploring of synonyms (words of like meaning) and antonyms (opposites) of words met in context enriches the meaning of words. Supplementary exercises like the following may be used:

1. Underline the word that means the same as <u>beautiful</u>:
   pale   pretty   lonely   thoughtful
2. Underline the word that means the opposite of <u>noisy</u>:
   boastful   tiny   quiet   rosy

A great variety of exercises for developing word knowledge along the lines discussed above can be found in Russell and Karp (145), Harris (94), Cole (37), Durrell (56), and Strang, McCullough and Traxler (161), as well as in the workbooks which accompany basic readers.

Use of the Dictionary

Proper use of a good dictionary can be an important aid in developing word meanings. Few children acquire the dictionary habit or know the wealth of fascinating information that can be found in a dictionary. Development of the dictionary habit depends upon a well-organized program of instruction carried out by a skilled and enthusiastic teacher. No child will enjoy using a dictionary to get word meanings until he has become skillful in finding a desired word quickly. Exercises for developing and testing this skill are given in Durrell (56), McKee (127), Harris (94), and in many workbook materials. After locating a word, the child must know how to select from the several meanings listed the one that fits the context from which the word came. This implies that the child must have a grasp of the meaning of the rest of the sentence or paragraph in which the unknown word occurs. Considerable training is required to develop skill in choosing correct dictionary meanings. Exercises found in such workbooks as those cited above are easily constructed. Another example follows:

Directions: Several numbered definitions are given for the word in heavy black type. Read the word and its definitions. Next read the sentences below the definitions. Write the number of the definition in front of the sentence in which the meaning of the word is used.

grate (1) grind off in small pieces   (2) rub with a harsh sound   (3) have an annoying or unpleasant effect

   _____ Please <u>grate</u> the cheese to put on the salad.
   _____ Mary's manners always <u>grate</u> on me.

In addition to developing skill in use of the dictionary for acquiring word meanings, this type of exercise provides further training in deriving meanings from context clues and in noting different meanings for the same word.

Experience with synonyms and antonyms enriches word meanings when the words dealt with are in meaningful context. Some dictionaries for children give synonyms for certain words but no antonyms. Ordinarily, exercises like those given above or like those below are employed for choosing words of like or opposite meanings.

Directions (synonyms): Read each sentence and note the underlined word in it. Select from the list of words below the sentences the word that means the same or nearly the same as the underlined word. Write the word selected on the line after the sentence.

Father had no reason to doubt Jim. _____

The automobile repair man needs many implements. _____

    trucks   tools   avoid   mistrust

Exercises for antonyms are constructed in a similar way. Here the child is asked to find the word that means the opposite or nearly the opposite.

General Statement

The acquisition of word meanings begins early and continues through school and beyond. Without a minimum meaning vocabulary, the child will not be able to think clearly, make satisfactory progress in learning to read, or carry on intelligible oral communication. As noted by Cole (37), there is no easy road to the acquisition of word meanings. She favors having children get intensive drill on words that have been isolated rather than having them lean on context for meanings. This drill involves analysis, study, use, and occasional review of the particular word. The stand of this book emphasizes an intermediate position. Drill on word meanings is employed but this drill is always to be associated with the use of the word in context. Furthermore, there are a number of approaches such as have been described above which should be employed in developing word meanings. It is important that all these approaches be integrated in the developmental program of vocabulary training. Each approach is to be co-ordinated and given proper emphasis in terms of the needs of the individual child. Building the habit of noticing new words, especially expressive words, noting an author's way of defining his words, appreciating how sensory words are employed, watching the semantic variations of words and the like are all important outcomes. It is by means of such habits as these that a child's vocabulary expands and clarifies.

SENTENCE COMPREHENSION

In addition to knowing the meaning of words, there are many other skills needed for satisfactorily understanding sentences. These include the grasping of relations between words and groups of words, reading by thought units, proper interpreting of punctuation, comprehending figures of speech and symbolic expressions. Retarded readers tend to be deficient in one or several of these skills.

Diagnosis and Remediation

Grade level in sentence comprehension is readily measured by means of standardized tests. Many silent reading tests include sections on sentence comprehension. Examples are: *The Gates Primary Reading Tests,* the Bond-Clymer-Hoyt *Developmental Reading Tests, Chicago Reading Tests* by Engelhart and Thurstone, and the elementary form of *Iowa Silent Reading Test.* (See Appendix I for comprehensive list of reading tests.)

Having ascertained the grade level for sentence comprehension, the next step is to determine to what degree a child has difficulty with the special skills involved in comprehending sentences. Ability to understand the relation between various parts of a sentence may be termed *sentence sense.* Various types of exercises may be employed both for diagnosing lack of sentence comprehension and for training in what may be called *sentence sense* or the ability to understand the relation between various parts of a sentence. The following are a few examples:

Directions: Read each sentence. Then decide whether the underlined part tells when, why, how, what, or where. Draw a line under the right one of the words which follow the sentence.

1. The large farm belongs to father.   when   why   how   what where

2. Because John was ill, he did not go to school.   when   why   how what   where

3. Uncle John went into the big barn.   when   why   how   what where

4. All the children came on the run.   when   why   how   what where

5. Mary's train will arrive at six o'clock.   when   why   how what   where

A variation from the above is to find and copy the word or words that answer the question, "who" or "where." After informing the pupil that the sentences answer the questions "who" and "where," he is directed to write below the sentences the word or words that answer the question:

1. The boy went to the blackboard to write the word.
2. From school to the park is only one-half mile, explained the teacher.

	Words that tell	
Sentence Number	Who?	Where?
1	___	___
2	___	___

The responses may be made by having the child draw a line under the words that answer the question, "where," etc.

In a similar manner, items may be constructed that answer the questions "when" and "what," or "why" and "how." The exercises may be varied by using sentences to answer other combinations of questions as "who" and "why." The sentences may be taken directly from books or made up from words in the child's reading vocabulary. Sample items may be found in Russell and Karp (145) and in such workbooks as those listed above.

The remedial teacher will need some sort of criterion to use in deciding whether a child is deficient in sentence sense. There is no standardized procedure that will serve as such a criterion. The following may be employed as a rough standard. If a child is able to recognize and understand all the words in a sentence, but is unable to identify the parts that answer the questions "who," or "where," or "why," etc., he should receive appropriate remedial instruction. It is well to begin with relatively easy sentences and gradually work up to reading material at what is in other respects the instructional level of the child.

Thought Units

It has already been noted that reading by thought units promotes comprehension of sentences. Many disabled readers are either word-by-word readers or they tend to group words inappropriately so that clear comprehension of the sentence as a whole is impossible. At the start of instruction in reading, the child must recognize each word separately. In the beginning, he is required by his immaturity to study each word closely in order to identify it at all, so there is little likelihood that he will be able to group several together for recognition as a thought unit. However, as the child becomes more adept at word identification and as he builds a stock of words that he can recognize at sight, he is able to group some together.

The first grouping by thought units rather than by individual words is in two-word combinations, as: "the cat"; "Daddy said"; or "to ride." Such grouping of words takes place only after the child is very familiar with each of the words and only when they are set off together by the typography. For example, in the sentence "Daddy said, 'We can stop,'" the punctuation makes the grouping of "Daddy said" a natural and easy thing to do. Later, at the primer level, when two-line sentences begin to appear, additional help is given to the child in order for him to learn to read in thought units. A sentence would be printed in a way such as the following:

> Judy said, "Put the duck
> in the water."

The child would almost be forced, by the format, to read by thought units. Still later, he is expected to be able to analyze a sentence into thought units rapidly as he progresses along the line of print. This is a mature sort of reading that must be predicated on recognizing the words and phrases involved at sight.

Inability to read in thought units can be diagnosed in several ways. The simplest method is to listen to the child read easy material orally. If he reads in a word-by-word manner or if he clusters words in meaningless groups, he is probably ineffective in recognizing thought units in his silent reading and he is certainly not reading by thought units orally. Another method of diagnosing this ability, is to flash phrases before the child for recognition. If he reads the phrases significantly less well than does the usual child of equal general reading ability, it is safe to assume that he has limited ability in recognizing thought units in isolation. It is then probable that he cannot locate and recognize thought units in a sentence. Such a test does not give any indication of the child's ability to analyze sentences into thought units. Therefore, both oral and flash appraisals should be made.

There are techniques for appraising eye movements in silent reading which also give evidence that is useful in diagnosing the ability of a child to read in thought units. Pictures of eye movements, such as those made by the Ophthalmograph, have been used. However, it is questionable whether any additional information obtained by using this device is worth the expense involved. In all probability, a pocket mirror would give almost as much information with practically no expense. If a pocket mirror is placed on the table between the child and the examiner the child's eye movements can be observed as he reads. The number of fixations he makes while reading each line of print can be observed and recorded. The examiner will not be able to tell whether the fixations the child makes are reasonable stops, i.e., whether a stop is made for each thought unit, but he can tell whether or not the number of fixations is the same or more than the number of thought units. Gates and Cason (84a), have shown that the oral reading diagnosis and the flash presentation of phrases are among the most practical and accurate appraisals of ability to read by thought units.

Remedial methods for the child who has been diagnosed as disabled in reading thought units must be based on the premise that ultimately he will have to learn to recognize meaningful groups of words as he silently reads consecutive printed matter. He will be reading sentences, not isolated thought units. Skill in reading by groups of words is dependent in part upon the child's ability to analyze the sentences into reasonable units. It is also necessary for him to encompass the group of words he separates as a single idea. The remedial work must teach the child to rapidly recognize thought units of several words and also to spot such groups of words in the sentences he reads. Many children are able to recognize isolated thought units flashed before them, but still they are incapable of reading silently or orally by thought units. Since they cannot readily divide a sentence into proper clusters of words, they must read each word separately.

Remedial instruction designed to enable a child to read in thought units should be done in contextual settings or the phrases learned in isolation should be immediately read in complete sentences. The following exercises will give the child instruction and experience in reading by thought units:

1. Whenever the teacher introduces new words in a selection, it is desirable to have them read in the phrases in which the child will see them.

2. After the selection has been read, the child can reread to locate certain expressive phrases as suggested by the teacher.

3. Preparing material to read orally provides excellent experience in reading by thought units.

4. Multiple-choice exercises in which phrases are used as answers and distractors may be used.

   a. Draw line under the correct phrase to complete the sentence.

                 over the fence.
     (1) The ball sailed down the hole.
                 under the water.

                 flew away.
     (2) The dog talked softly.
                 ran fast.

5. Rapidly finding phrases on given pages to answer specific questions.

   a. On the page I tell you, find the phrases that answer the following questions:

Question	*Phrase*
(1) Where was the rooster?	(near the barn)
(2) What did John see?	(a pink light)
(3) Who was happy?	(the white bear)
(4) When did the boys swim?	(one summer day)

6. Mark off the thought units in the following sentences and tell the *who,* or *what, did what, where, why* questions they answer.

   a. The large truck went slowly down the street.
   b. Billy and Frank quickly made a snow fort to hide behind.

7. Draw a line from the phrase to the word that has a similar meaning.

a big meal	stroke
to rub softly	feast
away from everybody	chop
to cut down	alone

8. Locate these phrases in your book on the page I give, and tell what they mean.

her grandson's father	with a splash
answer the knock	cry for help
bright as stars	pulls us out
break the horse	fine fishing country
white as snow	gift of sight

9. On the pages I tell you, find a phrase that makes you:

hear something	(the screaming gulls)
feel something	(the cool breeze)
see something	(colored autumn leaves)
smell something	(sweet-scented flowers)
taste something	(a sour apple)

10. The use of rapid exposure techniques, such as the tachistoscope described in the next chapter, will aid in teaching children to recognize a phrase or thought unit at one eye fixation. For group work, the Minneapolis North High School Reading Committee found that an opaque projector can be used as a tachistoscope. A piece of cardboard is placed before the lens and moved up and down to expose thought units for about one-half a second. The phrases for this work should be in the form of sentences, such as the following:

A brown beaver	at the bottom
was at work	of the pond
near the island	He swam
He was making	under the water
a tunnel	again and again

11. Sentences may be separated into thought units to be read by the children, as:

The old man	with the angry face	was happy now.
He had found	the one thing	he liked.

Sentence Structure

The inability of retarded readers to sort out and properly relate the meanings in different parts of a sentence is sometimes complicated by sentence structure. For instance, difficulties may arise when the subject is last, or between two parts of the predicate rather than at the beginning. Informal exercises for diagnosing such difficulties and for remedial instruction are similar to those described above for developing sentence sense. For example, what word answers the question "who" in each of the following sentences? "Hearing the low, rumbling sound again, Jack suddenly remembered something." "Then into the cool water went John."

Authors are not without fault in providing handicaps to sentence comprehension. Too frequently, sentences are excessively long and too complex for clear exposition. Sometimes they are just poorly written.

Pronouns

Sometimes difficulties arise when the thing or person referred to by a pronoun is not readily grasped. Retarded readers have this kind of difficulty more often. The following type of exercise may be used both for informal diagnosis of difficulties and for remedial instruction.

Directions: In the following sentences, the underlined word is used in place of the name of a person or thing already mentioned. Draw a circle around the word or words that tell who or what is meant by the underlined word.

1. After <u>he</u> arrived home from school, Jack shoveled the snow off the walk.
2. As the horses were freed, <u>they</u> galloped across the field.
3. Mary and Jane went to the store after <u>they</u> finished lunch.

Punctuation

Inadequate interpretation of punctuation or ignoring it altogether may also hinder sentence comprehension. Possibly the most common difficulty with punctuation among retarded readers is failure to appreciate the more common uses of the comma, i.e., to separate words and groups of words written as a series in a sentence, to set off an appositive, or set off a parenthetical expression in a sentence. These and other punctuation uses whose knowledge promotes comprehension are listed by McKee (127, p. 87).

Informal procedures must be employed to find out if a child is making proper use of punctuation. For instance, commas properly employed should aid in grouping words into thought units. Therefore, considerable information on the use of commas is gained by having the pupil read sentences aloud. If no use is made of commas to guide inflection and emphasis in phrasing, it is likely that the child has little appreciation of the function of the punctuation marks in what he read. Under these conditions, the child will have difficulty in comprehending the full meaning of a sentence. Test sentences such as the following may be taken from readers and used to illustrate the use of commas.

1. Deer, too, were there.
2. They stood still, heads up, listening.
3. Mary said, "Now we can go home."
4. After dark, when all was quiet, he slowly walked down the street.

A few children will need supervision to recognize that a capital letter is a clue to the beginning of a sentence and that a period or question mark signals the end of a sentence.

Remedial training for use of punctuation to facilitate comprehension will involve at least two things: (1) By discussion, attention of the pupil is directed to the use of punctuation within a sentence to indicate the relation between what has just been read and what follows. (2) The pupil is given ample practice with sentences from the context of his reading. The training should start with relatively simple sentences and gradually progress to more complex ones. In all cases, the sentences should be made up of words the child knows and can pronounce. In general, simple explanations and supervised practice will lead to improvement.

In a similar manner, as the child progresses in his reading, he may need help in the interpretation of semicolons, colons and dashes.

COMPREHENSION OF LONGER UNITS

Frequently, retarded readers are quite unable to understand the meaning of a paragraph. With such children, the tendency is to consider each sentence as a separate unit unrelated to the other sentences in the paragraph. It is possible for a child to read and understand words, thought units, and sentences and yet not comprehend fully the connected material in a paragraph. Similarly, some pupils are unable to sense the relation between paragraphs in stories and expository material of various kinds. Comprehension of paragraphs and development of story sense will be considered in this section. Additional attention will be given these matters in a later chapter on specific reading defects.

Paragraph Comprehension

Obviously, comprehension of a paragraph requires an understanding of the relations between sentences in that paragraph. Many readers retarded in all types of comprehension need guidance in identifying the topical sentence containing the key idea and in interpreting its relation to explanatory or amplifying sentences.

The evaluation of paragraph comprehension and remedial instruction is best accomplished by informal procedures. The same type of exercise may be used for both diagnosis and remedial work. Illustrative exercises may be found in Russell and Karp (145); McKee (127); Strang, McCullough, and Traxler (161); and in such workbooks as those cited above. The following discussion will explain how one may proceed when teaching paragraph comprehension to children.

To develop skill in finding the topical sentence which presents the key idea in a paragraph, the child is given illustrations and explanations. It is also pointed out that the topical sentence may be the first or the second sentence, or it may be a summary sentence at the end. After the examples and explanations, the child is asked to find and underline the topical sentence in new paragraphs. In addition to finding the topical sentence, the pupil should receive guidance in understanding how the other sentences in the paragraph develop the idea presented in the topical sentence: as by presenting details, by emphasizing importance, by explanations, by contrast, and by repetition of the same idea in other words. One technique of doing this is to number the sentences in a paragraph. Then through questions and analysis, bring out the role of each sentence in relation to the others.

A well-written paragraph is concerned with one central idea. Training to grasp this idea may be furthered in various ways: (1) Present a paragraph followed by three phrases, one of which is the headline or title that best expresses the topic of the material in the paragraph. The child is to indicate which one he considers most appropriate. (2) The child may be asked to write a headline (topic) for the paragraph, or write a sentence expressing the topic. (3) The pupil is given a topical sentence and asked to write a short paragraph by supplying appropriate supporting and amplifying sentences. (4) This time the paragraph is a good one except for one sentence. The child is asked to underline the topical sentence and then to cross out the sentence which does not belong in the paragraph.

Although the comprehension of paragraphs is important in all reading material, it becomes absolutely essential for clear understanding as the child moves into reading the content subjects. Some training for understanding paragraph unity is usually introduced at the time third-grade reading ability is reached. More formal training to develop paragraph comprehension becomes a regular part of reading instruction in the intermediate grade levels.

Larger Units

For full comprehension of longer units, the child should be able to sense the relation between the paragraphs which make up the unit. In good expository writing, as noted earlier, the introductory paragraphs usually state what the piece is about, or what is to be described or explained. The following paragraphs give the details of the explanation in logical sequence. And the final one or two paragraphs ordinarily state the outcomes or conclusion, or they sum up what has been said. In stories, there are ordinarily three parts also. (1) At the beginning are given either the time or the place of the story, or it may be both, and sometimes also the characters involved. (2) This introduction is followed by the main sequence of the story which tells what happens. (3) The final paragraphs usually relate how things turned out.

Teacher guidance aids in the development of the story sense so that children understand better the relation between paragraphs and are able to identify the three main parts of stories and expository materials. In teaching the relation between paragraphs the following may prove helpful: (1) Explain about the three main parts of a story, point out these parts in an illustrative sample, and make out a set of questions on each part. The questions should be organized to show the content that belongs to each part (introduction, what happened, outcome). (2) Teach the children to recognize the transitional expressions that often start a paragraph. Such expressions precede the main idea or topic of the new paragraph. These transitional expressions begin with such phrases as: (*a*) *But something else has happened* . . . (*b*) *Then he turned to John* . . . (*c*) *When this was done, he turned* . . . (3) Give the child practice in writing one sentence to express the main idea in each paragraph of a story or an article. Then have him attempt to link these sentences together in a co-ordinated pattern of thought, using transitional words or phrases where needed.

Comprehension in General

When a child is reading paragraphs and longer selections, his goal is to grasp the essential thread of the thought expressed in the material. The diagnosis of his proficiency in doing this is ordinarily made by presenting him with a selection to be read silently. After the reading is completed, his comprehension is checked by means of a series of questions. These may be asked one at a time by the teacher, or the pupil may do the exercises by himself, as in workbook materials. Or the teacher may ask the child to tell in his own words what the story is about. Although time-consuming, individual oral work of this kind with the retarded reader has distinct advantages. It furnishes direct information concerning his ability to understand and whatever difficulties interfere with his success. In addition, the teacher can provide guidance at appropriate places along the way.

In the remedial instruction, the pupil is first given plenty of experience in grasping the essential thought in relatively short and easy paragraphs. The program is gradually expanded to include longer and more complex paragraphs and then materials consisting of several paragraphs. At each step, materials on an appropriate level of difficulty should be introduced, avoiding any that are too difficult.

The major portion of the training for comprehending longer units and the adaptation of these basic comprehension abilities to meet specific purposes are ordinarily associated with development of the special comprehension abilities. These are considered in a later chapter.

SUMMARY

To read means to read with understanding. To accomplish this, there must be comprehension of words, thought units, sentences, paragraphs, and longer units. Instruction for developing comprehension involves coordination of all these into an integrated sequential program.

Listening comprehension runs ahead of reading comprehension in the early grades. As the mechanics of reading mature, reading comprehension tends to catch up with and soon equals listening comprehension. With still further progress in reading, reading comprehension becomes superior. The aim in reading instruction is to reach this level as soon as possible.

Standardized tests are useful for diagnosing grade level in word, sentence, and paragraph comprehension. For determining specific needs of a retarded reader, informal procedures are best.

Basically, comprehension depends upon a group of concepts or of meanings evolved through experience. Evaluation of a child's background of experience is best achieved through an informal inventory. Deficiencies discovered should be remedied as far as possible in the school. Firsthand experience is best. This should, however, be supplemented by vicarious or secondhand experience. The primary aim of such experiences is to develop concepts tied to meaningful words which can be used by the child in thinking, speaking, listening, writing, and reading.

Instructional techniques for developing word meanings include pointing out the use of context clues, insuring wide reading, encouraging the attitude of demanding understanding of words read and noting authors' definitions, teaching word meanings through systematic study of words and use of the dictionary. To be effective, all word study must be associated with the use of each word in context.

To comprehend sentences, the child must understand the words involved and the relations between these words and groups of words. He must also be able to read by thought units, interpret punctuation, and understand figures of speech, symbolic expressions, and semantic variations. Diagnosis and remedial instruction for sentence comprehension is based largely upon informal exercises such as have been described earlier.

Paragraph comprehension depends upon comprehension of the sentences involved and upon an understanding of the relation between these sentences. Similarly, the comprehension of larger units is based upon paragraph comprehension and an understanding of the relations between the paragraphs involved.

SELECTED READINGS

BOND, Guy L. and WAGNER, Eva B., *Teaching the child to read,* rev. ed. New York: The Macmillan Company, 1950, Chap. 9.

DOLCH, Edward W., *Psychology and teaching of reading,* 2nd ed. Champaign (Ill.): The Garrard Press, 1951, Chap. 9.

GATES, Arthur I., *The improvement of reading,* 3rd ed. New York: The Macmillan Company, 1947, Chaps. 9, 13.

McKEE, Paul, *The teaching of reading in the elementary school.* Boston: Houghton Mifflin Company, 1948, Chap. 3.

RUSSELL, David H., *Children learn to read.* Boston: Ginn and Company, 1949, Chap. 9.

TINKER, Miles A., *Teaching elementary reading.* New York: Appleton-Century-Crofts, Inc., 1952, Chaps. 9, 10.

YOAKAM, Gerald A., *Basal reading instruction.* New York: McGraw-Hill Book Company, Inc., 1955, Chap. 10.

12

CORRECTING
WORD-RECOGNITION
DIFFICULTIES

Skill in word recognition is a fundamental part of the equipment of a capable reader at any level. As the child matures in reading, the materials and methods used in teaching him gradually demand more and more independent word recognition. The child who has failed to establish effective means of identifying and recognizing words for his level of advancement, will be handicapped in all other aspects of reading. On the other hand, the mere ability to recognize and pronounce words is no guarantee that the child has become or will become a good reader, nor does it signify that he is associating meaning with the words.

Word study involves two types of outcomes. The first is expanding meaning vocabulary and teaching the word-recognition techniques so that meanings accompany the identification of the symbols. There is little use in the child's being able to recognize words if those words have no meaning. He must learn to associate meaning with the printed symbols. His meanings must be clear and precise if he is to comprehend the material he is reading. He must also be able to select, among all the meanings of a word, the one that is correct for the particular context in which the word is used. The word *run*, which is used in most pre-primers, has fifty-six different definitions even in a dictionary used in the elementary grades. The child must learn to use context as he recognizes the printed symbols to help him to select the correct meaning. For example, the meaning of *run* can be derived from the content in the statements "He was tired after the long run," and "All will turn out well in the long run." Often the sentence alone will not give the meaning of a word, only the gist of the passage will. For example, the precise meaning of *run* cannot be derived from the sentence "He was out of breath after he made the run." In order to understand the word *run,* the reader must know not only that the boy was playing baseball, but also that he scored rather than chased a fly ball. The development of word meaning has been discussed in the preceding chapter but it is important to teach the word-recognition techniques in such a way that words will be rapidly identified and proper meanings associated with them.

The second outcome of instruction in word study is the development of a set of flexible skills and knowledges that will enable the child to recognize words he already knows and identify new words with speed and understanding. It is with limitations in skillful performance in these achievements that this chapter will concern itself. If the child is unable to work out independently the pronunciation of a word he has not learned to identify or if he is unable to recognize it visually, he will be unable to understand its meaning. Therefore, instruction in effective word identification and recognition is basic to the whole art of reading. But just as ability to manipulate a brush does not make a creative artist, the development of word-study skills is not all that is involved in becoming a mature, diversified reader.

Word identification and word recognition are two closely related features of word perception. First contact with a new word form involves identification of the printed symbol in terms of its sound and meaning. Subsequent contacts develop recognition. In this text, the development of word recognition implies identification as the first step in the process. Until a printed symbol is grasped at a glance, i.e., until it has become what we term a *sight word,* recognition involves identification. Instruction in word recognition is designed to enable the child to do three interrelated tasks. *First,* he must be able to recognize known words rapidly with a minimum of analysis. For example, if he knows the word *think* as a sight word, he should not analyze it into *th-ink,* pronouncing each part and then blending it into the word *think.* Indeed to do so again and again would be most detrimental to his reading ability. There are children who are in difficulty in reading for just this reason. *Second,* he should be skilled in recognizing partially known words with little analysis. If the child knows the word *think,* he should be adept at identifying it in all of its variant forms. He should need but a glance at the word to enable him to recognize and know the meaning of *think, thinks, thinking,* and as he gains maturity, *unthinkable.* In such words, the child should learn to identify the root word, recognize the modified form rapidly, and understand the changed meaning. *Third,* the child must develop a flexible set of skills that will enable him to work out the recognition of new words independently. As he matures in reading, he should be able not only to pronounce the new words, but also be so skilled that he can recognize the words without interrupting the thought of the passage.

Instruction in word identification is complex indeed. It is small wonder that reading instruction has progressed through a series of methods from the spelling approach of the *Blue-Back Speller* days, to the whole word approach of the *Quincy Method,* to the phonetic emphasis of the *Beacon* and *Gordon* systems, to the sentence or context emphasis, to the modern composite methods which employ context, whole word, phonetic, and structural analysis as aids to word identification. The major problem in the modern approach is to teach the flexible set of skills needed so that none will be omitted or over- or underemphasized and so that the more analytical and time-consuming aids to recognition will be used only when needed. In order to teach the child the word-recognition techniques necessary to enable him to recognize known words and to identify new ones visually or phonetically, there are at least five sorts of "balance" that must be maintained.

First, a balance between the establishment of word-recognition techniques and the development of meaning vocabulary is desirable for reading growth. If there is too much isolated drill on word parts, the child may become a capable word-caller but he may not understand what he is reading. The child may be able to make a fairly accurate attempt at pronouncing new words, but unless what he pronounces has meaning accompanying it, the results may be erroneous. Even though the early lessons in reading employ very common words, the teacher who neglects to introduce the words in meaningful settings may encourage an overemphasis on analytical techniques at the expense of word meaning. Conversely, the teacher who neglects to teach the recognition skills may cause the child to make random attempts to say any word that comes to mind or it may make the child too dependent on her. The word-recognition skills, therefore, should be taught in meaningful situations and in words rather than in isolation. They must, however, be taught and learned as part of the co-ordinated program.

Second, a balance between the acquisition of sight vocabulary—words the child knows at a glance—and the establishment of word-recognition skills is essential. The child needs to learn to recognize at sight an ever-increasing number of words because it is on these that his fluency as a reader depends. It is also on these words that much of his ability to derive meaning from printed matter is based. If the child is led to place too much emphasis on either one of these learnings at the expense of the other, the results will be serious. The teacher may place so much emphasis upon building sight vocabulary that the child fails to establish the needed word-recognition techniques. Such a child may seem to progress well at the start, but he will soon become a disabled reader. He will lack independence, since he has no way of working out the pronunciation of new words nor of identifying them by himself. The teacher who stresses word recognition and neglects the building of sight vocabulary is encouraging the child to become a slow, laborious, and overanalytical reader. The child needs to build both an ever-increasing sight vocabulary and a more diversified set of word-recognition techniques. The child who excludes one in favor of the other will be in serious trouble in reading. This is one of the most difficult balances to achieve. As a result, there are many children who go to work employing analytical study on words that they really know at sight and other children are at a loss to work out the pronunciation of new words independently because they have never sufficiently learned it.

Third, there must be a balance between the meaning clues and the analytical aids, which are synthetic aids to word recognition. The child who depends too much upon meaning clues to recognition will make a great number of errors that have little relationship to the looks of the word he miscalls. These errors consist of substituting words that make sense though they are not the words of the author nor do they show his meaning. For example, such a reader might read the sentence "The ship sailed over the equator," as "The ship sailed over the seas." Such a reader is often inaccurate and misses out in comprehension. The child, on the other hand, who depends too much upon analytical and blending aids to the exclusion of meaning may also be inaccurate. The errors might be phonetically accurate, but they may make no real sense of any kind, perhaps are totally meaningless. For example, the sentence "The Scotch girl's dress was plaid," might be read "The Scotch girl's dress was played." In either this case or the former one, little or no understanding is the result. The child must develop both abilities and when he has done so he can use them to reinforce one another. The child who lacks the analytical techniques is handicapped because, many times, exact recognition is impossible from content alone; and the child who depends too much upon word analysis is unable to use context to speed recognition and to check the accuracy of his recognition through the sense it makes.

Fourth, a balance between the analytical techniques must be maintained. If the teacher places too much emphasis on phonetic training, the child may fail to develop the ability to use larger elements in recognizing words. The result may be a letter-by-letter sounding approach which is unfortunate as a major means of word recognition. Also such an emphasis may teach the child to separate words to such an extent that synthesis or blending of sounds into one word becomes impossible for many children. On the other hand, if the emphasis on larger structural and visual elements is too great, the child may not have skill in using smaller elements or letter sounds sufficiently developed to enable him to recognize certain words, such as unusual names that require sounding. Many children with reading disability have failed to establish this balance and hence have become either one type of overanalytical case or the kind of reading case who lacks sufficient phonetic knowledge.

Fifth, there must be a balance between the emphasis placed on knowledge of word parts and the orderly inspection of words along the line of print from left to right and from the beginning of the word to the end. If too much stress is placed, for example, on word families such as the *at* family in *cat, sat, fat, hat,* the child may neglect the beginning elements of words and thus make an unreasonable number of errors with the beginnings of words. Another child using this emphasis may become a difficult reversal case because he has established the habit of looking at the end of words to pick up his clues to recognition. When a child makes an excessive number of errors in any specific location within words, it usually indicates that knowledge of word parts has been emphasized at the expense of orderly inspection from beginning to end of each word he studies. In this respect, another balance is required in connection with the orderly inspection of words, which is that the child must develop flexibility in his visual analysis of the word he is trying to recognize. For example, suppose the word is *frighten;* the child selects *fri* as the first element he recognizes. Unless he quickly rejects this result of his visual analysis, he will be unable to work out the rest of the word, because *ght* will not be very helpful to him. He may try to sound each letter, *g—h—t,* and then get into marked confusion. A child who was more flexible in the visual analysis of words would reject the first separation of the word and break it into more suitable parts, such as *fr—ight—en.* Then, applying his knowledge of the elements, he would be able to pronounce the word with little difficulty.

Word recognition is much more complex than is assumed in programs that emphasize a single set of skills or in instruction that places the child in a stimulating reading environment and expects him to discover all the needed skills and maintain the needed balances between them. Word recognition entails too many related learnings to allow the program to be narrow or to be incidental. The necessary skills and knowledges can be classified into the following six basic learnings:

1. Associating the appropriate meanings with the printed symbols.
2. Using context clues and other meaning aids to anticipate the words to be recognized and then checking the accuracy of the recognitions.
3. Becoming flexible and efficient in visually analyzing the words into usable recognition elements.
4. Developing knowledges of visual, structural, and phonetic elements (knowledge such as what the visual element, *ight* says in *fright, right, night,* etc.), knowledge of consonant and vowel sounds, blends and digraphs, prefixes and suffixes, etc.
5. Learning skill in auditory blending and visually synthesizing word parts to rapidly pronounce or recognize the word as a whole.
6. Forming the habit of using the more analytical and the pronunciation techniques when and only when needed.

The major source of word-recognition difficulty will be found in the child's failure to establish any of these basic learnings or his overemphasis on any of them. A study in process by G. L. Bond and T. Clymer in which more than four thousand children were measured in these basic learnings shows that a child could not be a good reader if he remained inadequate in any one of them. The study also shows that competency in any one, or even in all of them, was no guarantee that the child would be a good reader. As complex as word recognition is, reading ability entails much more. A deficiency in any of the basic areas of word recognition will, however, make it almost certain that the child will become disabled in reading in general. Overemphasis on any of the areas to the point that others are not fully used will also make for poor reading in general.

Word-recognition problems are often found to be at the root of the difficulty of those disabled readers who fall into the descriptive categories *limiting* disability and *complex* disability. The more prevalent types of word-recognition disabilities are listed below. Each will be discussed, showing how it is diagnosed and the methods of correction that have been found helpful. The list follows:

1. Failure to associate meaning with printed symbols.
2. Insufficient sight vocabulary.
3. Failure to use meaning clues.
4. Ineffective visual analysis of words.
5. Limited knowledge of word parts.
6. Lack of ability in synthesizing.
7. Becoming an overanalytical reader.
8. Excessive locational errors.

FAILURE TO ASSOCIATE MEANING WITH PRINTED SYMBOLS

The real goal of all word recognition is to enable the child to identify words and to associate the appropriate meanings with them. Often programs of word recognition emphasize oral word study and pronunciation so strongly that the child fails to establish the habit or to sense the importance of understanding the meaning of printed symbols. The child may, therefore, give fairly close approximations to the pronunciation of the words he studies, but he may not have identified the word as one he knows in his listening or speaking vocabulary. Sometimes the teacher can detect mispronunciation that indicates that the word was almost, but not quite, recognized. At other times, it will be necessary to ask the child what the word means in order to detect whether he is having this basic difficulty. Of course, a relatively low level of performance by a child on oral vocabulary or meaning vocabulary tests, when compared with his skill in word-recognition techniques, such as knowledge of word elements and visual analysis of words, indicates this type of difficulty.

Remedial work for such cases should emphasize the basic comprehension abilities and reading for meaning as described in the preceding chapter. In addition, in all word-recognition exercises, the meanings of the words should be kept in the forefront. Drill on isolated word elements should be completely rejected for this type of case, as indeed it should be for most children, lest the development of this unfortunate disability be encouraged. The word-identification exercises should at all times be in meaningful, contextual settings so that there is the opportunity to recognize not only the word, but also its meaning as is necessary for general success.

There are methods closely related to the real reading act which will help the child to develop the habit and the ability of associating meanings with the word symbols. The child may, for example, be requested to draw illustrations for a story he is reading. In order to do so, it is necessary for him to attend to the meaning of descriptive words. If the child is expected to retell a story in his own words rather than to repeat the words in the book, he will soon learn to interpret the meaning of the word symbols. Any comprehension exercise which does not allow verbalism, by which we mean merely repeating the words of the book, will encourage the association of meaning with the words read.

In addition to emphasis on word meanings in all reading comprehension situations, the child must at all times develop his word-recognition techniques in meaningful settings, if he is to be encouraged to associate precise ideas with the printed symbols. The child who is limited in this ability may also profit from exercises such as the following:

1. Exercises to develop clear sensory impressions.

   a. What did you hear:

   when a stone hit the water?
   splash   cr-ack

   when the branch broke?
   bang   cr-ack

   when the gun went off?
   splash   bang

   b. An animal with stripes on it:

   elephant   horse   zebra

   c. Match the words with the phrase that tells the same thing.

   Put the number of the word before the phrase.

   1. lagged   _____flowed with force
   2. gushed   _____moved slowly
   3. gurgled   _____made a noise as it flowed
   4. rushed   _____moved rapidly along

   d. Put *J* before each word that would tell about a jolly person.

_____merry	_____laughing	_____joyful
_____sober	_____gay	_____droopy
_____beaming	_____bitter	_____dreary

2. Exercises to develop precise meanings.

   a. In each line, find the two words that have opposite meanings.

many	some	no	few
tall	slim	short	little
good	tired	sad	bad
right	bad	wrong	trouble
wet	dry	damp	moist

    b. Find the words that have a similar meaning.

glow	bright	shine	spark
rushed	walked	ran	hurried
replied	said	answered	wrote
center	middle	around	point

    c. Complete the sentences with the best word from those listed below it.

        1. When the boy saw the people far away he _____ to them.
        said   shouted   whispered   muttered

        2. The cruel boy rode the horse _____.
        roughly   glaringly   harshly   sharply

3. Exercises to develop extensiveness of meaning.

    a. Tell the difference in meaning of *pound* in these sentences.

        1. We ate a *pound* of candy.
        2. See him *pound* the nail.

    b. Tell the difference in the meaning of *roll* in the following sentences:

        (1) We ate a *roll* for lunch.
        (2) We watched the big waves *roll* along the beach.
        (3) Get a *roll* of paper.
        (4) Please *roll* the ball to Jim.
        (5) The dog could *roll* over.
        (6) The teacher called the *roll*.
        (7) We could see the *roll* of the hills.
        (8) We could hear the *roll* of drums.

    c. Put the number of the right definition in front of each sentence.

    trunk (1) The main stem of a tree.   ____He picked up a peanut with his trunk.

            (2) A box used to carry clothes.   ____The trunk of the oak was rough.

            (3) Part of an elephant.   ____He put the trunk on the train.

    bark (1) Cry of a dog.   ____He peeled some bark to make a rope.

            (2) Part of a tree.   ____He heard a loud bark across the bay.

            (3) A sailing boat.   ____He saw the bark on the sea.

Exercises such as those given above and the suggestions made in the preceding chapter will aid in building the habit of attending to word meanings and will also develop skill in associating meaning with word symbols. Many times a child makes a close approximation to a word by the use of phonetic and other word-recognition techniques, but unless he keeps the context in mind, the word will remain unidentified. In addition to exercises, extensive reading coupled with the habit of noticing expressive use of words will aid in encouraging the child to associate meaning with printed symbols. Since the goal of all reading is to derive meaning from the printed page and since this goal must be achieved by recognizing printed symbols and their meanings, all word-recognition exercises should demand not only the identification of words, but also an understanding of their meanings.

INSUFFICIENT SIGHT VOCABULARY

The importance of forming the habit of rapidly recognizing known words, rather than studying each word encountered as though it had never been seen before, cannot be emphasized too strongly. The child who fails to build a large sight vocabulary and who does not have the habit of recognizing these at a glance cannot hope to become an able reader. He will not only be limited in his ability to group words into thought units, so necessary for comprehension and fluency, but he will also be seriously handicapped in identifying new words. This latter limitation comes about in two ways. First, the child will be unable to use context clues effectively because the vocabulary load of unknown words will be too great. Second, he will be inefficient in the more mature methods of word study. Affixed words, for example, will be difficult to recognize because the child will not be able to identify the root word, since for him it is not a sight word. Compound words will also present him with a tough problem, since he has not developed the habit of sight recognition of the two smaller words from which such a compound is made. The child who does not have a substantial sight vocabulary, and who does not have the habit of recognizing those words as known units, will find learning to read a most confusing enterprise. For this reason, modern instruction in reading emphasizes the building of a sight vocabulary from the start.

There are children who get too early an introduction to analytical techniques or who are so thoroughly drilled on isolated word parts that all words fall to pieces before their eyes. Such children may become so adept at working out words that they fail to have an immediate need for building a sight vocabulary. In the early grades, the teacher may find it difficult to detect the fact that these children are not building a sight vocabulary. If, however, they are allowed to persist in this practice, the results will be disastrous to their reading growth. Either they will have to reject this detailed study of each word and build a sight vocabulary or they will become severe disability cases.

In other children, a limited sight vocabulary is easily detected. They may be word-by-word readers, making phonetic errors with words they should know at sight or they may fail to phrase well in oral reading. Another indication of failure to build a sight vocabulary of common words is a tendency for the child to make about an equal number of errors regardless of the difficulty of the material he is reading. If a child, for example, makes about the same percentage of errors in reading a first-grade reader as he makes in a fourth-grade reader, he is likely to be limited in his development of a sight vocabulary. If he tends to make more mistakes on small common words than he does on polysyllabic words, he is in all probability limited in sight vocabulary.

The teacher can easily measure sight vocabulary by rapid-exposure techniques. She can either flash words printed on cards or use a tachistoscope for the quick exposures. The child who cannot readily identify common words at a glance has failed to develop a sight vocabulary. An easily constructed and versatile tachistoscope can be made out of posterboard as indicated in Figure 12.

The basic frame of the tachistoscope (Part 1) is made by cutting a piece of posterboard 5″ by 10″ and pasting two strips of posterboard ¾″ by 10″ at each side. Then a shutter 1″ by 6″ is fastened on the right side with a paper fastener (A) so that it can swing freely up and down, as shown. This is the basic frame upon which various exercises will be placed. Part 2 is a drill slip cut from a manila folder on which is typed or printed, at the proper intervals, the word parts, words, or phrases to be used in the exercise. This printed list will be pulled up between the basic frame and the removable face (Part 3). The removable face is a piece of manila folder 5″ by 9″ with a slit about ⅜″ wide and 3½″ long across it with a notch to fit around the paper fastener (A) on the basic frame, as shown. It also has four holes (B) so that it may be fastened to the basic frame.

For certain exercises this removable face can be left on. For other exercises, different faces will need to be substituted. For all word and phrase drills, the face shown in the figure may be used. For drills on word parts, faces will need to be changed to fit the exercise. For example, if the initial blend *str* is being drilled upon, the face used will have *str* printed or typed on it at (X) just before the opening. Then the drill slip (Part 2) will have typed on it at appropriate intervals, *eet, ing, ong, ange, aw, ipe,* and other endings that make real words with *str* as the initial part of the word. Then as the drill slip is moved up, space by space, a quick up and down movement of the shutter will expose the word parts so that the child will see the different words, all of which begin with *str*. The shutter may be held open for a longer time when a more prolonged study of the word parts is desired, as suggested later in this chapter. A set of removable faces and drill slips to make exercises for many word elements can easily be made. Drill slips for sight words and for phrases can be typed and used with the removable face, as indicated in the figure. The remedial worker may wish to make two basic frames and use one for word and phrase exercises, in which case the face could remain attached; and the other for word element exercises, in which case the face would have to be changed according to the element being drilled upon.

When using such a tachistoscope, if the child makes a considerably greater number of errors when the shutter is used than he does when look-

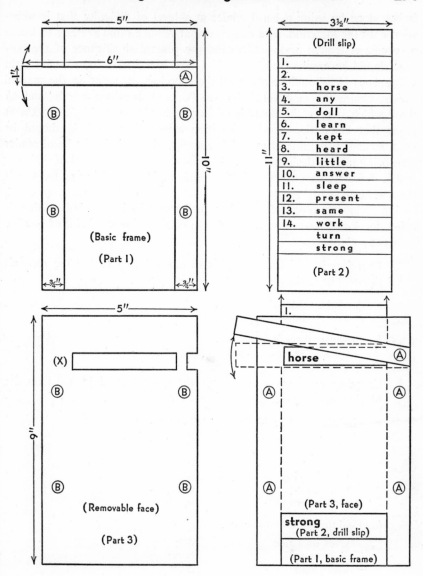

FIG. 12. Word and phrase tachistoscope.

ing at the words for an unlimited time, he can be assumed to have an insufficient sight vocabulary. A few such indications of limited ability in recognizing words at a glance would make remedial work in developing the habit of rapid identification and in building a larger sight vocabulary mandatory.

Remedial training for increasing the sight vocabulary of a disabled reader is best done by using a basal reader at a level of difficulty that is somewhat easy for the child. The exercises that require rapid reading to locate a specific statement or to understand the general significance of the passage should be emphasized for a child who is trying to increase his sight vocabulary. He should be given all the exercises suggested in the manual which require the new vocabulary to be read as whole words, and all those which require the analysis of words should be avoided. Workbook pages that emphasize word recognition rather than analysis should be used. Extensive reading of material related to the topic in the basal reader then being used is desirable. Such material should be at a level of difficulty that is definitely easy for the child, so that rapid recognition of the words is encouraged.

The following types of exercises, using the basic vocabulary that is being developed have proven effective in encouraging the habit of reading words at a glance.

1. Exercises in which the word is so much expected that the recognition will be rapid.

    a. A cowboy rides a _____.
    tree   horse   farm

    b. In winter there is _____.
    snow   house   well

2. Exercises in which a child finds the correct word in a list on the blackboard as the teacher gives the clue.

    a. Find the word in this list that tells us where we:

Clue	*Words*
buy food	farm
go swimming	table
find cows	store
eat dinner	beach

    b. Find the word that tells us what animal:

gives us a ride	dog
gives us milk	horse
barks loud	duck
swims under water	cow
says, "Quack"	fish

3. Exercises that require meaningful scanning of a list.

    a. See how fast you can draw a line around all the things that can run.

horse	house	girl	pig
tree	dog	road	man
cat	boy	store	window

b. See how fast you can draw a line around all the things that are good to eat.

candy	pie	trees	cake
mud	meat	nuts	pencils
soup	boards	fruit	dessert

4. Various word games that call for immediate responses and require sight recognition of words and their meanings.

a. Cards with names of animals printed on them can be used. Two children can play together. One child can flash the cards and the other one can respond. Such words as the following can be used:

chicken	elephant	bird	goose
dog	duck	pony	donkey
horse	goat	wren	fish

One child may tell the ones that name an animal with four feet as the cards are flashed. Then the other child may tell the ones that can fly.

b. Another set of cards could be made of verbs and the child could tell which words on the cards tell movement. The types of words that might be used are:

afraid	listen	march	walk
jump	roll	sleep	feel
think	skip	ride	guess
flew	know	slide	was

c. A fish pond game in which words are attached to paper clips and the child uses a pole with a magnet on the end of the line may be used. If the child can read the word that he fishes out of the pond at a glance, it is caught. If he has to study the word, that fish gets away, but he may be able to catch it at another time. Any words that caused the child trouble in the basal reader could be used in this game as well as other words that he knows well.

d. A game similar to "authors" can be played with words. The words are grouped in sets of four similar things, such as clothes, animals, trees, time, food, toys, people, and colors. Four children may play together. Each child gets eight cards and the remaining cards are placed in a pile in the center. The children take turns drawing one card from the center pile and then discarding one. The child who first gets two complete sets of four similar words wins the game. The sets of word cards for this game might be these:

Clothes	*Animals*	*Trees*	*Time*
coat	lion	oak	afternoon
hat	elephant	maple	spring
shoe	donkey	fir	tomorrow
dress	horse	willow	morning

Food	*Toys*	*People*	*Colors*
bread	doll	aunt	yellow
pudding	wagon	father	green
peanuts	football	uncle	blue
strawberries	balloon	mother	brown

Furniture	*Flowers*	*Fruit*	*Meals*
chair	pansy	peaches	breakfast
table	tulip	bananas	dinner
bed	daisy	apples	lunch
desk	poppy	pears	supper

e. Many other games such as Wordo (like Bingo), Old Maid, Spin the Wheel, Climb the Ladder, Dominoes with Words, and Grab Bag can be played.

f. The tachistoscope described above can be used to get rapid exposure for games such as those described in 3a and b, and 4a and b. However, the directions would have to be slightly modified. This device is especially suitable for the child who has not built a sight vocabulary because he has depended too strongly upon his ability to analyze words.

The exercises used in building sight vocabulary should be such that the child is encouraged to inspect the words rapidly rather than to resort to detailed study of them. The words should be presented in situations that require understanding of the word meanings.

The child should be reading material that introduces new words gradually and repeats them at well-spaced intervals. Basal readers are the most suitable material for expanding sight vocabulary. If the child is highly motivated to read the selection, if the new words are introduced before the selection is read, and if the purposes require rapid reading, the child should increase his sight vocabulary. When such basic instruction is reinforced with exercises such as those described above, using the words being emphasized, the gains should be even greater. In all of the reading and drill situations, recognizing the meaning of the words should be required and pronunciation held to a minimum. Permitting pronunciation of the words encourages a slower type of recognition than is desired. What the child with an insufficient sight vocabulary needs is experience in recognizing the word and its meaning at a glance.

FAILURE TO USE MEANING CLUES

Meaning clues are among the most important aids to word recognition. The effective adult reader uses these clues in all word identification and recognition. Meaning clues enable the reader to anticipate new or unfamiliar words before he actually sees them. No matter what other aids to recognition are used, the proficient reader always uses some form of meaning clue to aid him if there is one given, as there almost always is in ordinary prose. Many disabled readers have failed to acquire this ability and they are therefore to some extent ineffective in word recognition and even in the more detailed identifications. The failure to use meaning clues precludes the acquisition of such mature reading skills as grouping words in thought units. It also limits the development of accuracy in using the other word-recognition techniques. The ineffective use of meaning clues, moreover, forces the child to analyze carefully many words that should be identified with a minimum of inspection.

Meaning clues can be divided into two types. The first are expectancy clues which enable the mature reader to anticipate the sorts of words and concepts that he is likely to encounter when reading about a given topic. If, for example, a mature reader is reading about soil conservation, he might expect to meet such words as *erosion, soil, depletion, levee, irrigation, rotation, drainage,* and many others. This anticipation would make the recognition or identification of the words more rapid than if they unexpectedly appeared in prose on some other subject. The second type of meaning clue is the context clue, which is even more helpful. The use of context clues is a sort of rapid recognition technique in which a word or phrase is so completely anticipated from the meaning of the sentence or paragraph that the merest flick of a glance is all that is needed to confirm that it is that expected word or phrase. Even if the word symbol is unfamiliar, the context plus a minimum of inspection is all that is needed for its identification.

Weakness in Use of Expectancy Clues

The child who does not anticipate words that he is likely to meet when reading about a specific topic or within a specific field, is to some degree handicapped in word recognition. There are many children and even some adult readers who fail to use their knowledge of a subject as an aid to word identification and recognition. There are many adult readers, for example, who skip the graphic presentation of the facts discussed in the running comment. A brief study of the table, chart, or graph would enable them to anticipate the context and the words within the passage. The reader who uses the pictorial aids effectively becomes a more fluent and understanding reader of a passage, partly because he is prepared for those words. He, therefore, can identify them with ease and devote himself to the meaning of what is read rather than to the mere recognition of words. For the younger reader, picture clues operate in much the same way. A well-illustrated book builds expectancy clues. However, the child must be taught to use such pictures effectively. Modern basic reading programs use pictures as a means of building the habit of anticipating words and concepts. However, there is a possibility of danger in the overuse of pictures. If the picture tells too much of the story or if all the concepts are illustrated, they lose their value because they leave so little for the child to discover by reading. The readiness activities preceding reading on a topic, which include the planning, development of background, and introduction to new words, are a form of building expectancy clues for the youngsters. Programs that neglect such essentials of reading instruction predispose the child to be weak in using expectancy clues.

The ineffective use of expectancy clues in word recognition can be detected by noting unusual difficulty in recognizing the words specifically related to a topic. It can also be suspected of the child who is always weak in citing words he might expect to find in a passage about some given topic, whatever that topic may be. If, for example, a child is asked to tell what words might be used in a story about a rabbit and if he could not mention some such words as *jump, carrot, run, hop, long ears, cotton tail,* and *burrow,* he is probably weak in using expectancy clues.

The remedial work for such a child would be, for the most part, to place greater emphasis on the readiness development which precedes the reading of a topic and each selection within the topic. The child who is weak in using expectancy clues needs more attention given to the introductions of units and selections, more picture study prior to reading, more opportunity for vocabulary development on a particular topic or selection to be read, and more careful planning of the outcomes expected. Meaningful reading rather than just recall should be emphasized. Suggestions for the introduction and building of readiness can be found in most of the manuals that accompany basal readers. Basal readers which have such suggestions in their manuals would be good material in which to develop the habit of anticipating words and concepts. However, the instruction need not be limited to such material, even though the methods employed should be the same.

There are certain exercises which also help develop effective use of expectancy clues. The following illustrate some of the types that are useful:

1. Exercises using pictures to build expectancy clues.

   a. Look at the picture above. In it you will see some animals. They are doing funny things. Then look at the sentences below. Draw a line around the name of the animal that the sentence is about.

He is opening his mouth for a peanut.		
elephant	hippopotamus	monkey

He is walking back and forth.		
giraffe	elephant	kangaroo

He is in the water.		
elephant	hippopotamus	kangaroo

   b. Studying the picture illustrating a selection prior to reading it. The unit to be read may deal with various types of animals in the zoo. A study of the picture would enable the children to anticipate the names of the animals. Then before each selection is read, a review of the names of the animals in the selection can be made. The picture clues become a great aid to recognition of such difficult words as *baboon, kangaroo, hippopotamus, elephant, orangutan, zebra, panther,* and *crocodile.*

2. Exercises using knowledge of the topic to build expectancy clues.

   a. Mark the words you would expect to read about in a farm story, *F.* Mark those in a city story, *C.*

stores	cattle	tractor	streets
chickens	street car	escalator	traffic
crowds	hay stack	silo	meadow

   b. Which of the following phrases would you expect an old seafaring man to use? Put *S* before them.

   _____ a square-rigged ship
   _____ pretty autumn leaves
   _____ over the bulwarks
   _____ the larboard boats
   _____ the well-filled silo
   _____ port the helm
   _____ a ship of the desert

Failure to Use Context Clues

The child who has failed to develop ability in using context clues as an aid to word recognition is indeed in difficulty. This ability is one of the most important, if not the most important, means of word recognition. It is a rapid technique which enables the reader to identify a word immediately. For example, in the sentence "The man put his hat on his _____," it is not difficult for the child to know from the context that the missing word is *head*. At least the meaning of the sentence enables the child to anticipate the few words it could possibly be, rather than one of the 800,000 it might be if it were just any word, without regard to context. In addition, the use of context clues makes the selection of the correct meaning of the word possible. In the sentence used in the example above, the word *head* could only have been a part of the man, it could not have been the head of a stream nor a head of steam.

The reader who uses contextual aids is more likely to recognize a new word correctly than if he were using no such aid. He can frequently get a close approximation to the pronunciation of a word from his analytical techniques. The context clues enable him to identify the word even though he picked up only a close approximation to the actual word from his analysis. Context clues usually work in combination with other word-recognition techniques. These meaning clues make the application of analytical techniques much more rapid and accurate.

An equally, if not more, important use of context clues is that they act as a check on the application of all the other recognition techniques. Just as in subtraction, it pays to add afterwards, so as to check the answer, so in reading it pays to check the meaning of the sentence to see if the problem in word recognition has been correctly solved. When the child has figured out a word, he must be aware of whether or not it makes sense in the context in which it is found. If it does, he probably has found the correct solution. If it does not, he should reinspect the word because he has undoubtedly made a mistake. Without at least a fair degree of skill in the use of context clues, the child will be slow and inaccurate in word recognition. With such skill, he can be a good reader if he also has other word-recognition techniques well developed. A child who depends on contextual clues alone will also be inaccurate and become a disabled reader. It is important to know, however, that many children who are thought to be in difficulty in reading because of limited skill in analytical techniques or because they have insufficient knowledge of phonetic, structural, or visual elements are really in difficulty because they are not using context clues well.

The child who is limited in the use of context clues is easily spotted. If he makes as many errors when reading words in context as he does when he is reading a list of words, then he is not making sufficient use of the meaning of sentences or paragraphs as an aid to recognition. If the child's errors do not fit the meaning of the sentences and tend to be far afield, he is not using context clues. If, for example, the child reads the word *cat* as *sat* in the sentence "The dog ran after the cat," he is not using context because *sat* makes no sense at all. If, however, he read *cat* as *car,* he is probably using context because *car* would make sense. Another way of detecting this limitation is by comparing standardized test results. If, for example, the child makes a relatively high score on Test I, "Reading Words in Isolation" as compared with Test II, "Reading Words in Context" on the *Bond-Clymer-Hoyt Silent Reading Diagnostic Tests,* he would be making ineffective use of context clues. Ordinarily this difficulty is readily corrected.

Remedial training in the use of context clues should be based upon having the child read materials that are of such a level of difficulty that he encounters about one new word in every forty running words. He should be reading for purposes that demand thorough understanding of the content. In the more severe cases of this type, a separate and immediate purpose for each paragraph or sentence should be stated. This will emphasize reading for meaning and will enable the child to recognize known words at a glance and use context clues as an aid to other techniques in the identification of unfamiliar words. The teacher may need to ask the child from time to time what he thinks the word might be, or have the child use the context plus the initial sound to help him solve his word-recognition problems.

In addition to the above suggestions, the following more formal exercises will encourage the child to use context clues:

1. Exercises in which the meaning of the sentence indicates the word to be recognized.

   a. The boys rode over the snow on it. What was it?
   sleigh   store   peanut

   b. Mother put a candle on the cake for Bob's _____.
   football   birthday   ceiling

2. Exercises in which the child reads a paragraph, filling in the missing words, using the initial elements given. He does not need to write them but reads the sentences to himself. Comprehension questions can be asked.

   Billy caught the ball.
   Then he th_____ the ball to his father.
   Father c_____ the ball, too.
   Billy and his father were pl_____ catch.
   A dog came to play.
   He j_____ up and got the ball.
   Then he ran a_____ with it.

3. Exercises in which context plus initial elements are used as aids to word recognition.

   a. We will get some apples at the st_____.
   store   steep   farm

   b. The car went down the str_____.
   strong   road   street

4. Riddles in which the context gives the answer.

   It lives in a zoo.
   It hops about.
   It carries its baby in its pouch.
   It is a _____.
   elephant   crocodile   kangaroo

To sum up, it can be stated that meaning clues are helpful in word recognition in three ways. *First,* such clues enable the reader to anticipate the words he is to read. This makes the recognition of known words rapid and accurate and allows the reader to work out the identification of unfamiliar words with a minimum of study. *Second,* the use of such clues is essential as a check on the accuracy of his recognition. If the word recognized does not make sense, it should be his habit to devote further study to the word missed. *Third,* the application of other word-recognition techniques frequently gives the child only a close approximation of the word and then the meaning clues enable him to recognize the word correctly.

Proficiency in both the use of meaning clues and the application of analytical word-recognition techniques is required if the reader is to associate the correct semantic variation with the printed symbol recognized. Meaning clues alone are not enough for good reading at any level. They must be accompanied by the use of a flexible set of word-recognition skills. It is the interaction of all the word-study skills that forms the foundation on which a competent reader builds his reading structure.

INEFFECTIVE VISUAL ANALYSIS OF WORDS

The set of skills needed to reinforce the meaning clues to word recognition can be grouped under three types of learnings: (1) flexible visual analysis of words; (2) knowledge of word parts; and (3) fluent synthesis of word parts. Visual analysis of an unfamiliar word must always precede the application of knowledge of word parts. Both of these come before the final synthesis of the parts into recognition of a word. For example, a child unfamiliar with the word *something* might visually separate the word into *so—met—hing*. He would then apply his knowledge of the parts, pronouncing each in turn. Then he would blend the parts and find that he had failed in his attempt because his original visual separation of the word was wrong. He would quickly have to reject his first visual analysis and make another one. This time he might see the first of the two small words from which the word *something* is made and separate the word into *some—th—ing*. Then applying his knowledge of the parts and synthesizing them, he would be able to recognize the word. Of course, such an approach to recognizing the word *something* would have been a rather immature attempt. A more advanced reader would have visually analyzed the word into the largest known elements, *some* and *thing*. He would visually recognize these parts and then synthesize them. Aided by context clues, the separate parts would not have to be spoken and blended, but the whole word, *something,* would have been recognized at a glance. Nonetheless, the word would have been visually analyzed, knowledges applied and then synthesized, all with great rapidity. The visual analysis of words must be flexible and diversified if the child is to become an able reader.

In order for the child to become an effective reader, he needs to develop great skill in the visual analysis of words. He must, at a glance, be able to separate the word into elements that are going to be useful in recognizing it. An element that is useful in one word may not be suitable in another. For example, the element *on* in the word *upon* is useful, but separating *on* out of the word *portion* would prove detrimental in recognizing the whole word. The child, therefore, must achieve flexibility so that when one method does not work, he can quickly reappraise the word and reanalyze it visually. If he is to be effective, he must analyze a word only when he does not know it as a sight word, and even then, he should select the largest usable elements in the word rather than resort to piecemeal analysis.

The child who is disabled in the visual analysis of words can be identified in three ways. *First,* when orally working on words, he will select inappropriate elements to sound out and often he will try again and again to use the same analysis when it has proven ineffective. If when the examiner shows him how to analyze the word by covering up parts of it, the child is able to recognize it, then his major problem in word recognition is faulty visual analysis. *Second,* the child who is relatively poor in the Syllabication Test of *The Gates Reading Diagnostic Tests* in comparison with his performance on the other Visual Perception Tests is probably disabled in visual analysis of words. *Third,* if the child, in comparison with his general reading ability, does poorly in the Visual Analysis Sections of the *Bond-Clymer-Hoyt Silent Reading Diagnostic Tests,* he is in difficulty in visual analysis.

The remedial training for a child with this kind of disability must focus upon two outcomes. *First,* it should give the child help in locating the most useful structural, visual, and phonetic elements in words. *Second,* it must develop flexibility in the visual attack on words, teaching the child to use the larger elements first, but to change quickly from an analysis that does not work to one that does.

The most effective remedial measures are similar to those used by the teacher when she is developing this ability in the first place. Such training as finding similarities in known words like *fight* and *sight* or *three* and *throw* gives the child experience in visual analysis. The material used for such training should be rather difficult so that the child will be forced to analyze words visually. Help in finding parts of compound words or in locating root words in affixed words is excellent experience in visual analysis. Experience in syllabifying words is also effective. Exercises such as the following, first using known words and then having the child locate similar elements in unknown words, should be used liberally with a child seriously deficient in visual analysis of words:

1. Exercises involving finding the root word in words with variant ending forms:

   a. Find the root words from which these words are made.
(1) looks	looking	looked
(2) worker	worked	working
(3) washes	washing	washed

   b. Find the root words in words having variant endings, such as: *want* in *wanting; wait* in *waited; swim* in *swimming.*

2. Exercises having the child make choices between variant forms, such as:

        wanting

a. The bear   the honey.

        wanted

        talk

b. The man was talking to them.

        talked

        make

c. Mother is   a cake.

        making

3. Exercises that require the finding of similar blends:

    a. You see the picture of the clown, say clown. Look at the words here and put X on the ones that begin like clown and that tell something we can do.

clap	clean	clocks
come	clothes	play
climb	cook	clam

4. Exercises that emphasize seeing similar word parts

    a. Put X on the right word.

        (1) <u>She</u> wanted to _____ for joy.

            sing   shout   shoe

        (2) <u>String</u> is not as _____ as rope.

            street   big   strong

    b. Draw a line under the right word.

        (1) The sun cannot be seen at _____.

            fight   night   right   sight

        (2) The train runs on a _____.

            sack   black   track   tack

        (3) Baseball is a _____.

            game   same   came   tame

5. Exercises that teach syllabication

    a. Say the words below and think how many parts you hear. These parts are syllables. Write the number of syllables after each word.

about _____	surprise _____	something _____
rabbit _____	together _____	thermometer _____
cat _____	wonderful _____	banana _____

    b. Show the syllables in these words, as: dif/fer/ent.

ahead	forgotten	furniture
yellow	interested	tomorrow
after	moment	electricity

6. Exercises that emphasize seeing the two parts of compound words

    a. Find the two small words in each compound word and tell how they help us know what it means.

fireplace	baseball	sailboat	policeman
fireside	football	rowboat	fireman
firefly	basketball	ferryboat	fisherman

    b. Take one of the little words from each compound word below the sentence and make a new compound word to fill in the blank.

        (1) We were seated by the _____ to get warm.
            firehouse   outside

        (2) The wind makes the _____ go fast.
            sailfish   steamboat

7. Exercises that develop skill in analyzing affixed words

    a. Draw a line around the part of the word that says *again*.

relive	remake	retell
rework	replay	relearn

    b. Draw a line around the prefix and tell how it changes the meaning of the root word.

unhappy	retake	unknown
mistrust	displease	repay
unkind	dislike	mislead

    c. Draw a line around the suffix in these words. Put the right number after the words to show what the suffix means.

(1) without	(2) in that way	(3) full of
bravely _____	thoughtless _____	thoughtful _____
careless _____	wonderful _____	sadly _____
careful _____	strangely _____	thankful _____

    d. Draw a line around the root word, the word from which the larger word is made. Tell how the prefix and suffix change the meaning of the root word.

unfriendly	unthankful	distrustful
unkindly	unlikely	dishonestly
disagreeable	repayable	unkindness

The experience that the child gains from exercises given to improve his visual analysis of words must be used right away in meaningful settings. The child should be asked to put these words in sentences immediately or tell the derived meanings. This sort of drill should not be used in isolation but as a reinforcement of a broader program of word recognition. The words used in such exercises should be words with which the child is familiar or that will soon be introduced in the basic reading program.

The emphasis should be placed on developing flexibility and establishing the habit of dividing the words into the largest usable elements. The program should attempt to get the child to avoid faulty approaches to word recognition, such as letter-by-letter spelling or sounding. Sounding of individual letters, for example, may help a child to recognize a small word, such as *cat,* but it would be extremely confusing as a means of recognizing longer or more complicated words, such as *telephone* or *impatient.* Yet many children do this letter-by-letter sounding of all words that are unfamiliar because an isolated sounding method was employed in their early reading instruction.

Many children are in difficulty in word recognition because they place too much dependence on one technique or because they fail to use the most efficient ones. Such children, for example, may have developed the habit of searching for known little words in larger words. This technique is helpful in identifying compound words or affixed words, but it is detrimental in recognizing many other words. Finding *ear* in *bear* is of doubtful assistance, as is also finding *to—get—her* in the word, *together.* The exercises must be designed to develop a diversified and flexible attack on words. They must also emphasize orderly progression through the word from its beginning element to its end.

LIMITED KNOWLEDGE OF WORD PARTS

The child who is to become a capable, fluent, and independent reader must develop an extensive knowledge of word elements. There is little use in the child being skillful in visually analyzing words unless he knows what the parts say. It is of no use, for example, for the child to separate visually the word *spring* into *spr—ing* unless he knows what the initial blend *spr* and the ending *ing* say. The child needs to learn a vast number of word parts. The larger the elements he can use in recognizing words, the more fluent and understanding will be his reading. The more he uses context and meaning clues, the less he will need to analyze the words. It will often be necessary, however, for a child to break a word into small parts in order to recognize it. This will not aid him if he does not know the small elements. The child must master the knowledge of many phonetic, structural, and visual elements in words.

Limited knowledge of word parts can be detected by the diagnostician in several ways. Most of the diagnostic reading tests sample the more useful phonetic, structural, and visual elements. Any weakness shown on these tests in comparison with the child's general reading capability indicates that he may be limited in the number of elements with which he is familiar. Another means of spotting the presence of this weakness is manifest difficulty in associating sounds with word elements when the child is working out the pronunciation of words orally. If the child uses reasonable visual analysis of a word, but does not know letter sounds, common phonograms, or visual elements, he is limited in his knowledge of word parts. If he seems to be able to break a word into syllables but cannot pronounce many of them, he is limited in his knowledge of important word parts and should be given remedial training to increase his phonetic, structural, and visual knowledges.

When the teacher or remedial worker points out to a child the similarity between a new word and other words he knows, he is receiving instruction in word-element knowledges. Manuals accompanying basic reading programs give many suggestions for introducing new vocabulary to the child before he reads a selection. In presenting the new words, the teacher is not only supposed to make the meaning clear, but also is expected to show the child the most efficient visual analysis of each word and compare it, when necessary, with known words which contain the element causing the child difficulty. If, for example, the new word is *trouble,* the teacher might say that it begins like *train* and ends like *double.* The three words would be written on the blackboard. The teacher might also say it is something we would rather not have. The teacher would have given some instruction in the knowledge of what *tr* and *ouble* say.

Many exercises in manuals of basal readers give direct instruction to develop knowledge of word parts. These are especially suitable for the child who is limited in this area because the basic vocabulary in these readers is well controlled and the authors of the manuals know the words that have been taught previously. They can, therefore, use known words to teach the elements needed for recognizing new words. The authors can also keep an account of the word elements they are teaching so that they can develop the knowledges gradually with ample repetition to insure that they will be learned. It is, therefore, recommended that a child who is limited in word-element knowledge be given instruction in basal reading materials at the appropriate level of difficulty. The remedial teacher should emphasize the introduction of new vocabulary and the word-recognition exercises that are suggested after the reading of each selection. In addition, word-recognition exercises which are in the workbooks that accompany the readers should be used to the fullest.

All of the exercises suggested in the section above for improving visual analysis of words aid in teaching knowledge of visual, structural, and phonetic elements. Exercises such as the following will prove beneficial to the child who is limited in his knowledge of word parts. The words used should be words that have been or will soon be introduced in his basic reading book.

1. Exercises to teach initial consonant sounds.

   a. Say the words *can* and *come.* Put *C* before all the words that start like *can* and *come* and that also name an animal.

____cat	____candy	____cow	____cookies	____chicken
____duck	____eat	____chair	____elephant	____cake
____eel	____camel	____canary	____calf	____cub

b. Make a word naming something to eat by putting the first letter of a word on the left in the right blank. The first one is done for you.

soon	__eaches	but	__ake
cook	_s_ oup	people	__utter
puppy	__ookies	come	__eanuts

c. Write the first part of the word in the space. It starts like one of the words below the sentence.

    (1) The dog ran __ome.
       son   hope   cone

    (2) The cat wanted some __ilk.
       pig   like   mill

d. Draw a line to show which words start with the same sound as the thing in each picture. The first one is done for you.

                      donkey
                      like
                      dinner
(Picture of a dog)   duck   (Picture of a leaf)
                      looked
                      dish
                      letter

2. Exercises to teach initial blend sounds.

    a. Write in the blank the word that begins with the same blend as the word underlined.

        (1) The <u>branch</u> soon _____.
           bring   fell   broke

        (2) The <u>block</u> was painted _____.
           brown   blue   green

        (3) There was <u>plenty</u> to do at the _____.
           playground   school   park

        (4) The brown <u>string</u> was _____.
           street   strong   splashed

    b. Draw a line to show which words start with the same sound as the things in the pictures.

                      truck
                      string
(Picture of a train)   tried   (Picture of a street)
                      tree
                      straight

    c. Draw a line under the right word. It must start with the same blend as the key word.[1]

[1] These samples give most of the important initial blends.

(1) *black*

The sky is
> dark.
> blind.
> blue.

(2) *bring*

The tree has many
> bring.
> roots.
> branches.

(3) *clap*

The cat has
> feet.
> claws.
> close.

(4) *cross*

The bird was a
> crow.
> wren.
> crown.

(5) *draw*

The girl wore a
> coat.
> drove.
> dress.

(6) *flap*

Away the bird
> flat.
> flew.
> sailed.

(7) *frog*

We like to eat
> from.
> fruit.
> candy.

(8) *glad*

We put milk in a
> glass.
> cup.
> glue.

(9) *grand*

Cows like to eat
> leaves.
> gravel.
> grass.

(10) *plan*

We like to
> plate.
> sing.
> play.

(11) *screen*

We heard the witches
> scream.
> scale.
> scold.

(12) *skip*

The sun is in the
> window.
> skate.
> sky.

(13) *slap*

He went to
> sleep.
> school.
> sled.

(14) *smile*

The puppy was
> brown.
> small.
> smoke.

(15) *snake*

The sled can slide over the
> water.
> snap.
> snow.

(16) *spot*

We eat with a
> fork.
> spoon.
> spade.

(17) *stay*

We cook on a
> fire.
> story.
> stove.

(18) *strap*

The kite was on a
> rope.
> string.
> straw.

(19) *tree*

He did a good
> deed.
> true.
> trick.

3. Exercises to teach digraph sounds.

   a. Finish the words. They end like one of the words below the sentences. The first one is done for you.

   (1) Th_at_ cat can run.
   > boy   sing   hat

   (2) Th_____ is a big dog.
   > ran   his   ten

   (3) Wh_____ will we go?
   > hen   hat   pile

    (4) The ch____ was full of gold.
        shop   best   ship

    (5) We get wool from sh____.
        hot   fine   sleep

    (6) We sew with a needle and thr____.
        tree   bone   bread

b. Draw a line around the right word. It must start with the same digraph as the key word.[2]

    (1) *church*

                    chimney.
        We make butter in a   pail.
                    churn.

    (2) *ship*

                    coat.
        She put on her new   shoes.
                    sharp.

    (3) *they*

                    there.
        We will soon be   thing.
                  back.

    (4) *thick*

                    home.
        He was safe on   third.
                  thin.

    (5) *three*

                    truck.
        The king was on the   threw.
                  throne.

    (6) *whale*

                    white.
        The paper was   wheel.
                  warm.

    (7) *who*

                    whose ball this is.
        I don't know   white.
                  who.

4. Exercises to teach vowel sounds.

    a. The vowels *a, e, i, o, u* say their names in many words. This is their long sound. Write the vowel that is long after each word. Then use the word in a sentence.

age ____	dine ____	vase ____
like ____	cave ____	use ____
alone ____	home ____	rope ____
bite ____	white ____	mane ____

---

[2] All the important digraphs are included in these samples.

Call attention to the fact that each word has one consonant between the vowel and the final *e;* that usually makes the first vowel have a *long* sound. Some exceptions may be given, as:

give	love	come	where
some	live	whose	were

b. Write the vowel that is *long* after each word. Then use the word in a sentence.

peach ____	snail ____	heel ____	mail ____
reach ____	road ____	keep ____	trail ____
tease ____	bead ____	leaf ____	people ____
plains ____	boat ____	mean ____	praise ____

Call attention to the fact that many times when two vowels come together the first vowel takes the long sound and the second vowel is silent. Some exceptions may be given, as:

bread	heavy	meant	poem
break	great	house	piano
chief	head	piece	moon

c. Put in the right word. It must have a short vowel.

The boy ran after the _____.
boat   game   cat

Other exercises using context clues can be used because it is only by means of context clues that the child can tell whether a vowel is long or short in an unknown word.

5. Exercises to teach hard and soft consonant sounds.

    a. When *C* has the sound of *S* it has the soft sound. When it sounds like *K* it has the hard sound. Put *S* after the sentences in which *C* is soft and *H* when it is hard.

        (1) We went to the camp. ____
        (2) I saw his face. ____
        (3) We rode on a camel. ____
        (4) It sold for ten cents. ____
        (5) The calf was brown. ____
        (6) We eat our cereal. ____
        (7) It was a new act. ____

    b. Similar exercises can be used to teach the other hard and soft consonant sounds.

6. Exercises to teach variant endings.

    a. Draw a line under the right word.

                drink
        (1) The cat   her milk.
                drinks

                wanted
        (2) Now she   to run away.
                wanting

(3) The boys plays / played ball.

(4) He wishes / wishing to go.

(5) Let us go in swim. / swimming.

7. Exercises to teach common word elements.

   a. Put in the right word. It must end like the key word.

     (1) *talk*
      We had a brisk _____.
      chalk   walk   run

     (2) *light*
      It was a dark _____.
      right   room   night

   b. See how many words you can make that rhyme with the following words. Use each of them in a sentence.

     bat   street   bright   bank
     ball   house   sand   like

The exercises designed to increase knowledge of visual, structural, and phonetic elements should, as often as possible, be put in contextual settings. This is desirable because many times the true sound of an element can only be known from its use in context. For example, the vowel sound in *read* cannot be known out of context. Also, context makes for more rapid recognition of the parts being taught, which is desirable. In addition, context offers an immediate and independent check on the accuracy of the association of the printed symbols with the oral pronunciation. Nonetheless, there are certain drill devices that are used to increase the disabled child's knowledge of word parts. Such drill devices should be used sparingly and when used, the words drilled upon should be read in context so that the elements learned in the drill situation have a reasonable chance of being transferred into the reading situation.

These devices are for the most part adaptations of devices developed by Durrell (56). The following are the types frequently used:

1. Word wheels
2. Word slips
3. Word tachistoscopes

Word wheels are constructed by cutting two disks. One should be about 5 inches in diameter and the other slightly smaller. On the larger disk, words are printed with the initial element missing. These words should all start at the same distance from the center (about 1 inch) and progress toward the outer edge like the spokes of a wheel. On a single disk, only words that begin with the same word element should be used. The initial element should be left off. For example, if the initial blend *str* is to be

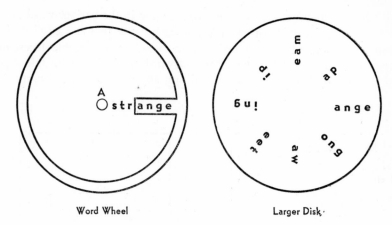

Word Wheel   Larger Disk·

FIG. 13. *str* Word Wheel.

taught, words such as *strap, strong, straw, string, strip, stream,* and *strange* could be used. The word endings only are printed on the larger disk (see Figure 13). In the smaller disk, cut a radial slit of the proper size and position to expose one word ending at a time. Print the initial blend *str* just to the left of the slit (see Figure 13). The two disks are fastened

FIG. 14. *ing* Word Wheel.

together at the center with a paper fastener (A), with the smaller disk on top. As the lower disk is rotated, the *str* on the smaller disk will make a word as it is combined with each ending on the larger disk (see Figure 13).

Other word parts may be taught in a like manner. If word endings, such as *ing, ake,* or *alk* are to be taught, the word wheel will need to be modified so that the ending is printed at the right of the slit cut in the smaller disk and the word beginnings are printed on the larger disk (see Figure 14).

Word slips may be developed to give training in the various word parts. They have an advantage over word wheels because they are easy to construct. A manila folder can be used to make the removable faces and slips. Figure 15 illustrates the use of a word slip. The removable faces and slips can be varied in order to drill on any particular word part. The

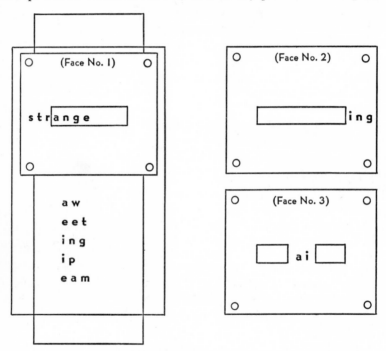

FIG. 15. Word slip device.

word slips and faces can be made by typing the word part to be drilled at the appropriate place on the face (see Figure 15 faces 1, 2, and 3). The remaining parts of the words can be typed or printed at convenient intervals on the slip. A permanent posterboard back can be used for all exercises, since the face is removable.

Word beginnings that could be typed on word slips to use with the *ing* ending on removable face No. 2 are: *th, s, br, r, str, wr,* and *k*. The following words could also be used with this face: *walk, talk, sing, jump, build, play, say, feed, hear,* etc. Root words ending in *e* or those that double the final consonant could also be used with face No. 2.

Slips and faces, such as face No. 1, could be made for all the important initial consonants, blends, and digraphs. No. 2 faces and slips could be made for all the important variant endings and visual and phonetic families. No. 3 faces and slips could be made to teach long and short vowels and vowel combinations. The words used in such exercises should be those that are being taught in the basal readers or from such lists of common words as compiled by Dale, Dolch, Gates, and Thorndike.

Word tachistoscopes such as the one illustrated in Figure 12, described earlier in this chapter, are really modifications of the *word slip* device and have the added feature that the exposure can be limited to one fixation. This is sometimes advisable for the child who has a tendency to dawdle or who tends to break words into too many parts. All that is needed to make any of the word slip faces into a tachistoscope is a shutter, which can be attached as indicated in Figure 12.

While drill on word parts with devices such as those discussed above has some merit for children who are limited in knowledge of visual, structural, and phonetic elements of words, it is more desirable to teach these in contextual exercises. Even these exercises are most effective when teaching the elements in words that come from a basal reading program. Under such circumstances, the child will not only be taught the elements in contextual settings in which he associates the printed symbols with oral pronunciation, but he will also get adequate review of the words introduced so that they can become a part of his permanent sight vocabulary. A more detailed method for teaching the child to relate word elements to sounds is the sound-tracing method. Such methods as those recommended by Fernald (70) and Monroe (131) prove beneficial with extremely disabled readers. These methods are highly individual and time-consuming, but they do aid the child who is severely limited in knowledge of word parts. Sound-tracing methods will be discussed in the chapter dealing with the specially handicapped child.

LACK OF ABILITY TO SYNTHESIZE

The child must be able to reassemble a word after he has visually separated it into parts and recognized them. Effective and rapid synthesis of the parts into the whole word is essential to word recognition. Many children are in difficulty with their reading because they lack ability in word synthesis. This ability to synthesize words is frequently called auditory blending. However, in actual reading situations, the word parts are neither thoroughly sounded nor auditorily blended. It is relatively infrequent that a mature reader resorts to auditory blending. He usually perceives the larger elements within a word visually and then synthesizes it visually without resorting to oral pronunciation at all. In the word *anytime,* for example, the able reader would see the words *any* and *time* in the larger word. He would not pronounce these parts nor would he pronounce the word as a whole, but he would see immediately that it was a compound word made up of two well-known words. The mature reader would identify the word *anytime* by visually synthesizing the known parts and would be aware of the meaning of the compound word. This form of visual analysis, perception, and synthesis takes place so rapidly that the mature reader is rarely aware of such perceptual acts. He immediately senses the meaning of the printed symbol without reflecting upon the symbol itself.

The mature reader, while reading silently, does not even sound out the parts of a broken word at the end of a line of print. He just looks at the part of the word on the upper line and then quickly glances down to the remainder of the word on the next line. He immediately identifies the word and its meaning. No oral pronunciation or auditory blending takes place.

The child who is beginning to learn to read or the child who is disabled in word synthesis cannot so readily synthesize words visually. Indeed, he often finds it difficult to blend a word auditorily once he has pronounced it part by part. In his early reading instruction, the child is often required to sound out words part by part and then blend the sound elements together. Sometimes he makes too great a separation of the parts when orally studying the word and he cannot auditorily reassemble it. The difficulty that children sometimes have in either auditory or visual synthesis of words is brought about by too early and too much emphasis on phonetic sounding of words. Other children may be in difficulty with word synthesis because they lack the capacity to blend sounds orally. This latter group of children constitute a troublesome problem to the teacher of word recognition. They are, for example, unable to tell what word an examiner is saying when he pronounces the word part by part. If he says the word *drink* as *dr—ink,* with about a second of time between the parts, the child cannot tell what the word is. In some cases, the child cannot even tell that the examiner is saying *drink* if he pronounces it normally a second time after he has dissociated it. Bond (18) has shown that a child who is as limited as this in this ability is much more likely to become a disabled reader when taught under methods that require him to use auditory blending than he would be if more emphasis were placed on visual recognition and synthesis.

Many children have difficulty in blending because the word parts were learned in isolation rather than in words or they were taught too often in drill exercises rather than in contextual settings. In such situations, the child learns to lean too heavily on oral pronunciation and auditory blending of word parts. Often the oral pronunciation of words, part by part, leads the child to introduce an interval between each part that makes blending difficult if not impossible. Frequently the child who resorts to letter-by-letter sounding has forgotten the beginning of the word before he has completed the parts. This does not necessarily indicate that the child has a synthesis difficulty, but rather, it suggests the presence of an erroneous technique of word recognition which should be corrected.

The diagnosis of inability to synthesize words is somewhat complex. Three judgments must be made. (1) Is the child's problem really one of poor synthesis or is it the result of ineffective analytical techniques? (2) Is the child's problem one of poor auditory blending or is it poor visual synthesis? (3) Is the child's difficulty the result of faulty learning or is he auditorily handicapped? These judgments can be made by a study of the results of the reading diagnostic tests. In the *Gates Diagnostic Test* (described in Chapter 9), the results of the tests of Visual Perception Techniques (blending letter sounds) and Auditory Techniques (blending letter sounds) will indicate whether the child has a real deficiency in synthesis and whether he is auditorily handicapped or not. A comparison between these test results and those obtained on the *Bond-Clymer-Hoyt Silent Reading Diagnostic Tests* will show whether the child's limitation is one of visual synthesis or of auditory blending.

The diagnostician may also observe the child's ability to reassemble words that have been correctly analyzed and pronounced, part by part. If the child is frequently unable to blend words analyzed, he lacks ability in auditory blending. The diagnostician can pronounce some words, part by part, to see if the child can blend the sounds he hears. If the child is able to blend a large percentage of the words and recognize them, the diagnostician can be sure that the child's difficulty is due to imperfect learning and not to an auditory handicap.

The remedial work that should be given to a child who is poor in the visual synthesis of words is to have him recognize words presented to him by rapid-exposure techniques. A slip of words correctly analyzed into syllables could be placed in the tachistoscope and the child could tell some fact about each word. For example, the following list could be used and the child could tell if the word named an animal or a food.

ba	boon		chip	munk	
but	ter		don	key	
buf	fa	lo	choc	o	late
ce	re	al	cook	ies	
bum	ble	bee	lem	on	ade
car	rot		let	tuce	
mon	key		rob	in	

Typed exercises with many words broken at the ends of the lines read under timed conditions will also aid in developing rapid visual synthesis of words.

For the child who lacks ability in auditory blending, any sounding out of words should be done in a smooth rather than an interrupted fashion. He should be given considerable experience in blending two-syllable words. In addition, he should be given oral blending training. The teacher could pronounce words with the syllables only slightly separated and the child could say the parts and blend. It would be best to start with two-syllable words and gradually build up to longer words. Then single syllable words could be separated and blended. For children who are in difficulty in blending because they have learned to separate the words so distinctly that they are unable to synthesize them, more attention should be given to exercises to develop sight vocabulary, to associate meanings with words, and to teach context clues. Also for children with this type of difficulty considerable reading of relatively easy material is recommended.

THE OVERANALYTICAL READER

The overanalytical reader results from too early an introduction of detailed oral-phonetic instruction in word recognition or from too much emphasis placed on the establishment of word-recognition techniques. This overemphasis results in an unfortunate lack of balance between the building of a sight vocabulary and word analysis. The result is that the child either fails to build a sight vocabulary and must, therefore, attack each word he meets or he forms the habit of analyzing all words, even those he knows at sight. Another condition that predisposes a child to become an overanalytical reader is too great a use of the artificial or isolated exercises for developing word-recognition techniques. Another source of overanalytical readers is too much emphasis on instruction with letter-by-letter sounding methods or other methods which encourage piecemeal observation of words. A fourth cause is too heavy a vocabulary burden brought about by failure of the reading program to use a basal reader with a nicely controlled vocabulary.

Overanalysis takes two forms. The child may have the tendency to analyze words that he knows at sight. This is not only a slow process which impedes thoughtful reading, but also it may lead the child to make unnecessary errors in word recognition. Some children have so thoroughly established the habit of analyzing known words that they make more errors when allowed unlimited time to pronounce a list of words than they do when the same list of words is flashed before them by means of a tachistoscope, which forces them to read the words at sight. It will be recalled that word-recognition techniques should be so learned that the child will identify known words without detailed study and that he will recognize rapidly the words he knows in any of their variant forms. He will resort to time-consuming, analytical procedures when and only when he is working out words he had not previously met. The characteristics of an effective reader are that he inspects a word in only as much detail as is required for its recognition. The overanalytical reader, in a way, reverses this process. He approaches the majority of words as though they were unfamiliar to him. He studies them in detail, isolates elements within them, applies his knowledge of word elements, and then synthesizes the elements back into a word only to find that it is a word with which he is already familiar. Such a pattern of reading is detrimental both to reading fluency and to comprehension. The child is so concerned with analyzing words he already knows that he has no time to attend to content. It takes him so long to recognize each word that he cannot group them into thought units, and so his comprehension suffers, as does his speed of reading of the connected material.

The second type of overanalytical reader is the one who breaks words into too many parts. Instead of using large elements known to him, he resorts too early and too often to a study of individual letter sounds. Such a habit of recognizing words is extremely inefficient and often confusing. For the majority of words, letter-by-letter sounding precludes recognition. Take the words in the previous sentence, for example, and try to sound each letter in the words and then blend them into the words. Only a few of the words could be recognized in this way and even for those few that could, it would be a time-consuming, inefficient method. It is foolish, for example, for a child who knows the word *talk* to resort to a letter-by-letter sounding of the word *talking*. Yet many overanalytical readers do this. It would be equally foolish and totally ineffective for the child who knew *tion* in *action* to try a letter-by-letter sounding of that element. Yet many children who have had drill on isolated letter sounds do just that. This is not to imply that they did not need such training, but it does mean that care must be taken to maintain proper balances in word recognition.

Some children who are overanalytical go to the extreme of a spelling attack on words. They try to remember each new word by spelling it out. For example, they encounter the unknown word *donkey,* and try to learn it by naming each letter. It is impossible for a child to remember all of the words he is expected to learn by trying to recall the sequence of letters through spelling. There are, however, many children who, when asked to work out a word aloud, will name each letter in turn and sometimes after calling the letters, can say the word. For example, such a child will see the word *horse,* which he doesn't identify. When asked to try to pronounce it, he will say, *"h—o—r—s—e, horse."* This type of word recognition is detrimental to reading growth. It results from two conditions. First, the child is taught by a spelling method, wherein the names of the letters are learned and then the child is expected to recognize the words by spelling them. The second condition that has produced a spelling attack on words is too early an emphasis on correct spelling.

The overanalytical reader can be detected by studying his relative effectiveness on timed and untimed word-recognition tests. He can also be identified by asking him to work on words orally when he gets into difficulty. A third way of detecting this type of difficulty is to note children who rank relatively high on tests of word elements, but who are low on tests of word recognition. They will also tend to be slow readers with poor comprehension.

The remedial treatment for children who tend to analyze words that are already known as sight words, is to give more training with the types of exercises that were discussed above for increasing sight vocabulary, associating words with meanings, and using context clues effectively. Flash techniques, such as employing the tachistoscope as described above, are helpful. Rapid exposure of word cards is useful in overcoming the tendency to analyze words that are well known. All of these exercises, however, should be used just to reinforce the emphases that should be applied during the other reading experiences of the child. The reading of material with few if any word difficulties, for purposes that require rapid reading, such as reading to get the general significance of a paragraph, reading to locate a specific bit of information, or reading to predict outcomes, will tend to overcome overanalytical tendencies.

The overanalytical reader who breaks words up into too many parts is corrected by emphasizing structural analysis and knowledge of the larger elements. Stress on syllabication rather than on sounding each letter is desirable. Noting root words, prefixes, suffixes, and variant endings will aid the child to establish the habit of analyzing words into larger elements. Instruction in word recognition should encourage the child to select as large elements as he can when he is working out the recognition of words that he does not know at sight. In the remedial work, weight should be put on the exercises for developing effective visual analysis that teach the child to isolate the larger structural and visual elements within words. In addition, it should be stressed that wide reading of relatively easy material will help the child who tends to resort to piecemeal observation of words.

EXCESSIVE LOCATIONAL ERRORS

Some children in difficulty in word recognition may not be readily classified in any of the above categories. Their mispronunciations tend, however, to form a consistent pattern that can be analyzed. These errors are classified in many ways by different workers in the field of reading. In general, the classifications are based on the location of the errors in the words in which they occur. For example, a child may make an excessive number of errors in the initial part of words, such as calling *house, mouse.* Another child might cluster his errors around the middle of words. He might call *house, horse.* A third child may make an unusually high percentage of errors toward the end of words. He might call *house, hour.*

With a given child, these errors tend to be most frequent in a specific part of the word because his word perception consistently neglects that part of the word. Roughly, these errors can be classified as Initial Errors,

Middle Errors, and Ending Errors. The child can also confuse the order of word parts and make Orientational Errors. The next chapter will suggest remedial methods for the orientational types of error.

Locational errors are diagnosed in two ways. First, a sample of errors made in word pronunciation can be assembled and classified. Second, the errors a child makes in multiple-choice test items, where the distractors are so selected that they represent error types, can indicate error patterns. The *Gates Reading Diagnostic Tests* utilize the first method of diagnosis, while the *Bond-Clymer-Hoyt Silent Reading Diagnostic Tests* employ the second. The diagnostician may also want to collect a sample of errors to classify informally. The disadvantage of doing this is that he cannot know the number of possibilities present in the sample he takes, nor can he judge how frequently, in general, a certain type of error should occur.

Initial errors indicate that the child as he inspects words is neglecting to notice the beginnings of words closely enough. He tends to make errors, such as calling *his, this* or *the, he.* Another type of initial error is calling the word *tall, fall* or *when, then.*

The remedial procedures used for correcting initial errors are similar to those described for developing more effective visual analysis of words and knowledge of initial elements. The difference lies in the matter of emphasis. For the child who tends to make an undue number of errors in the initial part of words, even though he knows initial elements, the exercises are designed to focus his attention more directly and systematically on the beginning of words. The building of a picture dictionary by the child will force him to look systematically at the words. Other exercises in alphabetizing words will make him pay greater attention to word beginnings. Sorting labeled pictures for filing will also help. The child should be shown the nature of his errors and a comparison should be made between the word he pronounced and the way it actually appeared in print. For example, if he calls *cat, eat,* he should be shown that he got the word almost right, but that he must pay closer attention to the beginning of the word. This sort of encouraging attitude toward the errors should be maintained. All the exercises on initial consonant blends and digraphs will aid in overcoming a child's tendency to neglect the beginnings of words. The following type of exercises will prove effective also:

1. Multiple-choice questions in which the child is forced to attend to the initial element.

                boat.
a. The man put on his goat.
                coat.

           way.
b. The dog ran away.
           play.

2. Classification exercises that emphasize initial sounds and word meanings.

   a. Find every word that starts like *crack* and is something we can eat.

crab	candy	cranberries
apple	crown	cradle
cracker	bread	crumbs
creep	cried	cream

3. Multiple-choice exercises in which the initial blend is given.

   a. The car went down the str____.
     strange   road   street

Middle errors result from insufficient inspection of words. These errors are brought about by two factors. First, the child may be hurrying his inspection of unfamiliar words to a point where he neglects the middles of words. Second, it may be the result of limited knowledge of vowel sounds. Exercises that teach the phonetic sounds of vowels will be helpful. Methods that encourage the child to inspect words in an orderly fashion will aid in correcting any tendency to neglect the middle of the word. Copying some of the words that cause difficulty may help, as would tracing the words also. The use of context as a check on accuracy will encourage the child to reinspect the words missed. A child using context clues, for example, could not very well call *cat, cot* in the sentence, "The cat climbed the tree," without rereading to find out what was wrong. The need for closer inspection of the middles of words should be pointed out to him and comparisons should be made between the error made and the printed word. Multiple-choice exercises, such as the following, will prove helpful in correcting this type of difficulty by forcing the child to attend to the middle parts of words.

                  pen.
1. The pig was in the pan.
                  pin.

                  children.
2. The egg was laid by the citizen.
                  chicken.

Ending errors are made quite frequently and it will be found that good readers make a higher percentage of these errors than do poor readers. An overemphasis on word endings may cause a neglect of the very important initial elements and it may also cause reversals and other orientational confusions. The mature reader starts at the beginning of an unfamiliar word and works systematically along it from left to right until it is completely inspected. All the exercises designed to increase knowledge of variant endings, families of words, and suffixes will aid in eliminating an extreme tendency to make errors in the final elements of words. If the exercises are in contextual settings, the child must attend both to beginnings and endings of words. Such exercises are helpful in calling attention to the final element without the hazard of creating more difficulties than are corrected. One type of exercise frequently used by teachers is unfortunate. Finding words in a list that belong to a *word family,* such as the *at* family or the *ay* family without using meaning as a check is detrimental because the child selects the words by the endings alone without recognizing what the words are. This forces the child to neglect the important initial element of the words and encourages him to avoid an orderly inspection of each word.

Exercises that may be used safely are:

1. Finish the word. It should rhyme with *call.*
   The boy was playing with a b_____.
   tall   back   ball

2. Find the words that end like *coat,* which you would like to play with.
   goat   doll   float
   gloat   boat   clock

SUMMARY

Word recognition is a difficult and complex learning. It involves the development of a highly integrated and flexible set of skills and abilities. In order to avoid some of the more serious types of word-recognition difficulties, well-organized instruction must be given at all levels. The child must be started by teaching him to build the habit of attempting to recognize words as words. The early training entails the use of context clues, picture clues, and teacher's questions. Then the child is taught to note similarities in initial elements and so gradually the whole hierarchy of word-recognition techniques is developed. These skills and knowledges fall roughly into five types: (1) the ability to recognize many words at sight and to associate meanings with printed symbols; (2) skill in using context clues and other meaning aids to anticipate the words to be recognized and to check on their accuracy; (3) skill in employing a flexible and efficient set of techniques in visually analyzing words into usable recognition elements; (4) knowledge of a wide variety of visual, structural, and phonetic elements; (5) skill in both auditory blending and visual synthesis of word parts into word wholes.

The major source of difficulty in word recognition is the failure to establish any of these basic learnings and the failure to maintain a balance among them. The best method for correcting difficulties in word recognition is to have the disabled reader develop these skills and knowledges in the course of reading meaningful material in a basal reading program. The remedial teacher should take great care in the methods she uses in introducing new words, so that the child's strengths may be utilized and any limitations in recognition may be corrected while the proper balances are maintained. The exercises suggested in the teacher's manuals that stress the skills needed by the child should be emphasized.

Workbook exercises that accompany basal readers are among the best for developing word-recognition skills and knowledges. In addition to these essential materials, the remedial teacher will need to work up supplementary exercises of her own devising. The various sorts that have proven helpful in correcting limitations in word recognition have been described in this chapter. They should, however, be used with caution and recognized as drill devices rather than as a complete solution to the disabled reader's word-recognition problems.

SELECTED READINGS

BOND, G. L., and WAGNER, E. B., *Teaching the child to read,* rev. ed. New York: The Macmillan Company, 1950, Chaps. 9, 10.

BRUECKNER, L. J. and BOND, G. L., *Diagnosis and treatment of learning difficulties.* New York: Appleton-Century-Crofts, Inc., 1955, Chaps. 6, 7.

DURRELL, Donald D., *Improvement of basic reading abilities.* Yonkers (N.Y.): World Book Company, 1940, Chaps. 8, 9.

GATES, Arthur I., *The improvement of reading,* 3rd ed. New York: The Macmillan Company, 1947, Chaps. 7, 8, 9.

HARRIS, Albert J., *How to increase reading ability,* 3rd ed. New York: Longmans, Green & Company, 1956, Chaps. 12, 13, 14.

McKEE, Paul, *The teaching of reading in the elementary school.* Boston: Houghton Mifflin Company, 1948, Chaps. 8, 9, 10.

McKIM, Margaret G., *Guiding growth in reading.* New York: The Macmillan Company, 1955, Chaps. 9, 12.

RUSSELL, David H., *Children learn to read.* Boston: Ginn and Company, 1949, Chaps. 9, 10.

TINKER, Miles A., *Teaching elementary reading.* New York: Appleton-Century-Crofts, Inc., 1952, Chaps. 8, 9.

YOAKAM, Gerald A., *Basal reading instruction.* New York: McGraw-Hill Book Company, Inc., 1955, Chaps. 8, 9.

13 TREATING ORIENTATIONAL DIFFICULTIES

DEVELOPMENT of proper directional habits in the reading situation involves two related instructional tasks. The first is concerned with acquisition of the left-to-right sequence of eye movements along a line of print. This is a somewhat gross orientation which nonetheless must be learned. The second task is establishment of the left-to-right direction of attack required for proficient word identification and recognition. This is a more precise and difficult skill to acquire. Contrary to one's first impression, these two aspects of sequential orientation in reading are only roughly related. It is true, of course, that both involve beginning at the left and progressing toward the right. But a child may have learned to begin at the left end of a line of print and in general move his eyes on toward the right without having mastered proper directional orientation within particular words. Extensive and continuing training is needed to develop the latter.

CHARACTERISTICS OF NORMAL GROWTH

An appreciation of the essential learnings in developing left-to-right orientation in reading depends upon a knowledge of pre-school perceptual habits, and of the proper developmental program of instruction in school.

Pre-school Perceptual Habits

During the pre-school years the child has learned to recognize people, landscapes, animals, and objects both from firsthand visual experience and from viewing pictures and diagrams. In all this, the direction of the perceptual sequences as revealed by eye movements is neither orderly nor oriented in a specific direction. Rather they involve a series of brief glances while the eyes rove in an irregular pattern of fixations over the object or picture. The directions of the movements are just as likely to be from right to left as left to right, or upward as downward, or obliquely in any direction. As the child looks over an object, noting points of interest or searching for familiar items, the direction of the eye movements is not only irregular but also unpredictable to a large degree. These habits of perception are thoroughly established prior to entering school. Unless appropriate systematic instruction is given by the time the child begins to read words and sentences, he is likely to continue the habit of examining

303

objects with irregular directional sequences in viewing words. In school, to be efficient, the child must read words in a sentence, one after another from left to right. And unless a word is recognized at a glance, he must proceed along the word from left to right to identify it correctly.

Pre-reading Instruction

Until a child arrives at school for the first time, he has had little or no experience that develops left-to-right perceptual sequences. He may have viewed comic strips while someone read them aloud. While this provides some training, it tends to be incidental and unsystematic. At school, during the pre-reading activities, a child is ordinarily given specific and systematic instruction so that he will develop the habit of orienting himself to the left-to-right direction in perceptual activities. To facilitate this, the child should be taught to identify his right and left hand, and to grasp the concept of right and left in relation to the sides of objects in the schoolroom such as the bulletin board, the blackboard, the desks, the pages of a picture book, and so on. This can be accomplished largely through incidental learning or games. Instruction of this kind, although systematic, is informal in nature rather than formal drill. For instance, the teacher can remark that she will write or draw something at the left side of the blackboard as she starts to do so. When the teacher asks the children to rearrange the material on the bulletin board, she can ask them to post the materials from left to right. Again, a sequence of action pictures can be drawn from left to right on the blackboard and interpreted in the same direction as the children follow. Certain materials in readiness workbooks are arranged to develop the habit of working from left to right. Some picture books are designed especially for this purpose. The resourceful teacher will frequently bring in the notion of left and right in instruction, in play, in arrangement of materials, and so on, so that the concept will become well established. Several useful exercises and games which may be used for this training are described by Hester (99). At every opportune place, therefore, as the child approaches the time when he will begin to read, the left-to-right sequence of perception should be emphasized. For example, as the teacher writes on the blackboard, the child can be shown that the words are formed from left to right, and that she then reads the material in the same order, following with a pointer. An essential aspect of pre-reading instruction is to set up this proper directional orientation.

Authors are not in agreement as to the value of this kind of training. Hildreth (102) states that extensive training in left-to-right orientation is not necessary prior to learning to read. She questions whether it contributes to reading readiness. According to her, the average child does equally well if he gets his directional training during regular practice in learning to read and write, provided sufficient attention is devoted to the proper orientation during the beginning lessons. Gates (79) holds a contrary view. He states that knowledge of the concepts of left and right and progression from left to right should be clearly established before reading is begun. Furthermore, he approves of observing materials other than words to give experience in the left-to-right sequence. Monroe (133) is another prominent writer who emphasizes the need for habituating the left-to-right sequence of perception by instruction in a variety of situations throughout the entire reading readiness program.

Although some writers have expressed reservations on the necessity of this training, we hold that it does have certain values. It is possible, of course, that some instruction designed to develop left-to-right directional habits may become artificial and ineffectual but this need not occur. It can be conceded also that pre-reading instruction in left-to-right orientation may not transfer readily to the reading situation. The alert teacher will expect this and consequently she gives additional instruction to facilitate the transfer as reading gets under way. It is undoubtedly helpful for the child to sense early that, in the reading situation, one progresses from left to right. When work to develop word recognition begins, the teacher's task is much easier if all the pupils have clear concepts of left, right, and progression from left to right. Even though the average pupil may without difficulty acquire the knack of proper directional orientation during reading instruction, a considerable number do not do so. Actually the time devoted to developing directional orientation is relatively small. The habit is effectively taught largely through incidental techniques. These incidental techniques can be reinforced by systematic use of readiness books while the children are developing such other readiness skills as ability to use books and other instructional materials, as working in groups, or following directions, or attending to sequences, etc. As the pre-reading training progresses, observation plus checking by means of informal exercises will identify those pupils who have no clear concept of left and right and who are failing to acquire the left-to-right orientation. These pupils should receive additional systematic instruction to overcome the deficiency.

Instruction During Reading

As soon as children begin to read words and lines of print, additional emphasis must be placed upon the development of proper directional orientation. Effective reading is achieved only when perceptual sequences, largely guided by eye movements, move from left to right. This requires systematic regimentation. Except in the case of sight words, those which are recognized at a glance, the children must be instructed to examine a word from left to right in working out its recognition. It will be necessary for the teacher to demonstrate repeatedly the proper directional orientation in perceiving words. She should be sure, before using these terms, that all pupils have learned through preliminary and partly incidental training the meaning of left and right.

Establishment of the left-to-right habit is by no means confined to beginning instruction in reading. The training is continued more or less throughout the instruction for development of the word-recognition techniques. Such training is effective only when correctly and systematically done (see chapter on word recognition). Working out word identification through proper attention to initial consonants, consonant substitution, phonetic analysis, structural analysis, syllabication, and proper use of the dictionary requires constant attention to the left-to-right orientation. Many pupils who have developed proper directional habits in the early stages of reading will lapse from the habit at later stages without additional instruction.

In addition to progressing from left to right in word recognition, the child must learn to move his eyes from left to right in reading a line of print. He must be shown that he looks at the first word at the left and then progresses systematically to the right with a long return sweep from the end of one line to the first word in the next line. The number of stops or fixations along the line and the duration of each fixation need not concern the teacher at this time. This is a matter that depends upon the thought processes and will automatically become more efficient as the child gains maturity in reading. The relation of eye movements to reading proficiency is considered in detail later.

The left-to-right direction in reading words and in reading lines of print is, of course, developed simultaneously in the co-ordinated reading program. Unless these directional habits are firmly fixed, the child may become a disabled reader.

BASES FOR INAPPROPRIATE DIRECTIONAL HABITS

Lack of proper orientation of the perceptual sequence in reading words results in errors of response due to observing letters in a reverse order or a partial reverse order. A full reversal is illustrated by reading *saw* for *was* or *on* for *no;* a partial reversal by reading *won* for *own.* Sometimes reversal of a single letter in perceiving a word produces an error as reading *big* for *dig.*

Studies by Davidson (43) and Teegarden (166) reveal that it is a very common occurrence for children to make some reversals when learning to read. As the child progresses through the primary grades, reversals ordinarily become less frequent. Even in the upper elementary grades, an occasional reversal error is normal. But when reversal errors do not decrease or even increase as time goes on, they become a serious handicap to progress in reading. According to the Teegarden study just cited, children with marked reversal tendencies do not make normal progress in reading. Monroe (131) found that reversals were fairly common among her reading defect cases. Tinker (170) noted that all severely retarded or nonreaders exhibit more or less difficulty in maintaining proper direction of perceptual sequences in the reading situation. Harris (94) points out that about 10 per cent of reading disability cases manifest prominent reversal tendencies. Where present, he states, they are very significant.

While reversal tendencies constitute only one of the manifestations of reading difficulty, they occur frequently enough to warrant closer examination. Apparently one or more of a number of factors may be involved in producing reversals. Two of these have been mentioned above: The first involves the transfer of earlier habits of perception to the reading situation, i.e., the attempt to study words with the irregular pattern of eye fixations used to examine objects and pictures. Without assistance, most children do not discover that the only effective procedure for identifying words is the left-to-right orientation of perception. The second is a lack of systematic instruction in left-to-right orientation during the pre-reading period and during the initial stages of reading instruction. Too frequently, a teacher may emphasize the left-to-right direction in reading lines of print but fail to give specific instruction for proper orientation in word recognition. As a result, children employ a variety of inappropriate methods of attack in attempting to work out the identification and recognition of the unfamiliar words encountered. Consequently, it is not only difficult for these children to recognize words properly, but also they tend to make reversal errors of one sort or another. Then there are also other causes of inappropriate directional orientation in observing words to which we will now turn. Several of these have been described by Gates (79).

Lateral Dominance

Laterality is the short term for *lateral dominance,* a phrase which applies equally to preferred use of right or left hand for skilled manual operations, or preferred use of one eye or the other for sighting. *Mixed* or *crossed dominance* is then the term for a combination of right-eyedness and left-handedness, or vice versa. And the phrase *lack of dominance* is applied when no consistent preference of one side over the other has been established.

The degree to which reversals are caused by laterality factors is not clear. After reviewing the evidence, Gates (79) suggests that in only a few cases is left-handedness or left-eyedness the basis of reversal errors. He also considers that mixed laterality and lack of hand dominance are unimportant in this respect. Dearborn (47) argues that it is easier for a left-eyed person to look from right to left than left to right, and that with mixed dominance or lack of dominance there is a confusion in direction of eye movements which results in reversals. Monroe (131) states that left-handed and left-eyed children, as well as those with mixed dominance, may become confused in directional responses. Her data reveal a slight tendency for left-eyed children to make more reversals than right-eyed children among her reading defect cases. Lack of consistent cerebral dominance, according to Orton's theory (136)—and we emphasize that it is a *theory*—leads to confusion and conflict in perceiving words so that reversal errors will be prevalent. A number of recent studies such as those of Gates and Bond (84), Gates and Bennett (81), Bennett (7), and Hildreth (100) fail to establish any significant relation between laterality and reversal tendencies. But all these studies did tend to find slightly more reversals among the left-handed group even though the differences were not statistically significant. We conclude, then, that although such differences do not seem important in group comparisons, laterality deviations *may* be crucial in an occasional specific case. Furthermore, the view of Carmichael and Dearborn (34) appears to have some merit. They point out that for left-handed children, the natural and easy movement of their skilled hand is right to left. Since the eyes tend to follow controlled hand movements, a similar perceptual orientation may be established. If the beginner in school who is left-handed tends to draw, scribble and write from right to left, his perceptual habits may be so formed as to produce reversals in word perception and interfere with his progress in reading. Although this is a possibility, it may or it may not occur for any given case.

Any conclusion about whether certain varieties of lateral dominance cause reversals in word perception must be tentative. Group studies seem to give a negative answer. But we must remember the practical reality that in reading disability, we are always dealing with specific clinical cases. The evidence suggests that in a relatively few cases, one of the factors involved in reversals may well be left-handedness, left-eyedness, mixed dominance, lack of dominance, or the behavioral habits due to one of these.

Visual Defects

Any condition which necessitates prolonged examination of a word in order to recognize it will produce numerous eye fixations, many of them being regressive or right-to-left movements. Among such conditions are visual defects, such as heterophoria, astigmatism, and hyperopia (Chapter 5), in which clear seeing of a word is impossible. It is inevitable that the to and fro movements employed in detailed examination of the unclear word image should include some inappropriate directional orientations in word perception, i.e., reversals. Experimental evidence of these is shown by Gates and Bennett (81) in their study of reversal tendencies among poor readers. The frequency of visual defects in the reversal group becomes twice as great as in the non-reversal group. They state that visual defects of one kind or another are the most conspicuous characteristic of the reversal group thus far found. In another evaluation, Betts (8) stresses the role of visual defects in causing reversals. Apparently the evidence that reversals are related to the presence of visual defects is indisputable.

Vocabulary Burden

Another condition which leads to prolonged examination of individual words is too heavy a vocabulary burden. Summaries (171, 174) of the literature dealing with eye movements and their causes list many studies showing that when a reader, either in the primary grades or later, encounters a word unfamiliar to him, he is forced to examine it in detail. Numerous fixations are made on the word as the reader moves his eyes forward and backward in irregular sequences. Too frequent encounters with unfamiliar words may have serious consequences for the beginning pupil. In addition to interrupting his regular left-to-right progressions along the lines of print, the frequent occurrences of regressions within words tend to develop inappropriate directional habits in word perception, so that reversals occur. To avoid this, there must be safeguards against accumulating too much new vocabulary during the early grades while the mechanics of reading are being developed.

Discrimination of Sound Sequences

Monroe (131) lists as a reversal cause, difficulty in discriminating the temporal sequences of speech sounds and difficulty in co-ordinating such sound sequences with the left-to-right direction of printed words. Thus in *stop* and *spot* the sounds are nearly the same but the order of occurrence of those sounds is different. It is necessary for the child to differentiate the sequence of sounds as well as the spatial pattern of letters in vision before he can develop an effective technique for identifying unfamiliar words.

Emphasis upon Word Endings

Reversals may be due to a misplaced emphasis on sounding in the development of techniques for word analysis. In acquiring the initial sight vocabulary, word recognition depends upon word-form clues. At the proper time, the preliminary aspects of sounding are introduced. As emphasized by Dolch (54), the most important aspect of sounding at any time during school life is use of the initial sounds, particularly initial consonants. This first step should be emphasized in reading instruction throughout the primary grades as the sequential program of word analysis unfolds. The habit should become so ingrained that the child will immediately use the initial sound when he encounters a word that he does not recognize as a "sight" word, i.e., perceive it as a whole. Furthermore, the initial consonants should be learned in words that are not in the same phonogram family. Thus *t* may be learned from *tell, take, turn,* etc. Further emphasis on the beginnings of words is achieved by teaching initial consonant-vowel combinations such as in *man, mat, may,* before the ending families are taken up. The more common practice, however, is to teach common ending families as in *man, ran, can.* Children are accustomed to listening to rhymes. Consequently it is relatively easy to teach the child to separate the initial consonant from the rhyming ending. Sometimes introducing instruction which emphasizes the endings of words prior to establishing firmly the habit of attending to word beginnings may interfere with or upset the left-to-right orientation necessary for accurate word recognition. Such instruction would tend to develop the bad habit of looking at ends of words first and middles or beginnings later. In this way, the child could become habituated to a word-recognition technique conducive to producing reversal errors.

Phonetic Analysis

Phonetics refers to a body of skills that must be learned. These skills are slow in developing and mastery of them is achieved only through an extended period of instruction continuing for several grades. Even the initial aspects of phonetic analysis (proper use of initial word sounds) can be learned satisfactorily only after the child has acquired what may be termed phonetic readiness. Too early introduction of sounding techniques and the teaching of too many principles all at once lead to trouble. The child becomes confused and fails to make satisfactory progress. When this is coupled with too great an emphasis on sounding with accompanying neglect of other word-recognition clues and techniques, a piecemeal type of word observation is acquired which hinders rather than promotes accurate recognition. The confusion accompanied by unsuccessful piecemeal observation leads to detailed examination and re-examination of a word. The errors of perception which occur usually include reversal tendencies, particularly part reversals.

Role of Eye Movements

In any reading situation when the vocabulary and comprehension load becomes too heavy, eye movements tend to fall into a random searching pattern, moving forward and backward in the attempt to recognize words and find meanings. As indicated above, this confused, random searching can lead to reversals in the order of words in a sentence as well as in letters within words. Some children, who have been subjected to too difficult a reading program, establish random eye-movement habits that persist even when they read materials with no difficulties. Nevertheless, at this point it is well to sound a caution. Eye-movement sequences tend to follow and indicate the presence of bad observational habits, not to cause them. It is the confusion in the central processes of perception and comprehension that leads to the random searching behavior. The irregular eye-movement patterns merely reflect this confusion. The situation is ordinarily remedied by clearing up these difficulties rather than by training the eye movements as such. This is done by providing materials well within the comprehension and word-recognition ability of the pupil. Other things being equal, the random searching type of eye movements will disappear when word recognition is not too difficult and when comprehension becomes clear and precise.

TECHNIQUES OF DIAGNOSIS

There are two aspects of inappropriate directional habits in reading that will need diagnosis: (1) inability to maintain left-to-right movements throughout a line of print, and (2) reversals in word perception.

Reading Lines of Print

Directional habits in reading a line of print are revealed by observation of eye movements, using apparatus, or by informal observation during oral reading. A complete survey of the techniques for studying eye movements is supplied by Tinker (171). Photographic records of eye movements during reading will reveal the sequence of fixations with regressions and inadequate back sweeps from the end of one line to the beginning of the next one. Study of these records will, therefore, reveal inappropriate directional habits. But such photographing of eye movements requires expensive apparatus and a trained operator. Direct observation by the teacher of the child's eye movements during reading ordinarily will reveal sufficiently well excessive regressions and inaccurate back sweeps. The teacher merely holds up a book or card with the printed material between her and the pupil and looks directly into the child's eyes while he reads. With some practice she will be able to note random back and forth eye movements within a line and when there is inability to hit accurately the beginning of the next line on the back sweep. The latter is shown when the child makes two or three moves to get back to the beginning of the correct new line. In general, the elaborate study of eye movements in the reading clinic involves much professional work with little profit except for research purposes. Tinker (169) has treated this problem and concluded that an elaborate study of eye movements in diagnostic and remedial reading can be dispensed with.

An equally satisfactory technique for discovering inappropriate directional habits in reading a line of print is to observe a pupil's responses during oral reading. A slow, stumbling performance with much repetition of words and transposition of words within the sentence will ordinarily indicate lack of consistent left-to-right progression along the line. Difficulty in finding quickly the beginning of a new line is shown by hesitation between lines or by reading a wrong word near the beginning of the new line. Lack of success in smoothly following typical paragraph material is another sign of difficulty in directional orientation.

Remedial Procedures

Methods for developing concepts of left and right and for giving children experience in observing materials in left-to-right sequence have been described above. Additional training of this kind should be provided for the few pupils who are still deficient in directional orientation.

The procedure for correcting inappropriate directional habits in progressing along a line of print are pretty much the same as those described above for beginning the development of proper orientation in reading. Demonstrations and explanations are given by the teacher during work at the blackboard and with experience charts and other printed materials. The pupil's attention is directed toward writing from left to right. Then the child is instructed to follow as a pointer or finger is moved along underneath the words when the sentences are read. In addition to explaining the procedure, demonstrations and exercises should be carefully organized, frequently repeated and emphasized. Finger pointing by the child during reading is encouraged in the early stages of remedial work. In such remedial work, the main difference from regular teaching is that the teacher is working with a single child. The training must be systematic and adjusted to the severity of the difficulty. Some cases will require much more extensive training than others.

Certain special aids are available for this corrective work. The first is to work with a single sentence that is confined to a single line of print. Its vocabulary and sentence structure should be well within the comprehension of the pupil. Additional spacing between words in the sentence sometimes helps. After considerable practice with a single line, a selection of two or three lines may be used with rather wide spacing between lines, even quadruple spacing, rather than the familiar double spacing of typed material. In teaching how to read this multiple-line material, emphasis must be put on going all the way back to the first word in the new line in the back sweep of the eyes after one line is finished. The teacher should demonstrate this by swinging a pointer or finger from the end of one line to the beginning of the next in a single continuous sweep. After an adequate amount of practice on this kind of spaced material, the child should be guided in transferring his new skill to reading regular book printing. Any basic reader of proper difficulty will be satisfactory for this. Instruction in following finger pointing along successive words in the line, in making the back sweep, etc., is continued in systematically organized periods of training until the left-to-right sequence of movements in reading words in sentences is firmly established. As the child gains skill, the training periods are resorted to less frequently until there is no longer need of them.

Word Perception

As noted above, inappropriate orientation in perceiving words results in reversal errors. Both diagnosis and remedial instruction for reversals are necessarily more elaborate than for directional habits in reading lines of print. The most satisfactory diagnosis of reversal tendencies is achieved through the use of standardized tests. Several of these tests have been described in Chapter 9. Parts of these tests which are employed for detecting and evaluating reversal errors are listed below:

1. *Durrell Analysis of Reading Difficulty:* Word Recognition and Word Analysis Test detects reversals of *b* and *d*, *p* and *q*, and of the sequences of letters within words.

2. *Monroe Diagnostic Reading Test:* Oral Reading Test, Iota Word Test, and Word Discrimination Test detect reversals of *b* and *d*, *p* and *q*, *u* and *n*, and of the sequences of letters within words and reversals of the order of words.

3. *Gates Reading Diagnostic Tests:* Oral Reading Test, Reversible Word Test, and Word Perception and Analysis Test detect reversals of the sequence of letters in words.

4. *Bond-Clymer-Hoyt Silent Reading Diagnostic Tests:* Recognition of Reversible Words in Context Test and the error classification in the Word Recognition Tests detect reversal of the sequences of letters in words.

It has already been noted that it is normal for beginners to make some reversals and that these are gradually eliminated by most children as they progress in reading. With each pupil who is a reading case, therefore, it has to be discovered whether reversals are common enough to cause trouble rather than being merely occasional incidents in ordinarily straight-ahead reading. In other words, it is necessary to decide whether the frequency of reversals is a sign merely of immature reading or is a genuine reading handicap. This evaluation is accomplished by consulting the norms which accompany the Gates, the Monroe, and the Bond-Clymer-Hoyt tests. In each instance, the frequency of reversals which constitutes a reading handicap and which must be corrected is indicated.

There are contrasting views concerning whether letter confusions, such as mistaking *b* for *d* and *p* for *q* are true reversals. Gates (79) states that he has evidence from unpublished data indicating that there is no close relationship between a pupil's confusing these letters with each other and a failure to employ a constant left-to-right orientation in observing words. Monroe (131), on the other hand, classifies the interchange of *b* for *d*, *p* for *q*, and *n* for *u* as regular reversal tendencies, e.g., reading *dig* for *big*. And Bond, Clymer, and Hoyt, when they organized their key for the *Silent Reading Diagnostic Tests,* found that reversal of these letters should be classified as regular reversal errors. In any case, if such errors persist with retarded readers, some corrective instruction seems indicated. Monroe, page 127, proposes using a tracing technique to achieve proper identification of such letters.

Remedial Procedures

In general, significant degrees of reversing the order of letters in words occur more frequently among the more severely retarded readers. This is not surprising when one refers back to the causes of reversals in word perception discussed above. The child who has severe eye defects, who has received inadequate training in left-to-right orientation, who has been taught so that he emphasizes word endings rather than beginnings, or who has been exposed to an improper program of phonetic training, not only develops reversals but also seldom progresses far in learning to read. Any analysis of the methods successfully employed to instruct nonreaders or severely retarded readers reveals that one procedure overshadows all others. Whether it is the *a-b-c* method of Hinshelwood (103), the sounding method of Monroe (131), and Kirk (114), or the tracing-sounding-writing method of Fernald (70), the instruction leads to habits of consecutive perception from left to right along the word, accompanied by a strong emphasis upon developing adequate apprehension of words as wholes, i.e., proper blending of letter sounds into word units.

The remedial teacher must not assume that correction of reversal tendencies constitutes the entire instruction program for any reversal case. Ordinarily, other difficulties are present and must be taken care of. But where reversals are present to a significant degree, as will be found in about 10 per cent of the disability cases, they are very important and require carefully organized and sometimes prolonged treatment.

In the beginning, the teacher gives a clear exposition of the need, in order to recognize a word, for examining it from left to right. She accompanies this explanation with a demonstration. After writing a word on the blackboard or on paper, she moves a pointer or her finger along the word as she pronounces it slowly. To emphasize the procedure when a restudy is needed, she then moves her finger quickly back to the very beginning of the word, and progresses to the right again as she reads it a second time. On the second time through, the teacher should put stress on the desirability of grasping the word as a unit after the difficult part is worked out. Next, the method of working out the recognition of an unfamiliar word encountered in the context of a sentence is explained and demonstrated in a similar manner. The finger is moved along underneath the words as they are read. After a slight pause on reaching the unfamiliar word, she moves her finger slowly along the word, pronouncing it as she did with the isolated word. The explanations and demonstrations are repeated as frequently as necessary while the pupil is practicing the left-to-right orientation in perceiving words. It is desirable for the pupil to practice with words in sentence context as soon as possible so that he may make maximum use of context clues to aid word recognition. In his practice with sentences he will become accustomed to employing the left-to-right progression along lines of print and to identifying unknown words in actual reading situations. Transfer of guided practice to sentences and paragraphs in book materials is made as soon as possible. It may be that this skill in proper perceptual orientation in reading isolated words and words in isolated sentences may not transfer automatically to book reading.

Although a child may be encouraged at first to use his finger to guide his perception along lines of print and along the successive letters in an unknown word, certain cautions are necessary. Such aid is definitely a crutch and should gradually be dispensed with when no longer needed. Furthermore, the teacher should instruct the pupil so that finger movements are used properly, i.e., not to point at one word after another with stops, but to use a consistent and *continuous* sliding movement from left to right to guide sequences of perception. Otherwise the finger may be used only to keep the place rather than to promote left-to-right progression. If the finger is moved forward and backward along a line or a word, or if it is held in one place while the reader examines a word in random order, nothing helpful will be accomplished. This use of the finger as a pointer will provide a ready means of developing proper directional movements in reading and will aid in correcting reversal tendencies only when it is carefully supervised by the teacher. But Monroe (131) has made it perfectly clear that proper use of this device is effective in preventing and in eliminating reversal errors.

Other Motor Aids

Many procedures employed with reversal cases to develop correct orientation in perceiving words are partly or largely motor in nature. One of these is the *Fernald* (70) *tracing-sounding-writing* method. A word is written by the teacher with crayola on paper in plain blackboard-sized script (or in print if child has used manuscript writing in this connection). The pupil then traces the word with finger contact, sounding aloud each part of the word as he traces it. This is repeated until he is able to write the word correctly *without looking at the copy*. The word should be traced with a continuous movement of the finger and the pronunciation should be done slowly, running the sounds together so the word is grasped as a unit. Thus the word *man* is spoken as the word is traced. Pronunciation of the separate letters without blending them into a word unit should be avoided. In a similar manner with a polysyllable word like *curtain, cur* is pronounced as it is traced and *tain* as it is traced, with the two syllables spoken so that they run together to make the whole word. The pronounceable parts of the word are sounded in a similar manner as the word is written without copy. The word should always be written and spoken as a unit. If the child fails on first attempt to write the word, he goes back to the copy, looks at the word, and perhaps traces it again with sounding as before. The child is never allowed to erase and patch up a word he is trying to write, for this would interrupt the steady left-to-right progression. After a word is written correctly, it is placed in a large file, alphabetized according to the first letter of the word. In addition to directing the child's attention to the beginning of words, this will prepare him for dictionary work.

The child should know the meaning of each word traced, and should experience its use in meaningful context as soon as he can write it. After a certain amount of tracing-sounding-writing, the child will be able to look at a word, pronounce it, and write it without looking at copy. A more detailed description of this method will be given in the chapter on the specially handicapped child. Here we are concerned primarily with its use for correcting reversal tendencies in perceiving words. In this, the emphasis is upon tracing and pronouncing a word as a unit, followed by writing and at the same time pronouncing the word as a unit. In addition, the phonetic knowledge gained gives the children a feeling of mastery in attacking unknown words. This is one of the most effective means of developing proper orientation in word perception.

Monroe (131) has worked out and successfully used a modification of the Fernald method. As employed by Monroe, it is actually a *combined phonetic and sounding-tracing method.* The procedure is illustrated by the following example: The word *man* is written in large cursive writing on a piece of paper. Attention is directed to the word and its pronunciation. The child is asked to say *man* as slowly as possible, as demonstrated by the teacher. He then takes a pencil and traces over the word while saying *man* slowly. He is encouraged to trace quickly and speak slowly, so as to come out even. The aim of this is to pronounce the word distinctly and slowly enough so that its sequence of sounds becomes evident. Further training has as its aim development of the knack of sliding the voice from one sound to the next so that the word is pronounced as a unit.

A sound-dictation method has been substituted as a variation of the tracing method. Here the child writes the words as the teacher dictates their sounds slowly, having first told the child he would hear the separate sounds, and asked him to say them slowly as he writes the letters for each sound. Thus, she pronounces *man,* having first asked the child to both say and write whatever word she says. In the case of *man,* the child is told that the *a* is short by hearing the teacher sound it that way. To use this method, the child must have learned the letters that correspond to the letter sounds and know how to write them. Children with second- and third-grade achievement usually do well on such drills. According to Monroe, writing from dictation with these directions is as helpful as the tracing, and some children prefer to write. Both the tracing-sounding and the writing-sounding techniques foster the discrimination of sound sequences in words and the coordination of these with visual sequences. Detailed exercises for doing this are given by Monroe.

Writing Words. Many children who are reversal cases have already had some experience in writing by the time they reach the reading clinic. The remedial teacher can make good use of writing to promote correct orientation in dealing with words. When writing, it is necessary to begin at the left and move to the right. So when writing is employed to develop left-to-right orientation, it should be free writing rather than the copying of material from the blackboard, a chart, or a book. The latter tends to become a piecemeal operation rather than a continuous sequence. The training can be started with simple words and sentences. Some polysyllabic words should be used as soon as the child can handle them. He should be encouraged to observe and pronounce aloud to himself each word as he writes it. This will call attention to the sequence of the word elements needed for correct perception. To become effective in correcting reversals, the child must observe the correct order of letters and letter sounds in the words he is writing. If hand printing or manuscript writing is used, the same precautionary instructing of the child is in order.

If there is any tendency to use mirror writing such as occurs in writing from right to left, it will immediately become obvious. Ordinarily, this reverse writing can be corrected by explaining to the child the need to move from left to right and by having him start writing words at the extreme left of the paper or blackboard. He will then readily move in the only direction possible, which is to the right. In extreme cases of this difficulty, the child may be told when writing sentences to write the separate words underneath each other, each word starting at the left margin of the paper. Or the teacher may make a short vertical line where the first letter of each succeeding word in a sentence is to begin. This special procedure can be discontinued after some practice.

Typing. The use of typing has been suggested as a technique for developing correct orientation in word perception. Presumably the child is forced to observe the proper sequence of letters in words as he types them. It is true that he will get some practice in noting the beginning of words on the copy as he types the first letter, then the second, then the third, and so on through the word. But if he is just learning to type, he is merely typing series of letters that happen to be in groups. He will be so engrossed in selecting and pressing each key corresponding to a particular letter that he is unable to devote attention to correct techniques of word perception either on the copy or in what he types. Studies of learning to typewrite reveal that words are typed as units only after a typist becomes fairly skilled. This would certainly not be the case with most young children. Furthermore, if it is beginning typing, there is likely to be very little understanding of what is being typed. The beginner's attention is devoted to the mechanics of typing letters, not to word units and meanings. Moreover, it is possible to type words and not recognize them. Left-to-right progression along a word must be combined with identification of the word in order to be effective in developing correct orientation in word perception. The teacher will find it exceedingly difficult to teach proper orientation for word perception in the typing situation. Other methods are less cumbersome and more effective.

Choral Reading and Motion Picture Aids. In choral reading, each member of the group and the teacher have copies of the reading material. All read aloud in unison, led by the teacher. This should help develop consistent progress along lines of print but has little value for promoting correct orientation within words. The use of special motion pictures composed wholly of lines of print, such as the Harvard Films developed by Dearborn and Anderson (49), also fosters left-to-right progression along lines of print. Obviously, films could be devised with a moving spot of light to guide the eyes along each successive line of print. Actually, choral reading and the motion picture devices now available are more useful for developing phrasing than left-to-right orientation.

Other Procedures

There are several other procedures for teaching the correct directional orientation in perceiving words. Of primary concern is the problem of developing the habit of initial attention to beginnings of words. Familiarity with and proper *use of initial consonants and consonant blends* as explained in the previous chapter is extremely important in this respect. A major portion of the children who are reversal cases have not acquired this ability. While deficiencies in knowledge of initial consonants are being remedied, a variety of exercises are available for habituating the child to attend first of all to word beginnings. The following are examples:

1. To direct attention to the *initial sounds of words and at the same time be sure that the whole word is read*. Sentences have been arranged with one word missing like those below. Beneath each sentence there are listed three words, only one of which may be correctly used to complete the sentence. One other of these three words besides the correct choice begins with the same sound as that which has been indicated in the sentence by underlining. To make the correct choice, therefore, the child must note both the beginning sound and the meaning of the correct word. Therefore, of course, he has to read the word. Words that have been used in reading lessons should be employed to make up the items. The child is instructed to read each sentence, to note the beginning sound that is underlined in one word of the sentence, and then to draw a circle around the word below the sentence that correctly completes the sentence. He is told that the correct word will begin with the same sound as that underlined in the sentence. And he is warned that this is true also of one other word below that is incorrect.

John wet his feet in the _____.
      wall   step   water

They shall go to see a _____.
      catch   show   shook

Mary's kitten likes to drink _____.
      milk   make   cotton

2. Another form of exercise that directs attention to *initial sounds of words* is illustrated below. Note that all the choices begin with the same sound. In addition to noting the initial sound, the child must read the whole

word to get the correct answer. The child is directed to read the sentence and to put a cross on the word that should go in the blank space.

After supper, Mary helped _____ the dishes.
     walk   wash   want   wait

3. *Training in consonant substitution* may be used for habituating attention to word beginnings. A few samples are given below:

a. To get contextual meaning, first show the child a sentence such as: "He came to see the new game." Ask him to read the sentence and find two words that look alike except for the first letter. Pronounce *came* and have the child point to the letter that stands for the first sound. Do the same for *game*. Then write the letters *t, s, n, g, c,* and have him give the sounds of the letters. Then write the word *came*. After the beginning letter is located correctly, erase *c* and substitute *t*. Pronounce the new word. Continue with the word *game*. Interchange initial consonants *s, n,* and *c* again, emphasizing the role of the initial letter and its sound in pronouncing the words.

b. Present to the child a word such as *may* or *last* or *pig*. Then ask him to tell you a word that looks and sounds like *may* except at the beginning. When he mentions a word like *day,* erase the *m* in *may* while he watches and substitute the initial consonant of the word mentioned. Ask the child to pronounce the new word and to note how changing just the first letter makes a new word.

c. A note of caution is in order at this point. When employing consonant substitution to accustom a child to attend to word beginnings, it is well to always emphasize initial letters and sounds. That is, avoid, for the most part, calling attention to rhyming ends and ending families of words, as groups of words ending in *-at* or *-all*.

For instance, in choosing one word out of two to complete a sentence, emphasize that the sound of the first letter in pronouncing the word will tell which is correct. Thus, if working with consonants *t* and *w,* say "which of the two words after the sentence should be used in the blank?"

Mary likes to _____ in the snow.   talk   walk

4. *Various games* may be employed for informal training in using initial consonants for directing attention to word beginnings. *Consonant Lotto* and the first part of *Group Sounding Game* in the Dolch materials (The Garrard Press, Champaign, Illinois) are designed for this purpose.

Adaptations of Durrell's devices (57) may be made for drill on initial consonants in emphasizing word beginnings. A word wheel described in the previous chapter may be used for this purpose. On a single disk, only words which begin with the same consonant should be used, with the consonant left off, as: *side, soap, silk, silly, sat, sash, seat, sea, sand, soft.* Write just to the left of the slit the initial consonant to be used, as *s.* The two disks may be rotated in such a manner that the *s* on the top disk will make a word with each ending as the latter is rotated into position.

In a similar manner, the words, with initial consonant missing, may be typed with triple spacing and in a column. An exposure card is prepared by cutting a slit of appropriate size in a piece of manila folder. Type the initial consonant just to the left of the slit. When the slit is moved into position, the initial consonant and the exposed ending make a word. A separate set of materials will be needed for each initial consonant or consonant blend. This device is illustrated in the previous chapter.

In all this work, the teacher should present the exercise in such a way that the child always attends to the initial consonant as the word is exposed. This can be accomplished by proceeding at a leisurely pace, by pointing to the initial consonant, and by having the child sound the consonant and blend it with the word ending. If this is not done, the child may tend to remember the initial sound and look first at the ending. The purpose is to habituate the child to always attending first to the beginning of the word.

5. It has been suggested that a *demonstration of reversal errors* is of value in discussing directional orientation in word perception. The purpose of doing this is to show a child what will happen when he starts reading at the end or the middle of a word rather than at the beginning. For instance, the teacher can write *war* and *raw,* one above the other. She then points out that the same letters are in both but they are different words so that he should always start at the left end of a word in reading it. Similarly, she calls attention to *left* and *felt,* or other partial or complete reversals. To convince the child that errors will occur unless he looks at a word in the right order is about all that can be accomplished by such demonstrations. In fact, any exercises of this kind are really of dubious value. For after such exercises and demonstrations, a child may acquire the habit of examining every unknown word one way and then another. If he does this, it will obstruct rather than assist elimination of reversal tendencies.

6. *Alphabetizing and dictionary exercises* promote left-to-right orientation in perceiving words. For early practice in alphabetizing, the child should have a file box or folder with the alphabet marked on the dividing cards. A single word that has been learned is written on a slip of paper. The word is then filed according to its initial letter. When the order of the alphabet has been learned, several words beginning with the same letter can be filed according to the sequence of letters within the word. All this develops the habit of looking first at the beginnings of words, and then progressing from left to right. Exercises for developing skill in alphabetizing and use of the dictionary are given in Durrell (57) and in various workbooks which accompany basic reader series.

Preparation of a picture dictionary is possible at a relatively immature reading level. This will teach a child the alphabet as used for classification.

Also, when he is writing a word for his dictionary, it will give him practice in going through a word from left to right.

Preventing Reversals

It is desirable, of course, to teach elementary reading so that severe reversal tendencies do not develop. From the outset, there should be emphasis upon proper orientation in word study as discussed in the early parts of this chapter and in the previous chapter. This becomes particularly important in teaching the various aspects of word analysis such as initial consonants, initial phonograms, and blending letter sounds into proper sequences. The first letter or letter group in a word should be sounded first, followed by an orderly progression to the right. A well-organized program of teaching word analysis (see preceding chapter) with attention to individual needs should help in establishing the normal left-to-right progression needed to prevent regressions.

General Statement

Various procedures have been described for correcting reversal tendencies in word perception. The remedial teacher should not use these procedures indiscriminately. After studying a particular child with some reversal difficulty carefully, she should choose the procedures and devices which seem most appropriate for correcting his difficulty. For instance, in one case, the difficulty may be due largely to inappropriate methods of word analysis. Another child may never have grasped the need for always starting at the left and progressing to the right, etc. Finally, the teacher should keep in mind that a child with severe reversal tendencies will probably have other difficulties which also require remedial instruction.

SUMMARY

In learning to read proficiently, the child must progress from left to right along a line of print, and follow a left-to-right sequence in working out the identification of unknown words. This directional orientation has to be taught. During the pre-school years, the child learns to examine objects visually with random sequences of eye fixations. Unless taught to do differently, he will carry these habits over to the reading situation in such a way as to slip into unfortunate reversals. Training to develop left-to-right sequences of perceiving should be begun in the readiness program and be continued after reading is started.

Inappropriate directional habits or reversals occur in about 10 per cent of reading disability cases. Various causes of reversals have been suggested: transfer of earlier habits of perception to the reading situation, lack of systematic instruction in the left-to-right orientation needed for reading, lateral dominance, visual defects, too heavy a vocabulary burden, inappropriate emphasis upon word endings, improper training in phonetic analysis, and inappropriate eye movements.

Inappropriate directional habits in reading a line of print are revealed by formal study of eye movements or by informal observation during oral reading. The latter is more satisfactory for use in the reading clinic. Systematic guidance is necessary to correct this form of difficulty.

Reversals in word perception are diagnosed best by the use of standardized tests. Norms which accompany such tests indicate whether the reversals are frequent enough to require remedial treatment.

A variety of methods which may be employed to eliminate reversal tendencies in word perception have been described. The more important include: explanation and demonstration of the left-to-right progression in studying unknown words, (2) the Fernald tracing-sounding-writing method, (3) the Monroe combined phonetic and sounding-tracing method, (4) writing words, (5) training in use of initial consonants and consonant substitution, and (6) alphabetizing and dictionary exercises.

The essential features of remedial instruction to correct reversal tendencies in word perception are to use methods which direct the pupil's attention to the beginning of a word and which lead to a consistent left-to-right progression in studying the word. Such training will establish habitual attention to the beginnings of words and then a visual left-to-right survey of word elements followed by sounding and blending of these elements into word wholes. The particular methods employed will depend upon the nature and severity of the difficulties revealed by diagnosis.

SELECTED READINGS

FERNALD, Grace M., *Remedial techniques in basic school subjects.* New York: McGraw-Hill Book Company, Inc., 1943, Chap. 5.

GATES, Arthur I., *The improvement of reading,* 3rd ed. New York: The Macmillan Company, 1947, Chap. 10.

MONROE, Marion, *Children who cannot read.* Chicago: University of Chicago Press, 1932, Chap. 6.

14 OVERCOMING SPECIFIC READING DEFECTS

THE PURPOSE of reading is to understand something that has been communicated in written symbols, to get an idea or a piece of information, or to share some experience. The reader may, at one time, read merely to find the answer to a question, at another, to understand some intricate relationships. The range and variety of reasons for reading are unlimited. A proficient reader must be able to adjust his reading skills and basic comprehension abilities to whatever is his purpose at a given time. There is little use in developing all the different skills we have been describing unless he is also taught to adapt these skills and abilities so that he can read effectively for many different purposes.

The development of comprehension abilities is a major goal of all reading instruction. The child should, at all times, be reading for a definite purpose which demands his understanding of the material read. Modern reading programs make it clear that both pupils and teachers should know the purposes for reading a selection before it is read. If the child is kept aware of the reasons why he is reading something, he can make progress in adjusting his skills and abilities to attain specific goals. By repeatedly doing this, the child develops a co-ordinated set of specific comprehension abilities and a variety of basic study skills. Such development, however, is relatively slow for most pupils.

Even though a child is skillful in recognizing words, has built a large sight vocabulary, and has grown adequately in basic comprehension abilities, he may be in difficulty because he has failed to acquire sufficient proficiency in some specific type of comprehension. When his word recognition is limited or his sight vocabulary, or his basic comprehension proficiencies, he will be ineffective in all types of comprehension. Under such circumstances, his case would be classified as "limiting" or "complex disability." There are, however, many children who are disabled readers, even though their handicaps are not in the basic capacities. These children are described as having some specific retardation, which has come about either by inexperience or by unfortunate training in particular types of comprehension. The child may be inexperienced in reading to organize the facts or concepts he has learned from reading. If this is the case, he may well be poor in establishing sequences, in classifying or listing facts into a reasonable organization, in following step-by-step directions, or in sensing major concepts and related ideas. These will all be recognized as specific forms of comprehension.

As is the case with all the skills and abilities, a balance must be kept in giving training in each of the specific comprehension abilities and the basic study skills. The child may be in serious trouble, even though described as a case with some specific retardation, because an unfortunate lack of balance has been permitted to continue. One child, for example, may in all his reading, be so concerned with getting the general idea that a writer is trying to develop, that he fails to note significant details. Such a child may carry this pattern into every reading situation and thereby become inaccurate, and a reader who can neither retain nor organize factual information. In a wide variety of reading situations, he would be inadequate. Another child may be overexacting in his reading and become so concerned with details that he fails to sense the author's true meaning. Perhaps he is so fearful of losing each detail in a passage, that he reads it with painful exactness which its significance does not warrant. He may search for information that is not contained in the selection. Such compulsive, over-detailed reading makes for a slow, laborious reader who frequently fails to understand the main ideas the author is presenting. Each of these children is in difficulty because he lacks flexibility in his reading approach.

Children, from the start of instruction, need reading programs that are well-rounded and that give them experience in the various types of comprehension and basic study skills. The reading program must develop balances between the specific comprehension abilities if children are not to become disabled readers. The programs also must include instruction in the basic study skills and oral reading if the children are not to become specific retardation cases. Among the more frequent types of difficulties in comprehension abilities, basic study skills, and oral reading are the following, which will be discussed in this chapter:

1. Limitations in specific comprehension abilities.
   a. Inability to locate and retain information read.
   b. Inadequate sense of organization of material.
   c. Limited ability in evaluating what is read.
   d. Immaturity in the ability to interpret content.
   e. Lack of appreciation abilities.
2. Insufficient development of basic study skills.
   a. Lack of skills needed to locate sources of information.
   b. Inefficiency in using basic references.
   c. Limited skill in interpreting pictorial and tabular materials.
   d. Lack of diversified techniques of organizing information.
3. Ineffective oral reading.
   a. Inappropriate eye-voice span.
   b. Inability to phrase properly.
   c. Unfortunate rate and timing.
   d. Emotional tenseness when reading orally.

LIMITATIONS IN SPECIFIC COMPREHENSION ABILITIES

The child who is ineffective in comprehension of a specific type needs to read for purposes which require the particular kind of comprehension in which he is deficient. Comprehension can be developed best in reading situations where the purposes of the reading have been carefully defined and in which the child will have to demonstrate that he has understood the material in the way required by the reasons for reading it. Obviously, what is read by the child in such a situation should be of the proper type and level of difficulty. In developing specific comprehension abilities, it is best if the child is given an opportunity to make some creative use of the results of reading. If, for example, a child has a specific limitation in the ability to follow directions, it is well to have him read some material that tells him how to make something and then have him go ahead and make it. It would be rather unwise to try to teach a child to read to follow directions with story-type material.

The information useful in diagnosing retardation in the various specific types of comprehension is obtained in several ways. *First,* there are many standardized tests which measure various kinds of comprehension. *The Gates Basic Reading Tests,* for example, which are suitable for children who read at third-grade level and higher, give evidence that is useful in diagnosing specific comprehension abilities. These tests measure four types of comprehension. Type A—Reading to Get the General Significance gives an indication of the child's ability to interpret content and arrive at the main idea of a passage. Type B—Reading to Predict the Outcomes of Given Events also is testing the child's ability to interpret the material read and to make a prediction of what is likely to occur on the basis of what has happened. Type C—Reading to Understand Precise Directions indicates to some degree the child's ability to sense the organization of a passage and to select its important details, while subordinating the nonessential ones. This is an exacting sort of reading that requires, at times, the sensing of relationships. Type D—Reading to Note Details gives evidence of the child's ability to locate and to retain specific bits of information. This type of reading requires attention to detail. The Gates tests, then, give evidence of the child's ability in three of the five categories of comprehension, namely, ability to locate and retain information read; ability to sense the organization of information; and ability to interpret the content read. The Gates tests do not indicate how well the child can read to evaluate or to what extent he has developed the comprehension abilities grouped under reading to appreciate.

The Developmental Reading Tests by G. L. Bond, T. Clymer, and C. J. Hoyt are also designed to measure types of comprehension abilities.

These tests provide measures of Vocabulary, General Comprehension, and Specific Comprehension at the primer, lower, and upper primary levels. The General Comprehension measures the ability of the child to interpret content to the point of arriving at the main idea or general significance of what is read. The Specific Comprehension measures more detailed knowledge and factual reading. At the intermediate level, *The Developmental Reading Tests* provide measures of Vocabulary and four specific types of Comprehension: Reading to Retain Information; Reading to Organize; Reading to Evaluate and Interpret; and Reading to Appreciate. These tests enable the teacher or diagnostician to locate areas of comprehension limitations. These and other reading tests that can be used in diagnosing specific types of reading comprehension will be found in Appendix I.

A second means of diagnosing difficulties in specific types of comprehension abilities is to study the child's relative success in doing workbook exercises. Modern workbooks have many lessons devoted to the development of each of the groups of comprehension abilities. An index of exercises to develop skills and abilities is given in the back of most of the workbooks that accompany basic reading programs. These exercises are not only excellent for remedial work, but they can also be used as models for exercises that the remedial teacher can develop for correcting specific types of comprehension abilities. In addition, these exercises can be used as work samples of the child's reading skills and abilities. The teacher can easily use them as a means of diagnosing the child's instructional needs. A sample index from *The Fun to Do Book for Days of Adventure* by Guy L. Bond and Marie C. Cuddy (24) [1] will illustrate this source of informal appraisal.

INDEX OF READING PROFICIENCIES [2]

I. COMPREHENSION ABILITIES
    A. *Reading to retain information*
        1. Isolate details: 5, 20, 54, 80
        2. Recall specific items: 17, 49, 60, 74, 83, 95
        3. Retain fundamental concepts: 5, 16, 17, 21, 47, 72
        4. Use facts to answer specific questions: 21, 29, 68, 80
    B. *Reading to organize*
        1. Classify: 6, 35, 51
        2. Establish a sequence: 5, 20, 51, 71, 83
        3. Follow directions: 4, 14, 19, 26, 31, 37, 40, 45, 59, 76, 79, 85
        4. Sense relationships: 23, 35
        5. Summarize and generalize: 23, 34, 52, 86
    C. *Reading to evaluate*
        1. Fact from opinion: 24, 28, 29, 55

[1] G. L. Bond and M. C. Cuddy, *The fun to do book for days of adventure.* Chicago: Lyons and Carnahan, 1951. Used with permission of the publisher.

[2] Numbers show pages on which specific experience is given.

   2. Judge reasonableness and relevancy: 2, 3, 17, 43, 49, 54, 55, 67, 69, 86, 89

   3. Sense implied meaning: 2, 3, 25, 49

   4. Establish cause and effect: 6, 23, 69, 82

D. *Reading to interpret*

   1. Main idea: 12, 47, 52, 72

   2. Draw inference or conclusion: 10, 24, 25, 68, 76, 79, 80, 87, 91

   3. Predict outcomes: 12, 24, 64, 66, 91

   4. Form an opinion: 8, 16, 63, 77, 87

E. *Reading for appreciation*

   1. Sense humor and plot: 43, 44, 54, 57, 89, 91, 92

   2. Form sensory impressions or feeling tone: 36, 39, 41, 43, 45, 56, 90, 93

   3. Understand characters: 16, 21, 42, 77

II. BASIC STUDY SKILLS

A. *Locating information*

   1. Table of contents: 1

   2. Alphabetized references: 7, 50

   3. Book parts: 1, 95

   4. Key words: 85

B. *Using general references*

   1. Dictionary: 7, 11, 22, 30, 62, 65, 73

   2. Encyclopedia: 50, 85

   3. Time tables: 31, 37

C. *Using visual material*

   1. Maps: 15, 19, 40, 59

   2. Pictorial and tabular: 10, 23, 26, 28, 29, 36, 39, 76, 79, 87

D. *Organizing*

   1. Outlining: 20, 35, 61, 74

   2. Grouping or categorizing: 9, 51, 60

III. BASIC MEANING DEVELOPMENT

A. *Paragraphing meaning and organization:* 34, 44, 52, 57, 58

B. *Sentence sense:* 82, 93, 94

C. *Phrase and word meaning*

   1. Author's definition or explanation: 50, 75

   2. Context clues to meaning: 2, 3, 11, 30, 32, 46, 48, 65, 67, 75, 88

   3. Dictionary and glossary: 11, 22, 30, 65, 73

   4. Antonyms, synonyms, and homonyms: 18, 32, 46, 58, 70, 81

   5. Semantic variations: 30, 65, 73, 89

   6. Enriching meanings (descriptive words, figures of speech, symbolic expressions): 27, 41, 42, 56, 77, 93, 94, 96

   7. Abbreviations: 31, 37

IV. WORD-RECOGNITION TECHNIQUES

A. *Meaning aids*

   1. Context clues to recognition: 4, 48, 53, 84

   2. Expectancy clues: 9, 35, 53

B. *Visual and structural aids*

   1. Root words: 4, 78

   2. Prefixes and suffixes: 4, 22, 78

      3. Syllabification: 14, 32
      4. Compound words: 4, 78
      5. Variant endings: 84
      6. Contractions: 33
   C. *Auditory and phonetic aids*
      1. Vowel and consonant sounds: 7, 13, 22, 32, 33, 62
      2. Blends, digraphs, and diphthongs: 13, 33, 62
      3. Diacritical markings and pronunciation aids: 13, 14, 22
      4. Synthesis (blending and accent): 14
      5. Dictionary: 11, 13, 14, 62

If it is found that a child's performance is poor in doing the exercises of a specific type of comprehension, he is in need of help in this area to correct the difficulty.

Another method of appraising the child's relative achievement in comprehension involves less formal procedures. The teacher may observe the child's ability to read for various purposes during regular reading instruction. If a specific weakness is noticed, the child should be given an informal test in this area. For example, if a child appears to be relatively competent in most of the reading in his class work, but becomes confused when he is expected to organize the material he reads, the various types of reading which require a sense of organization should be explored. The teacher may test the child's ability to select the important ideas and the information that is related to each. The child may be asked to classify under major headings some of the facts within a selection or to arrange some of the occurrences read about into a sequence of events. If in these respects his reading is below his general level of reading performance, he needs systematic instruction to develop a sense of organization.

The major method of correcting a specific type of comprehension difficulty is to have the child read material in a well-graded basic reader at the level of difficulty appropriate for him. The type of material to be read should be suitable to the type of comprehension ability being emphasized. The purposes for reading the material should be well defined prior to the reading. There should be a check made on the accuracy of comprehension at the end of the reading. However, the type of comprehension check used should reflect the nature of the specific comprehension ability stressed. For example, if the child is limited in his ability to read to get the general gist or significance of the paragraph, comprehension questions involving factual detail would be unwarranted. Such questions as "Which would be the most appropriate title for this selection?" or "Which of the following is the main idea of the selection?" would be the kind of comprehension check for this type of limitation. After the material has been read once, the child may reread it for new purposes, which will give him further experience in the specific comprehension ability that needs improving. The manuals accompanying basic readers have numerous suggestions for the development of the specific comprehension abilities.

The following sample page from the *Manual for Meeting New Friends* by Guy L. Bond and Marie C. Cuddy (22)[3] will illustrate the help that the teacher or remedial worker can get from using such manuals:

DEVELOPING SKILLS AND ABILITIES

COMPREHENSION

Main Idea of Paragraph: The teacher may give the main idea of a paragraph and let the children find the paragraph, as: The arrival of the caravan at the village (page 208, paragraph 3); the caravan is on its way to the city (page 210, paragraph 3); comparing the camel with the bus (page 212, paragraph 4; paragraphs 3-4 of Classmate Edition); reason for the city wall (page 212, last paragraph); selling articles (page 213, paragraph 1).

Sensing Relationship: Have the children tell what relationship there is between the climate of the desert and the kind of clothes worn by the people. (Protection from sun, heat, and dust).

Recalling and Using Facts to Answer Specific Questions: The questions on page 213 should be answered at this time. Some interesting facts may be brought out, as:

1. There is little or no rain in deserts, so flat roofs could be used; roof gave cool place to sleep. Roberto needed a sloping roof so heavy rain would run off, as well as stilts to keep house out of water. Desert people had few windows— did not want hot sun to shine into house—wanted a few openings because of dust storms.

2. Date palms need dry area with some irrigation; coconut palms need moisture.

3. Airplanes and long-range guns make walls obsolete.

4. The camel has pads on feet; requires little food or water during journey since it is able to store food and water in form of fat; carries heavy loads; hair and hide used for clothing, tents, rugs, etc.; flesh used for food.

WORD RECOGNITION

Phonetic Analysis: Have the children turn to *My Dictionary,* find *alligator* and note that, in the respelling, the ending *or* has an *er* sound. Then have them look for *anchor, harbor,* and *equator* to learn how the ending *or* is pronounced. Next have them find *record* and look for the marking of *or.* Write other words that contain *or* and have them pronounced correctly, as: *sailor, doctor, mayor, motor, favorite;* write other words that have the same sound, as: *collar, sweater, educator, weather, inventor.*

BASIC STUDY SKILL

Using General References: Have the children tell which things that were mentioned in the story they would like to know more about, as: dates and the way they are prepared and shipped; Arabian rugs; camels; cities in Arabia; Arabian nomads who use tent homes; goat's-milk cheese. Let them tell from what sources the information may be obtained. If possible, provide the sources from which the information or some of it may be obtained. Help should be given the less able readers in locating information. The more able readers should find information independently.

[3] From G. L. Bond and M. C. Cuddy, *Bond plan manual for meeting new friends.* Chicago: Lyons and Carnahan, 1954. Used with permission of the publisher.

Fun to Do Book, page 60, may now be used.

Modern manuals will have an index of exercises for developing skills and abilities. The index in the back of this manual will show that on the above page, for example, there are comprehension exercises dealing with *getting the main idea of a paragraph, sensing relationships,* and *recalling and using facts to answer specific questions.* It will also show that there is an exercise to teach *phonetic analysis* and a reading experience which will aid in developing the basic study skill of *using general references.*

Such materials give the classroom teacher or clinician a pool of exercises and experiences for developing all of the essential reading skills and abilities. These can be used to correct a difficulty as well as to develop the skills and abilities in the first place. Workbooks that accompany basic reading programs are replete in such suggestions (see Index of Reading Proficiencies given above). Usually in both of these references, there are indexes showing the pages upon which specific types of comprehension abilities are emphasized.

Many teachers and clinical workers prefer to use selections from library material, dealing with a topic of great interest to the child. Under such circumstances, it is highly important that the materials be of the proper level of difficulty and that care be taken to be sure that the type of material used is suitable to the form of comprehension one is trying to teach. In selecting material, the teacher has already in her mind the purposes for which it is to be used, i.e., in stressing a particular aspect of reading in which the child has shown that he is limited. She will also prepare comprehension questions to check the accuracy with which the child has read the selection, bearing in mind the present purpose.

Inability to Locate and Retain Information Read

This category of specific comprehension abilities requires exact, careful reading. The various comprehension abilities included in it are those like being able to: recall specific items of information, note the details within a passage, retain fundamental concepts, use facts to answer specific questions, and find statements to prove a point or to answer a question. These specific comprehension abilities start their development in the early reading assignments of the child and are continued as outcomes of instruction as long as systematic training is given. Many children, however, fail to establish a high degree of accuracy in the various forms of locating and retaining factual information. On the other hand, numerous other children are found to be overexacting. These latter should be encouraged to read relatively easy material for the purpose of enjoyment, for predicting what is going to happen next, or to get the general gist of a story or passage.

Children who are not exacting enough in their reading or who cannot attend to details within the passage when this is what is demanded by the purposes for reading, should be given reading experiences that require the collection of factual information with close attention to detail, and then require that this factual information be aired. The material used with children who have limited capacity for locating and retaining specific items of information should be material that has considerable factual content. For this, science material would be more suitable than narrative; or perhaps something from social studies, provided it is designed to give information rather than to give an over-all impression of some historical period. In other words, the material that will be found most useful in developing ability to read for informational purposes will be material that contains plenty of facts.

A chart should be kept showing the child's percentage of correct responses. Children at all levels of general reading competency may be inexperienced or ineffective in this specific type of reading comprehension. The exercises and materials in which the child is expected to get practice in attending to specific details should be at a level somewhat below his general reading capability, but it does not have to be as simple as would be indicated by his measured score in this one type of reading. By this we mean that if a child of fifth-grade age and mental ability has a general reading capability of 4.0 and measures 2.5 in reading to recall items of specific information, the remedial work would not ordinarily need to employ material of 2.5 level of difficulty, though it ought to be somewhat easier than 4.0 in difficulty.

A few samples of reading purposes that will give experience in reading to locate and retain factual information follow:

1. Read the story to see what facts it tells about robins.
2. Read the selection to find all the things a beaver uses in making his home.
3. Read the selection to find all the uses the plains Indians made of buffaloes.
4. Reread the selection to find additional facts to add to your list about the animals discussed in it.
5. Find and read sentences to prove or disprove these statements given orally.
   a. A big sea lion weighs about six hundred pounds.
   b. A big elephant may be eight feet high.
   c. A baby kangaroo sleeps in its mother's pouch.
   d. A full-grown kangaroo weighs more than a sea lion.
   e. Baboons like to swim.
6. Read to learn about the former home life of one of the major Indian groups in America: where they lived; what they ate; how they prepared their food; what they wore; what tools they used.

Inadequate Sense of Organization of Material

The specific types of comprehension included in this category have as their major distinguishing characteristic the ability to sense order or relationship among the facts read about. They include such abilities as: classifying and listing facts in a sensible manner; establishing a sequence of events; following a series of related directions; sensing relationships; and distinguishing between the major ideas and the related facts. These are exacting sorts of reading but they are of great importance. Reading to organize information has its start in the pre-reading exercises of children when they classify pictures of animals, for example, into those they would see on a farm and those they would see in a forest; or, when the child is expected to arrange a series of pictures in an orderly sequence of events. Some children fail to develop this ability to sense the organization and relationship among the ideas they are reading and this severely handicaps them in their use of printed material. These children need remedial work to develop proficiency in this vital area of comprehension abilities.

The material for developing ability to organize and sense relationships between facts, naturally must contain plenty of facts to organize and relate one to the other. The most suitable materials will be those units in some of the modern basic readers included to show the child how to go about reading the materials of science and social studies. The sections of the manuals related to these units of content matter will be found to contain many examples of exercises for developing ability to sense organization and relationships among the facts read. Other science and social studies materials of the proper level of difficulty for the child can be used to develop these specific abilities. The remedial teacher will need to use reasons for reading which require him to organize and will need to check on each child's effectiveness in carrying out such purposes. Below are some specific purposes that will help to teach the child to sense the organization of the ideas and information he is reading about:

1. Read about animals to make a summary chart showing: where they live; what they eat; how to recognize them; how they protect themselves; who their enemies are; how they get ready for winter.

2. Read to make a list of: (*a*) the kinds of damage done by floods; (*b*) means that are used to prevent damage.

3. Read to make an outline of three types of soil conservation problems discussed in the selection.

4. Read to summarize the information given about petroleum under the following headings: how petroleum was formed; how oil wells are located; how oil is obtained from below the ground; uses of petroleum; how we can conserve our petroleum resources.

5. Read the selection to find what is done first, second, and third in making a print of your hand.

6. Read to find and list in order the steps taken by Charles Hall in his experiments to find a quick and inexpensive way of changing alumina into aluminum.

7. Read to find out in what ways the life of a boy who lives by the sea in Brittany is the same and how it is different from that of a boy who lives in Bora Bora.

Limited Ability in Evaluating What Is Read

This group of comprehension abilities involves not only reading and understanding what the author said, but reflecting upon it so that critical judgments may be made. It includes such specific ways of comprehending as differentiating between fancy, fact, and opinion; judging the reasonableness and relevancy of ideas presented; sensing implied meanings; establishing cause-and-effect relationships; making comparisons; judging the authenticity of materials read; and critically appraising the validity of the author's presentation. Like all other comprehension abilities, these have their start in early reading lessons and develop as long as growth in reading continues. The time at which a child is asked if a fanciful tale could have really happened is the start of such instruction. Reading to evaluate includes some of the most important types of reading. For the person who is taught to read, but not to reflect upon what is read, is indeed frequently in danger of coming to faulty conclusions. The child who is unable to read critically and judge the reasonableness of material at his level of advancement, should be given remedial instruction to overcome this deficiency because reading to evaluate what is read is gradual in development and should not be left to chance learning.

The material most suitable for developing reading to evaluate is material that is written to influence people's opinions. During the early elementary school grades, such material is not readily available. Nevertheless, even there, certain types of evaluating reading can be done. Many times ideas are implied rather than directly stated. Frequently there are cause-and-effect relationships, even in first-grade material, and often statements of fact and opinion can be compared. Any material that is at the child's general reading level may be used to increase his ability to evaluate what is read. Many of the comprehension exercises in basal readers have the child reread material in order to evaluate it in a wide variety of ways. Some of the types of exercises that will teach the child to judge, reflect upon, and evaluate are illustrated by the following:

1. Have the child, after reading a somewhat fanciful story about animals, reread it to distinguish between the realistic and the fanciful statements.

2. Have the child decide from the titles of stories whether they are likely to be real or fanciful.

3. Have the children discuss whether a story read could have happened and give their reasons for their opinion.

4. Ask a child to judge which of given paragraphs in a fanciful story could have happened and which could not.

5. Ask him to judge the reasonableness of statements by indicating which probably are true and which probably are not true.

6. Have the child find and read orally just the part that proves a point and no more.

7. Have the children come to such conclusions from their reading as why pioneers might prefer to be paid in corn or other goods rather than in money.

8. Have the child judge the point of view of two people about a common happening read about.

9. Have him find facts that are relevant to a topic.

10. Have the children read to find statements which characters make that they know to be true and those that are their opinions.

Immaturity in the Ability to Interpret Content

This category of comprehension abilities is composed of types of reading that involve projecting the understanding of the selection beyond the statements of the author. It differs from organizing what is read in that it requires a child to derive new ideas from what he reads. Reading to interpret includes understanding the significance of a selection read, drawing an inference or conclusion not expressly stated, predicting an outcome of given events, forming one's own opinions, and inferring time and measurement relationships. These comprehension abilities require the reorganization of information and ideas expressed so that new relationships can be understood. In the pre-reading lessons, the child may be asked to study a set of related pictures and to select, from the two final pictures, the one that would best complete the series. Or, he may have to form an opinion about the thing he should do when a pet dog digs up the garden. From this meager beginning, the child gradually develops the ability to make judgments such as the real importance of the Constitution and the Bill of Rights to our way of life.

Some children who have good general reading ability find it difficult to interpret what is read. This type of reading ability is best developed in material that requires careful, considered reading. It is also developed by setting purposes for reading that necessitate reflecting upon what is read. The child must learn to take the facts and ideas presented, reorganize them, and sense new relationships among them that he did not find on the surface of what he read. The materials of social studies and science lend themselves to these sorts of reasoning, but well-written narrative material is also useful in developing the ability to interpret.

The main requirement of remedial instruction in this ability, for the child who is otherwise a capable reader, is to have him read for purposes that force him to reflect upon what he reads. Such purposes as the following illustrate the nature of reading assignments that will encourage interpretive reading:

1. Have the children anticipate the ending of the story.
2. Have the children read to find out why the signing of the Magna Carta is important to them.
3. The children may read to find which colony in America they would have preferred to live in, and why.
4. Have the children form an opinion about which of the two people they have read about they would prefer to have as a friend.
5. Have the children form their opinions about effects of various inventions such as movable type, electric light, and the reaper.

6. Have them form conclusions in regard to how climatic conditions have affected the ways in which people live.
7. Have them read to draw conclusions and form generalizations from the facts given in science.

Lack of Appreciation Abilities

This set of comprehension abilities is in some respects different than the others. The four types of specific limitations discussed previously dealt with noting and retaining factual information, organizing information, judging the authenticity of information, and interpreting it. The appreciation abilities deal more with the aesthetic qualities of the reading. Such reading abilities as understanding the feeling tone developed by the author; sensing the plot, humor, and action; forming various sensory impressions; and understanding the personal qualities of the characters are essential for appreciating what is read. The basic reading program and the program of guided literature reading are designed to develop these capabilities.

The child who cannot visualize the scene described, or sense the feeling of aloneness experienced by an early explorer, or appreciate the humor of an absurd situation, is in reading difficulty, although he may be able to do all of the factual types of reading. The materials best suited for developing reading to appreciate are the best children's books or the selections of a literary nature in basic readers. The child must read for reasons that will encourage him to develop the appreciation abilities. It would be unfortunate to force the factual types of reading such as are required for developing some of the other comprehension abilities upon the child when he is reading material that should be read for personal development, appreciation, or for the sheer beauty it affords.

An example of the effects of pursuing the wrong purposes at the wrong time can be seen in the quotation from Bond and Handlan (27):

An extreme example of formal recitation was observed in a class in which the children had read Alfred Noyes' romantic poem, "The Highwayman." For thirty-five minutes the teacher stood before the class and asked questions: "What was the girl's name? What color was her hair? What did the Highwayman wear?" More times than not, each question demanded only one or two words in response. If she failed to get the exact answer after four or five trials, she answered the question herself and went on to the next. Some of the period was spent in scolding the children for inattention and in moving two or three who grew restless under the barrage of questions. At no time during the lesson did the children have a chance to see that the rhythm of the poem showed how "the Highwayman came riding"; at no time did they have a chance to enjoy the story or to appreciate the beauty of some of the especially effective bits of description. It was difficult to see how this formal recitation helped the children either understand or enjoy the poem.[4]

[4] From G. L. Bond and B. Handlan, *Adapting instruction in reading to individual differences.* Series on individualization of instruction, No. 5. Minneapolis: University of Minnesota Press, 1948.

In order to build the abilities necessary for appreciation, the teacher must first find material that the child can read and that will be of intense interest to him. Fortunately, when the lack of ability to read for appreciation is a specific limitation, the child has capability in the basic skills and abilities and is in general a competent reader. He can read material at a level of difficulty that is near his level of general growth and development, but he does need special help in sensing the tone, plot, or action; in appreciating a characterization; or in visualizing a description. He can be taught the abilities necessary for appreciation, using material that is suitable to one of his age and in accordance with his interests. He is not limited in reading in general and he has no basic defects in his skills and abilities. If he were so limited, these basic defects would be his primary problem and would receive first attention.

While guiding children to read materials of quality that mean something to them is an essential element in improving reading to appreciate, there are certain other things that can be done to encourage it. The following illustrations indicate the kind of experiences that foster improvement in appreciation abilities where a child has failed to develop them:

1. Read a story to obtain the visual background needed to represent it on a mural.
2. Read a story to participate in a creative dramatic representation of one of the characters.
3. Read several stories to select one that would make a good play. (In order to do this, the child must sense the action, visualize the scenes, and understand the characters.)
4. Read to prepare a story for interpretive oral reading in book-sharing time.
5. Read to plan a radio or television presentation of a story.
6. Have the child discuss how he thinks someone in the story felt.
7. Have the child describe the sights, sounds, and smells encountered by the boy in the story who was adrift in New York harbor.
8. Locate some descriptive words within a story.
9. Read to share an adventure.
10. Read for the enjoyment of a good story.

INSUFFICIENT DEVELOPMENT OF BASIC STUDY SKILLS

Limitations in the basic study skills are specific in nature. The child can be an excellent reader in general, but at the same time be unable to (1) locate sources of information; (2) use basic references; (3) interpret pictorial and tabular materials; or (4) set findings down in a usable form of organization. A child who is limited in any of these skills has a specific difficulty in reading which should be corrected if he is to use the printed page effectively.

Two steps are needed to obtain the desired diagnostic information about a particular pupil. The first step is to use a standardized test. Some of the more useful standardized tests are described in Appendix I. For the most part, these tests will indicate only in which of the above areas his difficulty lies. They will define neither the nature of the problem nor the remedial work that is needed to correct it. The child may show on such tests, for example, that he is ineffective in locating sources of information, but this will not show whether his difficulty lies in lack of ability to alphabetize, inability to select appropriate key words, or lack of ability to judge the type of book in which he might find the subject about which he wants to read. A test of the basic study skills will give only a general diagnosis. It will reveal the skill that needs further and more analytical exploration by the diagnostician.

Each of the four categories of basic study skills listed above is composed of many parts. The teacher must know just wherein a child's difficulty lies if remedial treatment is to be effective and not waste time on elements of the total skill which have already been mastered. It would, of course, be wasteful to spend time teaching a child who is weak in locating sources of information to alphabetize if he already knows how to alphabetize. It would be equally undesirable to spend time and effort teaching him key words, when his real difficulty is that he doesn't know the type of book in which to look to find the information he wants. He is competent in selecting the key words, once he locates a book likely to contain the information.

The second step is to study the child as he works in the area in which the standardized test has shown that he has a weakness. This requires sampling the child's performance in that area. For example, if the child is weak in the use of basic references, it may be that he does not know whether the type of information he desires can be found in an encyclopedia, a dictionary, an atlas, an almanac, the telephone book, a standard text, or just where. By studying the selections he makes when answering such questions as "Where would you be likely to find information about: the time of the monsoons in India, the definition of a word, the address of another school, the population of a town, or the location of a country?" the diagnostician can narrow the problem.

A study of the child's efficiency in using the basic study skill in question is also needed. He may know which reference to use, under which heading to look for the information he wishes to find, and how to estimate pages within the reference, but still he may be slow and inefficient in using what he knows. The work sample will also give this necessary information.

Which remedial methods are proper is usually obvious when the nature of the difficulty is thoroughly diagnosed. The teacher needs to teach the child to do the things in which he has shown that he is limited. There are no real complexities involved in this. If the child does not know how to alphabetize, it is relatively easy to teach him the order of the letters and the fact that words are arranged in lists in this order by their first letters, then by the second letters, etc., and that it is always done in this way. This is a different and much simpler type of learning than is, for example, word recognition, in which few such rules apply.

Lack of Skills Needed to Locate Sources of Information

Skill in locating sources of information is helpful in most study activities. The child who knows how and when to use the table of contents, the index, and the card catalogue is better equipped to do independent study than is the child who does not think of doing these things or is not as skillful if he does do them. Among the most frequent limitations which produce difficulty in this basic study skill are: (1) inability to decide what types of books will contain the information wanted; (2) lack of knowing how to use such tools as the index, the table of contents, the card catalogue, the reader's guide, and the like; (3) limited skill in estimating the probable key words under which the information is classified or lack of flexibility in selecting other references when the first one does not contain the information wanted; (4) inefficiency in locating words in an alphabetical listing, especially in those lists which have major and subordinate subdivisions; (5) inability to estimate page locations within a book; (6) little skimming ability, making it hard to locate the exact information.

The teacher must find in which of these skills the child is behind and then give him reading assignments requiring the use of these skills in locating the information for a definite purpose. If the child shows poor judgment as to which book might contain the information that he desires, the teacher can teach him how to choose a good source by asking him questions. If his weakness is in not knowing whether to use the table of contents or the index, she can explain the use of each and give him experience in using them. If use of key words is the difficulty, several topics can be chosen to show how they are listed from general to specific, from common to unusual, from major headings to related ones.

If the child's weakness is in locating words in an alphabetical list, he must be drilled on the alphabet, in estimating how far through the alphabet one of the letters is, and in placing words in alphabetical order. The child who has insufficient skimming ability can be given many exercises that require the rapid location of specific facts within a page or a few pages on which the fact is known to be discussed. It might be well to start such exercises with the location of a date, since numbers on a page of print can readily be found.

Inefficiency in Using Basic References

The child who is capable in locating information in general, may find using basic reference material confusing. His difficulty is usually in not being clear as to what kind of information each reference contains. He does not know to which book he should refer to obtain the kind of information he desires. The teacher should find out which of the references the child is unfamiliar with and give him experience in using them. Many adults, for example, do not know all of the types of information that can be most readily found in a telephone book. The child is often uncertain as to the difference between an encyclopedia and a dictionary and which one should be used to get a specific bit of information. He may be equally confused about what can be obtained from other reference books. After the teacher locates the nature of the child's problem, an explanation of the contents of the different basic references and some experience in using each will usually correct the difficulty. At times it will be necessary to have the child tell in which of the common reference books he would look to find such things as the facts about Columbus, the meaning of the word *Tory,* the amount of wheat grown in Kansas last year—each time checking the accuracy of his answer by looking up that topic.

Limited Skill in Interpreting Pictorial and Tabular Materials

Skill in reading maps, graphs, charts, and tables is becoming increasingly important for understanding printed material. The child who fails to develop such skills will be handicapped in his reading in the content fields during his school years and also as an adult. If standardized tests show that a child is weak in this group of skills, the teacher should make a more analytical diagnosis to find which kinds of pictorial and tabular aids are causing him difficulty and to determine the exact nature of his trouble.

Again, as in most of the study skills, once the nature of the difficulty is known, the remedial work to be undertaken is definite. The child who has a specific disability in map reading, for example, may be in difficulty for a variety of reasons. He may be unaware of the fact that different maps use different scales. A map of his city may, for example, be larger than a map of his state, so he is troubled about distances and comparative sizes. He may get erroneous notions because he does not know that a flat map of a vast area must distort some things in order to show others. Many maps of the United States show Maine closer to the top than the state of Minnesota. Therefore many people think that Maine extends farther north than Minnesota, but in reality it does not. Because wall maps always have north at the top, many children think rivers flow downhill to the south and so they are surprised to learn that some rivers flow north and empty into Hudson Bay. There are many such faulty concepts that can become established in trying to read maps.

In reading each of the other types of pictorial and tabular materials, there are many possible kinds of confusion, also. The diagnostician should first locate the source of the difficulties and then give the child systematic instruction and purposeful experiences in order to overcome the weakness. The corrective work is best accomplished in the science and social studies units of those basic readers which systematically teach the study skills. They contain specific exercises to develop skill in interpretation of pictorial and tabular presentations. The principles these illustrate can be reinforced by the reading assignments in science and social studies classes. Krantz (116) has shown that each of these fields has its own specific study skills. The main feature of remedial instruction is that it is based upon a careful diagnosis which has determined the exact kind of instruction needed. It must be realized that these skills begin to form early in the reading experience of the child. Map reading may be started by interpreting a map which the teacher has made to show the children safe ways to go home from school. A chart showing daily temperatures at noon is often one of the child's early school experiences.

Remedial instruction for those children who are weak in these skills must progress from simple illustrative maps, graphs, charts, and tables to the more complex ones. It will prove helpful to progress from representations of things that the child has experienced to the more remote illustrative materials.

Lack of Diversified Techniques in Organizing Information

Skill in organizing information so that it can be understood and retained is essential. Many techniques are necessary in order to relate the facts learned from reading so that their interrelationships can be brought out for study. The comprehension abilities required in classifying, sensing relationships, understanding major concepts and subordinate ideas, and establishing a sequence are closely related to the basic study skills of organization. Without these comprehension abilities, the child would find it difficult indeed to learn the skills of organization. The child, for example, who cannot detect the difference between a major concept and the subordinate ideas, will find outlining difficult. The child who has not developed the ability to sense a sequence of events, will find making a time-line a confusing enterprise. If a child is unable to classify ideas into reasonable groupings, he will run into trouble trying to tabulate his information in a two-way chart for further study.

The difference between the comprehension abilities involved in sensing the organization of information and the basic study skills of organization is that the former involves reasoning and restructuring of information, while the latter is just the mechanics of ordering the information for further study.

In studying in the basic reader a science unit dealing with conservation of mineral resources, for example, the child may need to isolate and classify those ideas that deal with each of the resources discussed. He must also sense certain relationships between the nature of the mineral and the problem of conserving it. Uranium, coal, and petroleum are chemically changed in use, while aluminum, copper, and iron are not necessarily altered. The child may reason from these facts to certain generalizations concerning the conservation of each. This would be a high level of comprehension ability in the area of organization. The basic study skill may be that he arranges his findings in a two-way chart with each of the metals listed along the side and the various facts concerning it listed across the top, such as: where it is located, how it is mined, the way it is changed by use, and other facts. Then, each bit of information may be put in its proper cell for future study. Skill in making such a chart is a basic study skill. The generalizations made from studying the chart, as well as gathering the information to make the chart, would be the result of what we have throughout termed *comprehension*.

The child needs to develop many ways of arranging his information, if he is to think effectively about the ideas involved. Such basic study skills are taught in some reading programs from the start. When a child is told to record only the most important ideas for presentation to the class, he is making a rudimentary outline. He is making a two-way chart when he lists some animals he has read about in a first-grade reader along one side of his paper, while across the top of the paper, he puts such headings as: what its enemies are; how it protects itself; how it gets ready for winter; and what it eats. When the children list the order in which pictures for a box movie will be shown, they are establishing the forerunner of a time-line graph.

The remedial teacher who finds a child limited in this area of basic study skills needs only to suggest to the child reading purposes that require organization and then show him the most efficient mechanical methods to follow in recording his findings. He should be taught how to indicate major and subordinate ideas in an outline, how to make a time-line, how to make a classification chart, and the like. There is no doubt that much of the instruction will lie in the selection of the most efficient organization tool for the type of reasoning involved.

To summarize, the major problem for the remedial teacher when correcting some specific limitation in the basic study skills is to locate exactly the skill in which the child is not sufficiently tutored and then give him what he needs in the way of instruction. Care must be taken to follow a reasonable sequence in developing the skill. Most basic study skills can only be taught in material that is written in a style and is read for purposes that the study skill serves. It would not, for example, make sense to ask a child to make an outline of a poem. It would be unwise also to try to teach the study skills of science with some fanciful tale. Probably many teachers will find in some of the modern basic readers which have true content units the most suitable material available for developing diversified basic study skills. Some teachers may prefer to use texts from the content fields as materials. In either approach, the teacher must teach the child the skills and give him enough practice in using each of them so that they become a permanent part of his reading equipment.

INEFFECTIVE ORAL READING

Oral reading is a part of any well-rounded developmental program of reading instruction. There are close relationships between the development of oral and silent reading abilities, and as a result there is a need for carefully maintaining a balance between the two. If an undue amount of oral reading is used as a means of teaching silent reading in the early grades, growth in both oral and silent reading may be impeded. The child may become self-conscious about his oral reading and he may become an over-vocalizer, i.e., one who pronounces every word to himself in every silent reading situation. The tendency to have children read aloud from a basic reading book, one after another around the room, has little to justify it. A far better approach is to have the children, during instructional times, first read silently—a paragraph, a page, or a selection—in order to find the answer to a specific question or for some other well-defined purpose, and then read aloud the part of the selection that answers the question or fulfills the purpose they have in mind.

The development of oral reading is important enough to deserve a definite place in the program rather than be used as the mere handmaiden of the silent reading program. The reading curriculum, therefore, should include provision for developing oral reading in the manner that is best for the development of competence in this specific area and to avoid any unfortunate results to the child's silent reading. The ultimate aim of oral reading instruction is to enable the reader to interpret a selection to others. The effective oral reader learns to interpret printed material in a relaxed and fluent manner to an audience. At the start, all oral reading should be prepared oral reading, but as the child matures in both silent and oral reading ability, he will become more adept at reading orally at sight without first reading the material over silently. There are, then, sight and prepared oral reading, both of which can be interpretive. The amount of preparation needed for oral reading depends upon the nature of the circumstances and the maturity of the reader. The parent who reads a story to his child is probably reading it at sight. The sharing of a book by reading it aloud, in the New England reading circle manner, is also usually done at sight. In most other instances, oral reading is prepared, interpretive reading rather than sight reading. Both types of oral presentation should be outcomes of a reading program.

There are many adults who feel uncomfortable in oral reading situations and often rightly so in view of their lack of skill. This condition, in all likelihood, is the outcome of unfortunate early reading experiences and failure of their reading programs in school to develop oral reading as a specific ability. Just a few years ago, it was the custom for more of the child's reading time to be devoted to reading a selection at sight, while the rest of the class looked at it, each in his own book, than to any other phase of reading instruction. Unfortunately this method still persists in some classrooms. If some listening child lost his place because he got bored with the reader's slow pace and read ahead for himself silently, he was punished. Some teachers even went to the extreme of binding the books with rubber bands so that the children could not turn the pages and read ahead. Meanwhile the poor reader was stumbling along through his presentation with each of his errors apparent to all. The good reader either thought about something else or he followed along at the necessary slow pace which was most unfortunate for his own silent reading abilities. The results were both insecure and ineffective oral reading and slow and laborious silent reading.

Even though conditions have changed for the most part and oral reading is taught in a more effective way, there are still some children who are good silent readers and who have developed all of the basic reading proficiencies but are seriously retarded in oral reading ability. These children constitute a group having a specific retardation. If their poor oral reading is the result of some basic inadequacy, the major problem is to correct that difficulty. When there is no such underlying difficulty and the child is an ineffective oral reader, his problem should be diagnosed. The child who is poor in oral reading, but is otherwise an able reader for his general reading level may suffer from one of the following difficulties: (1) he may have an inappropriate eye-voice span; (2) he may lack proper phrasing in oral reading; (3) his rate and timing in oral reading may be unfortunate; (4) he may become emotionally tense while reading aloud.

Inappropriate Eye-Voice Span

Many children who are specifically retarded in oral reading are in difficulty because their eye-voice span is inappropriate. They may be focusing their attention directly on the word they are speaking or they may be trying to maintain an eye-voice span that is too great for their general reading maturity. If it is the former of these troubles, the child will read aloud in a halting and stumbling fashion with little expression and many pauses. He can not anticipate the meaning of what he is reading and therefore can not express it with his voice. He may very likely read along in a monotone. Each word that he does not recognize at sight will cause him to halt for inspecting it, whereas if his eye-voice span were longer, he would have time to identify words before he was required to say them orally.

If the latter is the trouble, i.e., if the child is trying to maintain too great an eye-voice span in oral reading, then he will in all probability be an exceptionally able silent reader who is transferring to the oral reading his silent reading habits. He is racing ahead silently, perhaps at the rate of 300 to 400 words a minute, but he can pronounce words orally at only 140 words a minute. Such a child may try to maintain an eye-voice span of 8 to 10 words. If he does this in his oral reading, he will be likely to omit many words or to read so rapidly that he can give but little expression to what he is reading aloud. He may lower his voice, enunciate poorly, and show little concern for his audience.

The diagnosis of eye-voice span is among the easiest appraisals for the diagnostician to make. The child is given a book at the appropriate level of difficulty for oral reading—a level at which he will encounter few word difficulties. He is given time to prepare the material and then he is asked to read it aloud to the examiner, who is at the child's right. As the child reads aloud, the examiner reads along silently with him. At intervals, the examiner covers the child's page with a three-by-five card in order to find out how many words the child is able to say after he can no longer see the print. Three or four trials of this should be made before the examiner starts keeping the actual record. The examiner should cover the rest of the line of print when the child is pronouncing a word that comes about one-third of the way through it. This testing should also be done with unprepared or sight oral reading. In this way, the examiner will have information on the eye-voice span of a child in both prepared and sight oral reading. It will be found that children in the early grades, with first- or second-grade reading ability, cannot maintain an eye-voice span of more than a word or two in unprepared oral reading. Therefore, in sight oral reading, they can be expected to be little more than oral word-callers. Instruction in sight oral reading should be delayed until they have acquired greater competency in reading. They will, however, tend to have a longer eye-voice span when reading aloud material that they have prepared for oral reading and therefore can be expected to interpret more effectively.

Remedial instruction for the child with a narrow eye-voice span should always be done in the prepared oral reading situation. The child should not be allowed to do any sight oral reading. Conversational passages are best for developing fluent oral reading for such a child. The material should be easy, with few if any unfamiliar words. The child should be encouraged to try to look ahead. Special attention should be given to phrasing. In certain cases, it will be profitable to use the method of testing eye-voice span as a device for teaching the child to lengthen his span. The purpose for his oral reading should be a real one, such as when he prepares to read something aloud that he knows he is actually going to read to others. He should rehearse until he is satisfied that he is ready for the oral reading.

The child who is trying to maintain too long an eye-voice span, needs to be taught to use one that is more appropriate to the oral reading situation. At the start of remedial training such a child should be given an opportunity to read prepared material before an audience. If a tape recorder is available, his oral reading should be recorded so that he can learn his oral reading pattern and think about how he could improve it. He should be taught the art of pausing from time to time while reading aloud and he should be encouraged to look at his audience frequently. The problem of teaching the child who has too long an eye-voice span, is one of getting him to use his superior reading ability effectively in oral reading situations.

Lack of Proper Phrasing Ability

A pupil who is a poor oral reader may lack proper phrasing ability and tend to read aloud either word by word, or by clustering words into groups disregarding the thought units involved. In either circumstance, attention to the meaning of what is read is neglected. The word-by-word reader can be immediately detected as he reads orally. Each word is pronounced as an unrelated entity. The words are read much in the manner that a mature reader might read a grocery list. When a child reads in this way, he may be directing his attention to the meaning of each word, but he is paying little attention to the interrelationships between them. The child who clusters words without regard to the real thought units is more difficult to detect when listening to his oral reading. What he reads may seem rather fluent, but it just doesn't seem to make sense. This kind of oral reading sounds as though someone were trying to read a grocery list four words at a time, and putting in expression not warranted by the dissociated content.

The remedial training for children who lack proper phrasing in oral reading is the same, no matter which of the two types is involved. The word-by-word reader was brought about in the first place by his having to read material with too large a vocabulary or by using content that repeated words in a mechanical and more or less senseless way. Early books should introduce words at a slow rate and these words should be used with great frequency, but always in meaningful content, avoiding nonsense repetition. Beginning books in reading that say, "Make, make, make it, John," or "See, see, oh, see," or "Look, look, oh look," are giving what is probably the best possible training in word-by-word reading.

The material used to correct the tendency to use inappropriate phrasing in oral reading should be material that is easy for the child, that avoids inane repetition, and that has a considerable amount of conversation in it. The use of dramatic readings, tape recordings, dummy or live microphone readings, and other such activities encourages proper phrasing. No sight oral reading should be attempted until growth in phrasing is well established.

Unfortunate Rate and Poor Timing in Oral Reading

Many children who lack ability in oral reading attempt to read too rapidly or have a poor sense of timing. They may start out reading at a reasonable rate but go continually faster until little of what is read can be understood. The good oral reader, at any level of advancement, reads at a rate that is relatively slow. He has a moderate degree of flexibility in his rate so that he may express different feeling tones by altering his rate of reading. He learns to use pauses effectively to hold the attention of his audience and also to emphasize important points.

One of the most helpful means of aiding the poor oral reader is to devote attention to his rate and timing. The child will profit from listening to good oral readers on the radio or on television and trying to emulate their performances. Tape recordings of the child's own reading will demonstrate his present pattern to him. The expert reader will set the child's goals. Oral reading situations best suited to the child's needs are those in which he shares findings related to class enterprises. Having such a child be the news commentator during sharing periods is excellent because the news is made up of short paragraphs giving accounts of different unrelated events. Each one is read and then the child pauses before going on to the next. The pauses are natural because of the change in content. The items are short enough so that the child does not accelerate his reading. The reading of long selections from a story should be avoided until after the child has his speed and timing under control.

The Emotionally Tense Oral Reader

Some children who have had frequent unfortunate experiences in oral reading become insecure or even frightened in such situations. The child who is experiencing emotional tensions about his oral reading can be detected by noting changes in the pitch of his voice while he reads. If his voice gets increasingly higher as he reads, he is becoming more and more tense. If his errors become more frequent as he reads, he is probably becoming emotionally blocked. There are few if any situations more highly emotionally charged than is oral reading for the poor reader. Everything that can be done to relieve his tension in oral reading situations should be done. Two things that will help him is to have him read material that is free from difficulties and that he has prepared so well that he can feel confident. Another aid to the emotionally tense reader is having the teacher near at hand and ready to prompt him if he gets into difficulty. Having the child read out of the sight of his audience seems to lessen some of his tension and will soon help him to establish confidence. Reading off-stage as a narrator in a play or reading behind the screen for a shadow show will often help the tense reader. A microphone placed in another room over which an announcement or a news report is read offers a good opportunity for the child to read, free from self-consciousness. If, under these conditions, the reading is well prepared and the material is relatively easy to read, great progress can be expected. As soon as possible, the child should discard these devices and learn to read before his audience.

There is much that is common among the four types of poor oral readers discussed above. As soon as children recognize their problem and are eager to improve their oral reading, a self-check-list of questions can be used. Each child will check the progress he is making in the phase of oral reading upon which he is working. One child may be working on his rate of reading, another may be working on phrasing, and a third on accuracy. The children may, under proper circumstances, judge the oral reading of one another. When this is done, they should tell what they liked, how well they think a child did in respect to what he was working on, and name any ways in which they think he might do still better. Such a list as the following adapted from Bond and Wagner (28), will prove helpful:

1. Did he select material that is of interest to his listeners?
2. Was he well enough prepared?
3. Did he read loud enough for all to hear?
4. Did he read as though he were telling the story?
5. Was he reading at a pleasant rate?
6. Did he express the meaning well?
7. Was he relaxed and did he have good posture?
8. Did he use the punctuation marks to help him?
9. Did he make us feel he wanted to read his story to us?

When the teaching of oral reading is done properly, not only is interpretive reading enhanced, but also oral language patterns are improved and better silent reading results. The child who is accustomed to reading aloud with pleasure will use some of the expressions he likes in his spoken language. He will gain feelings of confidence before groups and will sense the importance of adequate preparation. His silent reading will be improved because, in his preparation for oral reading, he will be concerned with the meaning, the characterizations, and the action which he is to interpret to others. His concern with thought units in oral reading will teach him to cluster words together properly in his silent reading. Modern programs of oral reading appear to be vastly superior to the 'round-the-room reading of bygone days which produced the many insecure oral readers among the adults of today.

SUMMARY

Three major groups of specific retardation problems are discussed in this chapter: The child who is limited in one or more types of comprehension, the child who has failed sufficiently to develop some of the basic study skills, and the child who is an ineffective oral reader but who is in all other respects a competent reader. Each of these children is in need of remedial help to overcome a specific defect.

The major method of correcting a specific type of comprehension difficulty, is to have the child read material in a well-graded, basic reader at the appropriate level of difficulty for him. The purposes for reading the material should be such that the ability in which the child is limited is stressed. The reasons for reading should be well understood by the child before the reading is done and there should be checks on the accuracy of the reading at the end. These check questions should reflect the specific comprehension ability being emphasized. The comprehension abilities discussed were reading to retain factual information, reading to sense the organization of information, judging the authenticity and relevance of information, interpreting the information given, and the appreciation abilities.

The methods suggested for correcting specific limitations in basic study skills were to find exactly the study skill in which the child was ineffective and then to teach that skill and give him enough practice to make it become part of his permanent reading equipment. The basic study skills discussed were location of sources of information, use of basic references, interpretation of pictorial and tabular materials, and methods of organizing information.

Ineffective oral readers need to be given material that is relatively easy for them to read and have ample opportunity to prepare it. The major problems in oral reading are: inappropriate eye-voice span, lack of proper phrasing, unfortunate rate and timing, and the emotionally tense oral reader.

SELECTED READINGS

BOND, G. L. and WAGNER, E. B., *Teaching the child to read,* rev. ed. New York: The Macmillan Company, 1950, Chaps. 11, 14, 15.

BRUECKNER, L. J., and BOND, G. L., *Diagnosis and treatment of learning difficulties.* New York: Appleton-Century-Crofts, Inc., 1955, Chap. 7.

GATES, Arthur I., *The improvement of reading,* 3rd ed. New York: The Macmillan Company, 1947, Chaps. 12, 13.

HARRIS, Albert J., *How to increase reading ability,* 3rd ed. New York: Longmans, Green & Company, 1956, Chaps. 8, 16.

McKEE, Paul, *The teaching of reading in the elementary school.* Boston: Houghton Mifflin Company, 1948, Chaps. 12, 13, 14, 15.

RUSSELL, David H., *Children learn to read.* Boston: Ginn and Company, 1949, Chap. 11.

STRANG, Ruth, McCULLOUGH, C. M., and TRAXLER, A. E., *Problems in the improvement of reading,* 2nd ed. New York: McGraw-Hill Book Company, Inc., 1955, Chap. 15.

TINKER, Miles A., *Teaching elementary reading.* New York: Appleton-Century-Crofts, Inc., 1952, Chaps. 14, 15.

WITTY, Paul, *Reading in modern education.* Boston: D. C. Heath & Company, 1949, Chap. 6.

YOAKIM, Gerald A., *Basal reading instruction.* New York: McGraw-Hill Book Company, Inc., 1955, Chap. 12.

15   IMPROVING READING IN THE CONTENT AREAS

As the child reads more skillfully, he is gaining proficiency in at least four interrelated capacities. He is gaining in his facility to understand more mature and complex reading materials. He is growing in his attitudes, interests, and tastes. This increases his desire to share the ideas, experiences, and imaginative creations of authors and he is becoming increasingly more demanding of the quality of these authors. He is gaining in his reading fluency. That is, he has become so familiar with print that his rate of reading can be adjusted to whatever purposes he brings to his reading. His reading is also now more and more differentiated according to the unique demands of the highly specialized materials to be found in different subject matters. This last is the phase of the child's reading growth which we will consider in this chapter.

As a child progresses through the grades, the range of materials he reads becomes ever wider. In modern instructional programs, reading in the content of subject matter fields is introduced during the primary school years. During these years, as children gradually make both more intensive and extensive use of printed materials, they are led to appreciate the fact that books are useful sources from which to obtain information. All sorts of items of special information are acquired by systematic use of readers and other printed materials. Progress in reading to study will be gradual during the first two grades. By the third grade, the child will be reading a considerable amount of informational material, particularly in relation to experience units and as he gets into elementary books on science and social studies. It is clear that the child's basic program cannot neglect the content fields right from the start. The basic program should itself reflect the kind of reading he is expected to do in the entire curriculum. Along with the reading of factual material there comes a need for every child to acquire both the purpose and the will to gain information on the specific problems which he meets either in a content subject or an experience unit. In connection with these, the child is introduced to special vocabularies and the new concepts they embody. Gradually the child is prepared for a smooth transition into the reading tasks of the intermediate grades where there is a rapidly stepped-up stress upon reading in various subject matter fields.

As the pupil advances into the intermediate grades, he meets a wide range of new reading material. He must learn to utilize all the abilities, skills, and procedures at his disposal in order to adjust to the specific purposes and requirements of each subject matter he encounters. It is during these grades that the foundations already established are made more solid, are refined and supplemented so that the pupil becomes well prepared for effective reading of the content materials. Basic reading instruction at this level will aid in the development not only of more independence but also of more flexibility in adjusting procedures and abilities to the distinct purposes and materials of each of the content areas.

The curricular materials of every field the child meets impose their own specific and unique demands upon his reading capabilities. Each field has unique reading problems. A fourth-grade child, for example, who has been reading story material for most of his three years of reading experience is suddenly confronted for the first time with a geography book. He has always read a story from the top of the first page on through several pages of the story uninterrupted. In the geography book, he starts at the top of the page in the customary manner. He reads about ten lines and then is told to look at Figure 1 on page 12. He looks at Figure 1 on page 12, and returning to the page he had just left, starts at the top of the page again. He has always done this. He reads ten lines that seem familiar and is asked to look at Figure 1 on page 12. He says to himself that he has already looked at Figure 1 on page 12, so he goes on reading down the page. Somewhat later he reads, "You noticed in Figure 1 that. . . ." He had noticed no such things. No one had told him to look for them and he was unfamiliar with the ways of the geographer. Such episodes constitute, of course, minor misunderstandings but many reading disability cases are caused by an accumulation of such misunderstandings or faulty learnings, each small in itself. How much easier and how much more profitable the reading experience would have been had these problems of organization been anticipated and readiness for reading geographic materials been developed earlier.

READING ABILITIES REQUIRED

Normal progress in acquiring the basic reading skills is essential for effective reading in the content areas. This involves development from grade to grade of the abilities necessary for adequately recognizing words, an adequate vocabulary, skill in reading by thought units, and finally both basic and special comprehension abilities as they occur in the developmental reading program. If a child has not hitherto made normal progress, this must be taken into account. For instance, no fifth-grade pupil with third-grade reading ability should be asked to read material in a geography book written for fifth-graders. Whatever books are used should be within the range of that pupil's ability to read and comprehend. To require a pupil to try to read a book he cannot read with understanding will only result in confusing him and probably developing in him a dislike for reading. Pupils who have failed to make satisfactory progress in learning the basic reading abilities are definitely handicapped in reading the materials in the different subject matters. After surveying the experimental literature, Fay (67) concludes that one of the first steps involved in improving reading in content fields is to build as good a foundation as possible in the basic habits, skills, and abilities in reading. It should be pointed out, however, that some of the basic skills and abilities cannot be developed in narrative material. Therefore, the basic program should reflect the actual reading requirements of a given grade so that the child can be taught the skills and abilities necessary for reading factual material.

Supplementary Abilities Needed

In addition to the basic abilities, other supplementary reading abilities are necessary for effective reading of the content subjects. To some degree, materials in each of these areas such as the social studies, the natural sciences, mathematics, and literature make unique demands upon the reader. Plenty of evidence to support this view is found in the experimental literature.

First, it should be noted that there is considerable overlapping among reading abilities in different subjects. In general, good readers in one area tend to be good readers in other areas. Swenson (164), employing 217 eighth-grade pupils, made group comparisons between those with high scores and those with low scores in reading and school achievement. There were 35 to 41 pupils in each group comparison. She found that those who rated high on vocabulary and comprehension in reading science material were also high in a general reading test, and vice versa. She also found that pupils high in vocabulary and comprehension, both of the general sort and in science materials, were high achievers in literature, history, and science. In a similar study of high and low groups, Shores (151) found that both general reading ability and historical reading ability *seem* to be closely related to achievement in literature, history, science, and geography. The results in these two studies, unfortunately, may lead to a misinterpretation. In group comparisons of this kind, only *general* trends are indicated. They demonstrate the existence of a relationship when a sizable group of pupils is studied, but they do not reveal the extent or the amount of the relationship in any one individual. It does not follow from these results that Mary Jones's score on a history reading test will predict her ability to read science material. Furthermore, the degree of relationship existing in the whole group could be shown only by obtaining a correlation. But no correlations were reported in these studies. Perhaps they were computed and if so, they would undoubtedly have been relatively low positive coefficients (see below). In such a situation, prediction of the relative standing of any one pupil from one measure to another is very precarious. Both Swenson and Shores, in the above studies, also came up with evidence that reading proficiency is to a considerable extent specific to the particular content field in which the reading is done. This must be borne in mind.

Tinker (168) has analyzed performance in reading various kinds of materials. Only when the materials in two reading tests are strictly comparable is performance in either comprehension or speed closely related ($r = .85$). When the subject matter of one test is different from that of another, the correlations are relatively low. For instance, the correlations, when one test is general comprehension and the other a test of the comprehension of poetry or of scientific materials, were, respectively, .38 and .35. Similarly, correlation between scores on speed of reading tests is low ($r = .46$) when contents of the two tests differ, the one being easy narrative and the other scientific prose.

The correlations between general reading tests and reading tests in the content fields range from about .30 to .50. The data collected by Eva Bond (17) indicate that reading abilities essential for achievement in various content subjects differ considerably. The reading abilities measured on standardized tests appear highly related to achievement in literature but not closely related to achievement in other content areas. Similarly, Elden Bond (16) found relatively low correlations between various measures of reading ability and scholastic achievement. He also found that good achievement in one subject matter does not necessarily mean good achievement in another. His suggestion, that highly significant relationships would be found to exist between reading and achievement if the reading measure were based upon reading within the content area in question, is sound.

The comparisons cited above plus other similar data indicate that there are many reading abilities somewhat independent of each other. Apparently there is no general silent reading ability or a general comprehension ability or a general speed of reading ability. Examination of all the relevant evidence shows convincingly that there are several types of reading ability, and that a person may be competent in some and not in others. Fay (67) states that the nature of reading in one area may differ radically from that in another. He concludes that specific instruction should be given for reading in the different content areas at every grade level above the second.

These data point up two problems in relation to reading content area materials. *First,* one must be concerned with rate and comprehension in specific subjects rather than any general rate or comprehension. For example, in the case of history, the two important things are rate of reading and degree of comprehension in history. The relation between these two measures will tend to be high only when the history material is well within the comprehension ability of the pupil. The attainment of a satisfactory grasp of a subject is possible only when the pupil possesses an adequate vocabulary, adequate concepts, and adequate skills in reading in this area.

The *second* problem concerns adjustment of rate of reading to the particular requirements in each subject field. As pointed out by Carlson (33), the two things about rate of reading in a content area to be kept in mind are the speed suitable for accomplishing the purpose for which the pupil is reading, and, second, the different speeds at which he can most effectively read materials of different degrees of difficulty. Versatility in the matter of speed is all-important. Instruction should be such that the pupil will understand that there is no one rate that is proper for reading all materials. To repeat, what is desired is that each pupil should read as rapidly as is appropriate for achieving his purpose and with proper allowance for the difficulty of the material he is reading. The child who has achieved this versatility so that as occasion demands he can change his pace, has learned an important procedure for reading in the content areas.

Appropriate speed of reading a particular story or article is often determined by the purpose for which the reading is done. For instance, reading a story for enjoyment would be done more rapidly than reading it so as to be able later to describe its characters. Or one would read an article in science more rapidly to gain a background of impressions than when reading it to select the relevant material for a written report embodying some generalization. One of these purposes is a matter of general ideas, the other of details. Some purposes are achieved best by rapid reading, others by careful, slow analytical procedures, and of course sometimes even rereading.

The nature and difficulty of materials require adjustment of rate for most effective reading. Where the pupil understands the vocabulary and concepts dealt with, and when other aspects of the material such as sentence length and organization are at a readability level which he can handle, the appropriate rate of reading is relatively rapid. Under these conditions, the thinking side of the reading proceeds unhampered. Comprehension is then achieved rapidly and smoothly.

The efficient reader demands understanding of what he is reading. Comprehension of material containing a vocabulary and concepts that are unfamiliar requires relatively slow reading. The child, in addition to working out recognition of the unfamiliar words, must take time to dig out meanings and clarify concepts. This thinking requires building up a background of meanings, and using the context before him, as well as analyzing the relations between words and between sentences. The more difficult the material, the slower it must be read in order to comprehend it. Any tendency to read difficult materials at too rapid a rate will have unfortunate results. Word meanings and concepts will not be understood. Such a passage can have little or no meaning for the child and from it he can only get incomplete or erroneous ideas. Furthermore, if he continues such practices, his ineffectual reading will tend to become habitual with him.

All this does not mean that rapid reading is unimportant. Any material should be read as rapidly as it can be comprehended while reading for a particular purpose. Speed of comprehension will be considered in detail in the next chapter.

Adjustment of instruction to individual differences of pupils is just as necessary in the content areas as elsewhere. (See Chapter 3.) In fact, this adjustment becomes doubly difficult in the subject matter fields because of the inherent difficulty of the materials and the poor way in which many authors write. Many teachers avoid this difficulty by using topically organized curricula and a range of material rather than a single textbook.

FOUR CONTENT AREAS

Learning to read effectively in the content fields is a difficult, complicated, and lengthy task. The range of the adjustments required for reading content subject matter and the ever increasing variety and specificity of material confronting the pupil is well illustrated by comparing excerpts of content area materials from basic books used in the primary grades and in the intermediate grades, as Bond and Wagner (28) have done. Any teacher may make her own similar comparisons. This contrast becomes more striking by noting the wide variety of subject matter material read in the many sources outside the basic books as the pupil progresses through the upper grades. To develop proficient reading in the social studies, science, mathematics, and literature, the teacher must know the reading problems and difficulties in each field with which she is concerned. Equipped with this information, every teacher will be better able to teach her pupils how to read material in each content field. There are ample data which show that instruction in reading materials in a specific content area produces significant gains in achievement in that area.

Certain features of the materials in the content areas cause reading difficulties. Fay (67) notes the following: (*a*) There is an unduly heavy load of facts and concepts. (*b*) The variations in typographical arrangement from one area to another may confuse the pupil. (*c*) All too frequently the materials are uninteresting to children. (*d*) The readability of materials is often harder than in basic readers. (*e*) Many writers tend to assume greater background than children possess. (*f*) All this emphasizes the need for carefully fitting materials to children and for carefully organizing instruction in reading such materials.

Brief consideration of the basic reading problems in four content areas is given in the following paragraphs. For additional details see Bond and Wagner (28) and Tinker (175).

Social Studies

A relatively large number of severe reading problems are encountered in the social studies. The pupil's understanding of historical, civic, economic, and geographic realities must ordinarily be gained through reading since his direct experience in these areas tends to be severely restricted. The variety and amount of reading required is great. Some of this reading may be done rapidly for the main idea. Other materials and purposes demand slow, careful reading with attention devoted to closely packed, sometimes intricate, details. The degree of precision required for satisfactory results in much of the reading will fall in between these two extremes.

Special Vocabulary. Commonly encountered stumbling blocks in reading social studies material are the specialized terms and their accompanying concepts. There are many unique words such as *cuneiform, plateau,* and *integration,* as well as proper names of people, places, and events. In addition there are words with specialized meanings attached when they occur in the context of certain social studies. These include such terms as *mouth, cape, run, court,* and *balance.* Especially difficult are such abstract terms as *democracy, culture,* and *civilization.* Although a pupil may be able to pronounce some of these words without special aid, many of the meanings are learned only gradually and with the teacher's aid.

Complex Concepts. The concept gives meaning to an item of vocabulary. Consequently the development of vocabulary meanings and the development of concepts progress hand in hand. In the social studies, many concepts, and consequently the word meanings, are very complex and difficult to learn. Extensive reading of appropriate materials is of major assistance in this but there should be proper restriction in the number of topics to be covered. The provision of incentives to dig out meanings, the clearing up of misconceptions, and developing effective methods of procedure are largely a matter of teacher guidance.

Selection, Evaluation, and *Organization.* The wide and extensive reading employed to achieve satisfactory progress in the social studies requires application of various kinds of comprehension and study skills. There must be acquaintance with source materials and techniques of using them in selecting pertinent information, an ability to do the critical reading involving judgment in evaluation of the selected materials, and skill in organizing the information which is wanted to use in reports or discussions. These special skills are considered in detail in an earlier chapter.

Readability. The style of writing employed in textbooks in the social studies frequently puts many hurdles in the way of the reader. One instance of this is numerous facts and ideas which are packed into relatively small space without enough organizational clues in the form of headings, subheadings, and boldface or italic type to bring out clearly the relative importance of the different facts and ideas. Hence there is little or no indication as to which ones are most worth learning. Yet to memorize all the detailed contents is neither possible nor desirable. Under such conditions the pupil is inclined to stumble along, learning indiscriminately some facts and ideas, or even to pick up no appreciable learning at all.

In addition, the writers of social studies books frequently introduce specialized words with no attempt, or an inadequate one, at defining them. Too often they inject new ideas without providing a sufficient context of meanings to clarify them. It should be noted, however, that in some recently published texts there has been distinct progress toward overcoming many of these shortcomings.

History. Certain reading problems in the social studies are particularly apparent in the field of history. Three of these are of prime importance: *first,* the materials in history make little allowance for the fact that the temporal order of events is not readily sensed by many pupils. *Secondly,* writers do not seem to appreciate that pupils have a marked tendency to interpret everything in terms of present-day conditions. Consequently it is difficult for pupils to see historical events in relation to the period when or the place where they occurred. This happens most frequently with the treatment of the historical predecessors of modern methods of communication, transportation, science, or living conditions in general. Good instruction requires that the pupils be furnished with as adequate a background as possible for interpreting past events in relation to the specific time and conditions in which they occurred. *Thirdly,* the reading and interpretation of pictures, charts, maps, and related materials constitute specialized kinds of reading which facilitate development of relevant word meanings and concepts as well as provide information. Details for developing these skills are given in an earlier chapter.

Geography. The reading problems common to the social studies considered above also occur in geography. Certain others more specifically related to reading geographical materials should be noted briefly. *First,* to read geographical material understandingly requires appreciation of such human conditions as housing, clothing, food, occupations, and traditions; of such material conditions as the physical features of landscapes, climate, and vegetation; and of the relation between the two sets of conditions. *Secondly,* it is necessary for a pupil to maintain his geographic set in absorbing the contents, in verbal or quantitative form, which are relevant to a geographical unit. This set is developed through preparation of the unit and definition of its purposes. A *third* problem lies in teaching the child to think concretely in terms of geographical location as he reads about different places and what goes on in them—such as methods of housing, transportation, and industry. *Fourth* is the problem of interrupted reading. This is brought about by the necessity of organizing a geography so that it refers the child to material on other pages.

Science

The reading of materials in science rightly constitutes an important segment of the kind of reading to expand one's knowledge that we have been talking about. For the child to understand the world in which he lives, he must learn some science. The variety of purposes for which science is read ranges from reading to gain general impressions and grasp relationships to reading to learn in detail the consecutive steps in an experiment, or to evaluate the conclusions arrived at in a class discussion. A considerable portion of the difficulties of reading science is due to the inherent difficulty of this material. Many of the problems encountered in reading science are similar to those met in the social studies. Others are relatively unique to the science material, such as its purposes and emphases. Because of this, somewhat different reading abilities, skills, and techniques are required.

Vocabulary. The language of science is precise and specific. Each branch of science—chemistry, biology or botany, etc.—uses vocabulary terms specific to itself, as well as drawing on the basic vocabulary employed in more general reading. Since these specific terms embody scientific concepts, it is necessary for the pupil to learn the minimum essentials of scientific vocabulary in any area if satisfactory comprehension is to be achieved. Examples of rather highly specialized scientific terms are *electromagnet, molecule, gravity,* and *lever.* The pupil must also learn specialized meanings of certain general words used in scientific context. Examples from physics are *scale, charge,* and the verb *conduct.*

Concepts. Even the elementary concepts in science are sometimes complex and difficult to understand. Two examples are the concepts represented by the terms *magnetism* and *photosynthesis.* The degree to which concepts in science are grasped will depend upon the capabilities of the individual pupils, the clarity of the context in which the hitherto unfamiliar item of vocabulary occurs, and the skill of the teacher in demonstrating and explaining it. Many reasonably concrete scientific concepts are readily demonstrated, explained, and understood, such as *electromagnetism,* and *surface tension,* which causes a drop of liquid to assume a spherical shape. Many other scientific concepts are not subject to direct demonstration and must therefore be handled by means of verbal description and abstract explanation. These are difficult for the pupil to understand. Diagrams and similes are sometimes helpful in explaining or clarifying such concepts.

Pictures and Diagrams. The reading and interpretation of pictures and diagrams in science tends to be inappropriate and inadequate without some form of systematic instruction. Ordinarily an explanation of these pictures and diagrams is supplied in the accompanying legend as well as in the discussion in the textual material of the facts and principles involved. Some children fail properly to relate this verbal discussion to the diagram or picture itself. Abstract schematic diagrams are still more difficult to read and interpret.

Following Directions. The directions to be followed in carrying out experiments in science are listed specifically. Both children and adults seem to have much difficulty in following such printed directions. Yet the successful performance of the experiment requires that the directions be followed very carefully. This reading should therefore be done slowly, meticulously, and thoughtfully in order that the sequential order of the steps described may be followed one after another. Ordinarily, difficulty does not arise because the pupil cannot read and understand the words and sentences; rather, because he does not follow them correctly, he omits steps or does them in the wrong order. Training in doing this better should receive more emphasis in instruction.

Comprehension Abilities and Study Skills. Remembering facts encountered constitutes, on the whole, a minor aspect of reading science materials. More important is the sensing of relationships and the formulation of generalizations. The higher levels of comprehension in reading science materials can be achieved only when the pupil has learned to perceive the proper relationships among the pertinent facts. When the knack of doing this has been acquired, the pupil can then proceed to formulate his own statement of these relationships, i.e., he makes a generalization. To achieve these ends, it is particularly important that the child learn to think while reading scientific materials. Skill in doing this is relatively slow in developing.

The abilities needed for comprehension and study are more or less constantly drawn upon in reading science materials. The particular skills employed in this will depend upon the nature of the material and the purpose for which the reading is done. The pupil must be prepared to vary his methods or procedures very flexibly in order to achieve the most effective reading in each situation. For instance, when working on a topical unit in science, he must select, evaluate, and organize, and these he cannot do unless he can grasp relationships and generalize.

Mathematics

Reading mathematical material presents a variety of problems, some of them highly specific. Frequently there are more reading problems per page in mathematics than in any other content subject. As was noted in the case of science, mathematics, too, has its own technical vocabulary (*numerator, quotient,* etc.). It also uses common words with a special meaning (*product, dividend, power*), employs complex concepts, and involves the study of relationships and the making of generalizations. Pictures and diagrams must be read and interpreted. Much of this reading is concerned with the exposition of processes, procedures, solving illustrative problems, and giving directions about assignments.

Meaning of Symbols. In arithmetic and other forms of mathematics, pupils must learn to attach meanings to highly abbreviated symbols such as $+$, $-$, $\div$, $=$, $\times$, $\perp$, and many others. At first the reading dealt with words as symbols; now they are condensed to "shorthand" signs. Thus, "is equal to" is represented by the symbol $=$. Also, pupils need to learn to recognize promptly many specialized abbreviations such as *lb., ft., yd., pk., min.,* to mention only a few. Meanings must also be assigned both to numbers encountered in verbal context and to those same numbers isolated in columns (problems in addition, subtraction, and multiplication). In this the pupil must comprehend the place value of numbers such as 429, the significance of 0 in such numbers as 30 and 0.4, and the meaning of common and decimal fractions. One prerequisite for a pupil's solving a mathematical problem is that he have as accurate a command of all the technical symbols it uses as if these concepts were all expressed in the uneconomical form of words. Without systematic instruction, many pupils make slow progress in acquiring sufficient skill to understand and properly manipulate these symbols, abbreviations, and numerals.

Verbal Problems. The statement of a verbal mathematical problem is ordinarily extremely compact, divorced from concrete context, and involves complex relationships. Satisfactory reading of such a problem is achieved by slow, careful, precise progress, together with rereading and thinking about it. In addition to a clear understanding of words and phrases, there must be a selection of relevant facts and a weighing of relationships between the pertinent words and phrases in the total pattern of the problem. Reading verbal mathematical problems is one of the most difficult reading tasks encountered in the content areas. Little success will be achieved without intensive concentration. The teacher should have a full realization of the reading difficulties the child is up against. A good method for handling verbal problems is outlined by Bond and Wagner (28). The child should adopt a pattern of procedure that will lead him to discern *first,* the information required in the answer; *second,* all the pertinent facts necessary to the solution; *third,* a sequential pattern of appropriate steps leading to the solution; and *fourth,* an evaluation of the answer he gets in terms of what is asked for.

Comprehension and Study Skills. Most of the specific comprehension abilities and study skills dealt with in a preceding chapter find application in reading mathematical materials.

Literature

Unlike such content areas as science, mathematics, and social studies, literature lacks a methodical regular sequence of content. Literary materials range from stories about men and women, as well as animals, and from historical novels on through poetry of various kinds to plays and essays. To a considerable degree, the primary concern of teaching literature has been the development of reading interests and tastes. These will be considered in a later chapter. There are, however, certain problems involved in the reading of literary materials that may be touched on here.

Ability to read literary materials with profit depends upon proficiency in a variety of basic reading abilities. Smith (154) has emphasized that a major function of teaching literature is to develop the reading skills necessary for intelligent interpretation of an author's meaning, for sharing in the moods he wishes his readers to feel, and for entering imaginatively into whatever experience he creates. These capabilities are in general those which are emphasized in the basic developmental reading program. They are refined, expanded, and perhaps supplemented under teacher guidance during the reading of literary materials. Proficiency in general reading ability is intimately related to success in literary achievement. The fundamental aspects of general reading ability as measured by standardized reading tests are concerned mainly with comprehension and vocabulary. Elden Bond (16) found that general comprehension (combined score from four tests) and general vocabulary (combined score from five tests) were closely related to literary acquaintance. In fact, this relationship (r of about .70) was much closer than that between literary acquaintance and any of the specialized reading abilities measured. We can state with a considerable degree of confidence, therefore, that the better a pupil's proficiency in general reading comprehension and the larger his vocabulary, the more success he will have in reading literary materials. This is because both the tests and the books previously read have been primarily narrative, and literature is primarily narrative material.

Basic Reading Abilities. In a way, general comprehension and vocabulary knowledge are products of progress in the reading abilities developed in the basic reading program. As the developmental program unfolds, pupils will make progress in acquiring word-recognition techniques, reading by thought units, techniques for increasing word knowledge, basic comprehension abilities, and special comprehension abilities. To do satisfactory work in reading literary materials at any grade level, the pupil should have made normal progress in acquiring these fundamental reading abilities taught in the basic course. In other words, the pupil will be able to read literary material satisfactorily at the reading level he has reached in the basic abilities, but not much higher.

In addition to the general level of reading ability, there are other factors important for reading literary material. Two of these are reading to appreciate the general significance of what is read and reading to follow events and foresee their outcomes as these are measured in Types A and B of *Gates Basic Reading Tests*. Skill in acquiring story sense, which is of high importance in certain literary reading, depends in no small degree upon these two abilities.

Other comprehension abilities and study skills are, at times, involved in reading literary materials. Purposes may vary from uncritical recreational reading employed in following the unfolding of a plot to critical evaluation of the deeper import of what is read.

Enrichment of Meanings. The profit gained from reading literary materials is in great part dependent upon the enrichment of meanings it brings. Important ways of enriching meanings are to be found almost anywhere we turn in literature. One of these is a full appreciation of descriptive words, especially words associated with sensory impressions, with sights, sounds, taste, touch, and smell. Meanings are also enhanced through skill in interpreting figures of speech and symbolic expressions. Or the reader may need to draw upon his previous experience to interpret an allusion and gain deeper insight into what is presented. Frequently the effects of writing depend upon the reader's imaginative penetration into mere hints and atmospheric suggestions. Another aspect of reading literary material is the arousal of moods. Smith's (153) example illustrates this:

> Alone in the night
> On a dark hill
> With pines around me
> Spicy and still.

Here the reader is asked to respond to the mood of the author.

General Comment. The foundations for successful reading of literature consist of the basic reading abilities and comprehension abilities presented in a broad developmental reading program. These are refined, expanded, and supplemented in reading literary materials. Only as children learn the appropriate techniques of reading literature under skillful teacher guidance can they be expected to engage in additional reading of literature with understanding and pleasure.

NECESSARY LEARNINGS

The material in the above sections has dealt with some of the fundamental aspects of reading in the content areas. In addition, attention was given to some of the special reading problems encountered in the social studies, science, mathematics, and literature. We are now ready to list the learnings necessary for proficient reading in these fields.

Application of Proper Comprehension Abilities to a Particular Field. General and specific comprehension abilities have been discussed in previous chapters. As already noted, the reading procedure, when reading subject matter, depends upon the nature and difficulty of the material and the purpose for which the reading is done. Application of comprehension abilities to the reading of specific content materials depends upon at least three things: *First,* there must be a satisfactory level of attainment in both the general and the specific comprehension abilities. This level will be reached when the child has made at least normal progress in a well-rounded developmental reading program. The pupil, if the basic reading program has included systematic instruction in reading in the content fields, will then be able to read content materials designed for his grade level. *Secondly,* the pupil will have to exercise discrimination in deciding what specific comprehension abilities are appropriate to apply in a given reading situation. *Finally,* the child must be flexible in adjusting reading procedures so that the appropriate comprehension abilities are applied effectively.

Special Vocabulary. The problem of technical vocabulary terms (i.e., words special to a field) begins in the later primary grades and increases through successive grades. To comprehend materials in each of the content areas, a child must understand the *essential* technical vocabulary in the field. In any area such as history, many technical words occur only infrequently and do not really contribute enough to the meaning to be worth learning. Other words are *essential* and should be learned. According to Cole (37), there are 328 such words in historical materials read by the end of the eighth grade. On the average, this would mean that the child would have to learn about 50 words a year to master the essential technical vocabulary, or between one and two words per week.

To teach the essential technical vocabulary, one must know which words are essential in a content field. The teacher may point out such terms as reading progresses, or she may find standardized lists such as those given by Cole (37a) very helpful. Cole presents the essential technical vocabularies for 13 different school subjects, including social studies subjects, science subjects, mathematical subjects, and American literature. In any subject, the essential technical vocabulary is accumulated gradually but at an accelerating rate by the pupil. The time to teach a child a technical term is when he is going to use it in context of the unit he is reading. Further treatment of teaching techniques will be found below.

Selecting the Proper Meaning to Fit the Context Where Words with Specialized Meanings Occur. A word with several meanings tends to be harder to learn than a word with only one meaning. The particular meaning of the former comes from the context in which it occurs. In a subject matter field, the meaning that fits may be highly specialized. And in some instances, the everyday meaning may interfere with sensing the technical meaning. Everyday terms which have special meanings in content subjects are illustrated by the use of *product* in arithmetic, and *cape* in geography. *Chord* has a variety of specialized meanings when found in music, engineering, and geometry. The pupil, therefore, must select and comprehend specialized meanings of common words to fit the context of a particular subject matter.

Concepts. As noted earlier, vocabulary terms are the symbols which stand for concepts. The clearness of concepts depends, therefore, upon the richness and preciseness of the word meanings which embody them.

In each of the content areas, the pupil is confronted with a bewildering array of concepts which belong primarily to that specific subject. The evolution of a concept to a satisfactory degree of clearness is slow and depends to a large extent upon a systematic program of instruction. Even the simpler concepts are often difficult for the child to master. Proficient reading in each of the content fields will be achieved in proportion to the progress in learning the specialized concepts encountered in reading materials peculiar to that field.

Symbols and Abbreviations. To read mathematical materials and much of science, the pupil must know and understand the use of a large number of extremely compact symbols. Some of these symbols as $+$ or $=$ stand for concepts involved in calculations; others stand for quantities: $a + b = 12$. In addition, the child must learn a large number of abbreviations such as those listed earlier. The abstract symbolic nature and the wide variety of these symbols together with a multitude of abbreviations provide an army of stumbling blocks to the reader. For many pupils, normal progress is achieved only through detailed instruction accompanied by sympathetic guidance.

Use of Pictures, Graphs, Maps, and Tables. Ordinarily, the reading, i.e., interpretation, of the pictures, graphs, maps, and tables in various content areas is not achieved incidentally. These devices are used to clarify the verbal discussion in the text. Effective understanding of these devices is seldom achieved without systematic instruction.

Adjustment to Differences in Organization. The organization of materials varies a great deal from one content area to another. We have literary material at one extreme and mathematics at the other. The first is on the levels we are talking about, pretty much straightforward narrative, the second is highly condensed and often abstract statements of factual and problem materials. The organization in any subject matter field depends largely upon the nature of its content, aims, and the relationships involved in it. The pupil must sense these factors and make the necessary adjustments. Discrimination in sensing organization and flexibility in adjusting reading procedures is greatly aided by teacher guidance.

DIAGNOSTIC AND INSTRUCTIONAL PROCEDURES

In any area of reading, the diagnosis of difficulties and the proper remedial instruction progress hand in hand, for as we have seen, the latter depends upon the former.

Although this section is concerned primarily with reading in the content areas, there is a preliminary problem which has to be reckoned with and which we have postponed until now. When a child is having difficulty in a content field, the very first step is to determine whether he is retarded in general reading attainments. This is done by using procedures described in previous chapters. If there proves to be a general reading deficiency, this has to be corrected before dealing with difficulties in the content fields. The correction of general reading deficiencies, however, does not of itself insure effective reading practices in the study of content subjects. A pupil who has developed his general reading abilities to a satisfactory level may still be handicapped by difficulties growing out of the specialized reading in the subject matter fields.

General Diagnostic Procedures in Content Fields

Initial indications that a pupil is having difficulty in reading materials in a subject matter field usually come from teacher observation of classroom performance. Difficulties due to retardation in general reading ability are checked and eliminated as indicated in the above section. The next steps are concerned with difficulties in the content fields.

Strang (160) has outlined certain diagnostic procedures common to all content areas. Some of her material is summarized below in modified form:

Self-appraisal. To a large degree, responsibility for improvement rests with the pupil. Initiative to help himself is promoted by self-appraisal. When a pupil realizes the reading potentialities and reading goals that it is possible and desirable for him to reach, he will tend to change his behavior so as to achieve them.

The teacher, acting as a sympathetic consultant, can aid the pupil in his appraisal. She raises questions about the pupil's reading tasks, his dissatisfactions with procedures, what reasons may exist for his inefficiency, and the ways to reach the desired improvement. The pupil is urged to discuss such questions freely with the teacher and to seek her aid in working out his reading problems. A frank discussion of the reading difficulty with an understanding listener usually clarifies it for both the pupil and the teacher. The best approach for beginning a face-to-face conference with a pupil is determined by what the teacher already knows about the child. The preparation for such a conference is important. To listen with understanding and to provide guidance when requested, the teacher should have organized all available relevant information about the pupil: school records, developmental history, school adjustment, test scores, interests, etc. The more complete the teacher's understanding of the pupil's abilities, needs, and interests, the more helpful she can be in guiding him to analyze his reading difficulty.

Observation of Classroom Activities. In any content field, diagnosis and remediation are intimately related to the instructional procedures. There is opportunity in nearly every class period to detect and correct reading difficulties. A well-conducted class period may well yield such information as one or more of the following: (1) whether the relevant reading was done with a well-defined purpose; (2) the degree to which the essential vocabulary is understood; (3) whether the discussion shows that the concepts incorporated in the reading are clearly comprehended; (4) difficulties in applying comprehension abilities and study skills to the particular subject matter; (5) difficulties in interpreting pictures, charts, graphs, and tables; (6) difficulties with symbols or abbreviations; and (7) whether proper adjustment in reading procedure was made to the specific organization of the subject matter. As each difficulty is discovered, suggestions are made by the teacher and the pupil for overcoming it. At times, evidence will appear indicating a need for individual corrective work with some pupils.

Use of Tests. A few standardized reading tests in subject matter fields are available at high school and college levels (see Appendix I). At the elementary grade levels, informal teacher-made tests can be used at appropriate times. The construction of informal teacher-made tests, with illustrative examples of objective and essay types, is described in detail by Ross (143). Other illustrative examples may be found in some of the workbooks that accompany basic reading series.

Informal tests modeled after standardized forms or made up like the illustrations in Ross or in workbooks are useful for measuring instructional outcomes. The test items should employ those kinds of passages that children are expected to read day by day. One form or another of informal test can be employed in a content subject to measure each of the essential learnings listed above.

Combination of Methods. Information from one or more diagnostic procedures is used by the teacher to guide her day-by-day instructional program and for getting a comprehensive picture of the difficulties of an individual pupil. Both the individual pupil and his reading teacher can learn a great deal in addition about the reading processes he uses in a content field by the following procedure: A passage is chosen from a textbook or reference book in the content field. The teacher sits beside the pupil and observes his method of procedure and notes his spontaneous comments. The meaning of the passage is discussed. When errors are made, the pupil is urged to think back and try to recollect where and how he went wrong in comprehending the material. As Strang (160) notes, the pupil's suggestions on how to surmount his difficulty are often sound and practical. Also, having made the suggestions himself, the pupil is generally motivated to carry them out. In this kind of diagnostic procedure, the teacher can do much to guide the pupil toward insight into his difficulty through unobtrusive shaping of the discussion and by suggesting questions he might think over. This technique, which is applicable in any content field, can be one of the best sources of diagnostic information.

General Nature of Remedial Instruction. Certain principles are basic for successful remedial reading instruction in all the various subjects. An interest and purpose for reading in each field must be developed. When interest is keen and purpose is clear, the pupil will be motivated to understand his difficulties and to undertake with some enthusiasm the practice necessary to produce improvement. The remedial instruction should begin at the child's present level of proficiency. Practice materials should be a regular part of the reading assignments in the field. From the beginning, guidance should make sure that the reading procedures used are appropriate to the material and to the purposes for which it is read. Motivation for improvement is increased when the pupil co-operates with the teacher in planning the remedial work. And motivation is maintained more easily when the child sees his own day-by-day progress.

The above principles and procedures of diagnosis and remedial instruction find general application in the content fields. We now turn to more specific procedures related to the necessary learnings listed above.

Application of Proper Comprehension Abilities to a Particular Field

To apply his ability to understand the reading of materials in the content fields, the pupil must have satisfactory command of this ability. As indicated above, a satisfactory command is achieved when the pupil has made normal progress in the developmental reading program which has taught the reading of factual as well as narrative content in purposeful situations from the beginning.

The next step is to check the pupil's ability to distinguish the particular comprehension abilities appropriate for use in reading a specific set of material in a content field. The comprehension abilities which are appropriate depend upon the nature of the material and the purpose for which the reading is done. How well a pupil can distinguish what comprehension abilities to employ may be determined by use of informal tests designed to appraise reading for different purposes as described in an earlier chapter, using content materials. An effective individual diagnostic procedure is the co-study method described above. The pupil and teacher sit down together and read the same passage. They then compare ideas gained and reading methods used.

The remedial program is devised in part from these discussions between pupil and teacher which accompany the informal testing or from the co-study method of appraisal. Such discussions spot difficulties and lay out the best methods of procedures for identifying and applying the comprehension abilities to a specific kind of material. The testing of the pupil's skill in identifying appropriate comprehension abilities in terms of purpose and kind of material is naturally followed by practice to develop versatility in applying the procedures in additional reading of similar materials. To know what procedures are appropriate does not guarantee that they will be employed properly.

Special Vocabulary

Teacher-made tests for diagnosing a pupil's proficiency in the special vocabulary of a content area are readily constructed, modeled after those found in standardized tests or in workbooks but using the words that occur in the unit being studied. Since the meanings of special vocabulary terms in content fields depend upon their context, each test item should be accompanied by a sentence in which the word is used. This sentence may be taken from a unit just completed, or made up to fit into the context of the unit. Thus, the following example would do for a common word, with special meaning, in a social studies unit on harvesting:

Cyrus McCormick thought it strange that after so many years men still used the *cradle* in harvesting wheat.
Cradle means: (1) a baby's bed on rockers; (2) a gold miner's rocking machine; (3) a frame fastened to a scythe; (4) the framework under a ship being repaired.

Or an example of a technical word in a science unit on metals:

German silver is an *alloy* frequently used for making drawing instruments and many other utensils.
Alloy means: (1) loyalty; (2) act of making easier; (3) mixture of two or more metals; (4) any metal that does not rust.

Another less formal technique of diagnosing a child's knowledge of special terms is by observing his use of them either in a conference with the pupil or in class discussion. Clear understanding of a word meaning should lead to proper use in discussion and writing.

Remedial instruction for correcting deficiencies in knowledge of special terms involves good classroom procedures and an emphasis upon individual needs revealed by testing and observation. Remedial work is in order for any pupil who has not learned the meanings of the essential special vocabulary terms of a unit in any content field.

One procedure for teaching the recognition and meanings of essential special words in introducing a unit is the following: The teacher makes a list of the important technical words in the unit. The meanings of these new words are explained through definitions, illustrations, and demonstrations. Attention may be directed to how they are spelled. Meaning in context is emphasized by reading aloud relevant sentences from the text. Any other means available may be used to stress the word meanings to the pupils. This is followed by reading the unit materials and by group discussion. The discussion provides opportunity to correct misapprehensions and to clarify meanings.

For those pupils who have not acquired adequate word meanings by the time the unit is completed, individual remedial instruction is in order. The difficulties discovered by diagnosis will guide the teacher in carrying out the remedial program. Additional experience with the object or action that the word represents is needed. Opportunity must be provided for additional reading of materials which include the words being taught. A better understanding of the more difficult abstract words is arrived at through teacher-pupil discussion. The teacher should realize that degree of vocabulary understanding finally achieved through class work plus remedial instruction will differ considerably from child to child.

Selecting the Proper Meaning to Fit the Context Where Common Words Have Special Meanings in a Content Field

The diagnosis of difficulties and remedial instruction is the same as described in Chapter 11 except that in the present instance we are dealing with materials in the content fields. The first example in the above section illustrates how diagnostic items may be constructed. Such testing should be supplemented by observation of performance in class discussions and if necessary by the sort of individual teacher-pupil co-study sessions described above. Pupils should be taught to be alert to the possibility that many common words have special meanings in the content fields and to make maximum use of the context in working out the special meanings. Otherwise the remedial instruction is the same as for developing the meaning of any vocabulary term.

Concepts

Earlier discussions have emphasized that the development of concepts is intimately associated with acquisition of word meanings. The richer a word's meaning, the clearer is the concept embodied in that word. The best way to assure clear and precise concepts in a content field, therefore, is to develop extensive and precise meanings for the essential scientific terms in the field. The dictionary meanings of such words as *photosynthesis* and *democracy* do not adequately represent the fullness of the concepts these words stand for. The concepts are developed to a proper degree of clearness and precision by many illustrations or demonstrations plus reading of materials containing the words followed by class discussions under teacher guidance. The diagnostic and remedial procedures are the same as described above for special vocabularies. In fact, vocabulary and concept development are part and parcel of a single program.

Symbols and Abbreviations

Diagnosis of proficiency in reading symbols and abbreviations has two aspects: The *first step* is to ascertain whether a pupil understands what a symbol or abbreviation stands for, i.e., that ÷ stands for *divided by,* and *qt.* stands for *quart.* The *second step* is to discover if the child understands the meaning of the terms represented by the symbol or abbreviation and how to use the symbols and abbreviations properly in reading context.

Teacher-made matching tests or a question-answer technique may be used to find out if a pupil knows what a symbol or an abbreviation stands for. In the matching test, the symbols or abbreviations are listed in one column and the words they stand for in a second column. The pupil draws lines connecting a symbol or abbreviation with the word or words it stands for. More effective perhaps is to write the symbol or abbreviation on a paper or blackboard and ask the pupil to state what it stands for. The more important symbols and abbreviations are quickly checked thus.

Understanding of meanings and appropriate usage is best evaluated by presenting the symbol or abbreviation in context of reading material. Then, by the co-study method described above, the teacher can readily discover difficulties and devise the proper remedial instructional procedures for correcting them. To teach the words which symbols and abbreviations stand for is merely a matter of drill. But to develop proper comprehension and usage, the pupil should encounter the symbols and abbreviations in context of the subject matter field. For the most part, they will occur in mathematics and science materials. The co-study method is effective for remediation as well as for diagnosis.

Use of Pictures, Graphs, Maps, and Tables

There are a few standardized tests for diagnosing proficiency in reading graphs, maps, and tables, such as the *SRA Reading Record* and *Iowa Every-Pupil Tests of Basic Skills.* Such tests are generally for junior and senior high school students. For the most part, the teacher will have to depend upon informal procedures for discovering difficulties in reading pictures, graphs, maps, and tables. Much information can be obtained from observation of pupil responses during class discussion. Most fruitful probably is the co-study method described above.

In well-written materials, the legend which accompanies a picture, graph, map, or table gives suggestions for interpreting it. In addition, the discussion in the accompanying text usually amplifies the information it gives. To read or interpret these devices properly involves reading the legend and the relevant text plus scrutiny of the picture, map, graph, or table to insure that all details and their implications have been grasped. The teacher will find that most of the difficulties in reading these materials consist either of inability to note the important details in pictures, etc., or neglecting to make proper use of legends and relevant text. Ordinarily all of these are involved.

The remedial instruction will consist of exercises to foster proper examination of a picture, graph, map, or table plus use of the legend and relevant text. Ordinarily the procedure runs about as follows: After a preliminary examination of the picture, the pupil reads the legend accompanying it. Meanings are clarified if he learns to put the content of the legend into his own words. Next he finds out what the text has to say about the picture.

The picture is now re-examined for the items suggested by the legend and explained in the text. In other words, the picture helps to clarify the textual material, and suggestions for interpreting the picture come from the legend and the text. Graphs, maps, and tables are read in a similar manner. (See also Chapter 14.)

Adjustment to Differences in Organization

As noted above, the organization of materials varies greatly within a subject matter field and from one field to another. The diagnosis of difficulties is a matter of discovering the pupil's ability to sense the nature of organization in a particular section of science, history, or some other area, and what facility he shows in adjusting his procedures in reading it. Possibly the best diagnosis is achieved by the co-study procedure already explained. The pupil and the teacher work together, comparing methods of sizing up the organization of the material, comparing the ways in which writers in various fields organize their materials, and the best methods of procedure for reading each. By this analysis, difficulties will be discovered and also the plans for improved procedures can be formulated. This will be followed by practice exercises on additional material employing the improved procedures. Subsequent teacher-pupil conferences should be held to check improvement, and to formulate modified reading procedures if necessary.

Interrelations

Although the learnings necessary for proficient reading in the content fields have been discussed separately, they are all co-ordinated in the practical instructional program. In a science unit, for instance, every one of the listed learnings may be involved. But in literature or some social studies units, the materials may not contain graphs, tables, symbols, and abbreviations. The teacher will readily discern the intimate relation of proper comprehension abilities and their application in reading procedures to differences in organization. Similarly, the learning of special vocabulary terms and the development of concepts are two aspects of the same process. In teaching the necessary learnings, therefore, the instructional program should be so organized that proper emphasis is given to each and to the end that the relation between them will be appreciated by the pupils in the class.

SUMMARY

Reading materials in the content fields are first used in the primary grades and become more prominent as the child progresses through subsequent grades, when the materials become more highly specialized. Proficient reading in these areas is based upon normal progress in a well-rounded basic reading program and in acquiring certain supplementary abilities and skills as occasion for their use arises in one or another field.

The abilities required for reading literature are closely related to general reading ability developed in the basic program. The reason for this may be because the basic program is frequently composed of predominantly narrative material. But the reading abilities used in the other areas are not intimately related to each other or to general or narrative reading ability, though of course there is some overlapping.

There is need for adjusting reading skills and abilities in each subject matter field. The comprehension abilities employed and the rate of reading depend upon the nature and organization of the material, its difficulty, and the purpose for which the reading is to be done.

Social studies, science, mathematics, and literature are the four content fields considered. They involve a wide range of materials to be read and somewhat different reading abilities are required in each field. Problems that arise in each were briefly considered.

The learnings necessary for proficient reading in the content fields were reviewed in some detail. They include application of proper comprehension abilities to a particular field, special vocabulary, common words with special meanings in a content field, concepts, symbols, and abbreviations, use of pictures, graphs, maps, and tables, and differences in organization.

Suggestions for diagnosis and remedial instruction with respect to each of the necessary learnings were given. To a large degree, diagnosis of difficulties in content fields depends upon teacher-made tests and other informal procedures such as observation of pupil responses in class discussions and in individual work with a pupil. The remedial instruction is based upon the diagnostic findings. The teacher should be alert to individual differences and adjust instruction to them.

Success of the remedial instruction depends upon maintaining good morale and motivation in the pupil. These are fostered by making the diagnosis and the organization of the remedial procedures a co-operative enterprise between the teacher and the pupil, as well as by making sure the child notices every sign of progress he is making.

SELECTED READINGS

ADAMS, Fay, GRAY, Lillian, and REESE, Dora, *Teaching children to read.* New York: The Ronald Press Company, 1949, Chap. 12.

ARTLEY, A. Sterl, ed., "Improving reading in the content areas," *The Reading Teacher*, Vol. 8, No. 2 (December, 1954).

BOND, Guy L., and BOND, Eva, *Developmental reading in high school.* New York: The Macmillan Company, 1941, Chap. 8.

——— and WAGNER, Eva B., *Teaching the child to read,* rev. ed. New York: The Macmillan Company, 1950, Chaps. 12, 13.

COLE, Luella, *The improvement of reading.* New York: Farrar and Rinehart, Inc., 1938, Chap. 9.

McCALLISTER, James M., *Remedial and corrective instruction in reading.* New York: D. Appleton-Century Company, Inc., 1936, Chaps. 11, 12, 13, 14, 15.

STRANG, Ruth, McCULLOUGH, Constance M., and TRAXLER, Arthur E., *Problems in the improvement of reading,* 2nd ed. New York: McGraw-Hill Book Company, Inc., 1955, Chaps. 7, 8, 9, 10.

TINKER, Miles A., *Teaching elementary reading.* New York: Appleton-Century-Crofts, Inc., 1952, Chap. 15.

WESLEY, Edgar B., *Teaching social studies in elementary schools,* rev. ed. Boston: D. C. Heath & Company, 1952, Chaps. 17, 18, 19.

16 INCREASING RATE OF COMPREHENSION

During recent years, teachers have become much concerned with techniques for improving the rate of reading of their pupils. In schoolroom practice this has frequently led to an overemphasis upon speed of reading per se. Pupils are told over and over of the need to increase their speed of reading and many exercises have been devoted to achieving faster reading. Several standardized tests encourage this stress on speed. Too frequently this emphasis has led to rapid reading with little understanding and also to a neglect of other more important aspects of the instructional program.

Speed of Reading or Rate of Comprehension

Certain writers have seemed to come close to believing that speed of reading is a valid measure of reading performance in itself, even when it is divorced from comprehension. Whereas the fact is, as anyone should see, that a measure of the rate with which words are recognized as words with no reference to apprehending their meanings and relationships, yields a score of little or no significance in real life. Put plainly, "reading" without comprehension is not reading. The only practical and adequate definition of rate of reading is to redefine it as the *rate of comprehension* of printed and written material. This is the definition adhered to in this book. To measure speed of reading, therefore, one must measure the rate with which material is comprehended. And we must also bear in mind that comprehension itself is always to be considered in relation to the purpose for which the reading is done. Thus, in practice, it becomes very important to know the rate at which a particular pupil grasps the general ideas in a story, or the rate at which he comprehends an exposition of history or science material, etc. And in the test situation, rate of reading is rate of comprehending as measured in the particular test. In consequence, standardized tests of speed of reading have certain limitations. The materials in such tests provide inadequate samples of all the different kinds of materials pupils must read; the speed of reading is measured in one situation only.

In some discussions, it is strangely assumed that speed of reading is a general ability that somehow transfers readily to the reading of a wide variety of materials. There is no such general speed of reading ability.

Even for the proficient reader, rate of reading is fairly specific to a particular reading situation.

Every teacher has to realize that rapid reading in itself is not a cause of better understanding. The fact is that a fast rate of comprehension is possible because the pupil possesses the abilities necessary for clear and rapid understanding.

DEVELOPING READING RATES APPROPRIATE TO MATERIALS AND PURPOSES

It has already been noted in previous chapters that *relatively* rapid reading is to be desired in any area of reading. That is, the reading should be at as fast a rate as the material can be comprehended properly. Although a proper fast rate of reading mathematical materials is relatively very slow, still some pupils read such materials at an undesirably slow rate. The same holds for areas such as science and social studies. Whatever the material and purpose, there can be an unnecessarily slow rate of progress or an appropriate fast rate. A rapid rate of reading in itself has no particular value. The proficient reader will have several speeds, each of which can be used as the occasion demands. An essential part of the instructional program is to see that pupils acquire these speeds and gain skill in using them appropriately. The emphasis should be upon developing as many pupils as possible into adaptable, versatile readers who are able to adjust their rates to the nature and difficulty of the material and to the purpose for which the reading is done. The goal is to *comprehend* at as fast a rate as possible. The best way to teach a child to comprehend at an appropriate rate is to furnish him with the skills and concepts to understand properly what he is to read. When this is done, he will ordinarily learn to understand rapidly what he attempts to read. Several aspects of this problem need attention.

Rate That Avoids Dawdling

Some children develop a congenial, meandering way of reading that is considerably below the rate at which they might read with both understanding and pleasure. When this becomes habitual, as frequently happens, it is a handicap to proficient reading. Such easygoing dawdling permits attention to wander and fosters daydreaming. In addition, of course, the child covers an inadequately small amount of material in an allotted time. When unduly slow reading is really dawdling on the part of the pupil, exercises to promote an appropriate faster rate should be provided. Dawdling is likely to be present when the slow reading is not due to one or another of the handicapping factors listed below. In any reading, the appropriate rate is the fastest rate that fits the situation and achieves proper comprehension.

Rate to Fit Material

To read effectively, rate must be appropriate to the nature and the difficulty of the material. The nature of materials varies widely. At one time, the pupils may be reading a fast-moving story, or an item of general interest in a newspaper. Here the appropriate rate of reading is relatively rapid. A short time later, the pupil may be reading geographic material concerned with the concept of erosion by wind and water. In this, a relatively slow rate of progress is necessary to grasp the ideas and relationships involved. Still later he may be reading the procedures for solving a mathematical or scientific problem which requires a very slow, analytical procedure and often rereading. The pupil needs to exercise discrimination in sizing up the nature of the materials so that he may adopt a rate appropriate for reading a particular kind of material with understanding.

Adjusting to variations in difficulty is somewhat similar. Variation in difficulty arises in many ways. Materials in some content areas are more difficult than in others, for example, science or mathematics as compared with literature. At times, there is marked variation in difficulty within the same unit in a single area. These difficulties may occur when unfamiliar vocabulary terms and concepts are encountered, or complex sentences and paragraphs, or any strange construction in language. A difficulty which requires increased attention to content necessitates slower reading for adequate understanding. The pupil should read just as slowly as he needs to in order to grasp what is said. Any pupil who attempts to read all materials at the same rate, irrespective of their nature or difficulty, will be in trouble. To read with understanding and at an effective rate, he must be able to modify his rate to fit both. Easy material should be read faster than difficult material. And familiar material should be read faster than unfamiliar material.

Rates for Different Purposes

Perhaps most important of all is adjustment of rate of reading to the purpose for which the reading is done. This has been stressed at various places in earlier discussions. If the pupil needs to get only a general impression or idea, or if he merely needs to look up a given item on a page, the speed should be relatively high. But if he needs to grasp the concepts in a given selection thoroughly, his pace will be relatively slow. This emphasizes the importance of purposeful reading. Prior to reading any unit, the child should be clear as to the purposes for which he is going to read. The most satisfactory purpose is one stated by the pupil himself. Where he cannot do this satisfactorily, the teacher's guidance should help provide him with a purpose *acceptable* to him. To be a really good reader, however, the pupil must have learned to set his own purpose. This requires discrimination and flexibility. That is, the pupil must be able to size up the materials and clearly understand the purpose. Then he must be flexible in choosing the appropriate rate for him to read with understanding. In other words, *the proficient reader is the adaptable, versatile reader.*

Relation to Comprehension

The relationship of speed of reading to comprehension is not certain. Numerous studies have been reported with correlations ranging from slightly negative to high positive. For lists of these studies and evaluation see Carlson (33), Eurich (63), and Tinker (168, 172, 173). Many of the coefficients are insignificantly small. Examination of the entire body of literature on the subject reveals the following trends: (1) When mature readers (high school and college) are involved and when rate of work and comprehension are measured on comparable materials, there is a significant positive relationship. This means that fast readers tend to comprehend more. (2) When speed and comprehension are measured on materials as different in content as easy narrative *vs.* geography, the relationship between the two tends to be low positive or negligible. (3) Elden Bond (16) notes that with high school students there is a highly significant relationship between speed of reading material from a specific content area and scholastic achievement in the area. (4) With elementary school children, the correlations between speed and comprehension tend to be negligible. However, as noted by Carlson (33), rapid readers are more efficient in comprehension at the upper levels of intelligence, and slow readers more efficient at lower levels of intelligence. This finding, together with the data cited above, suggests that one is more likely to find a positive relation between speed and comprehension among more mature readers. This would follow from the fact that more intelligent pupils as well as those in higher grades tend to be more mature readers. The lack of versatility of the immature reader in adjusting his speed to the requirements of different reading situations would tend to lower such correlations. (5) Factors which affect the size of the correlation between speed and comprehension include the nature of the reading tasks, techniques of measurement, difficulty of the material, and purpose for which the reading is done. Thus in reading mathematics there is little or no relationship; the relationship is lower for more difficult material; the relationship is lower in analytic reading than in reading for general ideas. (6) The teacher should realize that neither slow nor fast reading by itself produces proper understanding. To increase speed of reading as such does not improve comprehension. With some pupils, it may decrease comprehension. The best rate for a particular child to read a specific set of material is pretty much an individual matter to be determined by individual diagnosis. (7) It would seem that among the more mature readers, the fast readers usually comprehend better, although there are exceptions to this trend. The best indications are that a program to improve speed of reading would be advantageous for most pupils who are well advanced in acquiring the basic reading abilities, provided speed is not pushed to the point where adequate comprehension is impossible. Any general program for whipping up the speed of reading for all pupils in a class is inadvisable. (8) Finally, the true relationship may be that the child who has the necessary skills and abilities to comprehend well also has those necessary to read faster. So drill on speed of reading per se can be expected to do no good.

Role of Eye Movements

Much space in the literature has been devoted to the role of eye movements in reading. Surveys of all this material up to 1946 are given by Tinker (171, 174). Much emphasis has been placed upon the relation of eye-movement patterns to speed of reading. In particular, it has been pointed out that rapid reading is accompanied by few fixations and few regressions per line of print. This has led to the use of many gadgets and techniques to train eye movements in order to promote rapid reading. The training is designed to produce reading with few fixations and no regressions on each line read. This is a misplaced emphasis, for "good" eye-movement patterns are symptoms of reading efficiency, not fundamental contributors to it. Furthermore, exercises in "training" eye movements tend to be pretty mechanical and throw the emphasis upon speed of reading rather than upon rate of comprehension. In fact, when comprehension is improved by the fundamentally sound procedures described in this book, this improvement will be automatically reflected in improved eye-movement sequences and faster reading.

Norms for Speed of Reading

Taking into account what has been said above makes it appear hazardous to specify average rates of comprehension for the different grade levels. In a given grade, the average rate may be 290 words per minute for reading in one situation and only 140 words in another. It should be kept in mind that where average rates are given, they are for reading a specific kind of material for a set purpose. The published averages are usually for relatively easy material in some reading test. They are not to be interpreted as norms for all kinds of material read for different purposes.

GENERAL METHODS FOR DETERMINING DEFICIENCIES IN RATE

There are two aspects to be considered in diagnosing deficiencies in rate of comprehension. The first is concerned with measuring rate of reading for a specific set of material for a set purpose. The second consists of an analysis of the causal factors involved in the retardation. Rate of reading may be measured by either standardized or informal tests.

Standardized Tests

Numerous standardized tests provide measures of speed of reading (see Appendix I). Some, as the *Chapman-Cook Speed of Reading Test* are primarily concerned with speed. Others, as the *Iowa Silent Reading Test* have one section only devoted to measuring speed. In still other tests, such as the *Gates Basic Reading Tests,* a speed of reading score may be obtained by noting the number of exercises attempted within a set time limit. Inasmuch as the scores on these latter tests are number of items answered correctly in a given time, they can really be considered speed tests also.

Standardized tests designed for measuring reading ability in the primary grades ordinarily are not concerned with speed. In fact, it is unwise to stress speed of reading during the first three years in school. The emphasis should be upon developing such things as sight vocabulary, word-recognition techniques, reading by thought units, vocabulary knowledge, and comprehension. Any attempt to measure speed at these levels might lead to misplaced pressure for speeded reading, prior to the acquisition of the basic techniques upon which smooth, rapid reading depends.

Most standardized tests are designed to measure speed of reading of relatively easy materials for a set purpose. The vocabulary concepts and sentence structure are simple. These tests should provide an opportunity for pupils to show their maximum speed of reading *specific easy materials*. When the purpose is varied, as in the four types of *Gates Basic Reading Tests,* the speed scores will reveal to some degree the pupil's versatility in adapting speed to purpose when the material is easy.

Measures of speed of reading on standardized tests have specific limitations. As noted above, the tests use very simple specific materials, and the purpose for which the reading is done is limited. Earlier discussion has indicated that speed on such tests is not closely related to speed in reading other kinds of material. These tests are useful, therefore, only to gain some preliminary information about speed of reading. They are not appropriate for finding out the speed at which material in basic or supplementary texts will be read. Informal tests will be needed for this.

Informal Tests

For the most part, informal tests of reading rate will be found more useful for diagnostic purposes than standardized tests. When the test results are to be employed for guidance in instruction, the teacher will want to know the rate at which a pupil can read material in the basic text or in units on history, or science, or geography, or in some other field. She will also want to know how versatile the pupil is in adapting his speed to changes in difficulty and to the varying purposes for which the reading is done. These objectives can be achieved only through the use of teacher-made informal tests.

Informal rate-of-reading tests are easily constructed. The teacher merely selects from a text or a supplementary reader or a book employed in a unit, a series of consecutive paragraphs of the difficulty and complexity desired. The length of the test will vary with the type of material, the reading level of the child, and the difficulty of the material. Ordinarily, the selection will contain from about 400 to 800 words. The longer selections may be used for the more mature readers and for the less exacting reading tasks.

There should be a set of comprehension questions for the child to answer when the reading is completed. These questions may be modeled after those found in workbooks. The nature and number of the questions should be determined by the purpose for which the reading is done. When reading is for the purpose of getting the main idea, the pupil may be asked to check the correct answer out of five listed. But when reading to answer specific questions, there may be six or eight questions. If the purpose is to note the important details, there may be 10 or 12 questions. Unless comprehension is checked, a child may skip through the material to make a good record and not understand it adequately.

The purpose for which the reading is to be done should be clearly understood by the pupil before starting a selection. If individual testing is done, the child may read directly from a book. The number of words read per minute for two or three minutes of reading is computed.

If an entire class is to be tested at the same time, the selection should be mimeographed. A definite time limit, short enough so that fastest readers cannot quite finish, is set. Each pupil marks where he is when time is called and then counts the words read. Or all the pupils may be allowed to finish the selection. Each student copies down the last number, indicating elapsed time, that the teacher has listed on the blackboard. The teacher changes the figure on the blackboard at the end of each 10 seconds. This method of timing is preferred, since the questions to be answered cover the entire selection.

Interpretations

Grade or centile norms are usually given for standardized tests. By consulting these, the teacher is able to discover whether the pupil is reading unduly slowly for the type of material used and for the purpose set by the test. The four parts of the *Gates Basic Reading Tests* represent reading for four different purposes. The scores serve to identify pupils who are fast and accurate, fast and inaccurate, slow and accurate, slow and inaccurate, etc.

In using the informal rate tests, the teacher can also take into account both rate and degree of comprehension. After testing several children, both good and poor readers, the teacher will have data to show whether a child reads relatively slowly or fast in a specific reading situation. From the scores on comprehension she will also be able to note accuracy of comprehension. Good comprehension is represented by about 85 per cent accuracy; average comprehension by about 70 per cent; and poor comprehension by about 50 per cent or less.

Diagnosis should always consider comprehension along with rate. If the rate is high and comprehension low, or both rate and comprehension are low, exercises to increase rate are *not* indicated (see below). But when rate is average or low and comprehension high, the pupil will undoubtedly profit by a program to increase his speed of reading.

Versatility in Adjusting Rate. As already indicated, the proficient reader will adjust his rate to the difficulty of the material, to the nature of the material and to the purpose of the reading. The pupil who uses only one rate will encounter many difficulties. If the habitual rate is fast, it is not suitable for such situations as reading difficult materials in content areas; if it is a slow plodding rate, it is not suitable for story reading and other easy materials. Similarly when the purpose is to get the main idea, the rate should be faster than when the purpose is to note the important details.

Degree of versatility in adjusting rate may be ascertained as follows: (1) By use of informal tests, as described above, the rates for reading materials at several levels of difficulty and complexity may be determined. (2) Similarly, the rates for reading a single selection for different purposes may be measured. First, have the pupil read it to get the general idea, then reread it to find the answers to certain questions, then reread it again to note the important details. If about the same rate, either fast or slow, is employed for all reading, remedial instruction to develop the ability to adjust speed of reading to fit the situation is indicated.

Analysis of Causal Factors Involved

General methods of diagnosing inefficient rates of reading have been discussed in the above sections. In addition to discovering inappropriate rates, the diagnosis must take account of the possible causes. It has already been emphasized that the best way to promote the proper rate of reading is to equip the child with the abilities and skills necessary for quick recognition and clear understanding of what is to be read. Deficiencies in these abilities and skills should be eliminated prior to any exercises to increase rate. A number of the more important possible causes of unduly slow reading are discussed below. When these handicaps are eliminated, the child is more likely to grasp meanings accurately and as rapidly as is needed for a particular purpose. Or he can be trained to do so with a minimum of instruction.

It will be noted that some of the causes of slow reading listed below are involved in reading disability as discussed in earlier chapters. No disabled reader should receive instruction to speed up his reading until his basic difficulties have been corrected.

Small Sight Vocabulary

The pupil with a limited sight vocabulary is handicapped in developing an appropriate rate of reading. A measure of a child's sight vocabulary may be obtained from such tests as Test I in the *Bond-Clymer-Hoyt Silent Reading Diagnostic Tests* or Type I of the *Gates Advanced Primary Reading Test* and the *Dolch Basic Sight Vocabulary of 220 Service Words*. If the grade score obtained is relatively low, a program, such as described in earlier chapters, to increase the sight vocabulary should be initiated. An adequate sight vocabulary is one essential prerequisite for increasing speed of reading.

Vocabulary Knowledge and Comprehension

As noted above, a clear understanding of words and of materials in sentences and paragraphs is required for rapid reading. The clearer the meanings, the greater the possibility of increasing speed of reading. The extent of a pupil's knowledge of words, and the amount and quality of his comprehension is ascertained by use of standardized and informal tests. Diagnosis of these difficulties and techniques for remedial instruction are given in an earlier chapter.

Word Recognition

The pupil who is deficient in his techniques for identifying and recognizing words cannot increase his speed of reading. Only when words previously encountered are recognized quickly and accurately, and when he knows how to attack unknown words effectively, can speed of reading be improved. Techniques of diagnosing these difficulties and programs of remedial instruction are given in an earlier chapter.

Overanalysis

When, due to overemphasis on phonetic analysis, a pupil has acquired the habit of sounding out a large majority of the words encountered in his reading, his rate of progress is unduly slow. Rapid and oftentimes accurate word recognition are impossible. Observation of the oral reading performance will quickly reveal this unfortunate practice. Remedial instruction involves a de-emphasis of sounding. At the same time, the pupil should be provided with a balanced program of word-recognition techniques such as use of word form, context clues, and perhaps syllabication.

Insufficient Use of Context Clues

The rapid reader ordinarily makes maximum use of context clues for quick word recognition. Conversely, the pupil who makes little or no use of context clues is severely handicapped when he tries to increase his speed of reading. Too little use of context clues in word recognition is readily detected by observing oral reading performance. Also Test 2 in the *Bond-Clymer-Hoyt Silent Reading Diagnostic Tests* gives a measure of the child's ability to use context clues in word recognition. Details of diagnosis and remedial instruction have been discussed in an earlier chapter.

Lack of Phrasing

The child who is unable to read by thought units is the one who does not organize his reading material into logical phrases as he progresses through a sentence. Such a child is characterized as a slow, plodding word-by-word reader. Phrasing is just as important in silent as in oral reading. Until the knack of phrasing is acquired, the child will be severely handicapped in any attempt to increase his speed of reading. Details of diagnosis and remedial instruction are given in an earlier chapter.

Use of Crutches

Some children have developed the habit of moving the finger or a pointer along the line of print to guide their reading. Although justified with some children in early stages of learning or remedial work, the practice should be discarded as soon as feasible. Continued habitual use of such crutches will hinder development of appropriately rapid reading in many situations.

Vocalization

In the early stages of silent reading in the primary grades, many children tend to articulate words rather precisely and fully. At this level, the vocalization does not slow down speed of silent reading for the child can read no faster than he can talk. Later, as reading skill develops, vocalization becomes a handicap to improving speed of silent reading. With some children, the habit of pronouncing each word is so strong that it persists right through the grades if not corrected. The words may be whispered, or the lips and vocal organs may form the words without any sound, or the words may be formed mentally as inner speech with little or no movement of the speech organs. Whatever form the articulation or inner speech takes, time is consumed in forming the words. As long as the habit persists, silent reading can be no faster than the words can be articulated. Until the habit of vocalizing is eliminated at least in part, there can be little improvement in speed of reading. For most rapid reading, the vocalization must be either greatly reduced or eliminated.

Cole (37) has described in detail methods for diagnosing and eliminating the more obvious forms of vocalization. One method of diagnosis is to *time the reader*. Three successive pages of an easy unread story are selected, with an equal mount of material on each of the pages. The pupil reads the first page silently to get into the swing of the story. Time is then taken while the second page is read orally. The third page is read silently and also timed. In another similar set of three pages, and after the first page is read silently, the second page is read silently and timed. Then the third page is read orally and timed. By using this sequence of trials it is possible to eliminate any advantage due to position in the order of the reading. The average time is obtained for the two oral readings and for the two silent readings. If there is no vocalizing, the pupil in the intermediate or higher grades should read three to four times faster silently than orally. The closer the time for silent reading approaches that for oral, the more vocalization is taking place unless other factors are involved.

The teacher may detect vocalization by *direct observation*. The pupil reads a story silently while the teacher observes the amount of movement occurring in the speech mechanism. The pupil may whisper loudly, whisper faintly, move lips with no sound, or neither move lips nor whisper, but have movements of the throat in the region of the vocal cords. The whispering or lip movements are easily noted. Some practice is required to detect vibration in the vocal cords. The teacher places the tips of her fingers against the child's throat about half way between the chin and collar bone. Then she has the pupil read aloud and feels the movement. When the child reads silently without vocalizing, this movement should become so slight that it cannot be felt. If there is no observable whispering or lip movements or throat vibrations, ordinarily there is insufficient vocalization to interfere with development of a satisfactory rate of reading. However, if the pupil is employing inner speech to pronounce the words mentally, the vocalization must be inferred by the timing technique described above.

Decreasing Vocalization. One method of decreasing extreme vocalizing during silent reading is to make it impossible for the speech mechanism to pronounce words. An effective technique is to use some device so that the jaws are held apart and the tongue pressed down. A large eraser, a clean teaspoon, a tongue depresser, or a piece of wood of suitable size may be used to bite upon. Or the child may be allowed to chew vigorously on a large wad of gum during silent reading. A child cannot articulate words and chew gum simultaneously. None of these techniques should be continued longer than necessary. Ordinarily, such devices are not necessary, or they may interfere rather than help. It is better to inform the child that saying words to himself hinders rapid reading, and that such verbalization can be eliminated. He is told that, to read faster, he must not say the words to himself or move his lips or tongue. He must try to read fast.

A good technique for eliminating vocalization is to make available to the child a quantity of reading material which is very easy, extremely interesting, and unimportant. The material should be so easy and simple that there are practically no unfamiliar words, the kind of materials found two grades below the child's placement. If the material is interesting and exciting, there will be motivation for rapid reading. The motivation should be such that the child will want to tear through the story at a fast clip to find out what happens. He is urged to do this. Particularly at first, books with short stories should be used. To be unimportant, the reading must have no relation to regular school work. The so-called *Big Little Books* found in ten-cent stores are very useful for this purpose such as *G-Men on the Trail, Mickey Mouse in the Treasure Hunt,* etc. Such trivial materials are valuable only in the early stages of using fast reading to overcome vocalization. When a satisfactory rate of reading becomes habitual, the child can be guided to better materials.

A rapid reader cannot vocalize since it takes too long to articulate the words. When a child gets a good start in reading these easy stories, he should be encouraged in every way to race through them as rapidly as possible. For a while he may get little meaning, but at this stage, this is unimportant. With the rapid reading, vocalization will become less and less. When vocalization has been reduced to a minimum, better comprehension will return.

Oral Reading. Actually, vocalization during silent reading is oral reading without speaking the words out loud. In many cases it may be advisable to avoid regular oral reading while eliminating the vocalizing. This will help to de-emphasize articulation for the time being.

General Statement

The preliminary steps in organizing instruction for increasing rate of comprehension in reading are to discover and eliminate any of the handicaps listed above that may cause slowness. A pupil may be hindered by one or more of these factors such as lack of word-recognition skills, lack of phrasing, vocalization, or some other condition. When such obstacles are eliminated, the pupil may still read at too slow a rate. Or the teacher may discover none of the handicaps discussed above. The pupil may habitually employ an unnecessarily slow rate in all his reading because it is comfortable and because he has not been motivated to speed up. In either case, the instructional program should be organized to provide incentives for increasing speed of reading to the level appropriate for specific materials and purposes.

It is doubtful whether there should be any formal program for increasing speed of reading in the primary grades. These are the years during which the emphasis is upon developing such fundamentals as sight vocabulary, word-recognition techniques, and phrasing. But as the pupil progresses through the intermediate and higher grades, there should be some increase in rate of reading and in appropriate adjusting of rates to materials and purposes. When this does not occur, due to difficulties discussed above or because of habitual slowness, meandering, or dawdling, remedial instruction is in order. Suggestions for improving speed of reading are outlined in the next section.

PROGRAM FOR IMPROVING RATE

To be effective, a program for increasing speed of reading must be carefully organized and become the major instructional objective for the time being. The program should be confined to those pupils who show prospects of improving. Any attempt to increase the speed of reading of mentally dull children or of those who show they have stubborn cases of the deficiencies listed above, will only lead to confusion and discouragement rather than more efficient reading.

Materials

Relatively easy material should be employed, particularly in the early stages of the program. It should contain *very few* if any unfamiliar words. The difficulty level should be one to two grades below that in which the pupil is located. In general, the material should be selected from books other than the basic texts. For the time being, other kinds of reading should be curtailed or eliminated, such as study-type of reading, and especially oral reading. Only when there has been considerable improvement in speed of reading the easy materials is it safe to *gradually* introduce the more difficult types of reading. It is important to make this transition eventually in order to get the transfer to appropriately rapid reading of regular classroom materials. The transition should be made under teacher observation and guidance, otherwise it may prove to be only partial or nonexistent. It is entirely possible for a child to learn to read easy material rapidly and get little transfer to other instructional materials.

In the early stages of the speeded program, there should be little emphasis upon comprehension checks. Particularly, the comprehension exercises should not be such that they delay rapid perception or interrupt the flow of ideas. It is enough in the early stages of the program merely to ask the pupil what a story is about. When rapid recognition of words and smooth phrasing become habitual, comprehension will improve. It will then be safe to place more emphasis upon comprehension checks. Each exercise can be followed by five or six questions on its content. Rapid reading with adequate comprehension is, of course, the goal sought.

Motivation

In any program for increasing speed of reading, a variety of incentives is necessary if the pupil is to be motivated. Without motivation, a pupil will not feel any urgency to read faster and is not likely to do so. Factors which act as incentives and provide motivation include the following: (1) The reading material used should be highly interesting *to the pupil*. The interested child is a motivated child. Other things being equal, the child will be anxious to get through to the end of an interesting story rapidly to find out what happened. (2) A daily record of results should be kept. The teacher should greet any evidence of improvement with enthusiasm. Gains that are seen and appreciated will motivate the child to even greater effort. (3) Avoid fatigue and boredom. The exercises should be introduced with zest and in such a manner that the child will wish and expect to improve. Any sign that the child is tired or annoyed call for discontinuance of the exercises until he shows a more positive attitude. (4) Cheerful and sympathetic teacher guidance will help maintain motivation. At times, this will mean working alone with a pupil to provide just the help and encouragement he needs. This is particularly important during the periods when no discernible gains can be observed and the child becomes discouraged. (5) Allowing the child to participate with the teacher in organizing his remedial program will aid his motivation. The benefits he will enjoy when he can read faster are discussed with him. His special difficulties are talked over and the plans for improvement are worked out jointly by teacher and pupil. As obstacles arise or old hampering habits crop up, procedures for eliminating them are also worked out together. The more clearly the pupil understands his difficulties and the more he participates in the remedial planning, the better will be his motivation for overcoming the handicaps. (6) The purpose for which each exercise is to be read should be clearly understood. Reading without a purpose—and this means a clearly understood purpose—cannot be well-motivated reading. Sometimes pupils may be reading with more attention to details than is necessary for the purposes of the comprehension specified. A talk about this with the pupil will show him what he is doing wrong and how to correct it. (7) When improved speed has been acquired in special exercises, incentives should be provided to motivate a transfer of the faster reading to leisure reading and to school subjects. All sorts of encouragement should be employed. Examples are praise for the number of stories or books read for enjoyment, discussion of the benefits of fast reading, and emphasis on covering class assignments speedily. The carry-over of the new habits to all types of reading will be promoted by training in flexibility. (8) After the special instruction for increasing rate of reading is completed, the teacher must be alert to guard against relapses to the old slower rates. Motivation to maintain the appropriately fast reading may be provided by special speed tests at periodic intervals, together with class discussions on the importance of adjusting speed to purposes and materials.

Working Against Time

Practically everyone can read faster if he is inclined to, or if he has an incentive to do so. As already noted, most pupils coast along at a comfortable rate in their reading. With the proper setting which encourages a pupil to step up his speed of reading and with well-organized practice day by day, real progress can be achieved.

An effective and much used technique for increasing speed of reading is to work against time. Relatively easy material, a grade or so in difficulty below the pupil's grade placement, for example, is selected for the beginning exercises. These early exercises should be about 350 to 400 words in length. They may be mimeographed in a uniform manner on one page. When the teacher is working with a single pupil, his reading may be done directly from a book or magazine. Five or six comprehension questions are arranged on a separate sheet. These questions should be relatively easy, dealing with the general ideas in the story. Thus, for a story about certain animals seen on a trip through the woods: "What did Mary see in the woods?" "What were they doing?" After the story is finished, it is taken away and the questions answered. Comprehension will probably suffer during the early exercises but will improve as time goes on.

Each such exercise should be introduced under as favorable conditions as possible. The purpose of the reading is made clear to the pupil. The setting should be such that the pupil will be eager to read just as fast as possible with understanding. He should be led to expect to improve over previous exercises. The teacher times the reading and computes the number of words per minute as the pupil's score. The pupil should be shown how to plot his scores on a simple graph so that he will easily see his gains. When little or no gain is achieved for a time, the teacher should be sympathetic and encouraging. If several pupils are tested together, the teacher can mark the time on the blackboard every 10 seconds. As each pupil finishes, he notes on his paper the time shown on the blackboard.

Two exercises per day will provide enough pressure for this kind of work. And these two exercises should be separated by an hour or so. Such *spaced learning* will be more effective than giving several exercises, one after another. After the first few exercises, comprehension should prove to be adequate. But as the program gets well under way, no pupil should be pushed to read faster than he can comprehend.

As the program continues and the pupil has made appreciable gains in his speed for easy material, the teacher must help the pupil to make the transfer to regular school materials and to recreational reading. Gradually more and more of the materials for the exercises are taken from books comparable to those used in class work. The exercises should become longer. At the same time, standards of comprehension required are stepped up, but should always remain appropriate for the purpose for which the reading is done. At the same time the pupil should be urged to do all his reading at a faster pace, whether in school books, or in newspapers, magazines, or story books.

Mechanical Devices

A number of mechanical devices have been built and promoted vigorously for use in increasing speed of reading by pacing the reading through one means or another. The Metronoscope is a complex triple-shuttered device for exposing in succession three equal segments of a line of print followed in the same way by succeeding lines of the same story. The machine may be set for a slow rate of reading and gradually speeded up on successive readings to increase the rate of reading. Its aim is to encourage pupils to employ only three eye fixations for reading each line and to eliminate regressive eye movements. The Harvard Reading Films achieve a similar purpose by a motion picture method. The phrases, grouped in thought units, appear on the screen in bold face type on a faint printing of the whole page of connected material. The rate at which the phrases succeed one another can be varied by adjusting the speed control of the projector.

A variety of mechanical devices are available to pace the reader by moving a shutter, line by line, over the material being read. The reader is expected to keep ahead of the shutter. The rate of moving the shutter may be varied from slow to fast. In one variety of this type of machine, a shadow from a wire moves down the page of print. The reader tries to keep ahead of the shadow. The trade names of some of these machines are Reading Accelerator, Reading Rate Controller, Rate Reader, and Reading Board. The same end may be accomplished by a push-card method described by Blair (14). The teacher pushes a large card from top to bottom of a page while the reader is supposed to keep ahead of the card. The rate of moving the card can be varied to suit the needs of the particular pupil.

The Flashmeter and other short exposure devices known by the general name tachistoscopes are employed to flash number series and words upon a screen for a brief interval. The aim is to develop quick perception and to increase span of recognition. The same end may be accomplished by use of flash cards. Anderson and Dearborn (2) discount the value of tachistoscopic training to increase rate of reading. They conclude that time might better be spent on promoting growth in comprehension. Tachistoscopic training to improve rate of reading is of questionable value.

Value of Machines. In every study that has attempted to evaluate the use of machines, it has been found that they are no more effective in increasing speed of reading than are less complicated but sound classroom procedures. Cason (35), working with third-grade children, found significant gains: (*a*) by use of Metronoscope, (*b*) by well-motivated free reading in the library, and (*c*) by use of special exercises marked up into phrase units. The gains proved to be just as good by one method as any other. Her analysis indicated no benefit from use of the machine. Westover (182) found that college students who used ordinary materials and methods in a well-motivated speed-up program made just as good gains as students using a modified Metronoscope.

One argument usually advanced for use of machines is that pupils are tremendously interested in the use of the device and thus highly motivated. This is true. But even so, such children make no greater gains than those taught by regular methods. There is always a possibility that some child will improve with machine training but not by ordinary methods. However, no investigation has shown this to be so.

In general, it seems that programs for improving speed of reading can be just as satisfactory without use of elaborate machines. This assumes that the materials employed are carefully selected, the program of training properly organized, and the instruction effectively carried out. If the teacher is able to provide the incentives which will motivate the pupil, machines or other gadgets are not necessary to achieve satisfactory gains in speed of reading. In other words, use of certain machines does increase speed of reading but their use is not necessary to get equivalent gains.

There are two other drawbacks to use of mechanical gadgets to increase speed of reading: (1) the machines are expensive; (2) the use of machines too often becomes a ritual and tends toward an overemphasis upon the mechanical aspects of speeded reading to the sacrifice of proper attention on the more important processes of comprehension and the thinking that results from reading.

Developing Flexibility

As noted above, flexibility in adjusting rate of reading to the materials read and to the purpose for which the reading is done is the hallmark of a proficient reader. As the occasion demands, he can tear along at a very rapid rate, or he can employ a moderate rate if that is appropriate, or he can read very slowly in addition to rereading where a highly analytical procedure is in order. Too many students at all grade levels, even in high school and college, tend to read everything at approximately the same rate irrespective of the kind of material or the purpose for reading it. Even if some slight adjustment is made, frequently it is not of an appropriate sort.

To gain flexibility in rate of reading, the child must learn to choose the particular speed appropriate for a particular situation and learn to read at that rate with understanding. This requires teacher guidance because every pupil reads many kinds of materials for many purposes. The development of flexibility in speed of reading tends to be slow and difficult. It becomes a perennial problem at all levels from the third grade on. The teacher should not attempt to develop flexibility at just some one specific grade level. Training to develop flexibility must be a continuing part of the program of reading instruction throughout the school years. For the majority of pupils, flexibility in adjusting rate of reading is acquired slowly. But the pupil who achieves good flexibility possesses a fine asset.

Opportunities for guidance in adjusting speed of reading to the kind of materials are abundant in teaching units in the content areas. Preparation for every unit should include discussion of the right reading procedures to be employed.

Another guidance procedure is to have pupils read the same material several times, each successive time for a different specific purpose such as: (1) to grasp the main idea; (2) to note the important details; (3) to answer specific questions which they are told in advance; (4) to evaluate what is read; etc. Witty (186) presents a useful outline of examples of reading purposes, reading materials, and reading methods. In one column is listed "why you are reading," in another, "what you are reading," and in a third, "how you should read." In most workbooks which accompany basic readers, there are exercises to develop flexibility in rate of reading.

There is always opportunity to guide the development of flexibility when teaching the specific comprehension abilities and study skills described in an earlier chapter. That discussion need not be repeated here. Any instruction designed to develop comprehension in reading will necessarily involve guiding the pupils to discover the most effective rate at which to read a specific set of material.

SUMMARY

A good speed of reading is that rate at which material is comprehended according to the purpose for which it is being read. For the proficient reader especially, speed of reading is fairly specific to the particular reading situation. There is, therefore, need for developing rates appropriate to materials and purposes. In general, the goal is to comprehend at as fast a rate as possible. Some details discussed in relation to achieving this goal are: (*a*) rate of comprehension that avoids dawdling; (*b*) rate to fit material read; (*c*) rate to fit purpose; (*d*) flexibility in adapting rate to materials and purposes; (*e*) relation of rate to comprehension; (*f*) role of eye movements in different rates; and (*g*) norms for speed of reading. General methods for determining deficiencies in rate of reading include use of standardized tests and informal teacher-made tests. Each type of test should be used to supplement the other in diagnosis.

Complete diagnosis of difficulties in speed of reading must include an analysis of the possible causal factors at work such as small sight vocabulary, deficiency in word understanding and comprehension, difficulties in word recognition, overanalysis in word identification, insufficient use of context clues, lack of phrasing, and vocalization. A preliminary step in remedial work is to eliminate each of the difficulties listed above, if it is present. After this is taken care of, a program for improving rate may be carried out if needed.

The program for improving rate of reading must include the following: (*a*) use of appropriate materials; (*b*) proper incentives to develop and maintain motivation; and (*c*) appropriate techniques for increasing rate.

Two general techniques are employed to increase speed of reading. The first is working against time with proper materials and adequate motivation. The second consists of using machines of various kinds. Just as much gain in speed can be obtained by the well-organized, less complicated, and less expensive procedures as by use of machines.

An essential part of any program for speeding up reading is to develop flexibility in adjusting rate to materials and purposes.

In general, there has been too much emphasis upon speed of reading per se. The best way to teach a child to comprehend at an appropriate speed is to furnish him with the skills and concepts to understand properly and quickly what he is to read. When this is done, the child will ordinarily learn to understand rapidly whatever he attempts to read. If he has handicaps such as those discussed in this chapter, and does not improve his speed when these handicaps are removed, a speed-up program is in order. Similarly, dawdlers may profit from putting special emphasis upon speed. Perhaps the main problem in this area is to develop flexibility in adjusting speed to materials and purposes.

SELECTED READINGS

COLE, Luella, *The improvement of reading*. New York: Farrar and Rinehart, Inc., 1938, Chaps. 5, 6, 7.

GATES, Arthur I., *The improvement of reading,* 3rd ed. New York: The Macmillan Company, 1947, Chap. 14.

HARRIS, Albert J., *How to increase reading ability,* 3rd ed. New York: Longmans, Green & Company, 1956, Chap. 18.

PART V

Special Problems

17 IMPROVING INTERESTS AND TASTES

THE ACQUISITION of reading ability is of little value to a person unless he puts it to use in reading various types of material spontaneously and voluntarily. But this can be expected ordinarily only when the child has acquired at school the ability to read similar materials easily and with pleasure. In addition to acquiring mature reading skills, the school child must have become motivated to read lots of different things for his enjoyment, profit, and the enrichment of his personal and social life. Reading can contribute so very much to understanding oneself and others and the great wide world. It is up to the school to provide the child with broad and permanent interests and good tastes. Although growth in these things can only come gradually, much can be accomplished by the end of the elementary school.

READING INTERESTS

How much a child will read of his own accord depends upon his interests. These induce him to respond eagerly to certain features of his environment, as when he is playing, following some hobby, or reading a book. Interests can grow greatly in intensity and breadth, or they may fade and die out altogether. Ordinarily, a person will tire quickly of an interest in which his activity becomes restricted or in which he can do nothing at all.

Nothing is more important in teaching reading than maintaining strong motivation. This is especially true in remedial instruction. There is ample evidence from classroom and clinic to show that children make greater progress in their reading when they are able to read about things that are highly interesting to them. Larrick's (118) claim that under such conditions 50 per cent of the battle is won may well be an understatement.

Interest breeds motivation, the will to do something, including drive needed for learning. This is true in learning to read—the interested child becomes the well-motivated child, the habitual reader. Since the converse is true, we can be sure that without motivation a child with a reading disability, in particular, will learn little or nothing. But with good motivation, such a child will improve his reading under almost any method of remedial instruction.

When this is true, it is no wonder that authorities on reading emphasize a vital relationship between interest patterns and both reading activities and progress in reading. The modern trend is to base reading programs upon children's needs as these are reflected in interest patterns. These patterns can provide strong motivation to achieve in school reading and then to pursue wide and lasting recreational reading. The role of the teacher is twofold. To provide the most effective instruction in reading, it is necessary for her to make the most of the dynamic tendencies furnished by each child's interests. Secondly, the teacher should provide the lead in broadening the interests of her pupils and in stimulating new interests. In other words, the reading interests with which children arrive at school supply the teacher with her opportunity. But she must remember that the reading interests with which they leave school may be very largely her own creation.

To capitalize on the interest patterns of children, it is necessary to know what these patterns are. Summaries of interest studies are presented by Traxler and Townsend (177, 178, 179) in their periodic surveys of research in reading and by W. S. Gray in his summaries of reading investigations published yearly in the *Journal of Educational Research*. Representative studies are cited by Russell (144) and by Witty (185). These studies cover a wide range of areas. Several have been concerned with differences in sex and age with respect to reading interests as they occur in games and sports, making collections, in the use made of leisure time, and so on. Information from such studies is of some value to the teacher. For instance, the findings will indicate what types of books (adventure, mystery, romance, etc.) *tend* to appeal to children of a certain age and sex. Of course the usefulness of such information to the remedial teacher has its limits, since it can merely specify the areas within which the interests of a particular child *may* lie. But they can be suggestive to the teacher, for they name those interests which tend to be shared in common by many children of the same age and sex, information which will prove valuable when she is dealing, for example, with a nine-year-old boy. It would be absurd to expect such data to predict *exactly* what the interests of one particular child might turn out to be. It is well-known that some interests vary greatly from child to child of the same age and sex. In dealing with an individual case, it becomes necessary to identify and evaluate what are often his very specific interest patterns. This is one of the essential steps in diagnosing a reading disability case, for it can enter into organizing the remedial instruction for that child.

METHODS FOR STUDYING A CHILD'S INTERESTS

A number of procedures may be employed for studying the specific interest patterns of a child. Probably no one of these will give the maximum amount of information. Ordinarily the remedial teacher will resort to two or more procedures to secure enough information about a child's interests to guide her in organizing a program of remedial instruction for him.

Questionnaires. Detailed questionnaires are useful for accumulating data revealing the interest patterns of a child. Samples of interest blanks are given by Harris (94), Hildreth (101), and Witty (185). Questionnaires of this kind usually consist of check-lists of play and other forms of leisure activities, as well as different kinds of work. Preferences are indicated by checks. Also included are questions about reading interests and hobbies. These questionnaires may be used in a group testing situation with children who can read from the fourth grade up. With retarded readers in the elementary school, the teacher will ordinarily have to read off the items to each child individually and write in the responses for him.

After noting how these questionnaires are organized, the remedial teacher can readily prepare her own to use with her pupils. Or several teachers may enjoy co-operating in preparing such a questionnaire. A special advantage of the teacher-made questionnaire is that it can be changed at any time to make it more complete and more effective. A homemade questionnaire for studying interests of children can be as good or better than the printed commercial ones. See sample questionnaire in Chapter 11.

Interview. After the remedial teacher has established good rapport with a disabled reader, she should have a quiet, confidential interview with him. This interview may supplement the use of the questionnaire, or in some cases take the place of it. During the interview, every effort is made to make the child feel at ease so he will talk freely about his activities in and out of school, the kind of reading he likes, his favorite radio and TV programs, and so on. The teacher may use a mimeographed outline to advantage to guide her interview and to record the information. Such an outline should not be used if it interferes with rapport between teacher and pupil. Jotting down such items as favorite sports, movies, books, or suggestions for future reading will not ordinarily disturb a child. But sometimes the relaxed personal give and take of a quiet interview may be ruined by following a mimeographed schedule. Although an interview may be time-consuming, so much information is usually gained that it is very valuable.

Observation. A relatively simple and effective way to find out what a child's interests are is to watch his daily activities in school and out. In situations where children are free to express themselves in talk, play, drawing, and other activities, the alert teacher will find many opportunities to jot down an anecdotal note for later reference. Obviously, the child who draws dogs will be interested in reading about dogs. And the girl who loves to play nurse will enjoy reading about nurses. Many leads pointing to possible reading interests are discovered in this way.

Hobby Club. Teachers have found that a hobby club, a regularly scheduled period in which each pupil has the opportunity to relate the things he likes to do best with his leisure time, provides worthwhile information on interests. An enthusiastic report may start several other children following the same hobby. The teacher can usually suggest some special reading to deepen the hold that any hobby has on a child.

Although, in general, the interview will provide more information on interests than any other technique, the teacher will ordinarily wish to gather data from several sources.

Witty (185), page 306, provides a guide for evaluating data on a child's interests and activities. The first part deals with the pupil's attitude toward the interview, his responsiveness and co-operation. The rest is concerned with such evaluative items as whether the child's spending money is ample, average, or meager; whether his reading interests need stimulation, curbing, or direction; and whether he plays enough with other children or wants to do anything but play with them. At the end, suggestions are to be made on how to expand the child's interests, and on reading he needs to enrich and expand his interests. The remedial teacher should be able to construct readily an evaluative guide for use with each of her cases. The main use of such a guide is to co-ordinate the information obtained from various means. The evaluation will ordinarily reveal the areas where the development of interests will increase reading, and where the interests, already activated, should be further enriched and expanded.

DEVELOPING INTEREST IN READING

First of all, in order to develop an interest in reading, the situation in the classroom and at home or in both must be favorable to reading. Reading is promoted at home by such things as (1) encouraging attitudes of parents toward reading, (2) availability of books and magazines of the proper levels of difficulty and relevant to the child's interest patterns, (3) conversation about books, magazine stories, and articles in which the child takes a welcome part, and (4) story telling and story reading in the home. To be effective, activities of this kind in the home must be spontaneous, rather than something staged in an effort to snare the child into reading. Many children want to be like their parents, active in ways that are obviously genuine and worthwhile. Under such favorable conditions, most children will lengthen their leisure-time reading and broaden their reading interests.

The favorable physical setting at school will include a reading corner or classroom library. In this, the essentials will be one or two tables, enough chairs of appropriate size, book shelves and about 50 or more books, together with some children's magazines if possible. Such a reading corner should be attractive, colorful and comfortable. The range of difficulty of the reading materials should be wide enough to fit the abilities of each pupil and be of such a variety in content that each member of the class will find something interesting to read. All this is in addition to whatever special books have been brought into the classroom from the school library for the activity unit currently under way. If the reading corner is to count for much, time must be allotted from the daily class schedule for browsing and other silent reading. Even with a minimum of teacher guidance, proper use of the reading corner tends to stimulate and broaden reading interests of children.

The teacher who has a knack of reading stories aloud with real enthusiasm so that they fascinate the children will have little difficulty in stimulating interest in reading. An entertaining story which the teacher has read to the class will be reread by many pupils when it is placed in the classroom library and when attention is called to it. Similarly, some of the good readers among the pupils may read aloud to the group selections which have been carefully chosen and which they have prepared to read. When this is done the reader is motivated to do his or her best and the listeners become interested in stories they might otherwise have missed.

The scheduled *free* reading period should be one in which the pupils are *absolutely free* to enjoy reading any book or magazine they choose. Any pupil necessarily has to learn for himself how to use the school and community library facilities. If he needs help in choosing a book with the right subject and correct degree of difficulty, the teacher is available to help him.

Other methods employed at times to stimulate interest in reading include (1) displays of book jackets and book advertisements, (2) a book club with its own pupil officers, (3) carefully organized and regularly changed book exhibits in a corridor case, (4) an attractive wall chart on which each pupil can list books he has read, and (5) *very brief* book reports. In general, the enthusiastic teacher who plans systematically for developing interests just as she works for developing other aspects of reading will find she is rewarded.

The development of interest in reading should not be limited to providing the incentives which motivate the child to do a good amount of reading. He may be a boy who is interested primarily in animals, so he confines his reading to stories and articles in this area. The problem in his case is to draw his interests off into other lines, so he will want to read about many things besides his dogs and horses and all the rest. Guidance must step in so that such a child comes to realize that other types of material can also be very interesting. Perhaps the most effective incentives for broadening interests come from feeling the enthusiasm of the teacher and of other pupils for stories and books not dealing with what one thought was the only interesting area, such as animals. Judicious use of all the methods discussed above may be employed to expand reading interests as well as to deepen them. The alert teacher will sense the method or methods to emphasize with a particular pupil.

Reading disability cases, nearly all of whom dislike reading, present special difficulties. The first problem is to identify the pupil's interest patterns as described above. His introduction to voluntary reading should be through a book dealing with a topic prominent among his interests. The book should also be easy to read, short, well written, and have lots of pictures. Additional books are to be supplied as they are needed. The first several books may all be on one subject, perhaps animals if they are what he likes. It is important to keep within the area of his known interests until the habit of voluntary reading is well established, even when that may be exceedingly narrow. He may refuse to read anything but animal stories, or space stories, or gangster stories. But, in time, his interests may be gradually expanded by the techniques described above. The primary problem with retarded readers is to teach them to read at an appropriate level. Enrichment and expansion of interests can come gradually.

Some teachers consider it appropriate to give the child a book in line with his interest but a grade or so above his reading level. It is assumed that his interest will motivate him to read the book with profit. Such tactics are usually unfortunate. The child may persist in wading through the material but with great difficulty. His attempts to dig out the meaning and to identify the multitude of strange words will prevent his reading smoothly and with maximum understanding. As we emphasized in a previous chapter, *there should be no compromise with difficulty even to get material of high interest.*

Many children, who are reading at grade as measured by standardized reading tests, have relatively narrow reading interests. In such a case, after the teacher has first identified the pupil's interests, she may start in the reading she gives him where he now is and lead him forward by her wise and skillful guidance to broaden his old interests and to establish new and perhaps permanent ones.

READING TASTES

As noted in the above section, it is interest that determines largely the area or field in which a pupil tends to concentrate his reading and it is also the factor that decides the amount of reading he will do in it. But the character or quality of what he chooses for reading within that field of interest is what determines the level of his *taste.* For instance, whether he prefers the stories about pirates found in *Treasure Island* or in *Black Silver Pirate Crew,* which he got in a ten-cent store, certainly reveals his taste. The discrimination of what constitutes excellence in any area or field of reading, and a preference for it, spells out the difference between good and poor taste in reading.

To establish a criterion of excellence with regard to taste is not easy.

The quality of writing varies in any field. Whatever the subject matter, to improve one's taste requires a swing upward in preferred materials from a lower to a higher level of excellence. To prefer or choose the good implies discrimination. And discrimination is possible only when a child has had a rather wide range of reading experience. Tastes evolve or grow out of past experience and growth in this respect tends to be slow and irregular. It is entirely possible for a person's taste to be good in one area of reading and poor in another.

As pointed out by Tinker (175), a higher level of taste will be achieved when the pupil's background of experience has become broad enough to permit cultivated discrimination of those reading materials which contribute to the fulfillment of such needs as security, love, achievement, and the drive toward personal and social development. The kind of guidance that feels a child's need and sees to it that the right poem or story is available at the right time is what is most needed for improving his or her taste.

The use of any authoritative criterion of good taste with which to measure the level of a pupil's taste tends to be impossible. What is good taste and where the road to it lies are highly individual matters. Taste has to be evaluated in terms of the increased happiness, increased satisfactions, and the all-around increased welfare of the young person concerned. Evaluating improvement in taste must always be a matter of discovering his present level as compared with previous levels *of the same individual*. It must be in terms of this specific child's growth through experience. What is "good" literature for one child may not be at all worth reading by another.

Level of Reading Tastes

If we accept at face value the comments of many writers, the reading tastes of both children and adults in America are decidedly immature. These tastes are labeled with such terms as *appalling, deplorable,* or perhaps by the milder term *mediocre.* The great variety and numbers of comics and pulp magazines sold and the types of library books that are popular seem to indicate a relatively low level of discrimination in the choice of reading materials by many people. The desirability of guidance to broaden interests and to improve tastes in reading among both children and adults is generally recognized by thoughtful people.

Actually the conditions are probably not as black as often pictured. Furthermore, the chances for improvement with proper guidance are good. A surprising amount of reading gets done by a majority of the population even though there is much competition from other leisure-time activities such as using the car, movies, radio, television, and all sorts of things. The expectation that television would reduce the amount of reading done seems not to have been confirmed. In fact, there are signs that reading is on the increase. William Nichols, editor of *This Week* magazine with a circulation of eleven million, stated in a recent speech (1955) in Minneapolis that he has detected a resurgence of interest in the contents of the printed page—that the habit of reading is making a real comeback. This view is supported by the tremendous weekly and monthly circulation—in the millions—of many magazines. Further testimony to popularity of reading is revealed by the multitude of commercial book clubs, by the tremendous sale of inexpensive reprints of adult and children's books. In addition there are the public libraries and the commercial lending libraries located in stores. Taking into account all the competing activities, it is gratifying that so many people read so much. Furthermore, much that is read in books and magazines is of fair to good quality. For instance, discrimination is exercised in the choice of books for subscription book clubs, and many of the inexpensive reprints are of good quality.

The trend in the reading of children is equally promising. Nancy Larrick's article entitled "But Children Do Read Nowadays" in the November 14, 1954 issue of the *Saturday Review of Literature* in its issue for National Children's Book Week is illuminating. It is concerned with publication, sales, and circulation of children's books. While in 1920 there was one editor of children's books among the publishing companies of the United States, by 1954 there were 60, all working to see that our children get more and better books. Actually, there is ample evidence that American children never had so many good books as they have today, and never read so many. Still, a program of guidance is needed to increase the amount of voluntary reading, to broaden interests, and to improve tastes. Evidence shows that carefully organized programs for improving tastes produce gratifying results.

As pointed out by Tinker (175), it is quite probable that practically all reports on the reading habits of the population give an inadequate picture of the amount and the quality of reading done. The picture is not so dark when, as shown in one elaborate study, 50 per cent read books, and 37 per cent of these books are nonfiction. And the fact that more time is spent reading newspapers and magazines than books does not seem so bad when one remembers that much magazine and newspaper writing is of good quality.

The Comics Problem

Unquestionably the reading of the so-called comics presents problems relevant to reading interests and tastes. Fairly comprehensive analyses of survey data and views on the comics with implications for guidance in reading are given by Adams, Gray, and Reese (1), Russell (144), Smith (153), Tinker (175), and Witty (195). The comics are tremendously popular with elementary school children and are widely read by high school children and even adults. It is generally agreed, however, that what is needed is guidance rather than a denunciation or prohibition of comics. The effect of comics on the personality and adjustment of children is not unambiguous. Even among psychiatrists, juvenile-court judges, and child specialists there is a lack of agreement. Some claim that much juvenile delinquency and crime is caused by the crime and sex comics; others claim that this is doubtful. As Smith (153) points out, the possibly harmful effects of comics seem to depend upon which comics and which child we are thinking of. The child with a well-balanced, wholesome personality will probably be unharmed by any comic material. But excessive reading of the extreme sex and crime comics by severely maladjusted children may undeniably be harmful. It is also possible that the youngsters who are already emotionally disturbed and maladjusted are the very ones who are drawn to the gory crime and sex comics.

Ordinarily, the reading of comics is a problem when it becomes so excessive that it limits or prevents a broadening of interests and a wholesome development of tastes. Many children who read comics also read large numbers of books of different kinds and of good quality. Such children are not handicapped by reading many comic magazines each week. But children who do practically no voluntary leisure reading except of comics neglect reading the materials needed to enrich and extend their interests and the materials suitable for cultivating tastes.

There are several things the teacher can do about comic books. The first step in such guidance is to establish some degree of discrimination toward them so as to build up a preference for the better or more acceptable comics. A second step consists of relating the subject matter of comics to subject matter in books of recognized worth.

Guidance can lead to appraisal and discrimination in evaluation of comics by children in the intermediate grades. In Denecke's (51) study, the children examined comics for such items as interesting points, monotony, varieties of humor, degree of wholesomeness, accuracy, and relation to reality. The fifth-graders, through discrimination and evaluation, distinguished three relatively unique types of comics: those providing wholesome information; those providing humorous or amusing material; and those emphasizing crime, hatred, and revenge. Such discriminating analysis will provide a good basis for establishing children's preference for the more desirable comics.

Prominent among the elements that are attractive in comics are action, surprise, adventure, excitement, pictures, and sometimes humor. A second step in guidance should be concerned with furnishing the children with a variety of good literary sources which are rich in the same elements that attract them to the comics. There are short stories and books which have stood the test of time that contain characters, settings, and plots just as attractive, and depict episodes just as exciting as those in the comics. The almost universal interest in comics among children affords a unique opportunity to provide guidance for the development of tastes. The teacher who knows both comics and good literature can frequently stimulate a child to seek additional related stories in better books by calling attention to the intriguing plots and episodes in the latter. Moving from comics to other sources which yield satisfying reading experiences can be a first important move toward better tastes.

Development of Tastes

Tinker (175) has outlined conditions favoring growth in tastes and has suggested a sequential program for this growth. Incidental growth in reading tastes is seldom consistent or appreciable. Opportunities and guidance must be organized if they are to achieve satisfactory improvement. In the early primary grades, the teacher provides the stimulation that leads to enjoyment of good children's literature by reading aloud to the pupils carefully selected materials. With increase in reading proficiency, children more and more do leisure reading of materials they choose for themselves. The variety of materials in the basic text can initiate growth toward good tastes. But the availability of proper supplementary materials plus guidance are necessary for the continuation of this growth.

A child must be a proficient reader to achieve growth in reading tastes. Any given kind of material must be read with facility and a high degree of understanding to instill the enthusiasm and enjoyment so necessary for growth in taste. Since there are many more books of good quality available as difficulty of reading material increases, the more proficient the reader, the greater is his opportunity to read better books and so improve his taste. As in all reading programs, there must be adjustment to individual differences in any program for developing tastes.

The wider the reading and the broader the reading interests, the more favorable the conditions for improvement of tastes. Actually, the development of broad reading interests and the improvement of tastes occur hand in hand. In fact, some writers make no clear distinction between reading interests and tastes. Certainly, they are reciprocal in action. Progress in developing interests and tastes would be extremely difficult or outright impossible without wide reading experience.

Reading interests and tastes are more likely to develop when there are favorable environmental conditions. Two factors of prime importance may be mentioned: (1) *Appropriate* reading materials must be available. It is only common sense that children tend to read what is most readily obtained whether in school, at home or elsewhere. (2) The child must have sufficient time to read. There should be regular periods in school for leisure reading. Although there are many competing activities outside the school and at home, parents should encourage leisure reading and try to organize home life so there is plenty of time for it.

The role of the teacher is of prime importance in promoting growth in tastes. She should know her pupils, be well-read, and be enthusiastic in bringing children and books together. Smith (153) has stated this role well when she says that the understanding teacher senses the appropriate times for introducing books so that she will get the right book to the right child at the right time. Some of this reading material will meet the personal needs of children by providing imaginative experiences and enrichment of what is already familiar to them. At all grade levels, the enthusiastic teacher can encourage improved tastes and stimulate broadening of interests by telling and reading stories, and by reading poems aloud to her pupils. The teacher who has a wide knowledge of reading materials and shares this with her pupils through discussions, oral readings, and urging the reading of available books stands a good chance of developing interests and tastes in her pupils. The task is arduous, but the results will be highly rewarding and stimulating to the teacher.

The school has an important role in developing tastes. It is the school's obligation to provide books and library facilities so that appropriate materials are available to the pupils. Emphasis has already been placed upon the need for the schoolroom reading corner or library. The management of this should be co-ordinated with the school library if the school has a library. Loans of books from the city or county library at periodic intervals can also supplement the books in the school. An important aspect of guidance with regard to books is teaching children the use of both the school and public library. Co-operation between the librarian and the classroom teacher will facilitate getting appropriate books to children when they are needed. To assure a rich program of contacts with books, timing is important, particularly when a child is reading materials related to some of his own experiences. For instance, the proper time for a story about migration of birds could well be the time when the first robins arrive in the spring.

A variety of approaches may be employed to enhance appreciation and to stimulate interest in reading. Among these are puppet shows, recordings, selected radio and television programs, the use of slides and motion pictures. Another kind of approach which generates interest and promotes reading of desirable books consists of displays of book jackets and pictorial maps. All these techniques have been used to advantage to provide important stimulation in improving taste and broadening interests. The alert teacher will think of other things she can do.

Sequential Program in Taste

Building tastes is a continuous and long enduring process, one in which not much progress is to be expected in a day, a week, or a month. Continuous exposure to a variety of good materials is mandatory. This permits progress to occur, step by step, in a steady sequential order, gradual and sliding, one step into the other. Not until a child is ready for it will he read with pleasure such materials as *Tom Sawyer* or the poetry of A. A. Milne or children's books in science. Growth in discriminating taste accompanies the formation of good reading habits and interests.

A first step in any program to develop better tastes in reading involves appraisal of a child's present level of taste and pattern of interests. This is achieved, we have implied, through use of interviews, inventories, and any relevant materials in the pupil's cumulative record folder. To succeed, any program that seeks to expand interests and improve taste must start where a child now is. Present interests and tastes should be used as spring-boards for his future interests and tastes. If a child wants to read comic books, all right. Be thankful that he wants to read something. One must in a sense respect a child's taste at whatever level it is on. Try to discover what it is he likes about what he reads, such as plot, kind of adventure, and kind of characters. With this information, guide the youngster in selecting materials on a higher level along the same general lines as what he likes in the comic books or whatever he reads. In this way the guidance program, which is necessarily highly individualized, will lead the child by gradual steps to a sampling of a much wider variety of materials in order to awaken more fruitful interests and at the same time bring him into contact with materials of better quality. With this sort of program, the child gradually comes to feel the difference between the better and the poorer qualities of reading materials.

When a teacher undertakes a guidance program to broaden interests and cultivate tastes, she has to keep in mind what is desirable and what may be accomplished later when the child has been guided to the stage where he voluntarily reads extensively a wide variety of materials with under-standing. There will be gradual progress from relatively narrow interests to broader ones, and from a relatively low level of tastes to materials of better quality. With well-organized guidance, all children will make prog-ress. Naturally, some will advance farther than others. *The main objective is to get children to read widely with enjoyment.* What may be considered good taste will vary from child to child. It is neither possible nor desirable to set up one level of taste to be achieved by all children.

The Remedial Program

The remedial program for broadening interests and cultivating tastes in reading is essentially the sequential program organized for intensive work with a particular class, group, or individual. Interests and tastes of each child are evaluated according to techniques described above. This is fol-lowed by individualized guidance which will stimulate each child to read a wide variety of materials, moving gradually to a better and better quality. The sequential program is an integral part of the developmental reading program and continues throughout the grades. The remedial program is also an integral part of the reading program but it is more intensive and is more highly individualized. For instance, preliminary appraisal may indicate that certain members (few or many) of a fifth-grade class have relatively narrow reading interests and relatively poor reading tastes. The teacher may then organize for these pupils an intensive remedial program. Such a program may continue for a term or a year, or until the children reach a level appropriate for fifth-graders, i.e., they will be able to profit by the regular instruction in reading which includes or should include guidance for broadening interests and cultivating tastes. There is, fortunately, a wealth of well-written books which capture children's interests.

SUMMARY

Maturity in discrimination in his reading by a particular pupil has been achieved when through instruction he has acquired broad and permanent interests and an appropriate level of taste. Although growth in reading interests and tastes is gradual, proper guidance throughout the grades can accomplish much. In addition to providing strong motivation for learning to read, interests determine what is read and how much is read voluntarily. To a large degree, taste in reading depends upon interest patterns. Reading instruction should therefore make use of the dynamic tendencies provided by a child's interests. Guidance can broaden these interests and stimulate new ones. In order to do something for a child's interests, it is first necessary to find out what they are at present. Information is available on which interests tend to be shared in common by many children of the same age and sex. To identify and evaluate a child's specific interest patterns, use may be made of questionnaires, interviews, and observation of his behavior.

At home, interest in reading is fostered by favorable attitudes of parents, availability of books, conversation about books and reading, and story telling and story reading. At school, interest in books and reading is promoted by an attractive reading corner adequately supplied with books, by oral reading and story telling by the teacher, by free reading periods, by displays of book jackets and advertisements, and by pupil book clubs. Most important of all, perhaps, is the guidance provided by the enthusiastic and well-read teacher.

There is no such thing as a criterion of good taste which is applicable to all children. Improvement in taste is relative to the level at which a particular pupil finds himself. Although improvement is slow, well-organized guidance can lead to better discrimination and improved choice of reading materials for all children. The gains will be large for some pupils, small for others.

Factors which condition the development of tastes include reading ability, interest patterns, amount and variety of voluntary reading, availability of materials, time for leisure reading, and skill of the teacher. A program of guidance is essential. It has been demonstrated that well-organized and well-executed programs bring about remarkable improvement in reading tastes.

The reading of comics presents special problems in reading interests and tastes. Children who do practically no voluntary leisure reading except comics neglect reading the materials needed to enrich and extend their interests and cultivate taste. The teacher can provide guidance to instill some degree of discrimination toward comics so as to bring about a preference for the more acceptable ones. She can also guide pupils to similar subject matter in books of recognized worth.

There should be a sequential program for broadening interests and cultivating tastes. Such a program should be an integral part of the developmental program throughout the grades. Broadening interests and cultivating tastes is a gradual process. Continuous exposure to a variety of good materials is mandatory. The program for each child must start where he is. His present interests and tastes should serve as springboards for future improvement. The main objective is to get the child to read widely with enjoyment.

A remedial program to broaden interests and cultivate tastes is essentially the same as the sequential program. The main difference is that the remedial program is more intensive and more highly individualized.

SELECTED READINGS

ADAMS, Fay, GRAY, Lillian, and REESE, Dora, *Teaching children to read.* New York: The Ronald Press Company, 1949, Chap. 15.

BOND, Guy L., and WAGNER, Eva B., *Teaching the child to read,* rev. ed. New York: The Macmillan Company, 1950, Chap. 16.

GANS, Roma, *Reading is fun: Developing children's reading interests.* New York: Bureau of Publications, Teachers College, Columbia University, 1949.

HARRIS, Albert J., *How to increase reading ability,* 3rd ed. New York: Longmans, Green & Company, 1956, Chap. 17.

LAZAR, May, *Guiding the growth of reading interests.* Educational Research Bulletin No. 8. New York: Board of Education of the City of New York, 1945.

MCKEE, Paul, *The teaching of reading in the elementary school.* Boston: Houghton Mifflin Company, 1948, Chap. 17.

RUSSELL, David H., *Children learn to read.* Boston: Ginn and Company, 1949, Chaps. 12, 13.

SMITH, Dora V., Literature and personal reading. *Reading in the elementary school.* The forty-eighth yearbook of the National Society for the Study of Education, Part II. Chicago: University of Chicago Press, 1949, Chap. 10.

WITTY, Paul, *Reading in modern education.* Boston: D. C. Heath & Company, 1949, Chap. 2.

18

ADJUSTING TO THE SPECIALLY HANDICAPPED CHILD

PREVIOUS CHAPTERS have examined the remedial procedures appropriately used with the reading problems prevalent among the disability cases. In this chapter, brief attention will be given to methods for dealing with the complications introduced by various special handicaps. Although occurring relatively infrequently, these anomalies are important when present. Finally, in this chapter we shall talk about how to help the extremely disabled reader. The several types of disability reviewed here include emotionally disturbed children, slow learners, cases with extreme reading handicaps, children with poor eyesight, or poor hearing, speech impediments, and language handicaps.

Individualized Treatment. Throughout this book, emphasis has been placed upon individualized instruction. When dealing with such specially handicapped children as we shall describe in this chapter, there is need for even more individualized treatment. In order to obtain the best results, there must be a more careful and thorough probing of each individual's needs, and a more continuous and usually prolonged application of individualized remedial instruction. The fundamental principles of remedial instruction needed for the specially handicapped are not basically different from those discussed earlier. However, much depends upon skillful guidance. The fullest measure of success is achieved when an alert teacher senses every aspect of a pupil's difficulty and has at her command just the right procedures, demonstrations, materials, and instructional techniques to overcome or at least alleviate the discovered difficulty. She must know just what materials and procedures to select for a particular difficulty, and when to shift from one procedure to another in order to keep the pupil moving in the right direction. In other words, the teacher must be flexible in organizing her remedial programs, in beginning at the right point, and in introducing new materials and techniques to promote continuous progress toward learning to read better.

Especially relevant is the personality of the teacher, who must be a person who will patiently work to gain and keep good rapport with the child. For success, the child must like his teacher and firmly expect that she is going to help him. Only when there are close personal relations between pupil and teacher will it be possible for the teacher to provide the incentives which will maintain the level of motivation absolutely necessary to achieve lasting improvement in reading. Besides being well trained, the teacher must like children and be enthusiastic about her work. It is not too much to say that, in general, success in teaching these handicapped children depends largely upon the teacher.

It is probable that any single, narrow, or limited approach will be found inadequate for helping handicapped children out of their difficulties. Although one approach may be appropriate for initial remedial work with a case, it is likely that something new has to be tried every so often, as occasion demands. Certainly there is no one "sure-fire" method that will work best for all these pupils.

EMOTIONALLY DISTURBED CHILDREN

The role of emotional disturbances in reading disability was discussed in detail in Chapter 6. There, it was noted that most reading cases manifest more or less emotional maladjustment. Some children are maladjusted when they first arrive at school. Others develop emotional disturbances when frustrated in their futile attempts to learn to read. Whatever the roots of the trouble, it is certain that the remedial teacher has emotional maladjustment to deal with in most of her disability cases.

In many instances, the emotional maladjustment clears up when the child has gained appreciable success through remedial reading instruction. With the few who have deep-seated adjustment difficulties, more definite therapy is necessary. Authorities such as Bennett (7), Gates (77), and Witty and Kopel (190) note that many reading disability cases are characterized by a lack of persistence, tendencies to withdraw from the group, daydreaming, fears, and anxieties. Therapy aimed at the re-establishment of self-confidence and removal of these anxieties is what is needed. As suggested in reports by Axline (5), Bills (12), and Fisher (71), in addition to remedial instruction for correcting reading difficulties, the therapeutic role of the remedial teacher is also important in correcting reading disability. In fact, it is surely desirable that in every instance of remedial instruction, a psychotherapeutic relationship between teacher and pupil should be developed.

Fisher (72) tested the hypothesis that psychotherapeutic procedures will help to remove reading disabilities where emotional adjustment is involved. Twelve boys in an institution for delinquent boys were divided into two matched groups of six each. All were retarded more than three years in reading. They all had the same classroom teacher and all received remedial instruction for three hours per week given by the same remedial teacher. One group of six participated in nondirective or group-centered therapy for one hour per week. The other group received only the remedial instruction. The members in the therapy group and at the therapy meetings were encouraged to speak freely about their feelings, attitudes, and experiences. The program was continued for six months. Final testing revealed that the non-therapy group gained on the average 8.25 months in reading; those who had therapy gained 11.5 months, or 39.4 per cent more than the non-therapy group. It was concluded that the psychotherapeutic relationship established by the training was an important factor in the correction of reading disabilities in these delinquent boys.

Although the numbers in Fisher's groups were small and they were delinquent cases, the results appear to emphasize an important aspect of remedial instruction, particularly for cases with marked emotional maladjustments. In working with emotionally disturbed reading disability cases, psychotherapy is important. For that matter it is probable that all skillful remedial teachers bring some psychotherapy, however slight, into their relation with disability cases. With the more severely maladjusted cases, an organized program of psychotherapy in addition to reading instruction will very likely promote more rapid and lasting gains in reading. Furthermore, there will tend to be more improvement in emotional adjustment than arises from reading instruction alone. Psychotherapy is sometimes needed prior to any systematic reading instruction. For some of the severely maladjusted children, psychiatric help will be needed.

SLOW LEARNERS

Mentally retarded children with I.Q.'s from 50 to 89 are classified as slow learners. Children with I.Q.'s below 50 can learn only a few words. Reading instruction for them is futile. Those with I.Q.'s between 50 and 89 can, with proper instruction, make progress in reading up to the grade level corresponding to their mental age. The consensus of educators is that mentally retarded children should be started on a systematic reading program only when they reach a mental age of at least 6 years. As noted by Kirk (114), slow learners differ from normal children in learning to read because they cannot be expected to begin learning to read at chronological age 6, and even thereafter they naturally learn at a slower rate. They become discouraged in regular classrooms because of continued failure. This and their usually somewhat impoverished environmental and experiental background are reflected in poor language usage.

The slow learners will need a prolonged prereading and reading readiness period. On entering school, they will be more retarded than the normal child in the abilities and skills which form the basis for success in beginning reading. In fact, according to Gates (79), the readiness program for slow learners should be broader and richer than normal so as to reduce to a minimum the new learnings required when the pupil actually begins to read. The general aspects of reading readiness have been discussed in earlier chapters. Details of such programs may be found in Bond and Wagner (28), Tinker (175), Monroe (133), and Hildreth (102). During the prereading training and when the child's mental age is between 5 and 6, he will be able to learn to recognize his name and a few words used as labels and signs. Prior to reaching at least 6 years mental age, systematic reading instruction such as is ordinarily given will only result in a tremendous waste of time and energy on the part of the teacher, because so little is learned from it. Nevertheless, if special instructional methods (described later) are employed, these children can be given reading instruction with profit prior to 6 years mental age. Otherwise some of these children would not begin to read until 8 or 9 years old.

The mentally retarded child differs mainly from the normal in his reading progress by being a slower learner. He is ready to begin formal lessons at a somewhat later chronological age and he progresses at a slower rate. This means that at each succeeding level in the developmental program, he should have more materials and more individualized guidance than the normal child. Gates (75) has shown that the slow learner needs many more repetitions of a word in the context of basal reading materials before he can learn it. This is in addition to his encounters with such words in appropriate supplementary reading. The reading materials used are the same as those which have proved satisfactory with regular normal pupils. But there is more of the material, and the instruction is more highly individualized and more intensive. Repetition, explanation, demonstrations, provision of experience units, and amount of recreational reading should be extensive. In short, the program for the slow learner is broad, detailed, simplified, and *slow-moving*. In other respects, the program of reading instruction is the same as that employed for normal children. Programs devoted largely to drill exercises with little recreational reading tend to be less effective than the richer program just described. The interest and attention of slow learners is held and their motivation made greater by exposure to large amounts of interesting and exciting material pitched at an appropriate level of difficulty. Gates (75) and Huber (105) have shown that slow learners enjoy approximately the same kind of reading material as average and superior children of their age.

Reading Disability

When classroom reading instruction and materials are not adjusted to the slow learner, he may become a reading disability case. Such other causal factors described in Chapters 5 and 6 may also be involved. If a mentally retarded child fails to learn to read at the level indicated by his capacities he should be considered to be a disability case. The diagnosis of the extent and nature of his disability rests on the use of the techniques described for normal children in earlier chapters. According to evidence cited by Kirk (114), between 5 and 10 per cent of mentally retarded children are educable reading disability cases. By a curious coincidence, this is about the frequency of disability cases among mentally normal children.

Remedial Instruction

Results cited by Kirk (114) demonstrate beyond doubt that slow learners who become reading disability cases profit significantly from remedial instruction. For instance, in a group of 10 institutional children, with mean C.A. of 12-9 and mean I.Q. of 75, an average gain of 1.2 grades was achieved by 68 standard lessons, each 30 minutes long, over a period of about five months. This rate of progress was five times that of 100 unselected children in the same institutional school. Furthermore, five months after the remedial training ceased, these cases contined to progress in the regular classroom situation at a rate twice that of the 100 institutional children who had not had the remedial instruction. Most of the 10 remedial cases also showed better general adjustment and improved attitudes and behavior as they became more proficient in reading. Other data cited revealed similar gains. It was concluded that significant and satisfying results can be obtained from remedial instruction with mentally retarded children who are retarded in reading.

The Hegge-Kirk remedial method was devised primarily for use with mentally retarded and dull-normal children. The details of this method are given in *Remedial Reading Drills,* by Hegge, Kirk, and Kirk (97). The method in its initial stages is primarily a phonic method. It is more complete than conventional phonic systems. There is much drill and an emphasis on certain principles of learning, such as the concrete associative aids used to help the child learn a new sound. And retention is aided by having the child say the sound, write it, and then blend the sounds into words. Sentence reading, story reading, and teaching words as wholes are introduced at the appropriate places as the child progresses. *This method is successful.* Any teacher who plans to use the method should consult Kirk (114) and the pamphlet by Hegge, Kirk, and Kirk (97) for more complete details.

Gates (79) does not approve of the detailed drill and the heavy emphasis upon the phonetic approach outlined by Kirk. On the basis of his experiments with slow learners in the New York schools, Gates suggests a broader program of instruction. Although more inclusive and more highly individualized, the plan he adopted approximates the regular basic program used for normal pupils. Significant features are its informality, its wide range of approaches, and its freedom for activity according to individual interests. Gates gives the evidence that this method is successful. Gates and Bond (82) show that classes of 25 children taught by this approach gained 1.2 years in reading during a five-month training period. For details of the method, see Gates (79), pp. 503-509.

The following suggestions, adapted from Brueckner and Bond (31), pp. 188-190, give proven procedures for teaching slow-learning children to read:

1. Instruction in reading should begin later than for normal children. Due to limited intelligence, slow-learning children have not acquired the experience necessary for initial instruction in reading by the age of 6 years or 6 years and 6 months. Although it is not wise to wait for a mental age of 6 years and 6 months, initial instruction should be deferred as long as is required to make some progress in the prerequisite learnings.

2. Slow-learning children develop reading ability in much the same way as normal children but at a somewhat slower pace. This is true for their capability in word recognition, vocabulary readiness, and the setting of purposes. Any modifications in instruction necessary are more in the nature of a changed emphasis rather than a drastically different program.

3. A large amount of carefully controlled material must be used with slow learners. To make new words a permanent part of the child's sight vocabulary, he must be introduced to them more slowly than are brighter children. That is, vocabulary development is more gradual.

4. Slow-learners require more review of the basic words. This is achieved by use and re-use of workbook material, and by rereading a selection several times, and by reading much additional material involving the same vocabulary.

5. The slow-learning child has to be given more detailed and simplified explanations and he must also encounter simpler techniques. Frequently he finds directions in workbooks or in teacher-made exercises difficult to grasp. The teacher must be sure that each child understands what is expected of him in all his reading assignments.

6. More concrete illustrations of the things about which he is reading are needed. In contrast with the average child, the slow learner is handicapped in generalizing and in thinking abstractly about what he is reading. He should be given every opportunity, therefore, to come into direct contact with the things about which he is studying.

7. Reading goals should be relatively short-range, i.e., reached rather quickly. The slow learner cannot work effectively upon projects of long duration.

8. The slow learner requires more rereading before he can grasp the different purposes of what he reads. For example, if he is to read about a buffalo hunt, the first reading may be only to find out that the Indian boy shot a buffalo, the second reading to discover how the tribe prepared for the hunt, the third time to find out how the hunt was actually conducted, etc. Although the brighter child may achieve most of the purposes listed by just one reading, the slow learner cannot do this. Furthermore, the latter does not mind rereading because each new time helps him get a fuller understanding of the story.

9. There should be more experience and more guidance in exploring

the visual and auditory characteristics of words. For word-recognition skills to operate effectively, they must be applicable to a wide variety of words. These skills are difficult for slow learners to acquire. They profit from additional drill in analyzing words and in learning the sounds of the different word elements. Since rapid reading is not important for slow learners, a moderate degree of what might seem to be overanalysis is of little consequence provided it does not interfere with comprehension.

10. It is advisable to use more oral reading and oral prestudy in instructing slow-learning children. Many of them need to vocalize what they are reading before they can comprehend it well. The fact that vocalization slows the reading rate is of little significance with these children.

11. Slow-learning children should do more things, such as building models, cutting out pictures, etc., in connection with their reading than the brighter children.

12. Finally, the more able of the slow-learning children will profit by being in the same classroom with average and superior children provided the instruction is adjusted somewhat to their special needs. Although the slow learner will not be able to read much above his mental level, in many other respects his learning experiences may be similar to those of other children.

In the regular classroom situation, slow-learning children will ordinarily have I.Q.'s between 70 and 95. Those with lower I.Q.'s should be put in special classes. Brueckner and Bond (31), p. 187, give us data on the reading grade that may be expected of slow-learning children at age 16, under both average and superior instruction:

Stanford Binet I.Q.	Expected Reading Grade Under Average Instruction	Estimated Reading Grade Under Superior Instruction
95	8.6	9.5
90	7.7	8.3
85	7.0	7.5
80	6.2	6.7
75	5.4	5.8
70	4.8	5.2

These data for estimated reading grade at age 16 under superior instruction represents what may be expected when the instruction is adjusted to the needs of the slow-learning child. The above results, derived from a follow-up study, indicate that those children who were given special instruction could not maintain reading ability very far in advance of their mental grade. However, in *individual* follow-ups of the slow learners, it was found that some were able to acquire reading ability somewhat in excess of their mental level.

The remedial teacher who works with slow learners should be familiar with the Kirk, the Brueckner and Bond, and the Gates approaches. The teacher is likely to find that the Kirk method works best for institutional cases, and that the Gates or Brueckner and Bond procedure is more appropriate for dull-normals in the regular schoolroom situation. The Monroe (131) procedure which is largely phonetic with its emphasis upon drill, was also found by Monroe and Backus (134) to work well for remedial work with dull-normal school children. The well-trained remedial teacher will be versatile in selecting and applying the most appropriate of these techniques in adjusting instruction to the needs of each case.

EXTREME DISABILITY

Reading disability varies in degree. Some of these children have learned practically nothing, others read poorly and at a level significantly below what is expected of their mental age. Cases falling between these extremes may be graded in very small steps. Extreme disability cases, sometimes called nonreaders, are at the low end of the distribution. But they are not a distinct group. They are merely the most stubborn cases of disability who have failed to learn after fairly extended instruction. Furthermore, even these are not all alike, varying from one to another in background, attitudes, special difficulties, and other respects. Attention to these individual differences is necessary in organizing remedial instruction. No single formula of remediation can possibly work for all such cases.

Teaching skill is very important in helping these extreme cases. Besides having a good understanding of the reading process, the teacher should be familiar with a variety of diagnostic and remedial procedures. And she must be versatile in adapting these procedures both in accurate diagnosis of difficulties and in planning appropriate instruction for each particular case. Patience, sympathetic understanding of the pupil's difficulties, and skillful guidance throughout the instructional program are the key to aiding these extreme cases.

Certain methods of remedial instruction have been notably successful in teaching extreme cases to read. Three of these are briefly outlined in the following sections.

The Fernald Tracing Method

This method, sometimes termed the Fernald-Keller kinesthetic method, described in detail by Fernald (70), was originally designed for and used successfully with extremely disabled readers. The essential features of the technique are to teach the child to write words correctly, to motivate him to do this, to have him read the printed copy of what he has written, and to move on eventually to extensive reading of materials other than his own. The program consists of four stages.

Stage 1. The Child Learns by Tracing Words. In this initial stage, the child chooses some word he wishes to learn. The word is written for the child with crayola on paper in plain blackboard-sized script, or in print if manuscript writing is used. The child then traces the word with his finger touching the paper, pronouncing each part of the word as he traces it. This is repeated as many times as necessary until the child *can write the word without looking at the copy.* After writing the word once on scrap paper, he uses it in the story he is writing. When the story written by the child is finished, it is typed for him and he reads it in print. After a story is finished, the child files his newly learned words under the proper letters in his word file. To do this he must identify the letter in the file that is the same as the first letter of the word. In this way, the child learns the letters of the alphabet without any rote memorizing and without too much emphasis upon the individual letters in words. Points stressed in this first stage are that the finger contact is important in tracing, the child should always write the word without looking at the copy, the word should always be written as a unit (i.e., in case of error, the paper is taken away and after more tracing if that is needed, the child starts over again on a new piece), and the words should always be used in context. This last means that the child understands the words since they are employed in meaningful groups in sentences.

Stage 2 is the same as stage 1 except that tracing is no longer necessary. When this stage is reached, the child is able to learn any new word by merely looking at the word in *script,* saying it to himself as he looks at it, and then writing it without looking at the copy. He says each part of the word as he writes it. After each word is learned, it is filed as in stage 1. The child continues to write stories, longer and more complicated than before, and to read the typed copy of what he has written. Each word *must* be pronounced as it is written. The word should be said in the normal way, that is, it should be pronounced as it actually sounds rather than through sounding out the separate letters in such a way that the word as a whole is lost in the process. For instance, one-syllable words like *book* are spoken slowly, running the sounds together so that the natural sound of the complete word is maintained. In polysyllable words like *satisfy,* the child says *sat* as he writes the first syllable, *is* while he writes the second syllable, and *fy* as he writes the last syllable. That is, he pronounces each syllable as he writes it, running the syllables together to keep the whole word intact. After a little practice the child will achieve the knack of co-ordinating the slow pronouncing with the tracing (stage 1) and the writing.

Duration of Tracing Period. The length of the tracing period varies greatly from child to child. Tracing is omitted when the child is able to learn without it. In every case, the tracing drops out gradually. First, there is a decrease in number of tracings to learn a word, then some words are learned without tracing, and eventually tracing disappears altogether. On the average, the tracing period continues for about two months.

Material Used. Fernald worked only with children with average or superior intelligence. There was no attempt to simplify material so that it would fall below the intelligence level of the child. This applies both to vocabulary and subject matter. Any word and any sentence the child is capable of understanding and using properly in oral language can be learned so that it can be written and read. Actually, the longer words seem to be retained better for later recognition than shorter ones. The fact that complex materials can be used suggests that the Fernald method is especially useful for children with extreme reading disability who are chronologically older. For example, it is difficult to motivate a normal child of 12 to read ordinary primer material. But he will learn fairly rapidly to write and read material suited to his intelligence and interest level.

Stage 3. This stage dispenses with the use of script copy. The child now learns directly from the *printed* word without having it written in script for him. He merely looks at a printed word and says it to himself before he writes it. When this stage is reached, the child starts reading from books. He is permitted to read anything he wishes and as much as he likes. The teacher tells him words he does not know. After the reading, these new words are gone over and written by the child as explained above. This method might be even more successful if these early book-reading experiences were in material carefully selected in difficulty.

In *Stage 4* the child is able to recognize new words from their resemblance to words or parts of words he has already learned. Clues derived from meanings inferred from the context aid him in perceiving these. As in the previous stage, new words that cannot be worked out by the child are told him. He repeats the word as he looks at it and then writes it without looking at the printed word while he says it again to himself. Retention of words learned in this way is 80 to 95 per cent. By the fourth stage, the child is reading a wide variety of materials with considerable facility. Training is continued until the child is able to do the reading assigned in his classes.

During remedial instruction the child is not required to sound out any word when he is reading, nor is the word sounded out for him by the teacher. Nevertheless, the child does acquire phonetic skills through his tracing-sounding and writing-sounding training. Although Fernald's children knew no phonics at the beginning and were given no formal training in phonics they were able at the end of the training to pass phonics tests up to their age level.

Success of the Method. Fernald (70) reports rather phenomenal success with her tracing method. There is little doubt that application of the method by a well-trained remedial teacher will ordinarily achieve good success in teaching extreme cases.

Fernald considers that most extreme cases are children who have been unable to profit by the ordinary forms of classroom instruction, especially those methods which depend largely upon visual methods of presentation. She considers that the best way to overcome this extreme reading disability is to employ the kinesthetic method described above. This kinesthetic activity involved in the tracing and writing, combined with saying the word, appears to constitute the core of the technique.

Evaluation. When used by experienced clinicians, the Fernald method is undoubtedly successful. In the early stages it tends to be time-consuming. In an extreme case, the tracing may continue for eight months, although the average is only two months. But other methods require long periods of instruction also when dealing with instances of extreme disability. So the time factor can hardly be termed a drawback. When the instruction is properly carried out, the pupils can be as well motivated as with any other method.

It is worthwhile inquiring into the factors which are responsible for the success of this method. Fernald considers the *kinesthesis* coupled with enthusiastic and efficient teaching the keys to its success. It is possible that the kinesthesis as such is of minor importance. The method involves the following important features: (1) The child learns effectively the left-to-right sequences of perception by his simultaneous tracing-sounding and writing-sounding of words. (2) The visual structure of the word is associated with appropriate sounding of the pronounceable units of the word. (3) Skill in phonics is learned without having been taught formally. As part of this sounding, the child learns what is equivalent to consonant substitution in recognition of new words. After recognizing a familiar element in a word, the child attaches the proper beginning or ending sound. Meanings supplied by the verbal context are employed in choosing the proper ending or beginning to produce recognition of the new word. Thus in the sentence "Mary *took* the kitten home," the element *ook* may be associated with or recognized as part of the familiar word *book* or *look*. The context then helps to give the proper word *took*. Also through tracing-writing-sounding, many initial and final elements become known to the child so that he makes the substitution readily. (4) The very nature of the program leads to skill in syllabication. (5) The Fernald method, therefore, teaches left-to-right direction of word perception, the visual form of words, skill in phonics (including syllabication and the equivalent of consonant substitution), and use of context clues for identification and recognition of words. Added to all this, the child is strongly motivated by working with materials in which he is much interested. Whether or not kinesthesis constitutes another essential factor seems unimportant to the writers of this book. For in any case the five factors we have listed constitute by themselves a fairly well-balanced program for teaching word perception in remedial instruction.

In addition to word recognition, the Fernald method gives appropriate attention to vocabulary and concept development, and to comprehension.

The Monroe Method

The phonetic approach has been incorporated in a number of remedial procedures. The most comprehensive program among those which have been used very successfully in teaching excessively disabled readers is that of Monroe. This technique is essentially a phonetic method with emphasis upon patient, repetitive drill work, together with suggestions on how to introduce variety into it without losing the fundamental purposes of the drill. The remedial program is prescribed in all its details by the teacher to fit a particular case. We will describe its fundamental features here. To use the method, the teacher must familiarize herself with the details presented in Monroe's book (131).

Faulty Vowels and Consonants. These are major sources of difficulty with extreme cases. One case or another is sure to need instruction in the discrimination of specific speech sounds, in association of visual symbols with letter sounds, in observing that words of the same sounds often contain the same letters, and in co-ordinating the temporal sequence of sounds with the left-to-right sequence of letters in a word.

One of the first steps is to build up the ability to discriminate speech sounds. Pictures of several objects beginning with the same consonant, or containing the same vowel are mounted on cards. The pictures may be obtained from magazines or old books. Examples of typical initial consonants used are:

b as in boy, book	*m* as in man, moon
c as in coat, cat	*t* as in tiger, table, etc.

As far as possible, words which contain a vowel immediately after the initial consonant are chosen for this early drill. Single consonant sounds are learned more readily than consonant blends. Thus the *s* sound is learned more easily in *seed* than in *store*.

Cards with pictures are similarly arranged for the vowels, such as:

a as in man, cat	*o* as in box, top
e as in pen, hen	*i* as in fire, kite, etc.

To develop discrimination, the instruction is started with unlike sounds, as *m* compared with *s*. The cards for *m* and *s* are arranged in a row in mixed order, as:

man	soap	moon	seed

The child is instructed to sound the *m* and then name the object in the picture. After he succeeds with unlike sounds, the more difficult discriminations are taught as *s* and *sh* in seed and shell. These drills are varied by asking the child to give words beginning with a certain sound. A similar procedure is followed in the drills for vowels.

The next step consists in establishing associations between the letters and their most frequent sounds. Tracing is introduced as a reinforcement where necessary. The child traces over a letter written by the teacher. He sounds it as he traces. This is repeated until he can look at the letter and sound it correctly without tracing. Ordinarily, five or six consonant sounds can be learned at one sitting. After learning several consonant and vowel sounds, the child is taught blending letter sounds into words. The sounding-tracing method is an important aid in this. The sounding becomes a slow distinct articulation of the word as a unit while the tracing is being done. Monroe (131), pp. 121-123, gives a series of word lists to be learned in this manner. Recall is tested by presenting the words printed on cards. In this the child is encouraged to articulate the separate letter sounds and blend them. The phonetic skills the child acquires gives him a feeling of mastery in word recognition.

The child next progresses to reading specially prepared phonetic stories. The child is soon able to handle stories in ordinary primers and first readers. Nonphonetic words are learned by tracing-sounding. As the child gains in vocabulary and reading ability, the nonphonetic words are often identified from context.

Reversals. Monroe found it necessary to give the child a definite motor cue to the correct direction in developing the left-to-right sequence in perceiving words. This is accomplished by tracing-sounding as this is practiced by Fernald (see above). Monroe's adaptation of the method is described in detail in her Chapter 6.

Addition of Sounds. Failure to discriminate consonant blends and failure to discriminate word forms accurately frequently lead to adding sounds. The sounds more frequently added are *r* and *l*. When this tendency is persistent, drills are given on lists of words which are alike except for the presence of *r* or *l*. Examples are: *tack* and *track, fat* and *flat.*

Omission of Sounds. Omissions are often due to lack of accurate discrimination of the visual word patterns, or an overemphasis on speed. The correction of faulty consonants and vowels, described above, usually corrects tendencies to omit sounds. When omissions are due to undue stress on speed, the teacher should simply encourage a slower rate of speed until the errors disappear.

Substitution of Words. Substitutions are usually due to insufficient phonetic skill to identify words. Also the child recognizes too few words to get much aid from context clues. Excessive substitution is corrected by developing skill in analyzing words and by going back to easier reading material.

Repetition of Words. When repetitions are due to many mistakes in word recognition, the remedial treatment consists of instruction to reduce these errors in the ways described above. If they have become habitual, the teacher should try to make the habit so conspicuous to the child that he will attempt to avoid it. Oral reading by teacher and child together directs the child's attention to his mistakes in repeating words so he will try to stop. When repetition is due to stalling for sufficient time to recognize unknown words, it is best eliminated by developing word-analysis skills as described above.

Addition of Words. This is not a serious fault ordinarily. If the child is reading fluently and with comprehension, it is really best to ignore the addition of adjectives and adverbs. When the additions change the meaning, then the teacher should direct the child's attention to what is happening.

Omission of Words. When this is due to too much emphasis on speed, reading should be slowed down. Ordinarily, omission of a few words does not distort meanings and no remedial instruction is necessary. In the rare case where the omission distorts the meaning, concert-reading, as used to overcome repetition, will be found helpful.

Evaluation. The Monroe method is particularly successful with extreme disability cases. For the 27 children in her group whose reading ability would place them less than half-way through the first grade (1.0-1.4), the average gain was 1.3 grades after approximately 26 hours of remedial instruction over a period of about eight months. Her control group of 50 cases who received no remedial instruction gained only 0.14 grade in eight months. In other words, the children who had no remedial training made practically no gain, while those with instruction by her method gained over a year in reading.

The Monroe method is a definite, somewhat rigid, drill program that takes considerable time. The progress is from letter sounds to words in sentences. It delays reading of words longer than the Fernald method. However, the teaching of extremely disabled cases to read is bound to take time whatever the method used. The Monroe method probably takes no more time to get results with these cases than would other methods. Monroe has worked out an effective combination of the tracing-sounding method with phonetic training. She recognizes that drill in her method is somewhat mechanical and laborious in the early stages. But as the child progresses, much of his reading takes on the characteristics of normal performance, except when he encounters an unknown word. He may then employ tracing or sounding, or both until the word is recognized. He then proceeds with his reading. The view taken in this book is that the Monroe technique is a suitable method to employ with severely retarded readers. Although also successful with the less severely retarded cases, other methods tend to get quicker results.

The Gates Method

Gates (79) is not in favor of either the Fernald or the Monroe methods for teaching excessively retarded readers. He considers it advisable to use the same methods as the procedures and techniques taught to normal children in the best classroom programs. His argument is that one should try to give the extreme disability case just as useful equipment as a normal pupil. The normal program simply needs to be enriched (certainly not restricted) for these pupils. The extreme disability case, *somewhere in the course of his development,* should be taught the effective use of all the techniques employed by successful readers. It might be noted that neither Fernald nor Monroe deny this last recommendation.

Remedial instruction for extremely disabled readers, according to Gates, is like that for normal pupils except that the program of instruction is more carefully managed. Its adjustment to individual needs and individual instruction is emphasized. The teacher must be flexible in selecting just the technique or approach that will fit a particular case. This requires an intensive study of each child's abilities, difficulties, and needs. The teacher will have to spend more time and exercise more care in demonstrating and explaining the techniques employed. Additional explanations and suggestions are given as needed. Care is taken so that the pupil moves ahead at just the proper pace. When a method or device does not appear to be serviceable, the teacher shifts to some other devices or form of help.

If the more individualized teaching of the commonly used procedures does not bring success, the teacher may resort to some of the techniques ordinarily employed only with excessively disabled readers. First, a fair trial is given the customary methods of observing words, using context clues, visual and auditory analysis, and development of appropriate left-to-right orientation in word perception. If the child's responses then reveal inadequate progress in learning to read, the teacher may resort to the tracing and writing techniques as employed by Fernald. Even in this case, the tracing and writing is not continued for weeks and months. It is to be used merely as a means of getting the child started right so he will consistently maintain the left-to-right progression in reading words. According to Gates, once the child has begun to make headway by the tracing-writing technique, he should be shifted back to a program which covers the full range of reading activities for a normal child.

Gates claims that his procedure is more widely used with extreme disability cases than any other. As evidence of its success, he cites the city-wide program carried out in the New York City schools, beginning in 1934. The instruction was individual and intensive but by no means a narrow drill program. However, many gadgets and special devices were invented and used by the teachers. Special efforts were made to insure that each pupil received large amounts of interesting reading material and an opportunity to employ his artistic, dramatic, exploratory, constructive, and other interests in relation to his reading. A majority of teachers considered that best results were obtained with all types of cases, including extreme cases, by an intensive application of the same methods recommended for ordinary classroom use. A minority felt that best success with extremely disabled readers was obtained by spending some time in tracing-writing as in the Fernald Method. Still other teachers considered that a phonetic approach similar to Monroe's program produced the best results. Many of the teachers felt that a more intensive use of either the tracing or the phonetic procedure was best for *certain cases but not for others*. Gates states that intensive use of tracing and phonetics was employed as a last resort when satisfactory progress was not achieved by a more comprehensive program.

The results of the New York City remedial program undoubtedly were good. With two months of training, the average case gained over four times normal expectancy. Less than 5 per cent failed to make normal progress. Later results were even more promising.

It should be noted that Gates admits, although with some reluctance, that certain extremely disabled readers need special procedures such as tracing-writing. However, he insists that such procedures and other special devices should be abandoned as soon as possible.

Evaluation. The approach recommended by Gates for teaching extreme cases has certain advantages: (1) It is a flexible program. Provision is made for shifting temporarily to a more rigid drill technique when needed. Gates does not deny the usefulness at times of the tracing-writing or the phonetic method with certain difficult cases. (2) Many excessively disabled readers should reach the stage where reading takes on the characteristics of normal performance sooner with the Gates program than when a method calling for more rigid drill is used. (3) It would seem desirable to start the extremely disabled reader with the Gates program. If, after a fair trial, progress is not satisfactory, the teacher can turn to the Fernald or the Monroe technique, or a combination of the two. After a fair amount of progress is made with this more fixed procedure, a gradual transition toward the broader and less mechanical instruction employed with normal readers can be attempted.

General Statement. Almost any *expert* remedial teacher may be able to teach most of her extremely handicapped children to read by any of the methods discussed here. But to be really expert, she should be able on occasion to use each of the methods effectively. Then, after a thorough analysis of a case, she can apply the method most suitable for remedying the difficulties it presents. There is no single "sure-fire" method suitable for teaching every extremely disabled reader and the same is true even for cases with less severe retardation.

Probably the reason for the success of these methods which enjoy widespread use with extreme disability cases is that a high percentage of such cases would be classified after a really adequate diagnosis as word-recognition cases. The fact that such methods are successful in general does not mean that some one or two of them might not prove very unfortunate for an occasional individual case. For instance, they may be suitable for 70 per cent of the extreme cases but may be extremely detrimental to the others. In the opinion of the authors of this book, the best approach to the extreme cases appears to lie in a more careful diagnosis and then the application of the indicated remedial work, which in some cases might well be the Fernald or the Monroe procedure.

THE VISUALLY HANDICAPPED

Many visual defects such as ordinary myopia, hyperopia, astigmatism, and muscular imbalance can be remedied by properly fitted glasses. Children with properly corrected vision suffer no visual handicap when they learn to read. Every child should have an adequate eye examination before he receives any instruction in reading. Any correction called for must be provided by one means or another. There should be additional periodic checks of visual status throughout the school years to identify and correct any significant defects which may develop later. Methods for diagnosing visual defects are discussed in Chapter 5.

A small number of children have visual deficiencies which cannot be fully corrected by glasses. A sight conservation program should be set up to keep watch over all children who are specified as in need of it according to a competent eye specialist. When a child has visual acuity no better than 20/50 in the better eye after correction, he is ordinarily in need of the special care provided in sight-saving classes. Whether such a child spends all his time in a sight-saving class, or part of it in a regular class and part in the sight-saving classroom, depends upon local practice.

The main objective in teaching children with severe visual deficiencies to read is to put them in a situation that will promote as much progress in reading as possible without harm to their eyes. The reading periods should be brief enough not to cause undue fatigue or injure the eyes. The eye doctor should specify how much time may safely be devoted to reading activities.

Other factors to consider are typography and illumination. The consensus is that material for sight-saving classes should be printed in large size type. The size ordinarily used is 24 point print or typed material of about that size. There is no satisfactory experimental evidence on this. McNally (129) found that 12, 14, 18, and 24 point print were all read at approximately the same rate by pupils in sight-saving classes. This evidence is far from conclusive. It is questionable whether the speed with which a short selection can be read provides sufficient evidence of the influence of type size on visual fatigue for *visually handicapped children*. There is ample evidence that both normal and visually deficient people find that words in large type sizes are easier to perceive correctly. The goal in dealing with sight-saving pupils is *ease of seeing, not speed of reading.* Until further evidence is available, the printing used in sight-saving classes should be equivalent to not less than 18 point type. It is also advisable to use material printed in a moderate line length of about 24 to 27 picas (4 to 4½ inches) with ample leading or space between lines. The optimal amount of leading has to be an estimate since no experimental evidence is available.

The fact that relatively little material is printed in such large-sized type makes it difficult to provide an adequate amount of reading material for pupils in sight-saving classes. Typewriters with primer-sized type are available. Material typed on one of these may be used to supplement what is available in large print. Visually handicapped children should have a wide variety of reading materials and an ample amount of it.

There should be plentiful illumination in sight-saving classrooms. This means at least 50 foot-candles of light in any area where visual discrimination is required as for reading, art work, blackboard work, and writing. Pens and pencils which produce thick black lines should be used by the children.

In sight-conservation classes, the reading should be co-ordinated with other forms of learning so that much of the time is devoted to listening and discussing, or to creative activities of one sort or another. The teacher must carry a heavy load of reporting, oral reading to the class, story telling, guiding discussions, and supervising dramatic and artistic activities. Good use may be made of such auditory and visual aids as radio, recordings, sound motion pictures, and ordinary pictures.

According to Gates (79), these children are at no disadvantage in auditory discrimination of words or in learning phonetic procedures for word recognition. Phonics should not be overemphasized, however. Attention should be directed to the characteristic configuration of word forms, and to perceiving the larger pronounceable units of words such as syllables, word roots, prefixes, and suffixes. This will avoid to some extent the minute examination of the details of letters in sounding out words. Also the development of good skill in the use of verbal contexts and pictures to aid in word recognition will tend to reduce the need for close attention to the smaller details of letters and words. Another way to cut down on fine visual discrimination is to emphasize the recognition of words in thought units. Any procedure which leads to perceiving larger units of word wholes, groups of words, or parts of words will help to keep down to a desirable minimum the detailed visual work in reading.

Many children suffer from a mild degree of visual deficiency, making their problem less serious. Most such children can participate in the regular reading program provided for normal children. It is probably desirable for them to rest their eyes frequently and to do somewhat less extensive reading. As with the more serious cases, they should be taught to recognize words by phonetic analysis, combining this with attention to larger units and the use of context.

HEARING DEFICIENCY

Here the problems also differ, since hearing deficiency occurs in varying degrees. Deaf-mute children are those who are totally deaf. They are born without hearing or have lost their hearing before the age when children ordinarily learn to talk. Other children with hearing difficulties range from the slightly hard-of-hearing to the severely hard-of-hearing or the partly deaf.

All children should be given an adequate hearing test early in their school life. This is especially important since many cases of severe hearing disability can be prevented if there is early diagnosis and treatment. The measurement of hearing has been discussed in Chapter 5.

Mild Hearing Deficiency. With a moderate amount of special aid, the child having mild hearing deficiencies will ordinarily adjust rather readily to the normal classroom situation. Such a pupil should be given a favorable seat close to the place from which the teacher does most of her talking to the class. Special emphasis should be placed upon clear enunciation in all situations which involve the hard-of-hearing child. He will be able to follow oral discussions more accurately if he watches the lips of the person speaking. Some training in lip reading will be helpful. To avoid embarrassment to the hard-of-hearing child, the recitation or discussion group should be arranged so that he can watch the lips of each speaker without obviously turning his head. Seating the children in a semicircle or around a table does this nicely.

The child with a mild hearing defect is bound to have more or less difficulty in auditory discrimination. Because of this, the teaching of word perception should emphasize the visual approach to word identification and word recognition rather than phonetics. This does not imply a total neglect of word sounds but merely that more attention than usual is paid to the visual characteristics of words and to the use of visual analysis along with context clues for recognizing words previously met and for identifying unfamiliar words. The degree of this emphasis will depend upon how much difficulty the child has with auditory discrimination. If these precautions are taken, the child with a relatively mild hearing defect should be able to make normal progress in learning to read.

Partly Deaf Children. Hard-of-hearing children are under a severe handicap in learning to read in classes where oral reading and phonetics are stressed. They will need a greater emphasis upon silent reading and a visual approach to word perception. The techniques used with mild cases of hard-of-hearing discussed just above will need greater emphasis. Particularly, these children should receive special instruction in lip reading if that is available. Once a hard-of-hearing child has acquired skill in lip reading, he can usually participate in normal class activities without too much or even with very little difficulty.

The hard-of-hearing child is likely to develop some emotional maladjustment unless special care is taken. Such a child easily acquires feelings of inferiority and of persecution. Every effort should be exercised to make the child feel that he belongs to the group in his class work and his play activities.

The Deaf-Mute. Teaching reading to congenital deaf-mutes inevitably involves serious difficulties, since they have never developed language concepts. Thompson (167), under the direction of Gates, has carried out a successful experiment in teaching beginning reading to deaf-mutes. Gates (79) also describes in some detail the procedures she used. This program has to depend entirely upon visual teaching materials. Words are introduced in a variety of contexts, most of which include some connection with real concrete objects and by actions and demonstration. Extensive use is made of pictures accompanying the words and picture dictionary material. Mastery of each step is required before going on to the next. Progress is gradual from words to phrases to sentences to paragraphs.

This method is effective in teaching deaf-mutes to read. At the end of one year, those taught by this method were far ahead of those taught by the regular deaf-school methods. More convincing is the comparison with the progress of normal children in the first grade. On several measures of reading ability, the deaf-mute group did as well or slightly better than the normal children in Detroit and New York.

It might be noted parenthetically that a non-oral method for teaching reading to normal children has been developed. Buswell (32) has shown that this approach is fully as effective as ordinary methods which combine oral and silent reading. This method, or a modification of it, might well be used with deaf-mutes or hard-of-hearing children.

Teaching deaf-mutes to read is a highly specialized task which the ordinary remedial teacher will not encounter. Those who teach deaf-mutes will need very much more information than can be given in this book. They should consult such references as those of Thompson (167) and McLeod (128).

SPEECH DIFFICULTIES

Speech defects are occasionally present in reading disability cases. The role of such defects as causes of difficulties in reading has been reviewed in Chapter 5. Speech defects which interfere with clear enunciation may be associated with inadequate auditory discrimination and thus lead to difficulty in word recognition. For such children, the phonetic study of words should be minimized. For these cases, emphasis should be placed upon the study of the visual characteristics of words, especially during the early stages of learning to read. Also, silent rather than oral reading should be stressed.

Some children with speech defects are embarrassed when they are asked to read orally or to take part in discussion. To avoid aggravation of the child's emotional state, the teacher should be sympathetic and tactful in her requests and suggestions. But it is not wise to excuse such a child altogether from oral work. The problem of organizing the proper balance between oral and silent work is a delicate one.

A first step is to provide the child with proper speech training by a speech teacher. As the child makes progress in developing smoother and more fluent speech he gains confidence in himself. One of the procedures in correcting speech difficulties is oral reading. At first, the pupil should read some well-prepared selection orally to his teacher, in private. As the speech difficulty is overcome, the child will be ready and perhaps eager to do some oral reading in class. The teacher should encourage but not force the child to do this. At the same time, as the child becomes more sure of himself, remedial measures for correcting specific reading difficulties may be undertaken.

DEFICIENCIES IN UNDERSTANDING ENGLISH

Children who come from a home where a foreign language is spoken may have little or no command of English. They may be unable to understand or speak English well enough to participate much in ordinary classroom activities. The situation may be further complicated, in certain cases, by low intelligence. It is not easy to obtain a fair estimate of a child's intelligence when he can neither understand nor speak English, irrespective of the type of test used.

The reading difficulties of children who come from homes where a foreign language is spoken, tend to be due to their inability to understand or speak English. The procedures ordinarily used in teaching beginning reading in our schools assume that each child has already learned to understand and speak the language. Language-handicapped children need first of all a program designed to improve their knowledge of English. A preparatory instructional period ordinarily should be devoted to three simultaneous activities: first, to building up a basic vocabulary for understanding and speaking; second, improvement of facility in oral communication; and third, providing a background of meaningful experiences. Words and concepts associated with the experiences must be in English. Thus the child learns to speak and understand a vocabulary before he encounters it in reading. It is probable that much of the training in the understanding and use of oral English should be carried out in sessions not concerned with reading. In general, lessons in reading should not be complicated by simultaneous training in pronunciation. All this does not mean that no reading is done while the child is being taught English. Although the two can be done concurrently, they should be in separate class periods.

Language-handicapped children need not become reading disability cases if an appropriate teaching program is organized early in their school lives. Nevertheless, the development of an adequate background in English is pretty certain to be gradual. Until this is achieved, these children will be at a disadvantage in reading activities. The program for developing facility in the use of English may need to be continued throughout the elementary school years in some situations.

When a child with a meager knowledge of English continues in school without receiving special training to eliminate his handicap, he may become a disabled reader. If this happens, his facility in the use of English must be improved, prior to much remedial work in reading.

GENERAL STATEMENT

In this chapter, an attempt has been made to present the problems and to suggest in general terms the required instructional procedures for teaching reading to specially handicapped children. Much of the teaching must be done by specialists who have been trained to teach at least one of the following groups: the slow learners, the visually handicapped, the deaf, or the children with speech difficulties. In addition, the teacher should know the principles of diagnosis and remedial teaching discussed earlier in this book. The remedial teacher can then introduce the modifications needed to make special adjustments to the particular handicap of each child. What these children need is an adequate diagnosis and the kinds of instructional modifications we have been describing in the above discussion.

SUMMARY

Included among the specially handicapped children are emotionally disturbed children, slow learners, extremely disabled readers, those with poor vision, the hard-of-hearing, speech cases, and those with any real language handicaps. Highly individualized treatment is necessary with all these types. The role of the teacher is especially important in dealing with the specially handicapped. She must have great patience, be very sympathetic, and be highly skilled and versatile in the field of remedial reading. To use a narrow or limited approach for all cases will be inadequate.

The major portion of the children with reading disabilities are emotionally disturbed. When dealing with the more severe emotional cases, definite psychiatric therapy is necessary. Probably some psychotherapy would facilitate the improvement in the majority of disability cases, particularly the more severe cases.

Slow learners, as we have used the term, are mentally retarded children (I.Q.'s between 50 and 89) who can profit from reading instruction. The proportion of reading disability cases in this group is about the same as among normal children. With proper instructional procedures, the mentally retarded can learn to read and maintain their reading ability up to the level of their learning capacity. A modified phonetic approach with emphasis on drill has been employed successfully in remedial work with the slow-learning child. The Hegge-Kirk method, which is slow-moving and involves much phonetic drill, is probably best for institutional cases. A broader method, which is pretty close to ordinary good classroom instruction but is more highly individualized, seems appropriate for those dull-normal children found in regular classrooms.

The extreme disability case is the child who has learned little or no reading during one or more years in school. Three remedial methods have been especially successful in dealing with these children. Fernald employed with success a tracing-sounding-writing method, which she called the kinesthetic method. This procedure is effective in developing left-to-right orientation in word perception, directs attention to the visual characteristics of words, develops skill both in phonics, including syllabication, and in the use of context in recognizing words. Such teaching also gives appropriate emphasis to developing vocabulary, concepts, and comprehension, but it is detailed, time-consuming and must be done on a completely individual basis. The teacher employing this method can deal with only a few cases at a time because she has to prepare many materials.

The Monroe technique, which has been successfully used to help extreme cases, is essentially a phonetic method with emphasis upon the patient repetition of the necessary drill plus a program for introducing variety without losing sight of the fundamental purposes of the drill. Special procedures are used for correcting particular difficulties such as faulty vowels, consonants, reversals, and others. Tracing-sounding is employed at appropriate places. This method may overemphasize the reading defect of the child and should only be used after a careful diagnosis indicates that the child is not an overanalytical reader already.

Gates advises the use of a method that embodies all the procedures and techniques taught to normal children in good classroom programs. To do this, he has to put stress on intensive individual instruction. He would revert to the Fernald or the Monroe method only when the broader program fails to improve reading. The expert remedial teacher should be familiar with all the above methods so that she may apply just the right procedure to meet the needs of each specific case.

The present writers would suggest that a careful diagnosis can usually locate the area of difficulty and indicate the type of remedial instruction needed. Such a diagnosis may well indicate at particular times the suitability of any one or a combination of the approaches discussed above.

Children with moderate visual deficiencies should be taught by methods which emphasize the auditory approach. Those with severe visual handicaps should be enrolled in a sight-saving program which will avoid severe visual fatigue. They need plenty of light, print in large type, and short reading periods. Stress should be placed upon learning activities which do not require close visual work.

Children with mild hearing deficiencies get along well in normal classroom activities which emphasize the visual approach to reading. The phonetic approach should be avoided in teaching hard-of-hearing children. For them, the visual approach to word recognition should be stressed even more than for the children with mild hearing deficiencies. Deaf-mutes should be taught to read in special classes. Emphasis should be upon the visual characteristics of words and upon silent reading.

Children with speech difficulties should have corrective work in speech by a specialist. As their speech becomes more and more fluent and adequate, they may be successfully reintroduced to regular methods of remedial instruction.

The first steps in dealing with children deficient in English because their parents are of foreign extraction is to teach them to use English. Only when they can do that fairly well can they profit from ordinary reading instruction. However, as soon as the teacher considers it feasible, they can be taught reading concurrently while their English is being improved.

SELECTED READINGS

FERNALD, Grace M., *Remedial techniques in basic school subjects.* New York: McGraw-Hill Book Company, Inc., 1943, Chap. 5.

GATES, Arthur I., *The improvement of reading,* 3rd ed. New York: The Macmillan Company, 1947, Chap. 16.

KIRK, Samuel A., *Teaching reading to slow-learning children.* Boston: Houghton Mifflin Company, 1940, Chaps. 2-7.

MONROE, Marion, *Children who cannot read.* Chicago: University of Chicago Press, 1932, Chap. 6.

19 ILLUSTRATIVE CASE STUDIES

THROUGHOUT THIS BOOK, stress has been placed upon individual diagnosis and remedial instruction, especially when dealing with the more complex and severe cases of reading disability. Among the preceding chapters, some have described the general nature of diagnosis and the general nature of remedial instruction. Others have gone into the diagnosis and treatment of specific types of deficiencies such as the various disabilities connected with poor word recognition. We have repeatedly emphasized that a thorough case study is required for dealing with any child who is severely retarded in reading. The present chapter describes in some detail several cases of children who have a reading disability of one sort or another such as is often met by a remedial teacher or in a reading clinic to which the child has been referred.

These case reports are taken from the files of the Psycho-Educational Clinic at the University of Minnesota. The data about each child fill a thick folder in the clinic files. Necessarily, the materials as presented in this chapter are much condensed. Although each case description here is brief, it is sufficiently complete so that its pattern and chief features are brought out. This handful of cases, of course, represents only a few of the great variety of reading problems that a clinician will meet in his work.

The proper procedures to employ in making a case study, with examples, have been described in Chapter 8 and need not be repeated here. The diagnoses and remedial treatments of five additional cases are given below. The first case is described in more detail than the four that follow it.

Case 1. A gifted boy who persisted in using immature word-recognition techniques

When Allan was referred to the Psycho-Educational Clinic for study, he was an attractive boy from a fourth-grade classroom. He was large for a boy 10 years and 6 months old. He had puzzled his teacher for some time. His discussions of class enterprises and his way of expressing his ideas were very good. In certain class activities he was an eager participant, while in others he tended to withdraw. His teacher was well aware that there was a relationship between Allan's tendency to lose interest in an activity and the amount of reading involved in it. She also understood that he had to obtain most of his information from class discussions, but once he had got it, his

433

reasoning and judgment about what he had just learned were mature. She knew that Allan was a disabled reader. She had watched the difficulties he experienced whenever he was asked to read something orally.

On the basis of a study of Allan's cumulative record card and recent test scores, she had made the general diagnosis that his reading disability called for more detailed study. The general diagnosis showed that Allan had a reading grade score of 2.5. His arithmetic grade score was 3.5 for problem solving and 5.2 for computation. His score on a group intelligence test indicated that he had an I.Q. of 98. His previous school record showed that Allan had repeated the third grade and that during the second year in that grade, less reading growth took place than in the previous year.

Allan's teacher did not think that the 98 I.Q. represented his true intelligence even though it was in keeping with the level of his general school achievement. She based this judgment on the quality of his discussions of a topic when he knew something about it and on his score in the computation section of the arithmetic test. She had also noticed that when problems were read to him, his arithmetical reasoning seemed effective. On the basis of all of this information, she felt that a thorough study of Allan's educational problem was required. Since she was without specialized training, she referred Allan to the Psycho-Educational Clinic for further study.

At the Clinic, a more analytical diagnosis was made as the first step in studying Allan's problem. This phase of the diagnosis consisted of giving a revised *Stanford-Binet Mental Test* and the *Developmental Reading Test— Advanced Primary*. The mental test indicated that Allan had a mental age of 13-0 and an I.Q. of 124. The examiner stated that the true intelligence of this boy might even be somewhat higher since he would have based at year ten, had he not missed item 3, Reading and Report. At the eleven-year level, he missed only item 3, Abstract Words; and at the twelve-year level, items 1, Vocabulary, 5, Abstract Words, and 6, Minkus Completion. At year thirteen, the only item missed was number 5, Dissected Sentences. Allan received eight months credit at year fourteen and four months credit at the Average Adult level. All the items missed early in the test had a relationship to reading, so it was the examiner's judgment that Allan was a very able child with a severe reading disability. While it was suspected that Allan was considerably brighter than the 124 I.Q. indicated, all that could be said was that Allan had a mental age of at least 13-0 and that he should be expected to read, if everything else were normal, at (4.5×1.24) $+1.0$ or 6.6 grade level. (All the grade expectancies in this chapter are computed by this formula, as explained in Chapter 4.)

The reading test showed the following scores:

Vocabulary	2.3
General Comprehension	2.5
Specific Comprehension	2.7
Average Reading Score	2.5

A comparison between the scores obtained thus far showed that Allan was a bright boy who should be reading at about 6.6 level of difficulty on the basis of reading expectancy as calculated from the results of the Stanford-Binet Mental Test. His arithmetic scores of 3.5 for problem solving (written problems) and 5.2 for computation (no reading involved) showed that he was doing reasonably well in an area not directly related to reading. Allan's average reading achievement of only 2.5 showed that he was seriously disabled in reading. The pattern of scores in the three areas of reading measured showed that his problem was a basic one. A study of the comprehension sections of the test revealed accurate performance on the simple items of these power tests but such slow speed that the boy did not get very far through the tests, even though the time limits are ample for the usual child. It was felt, on the basis of all the information thus far obtained, that Allan was a case of *limiting disability* and his area of difficulty was in word recognition. A thorough case study was therefore undertaken.

We must now answer the questions raised in Chapter 8.

1. *Is Allan correctly classified as a disabled reader?* The case study showed that he was indeed a disabled reader and that there was not the slightest indication of any physical, mental, or neurological condition that would alter his classification to anything other than disability in reading. While Allan was tense and became blocked in oral reading situations, there was no evidence of any basic emotional problem. It appeared, however, that there was an emotional involvement with respect to his reading and some accompanying rejection of reading activities.

2. *Who can most effectively give remedial work?* On the basis of recommendations made after the clinical diagnosis was completed, it was decided that Allan could best be treated in the school reading center, since his case of limiting disability needed only a well-defined type of instruction and involved only a minor emotional rejection of reading.

3. *What is the nature of the training needed?* This is the most essential question involved in re-educating a child who has been correctly classified as a disabled reader. Allan's reading pattern on the Gates Diagnostic Tests and on the Silent Reading Diagnostic Tests showed the limiting conditions that were present. He could not be expected to become an effective reader until his basic reading problems were corrected. Allan's reading profile, obtained by using the *Silent Reading Diagnostic Tests* (see Chapter 9) is shown on page 436.

A study of Allan's profile indicates the following facts:

a. Allan is an extremely able boy who has a basic word-recognition problem.

b. The comparison between Allan's total items right, total errors, and total omitted on Tests 1 and 2 shows that he attempts to recognize words, but is ineffective. He is more than a grade higher in the tendency to omit words (3.0) than he is in number of errors made (1.8). Even though he is

SILENT READING DIAGNOSTIC TESTS—EXPERIMENTAL FORM
Graphic Profile

Name **Allan** School_____ Grade **4** Date_____

BASIC DATA	Pupil Score	Grade Equivalent
		1.5 2.0 2.5 3.0 3.5 4.0 4.5 5.0 5.5 6.0 6.5 7.0 7.5 8.0
Chronological Grade	5.5	
Mental Grade	6.6	
Grade in School	4.5	

READING ABILITIES

	Pupil Score
Vocabulary	2.3
Factual (General)	2.5
Organize (Specific)	2.7
Evaluate-Interpret	
Appreciate	
Average Reading	2.5

RECOGNITION PATTERN (Perfect Score)

	Pupil Score	Grade Equivalent values
Total Right (1+2)	34	1,0 2,4 3,4 4,8 6,6 7,2 7,7 7,9 8,0 8,2
Total Errors (1+2)	47	5,4 4,5 3,8 2,6 1,5 ,9 ,4 ,4 ,2 ,0
Total Omitted (1+2)	10	2,0 1,5 1,2 ,0 ,7 ,3 ,3 ,1 ,0 ,0
Words in Isolation (1)	26	,9 1,6 2,2 3,2 4,4 4,8 5,1 5,2 5,3 5,4
Words in Context (2)	8	,5 ,8 1,2 1,6 2,1 2,4 2,6 2,7 2,7 2,8
Orientation (3)	9	,4 ,6 1,0 1,6 2,0 2,1 2,1 2,2 2,2 2,3

ERROR ANALYSIS (1+2)

	Pupil Score	Grade Equivalent values
Initial Errors	12	1,2 ,9 ,7 ,5 ,2 ,1 ,0 ,0 ,0 ,0
Middle Errors	12	1,5 1,3 1,1 ,8 ,6 ,4 ,2 ,1 ,1 ,0
Ending Errors	11	1,4 1,2 ,1 ,7 ,5 ,3 ,2 ,1 ,1 ,0
Orientation Errors	12	1,3 1,1 ,9 ,6 ,2 ,1 ,0 ,0 ,0 ,0

RECOGNITION TECHNIQUES

	Pupil Score	Grade Equivalent values
Visual Analysis (4+5+6)	9	1,0 1,4 3,0 4,3 5,3 6,3 6,6 6,9 7,2 7,4
Locating Elements (4)	4	,6 ,8 1,6 2,3 2,8 3,4 3,4 3,5 3,6 3,6
Syllabication (5)	0	,2 ,3 ,5 ,7 ,9 1,0 1,1 1,1 1,2 1,2
Locating Root Word (6)	5	,2 ,3 ,9 1,3 1,6 1,9 2,1 2,3 2,4 2,6
Phonetic Kn. (7+8+9+10)	72	2,3 3,9 5,5 6,9 7,8 8,8 9,5 102 106 111
Word Elements (7)	20	,5 ,8 1,3 1,7 1,9 2,1 2,3 2,4 2,5 2,7
Beginning Sounds (8)	17	,8 1,2 1,6 2,0 2,2 2,4 2,5 2,6 2,7 2,8
Rhyming Sounds (9)	11	,0 ,3 ,6 ,8 1,3 1,8 2,2 2,5 2,7 2,8
Letter Sounds (10)	24	1,0 1,6 2,0 2,4 2,4 2,5 2,6 2,7 2,8 2,8

WORD SYNTHESIS (11)

	Pupil Score	Grade Equivalent values
	11	,1 ,2 ,4 ,7 1,3 1,8 2,0 2,2 2,3 2,4

MISCELLANEOUS DATA

Hearing O.K.   Other _____   *Lines of importance*

Vision O.K.

not beyond the line of importance in either of the above, the difference shows that he is attempting the items but is inaccurate.

c. The fact that his score (2.6) on Test 1, Words in Isolation, was higher than his score (2.0) on Test 2, Words in Context—though the difference is not great enough to guarantee its significance—does suggest that he was ineffective in using context clues.

d. The Orientation Test, Test 3, reveals no specific difficulty in orientation when reading contextual material.

e. The Error Analysis shows that Allan has a tendency to neglect the initial part of the word (1.5). In fact, this is a significant characteristic as it is outside of the lines of importance, as described in the manual for this test. Allan made a score of 2.6 on Ending Errors, which shows that he pays considerable attention to word endings as compared with the beginnings of words. This is an unfortunate pattern. He also shows some tendency toward Orientation Errors in these tests. However, this amount of orientational confusion could readily be accounted for by his tendency to study the ends of words and to neglect their beginnings. Because Allan did not demonstrate any orientational difficulty in Test 3, there is no reason to think that a significant reversal tendency is involved.

f. The section of these tests dealing with recognition techniques reveals an interesting and important condition. Allan is extremely poor in those phases of word recognition involving visual analysis of words into their larger, more useful elements. He is, however, extremely strong in his phonetic knowledges. His knowledge of word elements, for example, is at the 3.8 level, or over a year higher than his reading in general. In fact, Allan's phonetic knowledge (3.5) as compared with his visual analysis (1.5) shows that he was two years more advanced in his knowledge of word parts than he was in locating these elements within words. It should also be noted that his knowledge of beginning sounds (2.7) is more than a year behind his knowledge of word elements (3.8).

g. His Word Synthesis score of 3.4 indicates that there is no defect here.

h. In summary, this detailed study of Allan's reading pattern reveals that he needs the remedial training described in Chapter 12, under three headings: (1) Ineffective Visual Analysis of Words, (2) Failure to Use Meaning Clues, and (3) the second type of Overanalytical Reader, i.e., the reader who breaks words into too many parts.

The *Gates Reading Diagnostic Tests* were also given to this boy. A study of the tabulated results of Allan's diagnosis, shown on page 438, indicates that this test in every way verified the conclusions obtained from the *Silent Reading Diagnostic Tests*. It added the information that Allan has a relatively good sight vocabulary (3.1) and also that when he is given more time to study words, his overanalytical tendency gets in his way. This is shown by comparing the score of 2.5 on the untimed word-perception test with the score of 3.1 on the flash word-perception test.

GATES TEST SCORES

	Raw Scores	Grade Scores	Rating
Oral Reading		2.4	M
Mispronunciations	24		
Full Reversals	1		M
Reversal of Parts	0		M
Wrong Order	1		M
Wrong Beginnings	5		L
Wrong Middles	5		L
Wrong Endings	7		M+
Wrong Several Parts	6		M
Oral Vocabulary	13	5.4	M+
Reversal Test			
Total Errors	20	2.4	M
Per Cent Reversals	12	3.2	M+
Phrase Perception	10	2.8	M+
Word Perception			
Flash	17	3.1	M+
Untimed	22	2.5	M
Visual Perception			
Syllabication	0	1.5	V L
Recognition of Syllables	13	3.0	M+
Recognition of Phonograms	18	3.4	M+
Blending Letter Sounds	15	3.2	M+
Giving Letter Sounds	24	3.2	M+

4. *How can improvement be brought about most efficiently?* Allan was given remedial work in the school reading center for an hour a day in a basic reader at the beginning of second-grade level of difficulty. Workbook exercises and those suggested in the reader manual for employing larger elements of words, visual analysis of words, and context clues were emphasized. Short selections were used for rapid reading.

5. *Are there any limiting conditions within the child that must be considered?* Allan had no visual or hearing difficulties and no other limiting condition was identified.

6. *Are there any environmental conditions that might interfere with progress in reading?* His parents were very concerned about Allan's reading, as well they might be. His mother had given him some reading instruction at home. She had sat with Allan every day after school for a period of three months, helping him with his reading. After that she had felt that she and the boy were not getting anywhere, so she discontinued the instruction. The help she gave him was sounding out unknown words. This is just what Allan did not need, as he already had too much of a tendency to break words apart and sound each letter. His mother thought there was something wrong

with Allan's memory because the words they worked out one day were forgotten the next. She was eager to co-operate. She accepted the Clinic's suggestion to help him by discussing with him what he was reading at home and telling him words he did not know. The more technical teaching was left to the reading center.

Allan's classroom teacher was also informed about the nature of his reading difficulty. She already knew that he was a slow reader and an ineffective one. She was interested in the findings of the complete diagnosis and readily fell in with the idea that she could make adjustments to his level of reading capability in the regular classroom work.

At the end of six months of instruction in the reading center, Allan was measured again. His reading ability, as tested by the Gates Reading Survey, showed gratifying results.

Vocabulary	4.5
Speed	4.4
Level of Comprehension	4.9
Average	4.6

The average gain was more than two years. Allan will soon be released from the school reading center. He is still disabled in reading, but he has overcome much of his basic difficulty. It is felt that the classroom teacher can give him the additional instruction and experience he needs.

Case 2. A bright third-grade boy deficient in sight vocabulary, in word-identification and recognition skills, and in ability to read by thought units

John was referred to the Psycho-Educational Clinic for a thorough educational diagnosis because of difficulties in all phases of his school work during the middle of the third grade. He had attended the same school without interruption from beginning kindergarten to the time he was seen at the Clinic. At that time he was 8 years and 4 months old and was in the middle of grade three. John is the third child in a highly respected family living in a medium sized town. He has one brother 22 years old, a sister 13 years old, and a sister 2 years old. The home may be described as excellent. His father's occupational status is high and his mother devotes her time to the home.

The physical status of John is good. He appears well built and well nourished. His hearing, tested on the *Western Electric Audiometer,* was normal. No visual difficulties were detected when he was given the *Keystone Telebinocular Test.*

Adjustment. John manifested emotional tensions at home. He cried easily, was afraid of the dark, complained of bad dreams, and was excessively noisy. At school he was socially aggressive and generally irresponsible. Judgments of personality stressed excessive emotionality, a quarrelsome relation with other children, and some sibling rivalry. The negative personality factors were evident primarily in the school situation and especially those related to reading.

Abilities. Tests revealed high second-grade achievement in spelling and arithmetic: Grades 2.8 and 2.9 respectively. Other scores follow:

Intelligence: *Revised Stanford-Binet:*
   M.A., 10-5; I.Q., 126; Mental Grade, 4.2
Reading: *Gates Advanced Primary Reading Tests:*
   Word Recognition, Grade 2.7
   Paragraph Reading, Grade 2.4
   Average Silent Reading, Grade 2.55

Oral reading rated at grade 2.8. The *Gates Reading Diagnostic Tests* revealed the following difficulties: (1) very slow rate with word-by-word oral reading; (2) limited sight vocabulary; (3) little use of context for word recognition; (4) a tendency to make part reversals, as reading *spot* for *stop;* (5) difficulties with the final sounds of words; (6) frequent refusals to try to work out the pronunciation of unfamiliar words. Otherwise the boy's skills were what one would expect from his reading level. He read orally in an artificially high-pitched voice with signs of emotional tension. Observation of his behavior during silent reading revealed rather prominent articulation.

The average silent reading grade was 2.55. This is approximately one grade behind actual grade placement and almost two grades behind the mental grade, or school learning ability. Achievement in oral reading was only slightly better than in silent reading.

We must now answer the questions raised in Chapter 8:

1. *Is the child correctly classified as a disabled reader?* The answer is *yes.* He is about two years behind his capabilities. John is a bright child who should be reading around the beginning of the fourth grade instead of the middle of the second grade.

2. *Who can most effectively give the remedial work?* The clinician should do the remedial instruction. The child has special areas of difficulty (reversals, lack of phrasing, wrong endings, etc.) as well as general retardation in reading.

3. *What is the nature of the training needed?* The program of training should include: (*a*) extensive reading of materials at a comfortable level of difficulty (grade two at first); (*b*) emphasis upon development of a sight vocabulary; (*c*) experience in phrasing; (*d*) guidance in suppressing articulation during silent reading; (*e*) emphasis on left-to-right orientation in word perception; (*f*) improvement of word-recognition techniques with special stress upon use of context; (*g*) training in comprehending larger units; and (*h*) encouragement and planning for recreational reading at home. (See earlier chapters for remedial procedures.)

4. *How can the improvement be brought about most efficiently?* There

should be at least one hour of tutoring per day by an experienced clinical worker. This is best given during his attendance at a clinic.

5. *Are there any limiting conditions within the child that must be considered?* No, his vision, hearing, and physical condition are normal. His emotional reaction to frustration will probably disappear as he achieves success in reading.

6. *Are there any environmental conditions that might interfere with progress in reading?* No, the home environment seems satisfactory.

John came to the University Reading Clinic for two successive summer sessions of five weeks each. The program outlined above was carried out. At the end of the first session (18 lessons), John was given a second form of the *Gates Advanced Primary Reading Tests* with the following results:

> Word Recognition, Grade 4.1
> Paragraph Reading, Grade 4.4
> Average Reading Grade, 4.25

This represented an average gain of 1.7 grades during the five weeks. There was a correspondingly desirable change in the personality of John. He was easily motivated to full co-operation in the program and his attitude changed from indifference to friendliness. At home he began to pick up books and read them by himself. John was actually very pleased when his mother arranged to postpone the family's vacation so he could attend the Clinic school for the second five-week session. Apparently he was finding satisfaction in his reading growth.

The program for the second term was a continuation of the one begun during the first term. The reading program was broadened and John was advanced to third- and fourth-grade books. After the second five weeks of training, another form of the *Gates Advanced Primary Reading Tests* was given. Results were:

> Word Recognition, Grade 4.8
> Paragraph Reading, Grade 5.4
> Average Reading Grade, 5.1

The reading performance of John was now close to his mental grade. He had gained about 2½ years in reading grade during his 10 weeks at the clinic. His work habits and attitudes were much improved. His interest in school work was normal. He was now ready to handle his regular school work successfully. In fact, his reading was now a grade ahead of the fourth grade which he would enter in the fall.

The reasons for the marked improvement in reading proficiency achieved by John during his 10 weeks at the clinic appear to be the following: (1) He is a bright youngster. (2) There had been no unfortunate pressures at home. (3) His difficulties were in specific areas of word recognition and phrasing. They were readily detected by diagnosis and corrected by the remedial procedures that had been recommended.

Case 3. A boy with extreme disability in reading

Henry is a severe reading disability case. He was referred to the Psycho-Educational Clinic at age 11-7. At that time he was in the third month of the fifth grade. He had spent 2 years in the first grade. According to his school report, Henry had made no appreciable progress in reading or spelling.

Henry is the third of eight children. His father is totally disabled and consequently on public relief. The family lives in a deteriorated tenement in a slum area of a large city. The children in this family are allowed to roam the streets at will. They sleep four to five to a bed. Apparently there is little the school can do to help the home situation. A social worker should be able to provide some aid.

The general physical condition of Henry is satisfactory except for signs of undernourishment and the fact that he has a mangled left hand which was caught in a washer in early childhood. During the past year he was hit by an automobile and suffered a skull fracture and multiple abrasions. Recovery, however, from this accident seemed complete. Audiometer and visual tests (*Keystone Telebinocular*) revealed normal hearing and vision.

Adjustment. Henry shows evidences of insecurity and nervous tension. He feels that he is blamed unjustly for many things. His behavior tends to be disorganized and he suffers from enuresis. Even so, he is a friendly lad and persists in those activities he is able to do. It seems that Henry has made a fairly adequate adjustment to a bad home situation. He apparently accepts these conditions without hostility toward his family.

Abilities. On the *Wechsler Intelligence Scale* Henry obtained an I.Q. of 96 on each part and on the total score. At this time his chronological age was 11-7. His M.A. was 11-1 and mental grade, 6.1.

Arithmetic tests showed middle fourth-grade achievement. His performance on the *Gates Primary Reading Tests* revealed only chance scores. He could not spell the simplest words.

On the *Gates Oral Diagnostic Test,* Henry measured at the primer level. He recognized only four words (*he, the, a, was*). There was no evidence that he had acquired any word-analysis techniques. Henry knew the names of all the letters of the alphabet but only the sounds of *e, t, c, p, r, j,* and *k.* No syllables or phonograms were recognized. In all the visual and auditory techniques, Henry rated at beginning first-grade level. Although he did well on rhyming, he failed in giving words with specified initial sounds.

Answers to questions raised in Chapter 8:

1. *Is the child correctly classified as a disabled reader?* The answer is decidedly *yes.* He is more than five years behind his capabilities. He has normal intelligence (I.Q. of 96) and should be able to read early sixth-grade material.

2. *Who can most effectively give the remedial work?* A clinician should

give the remedial work. A long continued program of individual teaching will be necessary. Since the child's retardation extends to every reading skill, it constitutes too severe a problem to be handled in the classroom or at the school reading center.

3. *What is the nature of the training needed?* The program of instruction should include: (*a*) a highly individualized systematic program through use of a basic reader series as outlined in the accompanying teacher's manuals. In addition to the basic readers, the proper workbooks and supplementary readers must be used. (*b*) At appropriate intervals, supplementary materials should be employed to develop sight vocabulary, acquaintance with initial consonants, phrasing, phonetic analysis, and writing of sentences containing words learned in the teaching program. Construction of a picture dictionary is advisable. (*c*) All evidences of progress should be warmly commended.

4. *How can improvement be brought about most efficiently?* The teaching can be done best in a clinic. There should be close contact with the child's regular school work and with his home. Arrangements were made for Henry to come to the Clinic for tutoring for three hours weekly.

5. *Are there any limiting conditions within the child that must be considered?* There is nothing of great importance. His vision and hearing are normal. Since he appears undernourished, the teacher must be alert for signs of fatigue. His attitude is good. He seems anxious to learn to read "like other kids."

6. *Are there any environmental conditions that might interfere with progress in reading?* The home situation is deplorable but there is little the teacher can do about it. However, encouraging notes sent to the home and the help of the school visiting social worker has led to a much improved attitude on the part of the parents. Also the situation became better when Henry's work in the Clinic was made an enjoyable experience for him.

At the end of two months training a second form of the *Gates Primary Reading Tests* was given. The scores follow:

Word Recognition, Grade 2.3
Sentence Reading, Grade 3.0
Paragraph Reading, Grade 2.2
Average Grade Score, 2.5

This was gratifying progress. Henry was now exceedingly proud of his reading ability. Self-confidence was increasing at the Clinic, in school and at home. Motivation was high. He was anxious to continue with the tutoring.

Progress at each step was carefully evaluated. At the proper time, besides the continued use of the basic series of readers with supplementary materials, more emphasis was placed upon silent reading, the use of original stories, training for phrasing, the use of word-recognition techniques, and supplementary reading for pleasure.

Henry continued three lessons per week at the Clinic for two more months. Close contact was maintained with his schoolroom teacher and his home. At the end of the second two months, another form of the *Gates Primary Reading Tests* was given with the following results:

Word Recognition, Grade 2.9
Sentence Reading, Grade 3.0
Paragraph Reading, Grade 3.2
Average Grade Score, 3.03

Henry was now reading at beginning third-grade level. He still relied heavily on context clues, although he had improved in other word-recognition techniques, especially use of initial consonants. Despite his enthusiasm for his reading lessons, Henry tired frequently. The clinic program was continued for a third two-month period. At the end of this time, he was reading at grade 3.5. Henry still needs to have carefully individualized instruction continued. In time, he should be able to make the transfer to his regular classroom work with a minimum of difficulty.

Henry has been a child with extreme reading disability who is now responding well to a systematic program of remedial instruction. With three lessons per week over a period of six months, he has progressed from primer level to grade 3.5. He is the type of case that needs an extensive program of individualized tutoring to bring his achievement up to his capacity. Probably another four months in the Clinic will accomplish this.

Henry represents the type of case with extreme reading disability that is sometimes classified as a nonreader. For this type of case, the remedial work consists mainly of a basic course in reading with highly individualized instruction. The program must be flexible to allow for emphasis upon each special need as it arises.

Case 4. A sixth-grade boy with a general deficiency in all reading skills who has acquired a set of ineffective reading habits and has formed unfortunate attitudes toward reading

Dick was referred to the Psycho-Educational Clinic by his school because of reading difficulties. He was just beginning grade six (6.0). At that time, he was 10 years and 8 months old. Home conditions seemed normal.

Dick appeared well nourished and in good health. His vision (with glasses) and his hearing were normal as tested on the *Keystone Telebinocular Test* and an audiometer.

Adjustment. Dick gets along well with adults but feels insecure with children of his own age. He is particularly inadequate when participating socially in school tasks. His solution in such situations is withdrawal. His attitudes toward school work are poor, he lacks persistence, and he is inattentive.

Abilities. Dick was given the *Wechsler Intelligence Scale for Children.*

His I.Q. was 121 on the verbal scale, 106 on the performance scale, and 115 on the full scale. His M.A. was 12-3 and his Mental grade, 6.8. In arithmetic, he tested at grade 4.8; in language, 5.3; in spelling, 3.3. The *Gates Advanced Primary Reading Test* was given with the following results:

> Paragraph Reading, Grade 2.9
> Word Recognition, Grade 2.6
> Average Reading Grade, 2.75

Oral reading tested at grade 2.6. The *Gates Reading Diagnostic Tests* revealed a general retardation in all reading skills rather than any specific difficulties. Analysis of the oral reading performance and the special tests on visual and auditory techniques revealed grade scores in harmony with his silent reading level, i.e., not significantly different from grade 2.75. However, his sight vocabulary was inadequate. He read part of each sentence word by word and then guessed at the rest. He made no attempt to correct himself through use of context. When his first response was incorrect he seemed unable to work out any other. His attempts to use a spelling approach to word identification were usually unsuccessful. On an informal test, employing materials from a graded series of basic readers, Dick measured about grade 2.5 which corresponded well with his scores on the standardized reading tests.

Answers to questions raised in Chapter 8:

1. *Is the child correctly classified as a disabled reader?* Dick is reading about 3.7 grades below his capabilities (M.G., 6.8). This represents severe disability in reading. He should be able to read middle sixth-grade materials.

2. *Who can most effectively give the remedial work?* This case can, if necessary, be treated in the school reading center, but only if the remedial teacher has considerable time for individual work with this child. Since Dick's retardation is so great, it would probably be better to have him taught in a clinic.

3. *What is the nature of the training needed?* The program of instruction for Dick should include the following: (*a*) He should be given individual instruction in reading at the level of beginning second grade where he can experience real success. (*b*) There should be much supplementary reading at levels below the second grade where he will meet few problems in word recognition. This reading will help him to overcome his habit of reading word by word. Dick should have some systematic training in reading by thought units in both oral and silent reading. (*c*) The greatest emphasis should be upon a general developmental program of reading instruction to increase Dick's sight vocabulary, to enable him to learn better the techniques of word identification and recognition and to improve his skill in silent reading. Most of the materials for doing this will be found in a basic series of readers with the accompanying workbooks. Methods of teaching these materials are given in the teacher's manuals. (*d*) To correct Dick's

tendency to guess wildly after noting only the beginning of a word, (e.g., saying *short* for *shape*), he should have instruction in visual analysis of words and in the use of context to check his accuracy in word perception. (*e*) After some progress, there should be instruction in reading to note details, and in choosing topical sentences when reading paragraphs. (*f*) Since Dick prefers to read factual material, a special effort should be made to find materials of this sort that are pitched at a level of difficulty which he can handle.

4. *How can improvement be brought about most effectively?* Dick will need individual instruction over a period of several months. There should be three to four one-hour periods of tutoring per week, either by a remedial teacher in the school reading center or at a clinic. (Actually Dick came to the Minnesota Psycho-Educational Clinic four times per week for nine weeks.)

5. *Are there any limiting conditions within the child which must be considered?* Dick has definite feelings of insecurity, particularly in relation to school activities. He needs sympathy and understanding from both teachers and parents. It is especially important that he experience success in the remedial work from the beginning. The teacher should be patient and always ready to praise his progress.

6. *Are there any environmental conditions that might interfere with progress in reading?* The clinician should maintain close contacts with Dick's parents and his regular classroom teacher. While the parents have been sympathetic and co-operative from the beginning, the situation can be improved still more as the result of conferences with the clinician. Work in the clinic should be co-ordinated with Dick's work in his classroom in order to lessen emotional stress in his regular school work. Particularly, he should not be required to try to read material beyond his reading ability. The classroom teacher must co-operate fully in these arrangements and assure successful participation in class activities.

What happened was that Dick came to the clinic four times per week over a period of about nine weeks. The remedial program outlined above was carried out. He had 36 lessons in all. At the end of the tutoring, Dick was given another form of the *Gates Advanced Primary Reading Test* with the following results:

> Paragraph Reading, Grade 4.4
> Word Recognition, Grade 3.2
> Average Reading Grade, 3.8

These results show a gain of 1.05 grades in reading during the nine weeks of remedial training. At this time, Dick was still 3.0 grades behind his mental grade, and over two grades behind his grade placement. Although he has made some progress in acquiring word-recognition skills, Dick continues to have difficulty in word analysis. Specifically, he continues to be deficient in left-to-right orientation, use of context clues, visual analysis, blending, syllabication, and structural analysis (locating and using parts of compound words and word roots).

Although Dick has made noteworthy progress in reading, he is still a disability case. He is not yet ready to do the reading required in the sixth grade where he is located. There is need for continuing the individual tutoring for perhaps three or four months more.

In addition to his general retardation in reading, Dick is a child who has developed ineffective habits and unfortunate attitudes that are difficult to remedy. These difficulties have become thoroughly ingrained through years of neglect. In general, the longer a child remains a disability case, the longer the remedial training that is necessary to bring him up to his reading capacity will last.

Case 5. A beginning third-grade boy with immature techniques of word recognition

Harry was referred to the Psycho-Educational Clinic at the end of his second grade for help in reading. At that time he was 7 years, 9 months of age. He would be entering grade 3.0 in the following September. Harry comes from a good home. His father is a successful insurance salesman. The mother devotes herself to home-making. There is a sister two years older than Harry.

Harry appeared well nourished and healthy. Vision and hearing were normal. Although Harry was found to have mixed dominance (*Harris Tests of Lateral Dominance*), this did not seem related to the reading difficulty, since excessive reversals did not appear in his reading.

Adjustment. Harry seemed well adjusted at home although his mother was somewhat overprotective. Even though he showed signs of frustration in the reading situation, this did not transfer to other activities. In general, Harry was cheerful and co-operative in school and play activities. From the very beginning of the remedial tutoring, he had a fine attitude toward his reading problem. The school reported that he was socially immature for his age. The *Vineland Social Maturity Scale,* however, showed that Harry was average in social responsibility and self-care.

Abilities. Tests revealed beginning third-grade achievement in arithmetic (3.1), and grade 2.2 achievement in spelling. Harry was given the *Wechsler Intelligence Scale for Children.* His I.Q. was 119 on the verbal scale, 131 on the performance scale, and 127 on the full scale. Harry's mental age was 9-10 and his mental grade or reading expectancy was 3.5. The *Gates Primary Reading Tests* were given with the following results:

Word Recognition, Grade 1.5
Sentence Reading, Grade 2.3
Paragraph Reading, Grade 1.5
Average Reading Grade, 1.8

Oral reading was at grade 1.9. Scores on the *Gates Reading Diagnostic Tests* revealed the following difficulties: (1) a limited sight vocabulary; (2) an almost total lack of ability in word analysis; (3) inability to name the letters *u, y, w, r, f, v, h, j, q,* and *l,* and inability to give the sounds for the letters *u, y, i, x, f, r, m, l, g, j, w, h, n,* and *v;* (4) deficiency is listening to sounds given and in naming and rhyming them; (5) an unsuccessful spelling attack was used in attempts to identify words.

Answers to the questions raised in Chapter 8:

1. *Is the child correctly classified as a disabled reader?* Harry's reading performance at grade 1.8 is 1.7 grades behind his mental grade of 3.5. This indicates severe disability. He should be able to read material at middle third-grade level.

2. *Who can most effectively give the remedial work?* Harry will need individual tutoring which may extend over several weeks. This can best be done in a clinic.

3. *What is the nature of the training needed?* The program of instruction for Harry should include the following: (*a*) A basic reading program, beginning at the primer level. Stress should be placed upon the word-recognition activities which accompany each unit. (*b*) There should be a large amount of reading in supplementary materials that are easy enough for him to read with pleasure. (*c*) He should be encouraged to do leisure reading at home as the program gets under way. (*d*) Various special materials and devices may be used at appropriate times for drill on the names and sounds of letters, and on procedures employed in word recognition.

4. *How can improvement be brought about most effectively?* Remedial instruction for Harry is best done in a reading clinic or by a remedial teacher in the school reading center.

5. *Are there any limiting conditions within the child which must be considered?* For the most part, Harry is a happy, well-adjusted child. No special psychotherapy is indicated.

6. *Are there any environmental conditions that might interfere with progress in reading?* The parents should be less protective of Harry. There should be opportunities for him to become more self-reliant. For instance, the parents should provide Harry with small home responsibilities with stress on his obligations in these tasks.

Harry attended the University Psycho-Educational Clinic for 10 weeks during the summer. The program outlined above was carried out. A second form of the *Gates Primary Reading Tests* was administered at the end of the tutoring with the following results:

Word Recognition, Grade 2.65
Sentence Reading, Grade 2.90
Paragraph Reading, Grade 2.30
Average Reading Grade, 2.62.

This represents a gain of about 0.8 grade during the ten weeks. Since Harry is still a remedial case, he should have some additional individual instruction if he is to handle third-grade work satisfactorily. When Harry returns to the third grade in September, the reading materials should be adjusted to his needs. Unless the classroom teacher devotes some individual attention to Harry's reading problems, he is likely to continue to be in difficulty.

The progress made by Harry in the clinic appears to be due to these facts: (1) He is a relatively bright boy. (2) He worked conscientiously and thoroughly and with enthusiasm throughout the tutoring. (3) The well-rounded developmental reading program was effective. (4) The supplementary drills on letter names, letter sounds, and techniques of word recognition were effective. (5) The guidance in supplementary reading was successful in inducing him to read for pleasure.

SELECTED READINGS

Gates, Arthur I., *The improvement of reading,* 3rd ed. New York: The Macmillan Company, 1947, Chap. 17.

Harris, Albert J., *How to increase reading ability,* 3rd ed. New York: Longmans, Green & Company, 1956, Chap. 19.

Monroe, Marion, *Children who cannot read.* Chicago: University of Chicago Press, 1932, Chap. 8.

Robinson, Helen M., *Why pupils fail in reading.* Chicago: University of Chicago Press, 1946, Chap. 11.

Strang, Ruth, McCullough, Constance M., and Traxler, Arthur E., *Problems in the improvement of reading,* 2nd ed. New York: McGraw-Hill Book Company, Inc., 1955, Chap. 20.

Witty, Paul, and Kopel, David, *Reading and the educative process.* Boston: Ginn and Company, 1939, Chap. 9.

BIBLIOGRAPHY

1. ADAMS, F., GRAY, L., and REESE, D., *Teaching children to read*. New York: The Ronald Press Company, 1949.
2. ANDERSON, I. H., and DEARBORN, W. F., *The psychology of teaching reading*. New York: The Ronald Press Company, 1952.
3. ARTLEY, A. S., Teaching word meanings through context. *Elementary English Review*, 1943, 20, 68-74.
4. ————, A study of certain relationships between general reading comprehension and reading comprehension in a specific subject matter area. *Journal of Educational Research*, 1944, 37, 464-473.
5. AXLINE, V. M., Non-directive therapy for poor readers. *Journal of Consulting Psychology*, 1947, 11, 61-69.
6. BEAR, R. M., The Dartmouth program for diagnostic and remedial work with special reference to visual factors. *Educational Record*, Supplement No. 12, 1939, 20, 69-88.
7. BENNETT, C. C., *An inquiry into the genesis of poor reading*. New York: Bureau of Publications, Teachers College, Columbia University, 1938.
8. BETTS, E. A., *Foundations of reading instruction*. New York: American Book Company, 1946.
9. ———— (ed.) *The American adventure series*. Chicago: Wheeler Publishing Company, 1948.
10. ———— and AUSTIN, A. S., *Visual problems of school children*. Chicago: The Professional Press, Inc., 1941.
11. ———— and WELCH, C. M., *Study books* to accompany the *Betts basic readers*. New York: American Book Company, 1951-1953.
12. BILLS, R. E., Non-directive play therapy with retarded readers. *Journal of Consulting Psychology*, 1950, 14, 140-149.
13. BIRD, G. E., Personality factors in learning. *Personal Journal*, 1927, 6, 56-59.
14. BLAIR, G. M., *Diagnostic and remedial teaching*, rev. ed. New York: The Macmillan Company, 1956.
15. BLANCHARD, P., Reading disabilities in relation to maladjustment. *Mental Hygiene*, 1928, 12, 772-788.
16. BOND, Elden A., *Tenth-grade abilities and achievements*. New York: Bureau of Publications, Teachers College, Columbia University, 1940.
17. BOND, Eva, *Reading and ninth-grade achievement*. New York: Bureau of Publications, Teachers College, Columbia University, 1938.
18. BOND, G. L., *The auditory and speech characteristics of poor readers*. New York: Bureau of Publications, Teachers College, Columbia University, 1935.
19. ———— Goals of reading instruction. *Reading in the content subjects*. Kent State University Bulletin, No. 5, Vol. 39. Kent (Ohio): College of Education, Kent State University, 1951, 13-19.
20. ————, CLYMER, T., and HOYT, C. J., *Silent reading diagnostic tests*. Chicago: Lyons and Carnahan, 1955.

451

21. BOND, G. L., and CUDDY, M. C. (or BOND, G. L., DORSEY, G., CUDDY, M. C., and WISE, K.), *Fun to do books to accompany The development reading series.* Chicago: Lyons and Carnahan, 1949 and 1953.

22. ——— and CUDDY, M. C., *Bond plan manual for meeting new friends.* Chicago: Lyons and Carnahan, 1954.

23. ——— and CUDDY, M. C., *The developmental reading series* (Regular and Classmate Editions). Chicago: Lyons and Carnahan, 1955.

24. ——— and CUDDY, M. C., *Fun to do book for Days of adventure.* Chicago: Lyons and Carnahan, 1951.

25. ——— and FAY, L. C., A report of the University of Minnesota reading clinic. *Journal of Educational Research,* 1950, 43, 385-390.

26. ——— and FAY, L. C., A comparison of the performance of good and poor readers on the individual items of the Stanford-Binet Scale, Forms L and M. *Journal of Educational Research,* 1950, 43, 475-479.

27. ——— and HANDLAN, B., *Adapting instruction in reading to individual differences.* Series on individualization of instruction, No. 5. Minneapolis: University of Minnesota Press, 1948.

28. ——— and WAGNER, E. B., *Teaching the child to read,* rev. ed. New York: The Macmillan Company, 1950.

29. ——— and WAGNER, E. B., *Child growth in reading.* Chicago: Lyons and Carnahan, 1955.

30. BROOM, M. E., DUNCAN, M. A. A., EMIG, D., and STUEBER, J., *Effective reading instruction,* 2nd ed. New York: McGraw-Hill Book Company, Inc., 1951.

31. BRUECKNER, L. J., and BOND, G. L., *The diagnosis and treatment of learning difficulties.* New York: Appleton-Century-Crofts, Inc., 1955.

32. BUSWELL, G. T., *Non-oral reading: A Study of its use in the Chicago public schools.* Suppl. Educ. Monog. No. 60. Chicago: University of Chicago Press, 1945.

33. CARLSON, T. R., *The relationships between speed and accuracy of comprehension of reading.* Unpublished Ph.D. thesis, University of Minnesota, Minneapolis, 1946.

34. CARMICHAEL, L., EVANS, E., and DEARBORN, W. F., *Special disabilities in learning to read and write.* Cambridge: Harvard University Press, 1925, 1-6; 36-49.

35. CASON, E. B., *Mechanical methods for increasing the speed of reading.* New York: Bureau of Publications, Teachers College, Columbia University, 1943.

36. CLYMER, T. W., *The influence of reading ability on the validity of group intelligence tests.* Unpublished Ph.D. thesis, University of Minnesota, Minneapolis, 1952.

37. COLE, L., *The improvement of reading.* New York: Farrar and Rinehart, Inc., 1938.

37a. ——— *The teachers handbook of technical vocabulary.* Bloomington (Ill.): Public School Publishing Company, 1940.

38. COOK, Walter W., *Grouping and promotion in the elementary schools.* Series on individualization of instruction, No. 2. Minneapolis: University of Minnesota Press, 1941.

39. CRANE, J. A., *Reading difficulties as a social work problem.* Unpublished M.A. thesis, McGill University, Montreal, Quebec (Canada), 1950.

40. CROSLAND, H. R., Superior elementary-school readers contrasted with in-

ferior readers in letter-position, 'range of attention' scores. *Journal of Educational Research*, 1939, 32, 410-427.

41. DAHL, L. A., *Public school audiometry: principles and methods.* Danville (Ill.): The Interstate Printers and Publishers, 1949.

42. DALE, Edgar, and CHALL, Jeanne, Formula for predicting readability. *Educational Research Bulletin*, 27: 11-20 ff., 37-45, Ohio State University, Columbus (Ohio): January, February, 1948.

43. DAVIDSON, H. P., A study of the confusing letters, b, d, p, and q. *Journal of Genetic Psychology*, 1935, 47, 458-468.

44. DEARBORN, W. F., Teaching reading to non-readers. *Elementary School Journal*, 1929, 30, 266-269.

45. ———— The nature of special abilities and disabilities. *School and Society*, 1930, 31, 632-636.

46. ———— Ocular and manual dominance in dyslexia. *Psychological Bulletin*, 1931, 28, 704.

47. ———— Structural factors which condition special disability in reading. *Proceedings of the American Association of Mental Deficiency*, 1933, 38, 266-283.

48. ———— The nature and causation of disabilities in reading. *Recent trends in reading*, Suppl. Educ. Monog. No. 49. Chicago: University of Chicago Press, 1939.

49. ———— and ANDERSON, I. H., Controlled reading by means of a motion picture technique. *The Psychological Record*, 1938, 2, 219-227.

50. ———— and ANDERSON, I. H., Aniseikonia as related to disability in reading. *Journal of Experimental Psychology*, 1938, 23, 559-577.

51. DENECKE, L., Fifth-graders study the comic books. *Elementary English Review*, 1945, 22, 6-8.

52. DOLCH, E. W., *A manual for remedial reading,* 2nd ed. Champaign (Ill.): The Garrard Press, 1945.

53. ———— *Problems in reading.* Champaign (Ill.): The Garrard Press, 1948.

54. ———— *Teaching primary reading,* 2nd ed. Champaign (Ill.): The Garrard Press, 1950.

55. ———— *Psychology and teaching of reading,* 2nd ed. Champaign (Ill.): The Garrard Press, 1951.

56. DURRELL, D. D., *Improvement of basic reading abilities.* Yonkers (N. Y.): World Book Company, 1940.

57. ———— *Durrell analysis of reading difficulty,* rev. ed. Yonkers (N. Y.): World Book Company, 1955.

58. EAMES, T. H., A comparison of the ocular characteristics of unselected and reading disability groups. *Journal of Educational Research*, 1932, 25, 211-215.

59. ———— The anatomical basis of lateral dominance anomalies. *American Journal of Orthopsychiatry*, 1934, 4, 524-528.

60. ———— A frequency study of physical handicaps in reading disability and unselected groups. *Journal of Educational Research*, 1935, 29, 1-5.

61. ———— The reliability and validity of the Eames eye test. *Journal of Educational Research*, 1940, 33, 524-527.

62. EDSON, W. H., *A study of the relationships between visual characteristics and specific silent reading abilities.* Unpublished Ph.D. thesis, University of Minnesota, Minneapolis, 1950.

63. EURICH, A. C., The relation of speed of reading to comprehension. *School and Society*, 1930, 32, 404-406.

63a. *The Everyreader Series.* St. Louis: Webster Publishing Company.

64. FARRIS, L. P., Visual defects as factors influencing achievement in reading. *California Journal of Secondary Education,* 1934, 10, 50-51.

65. —— Visual defects as factors influencing achievement in reading. *Journal of Experimental Education,* 1936, 5, 58-60.

66. FAY, L. C., *The relationship between specific reading skills and selected areas of sixth-grade achievement.* Unpublished Ph.D. thesis, University of Minnesota, Minneapolis, 1948.

67. —— What research has to say about reading in the content areas. *The Reading Teacher,* 1954, 8, 68-72.

68. FENDRICK, P. A., *Visual characteristics of poor readers.* New York: Bureau of Publications, Teachers College, Columbia University, 1935.

69. —— and BOND, G. L., Delinquency and reading. *Pedagogical Seminary and Journal of Genetic Psychology,* 1936, 48, 236-243.

70. FERNALD, G. M., *Remedial techniques in basic school subjects.* New York: McGraw-Hill Book Company, Inc., 1943.

71. FISHER, B., A psychologist's evaluation of teachers' reports and suggestions for their improvement. *Educational Administration and Supervision,* 1952, 38, 175-179.

72. —— Group therapy with retarded readers. *Journal of Educational Psychology,* 1953, 44, 354-360.

73. FORD, F. R., *Diseases of the nervous system in infancy, childhood, and adolescence,* 2nd ed. Springfield (Ill.): Charles C. Thomas, 1944, 877-886.

74. GANN, E., *Reading difficulty and personality organization.* New York: King's Crown Press, 1945.

75. GATES, A. I., *Interest and ability in reading.* New York: The Macmillan Company, 1930.

76. —— Maladjustments due to failure in reading. *School Executive,* 1933, 55, 379-380.

77. —— Failure in reading and social maladjustment. *Journal of the National Education Association,* 1936, 25, 205-206.

78. —— The role of personality maladjustment in reading disability. *Journal of Genetic Psychology,* 1941, 59, 77-83.

79. —— *The improvement of reading,* 3rd ed. New York: The Macmillan Company, 1947.

80. —— *Gates reading diagnostic tests,* rev. ed. New York: Bureau of Publications, Teachers College, Columbia University, 1953.

81. —— and BENNETT, C. C., *Reversal tendencies in reading: Causes, diagnosis, prevention and correction.* New York: Bureau of Publications, Teachers College, Columbia University, 1933.

82. —— and BOND, G. L., Some outcomes of instruction in the Speyer Experimental School (P.S. 500). *Teachers College Record,* 1936, 38, 206-217.

83. —— and BOND, G. L., Failure in reading and social maladjustment. *Journal of the National Education Association,* 1936, 25, 205-207.

84. —— and BOND, G. L., Relation of handedness, eye-sighting, and acuity dominance to reading. *Journal of Educational Psychology,* 1936, 27, 455-456.

84a. —— and CASON, E. C., An evaluation of tests for diagnosis of ability to read by phrases or "thought units." *Elementary School Journal,* 1945, 46, 23-32.

85. —— and PEARDON, C. C., *Gates-Peardon practice exercises in reading.*

New York: Bureau of Publications, Teachers College, Columbia University.

86. GESELL, A., and AMATRUDA, C. S., *Developmental diagnosis: normal and abnormal child development.* New York: Paul B. Hoeber, Inc., 1941.

87. GILMORE, J. V., *Gilmore oral reading test.* Yonkers (N. Y.): World Book Company, 1952.

88. GOODENOUGH, F. L., *Mental Testing.* New York: Rinehart and Company, 1949.

89. GRAY, W. S., *Standardized oral reading paragraphs.* Bloomington (Ill.): Public School Publishing Company, 1916.

90. ———— Reading as an aid in learning. *Reading in the elementary school.* Forty-eighth Yearbook of the National Society for the Study of Education, Part II, Chicago: University of Chicago Press, 1949, 233-253.

91. ———— *On their own in reading.* Chicago: Scott, Foresman and Company, 1948.

92. HAEFNER, R., *The educational significance of left-handedness.* New York: Bureau of Publications, Teachers College, Columbia University, 1929.

93. HAMILTON, J. A., *Toward proficient reading.* Claremont (Calif.): Saunders Press, 1939.

94. HARRIS, A. J., *How to increase reading ability,* 3rd ed. New York: Longman's, Green & Company, 1956.

95. HARRISON, M. L., *Reading readiness,* rev. ed. Boston: Houghton Mifflin Company, 1939.

96. HAUGH, O. M., *The comparative value of reading and listening in the acquisition of information and the changing of attitudes of eleventh-grade students.* Unpublished Ph.D. thesis, University of Minnesota, Minneapolis, 1950.

97. HEGGE, T. G., KIRK, S. A., and KIRK, W. D., *Remedial reading drills.* Ann Arbor (Mich.): George Wahr, 1945.

98. HENRY, S., Children's audiograms in relation to reading attainment. *Journal of Genetic Psychology,* 1947, 70, 211-231; 1948, 71, 3-63.

99. HESTER, K. B., *Teaching every child to read.* New York: Harper and Brothers, 1955.

100. HILDRETH, G., Reversals in reading and writing. *Journal of Educational Psychology,* 1934, 25, 1-20.

101. ———— *Personality and interest inventory.* New York: Bureau of Publications, Teachers College, Columbia University, 1935.

102. ———— *Readiness for school beginners.* Yonkers (N. Y.): World Book Company, 1950.

103. HINSHELWOOD, J., *Congenital word-blindness.* London: H. K. Lewis and Company, Ltd., 1917.

104. HOLLINGSHEAD, A. D., *An evaluation of the use of certain educational and mental measurements for purposes of classifications.* New York: Bureau of Publications, Teachers College, Columbia University, 1928.

105. HUBER, M. B., *The influence of intelligence upon children's reading interest.* New York: Bureau of Publications, Teachers College, Columbia University, 1928.

106. HULL, Clark L., Variability in amount of different traits possessed by individuals. *Journal of Educational Psychology,* 1927, 18, 97-102.

107. IMUS, H. A., ROTHNEY, J. W. M., and BEAR, R. M., *An evaluation of visual factors in reading.* Hanover (N. H.): Dartmouth College Publications, 1938.

108. Iowa elementary teachers handbook, Vol. II, *Reading.* Des Moines: Department of Public Instruction, State of Iowa, 1943.
109. JASTAK, J., Interferences in reading. *Psychological Bulletin,* 1934, 31, 244-272.
110. JENSEN, M. B., Reading deficiency as related to cerebral injury and to neurotic behavior. *Journal of Applied Psychology,* 1944, 65, 67-88.
111. JOHNSON, E. M., *et al., Library of modern wonder books.* Columbus (Ohio): American Education Press.
112. KARLSEN, B., *A comparison of some educational and psychological characteristics of successful and unsuccessful readers at the elementary school level.* Unpublished Ph.D. thesis, University of Minnesota, Minneapolis, 1954.
113. KENNEDY, H., A study of children's hearing as it relates to reading. *Journal of Experimental Education,* 1942, 10, 238-251.
114. KIRK, S. A., *Teaching reading to slow-learning children.* Boston: Houghton Mifflin Company, 1940.
115. KNOX, G. E., Classroom symptoms of visual difficulty. *Clinical studies in reading:* II, Suppl. Educ. Monog. No. 77. Chicago: University of Chicago Press, 1953, 97-101.
116. KRANTZ, LaVern, *The relationship of reading abilities and basic skills of the elementary school to success in the interpretation of the content materials in the high school.* Unpublished Ph.D. thesis, University of Minnesota, Minneapolis, 1955.
117. LADD, M. R., *The relation of social, economic, and personal characteristics to reading ability.* New York: Bureau of Publications, Teachers College, Columbia University, 1933.
118. LARRICK, Nancy, Making the most of children's interests. *Education,* 1953, 73, 523-531.
119. LAZAR, May, *Individualization of instruction in reading.* Educational Research Bulletin No. 1. New York: Board of Education of the City of New York, 1941.
120. ———— ed. *The retarded reader in the junior high school,* Publication No. 31. New York: Board of Education of the City of New York, 1952.
121. LEE, D. M., *The importance of reading for achieving in grades four, five and six.* New York: Bureau of Publications, Teachers College, Columbia University, 1933.
122. Literature Committee of the Association for Childhood Education, *Told under the blue umbrella.* New York: The Macmillan Company, 1947, 158-159.
123. LORGE, Irving, Predicting readability. *Teachers College Record,* March 1944, 45, 404-419.
124. MATEER, F., *Glands and efficient behavior.* New York: Appleton-Century-Crofts, Inc., 1935.
125. MCCALLISTER, J. M., *Remedial and corrective instruction in reading.* New York: Appleton-Century-Crofts, Inc., 1936.
126. MCCULLOUGH, C. M., The recognition of context clues in reading. *Elementary English Review,* 1945, 22, 1-5.
127. MCKEE, P., *The teaching of reading in the elementary school.* Boston: Houghton Mifflin Company, 1948.
128. MCLEOD, B., *Teachers' problems with exceptional children, IV. Deaf and hard-of-hearing children.* Office of Education Pamphlet No. 54. Washington: U.S. Government Printing Office, 1934.

129. MCNALLY, H. J., *The readability of certain type sizes and forms in sight-saving classes.* New York: Bureau of Publications, Teachers College, Columbia University, 1943.

130. *Minnesota scale of parents opinions.* Minneapolis: Institute of Child Welfare, University of Minnesota.

131. MONROE, M., *Children who cannot read.* Chicago: University of Chicago Press, 1932.

132. ———— Diagnostic and remedial procedures in reading. *Educational Record*, Supplement No. 11, 1938, 105-113.

133. ———— *Growing into reading.* Chicago: Scott, Foresman and Company, 1951.

134. ———— and BACKUS, Bertie, *Remedial reading.* Boston: Houghton Mifflin Company, 1937.

135. OLSON, W. C., Reading as a function of total growth. *Reading in pupil development*, Suppl. Educ. Monog. No. 51. Chicago: University of Chicago Press, 1940, 233-237.

136. ORTON, S. T., *Reading, writing and speech problems in children.* New York: W. W. Norton & Company, Inc., 1937.

137. PARK, G. E., and BURRI, C., The relation of various eye conditions and reading achievement. *Journal of Educational Psychology*, 1943, 34, 290-299.

138. PERCIVAL, Walter P., *A study of the causes and subjects of school failure.* Unpublished Ph.D. thesis, Teachers College, Columbia University, New York, 1926.

139. POLMANTIER, P. C., *A comparative study of the reading interests and abilities of delinquent and nondelinquent boys.* Unpublished Ph.D. thesis, University of Minnesota, Minneapolis, 1941.

140. REYNOLDS, M. C., *A study of the relationships between auditory characteristics and specific silent reading abilities.* Unpublished Ph.D. thesis, University of Minnesota, Minneapolis, 1950.

141. ROBINSON, H. M., *Why pupils fail in reading.* Chicago: University of Chicago Press, 1946.

142. ———— and HUELSMAN, C. B., Jr., Visual efficiency and progress in learning to read. *Clinical studies in reading: II*, Suppl. Educ. Monog. No. 77. Chicago: University of Chicago Press, 1953, 31-63.

143. ROSS, C. C., *Measurement in today's schools*, 3rd ed. revised by J. C. Stanley. New York: Prentice-Hall, Inc., 1954.

144. RUSSELL, D. H., *Children learn to read.* Boston: Ginn and Company, 1949.

145. ———— and KARP, E. E., *Reading aids through the grades*, rev. ed. New York: Bureau of Publications, Teachers College, Columbia University, 1951.

146. ———— and MCCULLOUGH, C. M. (or WULFING, G., or OUSLEY, O.), *My do and learn books* to accompany the *Ginn basic readers.* Boston: Ginn and Company, 1948-1950.

147. SANDIN, A. A., *Social and emotional adjustments of regularly promoted and non-promoted pupils.* New York: Bureau of Publications, Teachers College, Columbia University, 1944.

148. SCHUMMERS, J. L., *A follow-up study of 52 clinical reading cases four years after clinical training.* Unpublished study, University of Minnesota Psycho-Educational Clinic, Minneapolis, 1955.

149. SELZER, C. A., *Lateral dominance and visual fusion: the application to*

differences in reading, writing, spelling, and speech. Harvard Monographs in Education, No. 12. Cambridge: Harvard University Press, 1933.

150. SHORES, J. H., *Reading and study skills as related to comprehension of science and history in the ninth grade.* Unpublished Ph.D. thesis, University of Minnesota, Minneapolis, 1940.

151. —— Skills related to the ability to read history and science. *Journal of Educational Research,* 1943, 36, 584-593.

152. SLOANE, A. E., Massachusetts vision test. *Archives of Ophthalmology,* 1940, 24, 924-939.

153. SMITH, D. V., Literature and personal reading. *Reading in the elementary school.* Forty-eighth Yearbook of the National Society for the Study of Education, Part II. Chicago: University of Chicago Press, 1949, 205-232.

154. —— The goals of the literature period and the grade sequence of desirable experiences. *Improving reading in all curriculum areas.* Suppl. Educ. Monog. No. 76. Chicago: University of Chicago Press, 1952, 188-194.

155. SORNSON, H. H., *A longitudinal study of the relationship between various child behavior ratings and success in reading.* Unpublished Ph.D. thesis, University of Minnesota, Minneapolis, 1950.

156. SPACHE, G., A binocular reading test. *Journal of Educational Psychology,* 1943, 34, 368-373.

157. —— A new readability formula for primary-grade reading. *Elementary School Journal,* March 1953, 52, 410-413.

158. STRANG, R., *Problems in the improvement of reading in high school and college,* rev. ed. Lancaster (Pa.): The Science Press, 1940.

159. —— Relationships between certain aspects of intelligence and certain aspects of reading. *Educational and Psychological Measurement,* 1943, 3, 355-359.

160. —— Diagnosis and remediation of reading difficulties in content fields. *Improving reading in content fields.* Suppl. Educ. Monog. No. 62, Chicago: University of Chicago Press, 1947, 197-201.

161. —— McCULLOUGH, C. M., and TRAXLER, A. E., *Problems in the improvement of reading,* 2nd ed. New York: McGraw-Hill Book Company, Inc., 1955.

162. STROMBERG, E. L., The relation of measures of visual acuity and ametropia to reading speed. *Journal of Applied Psychology,* 1938, 22, 70-78.

163. SWANSON, D. E., and TIFFIN, J., Betts' physiological approach to the analysis of reading disabilities as applied to the college level. *Journal of Educational Research,* 1936, 29, 447-448.

164. SWENSON, E. J., A study of the relationships among various types of reading scores on general and science material. *Journal of Educational Research,* 1942, 36, 81-90.

165. TAYLOR, E. A., *Controlled reading.* Chicago: University of Chicago Press, 1937.

166. TEEGARDEN, L., Clinical identification of the prospective non-reader. *Child Development,* 1932, 3, 346-358.

167. THOMPSON, Helen, *An experimental study of the beginning reading of deaf-mutes.* New York: Bureau of Publications, Teachers College, Columbia University, 1927.

168. TINKER, M. A., The relation of speed to comprehension in reading. *School and Society,* 1932, 36, 158-160.

169. —— The role of eye movements in diagnostic and remedial reading. *School and Society,* 1934, 39, 147-148.

170. TINKER, M. A., Remedial methods for non-readers. *School and Society,* 1934, 40, 524-526.

171. ——— Eye movements in reading. *Journal of Educational Research,* 1936, 30, 241-277.

172. ———Speed versus comprehension in reading as affected by level of difficulty. *Journal of Educational Psychology,* 1939, 30, 81-94.

173. ——— Rate of work in reading performance as measured in standardized tests. *Journal of Educational Psychology,* 1945, 36, 217-228.

174. ——— The study of eye movements in reading. *Psychological Bulletin,* 1946, 43, 93-120.

175. ——— *Teaching elementary reading.* New York: Appleton-Century-Crofts, Inc., 1952.

176. TRAXLER, A. E., A study of the California Test of Mental Maturity: Advanced Battery. *Journal of Educational Research,* 1939, 32, 329-335.

177. ——— with assistance of SEDER, Margaret, *Ten years of research in reading.* Bulletin No. 32. New York: Educational Records Bureau, 1941.

178. ——— and TOWNSEND, Agatha, *Another five years of research in reading.* Bulletin No. 46. New York: Educational Records Bureau, 1946.

179. ——— and TOWNSEND, Agatha, *Eight more years of research in reading.* Bulletin No. 64. New York: Educational Records Bureau, 1955.

180. WALDMAN, J. L., WADE, F. A., and ARETZ, C. W., *Hearing and the school child.* Philadelphia: Temple University, 1930, 68-90.

181. WATKINS, M., *A comparison of the reading proficiencies of normal-progress and reading disability cases of the same I.Q. and reading level.* Unpublished Ph.D. thesis, University of Minnesota, Minneapolis, 1953.

182. WESTOVER, F. L., *Controlled eye movements versus practice exercises in reading.* New York: Bureau of Publications, Teachers College, Columbia University, 1946.

183. WHEELER, L. R., and WHEELER, V. D., The relationship between reading ability and intelligence among university freshmen. *Journal of Educational Psychology,* 1949, 40, 230-238.

184. WILKING, S. V., Personality maladjustment as a causative factor in reading disability. *Elementary School Journal,* 1941, 42, 268-279.

185. WITTY, Paul, *Reading in modern education.* Boston: D. C. Heath & Company, 1949.

186. ——— *How to become a better reader.* Chicago: Science Research Associates, Inc., 1953.

187. ——— and GOLDBERG, S., The army's training program for illiterate, non-English-speaking, and educationally retarded men. *Elementary English Review,* 1943, 20, 306-311.

188. ——— and KOPEL, D., Factors associated with the etiology of reading disability. *Journal of Educational Research,* 1936, 29, 449-459.

189. ——— and KOPEL, D., Sinistrad and mixed manual-ocular behavior in reading disability. *Journal of Educational Psychology,* 1936, 27, 119-134.

190. ——— and KOPEL, D., *Reading and the educative process.* Boston: Ginn and Company, 1939.

191. ——— and SCHACTER, H. S., Hypothyroidism as a factor in maladjustment. *Journal of Psychology,* 1936, 2, 377-392.

APPENDIX I: TESTS

Note: Name of publisher is abbreviated. The key to abbreviations is given below. Prices may be obtained from the most recent catalogues which publishers will send upon request. The prices are not quoted here because they change frequently. Representative tests rather than a complete list are given.

KEY TO PUBLISHING COMPANIES

APC   Acorn Publishing Company, Inc., Rockville Center, N. Y.

BEM   Bureau of Educational Measurements, Kansas State Teachers College, Emporia, Kansas.

BP   Bureau of Publications, Teachers College, Columbia University, 525 W. 120 St., New York 27, N. Y.

CDRT   Committee on Diagnostic Reading Tests, Inc., Kingscote Apt. 3G, 419 W. 119 St., New York 27, N. Y.

CTB   California Test Bureau, 5916 Hollywood Blvd., Los Angeles 28, Calif.

CTD-ETS   Cooperative Test Division, Educational Testing Service, Princeton, N. J.

EMH   E. M. Hale and Co., 320 S. Barstow St., Eau Claire, Wis.

ERB   Educational Records Bureau, 21 Audubon Ave., New York 32, N. Y.

ETB   Educational Test Bureau, 720 Washington Ave. S.E., Minneapolis 14, Minn.

GP   Garrard Press, 119 W. Park Ave., Champaign, Ill.

HM   Houghton Mifflin Co., 2 Park St., Boston 7, Mass.

LC   Lyons and Carnahan, 2500 Prairie Ave., Chicago 16, Ill.

OSUP   Ohio State University Press, Columbus, Ohio.

PC   Psychological Corporation, 522 Fifth Ave., New York 18, N. Y.

PSP   Public School Publishing Co., 509-513 North East St., Bloomington, Ill.

SC   Stech Co., Austin, Tex.

SRA   Science Research Associates, Inc., 57 W. Grand Ave., Chicago 10, Ill.

ST   C. H. Stoelting Co., 424 N. Homan Ave., Chicago, Ill.

SUP   Stanford University Press, Stanford University, Calif.

VW   Van Wagenen, Psycho-Educational Research Laboratories, 1729 Irving Ave. S., Minneapolis 5, Minn.

WBC   World Book Co., 313 Park Hill Ave., Yonkers, N. Y.

WPC   Webster Publishing Co., 1808 Washington Ave., St. Louis 3, Mo.

A. REPRESENTATIVE INTELLIGENCE TESTS

American Council on Education Psychological Examination for High School Students prepared by publisher from materials developed by L. L. Thurstone and T. G. Thurstone. CTD-ETS, 1952. Grades 9-12. New form issued annually. Time: 65 minutes. Scores for quantitative reasoning, linguistic reasoning, and total. Group test.

Arthur Point Scale of Performance Tests by G. Arthur. ST, 1943 (form I), PC, 1947 (form II). Ages 4.5 or 5.5 to superior adults. Two forms. Time: 45-90 minutes. Individual test.

California Test of Mental Maturity by E. T. Sullivan, W. W. Clark and E. W. Tiegs. CTB, 1951. Grades: kgn-1, 1-3, 4-8, 7-10 and adults, 9-16 and adults. One form. Time: 65-105 minutes at different levels. Three scores: total mental, language, non-language. The language, the non-language, and a short-form combination (60 minutes) of the two are available as separate tests. Group test.

Chicago Non-Verbal Examination by A. W. Brown, S. P. Stein and P. L. Rohrer. PC, 1947. Age 6-adult. One form. Time: 40 minutes. Group test.

Chicago Tests of Primary Mental Abilities by L. L. Thurstone and T. G. Thurstone, SRA, 1941-48. Ages 11-17. One form for long test, two forms for shortened version. Time: 25 minutes for short form, 240 minutes for long form. Group test.

Detroit Intelligence Test by H. J. Baker, PSP, 1942. Grades 2-4, 5-9, 9-16. Two forms. Time: 30-45 minutes. Group test.

Henmon-Nelson Tests of Mental Ability: The Clapp-Young Self-Marking Tests by V. A. C. Henmon and M. J. Nelson. HM, 1950. Grades 3-8, 7-12, 12-16. Two forms. Time: 30 minutes. Group test.

Kuhlmann-Anderson Intelligence Tests, Sixth Edition by F. Kuhlmann and R. G. Anderson. ETB, 1952. Grades 1, 2, 3, 4, 5, 6, 7-8, 9-12. One form. Time: 30-45 minutes. Group test.

Kuhlmann-Finch Intelligence Tests by F. Kuhlmann and F. H. Finch (G. L. Betts, ed.). ETB, 1952. Grades 1, 2, 3, 4, 5, 6, junior high school, senior high school. Time: 25 minutes. Group test.

Modified Alpha Examination, Form 9 by F. L. Wells. PC, 1951. Grades 7-12 and adults. One form. Time: 24 minutes. Group test.

National Intelligence Tests by M. E. Haggerty, L. M. Terman, E. L. Thorndike, and G. M. Whipple. WBC, Grades 3-8. Three forms. Time: 20 minutes. Group test.

Otis Self-Administering Tests of Mental Ability by A. S. Otis. WBC, 1928. Grades 4-9, 9-16. Four forms. Time: 20 minutes. Group test.

Otis Quick-Scoring Mental Ability Tests by A. S. Otis. WBC, 1939. Grades 1.5-4, 4-9, 9-16. Two to four forms. Time: 20-30 minutes. Group test.

Pintner General Ability Tests: Verbal Series by R. Pintner, B. V. Cunningham, W. N. Durost. WBC, 1923-46. *Pintner-Cunningham Primary Test*, Grades kgn-2, three forms, 45 minutes. *Pintner-Durost Elementary Test*, Grades 2.5-4.5, two forms, 45 minutes. *Pintner Intermediate Test*, Grades 4.5-9.5, two forms, 45 minutes. *Pintner Advanced Test*, Grades 9+, two forms, 45 minutes. Group tests.

Pintner Non-Language Primary Mental Test by R. Pintner. BP, 1930. Grades kgn-2. One form. Untimed. Group test.

Revised Stanford-Binet Scale by L. M. Terman and M. A. Merrill. HM, 1937. Ages 2-maturity. Two forms. Time: 30-90 minutes. Individual test.

Terman-McNemar Test of Mental Ability by L. M. Terman and Q. McNemar. WBC, 1942. Grades 7-12. Two forms. Time: 40 minutes. Group test.

Wechsler-Bellevue Intelligence Scale by D. Wechsler. PC, 1947. Ages 10-70.

Verbal and performance scores. Two forms. Time: 40-60 minutes. Individual test.

✕*Wechsler Intelligence Scale for Children* by D. Wechsler. PC, 1949. Ages 5-15. Verbal and performance scores. One form. Time: 40-60 minutes. Individual test.

B. REPRESENTATIVE READING READINESS TESTS

American School Reading Readiness Test by R. V. Young, W. E. Pratt, and C. A. Witmer, PSP, 1941. Grade 1. One form. Time: about 45 minutes. Vocabulary, visual discrimination of various kinds, recognition of words, following directions, memory for geometric forms.

Binion-Beck Reading Readiness Test for Kindergarten and First Grade by H. S. Binion and R. L. Beck. APC, 1945. Grades kgn-1. One form. Time: about 40 minutes. Picture vocabulary and discrimination, following directions, memory for story, motor control.

Gates Reading Readiness Tests by A. I. Gates. BP, 1939. Grade 1. One form. Time: about 50 minutes. Five scores: picture directions, word matching, word-card matching, rhyming, letters, and numbers.

The Harrison-Stroud Reading Readiness Tests by M. L. Harrison and J. B. Stroud. HM, 1950. Grades kgn-1. One form. Time: 90 minutes in three sessions. Measures visual discrimination, using context; auditory discrimination, using context; and auditory clues, using symbols.

Lee-Clark Reading Readiness Test by J. M. Lee and W. W. Clark. CTB, 1951. Grades kgn-1. One form. Time: about 15 minutes. Letter symbols, concepts, word symbols.

Metropolitan Readiness Tests by G. H. Hildreth and N. L. Griffiths. WBC, 1950. Grades kgn-1. Two forms. Time: about 65-75 minutes. Measures reading readiness, number readiness, drawing-a-man.

Monroe Reading Aptitude Tests by M. Monroe. HM, 1935. Grade 1. One form. Time: about 50 minutes (two or three sittings). The 17 subtests include visual functions, auditory discrimination, memory for a story, motor control, articulation, vocabulary knowledge, length of sentences used and laterality preferences.

Murphy-Durrell Diagnostic Reading Readiness Test by H. A. Murphy and D. D. Durrell. WBC, 1949. Grade 1. One form. Time: part 1-2, about 60 minutes; part 3, about 35-50 minutes. Auditory, visual and learning rate scores.

Van Wagenen Reading Readiness Scales by M. L. G. Klaeger and M. J. Van Wagenen (Part I) and M. J. Van Wagenen (Part II). VW, 1954. Grade 1 or end of kindergarten. One form. Part I: Listening vocabulary; Part II: Range of information, perception of relations, opposites, memory span for ideas, word discrimination. Part I and Part II may be obtained separately.

C. REPRESENTATIVE READING AND STUDY SKILL TESTS

Ability to Interpret Reading Materials in the Natural Sciences: Iowa Tests of Educational Development, Test 6 by E. F. Lindquist (ed.) and K. W. Vaughn. SRA, 1951. Grades 9-13. One form. Time: 60 minutes. Interpreting reading materials in natural sciences.

Ability to Interpret Reading Materials in the Social Studies: Iowa Tests of Educational Development, Test 5 by E. F. Lindquist (ed.) and K. W.

Vaughn. SRA, 1951. Grades 9-13. One form. Time: 60 minutes. Interpreting reading materials in social studies.

Bennett Use of Library Test by A. Bennett and H. E. Schrammel. BEM, 1947. High school and college. Two forms. Time: 50 minutes. Questions concerning library rules and practices.

Brown-Carlsen Listening Comprehension Test by J. I. Brown and G. R. Carlsen. WBC, 1953. Grades 9-13. Two forms. Time: about 50 minutes. Immediate recall, following directions, recognizing transitions, word meanings, lecture comprehension.

California Reading Test by E. W. Tiegs and W. W. Clark. CTB, 1950. Grades: 1-4.5, 4-6, 7-9, 9-14. Four forms. Time: 35-50 minutes. Vocabulary, comprehension and total scores.

Chapman-Cook Speed of Reading Test by J. C. Chapman and S. A. Cook. ETB, 1924. Grades 4-8. Two forms. Time: 2½ minutes. Speed of reading easy material with comprehension constant.

Chicago Reading Tests by M. D. Engelhart and T. G. Thurstone. EMH, 1939-40. Grades: Test A, 1-2; Test B, 2-4; Test C, 4-6; Test D, 6-8. Three forms. Time: 31-45 minutes. Comprehension of words, sentences, and paragraphs. Comprehension of maps and graphs added in grades 4-8.

Cooperative Dictionary Test by S. D. Melville assisted by C. Derrick and A. W. Henry. CTD-ETS, 1951-52. Grades 7-12. One form. Time: 30 minutes. Alphabetizing, spelling, pronunciation, meaning.

Detroit Reading Tests by C. M. Parker and E. A. Waterbury. WBC, 1927. Grades 2-9. Two to four forms. Time: 5-8 minutes. Comprehension and rate.

Detroit Word Recognition Test by E. F. Oglesby. WBC, 1924. Grades 1-2. Four forms. Time: 5 minutes. Word recognition.

DeVault Primary Reading Test by N. M. DeVault. CTB, 1931. Grades 1-2. Two forms. Time: 15-20 minutes. Word recognition, sentence and story comprehension.

Developmental Reading Tests: Primary Reading by G. L. Bond, T. Clymer, and C. J. Hoyt. LC, 1955. Grades 1-3 (Three levels: primer reading, lower primary reading, upper primary reading). One form. Time: 10-15 minutes on each part. Part I, basic vocabulary; Part II, general comprehension; Part III, specific comprehension.

Developmental Reading Tests: Intermediate Reading by G. L. Bond, T. Clymer, and C. J. Hoyt. LC, 1956. Grades 4-6. One form. Part I, basic vocabulary; Part II, factual reading; Part III, reading to organize; Part IV, reading to evaluate-interpret; Part V, reading to appreciate.

Diagnostic Reading Tests by Committee on Diagnostic Reading Tests. CDRT, 1952. Grades: 4-6, 7-13. Survey test: lower level has two forms, higher level, 8 forms. Time: 40 minutes. Measures rate, narrative comprehension, vocabulary and textbook type comprehension. Diagnostic tests: two forms at each level. Time: 15-60 minutes on different parts. Measures vocabulary, comprehension, rate and word attack.

Dolch Basic Sight Word Test by E. W. Dolch. GP, 1943. Assigned to no particular grade. Untimed. Recognition of the 220 words of the Dolch Basic Word List.

Durost-Center Word Mastery Test by W. N. Durost and S. S. Center. WBC, 1952. Grades 9-13. Two forms. Time: two class periods. Meanings for isolated words and words in context.

Durrell Analysis of Reading Difficulty by D. D. Durrell. WBC, 1955. Grades

1-6. Time: 30-90 minutes. Materials for individual diagnosis of reading difficulties.

Durrell-Sullivan Reading Capacity and Achievement Tests by D. D. Durrell and H. B. Sullivan. WBC, 1945. Intermediate, grades 3-6. Two forms. Time: 30-45 minutes. Word and paragraph meaning, spelling and written recall. Primary test, grades 2.5-4.5, contains easier portions of intermediate test.

Dvorak-Van Wagenen Diagnostic Examination of Silent Reading Abilities by A. Dvorak and M. J. Van Wagenen. VW, 1953. Grades 4-6, 7-9, 10-12. One form. Untimed except rate test. Rate of comprehension, perception of vocabulary in isolation, range of information, paragraph comprehension. An I.Q. may be derived from Parts I and II. Each division and Part I, Part II, and I plus II may be obtained separately.

Garvey Primary Reading Test by H. S. Reed and M. V. Seagoe. CTB, 1936. Grades 1-3. Two forms. Time: about 40 minutes. Word and phrase recognition, vocabulary and comprehension.

Gates Advanced Primary Reading Test by A. I. Gates. BP, 1943. Grades 2-3. Three forms. Time: 40 minutes. Word recognition and paragraph reading.

Gates Basic Reading Tests by A. I. Gates. BP, 1943. Grades 3-8. Four forms. Time: about 35 minutes. Reading to appreciate general significance, predict outcomes, understand directions, and note details.

Gates Primary Reading Test by A. I. Gates. BP, 1943. Grades 1-2. Three forms. Time: 50 minutes. Word recognition, sentence and paragraph reading.

Gates Reading Diagnostic Tests by A. I. Gates. BP, 1945. Grades 1-8. Two forms. Time: 60-90 minutes. Materials for individual diagnosis of difficulties.

Gates Reading Survey by A. I. Gates. BP, 1939. Grades 3-10. Two forms. Time: 60-90 minutes. Vocabulary and comprehension plus measures of rate and accuracy.

Gilmore Oral Reading Test by J. V. Gilmore. WBC, 1952. Grades 1-8. Two forms. Time: 15-20 minutes. Comprehension, rate and accuracy of oral reading. Analysis of errors used to diagnose reading difficulties.

Gray Standardized Oral Reading Check Tests by W. S. Gray. PSP, 1922. Grades 1-8. Five forms. Time: about 1-3 minutes. Rate and accuracy of oral reading.

Gray Standardized Oral Reading Paragraph Test by W. S. Gray. PSP, 1915. Grades 1-8. One form. Time: about 5-10 minutes. Rate and accuracy of oral reading. Analysis of errors used to diagnose reading difficulties.

Haggerty Reading Examination by M. E. Haggerty. WBC, 1929. Grades 1-3 (Sigma 1), 6-12 (Sigma 3). One form for Sigma 1, 2 for Sigma 3. Time: 20-25 minutes. Sentence and paragraph comprehension, vocabulary.

High School Reading Test: National Achievement Tests by R. K. Speer and S. Smith. APC, 1952. Grades 7-12. Two forms. Time: 40 minutes. Vocabulary, word discrimination, sentence meaning, paragraph comprehension.

Ingraham-Clark Diagnostic Reading Tests by J. E. Ingraham and W. W. Clark. CTB, 1929. Grades 1-3, 4-8. Two forms. Time: 20-30 minutes. Each level measures word form and word meanings, sentence and paragraph comprehension.

Iowa Every-Pupil Tests of Basic Skills by H. F. Spitzer, E. Horn, M. McBroom, H. A. Greene and E. F. Lindquist. HM, 1940-47. Grades 3-5, 5-9. Four forms. Time: 55-90 minutes. Test A: vocabulary and paragraph comprehension. Test B: reading maps, use of references, index, dictionary, and alphabetizing (3-5) or reading graphs, charts, and tables (5-9).

Iowa Silent Reading Test by H. A. Greene, A. N. Jorgensen and V. H. Kelley. WBC, 1943. Grades 4-8, 9-13. Four forms. Time: 45-60 minutes. Comprehension of words, sentences, paragraphs, rate of reading, skill in alphabetizing and indexing.

Kansas Primary Reading Test by A. Hoag, E. Humble, B. Robinson, A. Wipf and H. E. Schrammel. BEM, 1935. Grades 1-3. Two forms. Time: 12 minutes. Word knowledge, sentence and paragraph comprehension.

Kelley-Greene Reading Comprehension Test by V. H. Kelley and H. A. Greene. WBC, 1953. Grades 9-13. Three forms. Time: 63 minutes, three sessions advised. Paragraph comprehension, directed reading (finding answers), retention of details, rate.

Lee-Clark Reading Test—First Reader by J. M. Lee and W. W. Clark. CTB, 1943. Grades 1-2. Two forms. Time: about 25 minutes. Auditory and visual stimuli, following directions, completion, inference.

Los Angeles Elementary Reading Test by J. E. Ingraham. CTB. Grades 3-9. Four forms. Time: 30 minutes. Paragraph comprehension.

Los Angeles Primary Reading Test by J. E. Ingraham, CTB, 1925. Grades 1-3. Four forms. Time: 10 minutes. Comprehension of sentences and paragraphs.

Manwiller Word Recognition Test by C. E. Manwiller. WBC, 1935. Grades 1-2. Two forms. Time: 10 minutes. Word recognition.

Metropolitan Reading Tests by R. D. Allen, H. H. Bixler, W. L. Connor, F. B. Graham, G. H. Hildreth and J. S. Orleans. WBC, 1940. Grades 1, 2, 3, 4-6, 7-8. Three forms. Time: 30-70 minutes. Word and phrase recognition and word meanings in grade one; comprehension and vocabulary in other grades.

Metropolitan Achievement Tests: Reading by R. D. Allen, H. H. Bixler, W. L. Connor, F. D. Graham and G. H. Hildreth. WBC, 1933-49. Grades 3-4, 5-7.5, 7-9.5. Three forms. Time: 35 minutes. Paragraph comprehension and vocabulary.

Michigan Speed of Reading Test by E. B. Greene. PC, 1937. Grades 6-16. Two forms. Time: 7 minutes. Rate of reading easy material.

Monroe Diagnostic Reading Examination by M. Monroe. ST, 1928. Grades 1-6. One form. Time: about 45 minutes. Materials for individual diagnosis of difficulties.

Monroe Standardized Silent Reading Tests by M. Monroe. PSP, 1928. Grades 3-5, 6-8, 9-12. Three forms. Time: 45 minutes. Comprehension and rate of reading.

Nelson Silent Reading Test by M. J. Nelson. HM, 1939. Grades 3-9. Two forms. Time: 30 minutes. Vocabulary and comprehension.

The Nelson-Denny Reading Test by M. J. Nelson and E. C. Denny. HM, 1938. Grades 9-16. Two forms. Time: 30 minutes. Vocabulary and paragraph comprehension.

Pressey Diagnostic Reading Tests by S. L. Pressey and L. C. Pressey. PSP, 1929. Grades 3-9. Two forms. Time: 35 minutes. Vocabulary, comprehension and rate.

Pressey Diagnostic Vocabulary Test by S. L. Pressey and L. C. Pressey. PSP, 1929. Grades 1-3. Two forms. Time: 2 minutes. Size of reading vocabulary.

Reading Comprehension: Cooperative English Test by F. B. Davis, H. V. King, M. Willis, C. Derrick, H. R. Neville, J. M. Bradford, and G. Spalding.

CTD-ETC, 1951. Grades 7-12, 11-16. Four forms. Time: 40 minutes. Vocabulary, speed, and level of comprehension.

Reading Test (Comprehension and Speed): Municipal Tests: National Achievement Tests by R. K. Speer and S. Smith. APC, 1950. Grades 3-6, 6-8. Two forms. Time: about 33 minutes. Following directions, sentence and paragraph meaning, rate.

Robinson-Hall Reading Tests by F. P. Robinson and P. Hall. OSUP, 1949. College level. One form. Time: 15 minutes for each of four tests. Reading ability for art, geology, history, fiction.

Schrammel-Gray High School and College Reading Test by H. E. Schrammel and W. H. Gray. PSP, 1942. Grades 7-13. Two forms. Time: 25 minutes. Paragraph comprehension.

Silent Reading Diagnostic Tests by G. L. Bond, T. Clymer, and C. J. Hoyt. LC, 1955. Grades 2.5-6, and for retarded pupils in junior and senior high school. One form. Time: about 90 minutes in two sessions. Measures recognition of words in isolation and in context, recognition of reversible words in context, locating elements, syllabication, locating root words, word elements, beginning sounds, rhyming sounds, letter sounds and word synthesis.

SRA Reading Record by G. T. Buswell. SRA, 1947. Grades 7-12. One form. Time: 40 minutes. Rate of reading, comprehension, sentence and paragraph meaning, general and technical vocabulary, graph and other specialized reading.

Stanford Achievement Test: Reading by T. L. Kelley, G. M. Ruch and L. M. Terman. WBC, 1943. Grades 2-3, 4-6, 7-9. Three (primary) to five forms. Time: 30-40 minutes. Paragraph and word meanings.

Stone Narrative Silent Reading Tests by C. R. Stone. PSP, 1922. Grades 3, 4, 5-6, 7, junior high school. One form. Time: 40-60 minutes. Rate and comprehension.

Stone-Webster Test in Beginning Reading by C. R. Stone. WBC, 1937. Grade 1. Two forms. Time: 40 minutes. Vocabulary and sentence meaning.

Study-Habits Inventory by C. G. Wrenn. SUP, 1941. Grades 12-16. One form. Time: 10-20 minutes. Check-list of study habits.

Survey of Study Habits, Experimental Edition by A. E. Traxler. ERB, 1944. Grades 8-14. One form. Time: 30 minutes. The 85 items provide a self-analysis of study habits.

Test of Study Skills by J. W. Edgar and H. T. Manuel. SC, 1940. Grades 4-9. Two forms. Time: 60 minutes. Use of references, reading graphs, tables, maps, critical inference.

Test on the Use of Books and Libraries: General Education Series by Ralph W. Tyler (Director). CTD-ETS, 1950. Grades 7-12. Two forms. Time: about 50 minutes. Use of library, books, an index, card catalog, dictionary and various kinds of reference sources.

Tests of Natural Sciences: Vocabulary and Interpretation of Reading Materials: Cooperative Inter-American Tests by H. T. Manuel (Director). CTD-ETS, 1950. Grades 8-13. Two forms. Time: 35 minutes. Vocabulary, interpretation of reading materials.

Tests of Reading: Cooperative Inter-American Tests by H. T. Manuel, Director of Test Construction. CTD-ETS, 1950. Grades 1-3, 4-7, 8-13. Two forms. Time: about 25-50 minutes. Vocabulary and comprehension.

Tests of Social Studies: Vocabulary and Interpretation of Reading Materials: Cooperative Inter-American Tests by H. T. Manuel (Director). CTD-ETS,

1950. Grades 8-13. Two forms. Time: 35 minutes. Vocabulary, interpretation of reading materials.

Tests of Study Skills by G. W. Edgar and H. T. Manuel. SC, 1940. Grades 4-9. Two forms. Time: 60 minutes. Use of reference books, indexes, and dictionary, reading of graphs, tables and maps, critical inference.

Thorndike-Lorge Reading Test by E. L. Thorndike and I. Lorge. BP, 1947. Grades 7-9. Two forms. Time: 40 minutes. Measures a variety of factors in silent reading including ability to interpret idioms and figures of speech.

Traxler High School Reading Test by A. E. Traxler, PSP, 1942. Grades 10-12. Two forms. Time: 50 minutes. Rate, story comprehension, main ideas, total comprehension.

Traxler Silent Reading Test by A. E. Traxler. PSP, 1942. Grades 7-10. Four forms. Time: 46 minutes. Rate, story comprehension, word meaning, paragraph meaning.

Unit Scales of Attainment in Reading by M. J. Van Wagenen. ETB, 1932. Grades 1-9. Three forms. Untimed. Paragraph comprehension.

The Use of Library and Study Materials by M. S. Kirkpatrick, L. R. Thompson, and H. Tomlinson. SC, 1941. Grades 9-16. Two forms. Time: 40 minutes. Finding and interpreting information.

Use of Sources of Information: Iowa Tests of Educational Development, Test 9 by E. F. Lindquist (ed.) and K. W. Vaughn. SRA, 1951. Grades 9-13. One form. Time: 27 minutes. Proficiency in use of sources of information.

Van Wagenen Analytical Reading Scales by M. J. Van Wagenen. VW, 1953. Grades 4-6, 7-9, 10-12. One form. Untimed. Comprehension: central thought, details, ideas spread over several sentences, inferences, and interpretation. Each division may be obtained separately.

Van Wagenen Comprehensive Reading Scales by M. J. Van Wagenen. VW, 1953. Grades 4-12 (separate for each grade 4-8, 9 and 10 in one, 11 and 12 in one). One form. Untimed. Paragraph comprehension: grasping central thought, noting details, ideas spread over several sentences, inferences and interpretation. Each division may be obtained separately.

Van Wagenen Listening Vocabulary Scales by M. J. Van Wagenen. VW, 1956. Grades 2-6 (separate for each grade). One form. Untimed. Listening vocabulary knowledge.

Van Wagenen Primary Reading Scales by M. J. Van Wagenen. VW, 1956. Grades 1, 2, and 3 (separate for each grade). One form. Untimed. Reading vocabulary and comprehension.

Williams Reading Tests by A. J. Williams. PSP, 1926. Grades 1-3. Two forms. Time: 20 minutes. Vocabulary and sentence comprehension.

Work-Study Skills: Iowa Every-Pupil Tests of Basic Skills, Test B, New Edition by H. F. Spitzer, E. Horn, M. McBroom, H. A. Greene, and E. F. Lindquist. HM, 1947. Grades 3-5, 5-9. Four forms. Time: 47-77 minutes. Map reading, alphabetizing (or graphing in advanced battery) and use of references, index, and dictionary.

APPENDIX II: TEXTS

A. LIST OF TEXTS ON TEACHING READING

ADAMS, F., GRAY, L., and REESE, D., *Teaching children to read.* New York: The Ronald Press Company, 1949.

ANDERSON, I. H., and DEARBORN, W. F., *The psychology of teaching reading.* New York: The Ronald Press Company, 1952.

ARTLEY, A. S., *Your child learns to read.* Chicago: Scott, Foresman and Company, 1952.

BETTS, E. A., *Foundations of reading instruction.* New York: American Book Company, 1946.

BOND, G. L., and BOND, E., *Developmental reading in high school.* New York: The Macmillan Company, 1941.

———— and WAGNER, E. B., *Teaching the child to read,* rev. ed. New York: The Macmillan Company, 1950.

———— and WAGNER, E. B., *Child growth in reading.* Chicago: Lyons & Carnahan, 1955.

BROOM, M. E., DUNCAN, M. A. A., EMIG, D., and STUEBER, J., *Effective reading instruction,* 2nd ed. New York: McGraw-Hill Book Company, Inc., 1951.

CARTER, H. L. J., and MCGINNIS, D. J., *Learning to read, a handbook for teachers.* New York: McGraw-Hill Book Company, Inc., 1953.

CENTER, S. S., and PERSONS, G. L., *Teaching high school students to read.* New York: Appleton-Century-Crofts, Inc., 1937.

DOLCH, E. W., *Psychology and teaching of reading,* 2nd ed. Champaign (Ill.): The Garrard Press, 1951.

———— *Teaching primary reading,* 2nd ed. Champaign (Ill.): The Garrard Press, 1950.

———— *Problems in reading.* Champaign (Ill.): The Garrard Press, 1948.

GRAY, W. S., *On their own in reading.* Chicago: Scott, Foresman and Company, 1948.

HESTER, K. B., *Teaching every child to read.* New York: Harper and Brothers, 1955.

HILDRETH, G., *Readiness for school beginners.* Yonkers (N. Y.): World Book Company, 1950.

MCKEE, P., *The teaching of reading in the elementary school.* Boston: Houghton Mifflin Company, 1948.

MCKIM, M. G., *Guiding growth in reading.* New York: The Macmillan Company, 1955.

MONROE, M., *Growing into reading.* Chicago: Scott, Foresman and Company, 1951.

Reading in high school and college. Forty-seventh Yearbook of the National Society for the Study of Education, Part II. Chicago: University of Chicago Press, 1948.

Reading in the elementary school. Forty-eighth Yearbook of the National Society for the Study of Education, Part II. Chicago: University of Chicago Press, 1949.

RUSSELL, D. H., *Children learn to read*. Boston: Ginn and Company, 1949.

SCHONELL, F. J., *The psychology and teaching of reading*, 3rd ed. London: Oliver and Boyd, 1951.

SHAW, P. B., *Effective reading and learning*. New York: Thomas Y. Crowell Company, 1955.

SIMPSON, E. A., *Helping high-school students read better*. Chicago: Science Research Associates, Inc., 1954.

STONE, C. R., *Better advanced reading*. St. Louis: Webster Publishing Company, 1937.

———*Progress in primary reading*. St. Louis: Webster Publishing Company, 1950.

STRANG, R., *Problems in the improvement of reading in high school and college*. Lancaster (Pa.): The Science Press, 1938.

——— MCCULLOUGH, C. M., and TRAXLER, A. E., *Problems in the improvement of reading*, 2nd ed. McGraw-Hill Book Company, Inc., 1955.

The teaching of reading: A second report. Thirty-sixth Yearbook of the National Society for the Study of Education, Part I. Bloomington, (Ill.): Public School Publishing Company, 1937.

TINKER, M. A., *Teaching elementary reading*. New York: Appleton-Century-Crofts, Inc., 1952.

WITTY, P., *Reading in modern education*. Boston: D. C. Heath & Company, 1949.

——— and KOPEL, D., *Reading and the educative process*. Boston: Ginn and Company, 1939.

YOAKAM, G. A., *Basal reading instruction*. McGraw-Hill Book Company, Inc., 1955.

B. LIST OF TEXTS ON REMEDIAL READING

BETTS, E. A., *The prevention and correction of reading difficulties*. Evanston (Ill.): Row, Peterson and Company, 1936.

BLAIR, G. M., *Diagnostic and remedial teaching*, rev. ed. New York: The Macmillan Company, 1956.

COLE, L., *The improvement of reading*. New York: Farrar and Rinehart, 1938.

DOLCH, E. W., *A manual of remedial reading*, 2nd ed. Champaign (Ill.): The Garrard Press, 1945.

DUNCAN, J., *Backwardness in reading*. London: George G. Harrap and Company, 1953.

DURRELL, D. D., *Improvement of basic reading abilities*. Yonkers (N. Y.): World Book Company, 1940.

FERNALD, G. M., *Remedial techniques in basic school subjects*. New York: McGraw-Hill Book Company, Inc., 1943.

GATES, A. I., *The improvement of reading*, 3rd ed. New York: The Macmillan Company, 1947.

HARRIS, A. J., *How to increase reading ability*, 3rd ed. New York: Longmans, Green & Company, 1956.

KIRK, S., *Teaching reading to slow-learning children*. Boston: Houghton Mifflin Company, 1940.

KOTTMEYER, W., *Handbook for remedial reading*. St. Louis: Webster Publishing Company, 1947.

LAZAR, M. (ed.), *The retarded reader in the junior high school.* Publication No. 31. New York: Board of Education, City of New York, Bureau of Educational Research, 1952.

MCCALLISTER, J. M., *Remedial and corrective instruction in reading.* New York: Appleton-Century-Crofts, Inc., 1936.

MONROE, M., *Children who cannot read.* Chicago: University of Chicago Press, 1932.

―――― and BACKUS, B., *Remedial reading.* Boston: Houghton Mifflin Company, 1937.

ORTON, S. T., *Reading, writing, and speech problems in children.* New York: W. W. Norton & Company, Inc., 1937.

ROBINSON, H. M. (ed.), *Clinical studies in reading, I.* Chicago: University of Chicago Press, Suppl. Educ. Monog. No. 68, 1949.

―――― (ed.), *Clinical studies in reading, II.* Chicago: University of Chicago Press, Suppl. Educ. Monog. No. 77, 1953.

―――― *Why pupils fail in reading.* Chicago: University of Chicago Press, 1946.

―――― (ed.), *Corrective reading in classroom and clinic.* Suppl. Educ. Monog. No. 79. Chicago: University of Chicago Press, 1953.

STANGER, M. A., and DONOHUE, E. K., *Prediction and prevention of reading difficulties.* New York: Oxford University Press, 1937.

APPENDIX III

SOURCES OF GRADED BOOK LISTS

BEUST, N. (compiler), *Graded list of books for children.* Chicago: American Library Association, 1936. Brief description of books for grades one to three, four to six, and seven to nine.

BLAIR, G. M., *Diagnostic and remedial teaching,* rev. ed. New York: The Macmillan Company, 1956, 180-198. Various book lists for retarded readers in high school.

CARPENTER, H. McC., *Gateways to American history: An annotated graded list of books for slow learners in junior high school.* New York: H. W. Wilson Company, 1942. List of 200 books for social studies and English.

CARTER, H. L. J., and McGINNIS, D. J., *Learning to read.* New York: McGraw-Hill Book Company, Inc., 1953, 92-114. Reading materials classified according to various grade and interest levels. Also a graded list of books of interest to retarded readers, pp. 115-118.

COOKE, D. E. (chairman), and FRIER, E. A. (co-ordinator), *The road to better reading.* Albany (N. Y.): New York State Education Department, 1953. Texts for reading classes, pp. 64-66; adapted, simplified editions, pp. 69-70.

DURRELL, D. D., *Improvement of basic reading abilities.* Yonkers (N. Y.): World Book Company, 1940, 86-97. Graded list of books for teaching units at various grade levels. Also a selected list of books for remedial reading with vocabulary level and interest level indicated, pp. 112-114.

HARRIS, A. J., *How to increase reading ability,* 3rd ed. New York: Longmans, Green & Company, 1956, 592-619. A graded list of books for remedial reading; levels: grades one through six.

HILL, M. K. (compiler), *A bibliography of reading lists for retarded readers.* Extension Bulletin, College of Education Series, No. 37. Iowa City: State University of Iowa, 1953.

KINGERY, R. E., *How-to-do-it books.* New York: R. R. Bowker Company, 1954. List of books arranged from easy to advanced reading levels.

KIRK, S. A., *Teaching reading to slow-learning children.* Boston: Houghton Mifflin Company, 1940, 195-210. A bibliography of children's books suitable for slow-learning children. Pre-primer level through grade four.

LAZAR, May (ed.), *The retarded reader in the junior high school.* Bureau of Educational Research Publication No. 31. New York: Board of Education, City of New York (110 Livingston St., Brooklyn 2, N. Y.), 1952, 122-124. Fiction, simplified classics, and information books listed by grade levels one through six.

McADOW, B., Ten years with slow readers. *The English Journal,* 1941, 30, 573-579. Two hundred and fifty books popular with slow learners. Also published in G. M. Blair, *Diagnostic and remedial teaching.* New York: The Macmillan Company, 1956, 189-193.

ROOS, J. C., *Patterns in reading: An annotated book list for young people.*

Chicago: American Library Association, 1954. Arranged according to interest areas and roughly as to difficulty.

RUE, E., *Subject index to books for primary grades.* Chicago: American Library Association, 1943. Arranged according to reading level, pre-primer to third grade. (First supplement of 225 additional titles in 1946.)

———— *America, past and present: An annotated bibliography of children's stories.* New York: H. W. Wilson Company, 1948. Books for normal, retarded, and accelerated readers in junior high school age groups.

———— *Subject index to books for intermediate grades.* Chicago: American Library Association, 1950. Books range from third to sixth grade in reading level.

SLATER, R., *Books for youth who dislike reading.* Columbus (Ohio): Ohio State University, 1941. A master list of lists.

SPACHE, G., *Basic reading materials graded by a new readability formula for primary materials* (mimeographed). Gainesville (Fla.): Reading Laboratory and Clinic, University of Florida. The primary levels of books in a large number of basic reading series are included. This is also a comprehensive list of basic series of readers.

———— *Good books for poor readers.* Gainesville (Fla.): The Author, 1954. Titles arranged according to reading and interest levels, pp. 1-36; narrative materials adapted for poor readers (graded), pp. 37-49; graded books for boys and girls, pp. 76-79.

STRANG, R., *et al., Gateways to readable books.* New York: H. W. Wilson Company, 1952. Graded list of books for retarded readers of high school age.

———— McCULLOUGH, C. M., and TRAXLER, A. E., *Problems in the improvement of reading,* 2nd ed. New York: McGraw-Hill Book Company, Inc., 1955, 322. A list of easiest books for beginners with adult interests.

WILKINSON, M. S., *et al., The right book for the right child.* New York: John Day Company, 1942. Lists of graded books, pre-primer to high school levels.

APPENDIX IV

SOURCES OF MATERIALS*

American Association of University Women, *Children's books around the world*. Washington: American Association of University Women. A list of 265 children's books from 52 different countries.

American Library Association, *Aids in selection of materials for children and young people*. Chicago: American Library Association.

——— *Books for adult beginners, grades 1-7*. Chicago: American Library Association, 1946.

——— and Winnetka Public Schools, *The right book for the right child*. New York: John Day Company, 1942.

ARBUTHNOT, May H., *Children and books*. Chicago: Scott, Foresman and Company, 1947, 580-617. The annotated bibliography provides an excellent selected list of books for children up to 15 years. Reviews and comments are given in the preceding chapters.

——— and others, *Children's books too good to miss*. Cleveland: Western Reserve University Press, 1948.

Association of Children's Book Editors, *A selected list of books for boys and girls*. New York: The Children's Book Council and the New York Times, 1948.

Association of Childhood Education, *Bibliography of books for children*. Washington (D.C.): Association for Childhood Education. An annual pamphlet.

The Booklist: A guide to new books. Chicago: American Library Association. This bimonthly journal has a section devoted to children's books.

Bulletin of Children's Book Center. Chicago: Center for Children's Books, University of Chicago Library. Issued monthly.

CARTER, H. L. J., and McGINNIS, D. J., *Learning to read*. New York: McGraw-Hill Book Company, Inc., 1953. Materials for developing reading readiness, pp. 71-74; word recognition and vocabulary, pp. 75-77; structural and phonetic analysis, pp. 78-80; correcting specific reading errors, pp. 81-82; reading interest, pp. 83-86; comprehension and rate of reading, pp. 87-89; work-study habits, pp. 90-91; choric or group speaking, pp. 119-120.

Children's Book Council, Twelve recommended booklists in *The world of children's books*. New York: Children's Book Council.

COLBURN, E., *Books and library reading for pupils of the intermediate grades*, Publication No. 10 of the Laboratory Schools. Chicago: University of Chicago, 1942.

COOK, D. E., EATON, A. T., and WEST, D. H. (compilers), *Standard catalog for high school libraries*, 5th ed. with supplements. New York: H. W. Wilson Company, 1947. Lists for grades 7-12.

COOKE, D. E. (chairman), and FRIER, E. A. (co-ordinator), *The road to better reading*. Albany (N.Y.): New York Education Department, 1953, Work-

———
* See also Appendix III.

books and other reading aids, pp. 66-69; book lists, pp. 71-72; films useful in developmental reading programs, pp. 77-83.

DOLCH, E. W., *Dolch materials for better teaching of reading.* Champaign (Ill.): The Garrard Press. A variety of devices and other materials for developing word recognition, sight vocabulary, phrasing, pleasure reading, etc. Request catalog from publisher.

DURRELL, D. D., and SULLIVAN, H. B., *High interest—low vocabulary book list.* Boston: Boston University, School of Education, 1950.

GILES, R., COOKE, D. E., WEST, D. H., and others (eds.), *Children's catalog,* 7th ed. with supplements. New York: H. W. Wilson Company, 1946. Book lists for all grades up through ninth.

GRAY, W. S., and LEARY, Bernice, *What makes a book readable?* Chicago: University of Chicago Press, 1935.

HEGGE, T. G., KIRK, S. A., and KIRK, W., *Remedial reading drills.* Ann Arbor (Mich.): George Wahr, 1936.

HOLLOWELL, Lillian, *A book of children's literature,* 2nd ed. New York: Rinehart and Company, 1950, 623-661. Extensive lists of classified books, magazines, dictionaries, book lists and indexes.

The Horn Book Magazine. Boston: Horn Book, Inc. A monthly magazine devoted to books and reading material for young children.

JACOBS, L. B., *Bibliography of books for children.* Washington: Association for Childhood Education International, 1952.

KIRK, S. A., *Manual of directions for use with the Hegge-Kirk remedial reading drills.* Ann Arbor (Mich.): George Wahr, 1936.

LAZAR, May (ed.), *The retarded reader in the junior high school.* Bureau of Educational Research, Publication No. 31. New York: Board of Education, City of New York (110 Livingstone St., Brooklyn 2, N. Y.), 1952, 121. Readers and practice materials; magazines and newspapers, pp. 124-125; pupil reference materials, p. 125.

LEARY, B. E., and SMITH, D. V., *Growing with books.* Eau Claire (Wis.): E. M. Hale and Company, 1951.

LOBAN, W. (chairman), N.C.T.E. Committee on Adolescent Reading. *High interest—low vocabulary book list,* B1158. Martinez (Calif.): Contra Costa County Schools, 1951.

MAIER, L. S., *Materials, supplies and equipment for remedial reading instruction* (mimeographed). St. Cloud (Minn.): Reading Center, St. Cloud State Teachers College, 1953.

MARTIN, L. K., *Magazines for school libraries.* New York: H. W. Wilson Company, 1950.

National Council of Teachers of English, *Adventures with books: A reading list for elementary schools.* Chicago: National Council of Teachers of English, 1950.

Remedial reading materials. Part I and II. Minneapolis: Minneapolis Public Schools, 1946.

RUSSELL, D. H. and KARP, E. E., *Reading aids through the grades: Three hundred developmental reading activities.* New York: Bureau of Publications, Teachers College, Columbia University, 1951.

SNOW, M. B. (chairman of Joint Committee of the American Library Association, the National Education Association, The Association for Childhood Education, and the National Council of Teachers of English), *A basic book collection for elementary grades.* Chicago: American Library Association, 1951.

SPACHE, G., *Good books for poor readers.* Gainesville (Fla.): The Author, Reading Laboratory and Clinic, University of Florida, 1954. Workbooks, textbooks and similar materials useful in developmental and remedial reading, pp. 50-72; books on personal problems, pp. 73-75.

———— *Resources in teaching reading.* Gainesville (Fla.): The Author, Reading Laboratory and Clinic, University of Florida, 1955. Periodical references, textbooks, bulletins, etc., pp. 1-65; indexes and reading lists, pp. 66-71· magazines and newspapers for pupils, pp. 72-77; parent education materials, pp. 78-80; service bulletins, pp. 81-82; visual and auditory aids, pp. 83-95.

STRANG, R., MCCULLOUGH, C. M., and TRAXLER, A. E., *Problems in the improvement of reading.* 2nd ed. New York: McGraw-Hill Book Company, Inc., 1955, 321-324. Information on book lists and their use. Texts with practice exercises are given on pp. 323-324, and 328-329. These are mostly for junior and senior high school pupils. See p. 328 for a list of teen-age and popular adult magazines.

SULLIVAN, H. B., *Selected vocabulary interest reading list.* Boston: Educational Clinic, Boston University, 1949.

WURTZ, C., SINDT, D., and KEYSTER, M. L., *A bibliography of reading lists for retarded readers.* Iowa City: Reading Clinic, University of Iowa, 1950.

APPENDIX V

BIBLIOGRAPHIES OF READING LITERATURE

BETTS, E. A., and BETTS, T. M., *An index to professional literature on reading and related topics.* New York: American Book Company, 1945.

DALE, E. (ed.), *Bibliography of vocabulary studies.* Columbus (Ohio): Bureau of Educational Research, Ohio State University, 1949.

GRAY, W. S., Summary of investigations relating to reading. *Supplementary Educational Monographs,* No. 28. Chicago: University of Chicago Press, 1925. All titles (436) appearing up to July 1, 1924.

——— Summary of reading investigations (July 1, 1924, to June 30, 1925). *Elementary School Journal,* 1926, 26, 449-459; 507-518; 574-584; 662-673. See also successive annual summaries in same journal up through 1932.

——— Summary of reading investigations (July 1, 1931, to June 30, 1932). *Journal of Education Research,* 1933, 26, 401-424. See also successive annual summaries in same journal up to present date.

TINKER, M. A., Eye movements in reading. *Journal of Educational Research,* 1936, 30, 241-277.

——— The study of eye movements in reading. *Psychological Bulletin,* 1946, 43, 93-120. (These two articles contain all materials in the field up to 1946.)

TRAXLER, A. E., and SEDER, M., *Ten years of research in reading: Summary and bibliography.* New York: Educational Records Bureau (21 Audubon Ave.), Bulletin No. 32, 1941.

——— and TOWNSEND, A., *Another five years of research in reading: Summary and bibliography.* New York: Educational Records Bureau (21 Audubon Ave.), Bulletin No. 46, 1946.

——— and TOWNSEND, A., *Eight more years of research in reading: Summary and bibliography.* New York: Educational Records Bureau (21 Audubon Ave.), Bulletin No. 64, 1955.

INDEX

479